THE COLLECTED LETTERS OF
JOSEPH CONRAD

GENERAL EDITOR
LAURENCE DAVIES

FOUNDING GENERAL EDITOR
FREDERICK R. KARL (1927–2004)

CONSULTING EDITOR
HANS van MARLE (1922–2001)

VOLUME 7

THE COLLECTED LETTERS
OF JOSEPH CONRAD

VOLUME 7

1920–1922

EDITED BY

LAURENCE DAVIES

AND

J. H. STAPE

CAMBRIDGE
UNIVERSITY PRESS

CAMBRIDGE UNIVERSITY PRESS

Cambridge, New York, Melbourne, Madrid, Cape Town, Singapore, São Paulo

Cambridge University Press
The Edinburgh Building, Cambridge CB2 2RU, UK

Published in the United States of America by Cambridge University Press, New York

www.cambridge.org
Information on this title: www.cambridge.org/9780521561969

First published 2005

Printed in the United Kingdom at the University Press, Cambridge

A catalogue record for this book is available from the British Library

ISBN-13 978-0-521-56196-9 hardback
ISBN-10 0-521-56196-5 hardback

This volume is dedicated to the memory of three Conradians:

Philip Conrad
Bruce Harkness
Frederick R. Karl

CONTENTS

PLATES

These plates appear by kind permission of: Baker-Berry Library, Dartmouth College (2, 6, 7, 8); British Library Newspaper Collection, Colindale (4); Cambridge University Library (1); National Maritime Museum, Greenwich (3).

ACKNOWLEDGMENTS

The editors are grateful to holders of manuscripts, listed separately, for their co-operation.

Special thanks are due to Mr Owen Knowles, the late Hans van Marle, and Dr Gene M. Moore whose gracious help and wise counsel greatly facilitated work on this volume.

Dr Keith Carabine, Dr Linda Dryden, Dr Robert Hampson, the late Hans van Marle, and Professor Zdzisław Najder generously shared letters they have discovered. Dr R. A. Gekoski, Bookseller, Mr Peter Grogan, and the Center for Conrad Studies at the Institute for Bibliography and Editing, Kent State University, also kindly assisted in the preparation of this volume.

The editors are grateful to the following individuals for answering inquiries or otherwise facilitating their work: Ms Wanda Bachmann, Mr Jamie Barnes (Curator, Keswick Museum and Art Gallery), Dr Katherine Baxter, the Revd J. S. Bell (Senior Chaplain, Tonbridge School), Dr Steve Bell (Her Majesty's Nautical Almanac Office), Dr Martin Bock, Dr Xavier Brice, Mr C. F. P. Chapman (Secretary, Old Oswestrian Society), Ms Claire Cross (Wellcome Institute for the History of Medicine), Dr Charles Cutter (Brandeis University Library), Ms Caroline Dalton (Archivist, New College, Oxford), Mr A. J. Essery, Ms Glenda Gale (Alexander Turnbull Library), the late Raymond Gauthier, Ms Lee Grady (McCormick-International Harvester Collection Archivist, State Historical Society of Wisconsin), Dr Richard J. Hand, Professor James Heffernan, Dr Susan Jones, Professor Joseph M. Kissane, Ms Pamela Painter, Professor Walter C. Putnam III, Professor S. W. Reid, Professor John Rassias, Ms Erin Schlumpf, Dr Patrick Scott (Thomas Cooper Library, University of South Carolina), Dr Allan H. Simmons, Dr Carl Spadoni (Russell Archivist, MacMaster University), Dr Mariuccia G. R. Sprenger, Professor Ray Stevens, Mr Asa Tapley, Ms Régine Tessier, Dr Anne N. Thomas, Dr Robert W. Trogdon, Mr Robert Warren (Royal Observatory, Greenwich), Professor Cedric Watts, and Dr Andrea White.

J. H. Stape is grateful to the Faculty of Letters of Kyoto University for a visiting professorship during spring 1997, which permitted his work on this volume to begin, and to Toru Sasaki for arrangements connected with it. Some of the early work of locating and copying the letters in this volume was funded by the National Endowment for the Humanities.

The late Frederick R. Karl began gathering texts of Conrad's correspondence in the 1970s, working at first in tandem with Professor Zdzisław Najder. When Cambridge took up the proposed collected edition of the letters, Frederick R. Karl became its founding general editor; a critic and biographer of many interests who always saw the broader cultural landscape, he delighted in Conrad's artistry and gravitas and left his inimitable mark on Conrad studies. The late Bruce Harkness was both a generous and genial mentor and a master of anticipation, alert to those rewarding mysteries that scholars often overlook. The unassuming pride that the late Philip Conrad took in his grandfather's life and work showed itself in many kindnesses to those who shared his admiration. All three of these Conradians, so different from each other yet bound by the same enthusiasm, died in the spring of 2004. We dedicate this volume to their memory.

HOLDERS OF LETTERS

Texas	Harry Ransom Humanities Research Center, University of Texas at Austin
Thomas	Mrs Beryl Thomas
Turnbull	Alexander Turnbull Library, National Library of New Zealand, Wellington
UCL	Library of University College, London
UNC	Special Collections, Wilson Library, University of North Carolina Library, Chapel Hill
Virginia	Special Collections Department, University of Virginia Library, Charlottesville
Wagner	Hormann Library, Wagner College, Staten Island, New York
Warsaw	State Archives of Poland, Warsaw
Williams	Chapin Library, Williams College, Williamstown, Massachusetts
Wright	Mrs Purd B. Wright III
Yale	Beinecke Rare Book and Manuscript Library, Yale University, New Haven, Connecticut
Zagayski	Mr Mieczysław Zagayski

PUBLISHED SOURCES
OF LETTERS

Books cited without place of publication originated in London.

Candler   Edmund Candler, *Youth and the East: An Unconventional Autobiography*. 2nd edn. Edinburgh: Blackwood, 1932
Curle   Richard Curle, ed., *Letters: Joseph Conrad to Richard Curle*. New York: Crosby Gaige, 1928
Dryden   Linda Dryden, ed., 'Joseph Conrad and William Mathie Parker: Three Unpublished Letters', *Notes and Queries*, 45 (June 1998), no. 2, 227–30
Egan   Maurice Francis Egan, 'Our Debt to Poland', *Outlook* (New York), 28 July 1920, 568–72
G.   Edward Garnett, ed., *Letters from Joseph Conrad, 1895–1924*. Nonesuch Press, 1928
G. & S.   John A. Gee and Paul J. Sturm, trans. and eds., *Letters of Joseph Conrad to Marguerite Poradowska*. New Haven: Yale University Press, 1940
Galsworthy   John Galsworthy, 'Introduction', *'Laughing Anne' and 'One Day More': Two Plays by Joseph Conrad*, ed. John Galsworthy. John Castle, 1924, 5–15
Głos   *Głos Prawdy*, nos 108 and 114 (1926)
H. & M.   Ton Hoenselaars and Gene M. Moore, 'Joseph Conrad and T. E. Lawrence', *Conradiana*, 27 (1995), 3–20
Herzberg   *Newark Evening News* (NJ), 3 November 1921, p. 6
Hunter (1985, 2)   Allan G. Hunter, ed., 'Letters from Conrad: 2', *Notes and Queries*, 32 (September 1985), no. 3, 500–5
Hunter (1985, 3)   Allan G. Hunter, ed., 'Some Unpublished Letters by Conrad to Arthur Symons', *Conradiana*, 17 (1985), 183–98
J-A   G. Jean-Aubry, ed., *Joseph Conrad: Life & Letters*. 2 vols. Garden City, NY: Doubleday, Page, 1927
Janta (1957)   Aleksander Janta, 'Pierwszy szkic *Lord Jim* i polskie listy Conrada wbiorach amerykańskich', *Conrad żywy*, ed. Wit Tarnawski. B. Świderski, 1957, 208–28
Janta (1972)   Alexander Janta, 'Conrad's "Famous Cablegram" in Support of a Polish Loan', *Polish Review*, 17 (1972), no. 2, 69–77

JCLW   Jessie Conrad, ed., *Joseph Conrad's Letters to His Wife*.
                Privately printed, 1927
Jellard   Janet Jellard, ed., 'Joseph Conrad to His Doctor: Nine
                Unpublished Letters 1909–1921', *Conradiana*, 19 (1987),
                87–98
Jones   Doris Arthur Jones, *The Life and Letters of Henry Arthur
                Jones*. Gollancz, 1930
Karl   Frederick R. Karl, *Joseph Conrad: The Three Lives*. New
                York: Farrar, Straus, Giroux, 1979
Keating   George T. Keating, comp., *A Conrad Memorial Library:
                The Collection of George T. Keating*. Garden City, NY:
                Doubleday, Doran, 1929
Knowles   Owen Knowles, ed., 'Conrad and David Bone: Some
                Unpublished Letters', *The Conradian*, 11 (1986), 116–35
Krzyżanowski   Ludwik Krzyżanowski, ed., 'Joseph Conrad: Some
(1958)   Polish Documents', *Polish Review*, 3 (1958), nos. 1–2, 59–85
Lawrence   A. W. Lawrence, ed., *Letters to T. E. Lawrence*. Jonathan
                Cape, 1962
L.fr.   G. Jean-Aubry, ed., *Lettres françaises*. Paris: Gallimard,
                1929
Listy   Zdzisław Najder, ed., *Joseph Conrad: Listy*, trans. Halina
                Carroll-Najder. Warsaw: Państwowy Instytut
                Wydawniczy, 1968
Listy do Conrada Róża Jabłkowska, ed., *Listy do Conrada*. Warsaw:
                Państwowy Instytut Wydawniczy, 1981
Lowes   John Livingston Lowes, *The Road to Xanadu: A Study in the
                Ways of the Imagination*. Cambridge, MA: Riverside Press,
                1927
Lucas   E. V. Lucas, *The Colvins and Their Friends*. Methuen, 1928
Marrot   H. V. Marrot, *The Life and Letters of John Galsworthy*.
                Heinemann, 1935
Moore   Gene M. Moore, 'Conrad Items in the Dent Archive in
                North Carolina', *Notes and Queries*, 43 (December 1996),
                no. 4, 438–9
Najder   Zdzisław Najder, ed., *Conrad's Polish Background: Letters to
                and from Polish friends*, trans. Halina Carroll-Najder.
                Oxford University Press, 1964.
Najder (1970)   Zdzisław Najder, ed., 'Joseph Conrad: A Selection of
                Unknown Letters', *Polish Perspectives* (Warsaw), 13 (1970),
                no. 2, 31–45

Najder (1978)	Zdzisław Najder, ed., *Congo Diary and Other Uncollected Pieces*. Garden City, NY: Doubleday, 1978
Najder (1983, 2)	Zdzisław Najder, ed., *Conrad under Familial Eyes*, trans. Halina Carroll-Najder. Cambridge University Press, 1983
NRF	G. Jean-Aubry, ed., 'Lettres françaises de Joseph Conrad', *Nouvelle Revue Française*, 135 (1 December 1924), 108–16
Oswestrian	'Correspondence', *The Oswestrian*, 35 (1922), no. 3, 37
P. & H.	Reginald Pound and Geoffrey Harmsworth, *Northcliffe*. Cassell, 1959
Partington	Wilfred G. Partington, 'Joseph Conrad behind the Scenes: Unpublished Notes on his Dramatisations', *The Bookman's Journal and Print Collector*, 3rd series, 15 (1927), no. 4, 179–84
Pion	'Listy Conrada-Korzeniowskiego do Karola Zagórskiego i Anieli Zagórskiej', *Pion*, 15 December 1934, 6
Putnam	Walter C. Putnam III, ed., 'A Translator's Correspondence: Philippe Neel to Joseph Conrad', *The Conradian*, 24 (1999), no. 1, 59–91
Randall	Dale B. J. Randall, ed., *Joseph Conrad and Warrington Dawson: The Record of a Friendship*. Durham, NC: Duke University Press, 1968
Rapin	René Rapin, ed., *Lettres de Joseph Conrad à Marguerite Poradowska*. Geneva: Droz, 1966
Rothenstein	William Rothenstein, *Men and Memories: Recollections of William Rothenstein 1900–1922*. 2 vols. Cambridge University Press, 1932
Ruch	*Ruch Literacki*, 1927, no. 5, 142–3
Rude (1983)	Donald W. Rude, ed., 'An Unpublished Conrad Letter in the Texas Tech University Library', *Conradiana*, 15 (1983), 145–6
Rude (1987)	Donald W. Rude, ed., 'Two New Conrad Letters: Recent Additions to the Texas Tech Conrad Collection', *The Conradian*, 12 (1987), 175–7
Russell	Bertrand Russell, *The Autobiography of Bertrand Russell*. Allen & Unwin, 1967
Scott Moncrieff	C. K. Scott Moncrieff, ed., *Marcel Proust, An English Tribute*. Chatto & Windus, 1923

Sheard   Robert F. Sheard, ed., 'An Unpublished Conrad Letter
                   concerning *Metropolitan Magazine*', *Conradiana*, 24 (1992),
                   47–8
Slade   Joseph W. Slade, 'The World's Greatest Fiction Writer:
                   An American Poet on Joseph Conrad', *Conradiana*, 5
                   (1973), 5–11
Sutherland   J. G. Sutherland, *At Sea with Joseph Conrad*. Richards, 1922
Vidan (1970–1)   Gabrijela and Ivo Vidan, eds., 'Further Correspondence
                   between Joseph Conrad and André Gide', *Studia
                   Romanica et Anglica Zagrabiensia*, 29–30 (1970–1), 523–35
Watts (1964)   C. T. Watts, 'Joseph Conrad and the Ranee of Sarawak',
                   Review of English Studies, n.s. 15 (1964), 404–7
Watts (1969)   C. T. Watts, ed., *Joseph Conrad's Letters to R. B. Cunninghame
                   Graham*. Cambridge University Press, 1969
Winawer   Bruno Winawer, *The Book of Job: A Satirical Comedy*, trans.
                   Joseph Conrad. Dent, 1931
Wise   Thomas James Wise, comp., *A Conrad Library: A Catalogue
                   of Printed Books, Manuscripts and Autograph Letters by Joseph
                   Conrad*. Privately printed, 1928
Wright   Edgar Wright, 'Joseph Conrad and Bertrand Russell',
                   Conradiana, 2 (1969–70), no. 1, 7–16

OTHER FREQUENTLY CITED WORKS

Documents	Gene M. Moore, Allan H. Simmons, and J. H. Stape, eds., *Conrad between the Lines: Documents in a Life.* Amsterdam: Rodopi, 2000.
Hallowes	Note Book of Joseph Conrad by L. M. Hallowes, *Documents*, pp. 205–44
Hand	Richard J. Hand, 'Conrad and the Reviewers: *The Secret Agent* on Stage', *The Conradian*, 26 (2001), no. 2, 1–68
John Conrad	John Conrad, *Joseph Conrad: Times Remembered.* Cambridge University Press, 1981.
Saunders	Max Saunders, *Ford Madox Ford: A Dual Life.* 2 vols. Oxford University Press, 1996.
Stape (2000)	J. H. Stape, ed., 'From "The Most Sympathetic of Friends": John Galsworthy's Letters to Joseph Conrad, 1906–1923', *Conradiana*, 32 (2000), no. 3, 229–46
Stape and Knowles	J. H. Stape and Owen Knowles, eds., *A Portrait in Letters: Correspondence to and about Conrad*, Amsterdam: Rodopi, 1996
Sherry	Norman Sherry, ed. *Conrad: The Critical Heritage.* Routledge & Kegan Paul, 1973.

Unless otherwise noted, citations of Conrad's work are from the Kent Edition, published by Doubleday, Page, in twenty-six volumes (Garden City, NY, 1925).

CHRONOLOGY, 1920–1922

Unless otherwise stated, dates are for book publication in Britain rather than the United States; dates and locations for essays in periodicals record only the first appearance.

January-February 1920	Corrected proofs for the book version of *The Rescue*.
30 January 1920	Serialisation of *The Rescue* began in *Land and Water* (completed 31 July).
February 1920	Serialisation of *The Arrow of Gold* in *Lloyd's Magazine* concluded.
27 February 1920	Karola Zagórska arrived at Oswalds for a six-month stay.
4 March 1920	Finished preface to *The Secret Agent*.
15 March 1920	Finished first draft of *The Secret Agent* dramatisation (begun October 1919).
9 April 1920	Finished preface to *A Set of Six*.
26 April 1920	Cabled Washington, D.C., in support of loan to the Polish Government.
May 1920	Wrote prefaces to *Under Western Eyes*, *Chance*, *Victory*, and *The Shadow-Line*.
21 May 1920	*The Rescue* published in book form in America (on 24 June in Britain).
7 June 1920	Visited the British Museum for research on *Suspense*.
20 June 1920	Began *Suspense*.
18 July 1920	T. E. Lawrence visited Oswalds.
c. 21–24 July 1920	Drafted 'Memorandum on the Scheme for Fitting out a Sailing Ship'.
August 1920	The Conrads visited Rudyard Kipling at Bateman's.
1–21 September 1920	In Deal, Kent, revised *Notes on Life and Letters* texts and worked with J. B. Pinker on 'Gaspar the Strong Man' film scenario.
Before 5 October 1920	Finished preface to *Arrow of Gold*.
5 October 1920	Death of William Heinemann.

8 October 1920	Finished 'Gaspar the Strong Man'.
9 October 1920	Finished preface to *Notes on Life and Letters*.
November 1920	Translated G. Jean-Aubry's 'Joseph Conrad's Confessions' into English.
November or December 1920	Sat for a Max Beerbohm caricature.
16 December 1920	Finished draft of *Laughing Anne*. Began correcting *Notes on Life and Letters* proofs.
January 1921	First volumes of collected edition published by Doubleday and Heinemann.
23 January 1921	Accompanied by Borys Conrad and G. Jean-Aubry, the Conrads left for Corsica.
25 February 1921	*Notes on Life and Letters* published (22 April in USA).
4 March 1921	*Notes on My Books* published in USA (19 May in Britain).
24 March 1921	The Conrads celebrated their silver wedding anniversary.
10 April 1921	The Conrads returned to England.
May 1921	Introductory Note to *A Hugh Walpole Anthology* published.
12–25 June 1921	Translated Bruno Winawer's play *The Book of Job*.
7 and 14 July 1921	Sat for a portrait medallion by Theodore Spicer-Simson.
27 July 1921	'The Dover Patrol' in *The Times*.
10 October 1921	Began *The Rover* (as short story).
November 1921	Foreword to Alice Kinkead's exhibition catalogue *Landscapes of Corsica and Ireland* published.
December 1921	'The Loss of the *Dalgonar*' in *London Mercury*.
12 December 1921	'The First Thing I Remember' in *John O'London's Weekly*.
Mid-January 1922	Corrected text of 'The Warrior's Soul' for eventual collection of short stories.
24 January 1922	Signed agreement with T. F. Unwin for two new novels and volume of short stories.
8 February 1922	Death of J. B. Pinker in New York.
22 February 1922	Completed proof-reading Jessie Conrad's *Simple Cooking Precepts for a Little House* for pamphlet publication.
June 1922	Captain J. G. Sutherland's *At Sea with Joseph Conrad* published, with Conrad's foreword.

late June 1922   Finished *The Rover*; revisions continued into July.
July 1922   Met Maurice Ravel through G. Jean-Aubry.
25 July 1922   Sat for his portrait by Walter Tittle.
1 August 1922   Finished foreword to Richard Curle's *Into the East*
                         (published 1923).
8 August 1922   Made his will; Richard Curle and Ralph
                         Wedgwood appointed executors.
14 August 1922   Death of Lord Northcliffe.
2 September 1922   Borys Conrad secretly married (revealed to
                         Conrad in summer 1923).
14–18 September 1922   The Conrads visited Sir Robert Jones in
                         Liverpool and toured North Wales.
2–11 November 1922   Stage adaptation of *The Secret Agent* at
                         Ambassadors Theatre, London.
5 November 1922   Paul Valéry visited Oswalds.
3 December 1922   Conrad's sixty-fifth birthday.
4 December 1922   'Outside Literature' in *Manchester Guardian*.
23 December 1922   Death of S. S. Pawling.

INTRODUCTION TO VOLUME SEVEN

According to the folklore of creativity, artists in their last years express a serenity, a wisdom, a mastery of their craft that shows them both at home in this world and ready to leave it. Austen's *Persuasion*, Shakespeare's *Winter's Tale* and *Tempest*, Goya's Bordeaux paintings, Beethoven's last quartets all supposedly display this ripeness, this readiness. Between 1920 and 1922, Conrad completed one novel and made substantial advances on another, left unfinished when he died in August 1924. Many readers of *The Rover* have seen in Peyrol's final voyage either one, last resounding gesture of sacrifice in a cause whose adherents have slighted the old freebooter or a tranquil coming to terms with death, or even both. For obvious reasons, *Suspense* is harder to assess, but the temptation to read it in a similar way remains, down to its concluding words. Such interpretations may be too sentimental for the tough of spirit or too naïve for the sceptic – Don't they depend on *post hoc ergo propter hoc* reasoning? Can't that touching quotation from *The Faerie Queene* gracing both *The Rover* and Conrad's grave also be taken as the voice of Despair? – but they have helped to shape his literary reputation. That he also chose in this period to dramatise his bleakest, most ironic novel, *The Secret Agent*, clouds this image of a poignant sunset, and so, even more, does the state of mind, whether playful or dejected, expressed in his correspondence.

Far from feeling any mastery of his art, Conrad still had the habit of discounting any and all of his achievements, as in this avowal to Pinker about *Suspense*, his 'Napoleonic novel':

I don't know that a great subject is an advantage. It increases one's sense of responsibility and awakens all that mistrust of oneself that has been my companion through all these literary years. Mine, my dear Pinker, is the only instance within my knowledge of practice not giving self-confidence. There is a strain of anxiousness in my character that even the encouragement of your friendship and sympathy cannot altogether overcome.   (14 June 1920)

Far from feeling serene about his life, he often seemed to flounder in a swamp of melancholy. During an attack of gout, he wrote to Walpole:

I have been in great pain and, what is worse, in the depth of dumps. Have dumps any depth? Anyway the impression was a most horrible nightmare – unable to think, afraid to move and only able to worry . . . The whole thing was so brutal and unexpected that I feel as if I had been robbed of the last shred of my confidence in the scheme of the Universe. It all appears one great chaotic worry.

(14 June 1920)

As readers of Conrad's earlier letters will know, these states of mind were not new – these passages could have been written in the 1890s – but were all the worse for never being banished by achievement or success. At times, he could make light of his own nervousness, for instance about attending rehearsals of *The Secret Agent*: 'My spirit became like unto that of the field-mouse palpitating in its hole, though my body (and a considerable proportion of my native irritability) went up twice to town' (to Ada and John Galsworthy, [7 November 1922]). At other times, wit and irreverence break in, as towards the end of the letter to Bertrand Russell of [22–23 October 1922] in which Conrad also mounts a spirited attack on political and philosophical self-assurance, but the tone is certainly not that of the wise and tranquil elder.

Periods of despondency, as so often before, had much to do with the uneven rhythms of his writing: 'I have done no work to speak of for months, – such is the dreadful truth which I conceal from as many people as possible' (to Ada Galsworthy, 9 February 1922). Over these three years, Conrad begrudged the time he spent on literary housekeeping. There were fugitive articles to be rescued for *Notes on Life and Letters* or reprinted as pamphlets, preparations for the collected edition, letters to answer from correspondents all over the world who wanted his opinions on this literary question or that, and attractive side projects such as translating Bruno Winawer's comedy *The Book of Job*. None of these activities was impossibly time-consuming, but, in concert, they interrupted the narrative momentum he needed for good financial and artistic reasons:

All I can leave to my people will be my copyrights – which are worth something now. But this is a precarious provision at the best. Meantime I must keep in at work. But I've had two hard lives – each in its way – physically and mentally and I feel the need of easing down a bit. I assure you that through all my writing life I have never had the time to "look round" so to speak. When I went away from the desk it was to be laid up. Such were my holidays. I don't complain.   (17 July 1920)

The last sentence was a reproach to John Quinn, the recipient, who complained at length about his own misfortunes, and the generally defensive tone is a response to Quinn's unhappiness at no longer being the preferred buyer of Conrad's manuscripts. Nevertheless, this letter does speak for Conrad's condition – and his decision to take a working holiday in Corsica only exacerbated his plight.

Before leaving, he told Agnes Ridgeway, his friend from the days of visits to the Sandersons at Elstree, about his hopes for *Suspense* and his recent dramatisation of *The Secret Agent*. By a macabre accident, Conrad gave the letter a posthumous date, 28 December '24', instead of 1920: 'I want to breathe the air of [the] Western Mediterranean where my young life began – and I hope I will be able to do some work on my new novel. For the last year I have done nothing except correcting the text of my Collected Edition and writing prefaces for the same. I have also written a 4-act play.' The prospects for this journey into the past had seemed alluring: escape from a soggy English winter, respite for Jessie Conrad from the strain of running a household while in miserable pain, the celebration of their silver wedding anniversary, and for Conrad new territory, wildly picturesque and associated with Dominique Cervoni, his mentor and co-conspirator in Marseilles, and Napoleon Bonaparte, the anything but grey eminence of Conrad's later, 'Mediterranean' fiction. The Conrads were going at just the right moment: 'All the vendettas have been settled or have died out and it is very quiet there, I am told. On the other hand no golf courses have been laid out yet and no invasion from the dismal tribe with clubs is to be feared – for this year at least' (to John Galsworthy, 17 January 1921). The island had been discovered, however. The company at the hotel in Ajaccio came straight out of an early E. M. Forster novel: 'An atmosphere of intense good form pervades the place. Low tones – polite smiles – kind inquiries – small groups. The only disreputable looking person is the unavoidable Clergyman of the C[hurch] of E[ngland] who looks as tho' he must have had a few adventures in his time' (to Eric Pinker, 5 February 1921). At least the expedition gave Jessie Conrad some pleasure, but, for her husband, the time was otherwise completely wasted. 'The truth of the matter is', he told Alice Kinkead, 'that I like Corsica incomparably more in your pictures than in nature' (10 October 1921) – and he made no headway on his writing.

The Pinkers' grand excursion to Kent was another such occasion. When they arrived at Oswalds in the last days of July 1921, they came by mail-coach with J. B. Pinker on the box, driving four horses. This was not a tranquil visit, and it lasted more than a week.[1] An overflow of kitchen, stable, and dining-room servants had to be billeted in local inns. Catered lunches had to be laid on: 'I am afraid that those lunches won't be tip-top . . . At any rate I intend to use all my powers of persuasion and fascination to get those Canterbury people to turn out decent things, whatever they may be' (to J. B. Pinker, 18 [or 19] July 1921). The occasion was the annual Cricket Week, and Canterbury's mediaeval streets could not accommodate with

---

[1] This account depends on passages in John Conrad's *Joseph Conrad: Times Remembered* as well as on letters written between 18 July and 2 August.

ease a massive vehicle designed for the broad and well-paved post roads of nineteenth-century England. At least once, a wrong turning landed the coach in a cul-de-sac, so that it had to be backed out in an atmosphere of polite exasperation. On the first day of play, the would-be stylish arrival at the Kent County Cricket Ground became a little too dashing when the horses stampeded and spectators had to scramble for their lives.

Conrad, who had been enticed into coming along on the two-day journey from Reigate, soon grew weary of Pinker's running commentary on the art of carriage driving and had little relish for the days ahead of cricketing and picnics, since his own idea of sports and pastimes did not extend beyond nocturnal games of chess with his younger son and the occasional shot at palatable birds. He was trapped in an irritating pastiche of what Yeats, around this time, was calling 'ceremony', and Conrad wanted to be writing.

Nevertheless, Conrad also had an ancestral streak of *grand seigneur*. At Oswalds, he commanded an extensive 'lower deck' crewed by indoor and outdoor servants and Audrey Seal, the cantankerous but much-needed nurse who would eventually marry 'Long Charlie' Vinten, the chauffeur. Living in this way required extensive credit or a steady income, neither of which comes frequently to a writer. Once again, in fact, Conrad relied upon Pinker as his banker, and this system was liable to crisis:

You cannot doubt that if I had been given a clear view of having doubled my expenditure between the years 1918–1919 I would not* have pulled myself together and prevented the doubling of it again between 1919–1920 – which is pretty near what in fact happened . . . Believe [me] my dear it is not good for a man (even of much steadier character than mine) to have money falling on him in envelopes as if from heaven without even a clear wiew* of the resources from which it flows and opportunity of comparing and checking. Especially if he's a man by nature not particularly given to counting pennies.   (to Pinker, 19 April 1921)[1]

Illness permitting, the Conrads liked to entertain. They played host to such regulars as Jean-Aubry and Curle, and to writers and academics from around the world. One of the sharpest and most original observers of the Conrads at home was Tadaichi Hidaka, a lecturer from Waseda University, Tokyo, who describes Conrad's greeting at the railway station, the drive to Oswalds, the tour of the gardens, the generous lunch, the chat in the study – a hospitality ceremonious but warm.[2] Although suffering through yet more surgery, painful and mostly ineffectual, Jessie Conrad took great pleasure in society and, when possible, in visits to London, which she found a more

---

[1] For the use of asterisks, see 'Editorial Procedures'.
[2] 'East Meets West: Tadaichi Hidaka's "A Visit to Conrad" ', translated and introduced by Yoko Okuda, *The Conradian*, 23, no. 2 (Autumn 1998), 73–86.

agreeable place than her husband did: 'Thank you dear people for being good to Jessie when she was in town. I couldn't face the racket (!) of it. Perfectly ridiculous – but I can't help it. I don't know what to say to people' (to Rothenstein, 17 December 1920). When the *Woman's Pictorial* serialised her cookery book, the recipes were flanked with photographs of her, her home, and her choicest dishes as featured at the Peter Pan Tearooms in Shaftesbury Avenue. The première of *The Secret Agent* was an alarming event for Conrad, one that he chose to avoid, but afterwards:

> Mrs C confessed to me with an agreeable grin that she had *the* evening of her life, having never seen anything like that before and being sure of never seeing it again. The crowd around her box the compliments, the courtly respects of Benrimo, the speeches on the stage after the last courtain* – a perfect Function, as the Spaniards say. (to Agnes Ridgeway, 7 November 1922)

Beyond the fuss of entering a new school, their younger son did not give the Conrads much anxiety. Despite a modest performance in the entrance exam, John took a place at Tonbridge, not too far from Oswalds, where he was to live under the friendly eye of Agnes Ridgeway, whose husband was his housemaster.

Borys Conrad was another matter. Reading the dismal catalogue of lying and concealment, debts unpaid, fugitive jobs, and edgy dealings with employers, one should remember that posts in the first few, economically depressed years after the war were hard to find and hard to keep, even (some veterans said especially) for ex-servicemen – and this ex-serviceman was still suffering from the effects of gas and high explosives. All the same, Borys Conrad caused his parents much distress. When a 'financial agent' called in a loan, Conrad wrote: 'I hope I received the shock with becoming fortitude. One does not want to quarrel with one's son as long as one still keeps some belief in him. It is a crippling affair for me. One could get the money by extra work but in this affair the element of time is important' (to Graham, 7 July 1922). Borys's affairs required much 'becoming fortitude', even when he was not in any serious way at fault, as when the Surrey Scientific Apparatus Co. failed, taking with it his job and his and his father's investment, and ending the latter's long-standing friendship with Dr Mackintosh.

Few members remained of Conrad's extended family. The most important to him were the Zagórska sisters, Karola and Aniela. For a while, he subsidised Karola's life in Italy, where she was training to become an opera singer. Aniela kept him in touch with Polish cultural affairs, worked on translating his books, and generally acted as his Polish representative and prophet. Especially in Cracow and Warsaw, artistic life was flourishing, but, politically and economically, this was a parlous time for Poland, menaced by a Bolshevik invasion, and bitter, sometimes bloody, quarrels with Germany, Lithuania, and Ukraine over national boundaries. To Prince Sapieha, who was keen to enlist him in the newly founded Anglo-Polish Society, Conrad professed ignorance: 'As to the actual events of the last three years I am absolutely in the dark, not so much perhaps as to facts themselves but as to their profounder significance' (20 February 1920). The 'profounder significance' puzzled most observers, but Conrad could hardly escape the 'facts themselves' since the London papers covered the violent aftermath of war and revolution in Eastern and Central Europe quite extensively. Passing references in Conrad's letters show that he grasped the paradoxes of ethnic hostility and irredentism and, like many other liberal or right-wing Britons, feared the westward spread of Bolshevism (to Miller, 26 January, to Chassé, 21 June 1922).

Amidst all the anxieties over health, family, sluggish writing, and post-war malaise, Conrad took comfort from his friends. Pinker's sudden death on a business trip to New York was one of the hardest losses of these years. Outwardly, Pinker seemed a stiff, intimidating man. In his perennial morning-dress, tail-coat and all, he made Conrad, always meticulous with his clothes, look almost informal (see Plate 8). Under his pseudonym, 'Simon Pure', Frank Swinnerton told the readers of the New York *Bookman* about Pinker's way of doing business: 'Pinker did not let the publisher become sentimental. His "yes" had extraordinary potence as an interjection. It was quiet, expressionless, and it pulled the publisher up short. It held all the significances of assent, deprecation, sarcasm, and baffling incomprehensibility. It is quite likely that some publishers were rather afraid of Pinker in his lifetime' (May 1922, p. 275). Yet Swinnerton also recalled Pinker's kindness to young authors, and Hugh Walpole's *Times* obituary (10 February 1922) brought out Pinker's admiration for Conrad and Henry James. Although Conrad's response to this obituary sounds rather lordly, his own letters to Pinker reveal a closer, warmer friendship:

Gradually since 1914 an intimacy developed between us in a strange way. He seemed to think that he had earned the right of laying his innermost thoughts and feelings before me. A peculiar but in its way a touching assertion of the right of good service and – no other word will do – of devotion . . . He had a pride in his work and in his power to help people in ways that from a cold business point of view could not be justified to common prudence.   (to Walpole, 10 February 1922)

I feel I must get away for a few hours and who could I want to see but you? I may also find perhaps something to say. I can hardly use the pen to-day. Sheer worry.

But you won't see me a wreck and you won't find me a great trial. I simply feel that a couple of hours with you will do me all the good in the world.

(to Pinker, 5 May 1920)

This friendship between author and agent was quite remarkable, especially in the early twentieth century, when the commercial aspect of the relationship was new enough to seem less 'natural' than it has become. All the more remarkably, the friendly feelings transferred after Pinker's death to his elder son, who soon became 'my dear' or 'Dearest Eric'.

Other than J. B. Pinker, only Dr Mackintosh and Lord Northcliffe left the roster of long-standing correspondents; the former vanished in a fog of monetary claims and counter-claims; the latter died a feared and ridiculed tycoon whose worldly power and Napoleonic fantasies had fascinated Conrad. Commiserating with Edward Garnett on the loss of W. H. Hudson, Conrad noticed something odd: 'Strange fellows these Harmsworths! It is as if they had found an Aladdin's lamp. Stranger still to think that I had been more intimate with N[orthcliffe] than with Hudson. Funny world this' (25 August 1922). Friendships do not, of course, inevitably overlap. Among Conrad's friends, for example, Garnett was close to Cunninghame Graham but not to Jean-Aubry. Although Jessie Conrad was to shape a book around the idea, there was not so much a 'Conrad circle' as a Conrad archipelago, replete with islands.

Friendship has, of course, its varying rhythms. Conrad saw individual friends more or less often than he had in the past, and his surviving correspondence establishes a similar fluctuation. The contents of this volume suggest a special closeness to Garnett, Curle, Jean-Aubry, and, strong as ever but less frequent, with Cunninghame Graham, that incurable peripatetic. A wider list would include among familiars Harriet Capes, Sir Hugh Clifford, Hugh Walpole, Gordon Gardiner, Christopher Sandeman, Allan Wade, Edmund Candler, André Gide, the Rothensteins, the Galsworthys, the Colvins, and the Sandersons. Then there are those who were involved in some way with the business side of Conrad's writing: such translators, collectors, publishers, or producers as Philippe Neel, Thomas. J. Wise, John Quinn, F. N. Doubleday, J. Harry Benrimo. Others concerned themselves with Conrad as a literary figure: George T. Keating, Wilfred G. Partington, Elbridge L. Adams, F. Tennyson Jesse, C. K. Scott Moncrieff, and many more. Some of this spate of correspondence flows through channels already opened. Jean-Aubry, for instance, continued to brief Conrad on events in the worlds of music and current French literature; Cunninghame Graham was travelling again, this time to Colombia, and adding to the stack of his books on Latin America.

Other correspondence flows in new directions, as, for example, in the discussions about staging *The Secret Agent* with Eric Pinker, Allan Wade, John Galsworthy, and Benrimo, or the exchanges over recent Polish literature with Bruno Winawer. The variety is such, however, that a brief sampling is more revealing than an inventory.

Because of its range, a collection of letters, incomplete thanks to the vagaries of survival as it must be, is not simply a heap of raw material for some hypothetical biography. It will certainly attract biographers and also critics of biographical inclination; the letter to Edmund Candler of 3 April 1922 gives the only known evidence that Conrad visited the Basque country during the Carlist Wars, a clue to his putative career as a gun-runner. A biographer drawn to cultural affairs would see in the letters to and about the sailor-artist John Everett and the Irish landscape-painter Alice Kinkead (familiarly known as 'Kinkie') signs of a fresh interest in the visual arts. The linguist, and perhaps the psychologist, will consider the abrupt changes of register, the Gallicisms and Polonisms, the slips of the pen, and the traces of Conrad's pronunciation in the letters dictated to Miss Hallowes. Yet Conrad's reactions to the strife in Poland, Russia, and Ukraine, the prospects for class conflict in Britain (to Adams, 20 November 1922), the flood of American visitors to Europe (to Lucas, 23 July 1920), the future of China (to Russell, [22–3 October 1922]), or the welfare of ex-servicemen (to Hatton, 14 July 1921) are matters for a historian as much as for a biographer. Similarly, the letter to Scott Moncrieff of 17 December 1922 with its echoes of nineteenth-century theories of 'analysis' in fiction and its awareness of Proust's deep originality belong to a moment in European cultural history as well as to the history of Conrad's own opinions. Yet other letters deserve to be read in their own right as unintended comedy, especially those to Wise and Quinn, competing for access to the slightest morsel of Conradiana. Some of the letters to Wise, the scholar, thief, and master-forger who warned collectors against spurious editions of Conrad, choice examples of ingenious marketing as they are, read like parodies of bibliographical scholarship: '*Three MS pages* consisting of a message cabled to the Polish Government Committee of the State Loan to be raised in U.S. . . . It is hardly literature but, at any rate, it is a public act of mine and very likely to be the only specimen of Conrad's cable style' (20 May 1920).

An episode in the correspondence with Richard Curle speaks to the insufficiencies of a narrowly biographical understanding. Curle helped Conrad with his finances – selling pamphlets, settling tax-demands, arranging publicity for his work. He also helped with more literary chores, such as assembling

Notes on Life and Letters. Moreover, Curle's presence, like Pinker's, reassured Conrad and sustained him:

> While revising the text [of *Notes on Life and Letters*] You were very vividly with me – your friendship, your kindness, your personality and I missed more than ever your voice, your characteristic turn of conversation, the downrightness of your mind and the warm genui[ne]ness of your feelings.   (9 October 1920)

> I have been doing nothing but thinking – absorbing myself in constant meditation – over *the* Novel [*Suspense*]. It's almost there! Almost to be grasped. Almost ready to flow over on the paper – but not quite yet. I am fighting off depression. A word from you would help.   (1 October 1922)

When Curle wrote up his older friend for an article in *Blue Peter*, however, he became proprietorial and dogmatic:

> Didn't it ever occur to you, my dear Curle, that I knew what I was doing in leaving the facts of my life and even my tales in the background. Explicitness, my dear fellow, is fatal to the glamour of all artistic work, robbing it of all suggestiveness, destroying all illusion. You seem to believe in literalness and explicitness, in facts and also in expression.   (24 April 1922)

Here we return to the gap between what Conrad thought and felt and what he wrote. The letters are not so much a key to the fiction as a multiple reflection of complex states of mind as, in another mode, are the novels. The oscillation in his novels and stories between the ironic and the operatic is audible too in the correspondence, and on a broader scale there is a comparable oscillation between the novels and the letters. The proportion of the operatic is higher than usual in the late fiction, a result of what one could call his turn to history, but it is easy enough to oversimplify the tonal variation in these novels. Referring to a visit to New York, Conrad told Pinker: 'you will be able to see personally how Doubleday and his fourteen partners go about the business of publishing a Conrad. According to what they say themselves it must be something as impressive almost as an earthquake, heaven and earth clashing together like a pair of cymbals, and all that sort of thing' (10 February 1920). In his advance publicity, Doubleday promoted an impression of *The Rescue* as one of the greatest of romances. Booksellers and reviewers eagerly assisted him in this aim. The Liberty Tower Bookstore took out full-page advertisements in the literary section of the *New York Times* (30 May 1920) offering free copies, returnable without obligation if the reader did not think this the most wonderfully romantic of all novels. In this spectacularly tropical light, the book's satirical touches such as Mr Travers's opinions about correct dress in low latitudes and its sharp-eyed observations of local politics were simply flattened out, and everything quotidian disappeared. The necessities of survival that Conrad describes in a letter to the Dowager Ranee of Sarawak were too trivial to register:

the Cage . . . I have lifted bodily from your palace in Kuching and transported on board the "Emma" – a great liberty; but I really had to do something to save Mrs Travers from mosquitos. Your Highness will see yourself that from the position of that old hulk, right against the edge of the forest and on a swampy shore, unless I had done something like this Mrs Travers would have been eaten alive long before the end of that bitterly romantic episode in her life.   (15 July 1920)

Nevertheless, the difference between the elegiac cadences of *The Rover*'s final pages and the wry grumpiness of passages like the following echo the distance between the 'explicitness' of everyday life and the 'glamour . . . of artistic work' as Conrad understood them:

Your letter reached me this morning, bringing warmth and light to my spirits gloomied by the November sky and chilled by the November temperature of this Blessed Isle. As to the story of this household, it is soon told: "*Nous avons vécu.*" This saying of a Frenchman (Abbé Sieyès, I think) may be supplemented and coloured by the saying of an American (name unknown): "Life is just one damned thing after another." The longer I live the more I feel that the above *est une très belle généralisation*. Children and savages are alone capable sometimes of such illuminative sayings.
                                        (to Christopher Sandeman, 21 November 1922)

One thinks of Conrad in the mail-coach, ill at ease, not wanting to be there, a believer in tradition – he sent his essay on that subject to the British Legion's magazine – an admirer of confidence (the subject of another essay) yet a writer who never ceased to disconcert, a writer whose favourite metaphor for his own sense of life was that of a man dropped into a dream.

Laurence Davies
Dartmouth College

CONRAD'S CORRESPONDENTS
1920–1922

A dagger before a name marks a tentative ascription.

Elbridge L(apham) ADAMS (1866–1934) was a New York City lawyer whose acquaintance with Conrad began in 1916. During the visit to the USA in 1923, Conrad spent two days at the Adams's country house in the Berkshire Hills of Massachusetts. 'Joseph Conrad – The Man', published in *Outlook* later in the same year, benefitted from Conrad's help with it. Adams also admired the works of Bernard Shaw and published his letters to Ellen Terry at his own Fountain Press.

Clarence Edward ANDREWS (1883–1932), a professor of literature at Ohio State University, specialised in verse, writing books on the seventeenth-century playwright Richard Brome, on Romantic and Victorian poetry, and the poetry of the 1890s. An avid traveller, he dedicated his book on Morocco to Conrad.

The New York publishing firm D. APPLETON & Co. was founded in 1838 by Daniel Appleton, who had been involved in publishing from 1831. Selling both fiction and non-fiction, the firm was a vital force until the 1930s. The publisher of Stephen Crane, Edward Bellamy, and Edith Wharton, Appleton brought out the first American edition of Conrad's *An Outcast of the Islands*.

Jean-Frédéric-Émile AUBRY (1882–1950), French music critic and writer on literature, wrote under the names G. or Gérard Jean-Aubry. An admirer and close friend during Conrad's later years, he became a one-man Conrad industry, promoting the writer's reputation in France, translating a number of his works, producing the first biography, and compiling the first edition of his letters. Among his other friends were many composers, including Debussy and Ravel; both Manuel de Falla and Roussel wrote settings of his poems. From 1919 to 1930, he lived in London, editing *The Chesterian*, a magazine published by a firm of musical instrument makers.

Thérèse AUBRY (née Contant), the mother of Conrad's friend Jean-Aubry, lived in Rouen with her husband Frédéric-Ferdinand Aubry.

Enoch Arnold BENNETT (1867–1931) won widespread recognition as the pro-lific chronicler of Staffordshire, London, and cosmopolitan life. His Naturalist approach to fiction and financial success made him the butt of Modernist writers such as Virginia Woolf and Ezra Pound, yet his taste in Conrad was impeccable. Bennett was also active as a playwright, and like Conrad was a client of J. B. Pinker.

Born in San Francisco, Joseph Henry ('Harry') BENRIMO (1874–1942) pursued an acting career in New York before appearing on the London stage in 1897. The author of popular plays, he was also a stage director and producer, mainly in America. He produced Conrad's dramatisation of *The Secret Agent* in November 1922.

Mr BLODGETT, an American admirer of Conrad's work, lived in Okla-homa.

Born in the Netherlands, the American editor, author, and philanthropist Edward William BOK (1863–1930) worked in the advertising department of Charles Scribner's Sons before becoming the editor of the *Ladies' Home Journal*, a position he held for thirty years. For a time he simultaneously directed the Bok Syndicate Press, which sold the work of prominent writers. The author of numerous articles and books, he also published an auto-biography. In Philadelphia, Bok donated generously to the arts, especially music.

Captain David William BONE (1874–1959; knighted 1946), a seaman-writer, corresponded with Conrad in 1910, though only met him in December 1919 during the Conrads' stay in Liverpool. Conrad at first disliked his novel *The Brassbounder* (1910) intensely, but his attitude eventually softened. When Conrad sailed in her to America in 1923, David Bone was captain of the *Tuscania*. Conrad also knew his brothers, Muirhead, the artist, and James, the newspaper editor.

An architect and theosophist, Ohio-born Claude Fayette BRAGDON (1866–1946) trained and practised in Rochester, New York, until 1923, when he moved to New York City to turn his attention to stage design. Bragdon wrote three books on architectural theory, *The Beautiful Necessity* (1910), *Architecture and Democracy* (1918), and *The Frozen Fountain* (1932), and also wrote on theosophy; in both fields he explored the implications of higher-dimensional geometry: see *A Primer of Higher Space* (1913).

Lady Margaret Alice Lily BROOKE, Dowager Ranee of Sarawak (née de Windt, 1849–1936), the estranged wife of Rajah Charles Brooke of Sarawak, mingled in London's literary and artistic circles, counting Henry James, Edmund Gosse, and R. B. Cunninghame Graham among her large acquaintance. Conrad drew on her *My Life in Sarawak* (1913) in *The Rescue*.

Novelist, traveller, a war correspondent and journalist in the Middle East and Tibet, and autobiographer, Edmund CANDLER (1874–1926) left England for India in 1896 in search of romance, living there until 1914. After 1906 he was Principal of Patiala College, where E. M. Forster met him during his first journey to the subcontinent. Candler's health, undermined by his experience in Asia, forced a return to Europe where he lived out his final years in the French Basque country.

Harriet Mary CAPES (1849–1936), who lived in Winchester, wrote inspirational stories for children and was involved in the Sunday School movement. A great admirer of Conrad's works, she 'selected and arranged' *Wisdom and Beauty from Conrad* (1915; reprinted 1922). He dedicated *A Set of Six* to her.

Charles CHASSÉ (1883–1965), a French writer on modern art, was particularly interested in the work of Gauguin and the Fauvists. He directed the Paris School of New York University, and in 1922 published *Les Sources d'Ubu roi* on Alfred Jarry's iconoclastic play.

Samuel Claggett CHEW (1888–1960), American university teacher, specialised in Romantic poetry and late nineteenth-century literature. Most of his career was spent as a professor of English at Bryn Mawr College, Pennsylvania. He won first prize in the *Saturday Review* contest to provide an ending to *Suspense*.

American-born George Herbert CLARKE (1873–1953) was educated in Canada and taught in various American universities before taking up a professorship at Queen's University in Ontario where he served as Head of the Department of English from 1925 until his retirement in 1943. The *Sewanee Review*, which he edited from 1920 to 1925, featured his article on Conrad in July 1922. He reviewed *The Rover* and *Suspense* for the same journal.

Born into an aristocratic West Country Roman Catholic family, the Cliffords of Ugbrooke, Hugh Charles CLIFFORD (1866–1941; knighted 1909) went out to Singapore as a cadet in 1883 and spent his life as a colonial administrator.

He was serving as British Resident in Pahang, Malaya, when he wrote one of the earliest general appreciations of Conrad's work. Later, he was appointed to the governorships of Labuan and North Borneo, the Gold Coast, Nigeria, Ceylon, and the Straits Settlements. He published many volumes of short stories and sketches, collaborated on a Malay dictionary with Frank Swettenham, and produced a Malay translation of the colonial penal code.

After a brief career as a coal merchant, Sydney Carlyle COCKERELL (1867–1962; knighted 1934) became secretary to William Morris and the Kelmscott Press. Director of the Fitzwilliam Museum, Cambridge, from 1908 to 1937, he was widely connected in artistic circles and counted among his literary friends not only Conrad but also W. S. Blunt and Thomas Hardy.

Frances, Lady COLVIN (née Fetherstonhaugh, 1838?–1924) was, with her husband Sidney, a friend of Conrad's later years. Her first marriage, to the Revd Albert Hurt Sitwell, ended with her husband's death, but she had long been separated from him, making a living as an essayist. She had been a devoted friend to Robert Louis Stevenson.

Sir Sidney COLVIN (1845–1927; knighted 1911) became a good friend to Conrad, as he had been to Robert Louis Stevenson. Colvin, who had been Slade Professor of Fine Arts at Cambridge, was Keeper of Prints and Drawings at the British Museum from 1884 to 1912. Among his literary works were editions of Stevenson's letters and biographies of Landor and Keats.

The elder of Conrad's sons, Alfred Borys CONRAD (1898–1978) was educated in a training-ship and later worked in the motor industry. Gassed and shell-shocked during the war, he suffered from poor health and emotional problems thereafter. His occasionally irresponsible behaviour, his entanglement in debt, and his marriage without Conrad's knowledge strained relations with his father.

Jessie Emmeline CONRAD (née George, 1873–1936), the second of nine children, probably met her future husband in 1894 when she was working as a typist and living with her widowed mother. The Conrads married in March 1896. Both biographers and those who knew her disagree about her personality; some disparage her stolidity or patronise her want of formal education, others admire her fortitude and her shrewd management of a somewhat cantankerous family. An accident to her knee in 1904 exacerbated a previous injury, leaving her lame and in pain for the rest of her life. She wrote two books about her husband, *Joseph Conrad as I Knew Him* (1926) and

Joseph Conrad and His Circle (1935). Her *Handbook of Cookery for a Little House,* accepted by a publisher in 1906, did not appear until 1923.

Frederic George COOPER (1876–1966) served in the war as a transport officer and was named Lieutenant Commander in 1915, leaving the service as Commander in 1921. His articles on Conrad, whom he met, appeared in the *Nautical Magazine* (1921), *Blue Peter* (1929), *Mariner's Mirror* (1940), and *Annual Dogwatch* (1953).

A journalist and writer, Richard Henry Parnell CURLE (1883–1968) was Scots by birth but English by residence and education. He left Wellington College in 1901, and began working in publishing in London in 1905. His passion for travel appears in such books as *Into the East: Notes on Burma and Malaya* (1923) and *Caravansary and Conversation* (1937); his psychological curiosity in *Women: An Analytical Study* (1947). His first book was *Aspects of George Meredith* (1908), and he published many studies of other writers, including Robert Browning, W. H. Hudson, Thomas Hardy, and Dostoevsky. In his relations with Conrad, about whom he wrote three books and many articles and pamphlets, Curle became both protégé and protector – a combination of sympathetic critic, bibliographer, collector, acolyte, entrepreneur, and friend.

Major Ernest DAWSON (1884–1960) was introduced to Conrad by W. H. Henley and H. G. Wells. He contributed reminiscences and stories of Burma and Australia to *Blackwood's Magazine*. He served in Burma as a magistrate and as an officer in the Rangoon Volunteer Rifles. A resident of Rye, after his retirement he spent long periods on the Continent. His brother A. J. Dawson was another of Conrad's friends.

(Francis) Warrington DAWSON (1878–1962), resident in Paris and Versailles, came from a family of former plantation owners in Charleston, South Carolina. He wrote prolifically – fiction, essays, newspaper stories – and covered strikes, wars, peace conferences, the French Senate, and the Chamber of Deputies. To quote Randall, 'he had a special taste and talent for conversing with the great and near-great' (p. 4). In 1909, while on a safari in East Africa with Theodore Roosevelt, he met Conrad's old friends the Sandersons, and when Dawson came to England in May 1910 to report the funeral of Edward VII, he carried an introduction to Conrad.

Hugh Railton DENT (1874–1938) Dent's eldest son, spent his professional life in the family publishing house, J. M. Dent & Sons, joining it in 1909. He took over the running of the firm as his father entered his last years and became its head on 'The Chief's' death. Interested in classical music, 'Mr Hugh', as Conrad called him, also sang.

Established in 1888, J. M. DENT & SONS was largely a literary house, but in time expanded its list to include children's, educational, and self-help books, as well as textbooks and travel guides. Conrad's principal English publisher in his late career, the house brought out *'Twixt Land and Sea* (1912), *Within the Tides* (1915), *The Shadow-Line* (1917), *The Rescue* (1920), and *Notes on Life and Letters* (1921), as well as the posthumous *Suspense* (1925) and *Last Essays* (1926). Its Uniform Edition made Conrad's collected works accessible to a popular audience.

Joseph Mallaby DENT (1849–1926) was thirteen when apprenticed to a printer, and, shortly after, turned to bookbinding. In 1867, he moved to London, where he set up his own bookbinding shop, quickly winning a reputation for fine craftsmanship. He turned to publishing in 1888, achieving success by marketing popularly priced editions of the classics in, notably, the Temple Classics, Temple Shakespeare, and Everyman's Library series. Conrad and 'The Chief' were on cordial terms, but management through Pinker discouraged the kind of intimacy Conrad enjoyed with some of his earlier publishers.

Belgian-born French literary journalist and editor Fernand-Jacques-Paul DIVOIRE (1883–1951) was associated with the journals *L'Intransigeant* and *Le Temps*. Among his enthusiasms were music, dance, and the occult.

Born in Brooklyn, Frank Nelson DOUBLEDAY (1862–1934) began his publishing career at Charles Scribner's Sons in 1877. He allied himself with S. S. McClure from 1897 before going into partnership with Walter Hines Page. Between 1912 and 1914, initially at Alfred A. Knopf's urging, his interest in Conrad changed from casual to serious. The American publication of *Chance* was Conrad's first financial success, and for the rest of his life his association with Doubleday was cordial and rewarding. When Conrad visited the USA in 1923, he made Effendi Hill, Doubleday's home on Long Island, his head-quarters.

Poet, dramatist, and critic John DRINKWATER (1882–1937) was a founding member of the Pilgrim Players and later managed the Birmingham Repertory Theatre. His interest in mounting *One Day More* brought him into contact with Conrad, who professed to admire his poetry.

Charles ('Charley') Seddon Evans (1883–1944), an employee in the publishing house of William Heinemann, was involved in seeing the collected edition of Conrad's works through press. When Doubleday assumed the chairmanship of Heinemann's in 1922, Evans became one of the firm's managers.

(Herbert Barnard) John Everett (1876–1949), marine and landscape painter and engraver, studied at the Slade School of Art and was a friend of Augustus John and William Orpen, who lodged in his mother's house. Conrad, who came to know Everett's drawings through Will Rothenstein, was keenly interested in publishing an edition of *The Mirror of the Sea* illustrated with them, but the project fell through. Everett sold none of his marine work, bequeathing all of it to the National Maritime Museum. For an example of his work, see Plate 3.

Novelist and short-story writer Jean Fayard (1902–78) was the grandson of the very successful French publisher Arthème Fayard. His life at Oxford provided material for *Oxford et Margaret* (1924) and *Deux ans à Oxford* (1924). In 1931, his novel *Mal d'amour* was awarded the Prix Goncourt.

Reynold Hall Fitz-Herbert (1890 – c.1937), a New Zealander from the Hawkes Bay region of the North Island, was interested in maritime affairs and shipping. He contributed articles to the journal of the Hawkes Bay Navy League and composed an unpublished work entitled 'A Ship-Lover's History of New Zealand'. He also privately published a pamphlet on the Battle of Jutland.

In his novels and memoirs, Ford Madox Ford (1873–1939) created some of the best English fiction of the twentieth century. He was also a poet and an inspired editor. His collaborations with Conrad included *The Inheritors* (1901), *Romance* (1903), and 'The Nature of a Crime' (*English Review*, April–May 1909). Conrad and Ford quarrelled in 1909; by the end of 1911 a rapprochement had begun, hastened by Ford's admiring essay in the *English Review*, but the friendship never regained its earlier closeness. He changed his surname from Hueffer in 1919.

†George Gordon Frisbee (1874–1949) lived in San Francisco.

Ada Nemesis Galsworthy (born Ada Pearson, 1864–1956) was adopted by Ernest Cooper, a Norwich doctor. As a teenager she studied the piano in Dresden; later, she composed songs. Conrad wrote a preface for her translations from Maupassant, *Yvette and Other Stories* (1904). Although involved with John Galsworthy, she had been unhappily married to his cousin Arthur until 1904, when the death of John, Senior, eased the threat of family sanctions and she and John Galsworthy were able to marry.

John GALSWORTHY (1867–1933) met Conrad in the *Torrens* in 1893. His early writing was tentative, but in 1932 he won a Nobel Prize (an honour denied his friend) for his fiction and plays. Like his fictional Forsytes, his family was well supplied with money, and he helped Conrad with many gifts and loans during the earlier period of his career, providing constant encouragement throughout it.

An Aberdonian, Theodore James Gordon GARDINER (1874–1937), though troubled by ill health, had been a civil servant in South Africa, a tea planter in Ceylon, and a student at Harvard. After the war, in which he was involved in spy-hunting and the surveillance of enemy aliens, he worked as an arbitrator of industrial disputes and as Secretary to the National Club, London. His posthumous *Notes of a Prison Visitor* (1938) records some of his experiences of befriending convicts; he also published novels, and at his death was at work on a study of Napoleon. Conrad's friendship began during visits to Scotland in 1916 and strengthened over the years.

The son of Constance and Edward, David ('Bunny') GARNETT (1892–1981), the author of *Lady into Fox* (1923) and many other novels, was also a bookseller. Married to Virginia Woolf's niece, Angelica Bell, he moved in Bloomsbury circles in the 1920s and 1930s. His *Great Friends: Portraits of Seventeen Writers* (1979) recalls the era of his father's friendship with Conrad.

Edward William GARNETT (1868–1937), a publisher's reader and critic, was the husband of Constance, the translator. He lived some (and Constance all) of the time at The Cearne, a meeting-place for writers, artists, anarchists, socialists, and Russian refugees. Garnett's encouragement of Conrad in the 1890s and beyond was typical of his generous and painstaking attention to writers new and old, among them Edward Thomas, Robert Frost, D. H. Lawrence, and Dorothy Richardson. Although Conrad disapproved of his pacifism and Russophilia, Garnett remained a close and loyal friend.

Robert Singleton GARNETT (1866–1932), Edward's elder brother, was a senior partner in the law firm of Darley, Cumberland. During Conrad's breach with Pinker in 1910, he handled the writer's literary, as well as legal, interests, as he had done for Ford Madox Ford and D. H. Lawrence. A keen book collector, he was an authority on Alexandre Dumas *père*.

Of all the literary friends of Conrad's later years, André-Paul-Guillaume GIDE (1869–1951) was the most distinguished and most artistically remarkable. A born-again pagan and a recidivist puritan, his strengths lay in intimate autobiography and ironic fiction. Among his works are *Les Nourritures terrestres* (1897), *L'Immoraliste* (1902), *La Porte étroite* (1909), *Les Caves du Vatican* (1914), and *Les Faux-monnayeurs* (1926). He first met Conrad in July 1911, translated *Typhoon*, directed the other translations of his work into French, and dedicated *Voyage au Congo* (1928) to his memory.

Harold GOODBURN (1891–1966), a school master in chemistry and biology from Liverpool, taught in Dorset, Argentina, and Brazil before taking up a post at the King's School, Canterbury, where he taught from 1919 to 1945. He then taught in the Midlands before retiring in Canterbury. He is recalled as the eccentric 'Captain Burnwell' in David Moreau's *More Wrestling than Dancing: An Autobiography* (1990). He tutored John Conrad in mathematics on a private basis.

Admiral William Edmund GOODENOUGH (1867–1945; knighted 1919), who began his career as a naval cadet in 1880, moved up through the ranks during service in North America, the West Indies, the Mediterranean, and South China waters. He became Captain of the naval training college at Dartmouth in 1905, but soon returned to active service. He served in the war, and in 1920 became Commander-in-Chief of the Africa station. In retirement he was President of the Royal Geographical Society (1930–3) and Chairman of the British Sailors' Society.

(Henry) Gontran (Redman) GOULDEN (1884–1970) went into partnership with his father Henry Goulden, Canterbury bookseller and stationer, in 1908. Goulden dealt with Conrad as a customer interested in antiquarian books on Kent and arranged for the private printing of some of his pamphlets and of the dramatic version of *The Secret Agent*. As a member of the Friends of Canterbury Cathedral, which commissioned plays for performance in the Chapter House, he was involved in the annual festival, and in 1935 saw into print the acting edition of T. S. Eliot's *Murder in the Cathedral*.

H. J. GOULDEN, LTD of 40, High Street, Canterbury, booksellers and stationers, continued a family business begun in 1840. Its early history, in addition to printing and bookbinding, involved proprietorship of various newspapers in Kent, including the *Kentish Gazette* (until 1905). Conrad dealt with the firm for the private printing of a few of his works, and it apparently also supplied his stationery.

Robert Bontine Cunninghame GRAHAM (1852–1936) began a lasting friendship with Conrad in 1897, the result of a letter praising 'An Outpost of Progress'. A socialist and (according to some scholars) rightful King of Scotland, Graham worked and travelled widely in the Americas. He drew on his experiences in many volumes of tales, sketches, and essays and also in his unorthodox histories of the Spanish conquest. From 1885 to 1892 he represented North-West Lanarkshire in Parliament; he spent four-and-a-half weeks in gaol for his part in the Bloody Sunday demonstration of 1887.

HAMMOND CLARK & DAMAN, of 11 Great St. Helens, Bishopsgate, was a partnership of London lawyers: Frederick Hammond Clark (1846–1921), a barrister and former colonial administrator, and Gerard William Daman, admitted as a solicitor in 1919.

Alfred Charles William HARMSWORTH: *see* VISCOUNT NORTHCLIFFE

A. P. HATTON edited the *British Legion*, the Legion's weekly magazine, from July to October 1921. Founded in June 1921 by an amalgamation of four veterans' organisations, the Legion campaigned for the welfare of ex-servicemen and women, lobbying for housing, jobs, medical care, equitable pension rights, and seeking to avoid another war.

William Henry HEINEMANN (1863–1920) established his well-known publishing firm in 1890, entering into partnership with S. S. Pawling in 1893. Particularly noted for its fiction list, the firm, in addition to bringing out early works by Conrad and, later, the collected edition, published Stephen Crane, H. G. Wells, Robert Louis Stevenson, and Rudyard Kipling.

Max John HERZBERG (1886–1958), an American secondary school teacher and anthologist, championed Crane's work as president of the Stephen Crane Association. His efforts to have a tablet erected to mark Crane's birthplace in Newark, New Jersey, received Conrad's support.

John Edmund HODGSON (1875–1952) was the director of the long-established London auction house Hodgson & Co., a firm dealing in literary manuscripts and fine books; he was also a historian of British aviation and aeronautics.

Before moving to Sussex in 1913, Michael James HOLLAND (1870–1956) had been a neighbour of the Conrads, at Smeeth Hill, near Aldington. In his earlier years he had lived adventurously in South Africa and British Columbia; he recollected his experiences in *Verse* (1937). He was also an avid book-collector.

Lawrence Durning HOLT (1882–1961), junior partner of the Liverpool family firm the Ocean Steam Ship Company, solicited Conrad's advice about setting up a Liverpool-based training-ship. The scheme was not realised, its only fruit being 'Memorandum on the Scheme for Fitting Out a Sailing Ship', published in *Last Essays*.

Conrad HOPE (1890–1963), named in honour of Conrad, was the youngest of the four children of G. F. W. Hope, Conrad's first friend in England. A motor engineer, he was the director of Candor Motors in Colchester.

A publisher, William Thomas Hildrup HOWE (1874–1939) headed the American Book Company of Cincinnati. He was also a noted collector of Americana, and early American glass, and eventually amassed one of the most distinguished rare book and manuscript collections in the USA. On his death, it was purchased by Albert A. Berg, from whom it eventually passed to the New York Public Library. He commissioned Theodore Spicer-Simson's medallion of Conrad.

Elizabeth ('Elsie') HUEFFER (née Martindale, 1876–1949) married Ford Madox Ford in 1894. Her translations of Maupassant appeared in 1903, and she published fiction as Elizabeth Martindale. After the quarrels of 1909, the Conrads kept their distance from her. She was separated from Ford but refused to give him a divorce. In 1920, Conrad firmly rebuffed her attempt to re-establish contact with him and his wife.

Ford Madox HUEFFER: see FORD

Editor, literary journalist, and bibliophile (George Henry) Holbrook JACKSON (1874–1948) was particularly involved with *T. P.'s Weekly* (where *Nostromo* first appeared) and edited *To-day*. As well as verse and essays, he wrote studies of the 1890s, of Edward Fitzgerald, and Bernard Shaw, and published a biography of William Morris.

Virginia-born Meredith JANVIER (1872–1936), after graduating in law from the University of Maryland, practised in a Baltimore firm for thirteen years, whereupon he abandoned law to become a photographer. He was also an amateur strongman. Some twenty years later he again changed professions, becoming a manuscript and rare-book dealer. A contributor to the *Baltimore Evening Sun*, he published two collections of essays, *Baltimore in the Eighties and Nineties* (1933) and the posthumous *Baltimore Yesterdays* (1937), the latter with a preface by his friend H. L. Mencken.

G. JEAN-AUBRY: see AUBRY, Jean-Frédéric-Émile.

F(ryniwyd) Tennyson JESSE (née Wynifried Margaret Jesse, 1889–1955), a prolific writer, was fascinated by criminal trials, whose transcripts she edited for publication. Her best-known novels are *The Lacquer Lady* (1929), set in nineteenth-century Burma, and *A Pin to See the Peepshow* (1934), a fictional rendering of the trial and execution of Edith Thompson and her lover Frederick Bywaters for the fatal stabbing of Mr Thompson in October 1922. The thoughts of the condemned woman, whom Jesse treats with considerable sympathy, echo Winnie Verloc's after she has knifed Adolf. A dramatist in her own right, Jesse collaborated with her husband, Harold Marsh Harwood, on a number of plays produced during the war and in the 1920s.

After a brief career in business Henry ('Harry') Arthur JONES (1851–1929) became a popular and prolific playwright whose work was regularly performed on the late-Victorian and Edwardian stage as well as in America. The author of music-hall sketches and a theatrical manager, he wrote *Patriotism and Popular Education* (1919) and engaged in lively controversies with Bernard Shaw and H. G. Wells.

Jenny Doris (or Dora) Arthur JONES: see THORNE

A leading British orthopaedic surgeon, Sir Robert Armstrong JONES (1858–1933; knighted 1917; baronet 1926) came from North Wales, and practised in Liverpool, where he was consulting surgeon to all the major hospitals. He was also a consultant at St Thomas's Hospital, and a member of the War Office's Medical Advisory Board. During the war, he held the rank of Major-General and took on the immense task of organising reconstructive surgery at home and in the field. From 1921 to 1924, he served as President of the British Orthopaedic Association, and was frequently honoured overseas. His monographs and textbooks on the surgery of joints, military orthopaedics, and general orthopaedics were widely used. The professional relationship that began, in 1917, with the care of Jessie Conrad developed into a warm friendship with the Conrads.

New-York-born George Thomas KEATING (1892–1976) amassed a rich collection of Conradiana from various sales as well as from Thomas J. Wise. He donated his collection, catalogued in *A Conrad Memorial Library: The Collection of George T. Keating* (1929), to Yale University in 1938. Keating worked his way up from errand-boy to the head of Moore and Munger, a New York firm dealing in paper and clay products, eventually retiring to California. He also collected operatic recordings and music manuscripts, the American author James Branch Cabell, and materials about the Spanish conquest of the New World.

A portraitist, landscape painter, and goldsmith, Alice Sarah KINKEAD (1871–1926) was born in Tuam, County Galway. She studied painting in Dublin, Paris, and London in the 1890s, and exhibitions of her work were held in Ireland and Scotland as well as in London, Liverpool, and Paris beginning in 1897. She met the Conrads during their Corsican sojourn, and painted portraits of both of them. Conrad provided a foreword to the exhibition catalogue of her Corsican and Irish landscape paintings held at the United Arts Gallery, London, in late 1921.

The precise identity of Dr A. KNAUR is unknown. There is no doctor of this name in the British medical registers; he may well have been a scientist, have lived on the Continent, or both.

While still an undergraduate Alfred Abraham KNOPF (1892–1984) had corresponded with the Galsworthys and visited them in Devon. On graduating from Columbia University in 1912, he went to work at Doubleday, Page, where he was responsible for orchestrating the highly successful publicity campaign for *Chance*. In 1915, he began his own firm. With his wife, Blanche Wolf Knopf, he built up an extraordinary list that included, over the years, Wallace Stevens, Willa Cather, Dashiel Hammett, Langston Hughes, Thomas Mann, Jean-Paul Sartre, Simone de Beauvoir, Albert Camus, Yukio Mishima, Yasunari Kawabata, Doris Lessing, and Toni Morrison. He remained with the firm when Random House acquired it in 1960.

Popularly known as 'Lawrence of Arabia', Thomas Edward LAWRENCE (né Shaw, 1888–1935) read History at Oxford, writing his thesis on Crusader castles. From 1910 to 1914 he worked on archaeological digs in the Euphrates Valley. During the First World War, he fought alongside Arabs in revolt against Turkish rule and co-ordinated their efforts with those of the British army and navy. Reports by the American journalist Lowell Thomas of Lawrence's role in the sabotage of the Hedjaz railway, the capture of Akaba after a bold desert traverse, and the advance on Damascus made him a celebrity in the English-speaking world. He admired Conrad's work. At the time of his visit to Oswalds in July 1920, Lawrence was reconstructing *The Seven Pillars of Wisdom* (1926) from his recollection of a draft stolen from him the previous year. Lawrence continued to support Arab hopes after the war and was bitterly disappointed by the Allies' reluctance to foster national independence beyond the boundaries of Europe.

Charles LEUDESDORF (1853–1924), a mathematician, was the Registrar of Oxford University to whom Conrad wrote to decline the University's offer of an honorary degree.

John Livingston LOWES (1867–1945), educated at Harvard, Oxford, and in Germany, taught at various American universities before becoming Professor of English at Harvard where he taught from 1918 to 1939. A specialist in poetry, he was particularly interested in Chaucer and the Romantics, his best-known book being *The Road to Xanadu* (1927), a study of the sources of Coleridge's *The Rime of the Ancient Mariner*.

Edward Verrall LUCAS (1868–1938), an essayist, journalist, critic, and biographer of Conrad's friends the Colvins, worked for various publishers, including Methuen, as a reader and editor. He probably met Conrad through their mutual friend Edward Garnett when Garnett was attempting to establish his find on the literary scene.

Robert Dunbar MACKINTOSH (1865–1934) practised as a physician in Barnes, south-west London. From 1909 to 1921, when the friendship ended in a falling out because of the collapse of Mackintosh's Surrey Scientific Apparatus Company in which he had invested, Conrad valued the companionship and advice of this Scottish doctor, an amateur playwright and inventor described by his grand-niece Janet Jellard as 'an unpractical enthusiast and dreamer'.

Charles Edwin MARKHAM (1852–1940), formerly shepherd, cowboy, blacksmith, and teacher, became an instant celebrity when the *San Francisco Examiner* published 'The Man with the Hoe', a poem inspired by Millet, in 1898. Markham produced five volumes of poetry, anthologies, books about California, and *Children in Bondage* (1914), a polemic against child labour.

A career civil servant, Tadeusz MARYNOWSKI (1892–1949) served as Polish consul in Milan from 1919 to 1923. He later held consular posts in Buffalo and

Prague and was consul-general in New York from 1947 to 1949, returning to Warsaw shortly before his death.

(James) Redfern MASON (died 1941) was music critic for the *San Francisco Examiner* for many years. In that role, he became an advocate for new music, especially Schoenberg's. Another passion was politics: he wrote *Rebel Ireland* (1923) and once ran for mayor on the United Labor ticket. His wife, Grace Sartwell Mason, wrote fiction and travelled to Europe as special correspondent for the *Ladies Home Journal*.

Robert B. MATIER, born in Ireland in 1885, had settled in the USA.

Rodolphe-Louis MÉGROZ (1891–1968), English literary journalist of French and East Anglian ancestry, was an anthologist (especially of poetry), essayist, and biographer. He published *A Talk with Joseph Conrad* (1926) and *Joseph Conrad's Mind and Method* (1931).

Mary St Lawrence, Lady MILLAIS (née Hope-Vere of the Marquesses of Linlithgow, 1861–1948; widowed 1897), a Scotswoman, lived in Ashford with her son Sir John Everett Millais (the painter's grandson), Conrad's sometime chess partner. She was a close friend of Jessie Conrad. In her later years, she served as a Justice of the Peace.

†Mr MILLER evidently worked for the Russian Relief Fund, a British charity set up late in 1921 in response to the Russian famine.

A Parisian physician, Philippe NEEL (1882–1941) had a keen interest in contemporary English writing and in addition to Conrad translated Thomas Hardy and Henry James. His Conrad translations, commissioned by André Gide, included *Lord Jim*, *Nostromo*, *Under Western Eyes*, and *Victory* (the latter with Isabelle Rivière). Conrad professed himself well content with the quality of Neel's work.

The original press lord, Irish-born Alfred Charles William Harmsworth (1865–1922) became a Baron in 1905 and Viscount NORTHCLIFFE in 1918. After preparing for life as a teenage reporter and copy-boy, he started the popular *Answers to Correspondents* in 1888. With his younger brother Harold (later Lord Rothermere) he went on to buy the London *Evening News* in 1894, gave the world the first halfpenny morning paper, the *Daily Mail*, in 1896, and founded the *Daily Mirror* in 1903. The Harmsworths used the latest publishing techniques to cater to a rapidly expanding readership eager for simple, vivid writing and aggressively presented opinion. In 1908, they acquired a controlling interest in *The Times*. There and in his popular newspapers, Northcliffe promoted his often alarmist political ideas. During the war, his strident criticisms of Kitchener and of Asquith's Liberal and Coalition governments were variously heard as patriotic or self-seeking, malicious or urgently necessary.

American journalist and travel writer Frederick o'BRIEN (1869–1932) covered the Russo-Japanese War for the *New York Herald*. His later adventures in the Pacific led to *White Shadows in the South Seas* (1919), a best-seller about the Marquesas, and *Mystic Isles of the South Seas* (1921) about Tahiti, where he met Gauguin.

Glasgow-born journalist William Mathie PARKER (1891–1973) published many books on Scottish literature and contributed frequently to the *Fortnightly Review*, *Glasgow Herald*, and *John O'London's*. Responsible for running the *Tuscania*'s 'High Seas Bookshop', he was in contact with Conrad on his 1923 journey to America and published a reminiscence of the voyage in *Blue Peter*.

Wilfred George PARTINGTON (1888–1955) worked in London and Birmingham before joining the *Bombay Gazette* in 1912. After serving in the war, he edited the *Bookman's Journal and Print Collector* until 1931. His books include an anthology in praise of tobacco (1924), works on Sir Walter Scott, and, with Hugh Walpole, *Famous Stories of Five Centuries* (1934). A book collector and bibliographer, he was instrumental in documenting and exposing Thomas J. Wise's forgery of literary rarities. He issued a privately printed edition of Conrad's *Laughing Anne* in 1923.

Sydney Southgate PAWLING (1862–1922), Heinemann's partner and an admirer and promoter of Conrad during the early years of Conrad's career; though in declining health, he oversaw the preparations for the Heinemann collected edition in 1921–2.

Eric Seabrooke PINKER (1891–1973) went to work for his father after leaving Westminster School. During the war, he won the Military Cross for bravery under fire. When J. B. Pinker died in 1922, he became the firm's senior partner and thus Conrad's principal agent, taking over the marketing of his work. He later moved to New York, and in 1939 earned $2\frac{1}{2}$–5 years in Sing Sing for appropriating \$37,000 from his client E. Phillips Oppenheim.

London-born, James Brand PINKER (1863–1922) was one of the first literary agents in Britain. Over the years his clients included Ford Madox Ford, Henry James, Stephen Crane, H. G. Wells, Arnold Bennett, and D. H. Lawrence. He began acting for Conrad in 1900 and helped him through many financial crises, but a serious quarrel in 1910 suspended their relationship for several months and strained it for many more. By the time Conrad had finished *Chance*, however, they were closer than ever before. They visited one another's homes and took holidays together, including the visit to Corsica in 1921. In autumn 1920, they collaborated on *Gaspar the Strong Man*, a film scenario of Conrad's story 'Gaspar Ruiz'.

Mary Elizabeth PINKER (née Seabrooke, 1862–1945), acquainted with Conrad through her husband, was Conrad's hostess on his occasional visits to the Pinkers' Essex and Surrey homes.

Marguerite PORADOWSKA (née Gachet, 1848–1937) was the widow of Conrad's distant cousin, and thus his 'Aunt' – but also his good friend in the 1890s and the first novelist of his acquaintance. She lived in France and Belgium; her novels of French, Belgian, and Polish life were well known in their day. Often serialised in the prestigious *Revue des Deux Mondes* before book publication, they include *Yaga* (1887), *Demoiselle Micia* (1888–9), and *Marylka* (1895).

After Balliol College, Oxford, and military training in St Petersburg, Count Józef Alfred POTOCKI (1895–1968) served during the war as an officer in the Russian and Polish armies. Secretary of the Polish Legation in London during 1919–22, he later became Director of the Anglo-American section and member of the Political Department of the Ministry of External Affairs in Warsaw. After the Second World War he was *chargé d'affaires* in Lisbon and Madrid. He was the grandson of the man who served as the model for Conrad's Prince Roman.

The son of Irish immigrants, John QUINN (1870–1924) came from Ohio. As a New York lawyer, he had a highly lucrative practice in commercial and financial law, particularly the law of tariffs. As a supporter of the arts, he won an exemption for artists from sales taxes and built up a great collection of modern painting and sculpture. He also amassed modern literary manuscripts, and among the writers he collected on a large scale were Yeats, Pound, Eliot, Joyce, and Conrad. When Quinn auctioned off his Conradiana in 1923, after relations between patron and author had chilled, the collection, bought for a total of $10,000, fetched $110,000.

Richard Lodowick Edward Montagu REES (1900–70; 2nd Baronet, 1922), writer and painter, edited the *Adelphi* from 1930 to 1936, wrote books on George Orwell (1961) and Simone Weil (1966), translated Weil's notebooks and essays, and edited a selection of J. Middleton Murry's writings (1960).

REGISTRAR OF OXFORD UNIVERSITY: see LEUDESDORF

Otolia ('Tola') RETINGER (née Zubrzycka, 1889–1984) and her husband the political activist Józef Retinger became friendly with Conrad in 1912 and accompanied the Conrads on their trip to Poland in the summer of 1914. After the breakdown of her marriage, she returned to Cracow, and after the First World War worked briefly in restoring goods to the dispossessed. She then taught French, English, and German privately and for a time at a lycée. With Olga Małkowska, she was active in the Polish scouting movement.

Agnes Mary Warner RIDGEWAY (née Sanderson, 1875–1936) was Ted Sanderson's second-oldest sister. The affectionate enmity between Conrad and 'Miss Agnes' began around 1894, the time of his first visit to the boisterous household at Elstree. In 1908, she married the Revd Neville Vibart Ridgeway, and helped to make Ferox Hall at Tonbridge School an especially successful house for many boys, including Conrad's son John.

Having graduated from Oxford, the Revd Neville Vibart RIDGEWAY (1883–1973) was ordained in 1905. He taught briefly at Elstree and then, from 1906 to 1940, at Tonbridge School, save for an absence during 1917–19 when he was a chaplain in France. During the 1940s, he was an assistant master at Merchant Taylors' School. He lectured at the University of Maryland in the 1960s and was attached to the diocese of Bermuda where he spent his last years.

(Edric) Cecil (Mornington) ROBERTS (1892–1976) was a best-selling novelist, acclaimed playwright, and cosmopolitan *bon vivant*. Among his books were *Pilgrim Cottage* (1933) and *Victoria Four Thirty* (1937). During the First World War, he was a correspondent with the Dover Patrol, the RAF, and the Allied armies in France while doubling as literary editor of the *Liverpool Post*. Between 1920 and 1925, he edited the *Nottingham Journal*. In 1922, he dedicated his play *A Tale of Young Lovers* to Conrad. Roberts's introduction to him came through Grace Willard.

As F. N. Doubleday's secretary, Lillian M. ROBINS, was occasionally in contact with Conrad about seeing his work through the press.

Stella Virginia RODERICK, a member of the editorial staff of the popular American periodicals *Everybody's Magazine* and *Metropolitan Magazine*, was herself the editor of sixteen issues of the *Women's Magazine*. In 1932, she became Secretary of the Nettie Fowler McCormick Biographical Association, and published a biography of that prominent Chicago businesswoman and philanthropist, widow of Cyrus McCormick, in 1956.

William ROTHENSTEIN (1872–1945; knighted 1931) was notable for his portrait graphics, paintings, and drawings. Max Beerbohm described him as a young phenomenon in 'Enoch Soames' (*Seven Men*): 'He wore spectacles that flashed more than any other pair ever seen. He was a wit. He was brimful of ideas . . . He knew everyone in Paris.'

The Hon. Bertrand Arthur William RUSSELL (1872–1970; 3rd Earl Russell, 1931) met Conrad through Lady Ottoline Morrell in 1913. A lecturer at Trinity College, Cambridge, he had written *Principles of Mathematics* (1903) and the three volumes of *Principia Mathematica* (with Alfred North Whitehead, 1910–13). He felt an intense admiration for Conrad and his work and named his son after him. His pacifism during the war resulted in the loss of his fellowship and a prison sentence; his willingness to take unpopular stands on moral and political questions persisted for the rest of his life. His later books included *The Analysis of Mind* (1921), *The ABC of Relativity* (1925), *Marriage and Morals* (1929), *A History of Western Philosophy* (1945), and his *Autobiography* (1967–9).

Rather than follow the family tradition of marketing port and sherry, Christopher ('Kit') SANDEMAN (1882–1951) became a journalist, lecturer, and author. Opera, politics, poetry, history, and botany all fascinated him, and he also wrote and translated plays. Between the wars he led several expeditions to Peru and Brazil, rafting on the headwaters of the Amazon and the Huallaga, and collecting orchids for British herbaria.

Edward Lancelot ('Ted') SANDERSON (1867–1939) travelled from Australia with John Galsworthy in the *Torrens* in 1893. On that voyage, Conrad, then serving as first mate, showed him a draft of *Almayer's Folly*. Sanderson, who had read Classics at King's College, Cambridge, taught at Elstree, his family's preparatory school in Hertfordshire. After service in the Boer War, he and his wife, Helen, remained in Africa, first in Johannesburg, then in Nairobi, where he served as town clerk. He returned to England in 1910 to become Elstree's headmaster.

Helen Mary SANDERSON (née Watson, 1874–1967), who married Ted in 1898, was a Scotswoman full of moral and intellectual vigour. As 'Janet Allardyce', she contributed sketches of East African life to *Scribner's Magazine*.

Prince Eustachy Kajetan Władisław SAPIEHA (Sapieha-Rożański, 1881–1963), Polish politician and diplomat, was Poland's first envoy to the United Kingdom.

Charles Kenneth SCOTT MONCRIEFF (1889–1930), authorised translator of Marcel Proust's *A la recherche du temps perdu* and of Luigi Pirandello, translated Stendhal as well as works from Latin, Old English, and Old French. An employee of *The Times*, he apparently came to know Conrad through Lord Northcliffe. Conrad contributed to his *Marcel Proust, An English Tribute* (1923).

Clement King SHORTER (1857–1926) edited the *Illustrated London News* from 1891, and the *Sketch* and the *English Illustrated Magazine* from 1893 to 1900. He gave up all three editorships to begin *Tatler* and the *Sphere*. His critical works include books on the Brontës. In 1898, as editor of the *Illustrated London News*, he had agreed to publish *The Rescue* as a serial, but Conrad could not meet the deadlines. A bibliophile, he published various Conrad works as privately printed pamphlets between 1917 and 1919, among them *One Day More*, 'The Tale', and some occasional essays.

After reading History at Oxford, Douglas Brooke Wheelton SLADEN (1856–1947) went on to hold the first chair of History at the University of Sydney. An avid traveller, he published a number of books on Australia, Japan, Italy, Egypt, and Persia. When living in London, he founded the After-Dinner Club, devoted to conversation, mainly with the objective of introducing new blood into literary society.

Daughter of the Bishop of Carlisle, Frances Elizabeth Wycliffe SPOONER (née Goodwin, *c*. 1853–1939) in 1878 married the Revd William Archibald Spooner, Warden of New College, Oxford, and originator of the 'spoonerism'. She raised their family of five children and was a notable hostess. In her later years she became interested in the rehabilitation of long-term hospital patients in Oxford.

On going down from Cambridge, John Collings SQUIRE (1884–1958; knighted 1933) went in for politics. His enthusiasms for sport and literature soon won out, however, and he became a 'Georgian' poet, essayist, anthologist, and occasional writings between December 1918 and January 1920. To the best of our knowledge, Wise did not fabricate anything Conradian, and, in an article for the *Bookman's Journal* (31 December 1920, p. 160), was good enough to warn collectors against fraudulent cancels in Conrad first editions.

(Mary Channing) 'Marina' WISTER (1899–1970), the eldest child of the American novelist Owen Wister and civic activist Mary Channing Wister, published three books of poems: *Helen and Others* (1924), *Night in the Valley* (1930), and *Fantasy and Fugue* (1937). Married to the New Mexico painter Andrew Dasburg in 1933, she settled in Taos, and in addition to writing poetry and music was involved in asserting the rights of native people. She separated from her husband in 1947, returning to Bryn Mawr, Pennsylvania.

Aniela ZAGÓRSKA (1881–1943), a daughter of Conrad's maternal second cousin once removed Karol Zagórski (died 1898), received an allowance from Conrad. With her sister Karola, she held the Polish and Russian translation rights to Conrad's work. She herself translated *Almayer's Folly*, *Lord Jim*, and *The Mirror of the Sea* into Polish.

Karola ZAGÓRSKA (c. 1885–1955), Aniela's sister, stayed at Oswalds from late February to late August 1920. The visit cemented Conrad's affectionate and active interest in her well-being and resulted in his paying her a regular allowance. A professional singer, she sometimes lived in Italy, and later in the United States where she sang in opera.

(Jan) Tadeusz ŻUK-SKARSZEWSKI (1858–1933), a Polish neo-Romantic novelist, was an acquaintance of the Zagórska sisters. He resided for some time in England, where in 1897 he married Kate Hadley, who returned to Poland with him and worked as a translator.

EDITORIAL PROCEDURES

Hoping to balance the comfort of the reader against the requirements of the scholar, we have adopted the following conventions:

1. The texts stay faithful to Conrad's spelling, accentuation, and punctuation, but letters missing from within words are usually supplied in square brackets. Rather than use *sic*, we mark words that might be taken as misprints with an asterisk. If they appear in *Chambers English Dictionary* or the *OED*, unusual (but typically Conradian) spellings such as 'negociation' and 'inclose' are not marked. In general, we neither restore nor mark missing or misplaced apostrophes, nor do we star lower-case days of the week or adjectives of nationality, like 'russian' or 'american', which reflect the influence of French or Polish.

2. Where absolutely necessary to the sense, missing pronouns, articles, prepositions, and auxiliary verbs are also supplied in square brackets. When we expand abbreviated words, we remove the punctuation Conrad uses to mark the shortening; thus 'Hein:' becomes 'Hein[emann]', 'D'day' becomes 'D[ouble]day', 'B.' becomes 'B[orys]'. Contracted words not marked with a stop (e.g. 'D. P & Co' normally stay as they are. Gaps in the text, such as those caused by damage to the MS, appear thus: [. . .]. [?] marks a doubtful reading.

3. Again when sense dictates, full stops are tacitly provided and quotation marks completed; words apparently repeated by accident have been deleted. A list of these silent emendations can be found at the end of the volume. Typing errors in letters dictated by Conrad appear in a separate list; unless of particular interest, such errors in letters from correspondents are corrected without further ado.

4. Especially for pronouns such as 'You', Conrad used capitals more profusely than other English writers of his time. We preserve his usage, but distinguishing between upper and lower case must often be a matter of judgment rather than certainty. The same is true of locating paragraph breaks.

5. For the letters in French we observe the same conventions, but use square brackets and asterisks more sparingly. Conrad's erratic accentuation

we leave as it is, except in texts from *L.fr.*, where some presumed misprints or misreadings have been altered.

6. For the convenience of those who do not read the letters in sequence, information in footnotes may appear more than once.

7. American readers should note that Conrad used the British system of abbreviating dates; thus 3.6 would mean 3 June, not 6 March.

8. The Nonesuch rather than the less reliable Bobbs-Merrill edition of the letters to Garnett provides the copy-text when no manuscript is available. In the same circumstances, we use the American rather than the British edition of the letters to Curle because the former is less likely to censor names. Texts taken from J-A (for example, the letter to Sir Robert Jones of 5 March 1920) lack the signature.

9. This edition collects all available letters, but only the more interesting telegrams; references to some others appear in the notes.

10. The heading TS/MS denotes a typed letter in which passages other than the salutation or farewell are handwritten.

11. In the provenance headings in letters to Bruno Winawer and Aniela and Karola Zagórska, the description 'MS copy' or 'TS copy' indicates a transcription by them of Conrad's now lost original. Where letters to these persons were translated by them from Polish into French, the document's designation is followed by the qualifier 'in French'; in such cases, only an English translation is provided.

12. In the provenance headings, letters that have appeared only in microfilmed dissertations, as disjointed fragments in books or articles, or only in translation are described as unpublished. Letters appearing in a fuller but still incomplete form are described as published in part. In general, the provenance headings record a letter's first appearance in its original language and, where appropriate, its first appearance in English; we note republication only when an editor offers a better text or fresh information about an existing one.

The headings and watermarks of Oswalds stationery sometimes help to place undated letters. Two forms of the telegraphic address appear in the course of this volume:

Type one, to 24 May 1922:

CENTER: TELEGRAMS:–CONRAD, BISHOPSBOURNE

(For this letterhead in full, see *Letters*, 6, Plate 1.)

Type two, from 27 May 1922:

TELEGRAMS:–CONRAD, BRIDGE

For the duration of both letterheads, full sheets are watermarked CHARTA SCRIPTORUM over the image of a mediaeval scholar. With two exceptions, half-sheets folded as letterhead notepaper are watermarked ROYAL LAN-CASTER PARCHMENT over a rose. In November and December 1921, the notepaper bears the watermark ANTIENT SCOTTISH VELLUM, and in April 1922 Conrad used what appear to be printer's cast-offs for some of his notes to Eric Pinker. All three kinds of watermark are accompanied by the maker's name: J. S[traker]. & CO LTD. Conrad also used note-cards bearing the letterhead

OSWALDS,
BISHOPSBOURNE

1920

To Edward Garnett

Text MS Bryn Mawr; G. 292–3

[letterhead: Oswalds]
New Year's day.
1920.

Dearest Edward[1]

I won't mock yours and mine* philosophy by a parade of good wishes. This is the first letter I write in 1920 and we all here old and young send you our love.

I ought to have written you immediately after our return[2] here – instead of which I became immediately ill with a beastly complaint (not gout)[3] which prevented me sitting up at the table and made me generally unwilling to stir as much as my little finger if it were to save my life.

I am better to-day. As to Mrs Jessie she is going on well and strong; and I see the time when she will become ungovernable. But even that prospect is cheering in comparison to a bedridden future which hung over our heads for the last 3 or 4 years.

I've done nothing for the last six weeks and I feel that I'll never do anything any more. Somehow I don't feel so happy about it as I ought to – for what could be more soothing than a sense of impotence?

Give my affectionate New Years greetings to your wife and to David.[4] I wish more power to his right arm; for he, at any rate, may yet hope for one (at least) lucky shot against some Philistine[5] or other, in his life.

May you live long enough to see him whirl his sling! As to me I have no such expectation. I admit that I am not buried (or incinerated) yet but I have a strong feeling that I ought to be.

Ever yours

J. Conrad.

---

[1] Edward Garnett (1868–1937), a publisher's reader and critic, was the husband of Constance, the translator. He lived some (and Constance all) of the time at The Cearne, a meeting-place for writers, artists, anarchists, socialists, and Russian refugees. Garnett's encouragement of Conrad in the 1890s and beyond was typical of his generous and painstaking attention to writers new and old, among them Edward Thomas, Robert Frost, D. H. Lawrence, and Dorothy Richardson. Although Conrad disapproved of his pacifism and Russophilia, Garnett remained a loyal and often close friend.

[2] From Liverpool, where the Conrads spent much of December 1919 for an operation on Mrs Conrad.

[3] Inflammation of the prostate; see the letter to Pinker of 29 December 1919, *Letters*, 6, p. 545.

[4] Constance Garnett (née Black, 1862–1946), a distinguished translator of Russian fiction, and David (1892–1981), future author of *Lady into Fox* (1923) and many other novels.

[5] A sparkish pairing of Goliath, the Philistine giant whom David kills with a well-aimed stone (1 Samuel 17) with the modern Philistine, as characterised by Matthew Arnold, who has little or no love for artistry or learning.

To G. Jean-Aubry
Text MS Yale; *L.fr.* 150–1

[letterhead: Oswalds]
Jour de l'An
1920.

Très cher ami.[1]
Il faut me pardonner mon silence. En arrivant ici j'ai du me mettre au lit. Je viens de me lever juste a temps pour vous envoyer de la part de tout le monde New Years wishes of all health and prosperity.

L'affaire de Arrow of Gold est arrangée.[2] Vous pouvez marcher. Le titre de En Marge des Marées plaît a Gide. J'ai trouvé une lettre de lui[3] en arrivant ici.

Nous sommes encore sans domestiques – en camp volant. Il faudra cependant que Vous veniez bientôt. Je vais Vous envoyer un petit mot dans quelques jours.

Je n'ai pas travaillé encore, et je m'en sens incapable. Il faudra bien s'y mettre quand Mlle H[allowes][4] arrivera – lundi prochain. J'ai le trac.

Toujours le Votre affectueusement
J. Conrad

Translation

New Year's Day
1920.

My very dear friend.
You must forgive my silence. On arriving here I had to take to bed. I have just got up in time to send you New Year's wishes of all health and prosperity from everybody here.

---

[1] Jean-Frédéric-Émile Aubry (1882–1950), French music critic and writer on literature, wrote under the names G. Jean-Aubry and Gérard Jean-Aubry. An admirer and close friend of Conrad during Conrad's later years, he became a one-man Conrad industry, promoting the writer's reputation in France, translating a number of his works, producing the first biography, and compiling the first edition of his letters. Among his other friends were many composers, including Debussy and Ravel; both Manuel de Falla and Roussel wrote settings of his poems. From 1919 to 1930, he lived in London, editing the *Chesterian*, a magazine published by a firm of musical instrument makers.

[2] Jean-Aubry was interested in translating the novel, already assigned; bowing to Conrad's wishes, Gide reassigned it to him (see *Letters*, 6, pp. 517, 535–6, and Stape and Knowles, pp. 145–9).

[3] Now lost; that of 21 November 1919 (Stape and Knowles, pp. 148–9) leaves the issue unresolved.

[4] Lilian Mary Hallowes (1870–1950), Conrad's secretary, who, hired in 1904 for a month, remained his 'typewriter', with interruptions, for the rest of his career.

The *Arrow of Gold* business is settled. You can go ahead. Gide is pleased with the title *En Marge des Marées*. I found a letter from him on returning here.

We are still without servants – camping. Nevertheless, you must come soon. I will drop you a line in a few days.

I still haven't done any work and feel unable to do any. I shall certainly have to get down to some when Miss H. arrives – next Monday. I'm nervous.

Always affectionately yours

J. Conrad

To Captain David Bone

Text MS Sprott; Knowles

[letterhead: Oswalds]
4.1.20

My dear Cap[t] Bone.[1]

I was laid up directly on arriving here, and this is the explanation of the delay in thanking You for the precious copy of the book.[2] Pray convey to your brother[3] my great appreciation of his signature on the fly leaf.

I am an old admirer of his art – of his great vision of the soul of things.

Between you, you have produced the very thing in the way of a memorial of the men and Ships of *the* Service. I can't tell you how glad I am that Fate has provided the right men for that work.

May all luck and every prosperity attend you and all yours this year and in the years to come. I hope that some day we shall meet again – perhaps on the deck of your new ship.[4]

I shall have a copy of my next book bound specially for you and send it to Your Glasgow address.

With most friendly regards believe me always yours

Joseph Conrad

[1] Captain David William Bone (1874–1959; knighted 1946), a seaman-writer, corresponded with Conrad in 1910, though only met him in December 1919 during the Conrads' stay in Liverpool. Conrad at first disliked his novel *The Brassbounder* (1910) intensely, but his attitude eventually softened. When Conrad sailed in her to America in 1923, David Bone was captain of the *Tuscania*. Conrad also knew his brothers, Muirhead, the artist, and James, the newspaper editor.

[2] *Merchantmen-at-Arms: The British Merchant Service in the War*, published in November 1919.

[3] Muirhead Bone (1876–1953; knighted 1937) had provided drawings for the book.

[4] They had both spoken at a University Club dinner in Liverpool in December 1919 to honour the Merchant Service. Bone had recently taken command of the *Tuscania*, in which Conrad sailed to America in 1923.

PS The wretches who undid the parcel lost the wrapper with the address of you[r] Glasgow home. So I send this to your publishers.[1]

To Richard Curle
Text Curle 56

Oswalds
Bishopsbourne,
Kent.
Tuesday [6 January 1920][2]

Dearest Dick,[3]

Ever so many thanks for your letter of yesterday inclosing the list of papers for the misce[llane]ous volume.[4] It seems to me absolutely complete. I don't think there can be a scrap of my writing hiding anywhere.[5] There is nothing I can remember, at any rate.

The questions you raise require a little thinking over; I want to consult you about my ideas on that matter. I will write to you soon, very soon, asking you to run down here. Just now the conditions are unspeakable – rather. I have been unable to work or even to think. I was plunged in gloom and obsessed by dismal forebodings.

It is true I wrote two prefaces in my life, one for Ada Gals[worthy] the other for Edward Garnett's book.[6] But they were not concerned with their work. In one I speak of Maupassant *only* – in the other of Turgeniev, almost exclusively. But writing for your book[7] would have been another matter altogether. It would have had to be a direct personal appreciation. You see the difference? The facts of our case: – you the author of the only serious Study of J. C. (a book well known and generally acknowledged);[8] the actual

---

[1] Chatto & Windus.
[2] Curle's letter to Conrad of the 4th (Stape and Knowles, pp. 150–1) fixes the date.
[3] A journalist and writer, Richard Henry Parnell Curle (1883–1968) was Scots by birth but English by residence and education. He left Wellington College in 1901, and began working in publishing in London in 1905. His passion for travel appears in such books as *Into the East: Notes on Burma and Malaya* (1923) and *Caravansary and Conversation* (1937); his psychological curiosity in *Women: An Analytical Study* (1947). His first book was *Aspects of George Meredith* (1908), and he published many studies of other writers, including Robert Browning, W. H. Hudson, Thomas Hardy, and Dostoevsky. In his relations with Conrad, about whom he wrote three books and many articles and pamphlets, Curle became both protégé and protector – a combination of sympathetic critic, bibliographer, collector, acolyte, entrepreneur, and friend.
[4] *Notes on Life and Letters.*
[5] Conrad's essay on Galsworthy had been missed out (see the letter of 8 June 1921).
[6] For *Yvette and Other Stories* (1904) and *Turgenev: A Study* (1917).
[7] *Wanderings: A Book of Travel and Reminiscence*, to appear in March.
[8] *Joseph Conrad: A Study* (1914).

dedication[1] staring people in the face – would have thrown a complexion of complimentary futility upon the most sincere expression of literary opinion and personal regard.

All this may be controverted, no doubt, – but I shrank from the risk, both for your sake and mine. It did not seem to me worth the occasion. On general grounds a laudatory preface is not a good thing. The critics react instinctively. No, I don't think it would be good for the book. Honestly I don't. It looks as if the author had not enough faith in himself. And in this instance there is a disadvantage that in a book of that sort (travel) there is no question of sheer art involved which could be taken up and treated in a preface abstractedly. It must be either personal backing up – or nothing. A most difficult thing to do and moreover extremely liable to defeat its own ends. It occurs to me, however, that the dedication might be cancelled and, in that case, I would – if you really want it – try to write you a letter which you could print. I would try – and that's all I can say. And even then I fear you would have to wait for it. My dear, I am unable just now to write prefaces for my own stuff! They are clamouring for them in U.S. I can't even tackle the text of the *Resc.*[2] My mental state is awful.

Ever yours,

J. Conrad.

To J. B. Pinker
Text MS Berg; Unpublished

[letterhead: Oswalds]
Mond. 13[12].1.20[3]

Dearest Pinker.[4]

This is the week of your visit – is it not?

Please drop Jessie a timely warning.

I've been laid up. Serious. I mean the situation is – or is growing so, at least.

---

[1] 'To Joseph Conrad whose genius and friendship have given me many of my happiest hours, I inscribe this book, which his unfailing interest and sympathy have encouraged me to write.'
[2] Serialisation of *The Rescue* in *Land and Water* was to begin on 30 January. Revision for book publication was next on Conrad's agenda.
[3] Conrad was more likely to confuse the date than the day.
[4] James Brand Pinker (1863–1922), a Londoner, was one of the first literary agents in Britain. Over the years his clients included Ford Madox Ford, Henry James, Stephen Crane, H. G. Wells, Arnold Bennett, and D. H. Lawrence. He began acting for Conrad in 1900 and helped him through many financial crises, but a serious quarrel in 1910 suspended their relationship for several months and strained it for many more. By the time Conrad had finished *Chance*, however, they were closer than ever before. They visited one another's homes and took holidays together, including the visit to Corsica in 1921. In autumn 1920, they collaborated on *Gaspar the Strong Man*, a film scenario of Conrad's story 'Gaspar Ruiz'.

I expect the best results from your visit. But even if you came with the worst intentions You couldn't do much in the way of flattening me out more than I am already.

The Lond Mercury thought fit to send me a fee of £10 for the Crane.[1] I've paid it to my acct so please debit me with the pound which belongs to you there.

Ever Yours

J. Conrad.

To J. B. Pinker
Text MS Berg; Unpublished

[letterhead: Oswalds]
Thursday. [15 January? 1920][2]

My dear Pinker.

Please settle this bill which I couldn't find this morning to give you. And may I ask for the six £1 notes as usual, by post.

I went for a little drive this afternoon after working all the forenoon at *R[escue]* to some good purpose.

Ever Yours

J. Conrad.

To Grace Willard
Text MS Colgate; Unpublished

[Oswalds]
[mid-January 1920][3]

Dear Mama Grace.[4]

Herewith the £100. You have such a clear conception of the scheme that I'll say nothing more about that. *Aubusson*[5] is the thing and as to colour in general we will tend towards amber or even frank yellow as much as possible.

N'est-ce pas?

Ever Yours

Joseph

---

[1] 'Stephen Crane: A Note without Dates' had appeared in the inaugural issue of the *London Mercury*, December 1919.

[2] The allusion to Pinker's presence at Oswalds (see the previous letter) and a quickened tempo of work on *The Rescue*, mentioned on the 19th and 20th, suggest the date. Requests for the servant's wages on the month's remaining Thursdays disallow those dates.

[3] The letter to Pinker of the 19th suggests this dating.

[4] Grace Robinson Willard (née Cameron, 1877–1933; Mrs James Struthers Willard) was born in Illinois. She had done some book-reviewing and journalism, but during her long residence in London mainly applied her talents to interior design. A visitor to the Conrads, she helped to decorate and furnish Oswalds. She reviewed *Last Essays*, *Tales of Hearsay*, and Jessie Conrad's *Joseph Conrad as I Knew Him* for the *New York Evening Post*.

[5] A flat-woven carpet, named after the French town of its manufacture.

To Richard Curle

Text TS Indiana; Curle 57

[letterhead: Oswalds]
Jan. 19th. 1920.

Dearest Richard

I am too slack and languid to sit up to the table and write with pen and ink. I am not too feeble to talk however and if you feel at all disposed perhaps you would run down on Wednesday to lunch and sleep.

I can't ask you for a few days because I am now engaged in correcting the text of *The Rescue* which I promised the publishers in England and America would be ready end of Jan.[y] As I have done nothing to it till the last three days Miss H[allowes] and I are slaving at it all the morning and often in the afternoon in order to get through, somewhere near the promised date.

It would do me good to see you, morally and intellectually and I hope you won't mind coming for such a short time. We will have a good long talk. Pray drop us a line by return. Jessie's love.

Ever Yours

J Conrad.

To G. Jean-Aubry

Text TS Yale; Unpublished

[letterhead: Oswalds]
Jan. 19th. 1920.

Très cher.

I won't wait till I am fit to sit up and write in order to explain to you why we passed through London[1] without letting you know. Jessie was thoroughly overcome with fatigue and stayed in bed with her eyes shut through the one day we spent at the hotel. I was not feeling well already then but my intention was to take Jessie home and then return to London the same week to see you, one or two other persons, and have a men's dinner. Instead of which it turned out that I had to go to bed through a very nasty and unexpected development of a local cold contracted in Liverpool. I had to keep indoors and be very careful, but I expected every day to feel better. However the beastly thing hung on to me, depressing me physically and mentally, and I didn't have the energy to write to anyone. In that respect I am getting better now, but the gout has come since; a very painful wrist and all the usual consequences.

[1] In late December 1919.

Yesterday I was in bed all day. Catherine came down for Borys' birthday[1] and we talked of you considerably. She is immensely gratified at your wish to give her a part in your play[2] and she spoke of your kindness on this and other occasions with great appreciation.

We have now a team of servants – since Saturday – and you would not be running an undue risk of perishing from hunger, cold and undue neglect if you managed to come here early on Saturday and stayed for Sunday. The drawing-room still empty except for the piano which has come into it the other day. We are all very much in love with it.

A vous de coeur

J. Conrad.

To J. B. Pinker
Text MS Berg; Unpublished

[letterhead: Oswalds]
19.1.20.

Dearest Old Friend.

Herewith I send you John's acc[t] for his next term. I have also drawn a cheque to Grace Willard for £100 to pay for the drawing-room furniture – since the room must be furnished. How much we'll get for that God only knows: a strip or two [of] carpet and a few seats of sorts – enough to show people into the room when they call.

Will you please then transfer that amount to my acc[t] and in this connection it occurs (very anxiously) to me that I don't know in the least how I stand with you. I don't imagine for a moment that you will you* think I want to bother you with accts or figures. But You have been financing me through all the evil days of my writing life and tho' the days now are good I always feel that I[3] ought to be told beforehand of the demands I may make on you. So I want to warn you that besides the income-tax 1/2 year now due, there will be accts coming in for curtains – floor coverings and some additional furniture – which have not yet been presented. I don't remember the exact

---

[1] Borys Conrad turned twenty-two on the 15th. Catherine is the actress Catherine Willard, Grace's daughter, who was either two years younger or three years older. For her biography, see the list of Conrad's correspondents.

[2] Thanks to her theatrical training in Paris, Catherine Willard spoke excellent French. In England, she made her name as a Shakespearean, touring as Katharina in *The Taming of the Shrew*, and then taking such roles as Hermione, Olivia, and Lady Macbeth at the Old Vic. Jean-Aubry wrote several plays, among them *L'Heure fantasque*, *Le Merveilleux Éveil*, and *L'École des vertus*.

[3] A slip for 'you'?

amounts now but in any case it will not be an immense sum. The bill for the moving has not come in yet either.

Ever Yours

J Conrad.

PS I was in bed two days but the corr[ecti]ons of Rescue are moving on. Mama Grace took your etching to town for framing. The more one looks at it the more lovely it seems. Jessic's love.

To J. B. Pinker
Text MS Berg;[1] Unpublished

[Oswalds]
[19? January 1920][2]

Will you let them? I've no copy. Perhaps you could tell them where to get one

JC

To Thomas J. Wise
Text TS BL Ashley 2953; Unpublished

[letterhead: Oswalds]
Jan. 19th. 1920.

My dear Mr Wise[3]

I ought to have answered your kind letter long before; but on arriving home I had to go to bed and I have been more or less ailing since. This letter

---

[1] Text on the verso of a letter to Conrad from The British Drama League (signed Geoffrey Whitworth, Honorary Secretary) of 13 January, asking to see a copy of *One Day More* for possible production by the Sheffield Playgoers Society.

[2] The note was possibly included with the letter of the 19th.

[3] Thomas James Wise (1859–1937) collected – and fabricated – literary rarities. Having prospered as a dealer in lavender and other essential oils, he built up a considerable collection of books and manuscripts, many of which are now in the British Library's Ashley Collection, and enjoyed a steady reputation as a bibliophile and bibliographer. Meanwhile he was forging and selling at high prices unique early editions of Wordsworth, Shelley, Tennyson, Charlotte Brontë, George Eliot, Swinburne, and the Brownings, all hitherto unknown to scholarship. In order to improve his own collection of Jacobean plays, he was also helping himself to leaves from copies in the British Museum. His career as forger was not exposed until three years before his death, and his side-line as literary thief and vandal came to light long after. In 1918, he began to purchase manuscripts and typescripts from Conrad, and in 1920 overtook John Quinn as principal purchaser. As Conrad's first bibliographer, he published *A Bibliography of the Writings of Joseph Conrad* (1920) and *A Conrad Library: A Catalogue of Printed Books, Manuscripts and Autograph Letters by Joseph Conrad* (1928). He also printed twenty limited-edition pamphlets of Conrad's occasional writings between December 1918 and January 1920. To the best of our knowledge, Wise did not fabricate anything Conradian, and, in an article for the *Bookman's Journal* (31 December 1920, p. 160), was good enough to warn collectors against fraudulent cancels in Conrad first editions.

is being dictated because I have a bad wrist still and I don't like to wait any longer.

I hope to be well enough some time next month to come up to town and, if I am at all fit for human society – which just now I am not – I shall certainly give myself the very great pleasure of calling upon you and being introduced to the treasures of your bookcase.

Believe me sincerely Yours

J. Conrad

To Mr Blodgett

Text TS/MS Yale; Unpublished

[letterhead: Oswalds]

Jan. 20th. 1920.

Dear Mr Blodgett[1]

Pray accept my thanks for your friendly letter and kind invitation. Life is short and Oklahoma is very far away, but the consciousness of the distance from the friends of my work there seems to add to the value of the appreciative words you have been good enough to write.

As to the autograph I suppose these lines will serve for a sample of my unlovely handwriting

Believe me with great regard

Yours

Joseph Conrad

16. Jany. 1919[2]

Oswalds

Bishopsbourne

n^r Canterbury

To Sir Sidney Colvin

Text MS Virginia; Lucas 306 (in part)

[letterhead: Oswalds]

20 Jan 20

Dearest Colvin.[3]

You will have to add to the many proofs of your affection for me yet another act of forgiveness for my usual sin of silence. I assure you that for a month

---

[1] An Oklahoman, but otherwise unknown.

[2] As so easily happens in January, Conrad wrote the wrong year.

[3] Sir Sidney Colvin (1845–1927; knighted 1911) became a good friend to Conrad, as he had been to Robert Louis Stevenson. Colvin, who had been Slade Professor of Fine Arts at Cambridge, was Keeper of Prints and Drawings at the British Museum from 1884 to 1912. Among his literary works were editions of Stevenson's letters and biographies of Landor and Keats.

very nearly I havent had the energy to command my thoughts and resolution enough to lift a pen and try. That I am able today to tell you that much is in itself strong evidence that I am getting better. I can't imagine what has brought on me that long fit of the very blackest depression unless it be a very beastly little ailment (of an inflammatory nature) the first touch of which I felt in London on our passage home. It is passing off now; but by this time my old friend the gout has come along to keep me company. That devil took lodgings in my wrist, has enlarged it considerably and is making himself at home inside in a way that causes me to gnash my teeth when I don't want to do it. I don't want to do anything. If you were to peep magically into my study you would see me sitting absolutely motionless like a crabbed, unasiatic-looking Buddha – and not even twirling my thumbs – all day long.

However the last 3 days I've managed to put in about an hour a day pruning the text of *The Rescue* with the utmost severity. I don't know when that work will be published, and I am not much interested in it generally. What however does interest me no end if* your statement about a forthcoming vol of yours.[1] I am more than delighted to know that those most distinguished *croquis des personnes*[2] out of your past are going to be collected. In that good company you enumerate, there will also be another homme du monde of the widest sympathies and beautifully controlled expression, scholar, artist, observer, judge of character and devoted friend. You don't name him; but I think that in that book where his name will only appear on the title-page much will be revealed to us of Sidney Colvin with son tour d'esprit très avisé et un peu mordant,[3] and expressed with a sort of fascinating quietness I have never met before in anybody. I am *so* p[l]eased you have made up your mind! I do really think too that the book may very well turn out a succès de librairie.[4] I won't expound to you my reasons for so thinking, here and now, because of "lack of space". But they are good, very good.

I kiss dear Lady Colvin's hands.[5]

Our dearest love to you both

Ever Yours

J. Conrad

Jessie is making a marvellous progress.

[1] *Memories & Notes of Persons & Places, 1852–1912* (1921).
[2] 'Sketches of remarkable people'.
[3] 'His very shrewd and somewhat caustic turn of mind'.
[4] A 'success at the bookshops'.
[5] For her biography, see the list of Conrad's correspondents.

To W. M. Parker

Text TS NLS 5892/6; Dryden

[letterhead: Oswalds]
Jan. 20th. 1920.

Dear Sir[1]

I have to thank you for sending me the cutting from the Glasgow Evening Citizen containing your contribution on "The Arrow of Gold".[2] I need not tell you that your appreciation and your letter have given me very great pleasure.

Yours

J. Conrad.

To J. B. Pinker

Text TS/MS Berg; Unpublished

Oswalds,
Bishopsbourne,
Kent.
Jan. 22nd. 1920

My dear Pinker

I thought that the question of dramatisation of the "Arrow" had been dropped; and I had some reason to think so because when Quinn made his proposal in August last, and I communicated it to you, all you said was (I remember the very words) "I had a letter from a man" in a tone which made me think that the matter was not to be followed up seriously. It served me to put Quinn off[3] and I did not give it a single thought since. My innermost feeling was and remains averse from all idea of dramatisation of this particular

---

[1] Glasgow-born journalist William Mathie Parker (1891–1973) published many books on Scottish literature and contributed frequently to the *Fortnightly Review*, *Glasgow Herald*, and *John O'London's*. Responsible for running the *Tuscania*'s 'High Seas Bookshop', he was in contact with Conrad on his 1923 journey to America and published a reminiscence of the voyage in *Blue Peter*.

[2] The novel had appeared in August 1919. Parker's unsolicited comment, printed on 15 January, acclaimed it as 'Perhaps of all Mr Conrad's works . . . his greatest achievement. When future historians record the literary annals of these times it is to be hoped they will chronicle the appearance of this novel as a landmark in the world of letters.'

[3] See the letter of 31 July 1919, *Letters*, 6, p. 451.

book. I had not the slightest notion that any negociation was in progress. I had accustomed myself to the thought that the question would not arise for a long time yet, if ever. You put here before me an agreement, the issue of a negotiation which I had no idea was proceeding, with a man of whose existence I was not aware and whose name tells me nothing, and dealing with work that as yet I feel most reluctant to let anybody paw over and pull about for the purpose of dramatisation. No doubt you know all about him but you don't tell me anything.

I don't like the agreement very much. By para. 4, Section f, it prevents us securing Cinema rights for (practically) four years from the present date; and *that* even if the man makes a very poor show with his dramatisation from a money point of view. The words "at all events" put that beyond all doubt. And in this connection I will confess to you that the filming of the "Arrow" would be much less repugnant to me than the dramatisation. After all, the film deals only with the visual aspects, and as superficially as an illustration in a magazine; whereas the dramatisation cuts into the quick and may mangle the very heart of the thing. Of course if you make it a personal matter, as being a negotiator with full powers you may well do, I will sign and make an end of it.

Of course I might have spared you all the above because by para. 3, I can by my disapproval bring the whole thing to nothing. In my present disposition it was open to me to sign this agreement without saying a word in the firm intention to reject the MS when presented within the agreed period. But I could not put my hand otherwise than in perfect good faith to anything negotiated by you. And besides I want you always to know what is in my mind. Neither diplomacy nor self-interest can stand in the way of my frankness with you. And naturally I expect you to believe that if I do sign it will be without any mental reservations and with the firm intention to carry out the transaction you put before me – no matter what my decision as to the adaptation may be ultimately. I keep the agreement (2 copies) till I hear from you.

Ever affct^{ly} Yours

J Conrad.

PS Thanks for you letter advising payments received yesterday.

I am going on with Rescue text as if there had been no new point raised as to dates. I have a horror of altering settled arrangements even if [I] didn't like them originally. Can we hold back D[ouble]day? I would like simult^{ous} pub^{on} very much. If you think of putting pressure on Dent perhaps we could make him a small concession in the matter of that confounded school-book[1] which he seems to have badly on the brain.

J. C.

If not too much trouble pray send me six £1 notes for wages.

To G. Jean-Aubry
Text TS/MS Yale; Unpublished

[letterhead: Oswalds]
Jan. 24th. 1920.

Très cher Ami.

We shall be delighted to see you next week, and we expect to hear from you in a couple of days.

I know the work of Paul Adam very little and all I have in the house is his Lettres de Malaisie;[2] but I quite understand what you say about the difficulty of a general and inclusive pronouncement on the whole of it. I didn't know he was such an old friend of yours. I am sure your mind will be able to get at the heart of the subject in your own illuminating manner.

Our kindest regards to Madame Alvar.[3] I have heard something of Madame Alvar in the Serva Padrona, from Catherine,[4] who was delight with the singing and quite impressed by the impersonating power revealed in the acting. I wish I could see it; and I hope I shall some day.

The image of you in the dentist's chair is too horrible for our sensibilities to contemplate. We feel for you but we try not to think of it.

Ever Yours

J. Conrad

PS Jessie sends her love. John is gone to school. Un grand vide!

---

[1] See the letter to Pinker of the 28th.

[2] At home in the milieux of Proust and the Symbolists, Adam (1862–1920) was particularly known for his series of novels dealing with French political life from the Revolution to the Third Empire. His interest in French colonial expansion also led to a number of works, including the novel *Lettres de Malaisie* (1898). An acquaintance of Conrad's correspondent Warrington Dawson, he wrote a preface to Dawson's *Le Nègre aux États-Unis* (1912); see Randall, p. 49.

[3] The professional name of Jean-Aubry's close friend the Swedish-born singer Louise Victoria ('Loulette') Woods Harding (née Beckman, 1883–1965). She and her husband, a wealthy barrister, held a literary and artistic salon at their house in Holland Park, Kensington; her circle included Ravel, Malipiero, Roussel, Falla, Saint-Saëns, Madariaga, Eliot, Hofmansthal, and Valéry.

[4] London saw no performances of Giovanni Battista Pergolesi's *La serva padrona* (1733) in 1920. The staging was possibly provincial or private, the forces required being small. Catherine is Catherine Willard.

To J. B. Pinker
Text TS Berg; Unpublished

Oswalds,
Bishopsbourne,
Kent.
Jan. 24th. 1920.

Dearest Friend

Its obvious that I do forget things. I only remembered the first mention, but I forgot our decision and accustomed myself to think that the "Arrow" was safe from desecration. I can't tell you how glad I am that you don't think better of the agreement than I do, and that you don't mind dropping the affair. In view of possible eventualities I say again that I contemplate without repugnance the mere visualising of the "Arrow" on the screen, if anybody wants to do that; though, personally, it seems impossible to me.

I am glad you have touched on the "Rescue" transaction. A doubt has arisen in my mind as to the absolute worth of Unwin's statement. It is his nature to find grievances and utter complaints.[1] How would it be if you asked him to give you some idea of the demand for and the prospects of the "Arrow" to bear out his statement for which there may be only the slightest foundation? What, for instance, are the present orders and the actual weekly sales? It seems to me only natural that before altering our arrangements we should want to have a good reason shown. After all we have a complete right to ask for facts and the refusal to disclose them would look extremely suspicious.

H[ugh] D[ent][2] who has a father-in-law lurking somewhere in this neighbourhood has asked permission to call on Tuesday with his wife. I didn't like to stop him. No doubt he will try to talk of all these matters and that's rather a nuisance because I don't want to talk on any matter. I will drop you a line when this is over. I am glad you agree as to a simultaneous publication. I am afraid you won't be able to rein-in Doubleday and his team without making them rear and kick all in a row. However, that's none of my circus and it will be amusing to watch your performance.

Ever affct[ly] Yours

J Conrad.

---

[1] T. Fisher Unwin (1848–1935) had been Conrad's first publisher, but Conrad always suspected him of parsimoniousness, and their dealings had become cool or even acrimonious, especially over copyrights for the collected editions. Unwin had published *The Arrow of Gold* in 1919.

[2] Hugh Railton Dent (1874–1938), who joined the family firm J. M. Dent & Sons in 1909.

To Sydney Cockerell

Text MS Rosenbach; Unpublished

[letterhead: Oswalds]

27.1.20

Dear Sir.[1]

It is very kind of you to invite me for the Purcell performances.[2] It is positive pain to have to tell you that I cannot come. Tho' not actually laid up I have been disabled more or less by gout for the last 3 weeks.

Travelling is out of question for me just now. I can only assure Mrs Cockerell and yourself of my sincere gratitude for your kind thought.

Yes. I would be glad of a sight of Blunt's 2 vol.[3]

My wife was operated[4] last Dec with complete success and we have every ground to believe that her 16 year old troubles are over at last. She asks to be remembered to you.

Believe me with warm regard

Yours

J Conrad.

Pardon this odious scrawl. I've a bad wrist.

To J. B. Pinker

Text TS/MS Berg; Unpublished

[letterhead: Oswalds]

Jan. 28th. 1920.

My dear Pinker

As I anticipated H[ugh] Dent talked about a school book or rather two school books. Without giving up the idea of the Mirror of the Sea selection he

---

[1] After a brief career as a coal merchant, Sydney Carlyle Cockerell (1867–1962; knighted 1934) became secretary to William Morris and the Kelmscott Press. Director of the Fitzwilliam Museum, Cambridge, from 1908 to 1937, he was widely connected in artistic circles and counted among his literary friends not only Conrad but also W. S. Blunt and Thomas Hardy.

[2] Henry Purcell's *The Faery Queene* (1692) was to be performed at Cambridge in mid-February.

[3] Wilfrid Scawen Blunt's *My Diaries: Being a Personal Narrative of Events, Pt. 1, 1888–1900* and *Pt. 2 1900–1914* (May 1919 and January 1920). Blunt (1840–1922), a friend of Cunninghame Graham, was a landowner, poet, horseman, anti-colonial politician, and adulterer. His diaries give a vivid account of campaigns against imperial rule in Ireland and Egypt. Cf. *Letters*, 6, p. 468.

[4] Although it may look strange to the modern reader, this use of 'operate' as a transitive verb was currently popular among medical people. The *OED*'s earliest citation comes from a 1908 issue of *The Practitioner*. Polish uses a similar construction.

has another in his mind composed of Youth and Gaspar Ruiz.[1] He wanted
to know if I objected. I don't object. Then he got on the three halfpence
question,[2] but as he said that he was going to see you on that very subject
there is no need for me to enlarge on his discourse. Apart from mentioning
that speaking generally I did not like the idea of school books and that you
were aware of my views I made no reply to his argument. Then he touched
on The Rescue, of which he told me he was going to print 20,000 copies to
begin with and made a statement about his trade arrangements, I suppose
in the same terms he used to you already. If he expected anything definite
from this visit he must feel disappointed.

I wonder what F. U[nwin] will say to the demand for a definite statement
about the Arrow. Please let me hear.

I keep on feeling seedy. R. text will be finished by Mond: next.

Ever Yours

J Conrad.

To J. B. Pinker
Text TS/MS Berg; Unpublished

[letterhead: Oswalds]
Jan. 29th. [1920][3]

Dearest Friend.

It seems to me that I didn't acknowledge receipt of the Income Tax paper
which you sent me to be completed and signed. I did so and posted it yesterday
to the Collector.

I think that by next Friday our drawing-room will be completed for something not exceeding £150, which will cover also the cost of upholstering with
some old Italian brocade two of the sofas and one or two chairs. It will also
cover the mending of two old Adams panels (torn out from some house of
the time) decorated with paintings of flowers and to be stuck on the walls of
that marvellous drawing-room, instead of pictures.[4] How they will look there
heaven only knows; but I am assured I could sell them for a price which would
cover the original cost *and* the mending. There will be also three Aubusson
bits of which one biggish square is very mellow with age but really quite
attractive; another much smaller is as bright as when it left the loom, one
would think, and is really a good-looking piece. The third I haven't seen yet.

---

[1] Conrad wrote an 'Introductory Note' to *Youth and Gaspar Ruiz*, published by Dent in their King's
Treasury series in the summer. Conrad did not sign the contract until May; see Hallowes.
[2] A question of royalties?   [3] The references to furnishing Oswalds fix the year.
[4] The Adam brothers, Robert (1728–92) and James (1730–94), were Scottish-born architects and
designers.

When I hear talk of that kind around me it seems to me I am dreaming a strange aesthetic dream in the atmosphere of a curio shop. It's very funny.

What is not funny is my persistent seediness. Drop me a line to say how you are – for I have my doubts! But that may be my morbid pessimism.

I am returning you the unsigned agreements, since this matter is dropped with your consent.

Pray send me £6 in notes if not too much trouble.

Ever Yours

J. Conrad

To J. B. Pinker
Text TS Berg; Unpublished

[letterhead: Oswalds]
Feb. 5th. 1920.

My dear Pinker

Thanks for forwarding the wire. I was expecting [it] just about this time. I surmise that the mysterious appearance and disappearance of Carola[1] last November was simply a case of impersonation, for whatever purpose it may have been intended, which did not come off. My aunt Poradowska[2] is well known in Poland and after all we cannot be sure that the girl who turned up in November and told the porteress that she would be back in half an hour was Carola, or even that she *said* she was Carola. I rather think that the porteress who was told to look out for a Polish lady jumped to that conclusion without ever asking for her name. At any rate whoever the November-woman was she could not have been a professional thief, or anything of that sort, because she refused the key of the apartment which the porteress was actually trying to force on her. Most likely it was some poor girl, probably in search of some sort of assistance and whose heart failed her at the last moment. Any way I am immensely relieved and I hope we will get the* word of this riddle in the letter which is promised in the wire and will probably be addressed to your care.

I am keeping Carola off for a week because there is a nurse in the house now who occupies the room which C. will have. Since yesterday afternoon I am better. I have no temperature this morning and the cough is easier. Of course I feel weak and I don't think it would be prudent for me even to attempt to get up for a few days yet. Of course all work, even proof correcting

[1] Karola Zagórska (*c.* 1885–1955), the daughter of Conrad's maternal second cousin once removed, Karol Zagórski, was to arrive at Oswalds in late February for a six-month stay.

[2] Marguerite Poradowska (née Gachet, 1848–1937), the widow of Conrad's distant cousin and thus his 'Aunt', lived in Paris. The first novelist of his acquaintance, she was a close friend in the early 1890s, but a hiatus in the second half of the decade suggests a temporary rupture.

is out of the question. This letter is as much as I can manage to-day. I will be sending instructions to my bank to forward a draft, £40, to Madame Poradowska for C., as I don't suppose the poor girl has much left of the £100, we forwarded to her last Sept. Please transfer that amount to my account.

I needn't tell you how much I would like to see you. I feel a good bit shaken up.

Jessie too has not been getting on so well. Her heart has been troublesome for the last fortnight and is the sort of thing to make one anxious.

Ever Yours
J Conrad.

To J. B. Pinker

Text TS Berg;[1] Unpublished

[early? February 1920][2]

P.S. This is for your eye only. We, here, could be ready for you and Heinemann[3] on Wednesday next. But the question is whether it wouldn't be much nicer if you came the afternoon before on your own visit, Heinemann being allowed to join us say on Thursday, strictly for the middle of the day. Please arrange all that as most convenient to you and deliver the invitation to H. in my name according to what you decide. The other way would be of course for you both to come together and for you to remain behind. Perhaps you may decide that I don't need to see H. personally. What I am anxious for of course is a talk with you before you leave; and, as a matter of fact, we can settle everything between us two on that or any other matter.

The miraculous furniture is supposed to arrive on Monday evening and so you shall inaugurate it by being the first guest who will sit on those sofas and put his feet on those Aubusson squares. I am marvellously limp, though people tell me I don't look like a dug up corpse. I feel something like it, wondering what I am doing still in this world.

If anything occurs to me I will drop you a line this week. Please send me six notes like last week.

[1] The body of the letter does not survive.
[2] Kept at the Berg with the letters of July 1920, but the contents do not match this date. It must precede the letter of 15 February scotching the idea of a visit from Heinemann. On 29 January, Conrad expected the furniture to arrive on Friday, 6 February. A brief delay in these plans would make the Monday referred to here the 9th, so Conrad must be writing a few days earlier. The improved health after his bout of illness reported on the 5th and the news about taxes in the letter of the 10th confirm the period.
[3] William Henry Heinemann (1863–1920), senior partner in the well-known firm he established in 1890, was one of Conrad's early publishers. He was now planning to bring out the British collected edition of Conrad's works.

You have done wonderfully well with the tax collector!!! I knew that it would not be very far from £100 saved on the two payments. Thanks for settling the bill.

All our loves

Yours

JC.

To J. B. Pinker
Text TS/MS Berg; Unpublished

[letterhead: Oswalds]
Feb. 10th. 1920.

My dear Pinker

I hasten to transmit to you the tax collector's note which shows that your claim on my behalf has worked very well. I don't remember the figures of the first assessment but at any rate I think the claim saves at least £50 on the two half-yearly payments, which is what a certain friend of mine would call "a good round sum". I sent you yesterday the demand note on the old scale as it's right that you should have all the documents that pass, but I don't suppose you have remitted yet.

My cousin's* C[arola]'s case was a case of impersonation right enough, but of such a silly nature that no reasonable person could have hit on the explanation. A young woman, the wife of a junior diplomatist, travelling from Brussels to Constantinople called that morning in Nov. on Madame P[oradowska] rather earlier than usual and the concierge asked her "You are no doubt the Warsaw niece that M[a]d[am]e de P. is expecting every day?" and that idiot thought it funny to say "Oh yes, I am the Warsaw niece, I am going to call on some friends at No. 32 and I will be back in the course of the morning." And so she went away and forgot all about it, lunched with her friends, went on shopping for two days and couldn't find time to call again on Mme P. Poor Aunt Margaret waited till next day and then sent to No. 32 asking those people whom she didn't know personally whether Mademoiselle C. Zagorska had called on them. They of course answered that they had never seen Miss C. Z. and that they didn't even know that such a person existed. Now that feather-headed imbecile writes from Constantinople telling the little tale and concluding "of course you must have guessed it was I". Mme. P. uses very strong language about her to me which opens my eyes as to the power of expression of old ladies of 80 when properly roused.

On the face of it Unwin's statement seems to justify his letter. But after all it isn't proved that the publication of *Rescue* would injure the further sale of the *Arrow*. I think in those matters nothing can be affirmed with certitude and you know what my feelings are about matters that have been already settled. And there is this, too, that, since your journey to U.S. is definitely decided on, you will be over there on or about the time when *R*. will be due for publication (if no change is made) and you will be able to see personally how Doubleday and his fourteen partners go about the business of publishing a Conrad. According to what they say themselves it must be something as impressive almost as an earthquake, heaven and earth clashing together like a pair of cymbals, and all that sort of thing.

What you write about Heinemann and his energetic proceedings in view of the English de luxe edition interests me very much. But its no good deluding oneself with the hope of me being able to come up to town before your departure for America. Of course I know, my dear fellow, you will come and see me here and I hope you will pick out one day early next week and spend the night and let me have a good look at you before your journey amongst the redskins. But apart from that if H. wishes very much to get on with that job perhaps you could bring him here for a day with all the documents. I don't know that the affair is big enough to call for this additional trouble on your part but as far as I am concerned I will be fit enough to go into the matter. For the last three days I have had no temperature and I came down yesterday to my study for the first time almost since your visit. I feel of course very weak yet and my left arm is still in a sling which is a nuisance apart from the pain.

I haven't been able to think much of anything, but the little thinking I did was connected mostly with the Vol. of miscellaneous writings which we have planned for issue in 1921. Most of the stuff itself is quite printable. The matter is very miscellaneous indeed. In length we may safely reckon on 70,000 words. There are four or five reviews of books which I wrote for the Daily Mail in 1910[1] which I am having hunted up in the B[ritish] M[useum] and will have transcribed. I think I could make something of that stuff though I don't particularly care to have it preserved. I won't say more about all this except that for the title I was thinking of: ESSAYS AND NOTES IN LIFE AND LETTERS. I offer this suggestion to your meditation and you will tell me what you think of it when we meet.

Jessie's rest in bed has done her good.

Ever Yours

J. Conrad.

---

[1] Of four reviews written, three were published, all in July 1910: 'A Happy Wanderer', 'The Life Beyond', and 'The Ascending Effort'.

I suppose you've had a corrected copy of *Set of Six* for transmission to US. Pray settle the encl^d bill connected with L'pool journey.

To Richard Curle
Text TS/MS Indiana; Unpublished

[letterhead: Oswalds]
Feb. 11th. 1920.

My dear Curle

I answer your letter formally here with a distinct request that you should interest me to the amount of £500 in any purchases of shares you may make speculatively, absolutely at your discretion and according to your sole judgment as to buying and selling – I keeping the above amount (£500) at your disposal whenever you call for it. I absolutely agree in your suggestion that all those transactions should be made in your name, this being the only way to relieve me from all personal participation in those speculations for which, as I explained to you in our conversation the last time you were here, I have neither time nor inclination. And I assure you, my dear Curle, that I am infinitely grateful to you for the opportunity you offer me and for taking all the trouble of the matter off my hands.

Always affectionately Yours
Joseph Conrad.

P.S. I am better. For the last three days I have had no temperature and at the present moment I am dictating in my study. It was a rather bad bout of bronchitis complicated with gout which still holds me by the wrist and makes it impossible for me to write more than a few lines in pen and ink. I am still very shaky and mentally tired, so I won't say anything about the other matters in your letter except that we rejoice to hear your health keeps up and that we will be delighted to see you here next week, any day after Tuesday. But I will write to your London address on Friday more extensively. Jessie (who is better) sends her love.

Ever yours

J. C.

B[orys] had an interesting ouverture* from a firm of aeroplane and motor-launch engine manufacturers in Windermere.[1] Old friends from the front.

---

[1] The Windermere Motor Launch Co. of Bowness-on-Windermere.

To J. B. Pinker

Text TS Berg; Unpublished

[letterhead: Oswalds]

Feb. 12th. 1920

My dear Pinker

Your letter gives one food for thought, but the first consideration is that your labour, your patience and your diplomacy in making the collected Edition possible should not be wasted. Mr Heinemann's point of view must be attended to. I think it will be possible to get within his scheme of 20 volumes. On the other hand I don't think it will be absolutely feasible to make all the volumes exactly the same size. There must be slight differences. After all a set of volumes is not a set of tea-cups and the literary aspect cannot be sacrificed to an exact uniformity of size, such as has been attained in Macmillan's selected edition of Henry James.[1]

I was never a great friend of the plan of dividing the long novels into two vols. It was one way out of the difficulty — that's all. I haven't the slightest idea what plan Doubleday is going to follow. The old scheme has been thrown overboard long ago. Of the new I have never heard a word. But I must say that my feeling towards an English edition is quite different. I shall await impatiently the amended scheme and the specimens you promised to send me. As Mr Heinemann's office has no doubt ascertained the number of words in every First Edition Vol. of my works I should like a note of that sent to me too. Before the war I had the words counted of everything then published but I can't lay my hands on the paper just now.

I should like to have submitted to me alternative bindings unless you and Mr Heinemann have already absolutely decided on that point. As to the arrangement of the text I am prepared to go any length short of absurdity. For instance Mr Heinemann must understand that the miscellaneous volume which ultimately must go into the set will be only of 70,000 words and that nothing will induce me to consent to have it eked out by, say, a couple of short stories torn out from their proper places.

I should like also to know what are the maximum and minimum limits to a vol. in Mr Heinemann's opinion.

I think it would be a very good thing if Mr Heinemann would consent to undertake a journey down here. There is a very good train at 10.45 from Victoria arriving at 12.42 in Canterbury, and if he would give us the pleasure to come down by this we could get three solid hours of talk after lunch, should

---

[1] Macmillan published the fourteen-volume 'Collective Edition of Henry James' (a selection from his published works) in 1883.

that much be necessary. I am afraid that me coming up to London within any reasonable time now is out of the question. I feel extremely weak and recovery after bronchitis takes a long time.

Ever yours

Joseph Conrad.

To J. B. Pinker
Text TS/MS Berg; Unpublished

[letterhead: Oswalds]
Feb. 15th. 1920.

My dearest Pinker

Thanks for your letter of the 13th which reached me only to-day. I agree to all you say. We certainly don't want Heinemann while we are discussing the terms of the contract. Your room will be ready for you on Tuesday but please drop us a wire stating day and train so that we can meet you in Canterbury.

Thanks for the notes.

Poor Jessie has shingles now! It's a very beastly and trying thing and how and why it came it's impossible to say as she [had] no mental or physical shock of any kind. On the contrary she was getting quite chirpy. Sheer bad luck.

As to myself: You will have to "wait and see."

Ever Yours

J Conrad

To J. B. Pinker
Text MS Berg; Unpublished

[Oswalds]
[mid-February 1920][1]

Dearest P.

This scheme[2] is such a concession to M^r H['s] view that I must insist on its adoption as it stands here. I could give my reasons for it but I don't want to explain. I may only state generally that in this particular matter my sense of the fitness of things is to [be] trusted rather more than Mr W. Heinemann's staff's.

---

[1] Conrad's letter to Pinker of the 12th and Pinker's scheduled visit for or after the 17th suggest the general dating.
[2] This letter is on a typed sheet headed 'A Scheme in 15 Volumes'. *The Rescue* and *Notes on Life and Letters* were added later in an unknown hand, and the list renumbered to twenty volumes.

I send you a duplicate for Mr H. with remarks and suggestions to which I
expect him to pay particular attention. Pray insist of* them inflexibly. They
have their reason and they are not either fantastic or difficult.

Ever Yours

C.

Put this in Your pocket when you come down please.

A Scheme in Fifteen Volumes

VOL. I	ALMAYER'S FOLLY,	65	
	TALES OF UNREST,	62	127
VOL. II	OUTCAST OF THE ISLANDS,	114	
VOL. III	N. OF NARCISSUS,	56	
	TYPHOON	88	144
VOL. IV	LORD JIM	130	
VOL. V	YOUTH	111	
VOL. VI	ROMANCE	185	
VOL. VII	NOSTROMO	170	
VOL. VIII	SECRET AGENT	98	
	INHERITORS	61	159
VOL. IX	SET OF SIX	88	
	TWIXT LAND & SEA	77	165
VOL. X	PERSONAL RECORD	49	
	MIRROR OF SEA	66	115
VOL. XI	WESTERN EYES	111	
VOL. XII	CHANCE	146	
VOL. XIII	SHADOW LINE	42	
	WITHIN TIDES	66	108
VOL. XIV	VICTORY	130	
VOL. XV	ARROW OF GOLD	120	

This scheme does away with Mr. W. Heinemann's objection to grotesque
differences of size. It isn't my fault if Romance is 185,000 words long and The
Outcast only 114,000 words long. Those are facts which cannot be schemed
away and therefore need not be discussed. Nothing can solve that difficulty
but the abandonment of the Collected Edition, which I suppose need not be
contemplated.

It is to be understood that the contents of Vols. I, III, VIII, IX, X, XIII,
are to preserve their absolute individuality as different works having no other

connection than the fact of being bound in one Vol. That is, that each of them, the first and the second, will have its proper pre[li]ms, viz: half-title, title page, dedication page (bearing on the verso the notification in italics, *First printed in* −). With the further proviso that a blank page will be inserted between the end of one work and the pre[li]ms of the other. I hope I have made myself understood clearly, I mean, for instance, that in Vol. IX, consisting of two collections of short stories (6 & 3) these must not be presented as a volume of nine short stories, but each of the two collections must have its individuality distinctly preserved by a full set of pre[li]ms as above.

I beg Mr Wm. Heinemann to agree to my request that the title pages should be in two colours, red and black, distributed in the usual way. The characters used should be Rom. caps. of a design to be decided upon. I should like it to approach as near as possible the form of letters cut on old Roman inscriptions and commemorative tablets. Two sizes also will have to be settled on, one for such short titles as Youth, Chance etc, and the smaller kind, perhaps, for the longer ones, such as The Nigger of the Narcissus. At any rate it seems so to me. (?)

I also wish (and indeed I think it *must* be done) that the backs of the books should bear the titles of all the works contained therein. For instance, Vol. IX should have at the back the two titles: *A Set of Six* − *Twixt Land and Sea*. I appeal insistently to Mr Heinemann when devising and planning the outward appearance of the set to bear in mind my great desire to affirm and emphasise the individuality of each included work.

JC.

To Richard Curle
Text MS Princeton; Unpublished

[Oswalds]
Tuesday. [17 February 1920?][1]

Dearest Dick.

Of course. We are expecting You. Car will meet your train at 6.18 Canter[y].
Our love

Yrs

J. C.

---

[1] Conrad's wish of the 11th to see Curle 'next week, any day after Tuesday' suggests a tentative date.

To Prince Eustachy Kajetan Sapieha

Text TS Warsaw, sygn. 1041; *Listy* 255–6; Najder (1983, 2), 249–50

[letterhead: Oswalds]
Feb. 20th. 1920.

His Excellency
The Polish Minister,
London.

Sir,[1]

I have long been aware of the state of ignorance of Western Europe as to the character, history, ideals and the very nature of the Polish Nation. I recognise fully the importance of the Association[2] proposed in your Excellency's letter. It is with the greater regret then that I feel myself compelled to state plainly that I am not the right sort of person to take the initiative in that matter. To set going and bring to a successful issue the organisation of such a Society is a task for a man of social connections, acquainted with influential people, and known personally to the wider world.

This is not the case with me. I have led a retired life. I have formed no social relations. My circle of intimates contains not a single influential personality either in the literary world or any other; and even with those my intercourse is made difficult and irregular by the unsatisfactory state of my health. The question of physical fitness has its importance. I am ill now. It is the reason why I am dictating this letter in English. I have been ill for nearly two months and it is impossible to say how long it will be before I am fit to come up to town. This sort of thing happens to me every year and often more than once a year.

There is another consideration which I must submit to your Excellency. I left Poland in the year 1874. My last visit (to the most distant part of Ukraine) was in 1892.[3] Since that time owing to the death of my uncle[4] I have not even had any letters that would have kept me in touch with the inner life of Poland, its problems and its perplexities. My accidental presence with my family in Cracow and Zakopane during the months of August and September, 1914, gave me really no further insight. In the general trouble of minds and consciences caused by the events which made the future of all mankind dark, it was impossible for me to learn much, and even to think connectedly, of the special problems of Poland. As to the actual events of the last three years I am absolutely in the dark, not so much perhaps as to facts

---

[1] Prince Eustachy Kajetan Władisław Sapieha (Sapieha-Rożański, 1881–1963), Polish politician and diplomat, was his country's first envoy to the United Kingdom.
[2] An English branch of the Anglo-Polish Society founded in Warsaw in November 1919.
[3] In fact, to the central part and in 1893.
[4] Tadeusz Bobrowski (1829–94), Conrad's maternal uncle and guardian.

themselves but as to their profounder significance. The plain truth is that I am not qualified to take the part your Excellency suggests, in an important undertaking which *must not* be exposed to the slightest chance of failure.

It remains for me only to apologise for the length of this letter. If I have enlarged to this extent in answer to your Excellency's communication it is only out of my deferential regard for the Representative of the Polish State.

I am, Sir, Your most obed[t] servant

Joseph Conrad

To Clement K. Shorter

Text MS BL Ashley B. 503; Unpublished

[letterhead: Oswalds]

21.2.20

Dear M[r] Shorter[1]

Absolute impossibility, nothing less, will prevent me from coming up on Monday. I've been laid up here 3 weeks with a very beastly sort of bronchitis and they won't hear of my putting my nose outside the door yet. If it had been mere gout I would have insisted on having my way.

I am no end sorry.

Best regards

Yours

J. Conrad.

To J. B. Pinker

Text TS Berg; Unpublished

[letterhead: Oswalds]

Feb. 24th. 1920.

My dear Pinker

I am sure you will be glad to know that yesterday I have finished my severe revision of "The Rescue". The last three pages were entirely re-written. I found the whole task extremely tiring and I am immensely relieved to think that it's done with. I had a sort of relapse and had to stay in bed yesterday. I finished the MS in bed last year. And now the revision had to be finished in bed too. A dismal coincidence which makes one anxious about the future.

---

[1] Clement King Shorter (1857–1926) edited the *Illustrated London News* from 1891, and the *Sketch* and the *English Illustrated Magazine* from 1893 to 1900. He gave up all three editorships to begin *Tatler* and the *Sphere*. His critical works include books on the Brontës. In 1898, as editor of the *Illustrated London News*, he had agreed to publish *The Rescue* as a serial, but Conrad could not meet the deadlines (*Letters*, 2, pp. 86–7). A bibliophile, he published various Conrad works as privately printed pamphlets between 1917 and 1919, among them *One Day More*, 'The Tale', and some occasional essays.

I will go on now to the question of the accounts coming in. I don't want during your absence to have to worry the Junior Partner.[1] (Give him my love). Talking with you a year or so ago I remember estimating the expense of coming in here at £500. That estimate suffers from the complaint of all the estimates I ever heard of: and that is a bad swelling. It isn't quite so bad as the swelling of Government estimates which I believe is three times the original size.[2] This one isn't even twice that. I have been looking over a note of bills coming in which I will send you in a day or two and I see that those actually relating to the house (including of course bills you have paid before) will total to about £700 – *and* the piano. Lee and Sons bill will come to about £300 or a few pounds more.[3] But then the estimate for moving had to be thrown overboard on account of the strike,[4] and I had to make special and eccentric arrangements to meet the emergency, for which Lee paid on my instructions, and so they come into his bill. Then all those floor coverings (a surprisingly big area in this small house), curtain stuff for a (surprisingly) great number of windows, were extremely expensive. Moreover in the inability of Jessie and myself to attend to it personally we had to give the order in bulk to Lee which is not an economical way but there really was no help for it. Then of course there was the labour of his men in laying down, fitting out etc, etc. and doing small internal repairs. However it will have to be settled. Then there is £100 which I will ask you to pay into my account to settle additional bills that will come through Mrs Willard for additional things in the drawing-room and some plated dishes and other necessaries of existence. For things we got from B. Ninnes Hythe:[5] (apart from the furniture bills you settled for me last year) a little glass, a little china and other necessaries of life, I have made an arrangement that I should pay him £25 a quarter beginning this next March, for which please my dear Pinker leave your instructions. Three such payments will settle him.

The above are the immediate payments connected with the fitting out of the new house. The only additional thing will be the account for drains and certain improvements to the bathrooms which has not come in yet and may reach £25 or thereabouts.

---

[1] Eric Pinker.
[2] In the 1919 budget, soon to be superseded, Austen Chamberlain, the Chancellor of the Exchequer, had seriously underestimated the post-war government's financial needs.
[3] Charles and Edward Lee of Canterbury dealt in antiques and furnishings.
[4] A railway strike, lasting from 1 to 6 October 1919.
[5] Frederick B. Ninnes kept an antique shop in Hythe; for a brief description, see John Conrad, p. 159.

The bill for putting the electric plant engine right is mixed up with the account of my motor engineers for petrol, oil, car repairs and such things, but I will provide for that myself with the proceeds of my set of the last eight pamphlets published by Wise. That engine and a couple of new cells will probably come to something like £40. Upon the whole and considering that I paid no fine on entering[1] and that there was neither much time nor inclination to haggle over all the innumerable points which arise with the taking of a new house, I don't think that the cost of this "beginning life afresh" has been very outrageous. Anyway you have got to finance me through it. You can't escape your fate. But you know the worst now.

We dispatched the revised slips of R[escue] without loss of time yesterday evening to Dent, who may pull off a proof now as soon as he likes. Doubleday's galley slips went addressed to Garden City by the same post. It is very obvious that they are in a state which may very well reduce a printer to despair but it is D.'s own fault. Why did he not wait for Dent's revised text in first proof to set up from, as indeed it was arranged with him? Why did he rush in and set up from typescript which he had been warned not to do? Of course once I got his slips (to my extreme dismay) I felt bound to correct them. Having been set from my typescript they had to be charged, first, with all the corrections that have been made on the Land & Water proofs and on top of that had to receive all the corrections of the revised text for book form. You may imagine in what state those Doubleday slips are! But what else could I do? I dared not disregard them altogether for fear they should start printing the book from them. In fact I had no option but to do what I have done, though I do honestly believe it would be easier for them to reset the whole directly they get the first proof from Dent. If the question is raised by Doubleday you will be able to deal with it personally; and whether they correct from slips or reset from Dent I am glad you will be there to tell them plainly that the text as amended by me *must* be followed exactly in the American 1st edition.

I have formed many resolutions to be very good during your absence and do something for which people will pay. Nevertheless I think I will begin by doing a Preface or two (for which nobody offers to pay) just to get my hand in at literary composition. Every morning I hope I will catch hold of a short story and I suppose that some morning I will. As to the Play that Fourth Act must be written if only to preserve my self-respect.[2] Oddly enough I have

---

[1] A 'fine' here means a fee rather than a criminal penalty – a relic of feudal law.
[2] Published by Goulden in 1921, the original version of the dramatised *Secret Agent* was in four acts, but Conrad then revised it down to three, that version being staged in 1922 and privately published in 1923.

had lately letters from various people who have just read or just re-read The Secret Agent and seem very much struck by it. If this goes on I will start hating the thing myself.

I hope, my dear Pinker, you will induce D. to put down cash promptly, for the Coll*ed* Edition, and in the way we touched upon when you were here last – that is to the name of the ultimate recipient. I should like you very much to see Quinn[1] if you are still disposed to do so. He may be a little put out just now but you will be able no doubt to smooth his feathers.[2] I have nothing but the most friendly sentiments towards Quinn, who I firmly believe has always meant well by me in all those transactions pecuniary and otherwise which have taken place between us.

I won't wish you here a prosperous journey because this is a strictly business communication. I will keep all the sentiment for the next letter. I suppose I ought to be glad at your getting at last the relief of a little change. As to rest I don't think that you will get much of it unless actually in your cabin at sea. Have you managed to get a single-berth one, I wonder?

Love from Mrs J. C.

Ever affect*ly* yours

Joseph Conrad.

To J. B. Pinker

Text TS/MS Berg; Unpublished

[letterhead: Oswalds]
Feb. 25th. 1920.

Dearest J. B. P.

I have this moment received the enclosed from Everitt,[3] which I pass on to you for your information.

Enclosed here also Lee's account.

The moneys required by me under the head New House are then as follows:

Lee's account, £*305.15.7*. – To my account in the Bank for other small bills, £*100*. – B. Ninnes, £*75* in three quarterly payments of £25 each beginning in March. – Plumber's and drainage account not rendered yet, but about £*30*.

(£512.15.7.)

I have just heard from Dent that he is going to put "Rescue" into pages as quickly as possible. Everitt writes like a man who has a mind. I answered

---

[1] The American lawyer and collector, John Quinn.

[2] Conrad had broken his promise about reserving the sale of manuscripts to him; as a result, relations with Quinn cooled. See *Letters*, 6, pp. 497–8.

[3] S(amuel) A(lexander) Everit (1871–1953) entered publishing after graduating from Yale and long worked for Doubleday's, becoming Treasurer and Executive Vice-President before retiring in 1930.

him generally on Rescue text and such things, and expressed my confident hope that you and he in the course of a talk or two will put C.'s affairs in America into perfect running order for years to come.

Yours

J. C.

PS I have some bills to pay not related to the House – Bookseller – cartage, Stationer. Will you pay in an add[ition]al £*50* to my acct so that I can settle them myself instead of sending them to you.

To Richard Curle
Text MS Indiana; Curle 58 (in part)[1]

[letterhead: Oswalds]
26.2.20

Dearest Dick.

I was glad to get a word from you.

Herewith ch: for £70. I hope you don't imagine I am startled or dismayed – or even surprised. I had a premonition. Perhaps you didn't know I was a man of premonitions?

Anyway we'll regard this transaction as if it had never been and I hope you will interest me in your next invest^t (up to £500) in the terms of my letter to you.[2]

We expect to see you on Sat for weekend by the 4.55 *Vic*.[3] Carola arrives to-morrow.

Revis^{on} of Resc: finished 2 days ago in bed. But I am up now and feeling better.

We'll have some talk and I want to hear how it stands with the pub^{on} of your book. My affair with H. $L^d Ed^{on}$ is settled. 1000 sets.

More viva voce

Regards from all

Yours

J. C.

To J. B. Pinker
Text MS Berg; Unpublished

[letterhead: Oswalds]
26.2.20

Dearest Pinker

I dont think I will distract you in the solemn moments of leaving your "native shore" by any letter after this one.

---

[1] Curle omits the second and third paragraphs.
[2] Of the 11th.   [3] The 4.55 from Victoria Station.

The preface for Sec. Ag^t is finished, but not finally in shape yet. I shall post it to D[oubleday] together with a copy of the Eng: Edition for them to set up from. I shall send it through your office, because his is the more official way[1] and anyhow all that business (I mean in all its details) should be left to your management.

I venture to remind you that end Mch there will be Miss H[allowes's] qu[art]er sal £25 – and a quar.^{er}'s rent to pay.

I've heard to-day from US that the sale of pamphlets is hung up for a time – therefore I must ask you to pay in another 100 to enable [me] to settle Haywards bill which with the repairs and the supplies for 6 mths is something over 80.[2]

Jessie will have to [be] taken to London to see Sir Robert.[3] I've no doubt that another (small) ab[s]cess has formed a little lower down the limb than the other. I am writing to Sir R to-day.

Is it from South[ampt]on that you are leaving? And is the ship's name *Adriatic*?

All our loves and all best wishes for Your journey, my dearest friend.

Ever Yours

J. Conrad.

To Eric Pinker
Text MS McGill; Unpublished

[letterhead: Oswalds]
26.2.20

Dear Eric.[4]

Writing to Father I forgot to ask for 6 £1 notes. Pray send them to me as before.

Yours

J Conrad.

---

[1] Because Doubleday liked everything to be done correctly? Alternatively, 'his' could be read as '[t]his'.
[2] C. Hayward & Son of Ashford attended to the Conrads' motoring needs.
[3] Sir Robert Jones: see the letter to him of 5 March.
[4] Eric Seabrooke Pinker (1891–1973) went to work for his father after leaving Westminster School. During the war, he won the Military Cross for bravery under fire. When J. B. Pinker died in 1922, he became the firm's senior partner and thus Conrad's principal agent, taking over the marketing of his work. He later moved to New York, and in 1939 earned $2\frac{1}{2}$–5 years in Sing Sing for appropriating $37,000 from his client E. Phillips Oppenheim.

To J. B. Pinker

Text MS Berg; Unpublished

[letterhead: Oswalds]

27.2.20

My dear Pinker

I return the Heinemann agreement duly signed. I haven't the slightest doubt you had very good reasons for the concession. This affair is sufficiently considerable from every point of view in any case. I have been making a small calculation which makes it come out like this

Roy^{ties} 3/- per vol. 20 vols. 1000 sets	£3,000.	
less F. M. H. proportion 1/2 roy^{ties} (1/6 per Vol. 2 vols. 1000 sets		
	−150	—
leaving for J. C. gross 2,850		
of which J. B. P.'s share as arranged	−570	—
	and J. C's	2,280
	{4. F. Unwin}	
less 5% on roy^{lties} on 10 vols.	{	
	{6. Methuen} (£1,500)	
		−75
leaving for J. C. nett proceeds		£*2,205*

I have deducted Hueffer's proportion[1] (which falls into your account with him, I suppose on the usual terms) to get the exact figures and not to complicate the statement; but I must ask you my dear Pinker to let me make up the comm[ission] which will be due to You from H[einemann] to the amount of our arrangement. It can be done by you debiting me with £15 in the general acct between us. The sum is small it is true but I have a particular desire that you should have the full *600* on this English edition.

---

[1] Ford Madox Ford's share of royalties on the collaborative novels, *Romance* and *The Inheritors*. Conrad continues to use Hueffer, Ford's pre-war surname, as in the days of their friendship and joint enterprise.

You don't imagine I expect you to answer this. I am not sure that you will even see it before you leave. I am improving – but I have had to give up the plan to run up and see you. Not improved enough – alas!

Ever most affect^ly yours

J. Conrad

To J. B. Pinker
Text MS Berg; Unpublished

[letterhead: Oswalds]
27.2.20
evening

Dearest friend.

I have just received (p.m.) your 2 letters of the 27th. Thanks for the six notes.

I am most compunctious at having unloaded such a lot on you at the last moment. But in truth I was not well enough to have looked into things before with any exactness – even if I had had the means to do so.

Prosperous journey and a safe return.

Ever gratefully Yours

J. Conrad.

To John Quinn
Text TS NYPL; *New York Tribune*, 5 April 1920, p. 10 (in part); J-A, 2, 237 (in part)[1]

[letterhead: Oswalds]
March. 2nd. 1920.

My dear Quinn.[2]

All that Doubleday matter[3] has been settled a long time ago by amicable agreement and belongs now to history. The trouble was not of my seeking. I simply raised objections as I was entitled to do on terms of freedom and equality without the slightest feeling of suspicion or antagonism but simply

[1] The previously printed extract runs from 'I confess' to 'more purposeful sort'. Jean-Aubry assigns the date [24 March].

[2] The son of Irish immigrants, John Quinn (1870–1924) came from Ohio. As a New York lawyer, he had a highly lucrative practice in commercial and financial law, particularly the law of tariffs. As a supporter of the arts, he won an exemption for artists from sales taxes and built up a great collection of modern painting and sculpture. He also amassed modern literary manuscripts, and among the writers he collected on a large scale were Yeats, Pound, Eliot, Joyce, and Conrad. When Quinn auctioned off his Conradiana in 1923, after relations between patron and author had chilled, the collection, bought for a total of $10,000, fetched $110,000.

[3] This responds to Quinn's letter of 20 January (TS carbon NYPL) about the number of sets in Doubleday's collected edition.

on the ground of my own view of my interests. However I have signed the formal agreement last week and I believe they are now going ahead in their usual whole-hearted manner.

Under the circumstances I will not answer the various statements and points of your letter of the 20th Jan. Pinker himself is leaving for America to-morrow. As his manners and moral character are good enough for men like Galsworthy, Bennett (the late Henry James too, who was not easy to please)[1] and a host of other men of worth and standing I answered his question "whether he might call on you?" affirmatively; giving him also messages from me personally of friendship and regard for you. That was before your two letters reached me; that of the 7th Feb. being delivered on the same day as the earlier one, for some reason best known to the Post Office.

My wife and I have been most sympathetically interested in the relation of your difficulties and the fine single-handed fight against adverse circumstances.[2] Our best wishes for a less strenuous but not unoccupied life in your distinguished position, in which you could find both material reward and the continued praise of men at less cost to your splendid vitality and your mental force. One does not like to think of a friend for whom one has a great regard and a man of an established great reputation, so hard driven by circumstances. But I note with pleasure that your health apparently has stood it extremely well and that you do not seem a bit jaded.

What you say of your changed attitude towards the Arrow of Gold gives me a certain amount of pleasure. I assure you it cost me some effort to pour cold water on your first proposal but I was so profoundly convinced of the story's unsuitability for the stage that I could not refrain from saying so to you.[3] I am pleased that your further reflection has brought you into agreement with my judgment.

I won't answer in detail that part of your letter which deals with our MS transactions.[4] Whatever promises may have passed between us in the years from 1911 to 1914 I plead that the conditions of the war, which has affected so many other transactions, apply to my action too. As I have said before, I wanted money in the first instance for a specific purpose which could suffer no delay. In the conditions of the unforeseen insecurity and disorganisation

---

[1] Writers for whom Pinker acted as agent.

[2] Quinn had been struggling with bad health and unreliable colleagues (Quinn to Conrad, 20 January and 5 February, TSS carbon, NYPL).

[3] Quinn had wanted to do his own dramatic adaptation of *The Arrow*. For Conrad's response, see *Letters*, 6, p. 454.

[4] Conrad may be referring to a comment in Quinn's letter of 5 February: 'You and I had an agreement that I was to have the first offer on all your MSS. I was not bound to take what you offered and you were at perfect freedom to put your own price upon what you offered. But I was to have the refusal at the price named by you.'

of all means of communications I went to the man on the spot; and under the prolongation of those same circumstances I went again to the man on the spot. The state of war brought unexpected calls on me, as on many others, and I was bound to attend to them. It so happened that this period coincided with my abandonment of handwriting. Thus you found yourself in possession of everything of mine drafted in pen and ink. You say, my dear Quinn, that you do not take that point; and, probably, from a collector's point of view there is nothing in it. But frankly I didn't advance it as any sort of excuse. I am an idealist in my way, and the fact that all MSS written completely by my hand will be in America while all the others, drafted differently, may remain in England seems (since division was unavoidable) to have a sort of fitness. In pursuance of that idea I have offered you the very last MS I have so far written in my own hand. It's most unlikely that there ever will be another. I am sending it to you, but the other I mentioned (that is some pages of Falk, typed and inter-lined) has got mislaid during our move from Spring Grove here. We changed houses at the time of the strike under the greatest difficulties and in some confusion – the professional mover, with whom I had a contract for the job, not being able to execute it as all his vans and men had been commandeered by the Government. Of course if that fragment ever turns up it shall be forwarded to you; but, really, it is not important enough to be in any sense a loss to your collection. Per contra a most unexpected lot of MS pages of *An Anarchist* turned up mysteriously. They are consecutive from page 46 to the end. I think you must have the beginning of that story[1] and I hope, if that is the case, that the two pieces will join properly. I've found also a few pages of *Romance* in mingled Conrad and Hueffer handwriting, which I must have preserved for a memento; but on coming on them during the search for that infernal Falk fragment I find that I don't seem to care very much for the associations of those old days. You will have to pay me something for those few things if you care for them at all, for you mustn't imagine that I have made my fortune as yet. I make an income; and of that the Government, to begin with, takes away one-fourth, that is 5 shillings in the pound, and if I have the imprudence to raise my income by another £500 that same hungry Government will promptly take 6 shillings in the pound. I don't speak of the so-called war-tax that hangs over all our heads (except of course The People's heads) and which will be in the nature of a levy on capital.[2] I don't say all this in a spirit of recrimination; but it is a fact that every unofficial bit will help, for I am already assessed for the current

---

[1] Quinn purchased the first part in 1913; see *Letters*, 6, pp. 230, 255.
[2] During the war, the standard rate of income tax had risen from 5.8% to 30%, but, on a graduated scale, those with high incomes could be liable for up to 50% or 60%. After the war, the government also increased the rates for death duties.

year. Next year I suppose I will have to make a clean breast of it because they assess one on an average of three years, and it would be unbecoming for such an idle plutocrat as I am to cheat The People.

Of European politics I know next to nothing, just a few bare facts on which it is hardly worth while to form an opinion. I confess to some little gratification at the thought that the unbroken Polish front keeps Bolshevism off and that apparently the re-born State has one heart and one soul, one indomitable will, from the poorest peasant to the highest magnate. Those same magnates, by the by, have now no more power and precious little more wealth than the poorest peasant, with whom they fight shoulder to shoulder against moral and physical pestilence bred in Russia, on a line from the Baltic Provinces to the present frontier of Roumania. The magic sense of independence is the cause of that union without reserves and regrets which enables that three times devastated and impoverished country to put forth its physical strength, and on the very morrow of rising from its grave to take up its old historical part of defender of civilisation against the dangers of barbarism, once Tartar and Turkish, and now even worse, because arising no longer from the mere savagery of nomad races but from an enormous seething mass of sheer moral corruption – generating violence of a more purposeful sort.[1]

Those, my dear Quinn, are the thoughts which cheer my not very laborious days. I seem to have lost the power to throw off my old enemy. The gout clings to me like ivy to a decaying tree. Since last July I haven't done a single bit of work that would bring money. All that I have managed to do is to write a few Prefaces for my collected edition and to revise with wholesome severity the text of *The Rescue* for book form. It was rather a wearisome task, requiring a lot of concentrated thinking, but I flatter myself I have improved that novel on its artistic side without interfering in the least with its popular qualities. Meantime I have been giving up my spare hours to turning round, speculating about, and trying to gauge the possible depth of the subject of my Mediterranean novel[2] which will be dedicated to you all right if I live long enough to finish it – and even if I don't. For even then the fragment would get published and I shall take good care that the dedication page shall be found amongst the precious papers left behind by the "late lamented". This promise, you will observe, is independent of circumstances less serious than a general earthquake or the end of the world.

[1] With virtually no help from other powers, Poland was fighting an invasion by the Red Army; this assault menaced the reborn country's boundaries as well as its political system.
[2] *Suspense.*

Well, I think, my dear Quinn, I have told you all I meant to tell you and even things I didn't mean to tell you when I began this letter. I hope you will receive all this verbiage in the spirit of friendship in which it is dispatched to you. May you ever prosper.

All here send you their warm regards

Very faithfully yours

Joseph Conrad.

To Eric Pinker
Text TS Berg; Unpublished

[letterhead: Oswalds]
March 3rd. 1920.

My dear Eric

Your letter of this morning was in the nature of a surprise as I understood I had to pay those people 5% on the amount of the royalties paid me on those books, not on their published price. This arrangement amounts to a shilling, a penny and a fraction of a penny per vol. But leaving the pence aside it will mean that I will have to pay Methuen 6,000 shillings and Fisher Unwin another 4,000 shs. if his conditions are the same: 10,000 out of the 60,000 which form my royalties on the whole thousand sets.

Whether it will be a thousand sets I don't know as yet. I wrote yesterday to Heinemann suggesting that he should come down here any day after the 8th of March and settle that matter after an exhaustive discussion. This is in accord with your father's letter which leaves that matter to me. I will of course let you know at once what happens.

I wired our goodbyes this morning to Southampton. I hope father left home looking fit and well.

Kindest regards

Yours

J. Conrad

To Thomas J. Wise
Text MS BL Ashley 2953; Unpublished

[letterhead: Oswalds]
Mch 3.'20

Dear Mr Wise

Looking through a drawer I found the pen and ink MS of my "Polish Question" paper, the one of which Mr Shorter was authorized to print a priv^{te} cir[culati]on booklet.[1]

---

[1] *The Polish Question: A Note on the Joint Protectorate of the Western Powers and Russia* (March 1919).

The paper was never intended for publication. It was written at a friend's request to be shown to the Foreign office (about June of the year 1916).[1] You must have seen the text. The MS consists of 15 pp foolscap.

I have also the *first draft* of two of my prefaces or Author's Notes. One is the Note for *The Secret Agent*. The other is for the "Mirror of the Sea". That one is double. That is there were 2 drafts one in *red* type corrected, from which the draft in *blue* type was taken, corrected in its turn, and it is from that blue type that clean copies for printers were taken. In fact the red type was suppressed.

Together 8 pp.

The Secret Agent is 10 pp.

If you care to give me £20 for the MS and £10 each for the other two (which is the price you paid for the prefaces in 1st draft now in your possession) I'll send them to you. I don't pretend to say these are important pieces, tho' the MS is my only attempt at anything lik[e] a state-paper.

I am still a prisoner, but the improvement in my health is not a sham this time I believe. I hope you've not been tormented by our common foe.[2]

With kind regards

Sincerely yours

J. Conrad.

To Jessie Conrad

Text MS Yale; *JCLW* 55–6

[letterhead: Oswalds]
Thursday [4 March 1920][3]
5.45. pm

Dearest of All Dear Girls That ever Were![4]

I have just got the wire in time to save me blowing the top of my head off with pent up worry. All my sympathy for the little girl that is going to be put

---

[1] Józef Hieronim Retinger (1888–1960), who was involved in Polish political affairs in London and Paris, delivered the note to the Foreign Office on 16 August 1916: see *Letters*, 5, pp. 638–40.

[2] Gout.

[3] *JCLW* places this in 1922. The 'Author's Note' to *The Secret Agent* (TS Yale), dated 3 March, and the letter to Sir Robert Jones of the 5th fix the date.

[4] Jessie Emmeline Conrad (née George, 1873–1936), the second of nine children, probably met her future husband in 1894 when she was working as a typist and living with her widowed mother. The Conrads married in March 1896. Both biographers and those who knew her disagree about her personality; some disparage her stolidity or patronise her want of formal education, others admire her fortitude and her shrewd management of a somewhat cantankerous family. An accident to her knee in 1904 exacerbated a previous injury, leaving her lame and in pain for the rest of her life. She wrote two books about her husband, *Joseph Conrad as I Knew Him* (1926) and *Joseph Conrad and His Circle* (1935). Her *Handbook of Cookery for a Little House*, accepted by a publisher in 1906, did not appear until 1923.

to bed for a fortnight. But I know that You (of all women!) are not going to be unreasonable about such a thing. Moreover Bobby[1] has spoken! That's enough. I wonder anxiously how much tired you are – and in what particular way – for you are a woman of considerable Varieties. It is only your sweetness and the grace that are in your heart which are always the same.

I worked all the morning. Note for S. Agent is finished *and* copied clean 1.30: At 2 oclock Dick wired that he was prevented coming by his boy developing influenza.[2] Wired back sympathy. You won't be surprised to hear that I couldn't sit at home twirling my thumbs while waiting for the wire. At 2.25 started for Hythe, nursing 3 wine glasses. Arrived 3.30. Old bandit very facetious pretending to drink strong waters from every pattern of glass in the shop.[3] Left 4.5 via Folk[esto]ne with a dozen claret glasses confined in a box. Am now very frightened at the purchase. A cut glass cup sat by my side on the back seat. Wants a job as a flower-holder in the window. Wages £3.10 forever. Arrived home 4.53. Tea. At 5.15 top of head lifting slightly. 5.28 wire. All pressure gone and a vague desire to go to bed and whistle tunes, but won't do that till after dinner. Great hugs for you and the boy. Love to K[arola].

Your own property

ever loving

J. C.

To Eric Pinker
Text MS Berg; Unpublished

[letterhead: Oswalds]
Thursday. [4 March 1920][4]

My dear Eric.

I return by Borys the signed agreement with Methuen (Coll*d* Ed*on*).[5] I've heard from H[einem]ann. I can see that he would prefer 1000 sets. We'll settle this next week.

Yours

J. Conrad

PS Please post me six £1 notes to day.

---

[1] Sir Robert Jones, her physician; see the letter to him of 5 March.
[2] Curle's son Adam was born in 1916.
[3] The 'bandit' being the proprietor, Frederick B. Ninnes.
[4] Dated by a note in Hallowes, which shows that Conrad signed the agreement with Methuen on 1 March. Conrad's Thursday is secure, this being the usual day when he requested the servants' wages.
[5] To include the books published by them in the collected editions.

To John Quinn
Text MS NYPL; Unpublished

Oswalds
Bishopsbourne
Kent
Eng^d
4 Mch. 1920.

Dear Quinn
  Herewith
  30 pp MS. Admiralty Paper.[1] Complete.
  say $5 per p.
  26 pp. MS. *An Anarchist.* To end of tale
  say $2 per p.
  12 miscellaneous pp MS. *Romance.* Mostly Hueffers 4 Conrads.
  no value.[2]
  Say $200 – if you care for the transaction

Yours

JC.

To Sir Robert Jones
Text J-A, 2, 236

Oswalds.
5.3.'20.

Dearest Sir Robert,[3]
  Ever so many thanks for the message for me you gave to the boy. I shall
certainly not worry now. And I don't think I worried much before. Weren't
you there? That thought was enough to keep worry off. Still a man somewhat
disabled for the common activities of life and feeling himself helpless, or, at
any rate, unhelpful, from that cause, is an easy prey to anxiety.

---

[1] 'The Unlighted Coast', written for the Admiralty in 1917.
[2] In fact, eleven leaves, three in Conrad's hand and eight in Ford's. They fetched $600 at Quinn's
sale.
[3] A leading British orthopaedic surgeon, Sir Robert Armstrong Jones (1858–1933; knighted 1917;
baronet 1926) came from North Wales, and practised in Liverpool, where he was consulting
surgeon to all the major hospitals. He was also a consultant at St Thomas's Hospital, and
a member of the War Office's Medical Advisory Board. During the war, he held the rank
of Major-General and took on the immense task of organising reconstructive surgery at
home and in the field. From 1921 to 1924, he served as President of the British Orthopaedic
Association, and was frequently honoured overseas. His monographs and textbooks on the
surgery of joints, military orthopaedics, and general orthopaedics were widely used. The
professional relationship that began, in 1917, with the care of Jessie Conrad developed into a
warm friendship with the Conrads.

I look forward to your arrival under our roof, – before very long, on some glorious day. My only concern now will be how to meet you with unbandaged hands, un-lame feet, un-aching back, un-anything of all these things that are as daily in my life as the daily bread of it. But for the last I have worked, whereas for the former I haven't even prayed. Why I should be thus privileged I can't imagine.

I hope all is well with your children and grandchildren. I don't know yet because I only expect my wife home this evening. I shall then also have reports of you.

I hope you will never dream even of taking any notice of this horrid scrawl. After all, – all I wanted to tell you is that I am and always shall be with the greatest regard

most affectionately yours.

To Eric Pinker
Text TS Berg; Unpublished

[letterhead: Oswalds]
March 5th. 1920.

My dear Eric.

I have just heard from H[einemann]. He will be in Birchington at the end of this month and will come over to see me then to discuss and settle the number of sets.

I have finished a Preface for The Secret Agent, which was the next in turn, and to save time have dispatched it direct from here to Garden City.

Have you an American copy of the *Set of Six* of either edition,[1] and does one or both of them have a Preface? I can't remember. If there is a Preface please send me the volume down here, so that I may see what it is like.

Regards.

Yours

J. Conrad.

To John Quinn
Text TS NYPL; Unpublished

[letterhead: Oswalds]
March 5th. 1920.

My dear Quinn.

I forgot to mention to you in my letter that your reference to some pamphlets[2] has given me the idea to write to Richard Curle, an intimate friend

---

[1] The Doubleday editions of 1915 and 1917.
[2] Quinn's letter of 5 February (TS carbon NYPL) had expressed a desire to own a complete run of the privately printed Conrad pamphlets

of mine, to whom I have confided a complete set of Wise's and my own pamphlets – two Series of 10 each – and also some done by Shorter, to dispose of for me. I don't know any dealers or amateurs, whereas Curle has very extensive relations amongst them. I won't conceal from you that I intend to make as much as I can out of the booklets. Curle's view is that the sets should be sold entire even if I have to wait some time for a good opportunity.

I haven't the slightest notion at the moment if he is in negotiation with anybody, or had any offers, or what he is doing at all; the matter not having been mentioned between us for a long time. In fact it was out of my mind completely when your letter came. I have asked him to drop you a line; and I write you personally on the subject only to let you know that he is not acting for himself but has taken the affair up to spare me the trouble of attending to it personally. I would not even have known how to conduct it to the best advantage.

As he has volunteered this kindness, amongst many others he is always ready to do for me, I could not, you understand, take the matter now out of his hands on any ground whatever.

I want also to tell you that I have decided to let no one publish any more of those booklets for some years to come – if I ever do. Neither will I do any myself.[1] I was drawn into this very unwillingly and want now to stop it dead.

You ought to be informed that there was a set of Wise (only) pamphlets (10) signed, which Curle has sold for me in U.S. to a dealer lately.

In sending you the items for your collection I forgot to say that one of the conditions is that you will send a typed copy of my "Admiralty Paper", as I find I have none by me.

I am my dear Quinn always sincerely Yours
J. Conrad

To Thomas J. Wise

Text TS BL Ashley 2953; Unpublished

[letterhead: Oswalds]
March 5th. 1920.

Dear Mʳ Wise.

Thanks for the good letter and the cheque, £40,[2] received this morning.

I am glad your health has been tolerable. Curle may come this week or not. The situation, as the newspapers say, is obscure. I have just had from him a

---

[1] He relented on this point, having 'The Dover Patrol' and 'John Galsworthy' printed in this format in 1922.

[2] For the items mentioned in the letter of the 3rd.

rather vague letter. Let me assure you of my deep sense of your kindness in letting him have those pamphlets to complete my set. It is extremely good of you.

I think you will find all the pieces signed at top and bottom and properly dated.

With kindest regards

yours faithfully

Joseph Conrad

To Major Ernest Dawson
Text MS Yale; Unpublished

[letterhead: Oswalds]
8. Mch 1920.

My dear Dawson.[1]

Your charming little inkstand-souvenir found us both in the profoundest dumps. I was laid up with bronchitis of a particularly disgusting sort – and gout in the wrists in addition. I didn't like to dictate you a typed letter – and so waiting from day to day for the power to hold the pen for more than a line and a signature I let the time slip. Why I didn't ask Miss Hallowes to drop you a line to say how things were with me I don't know. I was really too much flattened out to think of anything. These lines are the first evidence of improvement. B[orys] and I have been planning to tear the ink-bottle out and fit the box out as a petrol-lighter to be used in the drawing-room. An easy life.

For the photograph (excellent) let the lady thank you. That same lady has been to town to see her surgeon and has been ordered to bed for a fortnight. She has also managed to acquire a fairly complete bronchitis. To-day she is distinctly better and no doubt you'll hear from her before long.

I have begun working. Prepared my novel for the press (just before I went to bed with bronchitis) and am now devoting my languid attention to the play. We have had no one here since you left us. The season for visitors announces itself as very poor. Which is just as well; as we are not exactly an entertaining couple at present.

I hope you are resting, recuperating and taking a cheerful view of the future. With all our warmest regards

Yours always

J. Conrad

---

[1] Major Ernest Dawson (1884–1960) was introduced to Conrad by W. H. Henley and H. G. Wells. He contributed reminiscences and stories of Burma and Australia to *Blackwood's Magazine*. He served in Burma as a magistrate and as an officer in the Rangoon Volunteer Rifles. A resident of Rye, after his retirement he spent long periods on the Continent. His brother A. J. Dawson was another of Conrad's friends.

To Eric Pinker
Text TS Berg; Unpublished

[letterhead: Oswalds]
March 8th. 1920.

Dear Eric.

You may cheer up Vernon[1] by telling him on the 'phone or otherwise that I have been at the play ever since I could work at anything: that is the last two days; that the First of the Four Scenes which are to be presented in Act Four, according to his marvellous contrivance of a turning stage, is finished; and assure him that the whole horrible thing will be conducted exactly on the lines I told him of before, and which he seemed to approve. If it comes off, as I see it now, the audience won't get at the author to lynch him, because I don't intend to be there, but they will no doubt burn the theatre before they go home. But that of course is Vernon's affair.

I am anxious about the whereabouts of that Third Act. – If you have occasion you may mention to Vernon, as he is so much interested in the matter, that I admit that the Third Act may be altered to a certain extent as to phrasing and conduct of the stage action; but that the alteration of the scheme of the play is impossible, as he will see for himself on reading Act 4.

Kindest regards

Yours

J. Conrad.

To Richard Curle
Text TS/MS Indiana; Curle 59 (in part)[2]

[letterhead: Oswalds]
March 12th. 1920.

My dear Richard.

Sorry the visit didn't come off. Better luck next time; and if there is a genuine desire of the third party you may fix a date next week, if you like.

Books arrived this moment.[3] Many thanks for the affectionately inscribed copies, and the note of ages is interesting. I will talk to you about the two works with perfect and even offensive sincerity when we meet. My wrist is bad again. I am not anxious to write; and of dictating I swear to you I get enough with that ass Verloc and his tragic wife. That, however, will be done

---

[1] Frank Vernon (né Spicer, 1875–1940), actor and theatrical producer.
[2] Curle omits the third paragraph.
[3] According to Curle, his *Aspects of George Meredith* (1908) and *The Echo of Voices* (1917).

with by next Monday, unless there is a special curse on me of which I know nothing – as yet!

I am sorry for the poor little chap, with his incipient whooping-cough. It is a beastly thing to have and nearly as trying for the mother as for the child. Please give my kindest regards and true sympathy to your wife. I do hope it will be soon over, and Master Adam in great form again.

Jessie has taken a turn for the better.

All our love

Yours

J. Conrad.

To J. B. Pinker
Text TS/MS Berg; Unpublished

[letterhead: Oswalds]
March 12th. 1920.

Dearest Pinker.

To begin my first letter to "J. B. P. in America" I have the news that at this present moment of writing the Act Four of the S. A. is all but finished, there being nothing more to do but the last half of the last Scene. I won't pretend to say that it is the sort of job one can do while one whistles. What I can say is that the Play will be finished on the 15th; long before you read this.

Eric sent me word by B[orys] that Vernon has been inquiring as to how I got on, with a certain amount of interest. I dropped a line to E. asking him to tell Vernon that I was nearly through. The opening play of the season in the new Little Theatre seems to be something in the nature of a frost, and I wonder if they are thinking of putting on my horror in the spring.[1]

Of domestic news: Jessie returned from London on the 5th with orders to go to bed for a fortnight, at least, on account of the leg, which is receiving a certain treatment. Apart from that she has managed to catch a beastly bronchitis and, altogether, she has been looking a dismal object lately. She is, however, getting better. I have just had one of your birthday-chocolates, which are only distributed on special occasions.

As far as I could make out from the weather reports you must have had an average decent winter passage. I expect to see your arrival in to-morrow's paper.

---

[1] For more about the Little Theatre, then managed by J. E. Vedrenne and Frank Vernon, see the letter to Eric Pinker of 17 April. The 'horror' is the stage version of *The Secret Agent*. For the Little Theatre's transformation into a house that welcomed the horrific and became a possible venue for *Laughing Anne*, see the letter of 10 December.

Did you manage to get a rest? Next week I imagine you will have a conference with our friend Everitt and open to him many matters. But I really
don't know whether there are many or few matters to treat of in regard
of my affairs, tho' I have no doubt that you will have your hands full all
the time of your stay. Do you think it would be in order if I asked D. P &
Co. (through you of course) whether they would be kind enough to send
me a sort of synopsis up to the year 1919, showing the sale of each of my
books in both editions they run in the U.S., and of course, the proceeds.
It would amuse me to know, for I have often been asking myself how they
stood in respect of popularity as against each other. This can't give D. P &
C^o much trouble. I suppose it is just a matter of looking at the books and
taking out a few figures. As I grow older I think much more about my past
work in that and in other ways. When you drop me a line, perhaps you will
tell me, (what you will have heard of course) how the Arrow of Gold did in
the first eleven months of its public existence? Here belated notices drop in
still on the occasion of the Second Edition which F. U[nwin] advertised last
week; some of the writers taking it for a new publication altogether. Others
again giving it a friendly additional shove forward – which is very nice of
them.[1]

I don't think I will cable you on Monday to say that the Play is finished
according to plan. Let us be saving. And then I don't know your address;
though I suppose I wouldn't be far wrong if I picked out the smartest hotel in
New York. I am employing a third party[2] to try to do a deal with Quinn
in a set of private pamphlets. Something worth while! So, pray, handle
him like the fisherman his worm in Isaac Walton's book: "as if you loved
him".[3]

Jessie sends her love.

Ever affectiona^{ly} Yours

J. Conrad

PS. An Auth^{rs} Note for Sec^t Ag^t left for America last mail. I am going to write
one for a Set of Six next. *Do* please give me some news how, when, in what
form, they are going to pub^{sh} the Ltd Edition? I ought to know.
PPS Have arranged with H[einemann] to come down to see me here end
March for final decision as to the number of sets here.

---

[1] Lennox Robinson, for example, reviewed *The Arrow* for the *Irish Statesman* on 7 February.
[2] Richard Curle. See the letter of the 18th.
[3] Izaak Walton, *The Compleat Angler* (1653). The summary of a sentiment rather than a quotation.

To Grace Willard

Text MS Colgate; Unpublished

[letterhead: Oswalds]
[mid-March? 1920][1]

Dear Grace

Herewith the £50 of which I spoke. Please drop us a line as to when you'll want the van as it must be ordered a day or two in advance.

Love from us all to you and the Precious Child.

Yours always

J. Conrad

To G. Jean-Aubry

Text MS Yale; *L.fr.* 152–3

[letterhead: Oswalds]
[17 March 1920][2]

Cher Aubry.

Je crois que c'est juste. J'ai la moitié de serial rights. Du moins cela me semble aux termes de la note que j'ai prise a l'époque. Pour être certain il faudrait voir le contrat qui est chez Pinker. Voulez Vous que je le demande? Je m'imagine que le jeune homme saura le trouver dans l'absence de son père.

Merci du St Simon[3] arrivé ce matin a ma grande joie. J'ai fini le drame avant-hier.[4] Ce soir je finis la révision. Demain je me plonge en le St Simon. Une petite fête pour le travailleur – grâce a Votre bonne amitié.

Je retourne a l'Agent.

Tout à Vous

J. C.

On second thought[s] I am writing a Eric Pinker: de regarder le contrat et me dire ce que je reçois pour ma part des *serial rights*.

N'oubliez pas le libretto de Carmen si c'est possible. Une fois Vous en Espagne je pourrais courir après![5]

---

[1] Conrad's letter to Pinker of 24 February and the completion of Grace Willard's work at Oswalds by the end of March (see letter of the 26th) suggest the period.

[2] Jean-Aubry's date, confirmed by news that the adaptation of *The Secret Agent* was completed on the 15th (letter to Curle of the 18th).

[3] *Les Mémoires de Saint-Simon* by Louis de Rouvroy, duc de Saint-Simon (1675–1755), a gift from Jean-Aubry. Covering the years 1691–1751, the *Mémoires* give a brilliant picture of intrigues and personalities at the court of Louis XIV.

[4] The dramatisation of *The Secret Agent*.

[5] In Georges Bizet's opera *Carmen* (1875), set in Spain, Don José doggedly pursues Carmen after she leaves him for a new lover.

Et le Corsaire![1] – celui qui habite chez Vous – au Havre.

Translation

Dear Aubry.

I think that's correct. I get half the serial rights. At least that seems to me the terms of the agreement made at the time. To be certain one would have to see the contract at Pinker's. Do you want me to ask for it? I should think that the young man will know where to find it in his father's absence.

Thank you for the Saint-Simon, which to my great joy arrived this morning. I finished the play the day before yesterday. Tonight I finish revising. Tomorrow I plunge into Saint-Simon. A small reward for the labourer, which is owing to your good friendship.

I get back to *The Agent*.

Yours truly

J. C.

On second thought[s] I am writing to Eric Pinker: to look at the contract and tell me what my share of the *serial rights* is.

If possible, don't forget the libretto of *Carmen*. Once you are in Spain, I could chase you up!

And the Pirate! – the one who lives close by you – in Le Havre.

To Eric Pinker
Text TS/MS Berg; Unpublished

[letterhead: Oswalds]
March 17th. 1920.

My dear Eric.

I will keep the Spanish agreement[2] back for a bit, as it doesn't strike me as quite fair. £25 a book is very little considering the enormous South American market open to Spanish publishers – serials and books.

The second consideration is that I have had an unofficial hint that the newspaper "El Sol" wishes to publish the "Arrow of Gold" as a serial.

---

[1] According to Jean-Aubry, the poet 'Tristan Corbière', but a better match would be his father, Édouard (1793–1875), sailor, editor of the *Journal du Havre*, and marine novelist. Otherwise, the present tense suggests an allusion either to some old salt in Le Havre or to some upcoming performance of Hector Berlioz's concert overtrue *Le Corsaire* (1831).

[2] With the Madrid publishing house Atenea; the agreement would authorise the translation of *Almayer's Folly*. Atenea wanted to follow that with a translation of *Typhoon* (Atenea, S[ociedad] E[ditorial] to J. B. Pinker, 10 March, Berg).

Mr Madariaga,[1] the distinguished correspondent of "El Sol" in England, is leaving for Madrid shortly, and on his return I expect to hear something definite. What pleases me most is that Mr M. would undertake the translation himself if the affair comes off.

I would like to arrange this affair myself. As it is quite on the cards (in fact very probable) that I will retain the book right[s] of "Arrow of Gold" (El Sol is only a big daily with no publishing business), we could go to a Spanish Publisher later with a ready translation in hand, either ourselves or through Mr M. who would be personally interested in getting good terms for *that* book certainly, and by the same occasion probably for all the others.

A little delay then can't hurt us at all. If you really care for those people then you will use your diplomacy to keep the matter in suspense for a bit. Put it all on to me. I know nothing about them but I have the means, apart from Mr M., to discover the reputation of this and other Spanish publishing houses.

Kindest regards

Yours

J. Conrad.

Am expecting Your news by wire about V[ernon].
Pray send me the six notes to-morrow.

To Eric Pinker
Text MS Berg;[2] Unpublished

[letterhead: Oswalds]
Wednesday. [17 March 1920][3]

My dear Eric.

I forgot to ask you in my letter to look at my French contract with *La Nouvelle Revue Française* (signatory Gallimard) and send me word *what proportion of serial rights* I receive as my share under that agreement.

If it'll save you trouble send the document itself here so that I may look at it. But the above is the point I want to ascertain as I have forgotten completely what was fixed: 1/2 or 1/3.

Yours sincerely

J. Conrad.

---

[1] Salvador de Madariaga (1886–1978), man of letters, journalist, and writer on politics, an habitué of Mme Alvar's salon.
[2] Not in the main collection but the Gordan bequest of the 1990s.
[3] The previous letter fixes the date.

To Richard Curle

Text TS/MS Indiana; Curle 60 (in part)[1]

[letterhead: Oswalds]
March 18th. 1920.

My dear Curle.

Yes, next week will do, if you make it Friday. Saturday won't because the Shover[2] departs for weekend for amorous reasons.

I enclose you here a letter from Keating.[3] Do you think that what he means is that 500 dollars has been asked for *one* pamphlet?

Well! It is a startling bit of information, to be sure, if it is as I take it. I don't understand why K should be indignant at $500 being asked for a 10 set, since [he] has already paid $50 for single copies.

The first thought that comes into my head in any case is that if Q[uinn] doesn't jump at the set at 75 dollars a copy he will be a colossal ass. As to the rest I have answered Keating rather sharply, not liking quite that suggestion that I should "prevent" . . . Prevent what? How can I stop the dealers asking what they jolly well like, unless, indeed, I had my finger in that pie myself. That little word "prevent" raised my dander considerably.

It is quite conceivable you have done for the best by taking the Rectory. The sooner you are, and feel, settled the better I will be pleased. That's an excellent piece of news about the boy! I am heartily glad of it.

The first draft of the Play was finished on the 15th. I am now working at it, inking my fingers and ruffling my hair during the usual agonies. It is truly a damnable job but to be candid with you it isn't so bad this time – at any rate as yet. It's when I tackle the draft of the Third Act that the tug-of-war will come.

It is arranged that Vernon will come here some day after April 6th. I hear he is now busy rehearsing the next piece to be produced on the 6th. It may very well be that mine will follow; which would bring my production somewhere to the end of May. But devil only knows!

Aubry is going to translate, and our intention is to throw the thing at the pigeons in the Theatre du Vieux Colombier.[4] We may of course have it thrown back at us. Pigeons are wily birds.

Jessie sends her love. She spend her days in the chair now – upstairs. But really there is no change – and what we are most concerned at is the depressing effect of it on her. She worries herself with gloomy forebodings.

[1] Curle omits the fifth paragraph.   [2] Humorous or ironic version of 'chauffeur'.
[3] George Thomas Keating (1892–1976), a keen collector of Conradiana, then with Moore and Munger, a New York firm dealing in paper and clay products.
[4] Literally, the Old Dovecote Theatre (in Paris), and hence the play on pigeons. For Conrad's acquaintance with Jacques Copeau, the theatre's founder, see *Letters*, 4, p. 526.

Altogether life is pretty hard. Bills still come in – naturally. The grave is the only refuge from them. And in this connection do you think I could ask W[ise] £100 for the first draft of the play. It is a good piece, nearly half of it actual pen and ink, and generally interesting. About 140 pp.

Ever Yours

J. Conrad.

To Eric Pinker
Text TS/MS Berg; Unpublished

[letterhead: Oswalds]

March 18th. 1920.

My dear Eric.

Thanks for your letter. I had no idea V[ernon] was going to produce something new so soon. Any day after April 6th. will suit me if he only kindly gives me good notice, so that we are not intruded upon. As to him having the complete copy of Play:-

First of all please tell me whether you have the *clean* copy of *Act 1.* in your possession, or is it V. that has got it? I haven't got it. With that exception I have everything here, rough draft and clean copy, O.K.

Of course I have no objection to sending Vernon the complete play. I hoped he could come soon just because I wanted to consult him as to the conduct and actual wording of the Third Act before I started re-writing it in deference to his opinion. You know he jumped on that one with both feet – and such an (apparently) nice man too! I am still shaking with fright. However I propose to-morrow to drink half a bottle of neat whisky and then sit down to improve that Third Act. Therefore I think I will keep back the clean text till I have effected the above improvements. It will be done in time for him to read the whole before he comes down.

I expect to hear from you to-morrow, Friday, as I want badly the information, I asked you for, in the pen and ink letter. (French ser: rights share)

As to the Spanish business pray don't imagine that I am raising futile objections. I really don't think that it is quite good enough. If your father had been here I would have written to him exactly the same. I don't know whether, perhaps, you consider the immediate acceptance of pressing material importance. If so please tell me your mind right out and we shall see what can be done.

Cordially Yours

J Conrad

PS Give our joint loves to everybody at home – if you *ever* go home!

To G. Jean-Aubry
Text MS Yale; *L.fr.* 153–4

[letterhead: Oswalds]
Sunday
21.3.20

Mon cher Aubry.

Anglo-Saxonisme ici n'est pas de mise; laissez-moi vous embrasser a la façon Franco-Polonaise pour votre cadeau. C'est la plus aimable canne du monde. Elle sera ma compagne des mauvais jours – des jours ou je boite. Elle a l'air gai et un aspect charmant. Elle sera ma canne de salon ma canne d'intérieur – pas précisement une garde malade (beaucoup trop jolie pour cela) – mais enfin son sort est fixé.

Si vous avez le temps donnez moi votre avis:

La Maison Atenea S. E. de Campomanes 8. Principal Derecha. Madrid m'a fait une offre de £25 pour chaque ouvrage (trad^on) livre et *"serial rights"* compris. Au moins 2 ouvrages par an. etc etc Je n'ai rien signé encore et j'ai instruit Pinker, de suspendre les negotiations. Je voudrais savoir ce que El Sol dira – s'il dit quelque chose. Gallimard[1] est correct. C'est bien *la moitié* de serial rights en France.

à vous de coeur
J. Conrad.

Translation

My dear Aubry.

Anglo-Saxonism is not in order here. Allow me to embrace you in the Franco-Polish fashion for your gift. It is the finest walking-stick in the world. It will be my companion on bad days – days when I limp. It has a gay air and a charming look. It will be my salon stick, my at home stick – not exactly a nurse (much too pretty for that), but its fate is fixed.

If you have the time, give me your advice:

The house of Atenea Ltd, Campomanes 8, Front Door, Right, Madrid, has offered me £25 for each work (translation) delivered, *including serial rights*. At least two works per year, etc., etc. I have not yet signed anything, and I've instructed Pinker to suspend negotiations. I should like to know what *El Sol* will say, if anything. Gallimard is right. It is indeed *half* the serial rights in France.

Yours affectionately
J. Conrad

---

[1] The French literary publishing house established by Gaston Gallimard (1881–1975) in 1911.

To Richard Curle
Text MS Indiana; Curle 61

[letterhead: Oswalds]
23.3.20

My dear Richard.

Thanks for you[rs]. The car will meet the train on Friday. 12.42.

Can't ask you to stop for week end because Jessie is still laid up and the servants are going on leave. There is also trouble with the pump which will cause I am afraid 2 days' interruption of hot water supply when the repairs are taken in hand. The man may not turn up till Friday. Awfully sorry; but there are a good many of us and 2 girls will have their hands full. Also the cooking will be chancy as Dora will have to try her hand at it on Sund. You had better not risk it.

I am glad your book[1] is to be looked out for any day now. I am very impatient. Inscribe the copy to both of us as J[essie] will appreciate very much being associated in the presentation of the Vol.

All luck to it – and to you in every way.

You don't give your opinion as to what I may ask from W[ise] for MS of Play. 173 pp. 1/2 pen and ink. Unique, so far. I think 120 would not be extortionate. A very fine item.

Au revoir then

Yours ever

J. Conrad.

PS A full set of *corrected* galley slips of *Resc*[2] is awaiting your instructions to forward or keep.

To Richard Curle
Text MS Indiana; Curle 62

[letterhead: Oswalds]
Thursday. [25 March 1920][3]

Dear Richard

Just a line to thank you for the book.[4]

As I turn the pages my consideration for you grows to the proportions of respect.

There is a beauty of easy moving prose – charm of phrase – felicity of words which give the strongest possible impression of mastery of language and individual vision of things and men.

---

[1] *Wanderings.*
[2] The *Land and Water* proofs (Yale) used to set up the book text.
[3] Curle supplies the date.   [4] *Wanderings.*

My warmest congratulations.

Au revoir tomorrow

Yours

J. Conrad.

To G. Jean-Aubry

Text MS Yale; *L.fr.* 154

[letterhead: Oswalds]
Thursday. [25 March 1920][1]

Cher Aubry.

J'ai eu une lettre de Pinker fils.

Merci mille fois de la peine que Vs Voulez bien prendre. Je confesse que le feuilleton dans El Sol ou le Figaro me plairaît beaucoup – comme réclame si Vs Voulez.

Mais être bien traduit c'est ça qui me séduit le plus.

Nos meilleurs souhaits pour le succès de Votre voyage aux Espagnes.

Tout à Vous

J. Conrad.

Translation

Dear Aubry.

I had a letter from young Pinker.

Many thanks indeed for the trouble you are willing to take. I confess that serialisation in *El Sol* or *Le Figaro* would please me a good deal – as advertising, if you like.

But to be well translated, *that* is what attracts me most.

Best wishes for the success of your trip to Spanish parts.

Yours truly

J. Conrad

To Grace Willard

Text MS Colgate; Unpublished

[letterhead: Oswalds]
26 Mch '20

Dearest Grace.

Just a word of thanks for your more than friendly offices in getting the home together.

---

[1] Jean-Aubry supplies the date.

C[atherine] has been delightful and patient with her agèd friend. My love to her and best wishes for a good time on her holiday.

I enclose here a ch: for 50 to cover your out-of-pocket ex: which there *must* have been.

Pardon haste

All our loves

J. C.

To Thomas J. Wise
Text TS/MS BL Ashley 2946; Unpublished

[letterhead: Oswalds]
March 26th. 1920.

Dear Mr Wise.

I think I ought to let you know that I have a completed first draft of, what I may well call, my first play – with the exception of the One Act I did 16 years ago,[1] the first draft of which is either non-existent or in America. If it does exist it is not complete.[2]

I confess I would have liked to keep this MS. but I require some money for a specific purpose, so I will part with it – with some slight regret. It is an adaptation. The *Secret Agent*, A drama in Four Acts, pp. 173, for the most part heavily scored and corrected in pen and ink. Some pages are wholly re-written and not one of them is without some handwriting on it.

Whether there will be any more play MSS of mine I don't know. I feel at present that it is very unlikely. The labour is great; and now the task is done the satisfaction is imperfect. However it may be, this one I think is a good item and I suppose literarily interesting. *I want £150 for it.* It is absolutely the First Draft – the first creation. One copy of it exists called the *First Copy*, lightly corrected. Vedrenne[3] has got it now but I intend to get it back from him and leave in circulation only two perfectly *Clean Copies* (without any corrections) which will have to be made, one for England and one for America.

I don't send it to you for inspection, so as to avoid any unnecessary risk of loss, till I hear that you are inclined to consider the offer. I would be very reluctant for various reasons, delay being one of them, to have to send it to the United States. Indeed as I have said already I am very loth to part at all with this first attempt on my part to grapple seriously with dramatic art.

---

[1] *One Day More*, a dramatisation of 'To-morrow', written in 1904.
[2] The complete manuscript (Berg) appeared in Quinn's sale.
[3] J. E. Vedrenne (1867–1930) was a theatre manager, most notably in association with Harley Granville-Barker.

I hope you have benefited by your stay in Hastings. I am still seedy and find it still difficult to use the pen.

Kind regards

Sincerely yours

Joseph Conrad.

To Eric Pinker
Text TS/MS Berg; Unpublished

[letterhead: Oswalds]
March 27th. 1920.

My dear Eric.

On Thursday last the Play complete went to Vernon who has acknowledged it this morning. In all my communication and correspondence with him it is taken for granted that the Play *will* be produced by Vedrenne; therefore the question of agreement will crop up before long. I think however that it need not be solved before Father's return and therefore I refrain here from giving you my ideas on the subject. V[ernon] says he can't come down here till after the 9th. Ap. This will suit me all right. I imagine V. will read the play long before that, of course, and he may communicate his impression to you.

Thanks for the American proofs.[1] Miss H. has commenced reading them and has found already enough misprints to make it clear that a careful reading is absolutely necessary. I expect Heinemann will turn up here in a few days, according to plan, and I am determined not to let him go till the matter is fixed one way or another.

I expect that Doubleday has got Dent's proof[2] already by this time. The way Dent's people put in all the corrections without confusion or mistakes is perfectly wonderful. If you had seen the galley proofs as they went to Dent you would share my admiration.

I presume you got on all right with Aubry. His activity on the spot, over there, can't possibly do any harm and may do some good. You mustn't assume that he is a meddler. As a matter of fact he and I used to talk often about the Spanish affairs for some time past, so that when you sent me the agreement I felt in a measure bound to let him know that such a thing was in contemplation. Of course he volunteered to look into it purely as a friend.

---

[1] Given the reference to Heinemann in this paragraph, presumably of the first volume of the collected edition.
[2] Of *The Rescue*.

My poor wife has been getting steadily worse. She's all but completely crippled and in constant pain. It's extremely disquieting as it is a matter of great doubt what the cause is – or could be! This morning we have had a wire from Sir R. Jones announcing his visit for Wednesday next. I am worried about her extremely, for her endurance is over-tried and she begins to show it. It takes an uncommon firmness of mind to react against years of suffering and so many disappointments; and this last is very severe both on account of the favourable prospects after the operation and of the helplessness to which [she] has been reduced – worse than anything she has experienced before.

Thanks for giving B[orys] £5. He left home without his money. I have not received my notes so far. But the one o'clock post is not in yet.

Sincerely Yours

J. Conrad.

Thanks for pay[men]ts to Ninnes and Miss H[allowes]. The *rent was due on the 25.* – (£62-10-0)

To Stella V. Roderick

Text TS/MS Penn State; Sheard

[letterhead: Oswalds]
March 27th. 1920.

Dear Miss Roderick.[1]

I was very glad to hear from the Elder Brother of my friend *Romance*.[2]

My old friend and lit: agent, Mr James B. Pinker, is at this present moment in New York, but I am afraid that by the time you get this he will be already upon that inconvenient ocean which spreads between us. It is also just possible that he may have already called on you.

In his absence I don't really know very well how my engagements stand, but I have a notion amounting almost to certitude that I still owe two short stories to the Metropolitan Mag. on an old (1914) agreement. It was an agreement

---

[1] Stella Virginia Roderick, a member of the editorial staff of the popular American periodicals *Everybody's Magazine* and *Metropolitan Magazine*, was herself the editor of sixteen issues of the *Women's Magazine*. In 1932, she became Secretary of the Nettie Fowler McCormick Biographical Association, and published a biography of that prominent Chicago businesswoman and philanthropist, widow of Cyrus McCormick, in 1956.

[2] The magazine *Romance*, in which *The Rescue* was serialised from November 1919 to May 1920; it had grown out of *Everybody's Magazine*.

without dates, simply stipulating that the Met. Mag. should have the first six short stories I should write after the agreement had been signed.[1]

I will however communicate your letter to Mr Pinker on his return; but I must tell you at once that I have nothing in my drawers, long or short, (I never have), and that as a matter of fact my mind is for the present altogether off short stories. It is rather busy contemplating and, as it were, walking round a rather big subject – I don't say great – which will require a long book to work out. And when that will be done Heaven only knows!

I regret sending you such an inconclusive answer, but I wished to acknowledge your friendly and charming communication without delay.

Believe me very sincerely Yours
Joseph Conrad.

To John Galsworthy
Text MS Forbes; J-A, 2, 237–8

[letterhead: Oswalds]
28.3.'20

Best and dearest Friend.[2]

Thanks with all my heart for the dedication[3] you promise to us both. Jessie no doubt has written to you already. She is extremely delighted at having her existence acknowledged in that way.

Pray dear Jack drop us a line to say how dear Ada is after the journey.[4] I am afraid you will come in for the season of beastly spring winds mostly from the East. I dread their coming – tho' I don't see how they can make me much worse than I've been for the last 10 weeks.

Poor Jessie has been laid up for a month now. She's quite crippled again. The severe disappointment after the bright prospects of only 2 month[s] ago has affected her spirits – at last. I am very anxious about her. However Sir Robert has announced his arrival for Wed[y] next, and we shall know then what is to be done.

---

[1] The contract with this New York magazine offered £300 per short story. See *Letters*, 5, pp. 322, 441, and 6, p. 382.

[2] John Galsworthy (1867–1933) met Conrad in the *Torrens* in 1893. His early writing was tentative, but in 1932 he won a Nobel Prize (an honour denied his friend) for his fiction and plays. Like his fictional Forsytes, his family was well supplied with money, and he helped Conrad with many gifts and loans during the earlier period of his career, providing constant encouragement throughout it.

[3] To *In Chancery*, scheduled to appear in October.

[4] She suffered from chronic rheumatism and also had bronchial problems. The Galsworthys had been in France and Spain since December 1919.

You will be shocked to hear that I have just finished dramatising the Secret Agent. (Now the murder's out). It is very horrible. Vedrenne has got it to look at. If it ever gets on the stage the audience won't lynch the author because I don't intend to be there but I've warned V. that they will probably try to burn the theatre before they go home.

I've managed to ram everything in there except the actual cab-drive. It was very interesting to do – and perfectly useless.

In haste to catch post.

Our dear love.

Ever Yours

J. Conrad

To Thomas J. Wise
Text TS BL Ashley 2946; Unpublished

[letterhead: Oswalds]
March 28th. 1920.

Dear Mʳ Wise.

Thanks for your letter and enclosure received to-day.[1]

The *First Draft* will be posted to you, registered, to-morrow Monday. As to the *First Copy* as I've said Vernon has got it. I shall get it back from him some time in the course of the next month and shall send it to you directly the clean copies are made. As to these you must understand that I will not have them in my possession and very likely I will not even see them at all. They will bear no corrections in my hand and in any case if there are any corrections they would be only corrections of actual misprints which the office that will take the copies may make. They will disappear in the course of time, no doubt, after the acting copies have been taken from them and in any case they would be altogether different as to paper and type from the *F. D.* and *F. C.* which come from my work-table.

Hastings is rather far from us, so I didn't even attempt to ask you to come over, but if you ever think of giving Folkestone a turn don't forget that this house is only ten miles away and that we will be always very glad to see you here, and the pleasure would be all the greater if Mrs Wise[2] felt inclined to come too. Perhaps then my wife would be able to go about. The operation last December was quite successful in itself, but something has happened again and she has been laid up for the last month quite crippled and in a good deal of pain. We expect Sir Robert Jones here on Wednesday to see what's the matter and what there is to be done. All this is naturally a great

[1] A cheque for £150 for the stage adaptation of *The Secret Agent*, posted on the 27th.
[2] Frances Louise ('Louie') Wise (née Greenhalgh, 1875–1939).

worry and anxiety to me, so that I find any kind of work very trying and very difficult.

Believe me

very sincerely yours

Joseph Conrad.

To Lady Millais

Text MS Private collection; Unpublished

[letterhead: Oswalds]

31.3.20

Dear Lady Millais.[1]

To-day at Noon Sir R Jones operated Jessie, giving her instant relief. It was not a moment too soon. She was nearly at the end of her endurance. The prospect of this being the last of the trouble is very good and I have Sir Robert's assurance that nothing further can arise which he can not put right.

I saw Jessie at 4 pm. nearly recovered and trying to make little jokes in a feeble voice. She is in St George's Nursing Home where I feel she is safe. M[r] Whitehead Read*[2] is looking after her for Sir R. Jones as M[r] Fox[3] is really to[o] far away.

Jessie sends her love to you and Sir John.[4]

I am still seedy. I do hope I'll be able to run over before long.

With my most affectionate regards to Yourself and Sir John I am dear Lady Millais

always your most faithful friend & servant

Joseph Conrad

---

[1] Mary St Lawrence, Lady Millais (née Hope-Vere of the marquesses of Linlithgow, 1861–1948; widowed 1897), a Scotswoman, lived in Ashford with her son Sir John. She was a close friend of Jessie Conrad. In her later years, she served as a Justice of the Peace.

[2] After Cambridge, (Edwin) Douglas Ian Whitehead Reid (1883–1930) qualified as a surgeon and radiologist in 1909. He was senior surgeon at the Kent and Canterbury Hospital and St George's House nursing home, also in Canterbury.

[3] (Campbell) Tilbury Fox (*c.* 1870–1949), who qualified at University College, London, in 1901, practised in Ashford.

[4] John Everett Millais (1888–1920; 3rd baronet 1897), the painter's grandson and Conrad's sometime chess partner. He served in the war, held the rank of Lieutenant-Commander in the Royal Navy from which he was retired, and in 1919 had been a Justice of the Peace in Kent.

To Lady Colvin
Text MS Duke; Unpublished

[letterhead: Oswalds]
Thursday. [1 April 1920][1]

Dearest Lady Colvin.[2]

On returning from my morning visit to the Nursing Home in Canterbury I found your dear letter. I answer briefly, as you desire, by saying that Jessie had as good a night as could have been expected. She sends her dear love to you both.

The operation (40 min) was performed at noon and Sir Robert left here at 3.50 back for Scotland.

The relief given was instantaneous – and the prospect of this being the end of her troubles is very good.

I'll write in a day or two. I am feeling seedy and hop about in a gout-boot and with a bandaged wrist. (left)

What a life!

But nothing matters now that Jessie is relieved of all pain. The last 3 weeks were awful for her and for us who had to look on.

Come! I should think I would come — if I could only get away. I would run up on purpose to see you and dearest Colvin. Perhaps soon——but it's impossible to make any plans yet.

Always, dear Lady Colvin

your most affectionate and grateful friend and serv[t]
Joseph Conrad.

To Eric Pinker
Text MS Berg; Unpublished

[letterhead: Oswalds]
Thursday. [1 April 1920][3]

Dear Eric.

The Missus is going on very well.

I had a cable from Quinn saying he had Father to lunch and that he likes him immensely.[4] I hope it's mutual.

---

[1] The medical news indicates the Thursday in question.
[2] Frances, Lady Colvin (née Fetherstonhaugh, 1838?–1924) was, with her husband Sidney, a friend of Conrad's later years. Her first marriage, to the Revd Albert Hurt Sitwell, ended with her husband's death. She had been a devoted friend to Robert Louis Stevenson.
[3] Quinn's cable of 31 March (TS copy NYPL) fixes the date.
[4] Quinn wrote: 'Liked Pinker immensely not less because his long devotion your interests'.

Pray send me the usual 6 notes.

Yours

J. C.

To Grace Willard
Text MS Colgate; Unpublished

[letterhead: Oswalds]
2. Ap '20

Dear Mama Grace

When your letter arrived Jessie had just been operated by Sir Robert who came down from Scotland for the purpose. The operation gave Jessie instant relief and Sir R has very good hopes that this is the end of her troubles. She's going on very well indeed and has charged me to send you her best love.

You have been very good to us in the whole transaction. Jessie before leaving here for the S*George Nursing Home. Canterbury* (where she now is) had herself wheeled into the drawing-room and was delighted with the effect of the panel and the spanish carved frames.

We do hope the "dear child" will have a good time in France and come back refreshed. I won't see Vernon till after the 9th – and what he will say of the play when he comes I can't even guess.

No more at present

We all send our love to you

Yours

J. Conrad.

To Dr A. Knaur
Text MS Private collection; Unpublished

[letterhead: Oswalds]
3.4.20

Dear Sir.[1]

I am writing for my wife who has had a serious operation two days ago and is now in a Nursing Home.

My wife has been unable to trace the housekeeper in whose care M[r] & Mrs Retinger[2] left some of their things. The letter she wrote to her was returned through the dead-letter office.

Believe me very faithfully yours

Joseph Conrad.

---

[1] His identity is unknown, and the envelope, now missing, has also been read as addressed to Dr. A. Kranz. There is no doctor of either name in the British medical registers; he may well have been a scientist, have lived on the Continent, or both.

[2] On the Retingers, see the following letter.

To Otolia Retinger
Text MS Private collection; Unpublished

[letterhead: Oswalds]
3.4.20

Dear Mrs Retinger.[1]

Jessie has done what she could to trace the whereabouts of Mrs Vowles. I am afraid it really can't be done. I have written to D[r] A Knaur to that effect this evening.

Three days ago poor Jessie had to be operated again. We all hope that this will be [the] end of her troubles. She stood the operation (the third since June 1917) very well and is going quite satisfactorily.

We had a very anxious time with her ever since the middle of Jan[y] last. She suffered very much. At the same time I too was laid up with bronchitis and gout and altogether since New Year's day we have [had] a very dismal time.

I had a note from Joseph[2] (from Italy) which I answered by a postcard, as he was announcing his arrival in England for the end of March. We are very sorry to see from your letter that it is not to be.

Jessie sends her love and the two boys join me in the expression of my most affectionate regard and all possible good wishes.

I am dear Mrs Retinger ever your faithful friend and servt

Joseph Conrad.

To Sir Sidney Colvin
Text MS Hofstra; Lucas 306–7 (in part)[3]

[letterhead: Oswalds]
4.4.20.

My dearest Colvin.

Jessie is going on very well and everybody around her connected with the case seems determined to make it *the last time* as far as care and foresight can do it.

---

[1] Otolia ('Tola') Retinger (née Zubrzycka, 1889–1984) and her husband the political activist Józef Retinger became friendly with Conrad in 1912 and accompanied the Conrads on their trip to Poland in the summer of 1914. After the breakdown of her marriage, she returned to Cracow, and after the First World War worked briefly in restoring goods to the dispossessed. She then taught French, English, and German privately and for a time at a lycée. With Olga Małkowska, she was active in the Polish scouting movement.

[2] Józef Hieronim Retinger (1888–1960), who met Conrad in 1912, stimulated his interest in Polish affairs. The friendship, however, had largely faded by 1917.

[3] Lucas gives the wrong date, 21 April.

I may safely say that this is the first moment of moral and physical relief I
have tasted since our return from Liverpool just before Christmas. Perhaps
we both have "turned the corner" now! At any rate if Jessie has done so I
am likely to follow; – longo intervallo[1] – but still I will get round too, I think.
I may tell *you* that I feel very much shaken physically. Mental effort costs me
more than it ought to, I fancy. I have done some work however – not of a
very profitable kind tho' – three prefaces for my Coll[ed] Edition. I have also
finished a play – I don't know why. I mean I don't know why I have done
that thing at all. But it's done. I had also no end of a grind over the text of
the Rescue to make it fit for book-form.

Heavens! How I have slaved over that book! That prose!

And in this connection: I hope my dear Colvin you have understood that it
is only absolute impossibility which prevented me dedicating it to your wife.
I had promised it (*that* particular book) to Penfield[2] the last U.S Ambassador
to the late Empire of the East, in the year 1914, in commemoration of my
gratitude for his kindness to us – a kindness which had every appearance of
a *Rescue*.

Enough for to-day. I want to come up and talk – but I am afraid I would
only tire you both. You would forgive me no doubt but——

Truly I am growing a little odious to myself and yet I would put my trust
in You and Lady Colvin whose hands I kiss. Her letters are very precious to
Jessie.

Ever Yours

J. Conrad

To John Galsworthy
Text MS Forbes; Unpublished

[letterhead: Oswalds]
4.4.20.

Dearest Jack.

I wonder when you will reach these shores.[3] I wrote you to Grove Lodge
because it seemed you[r] direction.[4]

---

[1] A shortened version of the Latin tag 'Proximus sed longo intervallo': 'The next, but so far off'.
[2] Frederic Courtland Penfield (1855–1922) assisted the Conrads in Vienna, the United States
having undertaken to represent British interests in Austria-Hungary, the 'late Empire of the
East', on the outbreak of war.
[3] In fact, the Galsworthys had just returned from France and Spain.
[4] After 1917 the Galsworthy's home in The Grove, Hampstead. Conrad apparently had received
no reply to his letter of 28 March.

Now I add these few lines to say that on the 31 Mch Sir R Jones came from Scotland to see Jessie and decided on immediate operation. It was done in a Nurs^g Home in Canter^y, and the relief was instantaneous. Not a moment to[o] soon either. For the last 3 weeks she was growing desperate (her own word). We all had an awful time she suffering and we looking on.

Sir R. J. has every hope that this is the last time. We shall see.

I am less crippled now, but I feel shaken and mentally tired – and truly there is very little reason for the last. It isn't the toil. I don't toil now. I wonder how much longer I'll be able to spin?[1]

We do hope Ada is well by now. We expect a cheering word from you every day.

Our dearest love

Ever Yours

J. Conrad

To Edward Garnett

Text MS Indiana; G. 293–4

[letterhead: Oswalds]

4.4.20.

Dearest Edward.

I wonder whether you will condescend to look at my handwriting.

My dear fellow ever [since] we came home from L'pool[2] I have been more or less laid up with gout. Wrists – one after another ankles – then came bronchitis – days and days in bed.

Through it all I went on struggling with the text of the Rescue. You can have no idea in what close communion I felt myself to be with you. I think that every mark of your pen has been attended to.

It's over. Proofs read too. And for the rest I do not care.

Jessie meantime has been (after all these bright hopes following the L'pool operation) getting steadily worse, sinking into unbearable pain and still worse hopelessness.

Two days ago Sir R Jones came down from Scotland and operated again. The relief was instantaneous and now everybody connected with "the case" seems determined that it should be the *last time*. We shall see.

She is going on very well and sends you her love.

---

[1] 'Consider the lilies of the field, how they grow; they toil not, neither do they spin', Matthew 6.28 and Luke 12.27.
[2] In late December 1919.

I feel physically shaken. Mentally so-so. It's only my affection for you that remains unchanged from the old times.

Ever Yours

J Conrad.

To Major Ernest Dawson
Text MS Yale; Unpublished

[letterhead: Oswalds]

5.4.20

My dear Dawson.

I asked Miss Hallowes to acknowledge your letter at once and I am now writing myself to tell you that my wife has been operated again and that the prospects are good.

It was rather a shock to both [of] us to learn of you emigrating like this to France.[1] You are another victim of that all pervading official meanness which is characteristic of the times. Don't you regret not having been born, a member of the privileged classes – a miner, a railwayman, a plumber – or even a tramp. I admit that very little has been, so far, done for tramps; but still they are better off than public servants or officers of the King. Nobody cuts down their income (whatever it may be) on grounds of public policy.[2] They are sure of their position. They can afford to live (and tramp) at home. They need not care for the future . . .

I feel excessively embittered by this systematic slighting of all simple claims of merit and service, which I see going on shamelessly all round us.

Jessie whom I saw about an hour ago (in a Canter^y Nursing Home) sends you her love and her profound regret at losing the prospect of seeing you under her roof early this year. I suppose you will revisit your ungrateful country from time to time. Try to spare at least a day for us when you do.

I expect to have Jessie back here in about 3 weeks. We shan't move from here unless perhaps in Sept^er for a fortnight – that is if she is able to move with freedom. Everybody assures me she shall, by then – but it seems after so many disappointments, too good to be true.

Ever cordially yours

Joseph Conrad

[1] He did not, in fact, though he spent long periods on the Continent.
[2] Presumably, Dawson's pensions for military and civilian service had been trimmed by the government's refusal to honour multiple entitlements.

To Warrington Dawson
Text MS Duke; Randall 201

[letterhead: Oswalds]
5.4.20

My dear Dawson.[1]

I was very touched by your letter to B[orys]. Very remorseful too at my apparent neglect. But both Jessie and I ought to be excused. I have been more or less laid up since my last. As to Jessie after the bright prospects following the operation in Dec*er* last she needed all her fortitude to face the development of a new complication which crippled her completely again; in fact laid her up with horrible pain for some three weeks.

She was operated again on the 31 Mch, Sir Robert Jones coming down from Scotland on purpose, here. The relief was immediate – whether it is the last of her troubles we don't know. But the prospects are good and she is making a good recovery so far.

I won't say much more now. I am far from being well myself and we all had a horrid time of it for a month past looking at her sufferings. I am just beginning to recover my tone somewhat. 1919 was a bad year and 1920 looked as if it was going to be worse. But perhaps we have at last turned the corner.

Love from us all

Yours always

J. Conrad.

To John Galsworthy
Text MS Forbes; J-A, 2, 238

[letterhead: Oswalds]
Tuesday. [6? April 1920][2]

Dearest Jack

Thanks for your letter. We assume Ada is tolerably well by now.

---

[1] (Francis) Warrington Dawson (1878–1962), resident in Paris and Versailles, came from a family of former plantation owners in Charleston, South Carolina. He wrote prolifically – fiction, essays, newspaper stories – and covered strikes, wars, peace conferences, the French Senate, and the Chamber of Deputies. To quote Randall, 'he had a special taste and talent for conversing with the great and near-great' (p. 4). In 1909, while on safari in East Africa with Theodore Roosevelt, he met Conrad's old friends the Sandersons, and when Dawson came to England in May 1910 to report the funeral of Edward VII, he carried an introduction to Conrad.

[2] While the 13th cannot be discounted, Galsworthy seemingly replied to Conrad's hint in his letter of the 4th that he expected a word from him soon and replied immediately. His letter does not survive among those to Conrad held at Brandeis University.

Jessie is going on excellently. Had a fair night and is trying to make little jokes in a yet feeble voice.

I am a little awed by your mysterious warning as to *In Chancery* Dedi^{on}.[1]

I take it as an act of our old friendship and, God knows, I am glad that you have thought of it for us both. No other idea or consideration can intrude on my feelings there. I can't simply conceive that you of all people would do anything to shock my sensibilities. If I could not trust you who could I trust?

Of course I wanted to see the MS. But that was mere eagerness; and now you have roused my curiosity to the highest pitch I'll never forgive you if you dont send the MS instanter "to the above address".

My dear! I never knew (for certain) that you thought well of the Secret Ag^t. I wish to goodness I could come up to see your new play;[2] but I am still lame and existing so much on the verge of a heavy attack that I dare not trust myself in town for the night; especially just now with Jessie laid up in Canterbury.

Our dearest love to you both

Ever Yours

J. Conrad.

To Richard Curle
Text MS Indiana; Curle 63

[letterhead: Oswalds]
8.4.20

My dear Curle.

I'll be writing soon to you to ask you to come – but this week end is impossible.

Jessie sends her love. She's beginning to look more like herself.

Did I tell you I had a wire from Quinn apparently just to tell me he had P[inker] to lunch – and to acknowledge a few pp of MS I sent him (about £50)?[3]

Wise is quite a brick. He paid 150 for the *first draft* TS. of the play. God knows I wanted that cash.

Plumber's and drainage bill fell on my head this morning – also an enormous coal & coke. acc^t. I am still reeling from the blow.

---

[1] Published in October, it was dedicated: 'To Jessie and to Joseph Conrad'.
[2] *The Skin Game* was opening on the 21st at St Martin's Theatre. It ran until 29 January 1921, becoming Galsworthy's first commercial success.
[3] See the letter to Eric Pinker of [1 April].

Hein[ema]^{nn} was here for lunch yesterday. It will have to be 750 sets[1] I think. Some booksellers told his man that if 750 they will take 10 sets but if 1000 only three! However Hein^{nn} has enough paper for the greater num^{er}. Pink returns on Tuesday.[2]

I am still gouty in hand and foot but manage to crawl about. Miss H[allowes] returns from leave today and tomorrow I will try to start work.

Jessie's love. Mine too.

Yours

J. Conrad.

Imp[ortan]t I want to know what sort of reviews is your book getting? The more I look at it the more I think of it. But those reviewers are so superficial! I am quite anxious. Give me your impression.

To Eric Pinker

Text MS Berg; Unpublished

[letterhead: Oswalds]
8.4.20

My dear Eric.

Thanks for your sympathetic letter. My wife is going on very well and we hope that after this there will be no more complications.

Can you manage to pay in £100 to my acct at the bank. F. U[nwin] ought to have sent some cash I imagine.

Out of that I'll pay my plumber and drainage bill of which I warned your father. Of course it is more than the estimate. There is no end to these things. I mean bills.

H[einemann] was here yesterday. He showed me a dummy vol and specimens of printed pages. All that is quite satisfactory.

We have settled provisionally on 750 sets (and six sets for me). That number is certainly safer. However I told H that father was due back about Tuesday next and H proposed that we should hear what he has to say, before deciding finally. H. has secured enough paper for the larger edition and is ready to begin directly I give him copy.

Pray send me the usual notes. Last week's have been received safely.

Yours

J. Conrad.

---

[1] Of the collected edition. It was eventually 780, with thirty for presentation.
[2] From New York.

To Frances Spooner
Text MS Frewer; Unpublished

[letterhead: Oswalds]
9.4.20
Dear Mrs. Spooner,[1]
   I am writing this for my wife who is just now unable to answer your letter. She was operated again on the 31st. Sir R. Jones coming down here for the purpose. She is now in a Canterbury Nursing Home going on very well and desires me to convey to you her kind regards and her regret at not being able to answer you herself.
   Believe me, dear Mrs. Spooner, Your very faithful and ob[t]. servant,

Joseph Conrad.

To Aniela Zagórska
Text Pion; Najder 261-3[2]

Oswalds
10th April 1920.
My dearest Aniela,[3]
   I don't know what you must think of me! I trust you haven't given me up entirely. You will know from Karola how things are in this house. They do not excuse me, but perhaps will help you forgive me.
   I give you my best and completest authority and right to translate all my works into Polish. You are authorized to give or refuse permission and to decide all matters concerned therewith, using your own judgment and taking decisions in my name.
   I should be happiest if you yourself had the wish and the time to translate at least those books you like. I know from Karolcia[4] that you worked on *Almayer's Folly* – possibly even too conscientiously! My dear, don't trouble to be too scrupulous about it. I may tell you (in French) that in my opinion

---

[1] Daughter of the Bishop of Carlisle, Frances Elizabeth Wycliffe Spooner (née Goodwin, *c.* 1853–1939) in 1878 married the Revd William Archibald Spooner, Warden of New College, Oxford, and originator of the 'spoonerism'. She raised their family of five children and was a notable hostess. In her later years she became interested in the rehabilitation of long-term hospital patients in Oxford.

[2] Aside from the sections in French, text from Najder, with minor alterations.

[3] The daughter of Conrad's maternal second cousin once removed Karol Zagórski (d. 1898), Aniela Zagórska (1881–1943) received an allowance from Conrad and, with her sister Karola, shared the translations rights to his work into Polish and Russian. She herself translated *Almayer's Folly*, *Lord Jim*, and *The Mirror of the Sea* into Polish.

[4] An affectionate diminutive.

'il vaut mieux interpréter que traduire'.[1] My English is not at all literary. I write idiomatically. Je me sers des phrases courantes qui, après tout, sont celles avec lesquelles on se garde le mieux contre 'le cliché'. Il s'agit donc de trouver des équivalents. Et là, ma chère, je vous prie laissez vous guider plutôt par votre tempérament que par un conscience sévère. Je vous connais. J'ai foi en vous. Et vraiment Conrad vu à travers Angèle, ça ne sera pas déjà si mauvais. Inspirez vous bien de cette idée qui pourra peut-être alléger un peu la tâche ingrate que vous pensez entreprendre – si j'ai bien compris Karola.[2]

I will send you without delay my *A Personal Record*, *Nostromo*, and *The Arrow of Gold*. With respect to titles, what do you think of *Fantazja Almayera*? That is a possibility. In English the word folly may also be used of a building.[3] In Polish the word obłęd can't be used in the same way. 'A's Folly' is a stupid title that can't exactly be translated into any other language.

Jessie embraces you warmly and sends you her best love. She is going on very well, and I expect to have her home in a week to ten days. Thank you for the presents, and I kiss your hands for the two volumes si admirablement reliés[4] – and also for the pleasure of having Prus[5] in my home. Everybody says that Jan[6] is remarkably like his father; so one can expect that the time will come when he will write to you and thank you for the book and the drawing. Quel magnifique portrait![7]

Do forgive this short letter after such a long silence, and don't judge my attachment to you either by the one or the other, but only selon la charité de votre coeur et la largeur de votre esprit.[8] Sometimes, my dear, the thought itself takes the pen out of one's hand. But why explain. I repeat, j'ai foi en vous – en toutes choses.[9]

Yours affectionately

Konrad

---

[1] 'Interpretation is better than translating'.
[2] 'I use everyday expressions, which, after all, are the best defence against "cliché". It is, then, a question of finding equivalents. And there, my dear, I beg you to let yourself be guided more by your temperament than by strict conscience. I know you. I have confidence in you. And indeed Conrad seen through Aniela's eyes will by no means be bad. Take heart from this idea that may perhaps lighten a bit the thankless task you are considering taking up, if I understood Karola correctly.'
[3] Either a spurious ruin or, as in the case of Almayer's house, a real one whose sorry state becomes a monument to vanity.
[4] 'So handsomely bound'.
[5] Aleksander Głowacki ('Bolesław Prus', 1847–1912), a novelist whose work Conrad had read during his visit to Poland in 1914.
[6] I.e., John Conrad.
[7] Dr Kazimierz Górski's portrait of Conrad, painted 1914 in Zakopane.
[8] 'According to the kindness of your heart and the largeness of your spirit'.
[9] 'I have confidence in you – in all matters.'

To Lady Millais

Text MS Private collection; Unpublished

[letterhead: Oswalds]
Saturday. [10? April 1920][1]

Dear Lady Millais

Sir Robert has been and gone leaving us all in a much more cheerful frame of mind. There can be no doubt that the general condition of the limb has improved, though another incision may be necessary to help and accelerate complete recovery. To-day the local conditions were not yet sufficiently definite for him to think of using the knife. He promised to come next week if the surgeon in charge of the case (Read*) requires his presence. If not then he will put off his visit for a fortnight but he has definitely settled that in any case he will see Jessie before a month is out.

I do hope there has been no overfatigue from the run yesterday. We got home all right but the front tyre which caused me a lot of secret worry while we were wandering over the Marsh[2] gave up the ghost finally this morning.

Jessie sends to you and Sir John her very best love in which I beg to join, and [I] am always dear Lady Millais,

Your very faithful and obed[t] Servant
Joseph Conrad.

To R. B. Cunninghame Graham

Text MS Dartmouth; Watts (1969) 188

[letterhead: Oswalds]
15.4.'20.

Très cher et excellent ami.[3]

The photograph arrived this morning and is a great joy to me and a great acquisition for my study. Now I consider its fitting out as completed and not a single object, picture or effigy will be allowed to enter it after this. I am extremely proud to have you both – I mean you and your kind and wise-

---

[1] The 3rd is too soon after Jessie Conrad's operation, while unfavourable symptoms reported on the 27th rule out the 24th. Of the other two Saturdays, this seems the more plausible for a post-operative check-up.

[2] Romney Marsh, an area of sheep pastures crisscrossed by narrow lanes.

[3] Robert Bontine Cunninghame Graham (1852–1936) began a lasting friendship with Conrad in 1897, the result of a letter praising 'An Outpost of Progress'. A socialist and (according to some scholars) rightful King of Scotland, Graham worked and travelled widely in the Americas. He drew on his experiences in many volumes of tales, sketches, and essays and also in his unorthodox histories of the Spanish conquest. From 1885 to 1892 he represented North-West Lanarkshire in Parliament; he spent four and a half weeks in gaol for his part in the Bloody Sunday demonstration of 1887.

looking friend with the white face.[1] He looks most worthy of a place in your heart.

Ever so many thanks too for the *Life and Miracles* which I have just read for the second time. There is no one but you to render so poignantly the pathetic and desperate effects of human credulity.[2] It is a marvellous piece of sustained narrative and of intensely personal prose. Your large treatment makes the story intelligible both in its social origins and in its absurd and tragic psychology.

Very fine – very frightful too by the sort of reflections that only your writings have the power to suggest.

———————

Jessie is going on very well. She sends her love and reminds you earnestly of your promise to visit us again before long. I expect to be able to move her home in about a week.

Mes devoirs les plus respectueux a Mme Votre Mère.[3]

À Vous de coeur

Joseph Conrad.

To Michael Holland
Text MS Private collection; Unpublished

[letterhead: Oswalds]
15.4.'20

My dear Holland.[4]

It was a most delightful surprise to see your letter. I took it over at once to my wife who is now at a Canterbury Nursing Home (only 3. m. from here) recovering after a heavy operation on the knee – the third in the last two years. But we have great hopes that this will be the end of her troubles and that after 14 years or more of suffering she will be able at last to live without pain and to move about with comparative freedom.

---

[1] Watts suggests that this is Graham's horse, 'El Chaja'.

[2] Graham's *A Brazilian Mystic, Being the Life and Miracles of Antonio Conselheiro* had recently appeared. 'Antonio the Counsellor', a millenarian prophet, established the holy city of Canudos in one of the most desperate regions of Brazil. He and his followers were slaughtered by Brazilian troops in 1897.

[3] The Hon. Anne Elizabeth Bontine (née Elphinstone Fleeming, 1828–1925) took a well-informed interest in politics and the arts. Conrad's friendly relations with her went back to the 1890s.

[4] Before moving to Sussex in 1913, Michael James Holland (1870–1956), had been a neighbour of the Conrads at Smeeth Hill, near Aldington, Kent. In his earlier years he had lived adventurously in South Africa and British Columbia and would recollect his experiences there in *Verse* (1937). He was also an avid book collector.

Sir Robert Jones operated and Mr Whitehead Read* is looking after her now. As he knows your brother Bernard[1] we were about to take steps to learn something of your whereabouts through him when your letter arrived.

Yes. You are right. The old feel has gone. Your boys and mine will have to make the best of a very different world. Yet perhaps it will not be so intolerable as it appears to us in perspective. And they are young – they will adapt themselves (they jolly well will have to) to the changed atmosphere and to the new "sentiment of life" – for that they will be amongst those that will "*fully* survive". I will not and cannot doubt. And change, after all, is the rule of life. And in the last instance I put my trust in the genius not of any class but of the whole English people, in their political sagacity (hidden now under a lot of wild thinking) and in the great fact that by now the majority of the individuals[2] has got something to lose in the material sense and will think twice before rushing into a destructive policy.

My eldest boy was invalided out of the Army in July last. He joined in Sep[t] 1915 (I would [not] let him go sooner). From Jan 1916 he has served on the Western Front without a day's home duty or a day in hospital, till Oct 1918 when he was knocked out 1 1/2 miles from Menin[3] – during the advance. He is not quite himself yet but looks well. The small child that you were so good to at Smeeth Hill[4] is about to enter Tonbridge School. I am getting rather crippled with gout an[d] can only crawl about dismally. Our very kindest and warmest regard to you all.

                                                              Yours sincerely

                                                                    Joseph Conrad.

To Eric Pinker
Text TS/MS Berg; Unpublished

                                                              [letterhead: Oswalds]
                                                              April 17th. [1920]

My dear Eric

This is about what I expected. I am sorry for Vernon but I must say that I was surprised, after what he had told me of the aims and the idea

---

[1] Bernard Henry Holland (1856–1926) was called to the bar after Eton and Cambridge. He served in the Charity Commission Office and for other royal commissions, and was later active in local government in Kent. He edited Crabbe, wrote verse and biographies, and also wrote on politics.

[2] Conrad had originally written 'the nation' and in deleting it forgot to cut 'the'.

[3] A town in western Belgium.   [4] Holland's home near Aldington until 1913.

of the Little Theatre, that the first card played should be such a poor one as Knoblock,[1] who evidently could not deal in any fresh way with a war subject, being a characteristically commonplace mind. It looked to me like a deliberate attempt to sit on two stools. The Brighouse[2] card was a little better, but not much. It might have served if they had got out of Brighouse something characteristic instead of an imitation Barrie.[3] As soon as I read the first notice of it (and it was rather favourable) I foresaw what would happen. They would have done better if they had actually begun with J. Conrad where they would have been certain of a success of curiosity[4] and of a certain amount of controversy in the press which would have stimulated the public interest for some little time at least. However I was not ready and a success of curiosity would not be enough now to re-establish the fortunes of the Little Theatre. A six weeks' run would not do that. More one could not have expected perhaps, but it would have been a better and a more original and a more interesting start in any case; and, unless they have a "dead cert." in hand it would not perhaps be bad policy to put on J. C. even yet. However, you understand that all this is *strictly between ourselves*.

I am writing a few lines to Vernon asking him to send you the TS of the play, from which please have two copies made and return to me my own TS which I wish to preserve. I don't know what Vernon may have to say to J. B. but my own feeling is that whether they make a success or not with their next venture I do not care any longer to be associated with the fate of the Little Theatre. They have made a thoroughly bad start and I am afraid that they will have to throw their original ideas overboard and go on some other line to re-establish their finances. And in that case there is no reason why my play should go to the L. T. rather than to any other. But it's a great pity.

Thanks for the notes.

Yours

J. Conrad

---

[1] Edward Knoblock (1874–1945), actor, producer, and novelist, and, as a playwright, Arnold Bennett's sometime collaborator. Located in John Adam Street, off the Strand, the 250-seat theatre had been destroyed in an air-raid. When it reopened in 1919, its backers hoped to encourage artistic and social innovation, but, late in 1920, Jose Levy, the manager until his death in 1936, turned the house into the London home of Grand-Guignol (the Parisian 'theatre of horror') and persisted with the experiment until 1923. Bombed again in April 1941, the building was demolished in 1949.

[2] Harold Brighouse (1882–1958), playwright and novelist best known for his Lancashire comedy *Hobson's Choice* (1915).

[3] J. M. Barrie (1860–1937), popular Scottish playwright and novelist, now best known for *Peter Pan*. Conrad was friendly with him in his early career.

[4] A Gallicism: cf. 'succès de scandale' and 'succès de circonstance'.

PS Please show this letter to the long lost J. B. P. (if he ever turns up!) before he sees Vernon. I always want him to know my thoughts and feelings beforehand.

I am expecting to have Mrs J. C. back home on Wed^y next. It really looks my dear Eric as though the trick were done this time. Her regards to you.

To John Galsworthy
Text MS Forbes; J-A, 2, 238-9

[letterhead: Oswalds]
20.4.20

My dearest Jack

I finished your MS yesterday and am very much impressed by the ampleness of the scheme, the masterly ease in the handling [of] the subject and (in sober truth) the *sheer beauty* of these pages. Oh! my dear fellow it *is* good! A Great Saga. –[1]

And so poor James is gone at last. His: "Nobody tells me anything" has been for years a household phrase at which all my little family duly smiles – even John who knows James only from hearsay not having yet read the *M[an] of Property*. I miss him awfully. I broke the news to Jessie. She inquired about all the others. I told her of Soames' marriage and she was very much surprised. Who would have thought it! "But here it is" – and Soames is undeniable. His solidity is amazing. A great creation – and in this mainly that it fills completely the limits of possibility without ever raising a doubt in one's mind. Surprise is not doubt – you know. James' long meditation (in the dining room)[2] is what the French would call "saisissant". There is a quality in the life of all these Forsythes* that makes it more true in its imaginative force than the most scrupulously rendered actuality. Oeuvre de poète![3] There is no doubt about it my dear Jack.

I keep the MS for Jessie to read. She is coming home to-day. In the N[ursing] Home she could only read Tatterdemalion[4] which I have not yet seen. I didn't want to take it away from her even for an evening, as she seemed unable to tackle any other of the 12 vols she had in her room. She gave me her love for you both last night.

---

[1] *In Chancery* was the second volume of *The Forsyte Saga*; the first, *A Man of Property*, had appeared in 1906.
[2] Part One, Chapter 5.   [3] 'The work of a poet'.
[4] A collection of Galsworthy's short stories, published in March.

I am now off to Canterbury to see her put into the ambulance. – I am sorry for poor Ada with all the sincerity of a man "who knows what it is".[1] My loving duty to her.

Ever my dear Jack your affectionate and admiring

J. Conrad.

To Eric Pinker

Text TS/MS Berg; Unpublished

[letterhead: Oswalds]
April 20th. 1920.

My dear Eric.

I send you here a letter from J. B. P. which has reached me to-day at noon. I send it to you for your information and entertainment, but please return [it] to me for it is a very precious document. I have no doubt you will get as much pleasure from perusing it as I had.

Thanks for your letter. I am glad you take the same view of the L[ittle] T[heatre] muddle as I do. What your father says in his letter puts a different colour on the situation and I don't know whether it would not be an original stroke of business to have the play performed first in America – as there are people with open mouths over there. Anyway it would be better than hawking it about London. That is on the assumption that Vernon may be disposed, or perhaps even forced, to drop his end. I don't think he really wants to drop it, for I had a note from him asking for a clean copy to be sent to him as soon as you had them done. Pray do so, because we don't want to drop our end here till we know what Vernon is able or willing to do. I imagine this would be J. B. P.'s feeling too; but, after all, when it comes to the handling of that piece his view must be decisive.

To day at noon my wife arrived home in an ambulance and was carried upstairs by five men who had all their work cut out for them. She has stood the journey very well but it will be 3 weeks or so before she will be allowed to come downstairs "under her own steam". She sends her love to *all* the family.

I will be sending you the statement of which father speaks to-morrow. I will also write a letter to meet him on his arrival at Burys Court.[2] I suppose he may land on Sat next as I see the Caramania is advertised to sail from

---

[1] During a recent visit to Spain, Ada Galsworthy had had bronchitis and pneumonia (Stape, 2000).
[2] Pinker's home in Leigh, Surrey, near Reigate.

L'pool (outward bound) on the 1ˢᵗ of May, and those ships have generally a week at home. Kindest regards from us all here.

Yours

J. Conrad.

To J. B. Pinker

Text MS Berg; Unpublished

[letterhead: Oswalds]
23ᵈ. Ap '20.

My dear Pinker.

This is to thank you for Your delightful and amusing letter the herald of your return, and to welcome You home with affectionate greetings from us all.

Jessie returned home on the 20th inst. after her, I truly believe, *last* operation which was performed in Canterbury. Everything's going well with her – and I know you will share in our hopes and our sense of relief as the "truest of friends."

Eric will tell you of the transactions during his regency. I corresponded with him fully and he has been as nice and as wise as could be. Pray give our love to Mrs Pinker and Ralph.

The stock of Stout is being laid in to quench your thirst after your 40 days in the Desert. No fatted calf will be killed because in your case it would be an impertinence[1] – but a fat lobster and other things in good condition shall be procured for a "Family feast" directly you give us a date. And let it be soon.

I would have gone to meet you at the gate but I am still lame on 9 days out of ten – tho' of late I have begun to feel better in myself. It's about time I did.

Ever most affcᵗˡʸ yours

Joseph Conrad

To Eric Pinker

Text MS Berg; Unpublished

[Oswalds]
23.4.20.

My dear Eric.

I don't think there will be much for anybody in the transᵒⁿ of the *Nigger* into Italian, but of course I would like You to arrange the matter.[2]

---

[1] As if Pinker were a Prodigal Son whose return was being celebrated.
[2] No Italian translation appeared until Umberto Pittola's in 1926.

I've written to J. B. to Burys Court. I suppose you'll have him with you to-morrow.

Kindest regards

Yours

J Conrad.

To the Polish Government Loan Committee

Text MS draft Janta; Egan; Najder 263; Janta (1972) facsimile[1]

[Oswalds]
[26 April 1920]

For Poles the sense of duty and the imperishable feeling of Nationality preserved in the hearts and defended by the hands of their immediate ancestors in open struggles against the might of three Powers and in indomitable defiance of crushing oppression for more than a hundred years is sufficient inducement to come forward [to] assist in reconstructing the independence, dignity and usefulness of the reborn Republic investing generously[2] in honour of the unconquered dead in testimony of their own national faith and for the peace and happiness of future generations (stop)

To Americans one appeals for the recognition of that patriotism not of the flesh but of the spirit which has sustained them so well in the critical hours of their own history, in the name of common memories at the dawn of their own independent existence,[3] on the ground of pure humanity and as to lovers of perseverance and of courage in all its forms. (stop) They can't but feel sympathy for an idealism akin to their own in this example of unselfish union of all hearts and all hands in the work of reconstruction. For the only sound ground of Democracy is unselfish toil in a common cause. They would wish to help in rebuilding that outpost of Western civilization once overwhelmed[4] but never surrendered to the forces representing what they themselves most detest – inhumanity, tyranny and moral lawlessness (message ends)

Please edit as required (stop) Salutations (stop)

Joseph Conrad.

Dispatched on Monday 26 Ap. 1920.

---

[1] Text from facsimile.   [2] Janta (1972) gives a detailed history of the loan.
[3] The exemplary figure here is Tadeusz Kosciuśko (1746–1817), who fought in the American Revolution and took arms against Russian and Prussian domination of Poland.
[4] If not a reference to more recent events, then an allusion to the partitions of Poland in 1772, 1793, and 1795 by the empires of Russia, Prussia, and Austria.

To Lady Colvin
Text MS Duke; Unpublished

[letterhead: Oswalds]
27.4.20.

Dear Lady Colvin

We are grieved to hear your news. Do give our best love and sympathy to the sufferer. I had formed a plan to run up to-day but got a swollen foot during the night and apart from being dead lame, dare not trust myself away from home.

It is a miserable condition of perpetual funk to be in but it is infinitely worse to have to tell you that another complication is developing in the operated knee and poor Jessie is again confined to her room. The pain which has come on suddenly on Sat: is only made bearable by applications of ice. Sir Robert has been notified at once and we are now awaiting his reply. My only comfort is the assurance he has given me last time he was here that nothing can happen there which he cannot put right.

I am sorry I cannot write more cheerfully about ourselves. You and dear Colvin are daily in our thoughts. The first safe day I get I shall run up if only to see him for a moment – for it would be too tiring for him to have a visitor for any length of time. You, I know, would give me a few minutes more.

I have not been able to do any work lately and yet everybody tells me that I am looking well. But I know how I feel. Ceci entre-nous.[1]

Ever dear Lady Colvin

your most affectionate friend and servant
Joseph Conrad.

To Edward Garnett
Text MS Yale; G. 294-5

[letterhead: Oswalds]
[27 April 1920][2]

Dearest Edward.

Jessie was operated again on the 31 Mch. and after 3 weeks in a Canterbury Nur^g Home we brought her here. But unfavourable symptoms have set in again and there will be probably another operation.

---

[1] 'This between ourselves'.   [2] Date from postmark.

Meantime all we can do is to make her pain bearable by means of ice-bags and lotions.

This is our bumper of news and very beastly it is.

I ought to have thanked you long before for your dear letter.[1] My dear Edward! A set of the Ld Edition has been marked for your own in my thoughts ever since that affair has been planned.

The Eng^{sh} publ^m of Rescue will be delayed because of some muddle in the delivery of the paper. In US the date is 21st May and *if you like* I will send you a copy. But I can't imagine any one so impatient as that for JC's patched book.

I am feeling perpetually seedy and would gladly not trouble my head about it – if I only could.

I hope David will prosper in his adventure.[2] Give him my most friendly greeting.

Jessie sends you her love.

Yours ever

J. Conrad

To Harold Goodburn

Text MS Thomas; Unpublished

[letterhead: Oswalds]

27.4.20

Dear Sir.[3]

We are very glad to know that you will take John again after his birthday[4] as you so sympathetically stipulate.

My wife joins me in kindest regards

Yours faithfully

J. Conrad

---

[1] Of mid-April; see Stape and Knowles, pp. 154–5.

[2] David Garnett was setting up a bookshop.

[3] Harold Goodburn (1891–1966), a school master in chemistry and biology from Liverpool, taught in Dorset, Argentina, and Brazil before taking up a post at the King's School, Canterbury, where he taught from 1919 to 1945. He then taught in the Midlands before retiring in Canterbury. He is recalled as the eccentric 'Captain Burnwell' in David Moreau's *More Wrestling than Dancing: An Autobiography* (1990). He tutored John Conrad in mathematics on a private basis.

[4] 2 August.

To R. D. Mackintosh

Text MS Alberta; Jellard

[letterhead: Oswalds]

27.4.20

My dear Mackintosh.[1]

I suppose you know that Jessie was operated on the 31 of March in a Nurs^g Home in Canterbury. Sir R. Jones was very hopeful yet he was not quite positive as to all the trouble being over. We got her home just a week ago but last Friday night symptoms of [the] same old thing appeared and she is now in great pain which only the ice-bag over the knee makes bearable. Sir R was notified at once and we are now waiting for what he will say. He told me himself that this periostitis had a tendency towards a chronic state but he assured me at the same time that nothing could happen there which he could not put right ultimately.

I am telling you all these details at Jessie's express desire. I can't tell you how much we were grieved at your accident and how much we missed your promised visit. You know that nothing could be more welcome than your presence within our door.

Just put on you[r] considering cap and find out when you can give us that pleasure. Then drop a truthful line and open the throttle wide via M[aid]stone, Sittingbourne, Faversham, Can[terbu]ry. – The pub^on of Rescue is delayed because of the paper which isn't there.[2] But if you possess your soul in patience you shall get a set of the Lim^d Edition (either Eng: or Am) before you are a year older. More I cannot say.

Our affectionate regards

Your[s] always

J. Conrad

To J. B. Pinker

Text MS Berg; Unpublished

[letterhead: Oswalds]

Tuesday. [27 April 1920][3]

My dear Pinker.

I am sorry to say that since I wrote to you (at home) periostitis has set in again with every appearance of another ab[s]cess coming on and poor Jessie

---

[1] Robert Dunbar Mackintosh (1865–1934) practised as a physician in Barnes, south-west London. From 1909 to 1921, when the friendship ended in a falling out because of the collapse of MacKintosh's Surrey Scientific Apparatus Company in which he had invested, Conrad valued the companionship and advice of this Scottish doctor, an amateur playwright and inventor described by his grand-niece Janet Jellard as 'an unpractical enthusiast and dreamer'.

[2] Paper was still not as available as it had been before the war.

[3] Contents fix the date.

is laid up in great pain which only ice-applications make bearable. Sir Robert has been written to and we are awaiting his reply. It'll end no doubt in more knife-work. The whole thing is most distressing and looks serious enough.

She sends her love and begs you not to let this affect your plans as to your visit here – on any account.

I enclose here John['s] school acct. The boy worked 2 hours every day with one of the King's School masters in Canterbury and did very well in the master's opinion.

I send you here my message to Poles and Americans on the occasion of the P Gov^t Loan. The Comm^{ee} asked me to charge to them but the cost had to be paid here. H. Dent was here when I received the request and I asked him to get my message through by Marconi. Please repay him the sum named in the adjoined receipt of Marconi office.

Hugh Dent came mainly to talk of his desire to enter into some understanding with you as to my future work. My attitude was of benevolent reserve on that point. Neither did I row him on the paper-supply muddle (for Rescue) at which he was very crestfallen.

I felt tempted yesterday to run up and see you – and then I thought you would rather not be interrupted while busy getting hold of things afresh. To-day I have a swollen foot. 2 more prefaces go to D. P. & Co. Five more to do.

Ever affec^{ly} yours

J. Conrad.

To J. B. Pinker
Text MS Berg; Unpublished

[letterhead: Oswalds]
Friday. 30.4.[1920]^1

My dear Pinker.

On returning home I found your letter (arrived by the 1 o'clock delivery) announcing your visit for Tuesday next. We hold you to it. Please send us the train. 4.55 from Vic. is a good one. You will be in time if you wire from the station – I mean in time for us to meet you in Canterbury.

---

[1] Catalogued in Berg as from September 1921, but several clues point to 30 April 1920. Conrad speculates about the American prospects for *The Rescue* in its year of publication. At the end of April, Sir Sidney Colvin was seriously ill; Conrad was eager to see the Colvins, but an inflamed foot stopped him doing so on Tuesday the 27th. Since Jessie Conrad's recovery was in jeopardy, Sir Robert Jones had urgent reason to interrupt a visit to his daughter's, as he did on Saturday, 1 May ('tomorrow').

Miss Capes will be here; probably her last visit to us – for she is getting on.[1] She won't be in the way and You won't mind being given a room in the nursery flat to sleep in.

I had a rather painful hour with the Colvins. Lady C in utmost distress and then poor Colvin bursting into tears at seeing me. I suppose it is the beginning of the end with him.

Ever so many thanks for the statistical table of my sales in U.S. I studied it with interest and I see that if *Rescue* does even moderately well the *total* of sales is bound to be more than a quarter million copies up to August 1920. Considering that the first statement of *Febr^y 1910* is given as 695 copies and up to Aug^st 1912 as 1,678 copies only, this is not so bad.

We have had this moment a wire from Sir R. J[ones] who is staying with his daughter in Sussex. He will probably want to come see Jessie to-morrow or Sunday.

No more at present. Our loves.

Ever Yours

J. Conrad

To Nora Tattersall

Text MS Indiana; Unpublished

[letterhead: Oswalds]

2.5.20

Dear Mrs Tattersall[2]

My wife was very much distressed at her inability to see you the last time you were good enough to inquire personally about her health. She was going to write to you herself at the first sign of improvement for which we all hoped. However it did not come and she was operated again (this time at home) last Saturday: a four inch cut down to the bone but also involving a big nerve. In consequence of that she was in atrocious pain all day yesterday. She is easier to day and has asked me to tell you all about it in explanation of her silence and express her regret at not having seen you, together with her hope that you'll not give her up as an altogether invisible person. She will write to you directly she feels a little more fit.

---

[1] The children's writer Harriet Capes was born in 1849 and died in 1936. For the first letter to her in this volume, see 31 August.

[2] Nora Mary Dorothea Tattersall (née Beatson, 1867–1942) and her husband Major John Cecil de Veel Tattersall, whom she married in 1909, were acquaintances of the Conrads living in Charlton Place, Bishopsbourne.

I assure you, dear Mrs Tattersall that we are both very sensible of your kind and neighbourly interest and believe me, always,

Your very faithful and obed^t servant

Joseph Conrad.

To J. B. Pinker
Text MS Berg; Unpublished

[Oswalds]

Monday. 2[3]. 5.20.[1]

Dearest Pinker.

My wire has given you the information as to facts. As to my feelings they are simply horrible. Sir R. Jones arrived at noon on Sat. The operation was a four-inch cut below the knee down to the bone and unluckily it had to involve a big nerve. The consequence was that Jessie suffered horribly all day yesterday and a great part of the night. This morning she is a little easier. As the cut was left open on purpose we must have a nurse on the premises for the next few days, and there is no room vacant to put you up for the night. Jessie wants you to know she is very sorry and sends you her love.

I have had a letter from F. N. D[oubleday] which I enclose.

I have still an infinity of questions to ask you, but must leave them to my next or else till we meet. But pray tell me at once *when* and *how* D. P. & Co are going to pub^{sh} the L^d Ed^{on} that is whether *all at once* or so many vols. p. month; and in what month the pub^{on} is to begin or to take place in a lump.

I ask simply on account of the *prefaces* which I have still to write. D. P. & Co must not look on them as minor contributions. They have their importance – if any writings have any importance. They are short mainly because they are deeply meditated. It would have been no trouble to write a dozen pp of twaddle. They ought to be made a feature in advert^g the sets.

Ever Yours

J. Conrad

To Richard Curle
Text MS Indiana; Curle 64

[letterhead: Oswalds]

5 May. 20.

My dear Curle

Jessie was operated on Sat: last at home under local an[a]esth^c. A 4 inch cut down to the bone and involving a nerve. She had a most awful time of it

---

[1] Assuming, as usual, that the date is less reliable than the day.

with pain all Sunday and Mond^y. She is a little easier now. The worst of it is that all the trouble has not been removed. There is another inflamed region which will have to be treated – probably by an operation of a more serious nature. But not yet. Sir R. Jones will come again I suppose next week.

There being a Nurse in the house I must ask you to come only on Sat: ev^g instead of Friday – unless untoward developments take place; in which case I shall wire you to* Coleherne Court on Fr^y or Sat^y morng to stop you. But that is not likely.

I have cabled Quinn yesterday: *"Two sets of ten each and seven of Shorters will be sent to you next week in the terms of Curles letter." Conrad.*[1]

It would be nice if you could get Bumpus[2] or some of those people to dispatch the package in time for next Wednes^{ys} ship.

I don't feel very bright as you may imagine. Jessie sends her love.

Always Yours

J. Conrad.

To John Galsworthy
Text MS Forbes; Unpublished

[letterhead: Oswalds]

[5 May 1920][3]

Dearest Jack.

I am sending the MS of the admirable "Chancery" by this post.

Poor Jessie was operated at home last Sat. A four inch cut down to the bone and she had an infernal time of it with the pain afterwards for 3 days.

There is still another suspicious spot on the limb which will have to be treated in some way – perhaps by another operation.

All this is rather awful. I suppose there will be an end to it some day.

I am sincerely glad that the public takes to the play.[4] I can't leave home just now – and indeed I don't want to. But I mean to see it before long. I've done nothing for ever so long.

Our dearest love to you both.

Ever Yours

J. Conrad.

---

[1] Copy in the Quinn Collection (NYPL). Another cable of 12 May indicates that the package left in the *Mauritania* on the 8th.

[2] The long-established and well-known Oxford Street booksellers.

[3] Galsworthy's letter to Conrad of 4 May (Stape, 2000), requesting the manuscript's return and the information on the operation on the 1st fix the date. 'March' is typed under the letterhead but is not contemporary with the text.

[4] *The Skin Game.* See the letter of [6? April].

To Major Gordon Gardiner
Text MS Harvard; Unpublished

[letterhead: Oswalds]
5. May 20

My dear Gardiner.[1]

It will be too delightful to see you here whenever you can come.

Poor Jessie was operated on the 31 Mch. (in a Canterbury Nurs^g Home) and again here last Saturday. There is the prospect of another operation in the near future.

All this is rather awful. The trouble is pereostitis originating in the slight infection of the knee which Sir Robert Jones found already there when he operated for a stiff joint in 1918. The bones have grown together perfectly and it is only the recurrent inflammatory conditions that cause all this worry and pain and general misery of existence. I am getting quite anxious for the beastly thing is obstinate and she can't be carved indefinitely.

I have done no work to speak of and have been more or less gouty ever since the tenth of Jany. I only wish we could get a definitely good report of you – some day. But do come and let yourself be seen by those who, certainly, let no day pass without a thought for you.

Jessie's most affectionate regards. She was in horrid pain for two days but is much easier this morning.

Ever yours (notwithstanding the appearances)
Joseph Conrad.

To J. B. Pinker
Text MS Berg; Unpublished

[letterhead: Oswalds]
5 May '20

Dearest Pinker

Thanks for your letter. I had the £6 notes on Monday all right and cheque for B[orys] arrived to-day.

B. left early here to see John through London on his way to school. I asked him to ask you on [the] 'phone if you would see me to-morrow *Thursday*

---

[1] An Aberdonian, Theodore James Gordon Gardner (1874–1937), though troubled by ill health, had been a civil servant in South Africa, a tea planter in Ceylon, and a student at Harvard. After the war, in which he was involved in spy-hunting and the surveillance of enemy aliens, he worked as an arbitrator of industrial disputes and as Secretary to the National Club, London. His posthumous *Notes of a Prison Visitor* (1938) records some of his experiences of befriending convicts; he also published novels, and at his death was working on a study of Napoleon. Conrad's friendship began during visits to Scotland in 1916 and strengthened over the years.

about one. I feel I must get away for a few hours and who could I want to see but you? I may also find perhaps something to say. I can hardly use the pen to-day. Sheer worry.

But you won't see me a wreck and you won't find me a great trial. I simply feel that a couple of hours with you will do me all the good in the world.

Are you aware that Walpole is home?[1] Should he call on you in the morn[g] keep my arrival dark. Don't feel as if I wanted to see him or anybody else just at present – good fellows as they all are.

Ever Yours

J. Conrad.

PS Of course if you have engagements I shall try to take care of myself for a couple of hours and call again in the afternoon for a moment.

To G. Jean-Aubry
Text MS Yale; Unpublished

[letterhead: Oswalds]

Mardi. [11 May 1920][2]

Mon cher ami.

Je viens d'apprendre que Vous avez paru chez Pinker.[3] Se peut-il que Vous m'ayez* écrit et que je n'ai pas reçu Votre lettre.

Pendant Votre absence ma femme a eu deux operations une 31 mars et l'autre voilà 10 jours de cela. Et Sir Robert a annoncé son arrivée pour Samedi prochain pour voir ce qu'il y a a fair[e] – car ce n'est pas fini.

Elle souffre beaucoup. Mais il y a toujours l'espoir! Elle Vous envoie ces amitiés.

Je ne Vs parle pas de moi. Je suis desolé qu'a cause de Sir R nous ne pouvons pas Vous prier de venir pour le prochain week-end. Mais je désire bien fort de Vous voir. Les deux Nos du Correspondant (avec Le Planteur)[4] sont arrivés ce matin.

Je n'ai rien fait que finir ma pièce. Je n'ai pas la tête a moi.

Tout a Vous

J. Conrad.

---

[1] The novelist Hugh Walpole had been lecturing in America from late September 1919 to late April 1920. See the letter to him of 14 June.
[2] Postmarked 12 May.
[3] Literally, 'you were published at Pinker's', but the sense suggests a call on Pinker.
[4] Jean-Aubry's translation of 'The Planter of Malata' appeared in the 25 March and 10 April issues.

Translation

Tuesday.

My dear friend.

I just learned that you appeared at Pinker's office. Can it be that you wrote to me and that I didn't get your letter?

My wife had two operations while you were away – one on 31 March, the other ten days ago. And Sir Robert has announced his arrival for next Saturday to see what has to be done – because this is not over yet.

She is in a good deal of pain. But there is always hope! She sends you her friendly regards.

I won't speak to you about myself. I'm sorry we can't invite you to come next week-end because of Sir R. But I dearly wish to see you. The two issues of the *Correspondant* (containing 'The Planter') arrived this morning.

I have done nothing but finish my play. I'm not myself.

Yours truly

J. Conrad.

To J. B. Pinker
Text TS/MS Berg; Unpublished

[letterhead: Oswalds]
May 11th. 1920.

My dear Pinker

I return to you the precious Quinn's letter which of course now has only an historical interest. The everlasting pamphlets left U.K. by last Saturday's boat and the whole interest is concentrated now on Quinn's cheque, which will be due in about two weeks' time, I suppose.

The old car has been sold; and as I always said that I would take no less than three hundred pounds for it I am very pleased to tell you that I have got £305 clear after paying all the expenses and commissions. It was better to take it without waiting to get more, perhaps for a fortnight or so, with the expenses of advertisements and garage going on. Considering that the old car with all the repairs and alterations hadn't cost me more than £220 at the outside I think I have done fairly well with it after getting something like 16 months very hard wear out of the machine.

I enclose here [a] cheque for £100 in repayment of half the amount you transferred into my account. I will repay the other £100 out of Quinn's money directly it reaches me, if this arrangement suits you.

Jessie is a little easier but nothing decisive has happened so far. This morning I had a letter from Sir Robert announcing his visit for the end of the week but without naming a day. It is bound to be either Friday or Saturday however; and in any case it means my dear fellow that your visit must be put off till after next Sunday to Jessie's and my great regret. Whether there will be another operation and of what nature if there is to be one nobody can tell. But in this letter Sir R affirms again that there can be nothing which can not be put right with time and patience.

Jessie does not lack the virtue of patience. She sends You and Your house her best love. The nurse is to stay on for another fortnight, and all the preparations, sterilised dressings etc etc are to be made on Thursday in readiness for the Great Man's decision.

I am tackling in good earnest to-day the Elba novel[1] – and mean to continue from day to day if the heavens fall.

Ever Yours

J Conrad

To Sir Sidney Colvin
Text MS Yale; Unpublished

[letterhead: Oswalds]

13 May '20

Dearest Colvin.

I rejoiced at the sight of your handwriting.

Your letter was brought to me at the very moment I had picked up a telegram-form to send an inquiry about your progress. I would have been to see you but a confusedly worded message from Sir Robert Jones announcing his intention to come down to see Jessie kept me at home in continual expectation of a telegram. It appears now that he can not come till Saturday. There will very probably be another operation of a minor kind but more serious than the last.

I won't be able to run up tomorrow. Two of our servants are going away and I shall have to be out hunting for substitutes.

All worries would be like nothing if I could only see some signs of permanent improvement in Jessie's state. She suffers a great deal tho' perhaps a little less to-day than at the beginning of the week. But the strain is beginning to tell and she is not quite like herself.

I shall drop you a line on Sat: to tell you what has been done. These periods of waiting are beastly.

Jessie sends her dear love to you both. I kiss dear Lady Colvin's hands. Have you seen H[ugh] Walpole yet? We had only a telegram of arrival and I

---

[1] *Suspense.*

confess I have not written to him since his return. I haven't the heart to write to anybody or do anything or see any human being for social purposes.

Ever most affect^{ly} Yours

Joseph Conrad

To Lady Colvin
Text MS Rosenbach; Unpublished

[letterhead: Oswalds]

Sat. 15.5.20

Dear Lady Colvin.

As there was nothing done yesterday I did not wire the news – which, upon the whole, is good. Sir Robert found that the general state of the limb has improved. The trouble tends to become localised in one spot but the indications were not definite enough for making an incision at once. He will come again either this week or the next according to the report which will be sent to him by our local surgeon. This thing is *bound* to come right, as Sir Robert says, but it may take some time yet. He spent some 4 hours in the house and was most sympathetic and comforting. Jessie must not be moved yet from her long chair in which she has been lying night and day for 3 weeks now. She sends her dearest love to you both.

We have all been cheered by this visit.

After all there is nothing hopeless or mysterious about this. It is simply an acute pereostitis following a perfectly successful operation for a stiff joint. One could not expect to cure a bad knee of 16 years' standing without meeting with some trouble.

I was so happy to see dear Colvin's handwriting. We hope to hear of his further progress from you in a day or two. Do please tell us how you are. We are anxious still about you both.

I am not feeling particularly well. I am unable to tackle my work seriously. Meantime the days slip away! Jessie's indomitable cheerfulness keeps me going and if [I] could only see her period of suffering ended it seems to me I could do wonders.

I shall try to run up this week and see you. I have grown so stupidly nervous that at times the mere idea of a railway journey scares me out of my wits. I am confessing this to you under the seal of secrecy. I dont want the public to gain the notion of J. C. being a nervous wreck.

My love to You both.

Always Your most affectionate friend and Servant

Joseph Conrad

Jessie sends her love and hopes that by putting all together and with a will we shall bring off that visit this time.

To J. B. Pinker

Text MS Berg; Unpublished

[letterhead: Oswalds]
Saturday. [15 May 1920][1]

My dear Pinker.

Sir R. has just left the house. No incision was made to day as the local conditions are not definite enough as yet for the use of the knife. Perhaps there may be no occasion for it any more as there can be no doubt that the general state of the limb is much improved. The trouble instead of spreading shows a distinct tendency to localise itself in one spot. If another incision becomes necessary Sir Robert will come down again. Meantime the pain has eased and the future looks brighter in consequence – to us all.

Do you think you could manage to come and see us next Friday and carry out the whole programme according to plan? If you prefer any other day You've only to say so. "All the resources of the Establishment" (I believe this is the proper cliché phrase) will be put "entirely at your disposal." (another cliché. I verily believe I could write circulars all right)

A desire of industry is growing on me. I may yet do credit to your bringing up. What I am asking myself is – : why I should suffer from such a state of funk before that book?[2] I have tried my hand at a novel or two already, as you may remember. Then why——?

Unless things alter I shall have a sweet time of it for the next 10 months or so.

Ever Yours

J. Conrad

To Richard Curle

Text MS Indiana; Curle 65 (in part)[3]

[letterhead: Oswalds]
Sat. 15.5.'20

Dearest Richard.

Sir R. J. is just gone after declaring himself pleased with the general improvement in the state of the limb. The trouble tends to become localised in one spot but the appearances were not definite enough as yet to venture on

---

[1] Sir Robert's departure establishes the date.
[2] *Suspense.*   [3] Curle omits the last paragraph.

an incision. So nothing was done except a very thorough examination and Sir R. will come again to see Jessie either this week or the next – according to the report our local surgeon is to send him in a few days.

Mcantime hot fomentations and complete immobility in the long chair in which poor Jessie has been lying now night and day for 3 weeks. She is very cheerful and sends affectionate messages to your household and yourself.

I had to put off Pink's visit till next Friday. There are no news[1] of anything stirring in my affairs. I like you[r] travel book more and more both as personal expression and as individual prose-writing of a fascinating quality. (I can get no prose of any kind out of myself.)

Give my regards to your wife. I hope to be introduced soon to the man Adam[2] in that Oxfordshire paradise.

Yours ever

J. Conrad.

To J. B. Pinker
Text MS Berg;[3] Unpublished

[Oswalds]
[mid-May 1920]

My dear P –

What is the meaning of this par.?[4] I suppose a mistake. I had a copy of the Arrow in Swedish sent me last week. Its price was *11.50k* as stated on the book (*not one* krone).

Ever Yours

J. C.

To G. Jean-Aubry
Text MS Yale; Unpublished

[letterhead: Oswalds]
1920 17. Mai.

Très cher Aubry.

Nous vous remercions de tout notre coeur pour votre bonne lettre. Nous sommes impatients de vous voir.

Voudrez-Vous venir Jeudi prochain par le train de 10^h. 45^m (Victoria)?

---

[1] In French and Polish, the word is plural.   [2] Their infant son.

[3] Note on a postcard to Conrad from George T. Keating, postmarked 10 May 1920, New York.

[4] From an American press-cutting: 'Joseph Conrad's "The Rescue" has been translated into Swedish and published by Albert Bonnier, Stockholm. The Swedish edition sells for 1 krone, or about 28 cents. The novel will be published in this country by Doubleday, Page on May 21, who will sell it for $2.'

Sir Robert était ici le Samedi. Il a remis Jessie a la quinzaine. Voilà déja qu'elle a passé 2 semaines dans son fauteuil sans bouger, nuit et jour.

Mais l'état general de la jambe c'est amélioré et tout sera bien. Seulement cela sera long.

Comme deux de nos domestiques nous quittent nous ne pouvons pas Vous prier de passer la nuit cette fois ci.

Amitiés de la part de tout le monde.

Tout à Vous

J. Conrad

Translation

My very dear Aubry.

We thank you with all our hearts for your good letter. We are eager to see you.

Would you like to come next Thursday by the 10.45 train (Victoria)?

Sir Robert was here on Saturday. He has ordered another fortnight for Jessie – and she has already spent two weeks in her chair without stirring day or night.

But the general state of the limb has improved, and everything will be fine. Only it will take some time.

Since two of our servants are leaving us, we can't ask you to stay the night this time.

Friendly regards from everybody.

Yours truly

J. Conrad

To Thomas J. Wise

Text TS BL Ashley 2953; Unpublished

[letterhead: Oswalds]
May 20th. 1920.

Dear Mr Wise.

I am sending in accordance with your wishes six items as follows:

Author's Notes, 4: *Chance*; *Within the Tides*; *Twixt Land and Sea*; *Under Western Eyes*. Authentic First Drafts corrected by me in pen and ink pretty extensively, as you will see.

A *Short Introduction* written specially for a School-book which Dent is publishing, and relating to Gaspar Ruiz.

Three MS pages consisting of a message cabled to the Polish Government Committee of the State Loan to be raised in U.S. being an appeal for subscriptions to Poles and Americans. It is hardly literature but, at any rate, it is a public act of mine and very likely to be the only specimen of Conrad's cable style. If you don't care for the last two items pray send me £40 for the others, which would be, as it were, our agreed price for Author's Notes. If you keep the two last items then send me £50.

Our friend Curle said something to me about your wish to acquire for your collection such corrected First Proofs as there may be in the future. If that is the case I will preserve them for you when they are sent to me with the revise.

I hope you are keeping well.

Yours faithfully

Joseph Conrad.

To Richard Curle

Text MS Indiana; Curle 66

[letterhead: Oswalds]
24.5.20.

My dear Richard

I won't conceal from you that I am much affected by your last two letters.[1] I can't contemplate your possible departure for India[2] with equanimity. But you alone can judge of the proper conduct of *your* life. I can only feel that your decision is bound to affect *mine* intimately with a sense of loss in its deeper values. That much I had to say – tho' I daresay it is no news to you. For the rest – perhaps! Yes, perhaps it would be better for you to get away for a time. The great consideration is that such a move is bound to affect the complexion of your whole future. That is unavoidable. On the other hand the pressure of the material necessities may be irresistible in this case. I am thinking of all this with great and, I believe, quite unselfish anxiety.

Walpole has asked permission to come down on the 5th – for the week end. If you want to meet him this is an opportunity.

Enough for this time. Our love.

Yours

J. Conrad

---

[1] Announcing his departure for Burma to be temporary editor of the *Rangoon Times*.
[2] From 1885 to 1948, Burma was administered as a province of India.

To Thomas J. Wise
Text TS/MS Yale; Unpublished

[letterhead: Oswalds]
May 24th. 1920.

Dear Mʳ Wise.

Thank you very much for your letter and the cheque which I received yesterday. Since we sent you that batch another Author's Note (to Shadow Line) has been finished but has not been put into shape yet. When all the corrections are made I shall send to you the First Draft of it and also the one of Victory's Author's Note. That will bring the Notes to an end for a time, all the books, with the exception of the two last, being provided for.

I have also received my two papers: Tradition and Confidence, in their beautiful bindings. You are treating my productions in a princely fashion. It is a real pleasure to look at those bound copies in their high state of finish. I have, on the last page of each First Draft, certified their genuineness in the terms of the request contained in your letter. I am prepared to do anything in that way you may feel to be necessary. As to the corrected proofs I shall bear in mind your desire to possess them. A complete series of modifications my prose goes through till it gets finally to the printer and into the hands of the public would no doubt present some interest to a student of style. Of course you must not expect any future corrected proofs to look like the galley slips of *Rescue* which our friend Curle has probably shown you. They can be hardly called "proof corrections". They are fundamental corrections of the text, rather. I will mention to you here that this is at least the fifth severe cutting-down which the *Rescue* had got, and, even so, the text, pruned and trimmed and clipped, fills over 400 pages of the printed book. The comparison of the pen and ink text which you have got with the final text of the book would be a curious experience as showing how severe an author may be in his more mature period with the work of his early days.

Thanks for your kind inquiries about my wife. I regret to say that she is still laid up and still suffering a good deal of pain. Sir Robert Jones is coming again next week down here to see her. Though her condition is by *no means* hopeless yet the strain of suspense and of the successive disappointments begins to tell on me. My greatest support is her own patient serenity in this severe trial. She sends her kind regards and her thanks for your good wishes.

Believe me

very faithfully Yours
Joseph Conrad.

To J. B. Pinker
Text MS Yale; Unpublished

[letterhead: Oswalds]
26.5.20

My dear Pinker

We have just heard from R. J[ones] that he is not coming down this week. So if you like to carry out the programme of your visit on this Frid-Sat – as we planned, you have only to say so. The weather seems fixed and all things look fairly propitious.

If so please spend the famous Lloyd-Georgian Ninepence[1] on a wire *on receipt of this*. We take it you'll bring with you an aide-de-camp in the shape of Ralph.[2]

I would like too to mention to you a point or two as to mere affairs and ascertain what you think.

Yours ever

J. Conrad.

To J. B. Pinker
Text TS/MS Berg;[3] Unpublished

[letterhead: Oswalds]
May 31st. 1920.

Thank you for your letter and the cash which arrived safely.

I am writing to you on the machine[4] because I am sorry to say I have a bad elbow which the last three days has been painful enough to stop me working completely. Bad enough to stop me even reading and though I am not actually laid up I can't think of coming to London as I intended to do to look up some books in the British Museum. I am more vexed and distressed about this than I can tell you apart from the actual very severe pain because I did really hope to get a respite for two or three months at least. This physical worry on top of my continual anxiety about Jessie's state is about as much as

---

[1] Lloyd George's slogan 'ninepence for fourpence' was coined to garner support for the National Insurance Act of 1911. The weekly contribution was 3d (three pence) for women, and 4d for men; contributions from employers and the government brought the sum to 9d. (David) Lloyd George (1863–1945; 1st Earl Lloyd-George of Dwyfor 1945) was Prime Minister from 1916 to 1922.

[2] (James) Ralph Pinker (1900–59), who eventually joined the family firm.

[3] The greeting, usually added by hand to dictated letters, was here inadvertently omitted.

[4] I.e., dictating to Miss Hallowes.

I can stand just now. I can't think consecutively or concentrate on anything. All I could do was to finish the Prefaces for the De Luxe Edition of which the last two I managed to dictate last week but have been unable to correct as yet, for I can't use either my hand or my mind in an effective manner. I am better to-day so far that I am able to dictate this, but even this is an awful effort to stick to.

We could not have heard from Doubleday since the publication of The Rescue unless by cable for which I suppose there was not the slightest occasion. I hope the reception was good, though I feel beastly gloomy about that as about everything else.

Is it a fact that the Little Theatre is closed for the present, as I have heard from one or two people. If that is so I am very sorry for Vernon's disappointment, and though I have never built much on the play I consider it a piece of beastly bad luck for me. I did really hope to get a sympathetic presentation for that play but with Vernon out of it that hope falls to the ground. I imagine the thing is no good to him now and perhaps it will be just as well to get the copy back from him. I know there were two clean copies made but both may be useful to us. I presume you are dealing with the situation in some way or at least have some scheme in view and I confess I should like to know what is going on and what you think of the prospects.

Can you tell me what Dent is about. He hasn't written to me at all on the subject of The Rescue, and I don't want to write to him to be sure, but because you know whether there is any chance of early publication or whether the thing will have to be put off till next autumn.

I have had a letter from Heinemann asking for more copy for his limited Edition. I can't however send him more because he sets up from the American corrected proof and with the exception of Almayer's Folly, Outcast of the Islands, and Nigger of the Narcissus which I did send him no more books have reached me from Doubleday. I am dropping a line to H. to that effect and perhaps when you write to Doubleday you would mention that this side is waiting for them. Doubleday has a lot of corrected books to set up from as quick as he likes. He has got everything up to Chance, corrected text of English Editions and Prefaces all complete. Twixt Land and Sea and Within the Tides have been read through by Miss H[allowes] who has discovered a few misprints and corrected them. Those volumes with their proper Prefaces will leave by this Wednesday's packet. There will remain then from the old books Shadow Line and Victory, which will go next week, with their Prefaces. The Arrow of Gold and Rescue I consider new books for which there can't be any great hurry, for Arrow of Gold is not quite a year old as published in England and Rescue has not yet been published.

I wonder why I haven't had my copies of Rescue yet from America. They used to reach me here within the week of publication.

The local surgeon yesterday after seeing Jessie told me that it was time for him to report to Sir Robert Jones as the situation seems to require something further being done. Sir Robert will be in London on Wednesday and we expect to have a letter from him on Thursday as to his intentions. A diagram of the limb has been sent to him too so that he will be able to form an opinion.

My dear friend I can't trust myself to speak of it. There seems to be no end to this. She could not have better care skill and advice – and that is a comfort in a way, but the obstinacy of that thing begins to look ugly. Mrs Dummett[1] who was here yesterday with C. Graham told me that Robert Jones's daughter (Mrs Watson)[2] told her that her father expressed himself with the greatest confidence as to his ability to "get Mrs Conrad right" before very long.

Please my dear fellow send two £5 notes on receipt of this to Miss C. Zagórska 37–39 Gt Ormond St. Queen's Sq: W.C. She is gone to London for a week to get her old lace and certain objects of art (family possessions) valued with a view to selling them, and I could only give her 30/- when she left this morning. Our love.

Ever Yours

J Conrad.

To Thomas J. Wise
Text MS BL Ashley 2953; Unpublished

[letterhead: Oswalds]
1 June 1920

Dear Mr Wise.

I send you two prefaces called Authors Notes to:

Shadow Line

Victory to which I join hol[ogra]phs of two letters written to the press on the occasion of the controversy aroused by my article on the Empr^{ss} of Ireland collision pub^d in the Ill^d Lond News.[3] That article was published by you in booklet form.

---

[1] Elizabeth ('Toppie') Dummett (née Miéville, 1868–1940), Graham's companion for many years.
[2] Hilda Watson, like Mrs Dummett, a keen horsewoman.
[3] 'The Lesson of the Collision' (later 'Protection of Ocean Liners') had appeared on 6 June 1914. The collision, which occurred in the St Lawrence River in Quebec, led to enormous loss of life.

The two letters are the only example of J. C.'s style in controversy. If you keep these pen & ink pages pray send me £30.

In haste

Cordially yours

J. Conrad.

To Richard Curle
Text MS Indiana; Curle 67

[letterhead: Oswalds]
2 June '20

My dear Curle.

I will have to be out all day Saturday and for this reason and also for another connected with the servants we must ask you to come only on Sunday by the morning train – the one that arrives at Cant[y] East at 12.24 and will be met either by our car or Sneller's taxi. Awfully sorry to keep you off for a day but there has been a lot of complications – of the domestic order.

I don't think much of the temporary Editorship. If you go out you will stick out there I fear. However! . .

Au revoir then on Sunday, for I hope you'll be not so offended by this letter as to refuse to come.

Love from us all.

Yours ever

J Conrad.

To Count Józef Potocki
Text L.fr. 155; Najder 263–4

Oswalds
3 juin 1920

Je suis touché, Monsieur le Comte,[1] par l'idée vraiment amicale que vous avez eue de m'envoyer cette page.[2] Je n'ai gardé qu'une impression vaguement sinistre de ce temps-là. Mes souvenirs d'enfance ne remontent

---

[1] After Balliol College, Oxford, and military training in St Petersburg, Count Józef Alfred Potocki (1895–1968) served during the war as an officer in the Russian and Polish armies. Secretary of the Polish Legation in London during 1919–22, he later became Director of the Anglo-American section and member of the Political Department of the Ministry of External Affairs in Warsaw. After the Second World War he was *chargé d'affaires* in Lisbon and Madrid. He was the grandson of the man who served as the model for Conrad's Prince Roman.
[2] Najder identifies this as a document concerning Conrad's father Apollo Korzeniowski.

qu'à mon séjour chez le frère de ma mère (Bobrowski) à Nowofastow entre 1865 et 1869.[1] Ceux-là aussi ne sont pas joyeux.

J'ai vécu deux vies depuis. Tout cela est bien loin. *Pulvis et Umbra!*[2]

Veuillez accepter mes remerciements très sincères et l'assurance de ma haute estime.

Translation

I am touched, my dear Count, by the truly friendly idea you had of sending me that page. I have only a dimly sinister impression of those days. My childhood memories go no further back than a visit to my mother's brother (Bobrowski) at Nowofastów between 1865 and 1869. Those memories, too, are not happy ones.

I have lived two lives since. It is all so long ago. *Pulvis et Umbra!*

Pray accept my very sincere thanks and the assurance of my high esteem.

To Thomas J. Wise
Text MS BL Ashley 2953; Unpublished

[letterhead: Oswalds]
3. June '20

Dear M[r] Wise.

Thanks for your letter and encl[re].

I wrote a note in each book. I suppose it's what you wanted me to do. Pardon scrawl. Have a gouty elbow which makes writing difficult.

Certainly! We will be delighted to see you in July. Surgeon coming next week. My wife's thanks and regards

Yours

J. Conrad

PS Hand writing of notes fine specimen of Conrad's penmanship when gouty in the arm. But I wouldn't wait for God knows how long – perhaps.

---

[1] In fact, two visits: in summer 1866 and from the autumn of 1866 to the summer of 1867. An earlier visit dated to summer 1863.

[2] In *Odes*, 3, 7, Horace contrasts the unfailing renewal of nature and the heavens with the finality of our own deaths. When we join the illustrious dead, 'Pulvis et umbra sumus': 'we are dust and shadow.'

To Alfred A. Knopf
Text TS Texas; Unpublished

[letterhead: Oswalds]
June 8th. 1920.

Dear Mᵣ Knopf.[1]

My warm thanks for the charming copy of "Wild Oranges"[2] which it was a great pleasure to have in this interesting form. On this occasion you will perhaps be good enough, when you write, to give my most friendly regards to Hergesheimer[3] whose vital work combining strength of vision with delicate perception and masterly expression arouses my admiration and sympathy. I am immensely proud that *my* work should have found such a good friend in him. I had a long report about him from H. Walpole who was here yesterday.

We talked largely of you too and I showed him your reproachful letter which affected me, hardened sinner as I am in the matter of correspondence. If I failed to answer some of the communications you were good enough to send to me I can only apologise very sincerely and throw myself on your mercy. As to promising amendment for the future I won't do that because I know myself too well. The fact of the matter is that I have seldom anything interesting to say to my kind correspondents. I have not formed the habit of enlarging much on my feelings and thoughts, which apart from an artistic expression seem to me to have no exceptional value of any sort. Moreover I am often crippled and unable to hold a pen, which is the reason why in this instance I am answering your letter in type. I have done nothing worth mentioning for a good many months, and under such circumstances answering letters becomes a task which I find difficult to face.

You have ever been friendly to me and I beg you never to doubt that I reciprocate this feeling in full measure. I have been pleased and interested

---

[1] While still an undergraduate Alfred Abraham Knopf (1892–1984) had corresponded with the Galsworthys and visited them in Devon. On graduating from Columbia University in 1912, he went to work at Doubleday, Page, where he was responsible for orchestrating the highly successful publicity campaign for *Chance*. In 1915, he began his own firm. With his wife, Blanche Wolf Knopf, he built up an extraordinary list that included, over the years, Wallace Stevens, Willa Cather, Dashiel Hammett, Langston Hughes, Thomas Mann, Jean-Paul Sartre, Simone de Beauvoir, Albert Camus, Yukio Mishima, Yasunari Kawabata, Doris Lessing, and Toni Morrison. He remained with the firm when Random House acquired it in 1960.

[2] A limited edition of Joseph Hergesheimer's *Wild Oranges* published by Knopf in 1919.

[3] Joseph Hergesheimer (1880–1954), popular American novelist, short-story writer, biographer, and critic. *Java Head* (1919), his best-known novel, is about two ship-owning families from Salem, Massachusetts, who make their money in the China trade.

to hear from Pinker of the success and distinction of your publishing house and beg you to believe in my best wishes for its future increase in prosperity and reputation.

Believe me faithfully yours

Joseph Conrad.

To J. B. Pinker
Text MS Berg; Unpublished

[Oswalds]

Tuesday 8.6.'20

My dear Pinker.

I wired You this morning as I don't want to communicate direct with F. U[nwin] on any matter whatever.

Pray suggest (if you think it wise) to Hein[emann] he should set up Tales of U. (one vol with A Folly) from book. I'll correct in proof.

Also Typhoon (one vol with Nigger) could be set up from the book. The corrections I made are not many and I may be able to remember them.

I was yesterday in the B[riti]sh Museum all day. To-day I am getting on with *The Isle of Rest* provisional title for the Nap[oleonic] novel.

I have a bad wrist. Excuse the scrawl. I have a few bills to settle. Please pay in £80 to my acct and 20 to Jessie's due to her in lieu of pension.

I will let you know to-morrow what the surgeon says. Pardon this scrap of paper.

Ever Yours

J. Conrad

To Thomas J. Wise
Text MS BL Ashley 2953; Unpublished

[letterhead: Oswalds]

Monday [Tuesday, 8 June 1920][1]

Dear Mr Wise

Many thanks for your good letter. I've sent instructions to P[inker].

---

[1] Curle's visit to Oswalds of the 6–7th is likely that in question; 'yesterday' would thus be Monday. The book-signing mentioned to Wise on the 3rd confirms the period, although there were more signings later in the month (see the letter of the 24th).

Our friend R[ichard] C[urle] was here yesterday and I have signed your copy of S[hadow] L[ine]. I hope in the way you wished it.

Kindest regards

Yours

J. Conrad.

To Richard Curle
Text TS Indiana; Curle 68

[letterhead: Oswalds]
June 14th. 1920.

My dear Curle,

The announcement of the actual date[1] is quite a shock. You must know that after a very good afternoon in the B[ritish] M[useum] I returned home feeling very well and with most pleasant recollections of the day with you and Walpole, ended by profitable reading, but during the night a severe attack of gout came in the right wrist which notwithstanding my efforts to re-act laid me flat on my back in considerable pain and, what is worse, an extreme lowness of spirits. On Wednesday we heard that Sir R. J[ones] had decided to put off his visit for a week or more in consequence of the report from the local surgeon and partly owing to the pressing nature of his engagements for the past week. Of course he could have done nothing if he had come. How it was that I did not write to you on Wednesday evening you will guess. Just then I was not in a state to remember anything of what I had to do. Of course I might have asked Miss H[allowes] to drop you a line but I repeat again that I was not in a state to do anything.

As the attack was sharp so the recovery may be quick. I am certainly better now but I don't know whether it will be at all possible for me to travel up to town on Thursday. And then there will be this consideration, that Sir R. J. may select that particular day for coming down here. Upon the whole I think the prospect is hopeless, and yet I would like very much to do it. I understand quite well that your time is bound to be taken up by final arrangements for your departure and your prolonged absence from England, but really my dear Richard it is no use speculating on what *I* may be able to do. It would be much more to the purpose, from my point of view, to ask you direct – what are *you* able to do? Can you come down on Saturday and stay over Sunday, or perhaps (to save every hour of the first working day) you would go back to town on Sunday night.

[1] Of Curle's departure for Burma.

Please drop me a line at once and also let me know where you will be staying in London so that in case of developments of any kind I may write or wire to you in town. No more at present because even dictating requires a big effort.

Yours always,

J. Conrad

To G. Jean-Aubry
Text TS Yale; J-A, 2, 240–1

[letterhead: Oswalds]
June 14th. 1920.

My dear Aubry,

I am just getting over a most severe and unexpected attack of gout, which felled me last Monday night after my return from London, where I had spent a few hours in the B[ritish] M[useum] reading some of the works you have been good enough to discover for me more than a year ago.[1]

I feel fairly bad still and even the dictating of this insignificant letter is a great effort. Sir Robert Jones did not come last week, but he may visit my wife this week. It will all depend on the report of the local surgeon who will be writing to him to-day.

I have heard, so to speak unofficially, that Bennett either has read or is going to read, the play.[2] Ceci entre nous,[3] for I don't expect he will care for it and there is no need to take the world into one's confidence on so doubtful a matter. And in connection with this, do you still think it worth while to translate those Four Acts? If so I will ask Pinker to have a fresh copy made. There are two in existence now, I think, but one is in America and the other, I suppose, with Bennett. I do not know how long he may keep it and just now I am too depressed to care for the upshot of the whole affair. It is not very fascinating to me in any case.

Please, my dear fellow, thank Mrs Alvar from me for her good letter and tell her that I would really be grateful if she could let me know whether this Swedish translation is adequate.[4] I should like to produce a good impression

---

[1] Related to the Napoleonic background of *Suspense*.
[2] Arnold Bennett acknowledged receipt of *The Secret Agent* from Pinker on 8 June. Bennett was going to read it for the Lyric Theatre, of which he was a director (see *Letters of Arnold Bennett*, Vol. 1: *Letters to J. B. Pinker*, ed. James Hepburn, Oxford University Press, 1966, p. 284).
[3] 'This between ourselves'.
[4] Presumably E. Brusewitz's translation of *Chance*, published in Stockholm in 1919.

on any readers I may obtain in Sweden; it is not so much a matter of vanity as of actual sympathetic feeling for the country and the people.

Jessie sends you her warmest regards.

Tout à vous,

J. Conrad

To J. B. Pinker
Text TS Berg; Unpublished

[letterhead: Oswalds]
June 14th. 1920.

My dear Pinker,

Thank you for the six notes, which reached me only on Sunday morning.

I cannot tell you, my dear friend, how I value your Rescue letter. Indeed, you have had a great part in that book and your claim would have been undeniable and indeed unquestionable had I not disposed of the dedication before. But pray remember that when I flung out that promise lightly I was not at all certain that I would ever take the book up again. The fact of the matter is until you absolutely forced my hand with your usual ruthlessness I was not certain that I would take it up. It was all a matter of ten minutes as it were. I had to get up and fly round, and I cannot tell you how grateful I am to you for the magnificent move you made with that book, which indeed would have put life and resolution into a dead man.[1]

You[r] assurance that it has come off sets at rest whatever doubts I may have had. The only matter of great concern left just now is to keep up to the standard with the next one, for that will have a tremendous advantage in its subject. That is from the public point of view. From my own private point of view I don't know that a great subject is an advantage. It increases one's sense of responsibility and awakens all that mistrust of oneself that has been my companion through all these literary years. Mine, my dear Pinker, is the only instance within my knowledge of practice not giving self-confidence. There is a strain of anxiousness in my character that even the encouragement of your friendship and sympathy cannot altogether overcome.

No more now. I feel as flat (and as soft) as a pancake. Love and thanks from Jessie.

Yours ever,

J. Conrad

---

[1] Even by his own standards, Pinker worked exceptionally hard to place serial and book versions of *The Rescue* on both sides of the Atlantic, and Conrad paid close attention to the suggestions of the man he called his 'pilot' (*Letters*, 6, p. 367).

To Hugh Walpole
Text TS Texas; Unpublished

[letterhead: Oswalds]
June 14th. 1920.

My dear Walpole,[1]

Last Monday is the last pleasant day I am afraid I will have for a long time. The morning part of it was perfectly delightful in your company (under Curle's grave supervision) and the succeeding half of it was really profitable, for I got the books I wanted and discovered in them a few hints and suggestions that were helpful. I left the B[ritish] M[usuem] at six and got home at eight, feeling very well. But during the night a severe attack of gout in the right wrist began to develop notwithstanding my desperate efforts to re-act, and I was down on my back by the evening of Tuesday. I have been in great pain and, what is worse, in the depth of dumps. Have dumps any depth? Anyway the impression was a most horrible nightmare – unable to think, afraid to move and only able to worry. Luckily Sir R. J[ones] thought it advisable on the report of the local surgeon to put off his visit for a week at least, but by Wednesday I was not in a state to communicate with my friends to tell them this or anything else, for indeed I could not think of anything – not even of the obvious course of asking Miss H[allowes] to write for me. Even to-day I feel like a man returned from a visit to the infernal regions – both cowed and exhausted. The whole thing was so brutal and unexpected that I feel as if I had been robbed of the last shred of my confidence in the scheme of the Universe. It all appears one great chaotic worry. I think I have managed to keep a pretty good face on it before Jessie and that is about all I could do. Since Saturday morning the improvement, as far as pain is concerned, has been rapid; but otherwise the experience has dismalised me. Not dismayed. Observe the shade of meaning. The flatness of this piece of paper on which you read these words is like a mountain compared with the flatness of my spirits. I wonder whether Jessie has written to you. Perhaps she has, and she may even have told me so but I do not remember. It is 10–30 a.m. and I cannot remember anything, or think or anything, or contemplate any sort of exertion, physical or mental, without despair. I wish I could get

---

[1] Hugh Seymour Walpole (1884–1941; knighted 1937), a New-Zealand-born novelist, son of the Bishop of Durham, educated at Cambridge, was widely and well connected in the literary scene of his time, counting Arnold Bennett, Henry James, H. G. Wells, and Virginia Woolf among his friends and acquaintances. Although he was highly popular in his day, his reputation dwindled after his death. During the war, he was invested with the Order of Saint George for bravery under fire as an orderly with the Russian Red Cross. Before meeting Conrad, who was to treat him as a protégé, Walpole had already published his critical appreciation *Joseph Conrad* (1916; revised edition, 1924).

somebody to cut my liver out – I mean somebody competent – because I believe that nothing but an operation of that sort will do away with this horrible depression.

Enough of these details. I expect to get up and be clothed in my right mind by Wednesday, but as to coming up to town, as Curle wants me to do, on Thursday, it is out of the question. I had a letter from him this morning and it gave me a shock because I had forgotten completely all about his departure for Further India. I have just written to tell him that unless he comes down here for a day, or a night, or an hour, either Sat. or Sun. I won't be able to see him before he starts.

Jessie bears the delay, I won't say with a grin, but with a composure tempered by smiles. I have an idea that notwithstanding my efforts she was a little scared by this attack of mine. For myself I think it is over, but I know that the inner disturbance, physical and mental, will take some little time to quiet down and that there is no prospect of work or any ease of mind or body for a good many days.

Always yours,

J. Conrad

To J. B. Pinker
Text TS Berg; Unpublished

[letterhead: Oswalds]
June 17th. 1920. 10. AM.

Dearest Pinker

I have just received your cheerful note about The Rescue for which many thanks.

I enclose here tax demands for income (second half-year) and my local taxation. That last when taking the house I estimated at about £30; you will see that as a matter of fact it is £27.

Sir R. J[ones] is due to arrive here in a couple of hours. I am not in a state to do much this morning. If there is anything material to say I will drop you a line this evening.

Doubleday has sent me two reviews, one of the New York Times and one of the Evening Post. That last by Wilson Follett:[1] an enormous amount

[1] Follett's review was published in the *New York Evening Post Book Review* of 29 May (pp. 1, 13). Follett (1887–1963), the author of *Modern American Usage*, edited works by Thomas Beer and Stephen Crane. His *Joseph Conrad: A Short Study of his Intellectual and Emotional Attitude toward his Work and of the Chief Characteristics of his Novels* had appeared in 1915. The *New York Times* review by Louise Maunsell Field appeared in its literary section on 23 May (pp. 263–4) under the title 'Conrad's Art Spans Two Decades'. What particularly impressed the reviewer was the 'unity' of a work composed over so many years, 'so complete and perfectly rounded is the story it has to relate'.

of verbiage in which I presume there lurks somewhere a grain of meaning, but I have been incapable so far of finding it out. The other is plainer; and of course both reviews are most appreciative and, I suppose, *good* from a business point of view.

Have you got a copy to spare of the Secret Agent, play? Aubry writes me that he is ready to translate and take upon himself the worry of placing it in France if it can be placed at all. He would like to have a copy now so as to be ready with it in September. I think we could do no better than let him fly around and do his best because it is a fact that he has got very extensive connections in Paris.

Our dear love to you from us both

Ever Yours

J. Conrad.

To Thomas J. Wise

Text TS BL Ashley 2953; Unpublished

[letterhead: Oswalds]
June 21st. 1920.

Dear Mr Wise.

Am I mistaken in thinking that besides the First Draft of the drama The Secret Agent, you have also in your possession what, in our correspondence about typescripts, we always call the First Copy; that is the copy made at home of the corrected First Draft, also bearing some corrections by my own hand and from which the so-called Clean Copies (bearing no corrections by my hand) have been made.

If that is the case would you be good enough to let me have for a few days that First Copy. I don't think that this First Copy is bound with the First Draft which you sent me for signature; and the reason I ask for it is this: two clean copies were made for general purposes, of which one is gone to America and the other is now under consideration by Playfair, the manager of the Lyric Theatre, Hammersmith.[1] I have no idea how long he will keep it and meantime I am in need of another clean copy from which a French translation of the play could be made. I am anxious that the thing should be done as soon as possible and I don't know how long Playfair may keep his copy before he returns it, if he returns it at all, because should he accept the play he will no doubt stick to the copy which he will need to make prompt copies of the parts from.

---

[1] Nigel Playfair (1874–1934; knighted 1928), actor and producer, was the Lyric's manager from 1918 to 1932. His most recent successes there were his performance as Touchstone in *As You Like It* and his production of *The Beggar's Opera*.

The translator will be Mr Jean Aubry, whom you know and he is very anxious to begin.

If you are good enough to let me have that First Copy I shall have a clean copy made from it for Aubry and return it to you without the slightest delay.

I am sorry to trouble you but I have no text of any kind of the play in my possession, the only texts in existence being: First Draft, First Copy, and the two Clean Copies for public use. The copy made for Aubry would be the third Clean Copy and I shall suggest to Aubry that directly he has done his translation he should destroy it. Should however the First Copy be bound up in morocco with the First Draft (and I really can't remember whether it is so bound up or not) I will ask you to entrust me with the book, and, in that case, I can promise you that it will never leave my house as Miss Hallowes is ready to undertake the copying herself.

Kind regards from us both

Yours faithfully

Joseph Conrad

To Eric Pinker
Text TS Berg; Unpublished

[letterhead: Oswalds]
June 21st. 1920.

My dear Eric.

Thanks for your letter enclosing six notes. Will you please for the future send them off on Friday so that I can pay my people on Saturday. I can't always manage to cash a cheque here and they want the money to do their marketing with.

I have no text of the Play in my possession, but I have written to Wise who has got a copy in his collection, to send it to me. I shall forward it to you without delay and directly a clean type is made we will return Wise his copy.

I have also Doubleday's proof of Tales of Unrest, for which thanks. I hope he will be sending proofs of the other books as soon as possible, so that Heinemann may set up his edition from them.

Will you please thank your father for his letter advising me of the Doubleday cable. It is very comforting.

Sir Robert Jones was here on Thursday and I am glad to say that in consequence of an incision there is a marked improvement in the state of the patient.

Kind regards

Yours

J. Conrad.

To Richard Curle

Text MS Indiana; Curle 69

[letterhead: Oswalds]
Tuesday [22 June 1920][1]

My dear Richard

Thanks for your letter of farewell. This is only to wish you from us all God speed and the best of luck.

I will write to you c/o Rang[oon] Times in a fortnight, and give you general news of the house. I am most grateful to you for all the arrangements you've made for my vol of coll*ed* pieces.[2]

Whether I'll still be here to greet you in the spring I don't know; but I want you to take with you the assurance of my great regard for the writer and of my deep and constant affection for the man.

Yours always

Joseph Conrad.

To J. M. Dent

Text TS Berg; J-A, 2, 241–2[3]

[letterhead: Oswalds]
June 24th. 1920.

My dear Mr Dent.[4]

Many thanks for the advanced* copy of The Rescue which I received this morning and, as was only proper, inscribed at once to my wife.

You were good enough when I saw you last to undertake to have one copy bound in morocco for me for presentation to Penfield. I have another presentation of that sort to make. I must therefore ask you to have *two* copies instead of one bound in morocco for me in the same style in which the previous copies you have been good enough to have bound for me were done.

I am looking forward to getting my own six copies to-morrow morning but I must ask you to let me have one more at the special price as per agreement.

---

[1] Curle provides the date.   [2] *Notes on Life and Letters.*

[3] Jean-Aubry misidentifies the addressee as Hugh Dent. The next letter and the tone and contents here establish the recipient as his father.

[4] Joseph Mallaby Dent (1849–1926) was thirteen when apprenticed to a printer, and, shortly after, turned to bookbinding. In 1867, he moved to London, where he set up his own bookbinding shop, quickly winning a reputation for fine craftsmanship. He turned to publishing in 1888, achieving success by marketing popularly priced editions of the classics in, notably, the Temple Classics, Temple Shakespeare, and Everyman's Library series. Conrad and 'The Chief' were on cordial terms, but management through Pinker discouraged the kind of intimacy Conrad enjoyed with some of his earlier publishers.

And you mustn't be scandalised, either, at my gratuitous distributions. So many people send me their books that, with the few old friends who of course expect to have copies from me, a dozen doesn't go a very long way. And then there are copies that must go to France – three at least I think – and one or two to Poland. Upon the whole I think you had better send me a dozen (besides my six free copies) at your early convenience, because if such a distribution must be made it had better be made graciously, without undue delay which may look like carelessness or reluctance on my part.

I don't know whether I told you that there is a very fine review, very fine indeed, by Richard Curle, all ready, set up and proof corrected, for appearance in the New Statesman.[1] I don't know whether Desmond Mac[C]arthy[2] will be inspired to print it in this week's issue. I suppose it would not be very possible as I imagine the literary part of [the] New Statesman must be printed early in the week; but we may be sure of it on the Friday next after the day of publication.

I was very sorry to see you so crippled yesterday, but I trust that when you come down here on your promised visit you will be able to move as well as your friends would wish to see you.

Everybody I've met displays a great confidence in *The Rescue*'s success. I have been plunged in it too deep and for too long a time to have a clear sense of its quality. All the world *may* be wrong. Your own confident opinion is the one that has the most weight with me, and, after that, J. B. Pinker's, who, apart from his literary tastes, has, I have noticed, an almost unerring judgment as to the chances of a work of fiction.

On returning home yesterday I found an absurd wire from the Evening Standard asking me to say whether that forthcoming book of mine had in it any "message for the young". Could anything be more silly than such an inquiry and, especially, to a man like me who had never flapped any "messages" in the face of the world? I was sorely tempted to answer that it all depended whether the "young" in question was an ass or not. But I controlled my feelings and wired a reply to the effect: that "in a work exclusively artistic in aim to appeal to emotions there should be something for everybody, young

---

[1] Curle's review of *The Rescue* appeared on 3 July (pp. 368–9). After praising the consistency of his oeuvre ('His twenty and more volumes are neither dated by youth nor by some outworn phase'), Curle settles down to a florid description of Conrad's new novel: 'The whole story is incredible, real, moving, and tremendous. The currents of the visible plot, staged on a langorous tropic shore, intricate in variety of motive and in the strange play of barbaric psychology, serve to throw upon the two central figures, caught in that web of sinister plans, a gigantic shadow of impending doom' (p. 368).

[2] Charles Otto Desmond MacCarthy (1877–1952; knighted 1951), literary journalist, then the *New Statesman*'s literary editor.

or old, who was at all susceptible to [a]esthetic impressions."[1] – I don't know what else I could have said and remained polite at the same time. I hope you will approve of what I have done.

Please tell me whether Sir Sidney Colvin sent you back the copy of bound proofs you forwarded to him (I suppose) for reviewing purposes. I should like to know that.

Our kind regards

Yours sincerely

Joseph Conrad.

To J. B. Pinker
Text TS Berg; Unpublished

[letterhead: Oswalds]
June 24th. 1920.

My dear Pinker

I got a copy of the Play from Wise this morning and I pass it on to you so that you should have one copy *and carbon* made of it. Please ask the typewriting office to be very careful of Wise's copy which is part of his collection and for which he paid me £10.[2] When you send it back to me, please my dear fellow, have it registered to avoid any possible mischance.

This morning I had one advance copy of R[escue] from old D[ent] which of course I inscribed at once for Jessie.

I have given her and the nurse the message about your tooth and they made faces of retrospective sympathy in answer to it. You may rest assured that whenever you come you will be taken special care of on that ground.

I hope Eric clinched his business at lunch yesterday, the more so that he told me that it was a man-author whom he had in hand. I must confess that my sympathies for women authors are of a much cooler kind.

I hope you will let me know directly you hear from Playfair one way or another. I have just looked at the Play in Wise's copy and it seemed to me quite good enough from an abstract point of view. As to the scenic quality all I can say is that I tried very hard to put it in and that I had moments when, really, I *did* think I had managed to do it. But now I don't know.

Love from us all here to you and your House.

Ever Yours

J. Conrad.

---

[1] The *Evening Standard*'s reviewer quotes these remarks almost verbatim (25 June, p. 11).
[2] An error for £150; see the letter to Wise of 26 March.

To Thomas J. Wise

Text TS/MS BL Ashley 2953; Unpublished

[letterhead: Oswalds]
June 24th. 1920.

Dear Mr Wise

I hasten to thank you for the First Copy of The Secret Agent which you have been good enough to send me so promptly. It shall be returned to you directly one more copy is taken, without a moment's delay.

I have written notes in the two volumes you have sent me for the purpose and I hope they are what you wanted me to do.

It is very kind of you to concern yourself in this friendly manner about my occasional writings. I return to you the list you have sent me with two items, which I have in my possession already, crossed out. I will be infinitely grateful to you if you will have the others copied for me,[1] instructing the copyist to send the account to me.

I think you may like (as a curiosity) to have my reply to a rather absurd enquiry from the Evening Standard. So I send you both the wire and the draft of my reply as jotted down before being copied on to a telegraph form. Perhaps you will put it away together with the MS of The Rescue as my last pronouncement on it before publication.

Thank you for your kind enquiries. There's a slight improv^t in my wife's state. I am feeling horribly seedy and my wrist remains gouty.

Sincerely yours

J. Conrad.

To J. B. Pinker

Text TS/MS Berg; Unpublished

[letterhead: Oswalds]
June 28th. 1920.

My dear Pinker

There were seven reviews on the day of publication, as far as I know, and all what one would call good, though the only one deserving attention was in the *Morning Post*.[2] Courtney in the *D[aily] T[elegraph]* was dreary, *Westminster*

---

[1] For inclusion in *Notes on Life and Letters*.
[2] Of 25 June 1920, p. 4 (reprinted in Sherry, pp. 329–31). The reviewer wrote: 'It is difficult to write judiciously of a new novel by Mr. Conrad while still fresh from its magic . . . He thrills us, and always the last time he seems to thrill us as never before . . . It is probably true to say that Mr. Conrad has never more than in *The Rescue* made a determined attempt at this enthralment of our imaginations.'

Gazette man would have liked to be very sympathetic but didn't know how.[1] *Daily News* simply silly; *Chronicle, Express* and *Evening Standard* were the usual kind of thing, fair, selling notices.[2] Yesterday the *Observer* had rather more than half a column, a rather interesting attempt at an all round appreciation of the quality of the book. I don't know whether the Sunday Times had anything from the hand of Gosse or anyone else.[3]

Upon the whole it was a good send off, with the Morning Post striking the highest note; and if that is adopted by the majority of the provincial press then I won't have anything to complain of. Of course the *Man. Guard.* will take its own line and I am curious to see what it will turn out to be.[4] The *Scotsman* too will have his own opinion; and as to the *Glasgow Herald* I feel confident that Neil Munro will see to it that I am not wronged.[5] As far as the reception by the press is concerned we may feel pretty confident. From America no cuttings have reached me as yet, except the *New York Times* and *N.Y. Evening Post.*

---

[1] William Leonard Courtney (1850–1928), editor and reviewer of conservative tastes, was never inclined to Conrad. His review appeared on the 25th (p. 16). The reviewer for the *Westminster Gazette* ranked *The Rescue* not merely among the best of Conrad's books but among the 'supreme works of art', which are imbued with 'the essence of divinity' (25 June, p. 8).

[2] R. Ellis Roberts, the reviewer for the *Daily News*, read the novel as an attack on the 'stuffy folly' of Victorianism, but rather spoiled his case by referring to the Malay characters as 'black men' (25 June, p. 6). Also on the 25th, the *Daily Express* (p. 4, by Louis J. McQuillard), *Evening Standard* (p. 11), and *Daily Chronicle* (p. 7) all found the central theme to be what the *Standard* called 'The red blood's pulse' of passion, though the reviewers differed on the portrayal of Edith Travers, the *Chronicle* placing her in 'the gallery of Mr. Conrad's wonderful women', and the *Express* taking her as an example of Conrad's inability to imagine nuanced female characters: 'For him (as writer) woman is baffling as the Sphinx and cruel as the grave. Her lightest utterances he regards as things cryptic and fateful.'

[3] The literary historian, autobiographer, and critic Edmund Gosse (1849–1928) was an early admirer who did much to further Conrad's career, but the *Sunday Times* review of the 27th (p. 7) bears the initials 'H. C. R.'. The anonymous reviewer for the *Observer* sums up the novel's qualities as follows: 'We seem to absorb at once the stimulus of a personal drama, the philosophic interest of collision between the primitive and the conventional, and the privileged vision of art making its judgment of what is salient in each and bringing about the impact that shall reveal their significance' (27 June, p. 5).

[4] 'A. S. W[alkley]' was pleased to find *The Rescue* less demanding than some of its precursors: 'one thinks that Mr Conrad's technique gains in simplicity and his style in clarity as the years pass. Here there are none of those baffling changes in the narration that so piqued us of old, and though twice he jumps to the climax of an episode before recounting how it was reached, the device is in each case well justified . . . There is no fulsome splashing about in the language like that of a frivolous bather in familiar shallow waters, but the measured stroke of the strong and careful swimmer' (25 June, p. 5).

[5] The *Scotsman*'s brief notice was mostly plot summary (28 June, p. 2). Surprisingly, the *Glasgow Herald* made only passing allusions to the book. Neil Munro (1864–1930) was a Scottish poet, novelist, and critic. Conrad met him in Scotland in September 1898.

If this, as you so confidently predict, is the rising tide then we shall mark its height say in three month's time by means of that little dinner for intimates, of which we have spoken before. On the other hand if the *Play* ever makes a success there will be nothing for it but a solemn thanksgiving service. For, observe, that would be a miracle; and one can't celebrate a miracle by a dinner. That would be impious. Therefore you and I will go in state to St. Paul's.[1] The above is simply to give you a delicate hint that I am anxious to hear about Playfair. The delay doesn't seem to me a particularly good omen. However I can assure you that I won't tear my hair. Some time ago I forwarded to you a Bellasco*[2] letter of inquiry. Did you consider that opening to be worth looking into?

Mrs Meloney[3] came to lunch on Saturday and stayed till nearly six o'clock. She is so American that I found it as difficult to get on terms with her as with a phonograph. However I don't suppose she was dissatisfied with her visit. She tried to talk business about the next novel, of which of course I spoke openly as a piece of work on which I was engaged. I was also open as to the business part by frankly confessing that I knew nothing about it and did not interfere with the arrangements you made on my behalf. I am afraid she took me for an affected ass or perhaps an unaffected liar. She ended by assuring me that her relations with you were of the most friendly kind. Shortly afterwards she began to talk about an offer (apparently for Rescue) which some Cinema people either are prepared to make or have made already. I have forgotten the name she mentioned and all I remember distinctly is the stress she put on the remark that a 50% royalty was a remarkably good thing. Remembering your general view of the cinema business I didn't say anything to that, though I certainly think that a 50% royalty *looks* like a good thing, and is perhaps worth considering if there are means of keeping the execution of such an agreement under some sort of control. At any rate an offer like that would serve to put a gentle and reasonable pressure on our old friends.[4] It would be really deplorable if they kept us hung up for a full twelvemonth and then dropped us.

---

[1] St. Paul's Cathedral, in the City of London, the scene of national solemnities such as the recent service of thanksgiving to mark the end of the war.

[2] David Belasco (1859–1931), American actor, manager and playwright. His plays were a favourite source of opera libretti, including those of Puccini's *Madama Butterfly* and *La fanciulla del West*.

[3] Marie Mattingley Meloney (1883–1943; Mrs William Brown Meloney), journalist and editor of the *Delineator* (1920–6) and of the *New York Herald Tribune Sunday Magazine* (1926–43). She published a short article on the Conrads in the *Delineator* (11 August 1922).

[4] Either the Famous Players-Lasky film company or the Alice Kauser agency, which had acted for them in 1919, acquiring world cinema rights to four novels for $22,500 (*Letters*, 6, pp. 422, 434, 436).

I have various notions in that matter which I won't put on paper here because I have a scheme to come up to London on Friday next, proceeding thence to see John (and also John's headmaster in reference to his examination for Tonbridge). I propose to be back in London before 5 p.m. and to carry you off (with your consent of course) to have some tea, say at the Carlton Hotel, proceeding then at 5.30 together with you (and Ralph of course if he cares to have another try) by road via Wrotham, Maidstone, Sittingbourne, to Oswalds in time for 8.30 dinner. Like this we could have a quiet, short evening and a nice long talkative morning together and we could run you then to Ashford for any convenient afternoon train in the direction of Redhill, so that you could get home in good time to apply the master's eye to your domain. There is a certain charm in a late afternoon run of some 2 1/2 to 3 hours, at least for any man whose confidence is not utterly destroyed. If you are inclined to sign the above agreement we will insert a proviso excluding a *real* rainy day, for there is nothing less charming than a run in the rain whether early or late.

Pray give the above your favourable consideration and drop me a line.

Jessie's state marks a decided if partial improvement. There will have to be at least one more incision – perhaps two – but not till next week. She sends her love.

My grip on the novel[1] grows with every added page. My wrist is still painful, and my spirits nothing to boast of.

Ever Yours

J. Conrad

Please settle the enc^d acct for me

To Hugh Walpole
Text MS Texas; Unpublished

[letterhead: Oswalds]
Monday [28 June? 1920][2]

Dear Walpole.

Just to say I will have for you a copy of Eng first edition in a few days. All our loves

Yours

J. Conrad

Rem[em]ber you are booked for week end round 18th July here.

---

[1] *Suspense.*

[2] A June date has been scratched out; however, *The Rescue*'s publication date and mention of July rather than simply the day of the month suggest this placement.

To Lord Northcliffe
Text MS Neilson; Unpublished

[letterhead: Oswalds]
29 June 1920

Pray forgive me my dear Lord[1] this awful scrawl (with a gouty wrist), which is just to say that my wife and I will be waiting eagerly to hear of the day you promise to give us here.

It is a great honour for the Rescue to be allowed to accompany you to the country. It was sent to you not from vanity but from another and more genuine feeling the constancy of which I trust you will never doubt.

Yours sincerely

Joseph Conrad.

To J. B. Pinker
Text MS Berg; Unpublished

[Oswalds]
29.6.20

My dear Pinker

I have attended to Eric's request for J. Milne.[2] The photo goes directly to [the] Graphic.

Please send R. Tanner ch: for rent £*62.10* made out as before – I *think* to Col. Matthew Bell.[3] (Estate Office Bishopsbourne)

---

[1] The original press lord, Irish-born Alfred Charles William Harmsworth (1865–1922; Baron Northcliffe, 1905; Viscount, 1918), after preparing for life as a teenage reporter and copy-boy, started the popular *Answers to Correspondents* in 1888. With his younger brother Harold (later Lord Rothermere) he went on to buy the London *Evening News* in 1894, gave the world the first halfpenny morning paper, the *Daily Mail*, in 1896, and founded the *Daily Mirror* in 1903. The Harmsworths used the latest publishing techniques to cater to a rapidly expanding readership eager for simple, vivid writing and aggressively presented opinion. In 1908, they acquired a controlling interest in *The Times*. There and in his popular newspapers, Northcliffe promoted his often alarmist political ideas. During the war, his strident criticisms of Kitchener and of Asquith's Liberal and Coalition governments were variously heard as patriotic or self-seeking, malicious or urgently necessary.

[2] James Milne (1865–1951), journalist, critic, and editor, wrote on *The Rescue* for the *Graphic* (10 July, 66); an illustrated weekly, the *Graphic* regularly published photographs of the authors under review.

[3] Matthew Gerald Edward Bell (1871–1927), the owner of Bourne Park, Canterbury, and thus of Oswalds. He had served in India and Somalia. Richard Tanner was his agent.

There is also Miss H[allowes]'s quarter 25 – and £25 to B. Ninnes High St Hythe Kent under the arrangement covering this year (first pay^t was made in March).

Ever Yours
J. Conrad

To Claude Bragdon
Text Christie's, 24.11.1998

[letterhead: Oswalds]
June 30th. 1920.

Dear Mr Bragdon[1]

I hasten to thank you warmly for the book with the formidable title[2] and the very fascinating table of contents. Generally speaking I am singularly inapt to embrace metaphysical speculation. I am also a little afraid of them and to tell you the truth I never trouble my head about the Fourth Dimension, though, as a fact, it was indeed played with in The Inheritors. But that was indeed the play of an utterly unenlightened mind and anyhow most of this profane feeling was done by Hueffer. Also it was not very well done because, if you remember, essentially there was nothing really to differentiate the Fourth Dimension woman from the other poor, wretched, three dimension mortals.[3] I will of course read the book seriously, applying to it my intelligence as far as my intelligence will go. Meantime I appreciate warmly your gift as a sign of your friendliness to my work which I prize the more because I venture to think that it is also extended to the man.

In a day or two I will be sending you an inscribed copy of first English edition of The Rescue, which has just appeared here. Pray find for it a place

---

[1] An architect and theosophist, Ohio-born Claude Fayette Bragdon (1866–1946) trained and practised in Rochester, New York, until 1923, when he moved to New York City to turn his attention wholly to stage design. Bragdon wrote three books on architectural theory, *The Beautiful Necessity* (1910), *Architecture and Democracy* (1918), and *The Frozen Fountain* (1932), and also wrote on theosophy; in both fields he explored the implications of higher-dimensional geometry: see *A Primer of Higher Space* (1913).

[2] *Four-Dimensional Vistas* (1916).

[3] Inspired by E. A. Abbott's *Flatland; A Romance of Many Dimensions* (1884), stories about the paradoxes and possibilities of four-dimensional geometry were popular around the turn of the century: see, e.g., H. G. Wells's 'The Plattner Story' (1897) in the collection of that name; Wells presented Conrad with an inscribed copy. For Conrad and Ford, however, the fourth dimension is the space of ruthless modernity – the contrary of Wells's *The Wonderful Visit* (1895), where it is the home of angels.

on your bookshelf, to remind you now and then of the author's sincere regard and good-will to yourself.

Yrs sincerely

Joseph Conrad

To Edwin Markham
Text TS Wagner; Slade

[letterhead: Oswalds]
June 30th. 1920.

Dear Mr Edwin Markham[1]

I hate to send you a dictated letter but I have been held back by my lame wrist too long and I must convey to you my warmest thanks for your sympathetic, informative and more than indulgent article on me,[2] the best way I can. That those words so marked by friendliness and understanding should come from you is a great compliment and a great good fortune. This is my feeling, though you are pleased to talk of it as an "indiscretion".

Of course much must be forgiven to youth but you needn't boast so much of yours. I am on in my sixties too, and two such youthful individuals as you and I ought to be able to understand each other without many words. So please accept a warm handshake and the expression of my highest regard, and believe me

Always very faithfully Yours

Joseph Conrad.

To J. B. Pinker
Text TS/MS Berg;[3] Unpublished

Oswalds,
Bishopsbourne,
Kent.
June 30th. 1920.

Dear old friend

Thank you ever so much for the cuttings, the letter, and your readiness to do business on Friday. I conveyed your message to Jessie and hope to be at the door of the office the day after to-morrow, between four and five.

---

[1] Charles Edwin Markham (1852–1940), formerly shepherd, cowboy, blacksmith, and teacher, became an instant celebrity when the *San Francisco Examiner* published 'The Man with the Hoe', a poem inspired by Millet, in 1898. Markham produced five volumes of poetry, anthologies, books about California, and *Children in Bondage* (1914), a polemic against child labour.
[2] Slade indicates that the article (proofs at Wagner) was apparently intended for New York's *The International* but not printed. Markham would have sent Conrad proofs or a typescript.
[3] Postscript in Miss Hallowes's hand.

As to Doubleday clamouring by cable for more text I can assure you that he has got all the books for which he asks, except Victory which will go to him this week. I also repeat that he has got all the new Author's Notes for all the books up to and including the Victory volume. As to the Notes for Arrow and Rescue there can be no hurry for that. Let him get on with what he has on his hands now and I shall have both the Notes and the text for those two books ready for him when he is ready for them.

Hein[ema]*nn* is doing his part extremely well and with a care for which I am really grateful to him and his people.

Ever yours

J. Conrad

P. S. M*r*. Conrad says will you kindly settle these accounts –

To J. B. Pinker

Text TS/MS Berg; Unpublished

Oswalds,
Bishopsbourne.
July 1st. 1920.

Dearest Pinker

Thank you for the letter advising of various payments and enclosing a cheque for Miss H[allowes].

To-day is neither rain nor fine but the glass keeps up and if it is no worse to-morrow I will of course turn up. Will you please let me see (when I call on you) the agreement with the Cinema people. I have heard a lot about that side of the business and as I will have some remarks to offer we had better both refresh our memory.

I will drop B[orys] in London and proceed on to Ripley hoping to be in time there to take John out to lunch and then have a little talk with Mrs Pearce.[1] I will try to be with you as soon after four as possible and then we will pick up Borys and have a cup of tea before we start.

Though I hope it will be a different day to this one I intend to bring along the famous havelock that really seems to have been made (22 years ago) for you, not for me.[2] I regard that garment with particular affection since we got into the way of sharing it between us as though we were both young and penniless and with our way to make in a world full of hopes.

---

[1] The owner of Ripley Court in Surrey, John Conrad's school.
[2] A generously cut overcoat with a shawl collar. For a picture of Conrad wearing it, see John Conrad, p. 51.

We have received the envelope with proofs from Doubleday. I can see that the set of galleys of "One Day More" is complete. Can you tell me where that preposterous D. is going to ram it in the *de luxe* edition? I can't conceive. The thing is not big enough for a volume by itself. Has he got the wild idea of printing it at the end of the Typhoon volume cheek by jowl with the story "To-morrow"? If that is so, for goodness sake saw at his mouth as hard as you can[1] and try to stop him. If he means it for the *Miscellaneous* volume[2] then why this hurry? The *Misc*: vol: is not officially born yet. To deal with D. is like having a nightmare, a sort of slow, inconclusive, fatuous nightmare.

So long

Yours

J. C.

PS I am glad the date of the Ed^{on} is fixed for October.[3]

To F. N. Doubleday

Text TS/MS Princeton; Unpublished

[letterhead: Oswalds]
July 5th. 1920.

My dear Mr Doubleday.[4]

I return to you the corrected proof-slips of the play: "One Day More".[5] I understand from J. B. Pinker that these proofs are not for the de luxe edition but for another issue for general sale. I was very glad to hear it, not being able to conceive how that play could have found its place in the de luxe edition.

As a matter of fact this play, the three-act play founded on The Secret Agent, and any other play I may write in future, will have to form a separate volume of the de luxe edition for later issue to the subscribers. I don't think that it would be exactly fitting to include them in the volume of Miscellaneous writings, (No. 23 on your list) which I intend to call *Notes on Life and Letters*. It

---

[1] As if checking an impetuous horse.   [2] *Notes on Life and Letters*.

[3] The collected edition began publication in January 1921.

[4] Born in Brooklyn, Frank Nelson Doubleday (1862–1934) began his publishing career at Charles Scribner's Sons in 1877. He allied himself with S. S. McClure from 1897 before going into partnership with Walter Hines Page. Between 1912 and 1914, initially at Alfred A. Knopf's urging, his interest in Conrad changed from casual to serious. The American publication of *Chance* was Conrad's first financial success, and for the rest of his life his association with Doubleday was cordial and rewarding. When Conrad visited the United States in 1923, he made Effendi Hill, Doubleday's home on Long Island, his headquarters.

[5] Published by Doubleday in a limited edition of 377 copies in 1920.

is not ready yet and won't be ready for some little time, as, just now, I am devoting all my thoughts to the Napoleonic novel of which the provisional title for purposes of reference is *The Island of Rest*.[1]

I have been much cheered and encouraged by the excellent reports regarding the prospects of the *Rescue*. Thanks very much for the press-cuttings and specimens of advertisements you sent me through Pinker. The reception here was searchingly critical but sympathetic and upon the whole *most* favourable.

My wife joins me in the expression of warm regard.

Sincerely yours

Joseph Conrad

To John Quinn
Text TS/MS NYPL; Unpublished

[letterhead: Oswalds]
July 5th. 1920.

My dear Quinn.

I sent you my cable of enquiry[2] because I was anxious as to the fate of the parcel which Quaritch[3] undertook to send for me to you properly packed and insured. Nowadays one has not the same confidence in postal arrangements as one had before the war.

Thank you very much for your cable and the £50 remitted through the Canterbury Branch of Lloyd's Bank, of which I was advised by the Manager two days ago.

Your cable I have answered as follows on July 3rd:

"Thanks for cable and remittance by Lloyd's Bank. Reference was to Curle's letter stating terms for twenty booklets at 75 dollars each and five at fifty each which you acknowledged by cable 28 April to me as follows: Tell Curle glad to purchase both series pamphlets ten each also Shorters. Regards. Conrad."

The fact is that in my previous cable (May 3d) announcing to you the dispatch of the parcel of two sets of ten and one of five, *"in terms of Curle's letter"* the reference was to Curle's first letter to you offering you the pamphlets,

---

[1] It became *Suspense*.
[2] Of 30 June: 'Have you received pamphlets two sets of ten and one of five I sent you through Quaritch sixth May Neither had I cheque for manuscripts acknowledged in your cable first April as possibly letters gone astray Please cable' (NYPL).
[3] Bernard Quaritch, Ltd (established 1847), the antiquarian bookseller and dealer in manuscripts.

two sets of ten at 75 dollars each and five of Shorters at 50 dollars each, which you acknowledged by a cable addressed to me on the 28th of April, which I partly quote in my last cable to you and the whole text of which is as follows:

"Thanks letter regarding Pamphlets. Tell Curle glad purchase both series pamphlets ten each also Shorter's pamphlets. Writing. Quinn."

In consequence of the above I dispatched to you on May 3rd the announcement that the parcel was dispatched. I am sorry that through my wording this confusion should arise. There was no occasion for a further letter from Curle since in the first one in which he advised you of having those sets of pamphlets for sale he had stated my terms and asked you to make the payment direct to me.

I hope I have made myself clear in this matter of the letter which referred to the past and not to the future. Curle has left for Rangoon some time ago to take the editorship of the Rangoon Times for six months to oblige a friend who owns the paper and could not get a competent man to go out there and take charge in an emergency. C.'s book of Travels[1] was very well received here by the press but I won't go so far as to say that it sold very well. It certainly is not a production for the man in the street who has no time for abstract reading. But there is no doubt of his gift of personal vision and of his faculty of expressing it in very fine prose, to read which is a very great pleasure to anybody with a cultivated sense of language.

I will be presently dispatching to you an inscribed copy of the First English Edition of The Rescue. Its appearance here was delayed by some silly muddle about the paper supply Dent got into. In the end he had to take what paper he could get and perform the feat of getting 20,000 copies ready and put on the market in something like 22 days. It must have cut considerably into his share of profits, for the cost of any extraordinary labour is enormous here now. That of course does not affect me in any way and I must say that considering the short time, of the production, both printing and binding, has been done surprisingly well.

The book has been very well received, the criticisms being sympathetic in their rather minute analysis and the appreciations being many-sided and warmly expressed. The London Times review was headed "A Disillusioned Romantic"[2] but I think that if you saw it you would agree with me that it makes a very poor case for the theory of my disillusion. As a matter of fact I have never been so truly and whole-heartedly romantic as in conducting the

[1] *Wanderings.*   [2] *Times Literary Supplement,* 1 July, p. 419.

story of Lingard and Edith Travers to its inevitable end. In verisimilitude, in commonsense and even in cold reason that end could not be other than it is. The reviewer obviously doesn't like it and ascribes it to disillusion. But he is wrong. The romantic note is sustained to the very end; for my romanticism consists in the presentation of facts, not in tampering with the truth of any given situation.

However by this time you have no doubt formed your own opinion as to all that. I suppose Doubleday sent you an advance copy. If he hasn't then it is an outrage. Mine reached me here I believe on the day of publication in America.

I haven't seen enough of American criticisms to form an idea of the general attitude towards the book. Wilson Follett's long appreciation in the Evening Post[1] is very good and friendly, and interested me personally very much. The N.Y. Times article struck me as charmingly sympathetic. The two or three others I have had sent me are mere notices of the usual sort but favourable. There is in Chicago a paper which habitually jumps on my books with both feet, but this time I must say that the jump is rather lighter than the previous ones. Its final conclusion is that the book is insignificant and from a certain point of view it is no doubt true. The epithet may be applied to anything in the world including even that critical article itself. As to the sales Pinker had already very good news from Doubleday.

My poor wife who sends you her most friendly regards had a severe set-back in the recovery of her power of walking. But I am assured that it is bound to come all right in the end. Meantime she has been laid up for nearly 3 months! It is rather awful.

I've had a rather bad winter – bronchitis gout – general seediness – no work to speak of done since Jan[y] last. A week ago I made a beginning with my new novel but I see it will be a heavy pull at first.

It distresses me too much to read, talk or even think of politics.[2] I've withdrawn into my shell and say "nothing to nobody" – not even to you.

Believe me sincerely Yours

Joseph Conrad.

---

[1] For Follett's review, see the letter to Pinker of 17 June. The reviews in the *New York Times* and *Chicago Daily Tribune* appeared on 23 May (pp. 236–4) and 12 June (p. 13), respectively.

[2] In his letter of 17 April (TS carbon NYPL), Quinn denounced Woodrow Wilson, a fellow Democrat, as 'a colossal bluffer and cheat and charlatan... not only ignorant but... mendacious', insisted that all Germans should be held responsible for their country's conduct before and during the war, and recommended a calm and dispassionate approach to political life.

To Thomas J. Wise

Text MS BL Ashley A. 493; Unpublished

[letterhead: Oswalds]

5. July. 20

Dear Mr Wise

Many thanks for the copies.[1] It is very kind of you to help me like this. I have written a note bearing on serial pub*on* in the two american copies you sent me to sign.

I hope you haven't bought a copy of Rescue Eng. Ed. I am sending you an inscribed one. I had a difficulty in obtaining my author's copies because Dent is full of trade orders and naturally puts me off.

Kind regards

Sincerely yours

Joseph Conrad.

PS Miss Hallowes has just ascertained that we have the texts of *all* Shorters pamph*ts* that will be included in the vol.[2]

To J. B. Pinker

Text MS/TS Berg;[3] Unpublished

[letterhead: Oswalds]

6.7.20

Dearest Pinker

The tapestries are a fine gift. Our thanks to you both and especially mine to Your wife for her friendly letter.

I feel now under urgent moral obligation to do up the whole hall-space worthily. Awful responsibility!

With our love to all

Ever Yours

J. Conrad

P.S. I am such a damfool in those matters that it never occurred to me to propose to you to have cuttings – if that's the right term for it – from all those plants whose names you took down as if you were a constable wanting to drag them into the police court. Everybody in the house is scandalised

---

[1] See the letter to Wise of 24 June.

[2] For the volume's textual history and production, see 'The Texts: An Essay', *Notes on Life and Letters*, ed. J. H. Stape (Cambridge University Press, 2004), pp. 209–308.

[3] A typed postscript attached to a manuscript letter – the opposite of the usual pattern.

with me. For goodness sake send the list down here and I will hand it over to Burchett[1] who will know what to do at once, or in the autumn, whichever is the proper time for those operations.

To Warrington Dawson
Text TS/MS Duke; Randall 201–2

[letterhead: Oswalds]
July 9th. 1920.

My dear Warrington

Only the other day I dispatched to you a copy of my latest book. Powell[2] spent the night here, was perfectly delightful as usual; and, we thought, very little changed as far as appearance goes. As to the rest he is the dear fellow he always was. He carried off a copy of the American edition of The Rescue, but the one I sent you is the first Eng.

I shall this evening begin reading the typescript[3] Powell left with me. I assure you, my dear fellow, that I have grown so slow in everything I do that I have the greatest difficulty to find time, real free time, for anything beyond the daily task. But I have now found time for you and shall drop you a line when I have finished. At a cursory glance the beginning pages seem certainly arresting.

I will say no more because I hate dictating a letter to you and my wrist won't allow me to write more than a few lines at a time.

Jessie who's improving slowly (but still laid up) sends her love in which I join.

Ever Yours

J Conrad

To J. B. Pinker
Text TS/MS Berg; Unpublished

[letterhead: Oswalds]
July 9th. 1920.

My dearest Pinker

Wise is a very obliging fellow and I am just now under rather an obligation to him as he had several papers of mine (contributed to the press) copied by

[1] Jack Burchett, the gardener.
[2] John Powell (1882–1963), American pianist and composer.
[3] Of Dawson's 'The Manor', the genesis, Randall suggests (p. 202, n. 3), of *Adventure in the Night*, published in 1924 and dedicated to Conrad.

his own copyist at the Brit. Museum and wouldn't hear of my paying for the work. To ask him for advance sheets of his bibliography[1] is rather a delicate matter, especially as it is for public use and of that of course I would have to inform him beforehand. Of course I will ask him if you make a point of it, but it occurs to me that as you intend to check his proof it would involve looking through your records; and the only thing Wise would save us is the actual trouble of transcribing the entries. I would gladly pay for the additional work anybody you may employ for that task, rather than have Wise saying that he had contributed the bibliography to the English limited edition, or at any rate giving him the right to say so; and especially as a matter of favour. I will not therefore write to Wise to-day but shall wait for the further expression of your wishes in that matter.

(Apart from that I don't see why Heinemann should insert a bibliography in the Edition. It seems to me out of tone with the object of it, which is to present in a worthy form the text itself of my literary production, quite apart from all uses as a work of reference. I ask myself also in what particular place in the Edition is he going to insert that bibliography? The proper place for it of course would be the last Vol. It wouldn't look rational anywhere else. But the date of the appearance of the last volume cannot be determined till my literary activity has ceased, and I have a feeling that it will go on long enough to give Wise time to issue his bibliography of which I am promised a copy, an extract from which I would feel at liberty to communicate to Heinemann for inclusion later.)

I would have asked you for the name of your American if I had had anything in the way of MS by me, but I have not. Every scrap, down to rough drafts of cablegrams and letters to the press (on the occasion of the Empress of Ireland disaster) and small things of that sort, is gone to my two collectors. I am afraid there will be no more of my MSS, owing mostly to the bad wrist and new mental habits, except perhaps at times an odd letter to you in pen and ink, or on special occasions to some other correspondent. All my real MSS are now in the possession of John Quinn, and all the First Drafts in type are gone to Wise to whom the next original corrected typed copy has been promised, absolutely, in writing over my signature. How to get out of this unless by brutally breaking my word I can't see, and I couldn't do that except in the one case – if you were to ask for it yourself, to keep. But you are too sensible to attach either a collector's or a sentimentalist value to such things, the mere litter of a man's workshop. And besides, when it comes to

---

[1] *A Bibliography of the Writings of Joseph Conrad (1895–1920).*

MS you have something that no money could have bought, my letters to you, forming I should say a unique document. Believe me, my dear fellow, that the merest hint from you while it was still in my power would have secured for you as many MSS as you wanted. If I didn't offer any (or all of them) to you it was because I didn't think anything of them. I assure you that several of those now in Quinn's possession have been rescued from the coal lodge at Capel House. Amongst them the actual MS of Almayer's Folly, but not before the tenth chapter of it had gone up the chimney.

Thanks for the £6 in notes and for the copy (Wise's) of the play. Please send me one of the clean copies or even both as I want also a Polish translation to be made.[1] I am making a better pace with the novel. Further prov[inci]*al* and London reviews of R[escue] very good. Head not anything as swelled as the damned wrist, though.

With our love

Ever Yours

J. Conrad

PS Very pleased to hear Eric and Ralph think of coming here for day or two during Cricket Week.[2]

To Thomas J. Wise

Text TS/MS BL Ashley 2953; Unpublished

[letterhead: Oswalds]
July 9th. 1920.

Dear Mr Wise.

Many thanks for the copy with your bookplate. It was a very kind idea of yours to send it to me and indeed it is very acceptable.

I am afraid I won't be able to come to town soon. The fact is I don't like to go about amongst people with a bandaged wrist, apart from the feeling of seediness which is associated with it. I have also begun work on my next novel – a time when I need solitude in a mental sense.

My wife joins me in kindest regards

Joseph Conrad.

---

[1] Bruno Winawer's translation was premièred and published in 1923.
[2] Canterbury's annual Cricket Week, in early August.

To J. B. Pinker

Text TS Berg; J-A, 2, 242–3

[Oswalds]
July 10th. 1920.

My dear Pinker.

I answer your enquiry at once as to the MS of *The Duel*. I don't recollect whether it has been preserved at all, but if so it is in the possession of John Quinn of New York, 31, Nassau Street.[1]

Those enquirers seem to think that I have set up a shop of those things. If any of those MS hunters worry you in the future the following statement may be shown to them:

All my MSS in pen-and-ink are as far as they have been preserved, (complete or incomplete) in the possession of the aforesaid John Quinn, with the exception of the MS of *Rescue* (pen-and-ink, 602 pp, incomplete) the last of them being the MS of *Shadow Line*.

After that book all the First Drafts of my novels, typed and corrected by my own hand, are in the possession of T. J. Wise, of London, who has also acquired the pen-and-ink pages of the *Rescue* as above, with the complementary typed Draft, (corrected) to the end.

No MSS or TSS of mine are or are likely to be on the market for some considerable time, if I am to trust the voluntary statements of the above two collectors.

It may be added that a few short MS items (not novels) have been given away to be sold for charitable purposes during the war.[2] In whose hands these are of course I cannot tell.

Ever Yours

Joseph Conrad.

To Edward Garnett

Text MS Virginia; J-A, 2, 243–4; G. 295–6

[letterhead: Oswalds]
11 July 20

Dearest Edward

On some days my wrist is so disabled that I can't write at all – and dict^g letters is a horror.

---

[1] Some of it typewritten, the MS is now at the Free Library of Philadelphia. It appeared in Hodgson's sale of Conrad's papers on 6 December 1923 and thus never belonged to Quinn.

[2] Conrad donated the manuscript of 'Poland Revisited' to Edith Wharton's Belgian Fund Sale, held in New York on 25 January 1916, where Quinn bought it.

Thanks for your letter and the interesting inclosure. Now the thing[1] is done I am ready to forget all about it – all except your interest, the thought and time you've given to it, the great constancy of your friendship. This my dear Edward is what these pages will always mean to me. I tried to make the best of your advice in the general conduct of the last half; and, as to details, all your remarks and suggestions (in the margin of the *L & W* text) have been adopted and followed except in one instance amounting to about a line and a half.

Please tell the writer of the critical note on Mrs Travers that speaking in all sincerity I am immensely gratified by her appreciation and very much impressed by the acuteness of her analysis. One or two notice writers felt that there was something wrong. And my answer is *to them* that if I had hung Mrs Travers for 5 minutes on Lingards neck (at the last meeting) they would have been perfectly satisfied. To her I would only advance in palliation that one must take account of facts. The blowing-up of the Emma was a fact. It destroyed suddenly the whole emotional situation not only for them all but also for me. To go on after that was no joke. And yet something had to be done at once! I cared too much for Mrs Travers to play pranks with her on the line of heroics or tenderness; and being afraid of striking a false note I failed to do her justice – not so much in action, I think, as in expression.

After the last incision two weeks ago there is a distinct improvement in Jessie's state. But it will be a long, long job. Our love to you. I'll write again soon.

yours ever

J Conrad.

To J. B. Pinker
Text TS/MS Berg; Unpublished

Oswalds,
Bishopsbourne,
Kent.
July 13th. 1920.

Dear old Friend

Thanks for the two copies of the Play received to-day and for your good letter.

I am sorry I misunderstood Heinemann's intention. It's entirely my fault, as on re-reading I find your letter quite clear on the point. Lately I don't

---

[1] *The Rescue.*

seem to have all my wits about me, the effect perhaps of absorption in the new novel.

Dent sent me an advance copy of the school-book containing Youth and Gaspar Ruiz. The get-up and the print are very nice, in fact much better than I thought could be done for the money. I at once spotted two misprints, one of them serious, being the substitution of one word for another, enough to puzzle and mislead any intelligent child. The stupid ones of course don't know whether what they read makes sense or not. I wrote at once to H. D[ent] suggesting the insertion of an errata slip. I wrote you on the same day in reference to a collector's enquiry about the disposal of my MSS, a sort of official statement, calculated to dash their hopes to the ground and as I gather from your letter that you got it on Monday my warning to Dent may be in time.

I send you here chemist's bill for the quarter (Bing & Son) and the iron-monger's acct (Tyce*)[1] for settlement. The last is non-recurrent but as to the chemist – God only knows when *that* will subside! R. Jones may be down this week again as the swelling is well characterised now and it may be time for another incision. If that does as much good as the last then she will be well on the way to recovery. About time. I am beginning to feel distracted with worry.

Our love.

Ever Yours

J. Conrad.

To Clement K. Shorter

Text TS/MS Colgate; Unpublished

[letterhead: Oswalds]
July 13th. 1920.

Dear Mr Shorter

In answer to your enquiry about The Rescue I have to say that it is indeed the book of which Part I was seen by you in '99 and which you thought of publishing as a serial in the Illustrated London News. The thing went even so far that you sent me proof of the whole, I think, of Part I. For many years I preserved that proof (on rather shiny paper) but a year or so ago when I wanted to look at it I could no longer find it amongst my papers. Thus I have no memento but only a very vivid memory of that transaction.

I have not the slightest doubt that you must have read through the original text of that Part I, then. It was considerably longer than what now appears in

---

[1] Tice & Co. of 3, and E. Bing & Son of 41, St George's St, Canterbury.

book form. When after considerably more than twenty years I went back to that novel, my revision of the old work took the form of a very severe pruning. It needed it badly for, after all this cutting down of its first half, the volume has over 400 pages. I did not however touch the style as I was afraid that if I once began I would have to re-write the whole and alter the character of the book. Such changes as were made were merely verbal to avoid repetitions of certain words and suchlike blemishes.

I have been prevented from coming to town lately except just for a few hours, and that is why you have not seen me yet.

Kindest regards

Yours faithfully

Joseph Conrad.

To Lady Brooke, Dowager Ranee of Sarawak
Text TS/MS Lubbock; Watts (1964)

[letterhead: Oswalds]
July 15th. 1920.

Madam[1]

I am immensely gratified and touched by the letter you have been good enough to write to me. The first Rajah Brooke[2] has been one of my boyish admirations, a feeling I have kept to this day strengthened by the better understanding of the greatness of his character and the unstained rectitude of his purpose. The book which has found favour in your eyes has been inspired in a great measure by the history of the first Rajah's enterprise and even by the lecture[3] of his journals as partly reproduced by Captain Mundy and others.[4] Even the very name of the messenger whom you so sympathetically appreciate was taken from that source. Jaffir, if you remember, was the name of the follower and favourite servant of Pangeran Budrudin, who brought to

---

[1] Margaret Alice Lily, Lady Brooke, Dowager Ranee of Sarawak (née de Windt, 1849–1936), the estranged wife of Rajah Charles Brooke of Sarawak, mingled in London's literary and artistic circles, counting Henry James, Edmund Gosse, and R. B. Cunninghame Graham among her large acquaintance.

[2] James Brooke (1803–68; knighted 1848) became Rajah of Sarawak in 1841, having assisted Muda Hassim, chief officer of the Sultanate of Brunei, in wars against the Sea Dyaks. Conrad drew on his life in *Lord Jim* as well as *The Rescue*.

[3] A Gallicism: 'reading'.

[4] Rodney Mundy's *Narrative of Events in Borneo and Celebes Down to the Occupation of Labuan, from the Journals of James Brooke* (2 vols., 1848). The 'others' would include Henry Keppel's *The Expedition to Borneo and Celebes of HMS 'Dido' for the Suppression of Piracy; with Extracts from the Journal of James Brooke, Esq.* (1846) and his *A Visit to the Indian Archipelago in HM Ship 'Meander' with Portions of the Private Journal of Sir James Brooke, K.C.B.* (1853).

the Rajah his master's ring and his last words after that prince with Muda
Hassim and others had been treacherously attacked and murdered in Bruni.[1]

Your Highness is not mistaken as to my feelings towards the people of the
islands she knows so well and has presented so intimately in the volume of her
Life in Sarawak.[2] It was never my good fortune to see Kuching; and indeed
my time in the Archipelago was short, though it left most vivid impressions
and some highly valued memories.

It was a very great pleasure to read "My Life in Sarawak", recalling so
many things (which, I, myself, have only half seen) with so much charm
and freshness and a loving understanding of the land and the people. I have
looked into that book many times since. My thanks are due to Your Highness
for the renewed pleasure of it, and also, more especially, for the Cage which
I have lifted bodily from your palace in Kuching and transported on board
the "Emma" – a great liberty; but I really had to do something to save
Mrs Travers from mosquitos. Your Highness will see yourself that from the
position of that old hulk, right against the edge of the forest and on a swampy
shore, unless I had done something like this Mrs Travers would have been
eaten alive long before the end of that bitterly romantic episode in her life. I
hope I will be forgiven the liberty I have taken.

For all my admiration for and mental familiarity with the Great Rajah
the only concrete object I ever saw connected with him was the old steamer
"Royalist" which was still in 1887 running between Kuching and Singapore.
She was a venerable relic of the past and the legend, I don't know how far
true, amongst all the officers in the Port of Singapore was that she had been
presented to Rajah Brooke by some great lady in London.[3]

I have dictated this letter so far to inflict as little as possible of my horrible
scrawl on Your Highness. I have had a gouty wrist for the last month, a very
disconcerting thing to me for I agree with Your Highness as to the difficulty
of saying things in "type".

With renewed thanks for the letter Your Highness has worded so charmingly and in such a kindly spirit of appreciation I beg to subscribe myself
Your Higheness'*

most faithful and obedient Servant
Joseph Conrad.

---

[1] See Mundy, 2, p. 136, who uses this spelling for present-day Brunei.
[2] *My Life in Sarawak.*
[3] Brooke had purchased the *Royalist* in 1836. The steamer *Rainbow* was a gift from Angela,
Lady Burdett-Coutts (1814–1906), a major philanthropist and a possible model for the 'lady
patroness' in *The Secret Agent.*

To J. B. Pinker
Text TS/MS Berg; Unpublished

Oswalds,
Bishopsbourne,
Kent.
July 15th. 1920.

My dearest Pinker

Jessie will be writing to you herself; but the subject matter of your letter which she communicated to me has interested me very much. Apart from our affection for the boy it would please me very much if Ralph were, after all, to learn farming on the Bell estate.[1]

At present however the situation is not sufficiently well defined here. Bell intends actually to farm the whole estate himself. All the small tenants have had notice apparently for next Michaelmas.[2] At least so I am told, but there is still a doubt in my mind whether it can be for next Michaelmas or for Michaelmas after next? It seems to me that a year's notice is necessary, but of course those notices might have been given last Michaelmas though there has been no general talk about it till quite lately.

The Colonel being very full of his Great Adventure has been talking to me about it but purely in a conversational manner which struck me as rather grandiose. There apparently is going to be a cattle-farm, a chicken breeding establishment, and so on; and for each of them a specialist is going to be engaged. The last time I was at Bourne, when I went over there to see Sir William Hart Dyke,[3] (a youthful creature of 83 or so) Mrs Bell's[4] father, the Colonel told me that he was going to have also a milk-farm. I asked him if he had already secured any important contracts. He said he had not done so yet. This is the last news I have had of what is planned in the way of working Bishopsbourne Estate.

The point is now to find out whether Bell is going to have a general bailif[f] to direct all those things and the agricultural working of all his land, or whether he is going to supervise and direct the whole exploitation himself. I believe he is quite capable of thinking of it and I have an idea that he may yet make a success of it. It has struck me that he is more able than people give him

---

[1] He had been studying Agriculture at Wye College.
[2] The feast of St Michael, 29 September, one of the quarter days on which rent fell due and tenancies might change. The MS corrections on the TS read variously 'Michelmas' and 'Michalmas' and are changed here to 'Michaelmas'.
[3] William Hart Dyke (1837–1931; 7th Baronet of Horeham, Sussex, 1875) had sat as MP for Kent and Mid-Kent and been Secretary to the Treasury and Chief Secretary for Ireland.
[4] Mary Bell (born 1875), maid of honour to Queen Alexandra 1901–5, married the then Captain Matthew Bell in 1905.

credit for. The difficulty is that Jessie not being about and the establishment here working very casually it's difficult to ask people to lunch or dinner. But Mrs Bell drops in now and then for a few minutes to see Jessie and I on my side will try to get in touch with the Colonel and get some definite idea of his future arrangements. This, however, may take some little time. It would be advisable not only to discover whether he will have a general bailif[f] but to get also an idea what sort of man he has in view. Once we know that we may broach the subject with the Bells, because your plan amounts really to Ralph learning farming with Bell; since, obviously, the bailif[f] would have to get Bell's permission for anything of the sort (which a farmer would not have to do) and the general direction of course will rest with Bell, so that in that respect, at least, Ralph is bound to be in a sense Bell's pupil.

I must tell you also that, so far, though those people are very friendly and Mrs Bell is very nice to B[orys] and his young friends we are in no sense on a footing of intimacy with Bourne Park.

A small matter has cropped up relating to Hewison's cottage which has been practically settled between my wife and Mrs Bell, but I will take this opportunity to write to the Colonel just to keep in touch with him.

Pray give my love to Mrs Pinker and all the family.

Ever Yours

J. Conrad

PS. Northcliffe has just wired asking to come down here on Monday for a couple of hours – on his way to town I suppose.

To John Quinn

Text MS NYPL; Unpublished

[letterhead: Oswalds]
July 16th '20.
6.30 pm.

Dear Quinn.

Your letters (Ap. 17 & June 30)[1] have been this moment delivered. I have a very painful wrist but I'll try to answer you by tomorrow's packet if I can catch our post this evening.

My cable in answer to yours and a letter (which has crossed yours) clear up the imbroglio of Curle's letter. It was the letter offering the pamphlets. The terms he asked, or was to ask you, were fixed with my consent. If that

---

[1] Quinn had held back the 17 April letter; carbon copies of both are in NYPL.

communication missed you you have them now restated in my last wire and confirmed in my letter.

I note you have received two sets of 10 each – and one set of five issued by Shorter.

The extra two pamphlets (duplicates) I asked Curle to enclose in the parcel *outside the bargain altogether*. I thought you could make use of them as a collector either to exchange for something you would wish to have in your collection or in any other way. They are yours – the 2 duplicates unconditionally and irrespective of the sale of the other 25 which alone were the subject of negociation. Sorry I did not make this clear before.

Mail time! In haste

always very sincerely Yours

Joseph Conrad.

To John Quinn
Text TS/MS NYPL; Unpublished

[letterhead: Oswalds]
July 17th. 1920.

My dear Quinn.

I scrawled you a note in the greatest possible haste yesterday to catch the mail but I doubt whether I caught it, and very likely you will get that note and this more coherent letter by the same delivery.

I see on re-reading your letter that as a matter of fact there are only three Shorter pamphlets that you need for completion, the four others being duplicates. I thought that there were five *various* and two *duplicating*. This muddle is Curle's fault but just at that time he was in domestic trouble and had just acquired a house in the country to settle his wife and child in, which was absorbing his thoughts, and altogether he was in a state bordering on distraction. And now he is somewhere afloat on his way to Burma so that we can't haul him over the coals and obtain an apology. When I write to him in a few days I shall simply tell him that the transaction between us is completed, for he is of a worrying temperament and makes much of all those things and he has got enough troubles of his own.

In respect then of the superfluous copies of the Shorter pamphlets (of which I thought there were only two) I can only say that I wish you to have the four for your use, in any way that you may think fit, outside the terms of the bargain as stated to you in my cable of July 3rd and the letter which followed on July 5th. What you will have to pay me for, therefore, are the *two sets* of *ten* and only three pamphlets of Shorters. – I was much concerned at all the troubles you have had in your life of affections as well as in your business life.[1] Your relation of them ends, as usual with you, on a hopeful note; and I hope with all my heart that your "toughness" will not be tried much longer and that the doctor's opinion has set at rest those feelings of anxiety about those who are dear to one which are such a heavy burden to bear, even for the strongest character.

I hope to be able to take my wife up to Scotland some time in September. But it is only a hope and not a very strong one. She is still laid up with recurring complications but there is a marked improvement in general, and in certain particular symptoms as well. She sends you her best regards and hopes to make your acquaintance *de visu*[2] when you manage to take your long deferred holiday.

I am glad that you take my arrangements as to the MS. so well. I had many claims on me – and I have some still (in another country now)[3] – not to speak of my wife['s] prolonged disablement which is expensive. My most ardent wish is to see her recovered and sound before I "hand in my checks". There's nothing I dread more than an impotent old age, and I hope that experience will be spared to me.

But if so, then my time cannot be very long now; and you with your knowledge of life know well that a man unsuccessful (in the market) for 20 years can not attain a brilliant position at the end of his time. All I can leave to my people will be my copyrights – which are worth something now. But this is a precarious provision at the best. Meantime I must keep in at work. But I've had two hard lives – each in its way – physically and mentally and I feel the need of easing down a bit. I assure you that through all my writing life I have never had the time to "look round" so to speak. When I went away from the desk it was to be laid up. Such were my holidays. I don't complain. It is a mere statement of fact which explains many of my actions and many of my shortcomings.

With highest regard I am always my dear Quinn

Yours Sincerely

Joseph Conrad

PS Yes my resolve is not to have any more pamph[s] printed for many years if ever.

---

[1] Quinn's letter of 30 June (TS carbon NYPL) mentions problems with a member of his firm and his sister's need to take a rest cure.
[2] Face to face.   [3] Conrad regularly provided monies to the Zagórska sisters.

To J. B. Pinker

Text MS Berg; Unpublished

[letterhead: Oswalds]

19. July. [1920] Monday morning[1]

My dear Pinker.

Will you pay in £100 to Borys acct in our bank. As a matter of fact last night our Doc: put two car-deals in his way and I am quite willing he should make the amount of his Father's bills – or so – out of them.

This is – officially and actually – to be an advance on the money promised him when D[ouble]day pays ad^{ce} royalty on de Luxe Ed^{on}.

Col. Lawrence[2] was delightful yesterday and I'm sure N-ffe won't be tooday.*

Ever Yours

J. Conrad

To Thomas J. Wise

Text MS BL Ashley 2953; Unpublished

[letterhead: Oswalds]

19.7.20

Dear Sir

I've posted reg:^{d} the copy of the *O[utcast] of the I[slands]* duly signed. It is a very fine one – the price too is very fine!

I am correcting proof of the bib^{phy}. The arrangement and the quotes are excellent. I have made certain remarks in margin. The second lot of slips arrived yesterday.

The pages of Rescue in MS (Part 1st) were typed by my wife 1897 on purpose to be sent to Mr Shorter. They have disappeared together with proof-slips from the Ill^{d}. Lond: News – years ago.

In haste

Yours sincerely

J Conrad.

---

[1] The day after Lawrence's visit.

[2] Thomas Edward Lawrence (né Shaw, 1888–1935), 'Lawrence of Arabia', the author of *The Seven Pillars of Wisdom* (1926). For his visit accompanied by Cunninghame Graham, see H. & M. For a letter to him, see p. 538.

To Lord Northcliffe

Text MS BL Add. MSS. 62356; Unpublished

[letterhead: Oswalds]
20.7.20.

Dear Lord Northcliffe.

It was extremely good of you to send me that telegram. J'en reste tout confus[1] – to have unloaded my absurd perplexity on you like this!

Your visit has lightened the anxious murkiness of our life here. Never has time passed so quickly! Your passage amongst us seems now to have been like one of those delightful and evanescent dreams one remembers for a long time.

My wife sends her kindest regards and looks forward to the time when she will be able to receive you in a becoming vertical attitude. Sir Robert is coming on Friday for the night and will operate on Saturday morning.

Believe me, my dear Lord, always faithfully yours
Joseph Conrad.

To Lawrence Holt

Text MS Private collection; J-A, 2, 244–5

[letterhead: Oswalds]
20.7.20

Dear Mr Holt.[2]

To be still recognised, after all these years, as a seaman by the head of a House known so long and so highly honoured on the wide seas touches me deeply. I wish to thank you warmly for a moment of sincere emotion of a kind I did not think life could yet hold for me in store.

I will confess to you my diffidence – as a man of the port of London honoured by being called into counsel on a Liverpool scheme. In your great Sea-City, which always has been regarded in my time as the premier port of the United Kingdom, You have round you all the assistance that experience, knowledge and native sagacity can give.

It would however be a gross ingratitude to answer your request conveyed in such flattering terms by anything short of a perfectly frank statement of my ideas. The problem of education and training for Merchant Officers has been always very near my heart. I don't mind telling you on this occasion that ever since I became officer of a ship (3^d of the "Loch Etive" Glasgow

---

[1] 'I am quite embarrassed'.

[2] Lawrence Durning Holt (1882–1961), junior partner of the Liverpool family firm the Ocean Steam Ship Company. For his letter seeking Conrad's advice on fitting out a sailing ship to train cadets, see Stape and Knowles, pp. 159–60.

Genl Shipp^g C^o – in 1880) I have tried to do my duty by the boys. Good many passed through my hands when I became chief officer; some Conway boys,[1] others coming from schools on shore. I am proud to say that some of them (of various social grades and different upbringings) still remember keeping watch with "the Mate" and drop him a line now and then.

Thanks very much for your most kind invitation which I am sorry I cannot accept. Apart from arrears of work, there is the health of my wife. Your distinguished fellow townsman Sir Robert Jones is coming here to see her at the end of this week and of course I must be at hand.

In a day or two I will send you a short memoir[2] expressing only a general view of the matter under consideration for indeed I have no competence for dealing with Particulars. Conditions do change. The great point is to keep the continuity of the spirit of ungrudging service.

Believe me, my dear Sir, very sincerely Yours
Joseph Conrad.

To J. B. Pinker

Text TS/MS Berg; Unpublished

Oswalds, Bishopsbourne, Kent.
July 20th. 1920.

My dear Pinker

In the matter of title-pages for the Coll^d Ed^{on} as far as I remember I have talked over tentatively with Mr Heinemann the scheme of these title-pages and if my memory serves me right I proposed that they should be in red and black – red for the actual title of the book and the imprint of the publishing house at the bottom, the rest being black. Something on the lines of Fisher Unwin's earliest publications, that is, Almayer's Folly or the Outcast of the Islands which strike me as certainly very good-looking title-pages. However I would not insist on that or anything else, but I should like if possible Mr Heinemann to send me a specimen or two of his idea of what a title-page of a Collected Edition should be and then I would make my choice or offer my remarks. As to the actual *wording* of the title-pages I wish it to be the exact reproduction of the First Edition titles, including the motto, in such books as have it, which should be printed in italics, with the name of the author or the

---

[1] Between 1859 and 1941, three successive vessels were moored off Liverpool under the name HM School Ship *Conway*. Cadets served a year in her followed by three years at sea. Both Leggatt and the narrator of 'The Secret Sharer' were once 'Conways', and the veiled description of Liverpool and the Mersey in ch. 1 of *Lord Jim* hint that Jim is one as well.

[2] Eventually the 'Memorandum on the Scheme for Fitting out a Sailing Ship', printed in *Last Essays*.

work quoted from in small roms. The dedications too are to be preserved in the form they have in the First Edition.

I expect, all being well here, to call on you tomorrow (Wednesday), between 12 and 1, and will leave various matters of which I could have written, till then. But do not let this announcement affect in the least your engagements. I will just take my chance. I have just now a fit of worrying on me not utterly without cause but bigger than need be.

Sir R. Jones is coming on Friday 11.30 to make what they all hope to be the last incision.

Northcliffe yesterday was geniality itself – a sort of "dear fellow". Wonders will never cease! I'll tell you more tomorrow.

Ever Yours

J. Conrad

PS I had the £6 in notes. Thanks.

To G. Jean-Aubry
Text MS Yale; *L.fr.* 155–6

[letterhead: Oswalds]

22.7.20

Cher Ami.

Mille fois merci pour Votre lettre qui m'a donné une bien douce emotion. C'est que voyez Vous je crois en Jean Aubry, je fais grand cas de son opinion et il y a beau temps que mon amitié pour lui est devenue une vraie affection.

Ma femme Vous envoie un petit mot de bienvenue mais nous ne pouvons Vous prier de venir nous voir cette fin de semaine. Sir R. Jones (Lui – toujours!) arrive demain (Vendredi) pour passer la nuit ici. Il operera le Samedi. Il paraît que la chose est au point pour l'incision – celle qui doit guérir!.?

A partir de Mardi prochain nous vous recevrons avec joie tel jour qu'il vous plaira. Envoyez nous un petit mot. Et le Samedi, donnez nous une pensée d'ami – à tous les deux.

Toujours le Votre

J. Conrad.

Translation

Dear Friend.

Many thanks indeed for your letter which moved me a good deal. You see, I believe in Jean Aubry, I think highly of his opinion, and a long time ago my friendship for him became genuine affection.

My wife sends you a word of welcome but we can't invite you to come and see us this week-end. Sir R. Jones (yes, always!) is coming to-morrow (Friday) to stay the night. He will operate on Saturday. It seems the time is right for the incision – the one that should effect a cure!..?

After next Tuesday we will gladly welcome you on any day that suits you. Drop us a line. And on Saturday, do give a friendly thought – to both of us.

Ever Yours

J. Conrad.

To E. V. Lucas
Text MS Hofstra; Unpublished

[letterhead: Oswalds]
23^d.7.20

My dear Lucas[1]

I want to explain that the American critic's[2] letter enclosing your testimonial arrived here when I was in bed with a swollen ankle. I really could not see anybody. I got better very quickly this time but it was no use writing to our man as he told me he was going on to Paris in a very few days. They are all going on to Paris – invariably – in a few days. I never yet got a letter from one of them who wasn't "going on to Paris" in anything from 3 days to a week. Tell me my dear Lucas *is* there really a devil that is after them or it is a mere formula adopted to dazzle, to scare, to hustle one into a quick reply?

I often thought of you encompassing the world. I hope we will meet some day before long. I intend to explore the gloomy recesses of the Athen[a]eum[3] for you next time I am in town.

Till then (and after) believe me always yours

Joseph Conrad.

---

[1] Edward Verrall Lucas (1868–1938), an essayist, journalist, critic, and biographer of Conrad's friends the Colvins, worked for various publishers, including Methuen, as a reader and editor. He probably met Conrad through their mutual friend Edward Garnett when Garnett was attempting to establish his find on the literary scene.

[2] Identified by his letter to Conrad of 27 July (MS Berg): Charles Henry Meltzer (1852–1936), editor, dramatist, translator of opera libretti, and foreign correspondent and drama and music critic for the *New York Herald*. Galsworthy also wrote to Conrad about him; see Stape and Knowles, p. 160.

[3] Conrad was elected to this august London club in 1918.

To Lady Colvin

Text MS Duke; Unpublished

[Oswalds]
Sat. 24.7.[1920][1]

Dear Lady Colvin.

Pardon this scrap of paper. The operation this morning did not bring much immediate relief but we all expect considerable improvement in a few days.

Jessie sends her dear love in which all join to You and dear Colvin. You have been incessantly in my thoughts. I shall try to run up soon to You[r] Hampstead residence.

Always dear Lady Colvin Your most affectionate friend and Servant

Joseph Conrad.

To Lawrence Holt

Text MS Private collection; J-A, 2, 245

[letterhead: Oswalds]
Satu[r]day. 24.7.20

My dear Sir.

My secretary has just returned from leave and is engaged in typing the memorandum which will consist of about 14 pp and a covering (open) letter to you bringing forward the idea of "classical training" on which the whole argument of the memorandum is founded.

I know you will give it a patient reading though the very first postulate may shock you as being wrongheaded and altogether "impossible".

As to the "impossibility" I am ready to admit it at once – if you say so. As to "wrongheaded" I dont think I am that. I am only consistent – but perhaps to an impracticable degree.

I am concerned mostly in the Memorandum with the spirit of the scheme. I know it will be embodied worthily – whatever shape it may take.

It would be a great, a very great, pleasure to have you here for lunch and the afternoon (with the designer of course).[2] But I have a consciousness of the value of your time. It would take up the whole of your day, and the railway journey to and fro is a horrid grind. This much I had to say – and now I can only assure you that the car will meet any train you name in Canterbury (which is our Rway station for our friends) on the 3^d of Augst – or any other day.

---

[1] The only year in which Jessie Conrad endured an operation in July.
[2] Holt proposed the visit in his letter to Conrad of 23 July; see Stape and Knowles, pp. 160–1.

Of course if after seeing the Memo^{um} you still think a talk with me may be of the slightest use I will do my best to come up to town for the purpose. But I am a miserable slave to gout and may be prevented at the very last moment.

PS The Mem^{um} will be posted on Monday mor^{ng} at the latest.

To Lord Northcliffe

Text MS BL Add. MSS. 62356; Unpublished

[letterhead: Oswalds]
Sunday. 25. July [1920]

Dear Lord Northcliffe

The wire I wrote out in the morning for you did not get sent off and I found it amongst the blank forms when wiring you John's thanks.

The operation did not bring much *immediate* relief. Still it is a step on the road to recovery which had to [be] taken, and we all expect signs of improvement in a day or two.

Pardon this long screed. The patient sends you her thanks for your kind interest in her fate and her affectionate regards with her warmest wishes (in which we all share) for the complete re-establishment of your own health.

I am my dear Lord always your very faithful
Joseph Conrad.

To Lawrence Holt

Text TS Private collection; TS/MS draft Yale; J-A, 2, 245–7

[letterhead: Oswalds]
July 25th 1920.[1]

Dear Mr Holt

As I have told you before the education and the training of Merchant Service Officers has been always a matter of extreme personal interest to me. In my time I did my best in my small way to instil a definite conception of their calling into the minds of the boys I had with me in various ships. Since then the problem has been often in my thoughts, especially as regards the actual *training* as distinguished from mere imparting of knowledge in a theoretical way, which is under the more or less efficient control of the Board of Trade.

In view of the radical change which has come over the Merchant Service in my time, the scheme which the patriotism and the national sea-spirit

---

[1] Miss Hallowes wrote in the date.

has suggested to the Liverpool shipowners must naturally be, as it were, an embodied inheritance of the past. The principle underlying the processes of my thought applied to this practical matter is in a sense the same which lies at the basis of classical education. The public school man, even if he devotes himself to literature afterwards, has no immediate practical and as it were, *material* use for the classical lore he has acquired. He cannot toil slavishly in the track of Homer and Virgil or conduct his public life in rigid adherence to the political views of Thucidides* or the opportunism of Cicero. Indeed it would be very fatal for him to do so. He will only have gained a more liberal conception of his attitude to life and a strong inner feeling of that continuity of human thought, effort and achievement which is such an inspiring and at the same time such a steadying element in national existence, and in the corporate life of any body of men pursuing a special calling.

A year or a year and a half of training in a seagoing sailing ship I would regard for a boy destined for the sea as a course in classical practice of the sea. What he will actually learn on board that ship he will leave behind him directly he steps on the deck of a modern steamship. But he will have acquired the old lore of the sea which has fashioned so many generations, down to his very fathers, and in its essence will remain with the future generations of seamen even after the day when the last sail and the last oar have vanished from the waters of our globe.

Fortunately to reach antiquity in this case we need not go back very far. The evolution has been so swift that the classic time, though gone for ever, is still at our door. The sailing ship as evolved by the needs and enterprise of shipowners, the imagination of shipbuilders and the requirements of seamen reached its perfection of design in the years between '50 and '80. Like a good many other human inventions this hour of perfection was, so to speak, its last hour. After 1880 there was strictly speaking no evolution, there was only growth in a literal sense, in the mere size of ships, implying a loss in other directions. I put this point of view plainly before you as the remarks I will have to offer will be guided by it in their relation to the tonnage, rigging, handling and management of the vessel destined in the view of the Liverpool mercantile community to give, what I call, a course of classical training to the seamen of that port where so many maritime enterprises have been conceived with audacity and success; bringing with them also those changes which have so profoundly affected the sea life of to-day.

I am dear Mr Holt

very faithfully Yours

Joseph Conrad.

To J. B. Pinker
Text MS Berg; Unpublished

[Oswalds]
[25 or 26? July 1920][1]

Dearest Pinker

Meltzer was here and left enclosed particulars of a sort of Little Theatre his son has been running in N-York.[2] He may want to look at the play – and it even may suit him.

Perhaps it would be well to see.

Ever Yours

J. C.

To the Polish Legation, London
Text TS Warsaw, sygn. 1041; *Listy* 268–9; Najder (1983, 2), 251

[letterhead: Oswalds]
July 28th. 1920.

Mr Joseph Conrad presents his compliments and hopes this communication will be passed on to the Legal Councillor of the Polish Legation, or the favour may be done to him of advising him how to proceed in the matter in which he seeks advice, on the ground that the act he contemplates would benefit two ladies of Polish nationality at present domiciled in Warsaw. Mr Joseph Conrad is desirous of conveying the complete ownership of the copyright of all his works for translation and publication in the territories of the Republic of Poland (and eventually in all the territories which composed the late Empire of Russia) to Miss Angela Zagorska, for the joint benefit of herself and her sister, Carola Zagorska, absolutely, and for as long as his rights of copyrights endure under the laws of the Republic of Poland; the above gift being made in consideration of his affection for the aforesaid ladies and of the bond of relationship existing between them and himself.

Mr Joseph Conrad wishes to execute this deed in the strictest form of legal conveyance so as to make it absolutely valid in the courts of the Polish Republic and establish the right of the above persons beyond any question.

---

[1] Introduced through Lucas, Meltzer wrote to Conrad on the 27th (MS Berg) after a visit to Oswalds. Jessie Conrad's operation makes the 24th improbable, placing the visit on the 25th or 26th.

[2] The Greenwich Village Theatre at 4th Street and 7th Avenue, managed by Frank Conroy and Harold Meltzer.

Mr Joseph Conrad offers his apologies and begs to offer his thanks in anticipation for the Legation's assistance in this matter.

The Polish Legation.
London.

To J. B. Pinker
Text TS/MS Berg; Unpublished

Oswalds Bishopsbourne Kent
[30? July 1920][1]

My dear Pinker

I have received to-day the filled in Income Tax form and the typescript of the First Chapter of the Novel,[2] together with two letters relating to the Income tax figures and to your interview with Dent. Many thanks for all this and also the six pounds in notes which have duly reached me this morning.

All you say about Dent is very satisfactory and it was very good of you to lay so quickly at rest my fanciful apprehensions.

I have received the enclosed letter from Meltzer. The man produced a very favourable impression on me. I cannot however do anything in this matter till you answer my query in red pencil[3] and generally express your opinion upon the advisability of letting him see the Play here. This supposed American is a natural-born Britisher, educated partly in Paris and quite a civilised person, though most of his life was devoted to American journalism. He was in the '80s one of Gordon Bennett's[4] special travelling correspondents for European work, and told me a lot of interesting things about his various missions for the New York Herald.

I enclose here also a letter from S. S. Pawling, who apparently accepts our collaborated work on the Prospectus,[5] taking exception only to the time allowed for the completion of the set. In that I suppose Heinemann must have his way. I will write to S. S. on the social side but I should like you to answer on the point of publication, officially, from your office and over your signature. I have been this moment told by Borys that Ralph arrives at

---

[1] Meltzer's letter to Conrad of 27 July, Conrad's letter to Pinker of 3 August establishing the Sunday of Ralph Pinker's departure as the 1st, and Conrad's request of 21 June to have the weekly £6 posted on Fridays suggest the date.

[2] *Suspense*.

[3] On Meltzer's letter: 'shall I send him one of my copies?' referring to Meltzer's request for a copy of *The Secret Agent*.

[4] (James) Gordon Bennett, Jr, (1841–1918), the *New York Herald*'s editor and proprietor.

[5] Fot the collected edition.

3 o'clock. The weather looks adverse and I am afraid that he won't see much cricket,[1] especially as he must leave us on Sunday.

I hope you will not mind my sending this to your home, but whatever business there may be in it is not of a worrying kind – and it seems such a long time before I can communicate with you in London, owing to the bank holiday. But if you don't like it I'll never do it again.

Love from all here to all Burys Court

Ever Yours

J. Conrad.

To S. S. Pawling
Text TS/MS Heinemann; Unpublished

[letterhead: Oswalds]
July 31st. 1920.

My dear Pawling[2]

Thank you very much for the revised proofs of title pages and preliminary matter. I am returning you the set marked "A", and I must say that I am very pleased with its appearance. Will you, before you finally pass it for the printers, have another look at it in respect of the top margin. The body of the letter-press seems to me a little bit too high on the page, but I am not at all certain that it is so and I just call your attention to the point which must be decided by you.

Personally I think that the letters W and H should be put on each side of the windmill.[3] As you suggest the year may be printed on the verso of the title page where, unobtrusively, it will give all the necessary information. I have made the following corrections: transposition of a comma in the last paragraph of the Author's Note to Almayer's Folly, also correction of the date at the foot of the same Author's Note.

In Author's Note to "Tales of Unrest" I have made a correction in the top line of page X which is not absolutely indispensable but which I would like to be made.

My wife sends her kindest regards. She is again laid up after another minor operation. This worry has been going on for more than 2 years now. Of course we will be delighted to see you here and we shall hold you to your

---

[1] During the annual Canterbury Cricket Week.
[2] Sydney Southgate Pawling (1862–1922), Heinemann's partner and an admirer and promoter of Conrad during the early years of Conrad's career; despite rapidly declining health, he was overseeing the Heinemann collected edition.
[3] The Heinemann emblem, featured on title-pages.

promise directly the situation brightens up a little. Many thanks for your friendly personal interest in the Edition.

Believe me very sincerely yours
Joseph Conrad.

To Lawrence Holt
Text MS Private collection; Unpublished

[letterhead: Oswalds]
1st Aug 1920

Dear Mr Holt.

Your letter having reached me only today I am addressing this to London. I am very glad to hear you intend to come by the 9.15. It will give us 1 1/2 hours for a talk before lunch.

The car will meet the 11.7 at Cant. East and I hope the day will turn out decent.

Our regards.

Yours sincerely
Joseph Conrad

To the Polish Legation, London
Text MS Warsaw, sygn. 1041; *Listy do Conrada* 271; Najder (1983, 2), 251

[letterhead: Oswalds]
1. Augst. 1920.

Mr Joseph Conrad begs to present his warm thanks to the Polish Chargé d'Affaires for his ready response to Mr Conrad's request.

To Thomas J. Wise
Text MS BL Ashley 2953; Unpublished

[letterhead: Oswalds]
1.8.20

Dear Mr Wise.

Slips of Bib^{phy} received to-day.

I keep the bound MS (perfectly beautiful) till you come to claim it. I'll also write then the *note* according to your wishes.

Will you lunch on Thursday? One o'clock.

My wife is having a rather bad time just now but she hopes she will be able to see you.

This, just now, is a bachelor establishment and not particularly cheerful. Our regards

Yours faithfully

J. Conrad.

To J. B. Pinker
Text TS/MS Berg; Unpublished

Oswalds,
Bishopsbourne.
Kent.
Aug. 3rd. [1920]¹

4.15. p. m.

My dear Pinker.

I hope Ralph got home all right and at the proper time and not too much bored by his stay. It's a great pity he had to go away on Sunday because the private ball on Monday to which Borys went was an extremely successful affair and Ralph would have been sure to enjoy it.

Will you please settle the enclosed surgeon's account. It looks big on the face of it but it covers four months and, as its particulars show, includes five consultations with Sir Robert Jones, besides the long list of attendances. Anyway here it is and we can only hope that this item of expenditure will soon come to an end.

Lawrence Holt and his designer have just left the house, having arrived here about eleven this morning, with plans, specification[s] and all other details of the training ship. I had a very interesting day, though I can't call it profitable. Incidentally I have learned that the news of the Heinemann Edition is current in Liverpool amongst people who are likely to buy that sort of thing. I have had a letter from Sydney S. Pawling telling me what I had already heard from you that the Edition may be looked upon as practically sold out. I have also had the title pages of the two works which will form Vol. I. They look very well, both as to disposition and colour, the actual name of the book being printed in red. Miss H[allowes] has most carefully copied all the First Edition title pages and sent them on to Bedford St. last Friday, so there is nothing to prevent them setting up and printing all the title pages if they like.

I have asked Ralph to come here on Friday and I hope you will let him come, because this invitation has been given him specially as likely to forward the plan of having him as a pupil on the Bishopsbourne Estate. Mrs Bell had

---

¹ The year of Holt's visit.

a conversation with Borys which, so to speak naturally, turned on Ralph's stay with the hateful Tanner and the suggestion of the very thing you have in your mind did come from the lady. So the affair looks quite promising just now.

Our love

Yours ever

J. Conrad

PS Jessie easier since Sunday evening.

To William Heinemann
Text MS Lubbock; Unpublished

[letterhead: Oswalds]
4.8.'20

Dear Heinemann.[1]

Thanks for your letter. Every attention of which I am capable will be given to the proofs – but indeed I am a great duffer at that work. Jean Aubry wants to write an article on my Authors notes (in French I suppose?) as he considers that collectively they throw a light on my literary activity. I hear that E. Shanks[2] is disposed to write an article on the Coll^ed Edition at the proper time.

My wife thanks you for your friendly inquiry and sends her kind regards. She has been laid up at home since the end of April and had to stand 3 operations of a minor order it is true but trying nevertheless. We both hope that the waters of Harrogate like the waters of Lethe will make you forget that you had ever been ill.

I saw the two little pages of the Vol I. Excellent in every respect – what my younger boy would call "top hole".

Many thanks my dear Heinemann for your personal interest in the text – and everything else connected with the Edition.

Believe me very sincerely

Yours

Joseph Conrad.

---

[1] William Henry Heinemann (1863–1920) established his well-known publishing firm in 1890, entering into partnership with S. S. Pawling in 1893. Particularly noted for its fiction list, the firm, in addition to bringing out early works by Conrad and the collected edition, published Stephen Crane, H. G. Wells, Robert Louis Stevenson, and Rudyard Kipling.

[2] Edward Richard Buxton Shanks (1892–1953), critic and literary journalist, also a novelist and writer of verse.

To Arthur Symons

Text MS Morgan; Unpublished

[letterhead: Oswalds]
Thurs. 7[5]. 8.20[1]

My dear Symons,[2]

Impossible not to keep the lunch engagement on Sunday – but as I have wired I'll be back home by 1/2 past 3 or thereabouts. So if you don't mind coming about then for a cup of tea and a talk it would be a great pleasure for us all to have a glimpse of you. Proceed to Canter^y then to the village of Bridge (Dover R^d) 3m[iles] where inquire at the gate lodge of a park to right, close to church for Oswalds.

Tell your friend that the roads between Ashford and Cant^y are tolerable. Your best way is: Tenterden – Ashford – Canter^y – Bridge –[3]

Tout à Vous,

J. Conrad

To J. B. Pinker

Text MS Berg; Unpublished

[letterhead: Oswalds]
7.8.20

Dearest Pinker

This is only to thank you for your letter received this morning and to tell you that I respond to every[thing] in it which your old friendship has prompted you to write.

We hope R[alph] will turn up early to-morrow and see the last of the cricket. He will have to be put into a cottage-room for one night. But he already knows his fate.

Our love

Yours ever

J. Conrad

---

[1] Conrad more likely mistook the date rather than the day.
[2] Welsh-born Arthur William Symons (1865–1945) wrote poetry, essays, and fiction. As a critic he showed broad tastes in literature, music, and painting, and spoke up for such then-neglected figures as Baudelaire and Blake. In 1896, Symons took 'The Idiots', the first short story Conrad ever sold, for the *Savoy*. Symons suffered a severe mental breakdown in 1908 and could not return to his Kentish home until 1910. In 1925, he published *Notes on Joseph Conrad*.
[3] Symons would be coming from Wittersham, Kent.

To Thomas J. Wise

Text MS BL Ashley 2953; Unpublished

[letterhead: Oswalds]
Saturday [7 August 1920][1]

Dear Mr Wise.

Many thanks for your letter and enclosure. Your visit has been a great pleasure for us all.

I have many engagements ahead just now. It is also necessary I should do some work in the intervals of dissipation. I do not know how long you propose to stay in Folkestone, but I shall certainly try to find a day to run down there if only for an hour in the afternoon to be introduced to Mrs Wise.

Believe me with regards from all here

Yours sincerely

Joseph Conrad.

To J. B. Pinker

Text MS Berg; Unpublished

[letterhead: Oswalds]
11.8.20

Dearest Pinker.

I don't think there will be an occasion for me to come up this week. Friday then is the day on which we will meet. Drop us a line to say at what time you intend to leave town.

Karola proposes to leave here for London (on her way to Italy) on Sat: morning.

Will you please *if not too much trouble* bring her supplies with you in notes – £50 for travelling and getting a few things (as I promised her) and £30 for the quarter allowance beginning in Sept[er] – that is up to Dec. next, when such another sum will be sent her wherever she is. With about 6/8 per day[2] she will be able to live just decently in Italy – or later in Poland. Less wouldn't perhaps do. When it comes to the matter of mere necessities a few pence make a great difference. I leave all other matters till we meet but I enclose a letter I received this morning which perhaps you will answer.

Our love.

Yours ever

J. Conrad

---

[1] Presumably the Saturday following Wise's visit of the 5th (see the letter of the 1st).
[2] Six shillings and eight pence – a third of a pound.

To J. B. Pinker
Text MS Berg; Unpublished

[letterhead: Oswalds]
11.8.20.

Dearest Pinker

Pardon me worrying you everlastingly but would you phone Meth[uen]'s asking them to send me a copy of *Victory* and one of *Chance*. Also to Dent asking for immediate despatch to me of *Lord Jim* – and to Heinemann for one copy of *Typhoon* – the complete book not only the story.

I have promised to give all these books and then forgotten all about it.

Ever affect^{ly} yours

J. C.

To William Rothenstein
Text MS Harvard; Unpublished

[letterhead: Oswalds]
11.8.20.

My dear Will.[1]

Thanks for your good letter.

I hope you won't be annoyed if I say that it is altogether impossible for me to write anything for John Galsworthy's portrait.[2] I simply wouldn't know how to begin that sort of thing. We, that is Jack and I, are too old and intimate friends for me to attempt anything of the kind. But I daresay you'll understand.

Jessie has been 4 months in bed; but at last there is a turn for the better and we may expect her to improve very rapidly now.

We will be delighted to see you here. Do give us an idea when you can best spare the time for your most welcome visit and then we'll fix a date. With our love to you all.

Yours affect^{ly}

J. Conrad

---

[1] William Rothenstein (1872–1945; knighted 1931) was notable for his portrait graphics, paintings, and drawings. Max Beerbohm described him as a young phenomenon in 'Enoch Soames' (*Seven Men*): 'He wore spectacles that flashed more than any other pair ever seen. He was a wit. He was brimful of ideas . . . He knew everyone in Paris.'

[2] For Rothenstein's *Twenty-Four Portraits* (1920).

To Jenny Doris Thorne
Text MS Duke; Unpublished

[letterhead: Oswalds]
11.8.20

Dear Mrs Thorne.[1]

Thank you for your friendly letter. Just now I am waiting on the surgeon's pleasure and presently there will be a procession of people coming here. How I am to do any work I don't know!

Pardon this groan and also the apparent (only apparent) lack of alacrity in responding to your invitation. It is nothing in me; it is the outward (and stupid) force des choses which prevents me asking you at once to fix the day.

May I be permitted to write again in say 10 days' time? I hope by then to be more or less master of my movements and ready to attend all your commands.

Please give your Father[2] the expression of my warm regard – and a preliminary greeting to Mr Thorne[3] till we meet – under your wing, so to speak.

I am dear Mrs Thorne

your very faithful and obed^t Servant
Joseph Conrad

To Thomas J. Wise
Text TS/MS BL Ashley 2953; Unpublished

[letterhead: Oswalds]
Aug. 16th. 1920.

Dear Mr Wise

Thank you very much for your letter and enclosure which I received this morning.

I really don't see why Dent should have gone with this suggestion to you, putting in his oar where he wasn't wanted. I am very sensible of the kind way in which you express yourself about what you suppose to be my wish, and, indeed, I have so much confidence in the friendliness of your feelings towards me that I would not have gone in a round-about way to approach you, but in a matter of that kind would have addressed myself to you directly. It never occurred to me for a moment to have a Bibliography joined to the complete Edition of my works. The whole plan is settled, the prospectus is drafted and

---

[1] Jenny Doris (or Dora) Arthur Thorne (née Jones, 1888–1947) mingled in theatrical and literary circles when not in Cyprus, Morocco, Egypt, or Greece with her husband. After her divorce in 1923, she wrote sketches for dailies and magazines and did voluntary work, living with her father, Henry Arthur Jones, whose biography she published in 1930. Her autobiography, *What a Life!*, appeared in 1932.

[2] The playwright Henry Arthur Jones; see Conrad's letter to him of 3 November 1922.

[3] William Hobart Houghton Thorne (1875–1929), civil servant and judge.

probably printed by this time, and I don't want to introduce anything that was not in the original scheme.

I am none the less very touched by your readiness to fall in with what you naturally thought was my desire and thank you heartily for this fresh proof of you[r] good will towards

Yours sincerely

Joseph Conrad.

To Richard Curle

Text MS Indiana; Curle 70

[letterhead: Oswalds]

18[18–23].8.20[1]

Dearest Richard.

I had two letter[s] from you one from P[or][t] Said and 3 days ago one from Colombo – and I thought of you reposing under the shadow of Adam's Peak in the Garden Island of the tropics.[2]

Things here are pretty well. Jessie is having another try at resuming walking exercise. Sir Robert went away yesterday very pleased with the state of affairs tho' not quite certain whether another incision will not have to be made in a month's time. But we all hope that the patch of pain will subside gradually under a course of massage. On the 1st of Sep[t] we are going to Deal where I have taken "a suite" in a hotel for three weeks – while Miss H[allowes] departs (to the Lakes) on her holiday. I shall busy myself there with the text of *Notes on Life & Letters* vol which we have decided to fling out to the public next Spring. The Nap[ic] novel is in its 3 chap. All very lame and unsatisfactory – so far.

John works two hours per day and seems anxious as to his comm[on] entrance exam for Tonbridge.[3] The cricket week was attended by immense crowds. We had nobody but Ralph staying with us. I did not go once.

But I went to lunch with Lady Northcote[4] at Eastwell Park. The Duchess of Albany[5] was there and also Lady Gwendolen Cecil[6] – and *she* was very interesting and friendly. But the other too was very good, full of sense and

---

[1] The date at the end of this letter implies that Conrad finished it on the 23rd. A pause in the writing would account for the uncharacteristic repetition of news about Borys and John.

[2] Ceylon, now Sri Lanka.

[3] A reasonable performance in the Common Entrance Exam was the standard means of access to public schools such as Tonbridge. Candidates usually sat the exam at thirteen or fourteen.

[4] Lady (Alice) Northcote (1853–1934) was the widow of Henry Stafford, Baron Northcote, who had been MP for Exeter, Governor of Bombay, and Governor General of Australia. In 1919, she was made a DBE (Dame of the British Empire) for her services to hospitals.

[5] HRH the Duchess of Albany (1861–1922), the widow of Queen Victoria's son, the first Duke of Albany, and the King's aunt, was active in charity work.

[6] Gwendolen, Lady Cecil (1860–1945), author of a four-volume *Life of Robert, Marquess of Salisbury* (1921–32).

sympathy in her talk about the European situation. Altogether a very pleasant experience. B[orys] was invited too and drove me over.

Next event was T. J. W[ise] turning up for lunch and holding us spellbound by the flow of his utterance. It was most amusing! A very friendly person indeed – got on with Jessie very well. So did Old Dent who came with his son for one night and looked most venerable sitting in the big gilded armchair in his black coat which showed off his white beard while his child (Hugh D) sang to us Elizabethean* love songs. Très chic.

Afterwards General Gunter[1] – but that is a long story which may be told later – in the next dispatch.

B's laid up with a beastly bad throat. Karola has departed for Italy. I make her an allowance of £130 p.y. for 2 years certain with Pink's approval. That same P was 3 days with us, enjoying – as he said – my prosperity and planning ways and means to sustain all this splendour.

The Quinn deal has been closed satisfactorily by a draft for 1650 doll[ar]s = £450.1.1 – and many thanks to you dear Richard for it.

The only trouble is that there are no more such transactions to look forward to. I am spending more than I ought to – and I am constitutionally unable to put on the brake, unless in such a manner as to smash everything. You know what I mean – because you *do* know me.

John is working quite hard (for him) that is about 3 hrs p. day. There has turned up a prospect of a very good post for B in connection with Richborough, which has been bought from the Gov[t] by the firm of Alvan* Richards[2] (£6.000.000). B just now is laid up with a very nasty throat and is in great trouble about it. However the thing is by no means certain and anyhow looks much too good to be true – as it were.

There was no one here during the first part of Aug[t]. Walp[ole] is in Cornwall. Pinker is the only one who came for the night; and my oldest friend G. F. W. Hope[3] is just gone (23[d] Aug) after spending the week end with us.

On the *first of Sept.* we are all going to Deal for 3 weeks. We will go by car which I intend to keep there during our stay. The dist[an]ce from here is only

---

[1] No one of this rank appears in the *Army List*. Conrad may have known that colonels were often given the honorary rank of general upon retirement. If so, two individuals are possible: Lt-Col. Francis Ernest Gunter (1869–1936), who served in the Royal Medical Corps and published articles on tuberculosis, and Col. Clarence Preston Gunter (born 1873) of the Royal Engineers.

[2] W. Alban Richards & Co., a London firm of contractors and engineers.

[3] Conrad met G(eorge) F(ountaine) W(eare) Hope (1854–1930) in 1880. A *Conway* boy, Hope had served in the *Duke of Sutherland* (but not with Conrad) and owned a yacht in which he and Conrad made excursions on the Thames. He was a model for the Director of Companies in 'Heart of Darkness'.

19 miles but the change for Jessie will be considerable all the same.[1] Nurse goes with us of course. While we are there I will try to pull together the text of the vol of Notes on Life & Letters and also write a cinema scenario of Gaspar Ruiz. I am ashamed to tell you this – but one must live! Pinker himself is coming over to help me with it!!! Notwithstanding his funny secretiveness I fancy he had the offer of a large sum from some good quarter for a Conrad scenario.[2]

If one is to condescend to that sort of thing well then, all considered, I prefer Cinema to Stage. The Movie is just a silly stunt for silly people – but the theatre is more compromising since it is capable of falsifying the very soul of one's work both on the imaginative and on the intellectual side – besides having some sort of inferior poetics of its own which is bound to play havoc with that imponderable quality of creative literary expression which depends on one's individuality.

I don't write this in the way of excuse for my villainy. I believe that I am right in what I've said. I will stop short here – to be continued in my next in about a month's time. Love from my wife and the boys

Always yours most affectionately

Joseph Conrad

23 Aug^t

To J. M. Dent
Text MS Berg; Unpublished

[letterhead: Oswalds]
19.8.20

Dear Mr Dent.

I ought to have thanked you before for the Grey book[3] – you being a man of your word – have sent me the other day.

The House of Dent is spoiling the House of Conrad. This morning some more books arrived from Aldine House – this time for my wife.

She sends your* her friendly regards and wants me to tell you that she is improving and that she hopes with all her heart that you, too, are getting free of pain and able to move more freely about.

---

[1] Especially since Deal is on the coast.
[2] Famous Players-Lasky had offered $1,500 for an original screenplay. For the history of 'Gaspar the Strong Man', see Gene M. Moore's essay in Owen Knowles, Gene M. Moore, and J. H. Stape, eds., *Conrad: Intertexts & Appropriations. Essays in Memory of Yves Hervouet* (Amsterdam: Rodopi, 1997), pp. 31–47.
[3] Edward Grey, Viscount Falloden. His *Recreation* appeared in June.

E. Grey's book, of which I have already read a considerable portion, has certainly the charm of a genuine feeling expressed in plain language worthy of a great fisherman.

Yours sincerely

J. Conrad

To J. B. Pinker
Text MS Williams; Unpublished

[letterhead: Oswalds]
23.8.'20

Dearest Pinker.

Sandeman[1] having asked me to meet him on Friday I shall proceed to your place via London, by any train and from any station you may suggest as convenient to you. I'll be free for the 5.20 – or even for the 4.27 (Cannon St) if you like. Should you not be in Town I'll take the 5.20.

Please drop me a line.

Jessie's progressing remarkably. Jones was very pleased and this really looks like the end of trouble for her and for me.

She sends her love and looks forward to seeing you in Deal as per plan.

Ever Yours

J. C.

To William Rothenstein
Text MS Harvard; Unpublished

[letterhead: Oswalds]
23.8.20

My dear Will.

The surgeon was here two days ago and found Jessie sufficiently improved to advise me to give her a holiday by the sea. We are therefore leaving here on the 30 for Deal where we shall remain till the 21st of Sept[er].

We are no end sorry to hear that Billy is not well. Perhaps by the time we return home Alice[2] will not be so tied, and will come with you.

---

[1] Christopher ('Kit') Sandeman (1882–1951), who belonged to the sherry-making branch of the family, was a journalist, lecturer, and author.

[2] Alice Rothenstein (née Knewstub, 1867–1957) had acted under the name Alice Kingsley. Billy was the youngest child.

There are a few windmills here but not of a very distinguished appearance. However I shall introduce you to them when you come. The *R*[*escue*] (which, I am happy to see, has pleased you) is going fairly well in this country.

Our love to you all big and little.

Ever Yours

J Conrad.

To Marina Wister

Text MS Indiana; Unpublished

[letterhead: Oswalds]

23.8.20

Dear Miss Wister.[1]

It is extremely difficult to answer a letter like yours which reached me a few days ago. Nothing that I could say in the way of thanks could be adequate to the intense pleasure you have given me by your warm appreciation so charming in expression, so generous in spirit, so exceptional in understanding so precious in its sympathy.

Indeed I think you make too much of my achievement which seems to me very small and as if already lost in the night of ages. You – but I won't argue with you. Who am I to quarrel with a gift from the gods? And a reader like you is a gift from the gods who sometimes do overwhelm an undeserving mortal with a fearful joy tempered by a little sadness.

Pray give to your father[2] the expression of my very great, very grateful regard. I remember very well meeting him [at] H James' house.[3] He's is* not one of those men one forgets. And you too shall never be forgotten by the gratitude of him whom you have made your friend and most faithful servant

Joseph Conrad

---

[1] (Mary Channing) 'Marina' Wister (1899–1970), the eldest child of the American novelist Owen Wister and civic activist Mary Channing Wister, published three books of poems: *Helen and Others* (1924), *Night in the Valley* (1930), and *Fantasy and Fugue* (1937). Married to the New Mexico painter Andrew Dasburg in 1933, she settled in Taos, and in addition to writing poetry and music was involved in asserting the rights of native people. She separated from her husband in 1947, returning to Bryn Mawr, Pennsylvania.

[2] Owen Wister (1860–1938), a writer of westerns, best known for *The Virginian* (1902).

[3] During Wister's visit to Lamb House, Rye, Sussex, of 16–17 July 1914?

To J. B. Pinker
Text MS Berg; Unpublished

[Oswalds]
24.8.[1920]¹ Tuesday

Dearest P.

Will you pay £150 to my acct. I have all sorts of bills to settle.

Miss Hallowes departs on Sat next to begin her holiday. Please send her the quarter's salary beginning in Sep^t. That will settle her till end of Dec^er. I think it may be convenient for her to have the money now.

I will have her board and lodging bill on Sat: when her week ends in Cant^y. Please address your letter to her here.

Yours ever

C.

To Edward Garnett
Text MS Berg; G. 296–7

[letterhead: Oswalds]
26.8.20

Dearest Edward.

Thank you for your good letter and enclosure.

There was a Kniep[p]² establishment near Dresden (in 1886) when I went to meet my uncle in Marienbad.

Frankly I have no faith in all these things and I don't want to go to these places (Kniep[p] was a Bavarian illuminé³) which are odious to me, with their pathetic population hypnotised into going through all these tricks and ceremonies, by mere senseless verbiage. Have you read (calmly) the pages you have sent me? or any other "healer's literature"?

I am taking Jessie for a change to Deal from the 1st to 21st of Sept. She is beginning to walk (about the house) and sends you her love. Will you name any day, say after the 22^d, for a visit here – as long as you can spare time for.

Ever yours

J. Conrad.

PS Write here – Deal is only 18 miles off and letters will be forwarded.

---

¹ The holiday plans establish the year.
² Sebastian Kniepp or Kneipp (1821–97), a priest who had studied medicine and treated mountain folk with cold water and 'grass' cures in Wörishofen, Bavaria, had a devoted following by the 1890s, particularly in Germany and Austria where his *Meine Wasser-Kur* (1890) was popular. The water-cures that Conrad himself underwent at Champel, Switzerland, were less excruciating.
³ A member of the Illuminati (Enlightened Ones), the free-thinking esoteric society founded at the University of Ingolstadt, Bavaria, in 1776, suppressed in 1784 but credited by conspiracy theorists with amazing powers of underground survival.

To G. Jean-Aubry
Text TS/MS Yale; *L.fr.* 156–8

Oswalds
Bishopsbourne
Kent.
Aug. 26th. 1920.

Cher Aubry

J'entre en matière sans préliminaires.

Et d'abord au sujet de Part V. Je commence cette partie là de cette manière pour faire connaitre d'avance la situation psychologique qui est la plus importante dans toute cette histoire. Il est évident que de cette manière là j'évite des longues explications sur l'état d'âme de M. et Mme. Travers, de Lingard, et même de Jorgenson; car la scene entre M. et Mme. Travers qui commence Part V. jette une lumiére particulière sur la scene de la négociation dans l'estacade de Belarab, et lui donne une allure dramatique au lieu d'en faire simplement un morceau de prose discriptive*. Cela saute aux yeux il me semble; et en meme temps ce procédé de narration raccourcit le récit. Il le corse aussi, en tenant la question principale, l'intérêt psychologique, au premier plan. Voilà tout ce que je pense vous dire, et je pense que j'ai raison.

"Le roman est un art *trop* difficile".[1] Cette phrase a été dite par A. Daudet a Henry James au cours d'une discussion, plus ou moins technique, qu'ils ont eu[e] pendant la visite d'Alphonse Daudet en Angleterre[2] – et, ma foi, j'ai bien envie de la répéter ici en l'appliquant justement a la composition de la "Rescue". Oh! que j'envie le technicien ou le savant qui écrivent pour des gens qui non seulement comprennent le sujet mais sont aussi, pour la plupart, capable de comprehendre* la methode.

Je connais le conte de Merimée d'ont* vous parlez. C'est "Tamango". Cela est assez bien. Quant a moi je n'aurai[s] jamais pu l'écrire ni de cette façon là ni d'aucune autre. Je me serai[s] perdu dans les technicalités de la situation. Du reste je pense que "Tamango" est plutôt un morceau philosophique dans le genre des écrivains du 18me siècle. Du moins c'est l'impression qui m'est restée depuis des années qui j'ai lu cela.[3]

---

[1] Conrad uses the phrase in his essay 'Henry James: An Appreciation', collected in *Notes on Life and Letters*, and in the prefaces to *Chance* and *Within the Tides*.
[2] Daudet's visit occurred 6–27 May 1895.
[3] Prosper Mérimée's 'Tamango' (1829) indicts the slave trade, already illegal but still flourishing clandestinely. The narrative traces the fate of a group of Wolof slaves bought by a French skipper from Tamango, an African dealer, who himself becomes enslaved along with his wife. The slaves revolt, kill the European crew, but cannot work the ship themselves. Only Tamango survives to live out his days as a military musician in Jamaica. Eighteenth-century philosophical tales include Samuel Johnson's *Rasselas* and Voltaire's *Candide* and *Zadig*.

Je garde la traduction de la Note pour "En Marge des Marées" pour le moment.[1] J'ai des tas des choses a faire aujour'dhui car demain, je pars en visite chez Pinker jusqu'a lundi. Je reviens ici ce jour là (le 29) et le 1er Sep' nous partons tous pour Deal ou nous allons rester jusqu'au 21. Ma femme commence a marcher. Sir Robert a été très content. Il y a bien encore un endroit douleureux mais ils pensent tous qu'il y aura reabsorption dans le courant de deux ou trois semaines et la guérison sera alors complète. Elle Vous envoit ces amitiés ainsi que les garçons. B[orys] a souffert de la gorge. Jean va bien. Ecrivez moi a Great Eastern Hotel – Deal. Kent.

Miss H[allowes] prend son congé pour un mois. J'ai l'intention de m'occuper a corriger le texte de mon vol: des *Notes on Life and Letters* pendant notre séjour a Deal.

Mes devoirs a Mme Alvar.

A Vous affectueusement

Joseph Conrad.

PS important Je vous prie renvoyer moi le[s] Notes pour Youth and Nostromo.

Translation

Dear Aubry

I get down to business directly.

First, as to Part V. I begin the section that way to establish in advance the psychological situation, which is the most important in the whole story. Obviously I thus avoid long explanations about the state of mind of Mr and Mrs Travers, Lingard, and even Jörgenson, because the scene between Mr and Mrs Travers that begins Part V throws a particular light on the negotiation scene in Belarab's stockade, and gives it a dramatic quality rather than making it simply a piece of descriptive prose. This ought, it seems to me, to be quite obvious, and at the same time this narrative strategy shortens the tale. It also strengthens it by keeping the main issue, the psychological interest, in the foreground. That is all I want to tell you, and I think I am right.

'The novel is *too* difficult an art'. A. Daudet said this to Henry James during a somewhat technical discussion which they had during Alphonse Daudet's visit to England – and, oh, yes, I am very tempted to repeat it here in applying it precisely to the writing of *The Rescue*. How greatly I envy the technician or the scientist who writes for people who not only understand the subject but who also, in the main, can understand the method.

I do know the Merimée story you speak of. It is 'Tamango'. A rather good piece of work. I myself would not have been able to write it in that way or in

[1] Jean-Aubry's translation of *Within the Tides* appeared in 1921.

any other. I would have lost myself in the situation's technicalities. Moreover, I think that 'Tamango' is more like a philosophical piece in the manner of eighteenth-century writers. At least, that's the impression that has stayed with me since I read it years ago.

I am holding on to the translation of the Note to *Within the Tides* for the time being. I have much to do today because tomorrow I leave to stay with Pinker until Monday. I come back here on that day (the 29th), and on 1 Sept we are all leaving for Deal where we stay until the 21st. My wife has begun to walk. Sir Robert was very pleased. There is still a painful spot, but they all think a reabsorption will occur within the next two or three weeks and that the healing will then be complete. She sends you her regards as well as those of the boys. B has had a sore throat. John is well. Write to me at the Great Eastern Hotel, Deal, Kent.

Miss H. is going on leave for a month. I plan to busy myself with correcting the text of my volume of *Notes on Life and Letters* during our stay at Deal.

My duty to Madame Alvar.

Yours affectionately

Joseph Conrad

PS important Pray send me back the Notes for *Youth* and *Nostromo*.

To J. B. Pinker

Text MS Berg; Unpublished

[letterhead: Oswalds]
26.8.20 Thursday.

My dearest P.

It strikes me I could get away from Sandeman by 3 o'clock.

What say you if we went together to Stoll's picture Theatre in Kingsway for an hour or so before catching our 5.20 train?[1]

I will ring you up on my arrival in town about noon to hear what you say to it – and if *yes* I would call at your office early. (say 3.20) I have really no idea how a moving pictures story is composed – and I suggest the Stoll house (Kingsway) because they run from 2.30 and are doing now Les Misérables of V. Hugo a subject from which something may be learned.[2]

Ever Yours

J. C.

---

[1] The start of the visit to Burys Court.
[2] Frank Lloyd had directed the most recent version for Twentieth Century Fox in 1918. The film was not at Stoll's but at the London Pavilion, Piccadilly, where only the Saturday performances began at 2.30.

To Harriet Mary Capes
Text MS Yale; Unpublished

[letterhead: Oswalds]
Tuesday. 31.8.'20

Dearest Harriet[1]

You must forgive for the sake of our old friendship what has the appearance of unpardonable neglect. It was neither that not yet forgetfulness. We were both somewhat depressed (the darkest hour before the dawn) and had not the heart to write of hopes which had been deceived so many times. But this time it really looks as if Jessie's troubles were at an end. She has been coming downstairs regularly every day for the last week; and to-morrow I shall take her to Deal (only 18 m[iles] from here) for a change, which she needs badly after being confined to her room so long.

Many thanks for the letter you have sent me to read. It was a very great pleasure. Pray express my intense gratification on the generous praise. An artist in words lives on the generosity of his readers.

Jessie will be writing to you in a day or two. I am now about to tackle in earnest the arrears of my work. It's simply awful.

Ever my dear Harriet

Your most affectionate and obedient friend
J. Conrad

To G. Jean-Aubry
Text MS Yale; *L.fr.* 158–9

[letterhead: Oswalds]
Mardi. 31.8.'20

Mon cher Aubry.

Le photo n'est pas déjà si mauvais, quoique Votre physiognomie est plus fine que ça. Mais enfin cela Vous rap[p]elle. C'est mieux que rien.

Faut pas faire des excuses. Vous savez bien qu'en vertu de notre affection réciproque nous pouvons nous dire tout ce qui nous passe par la tête sans danger d'être indiscret.

Je suis content de savoir que l'Agent Sec^t marche.[2]

---

[1] Harriet Mary Capes (1849–1936), who lived in Winchester, wrote inspirational stories for children and was involved in the Sunday School movement. A great admirer of Conrad's works, she 'selected and arranged' *Wisdom and Beauty from Conrad* (1915; reprinted 1922). He dedicated *A Set of Six* to her.
[2] That is, his translation of the stage adaptation.

Carola est en route pour la Pologne.[1] Nous quittons Oswalds pour le *Great Eastern Hotel. Deal.* demain. Nous serons de retour le 21 Sep^t.

Amitiés affectueuses de la part de tout le monde ici.

Tout à Vous

J. Conrad.

Je suis touché de l'inscription que vous avez mise au bas de Votre portrait. J'attache un prix particulier au sentiment qui nous unit.

Translation

Tuesday.

My dear Aubry.

The photograph isn't all that bad, although your physiognomy is more refined than that. In any case, it reminds one of you and is better than nothing.

Mustn't make excuses. You well know that our mutual affection permits us to say whatever comes into our heads without risking indiscretion.

I am pleased to hear that *The Secret Agent* is progressing.

Karola is on her way to Poland. To-morrow we leave Oswalds for the *Great Eastern Hotel. Deal.* We return on 21 Sept.

Affectionate regards from everybody here.

Yours truly

J. Conrad

I am touched by the inscription you put at the bottom of your portrait. I place particular value on the bond that links us.

To J. B. Pinker

Text MS Berg; Unpublished

[Oswalds][2]
Great Eastern Hotel
Deal.
Kent.
31.8.'20

Dearest Pinker.

I forward you this sweet communication as by myself I wouldn't know how to answer it adequately, my feelings being too deep for words. (I've signed the damned thing.)[3]——

---

[1] Karola Zagórska was on her homeward journey after six months at Oswalds.

[2] Still at home, Conrad crossed out the Oswalds address and added that of the hotel in Deal.

[3] The agreement with Unwin to include *Almayer's Folly* in the collected editions?

I've had a great time in Your house from every point of view, even purely mental – for, as I dare say you know, my mentality depends on the emotional state of my being more perhaps than is the case with other men. You will be glad (or is it sorry?) to hear that your wine had nothing to do with the wrist trouble. It is no longer painful and the swelling is going down. Without depreciating the charm of your drinks it's evident that, this time, the cause was purely mechanical.

Would you ask our solicitor (can't find his address) to draw up a document in the sense of the enclosed note?[1] Pray cast your eye over it yourself. – My idea is to have it officially translated and duly stamped at the Polish Legation and then send it on to Angela in Warsaw. I have already consulted you on the subject of this – you may remember.

Ever Yours

J. Conrad.

To Mary Pinker

Text MS Private collection; Unpublished

[letterhead: Oswalds]
31.8.'20

Dear Mrs Pinker.[2]

I arrived here after my most delightful visit at your house greatly refreshed and with my wrist rapidly improving. It is nearly well now. There is nothing to mar the charming impression of my sojourn amongst you all and of the good time I've had in the friendly atmosphere of your home.

Let me thank you here for Your friendly reception which I prize most highly and in which your charming (even after her hair was bobbed) daughter[3] has assisted you so ably. She was perfectly sweet to me all the time and I have developed a real affection for her.

---

[1] The solicitors were Withers, Bensons, Currie, Williams & Co. The note reads: 'In consideration of our relationship and of the affection I bear to them I wish to make over absolutely all the translation, publication and the consequent copy-right rights in The Rep[ubli]c of Poland and the territories of the late Russian Empire in all my works to Miss Angela Zagorska (now domiciled in Warsaw) for the joint benefit of herself and her sister Karola Zagorska in equal shares – *Query*. How do I stand as to disposal as above of Almayer (Fisher Unwin) and Typhoon (Wm Heinemann)? Must these be excepted? Or have I the power to transfer trans^{on} rights?'

[2] Mary Elizabeth Pinker (née Seabrooke, 1862–1945) was Conrad's hostess on his occasional visits to the Pinkers' Essex and Surrey homes.

[3] (Mary) Oenone, who was born in 1903. Cutting the hair short was a new (and controversial) fashion.

My wife sends her love to you and to her and to all the house. This time Ralph is specifically include[d] by name in this message – in which I join with all my heart.

Pray believe me, always Your most faithful and obedt friend and Servant.

Joseph Conrad.

PS I hope you've had the box from F[ortnum] & M[ason].[1] I gave the address Burys Court N^r Reigate. I hope its all right – but I tremble. Out of regard for your and Miss Pinker's feelings I selected the *smallest* chocolates I could see in the shop and the "young lady" there seemed to think me a perfect idiot.

To J. B. Pinker
Text MS Berg; Unpublished

[letterhead: Oswalds]
Wednesday. [1 September 1920][2]
9.30 AM

Dearest Pinker.

I have just received Your letter about Wells. The fellow is on the make. Of course I can have no objection but if you like to send me the letters you select I'll be very glad to see them as a matter of simple curiosity.[3] By the by the Hotel is *South Eastern* not G^t Eastern as I think I told you in error.

Please pay £25 more to my acct. I had no end of bills. This outing too will cost something! Jessie will contribute 1/2 her weekly money but indeed £7 a week will not go very far. It's more for the principle.

But I hope that the Notes on Life and Letters at which I am going to work there will more than pay for it.

Ever Yours

J. Conrad.

[1] Of 181 Piccadilly, Conrad's favourite purveyors of fine foods.
[2] Contents suggest the Wednesday in question, the note being written before the Conrads' departure from Deal.
[3] Gabriel Wells (1862–1946), a New York bibliophile and dealer in rare books and manuscripts, was interested in buying Conrad MSS, including correspondence. On 28 December, he sent Pinker $400 in payment for a batch of Conrad's letters (TS Berg). Frank Doubleday made the original introduction; on 30 July, he wrote to Pinker in the hope of a meeting between Conrad and Wells, 'the most valuable friend that any author can have in this country when it comes to selling limited editions' (TS Berg).

To C. S. Evans

Text MS Yale; J-A, 2, 248 (in part)[1]

[Deal]

[3? September 1920][2]

Dear Mr Evans.[3]

A. I don't know really how Donkin[4] pronounces *minnyt* – but I know that the phonetic spelling of the Oxd. Dictionary is a mere phantasy; for no one says *minit*, giving exactly the same sound to both i's in that word.

B. All the phonetics of Donkin's speech are wrong, alas! A real cockney drops his aspirates – but he *never* adds one. Its the country people who do that. I have for this the undeniable authority of Mr Edwin Pugh.[5] A cockney will naturally say *'ome* for *home* but he would *never* say (for instance) *hoperation* for *operation*. What I ought to have done was to take out *every* initial *h* out of his speeches, since I called him a cockney. But God only knows what Donkin is! It's too late now to chase all those *h's* out of the text, I fear.

Yer – You should be adhered to as printed [in] my first ed.

Many thanks for Your good care.

Yours gratefully

J. Conrad.

I have written add^al par. to *Almayer's* preface.[6] Pp 241–256 of *Outcast* returned.

PS Pre[li]ms of Alms: enclosed with apologies for the delay. More pre[li]ms of Tales of Unrest. (3 corre^ns in Authors note).

---

[1] Jean-Aubry omits part of the first postscript and the whole of the second.

[2] Conrad's wrote on the verso of Evans's letter to him of 2 September (J-A, 2, 247–8; Stape and Knowles, pp. 161–2). Jean-Aubry's conjecture of a reply on the day of receipt is reasonable but only if Evans's letter was sent directly to Deal.

[3] Charles ('Charley') Seddon Evans (1883–1944), an employee in the publishing house of William Heinemann, was involved in seeing the collected edition of Conrad's works through press. When Doubleday assumed the chairmanship of Heinemann's in 1922, Evans became one of the firm's managers.

[4] The Cockney malcontent of *The Nigger of the 'Narcissus'*, the text now being prepared for Heinemann's collected edition.

[5] Edwin Pugh (1874–1930), novelist of London life, was a friend of Conrad in his early career.

[6] Three sentences added to the 1895 preface; for the text, see *Almayer's Folly*, ed. Floyd Eugene Eddleman and David Leon Higdon (Cambridge University Press, 1994), p. 200.

To C. S. Evans
Text MS Texas; Unpublished

[Deal?]
[early September? 1920][1]

Dear Mr Evans.

The matter of the name for the Edition was settled when Mr Heinemann was here. There was to be *no* special name for this first Comp^te and Limited Edition. We retained the White Horse on purely decorative grounds.

Of course if Mr Heinemann insists he must have his way.

For end paper. I prefer much the Rom Caps.

I send you the only pp of the Youth vol in my possession. Miss H[allowes] sent them to me to look over her corrections.

Kindest regards

Yours

J. Conrad.

To J. B. Pinker
Text MS Berg; Unpublished

[letterhead: South Eastern Hotel, Deal]
Sunday [5 September 1920][2]

My dear Pinker

I have just read through the letters you have sent me. The handwriting of some of them is awful!

I don't know that I could formulate any distinct objections even if I wanted to. There is however a point or two – not worth enlarging upon in writing which I could show you in the actual correspondence. Will Mr Wells wait for your decision till after your arrival here? After all you are doing him a favour.

We shall expect you on Monday the 13th. I am getting on with the Vol of scraps,[3] and shall have that thing ready by the time you arrive here.

Give our love to everybody

Ever Yours

J Conrad.

Thanks for the £6 in notes duly received.

---

[1] The tempo of work on the Heinemann collected edition and Miss Hallowes's departure for her holiday on 28 August (see the letter of 24 August) suggest the general period.
[2] The 12th would be too close to Pinker's intended visit; the 5th was the only earlier Sunday spent in Deal.
[3] *Notes on Life and Letters*, then being revised.

To George T. Keating

Text MS Yale; Keating 118

[letterhead: South Eastern Hotel, Deal]
6.9.20

Dear M[r] Keating[1]

As you will see from this we are away from home. We left it on the 1st of this month at which date no parcel from you has reached Oswalds.

Miss Hallowes (my secretary) is also away on her annual holiday.

I am afraid Your business (of the pamphlets) can not be attended to till the end of this month.

in haste

Yours

J. Conrad

To J. B. Pinker

Text MS Berg; Unpublished

[letterhead: South Eastern Hotel, Deal]
Wed: 8.9.20

Dearest P.

I send you the enclosed for settlement in due course.

I hear from B[orys] that you are coming to Deal (on Sat next) *through London* by the train arriving here 6.18.

It shall be met – if that is so. But is it so?

Ever Yours

J. C.

To Edward Garnett

Text MS Private collection; G. 297

[letterhead: South Eastern Hotel, Deal]
9 Sep[r] '20

My *very* dear Edward

We rejoice at your promise to come to us on the 4 Oct. You must let us know the train which we will meet in *Canterbury* (*not* Bishopsbourne).

---

[1] New-York-born George Thomas Keating (1892–1976) amassed a rich collection of Conradiana from various sales as well as from Thomas J. Wise. He donated his collection, catalogued in *A Conrad Memorial Library: The Collection of George T. Keating* (1929), to Yale University in 1938. Keating worked his way up from errand-boy to head of Moore and Munger, a New York firm dealing in paper and clay products, eventually retiring to California. He also collected operatic recordings and music manuscripts, the works of the American author James Branch Cabell, and materials about the Spanish conquest of the New World.

I can't tell you how glad I am to hear that you are going to bring out some critical essays.[1] Their value will endure long, long after the "old timepiece" has really stopped. For, as to the present, those who say it does no longer go are simply unable to hear the golden tick.

Jessie's love.

Ever Yours

J. Conrad

To Harold Goodburn

Text MS Indiana; Unpublished

[letterhead: South Eastern Hotel, Deal]
15.9.'20

Dear Mr Goodburn

This will be John's last lesson and I must convey to you my wife's and my thanks for the pains you have taken with the boy. Let us hope that your toil and care are not [to] be wasted.

Pray send me just a note as to the amount of my indebt[ed]ness to you.

With kind regards from us both to Mrs Goodburn and yourself

Yours sincerely

Joseph Conrad.

To Harold Goodburn

Text MS Private collection; Unpublished

[letterhead: South Eastern Hotel, Deal]
18.9.'20

Dear Mr Goodburn

Enclosed the cheque.

I am glad the little girls like the pictures.[2]

With our kindest regards

Sincerely Yours

J. Conrad.

---

[1] Garnett's *Friday Nights: Literary Criticisms and Appreciations* eventually appeared in June 1922.
[2] Edward Lear's *Nonsense Songs*, Conrad gift to Goodburn's children, is inscribed 'For the Nursery Library of the Misses Goodburn from Joseph Conrad 1920'. Goodburn's family then comprised twin girls born in Buenos Aires in 1917, a girl born in Rio de Janeiro in 1918, and another born in Canterbury in January 1920.

To G. Jean-Aubry

Text MS Yale; *L.fr.* 159–60

[letterhead: South Eastern Hotel, Deal]

[18 September 1920][1]

Mon cher ami.

Pardonnez moi d'avoir détenu Votre article sur Merimée si longtemps.[2] Je l'ai lu aussitôt son arrivée et puis je l'ai relu – hier. C'est un des meilleurs morceaus* que j'ai lu de Vous – quoique Vous me plaisez toujours. Mais ceci m'a donné un plaisir tout particulier par la maîtrise de Votre sujet (qui est *l'homme* lui même) et le style précis et interéssant dans lequel vous poursuivez cette étude psychologique qui certainement valait bien la peine d'être faite. Mes félicitations! Je ne crois pas qu'on puisse faire mieux dans ce genre là. C'est bien gentil a vous de m'avoir envoyé ces pages si parfaitement réussies.

Nous revenons à Oswalds Mardi prochain. Pas de domestiques. Enfin on verra! Jessie Vs envoit ces* amitiés. Elle s'éxerce a marcher et de ce côté tout va assez bien. Moi j'ai travaillé – dans un genre que Vs étonnera[3] – et même assez bien. Mais je ne peux pas secouer ce pavé que j'ai sur la poitrine. Et, Vous savez il n'y a aucune cause pour cela!

Il faudra venir nous voir bientôt. Je vais vous envoyer un petit mot dans le courant de la semaine.

Votre affectueusement

J. Conrad.

PS Pinker qui est ici vient de recevoir par telephone de son bureau la demande d'une copie de la pièce pour Norman McKinnel[4] qui veut la lire. Je n'ai pas d'exemplaire. Pouvez vous nous preter celui que Vous avez, pour quelques jours? Envoyez directement a *J. B. Pinker. Talbot House. Arundel S*ᵗ. *Strand.*

Translation

My dear friend.

Pray forgive my keeping your article on Merimée so long. I read it as soon as it arrived and then re-read it – yesterday. It is one of the best pieces by you I've read, although your work never fails to delight me. But this gave

---

[1] In Jean-Aubry's hand on MS and confirmed by the postmark.
[2] A typescript of 'Mérimée', published in *La Revue de Genève*, 4 (October 1920), pp. 483–500.
[3] The film scenario of 'Gaspar Ruiz'.
[4] Scots-born actor, director, and manager (1870–1932), McKinnel débuted in 1896. He appeared in a variety of roles in the West End, playing alongside H. Beerbohm-Tree and Henry Irving. In March 1921, he took over the management of the Comedy Theatre.

a special pleasure in its mastery of your subject (the very *man* himself) and in the precise and interesting style in which you pursue this psychological study, which was certainly well worth doing. My congratulations! I don't think one could do anything of the sort better. How kind of you to have sent me those so perfectly achieved pages.

We return to Oswalds next Tuesday. No servants. Well, we shall see! Jessie sends her regards. She is trying to walk and that is going well enough. As for myself, I did some work in a form that will surprise you and made a pretty good job of it. But I can't shake off the weight that sits on my chest. And you know there is no reason for that!

You must come to see us soon. I'll send you a word during the course of the week.

Yours affectionately

J. Conrad

PS Pinker, who is here, has just had a telephone call from his office asking for a copy of the play for Norman McKinnel who wants to read it. I don't have one. Could you lend us yours for a few days? Send it directly to *J. B. Pinker. Talbot House. Arundel St. Strand.*

To J. B. Pinker

Text MS Berg; Unpublished

[letterhead: Oswalds]

21.9.20

5 pm

Dearest J. B.

We arrived here all well about an hour ago – and the post has just come in bringing the Doubleday Ed[on] pages for signature. Please tell Eric I will attend to it to-morrow.

I have a horribly swollen face and have had a hellish night. Easier now, but feeling very cheap.

Thanks for particulars of Goodenough's[1] rank and decorations. You are a great person for *not* forgetting.

I hope you had a good journey home.

Your phone message was very satisfactory to B[orys]. Sir John (or James) Perry[2] is the very person N'cliffe has influence with.

B will write to-morrow to Lord N.

---

[1] See the letter of the 25th.

[2] The naval architect Sir William John Berry (1865–1937), who was Director of Warship Production?

I shall see Col. Bell as soon as my old muzzle returns to a presentable condition[1].

Love to you all

Ever Yours

J Conrad.

To the Polish Legation, London

Text MS Warsaw, sygn. 1041; *Listy* 274–5; Najder (1983, 2), 252

[letterhead: Oswalds]
22 Sep. 1920

Ref. N° 4439.

Mr Joseph Conrad presents his compliments and thanks to the Chargé d'Affaires of Poland.

Mr Conrad while awaiting the reply from Poland has instructed his solicitor to prepare a formal Deed of Gift according to English procedure. This document together with a translation into Polish, which perhaps the Legation will consent to certify as in all points correct, he intends to send to Miss Angela Zagorska. With this legal expression of Mr Conrad's will and act Miss Zagórska could address herself to an advocate who would know what steps to take to make the instrument valid in Polish Courts – or should that be legally impossible, would prepare a corresponding deed in accordance with Polish procedure which he could send over here for Mr Conrad's signature to be witnessed and legalised at the Polish Legation in London.

This course will have the advantage of making Miss Zagorska's rights secure before any English court. This may be of some importance as Mr Conrad's testamentary dispositions direct the sale of his copyrights outright on the best conditions obtainable 20 years after his death.[2]

Mr Joseph Conrad wishes to convey his deep sense of the attention given by the Legation of the Republic to his request and begs the Polish Chargé d'Affaires to accept the assurance of his highest regard.

The Polish Legation.
London.

---

[1] He had a painful swelling of the face; see the letter of the 23rd.

[2] No such clause appears in Conrad's will of 8 August 1922 (*Documents*, pp. 247–51).

To J. B. Pinker
Text MS Berg; Unpublished

[letterhead: Oswalds]

23.9.20

My dear Pinker

B[orys] is taking John to school. Pray give him £8 for expenses and for himself.

Jessie wants me to tell You that whenever Bell calls for Ralph we are ready for him now. There are two women, the head gardener cleans boots & knives the second gard: tunes the piano and dusts the drawing room, and the shover[1] looks after the study ... etc, etc.

I can't keep on being funny because my physiognomy still has a bulge which pains all over, and causes me to mope and sulk instead [of] attending to business in a spirit of cheerful alacrity.

Love from the Missus

Ever Yours

J. Conrad.

To Admiral Sir William Goodenough
Text TS copy Yale; J-A, 2, 248–9

Oswalds,
Bishopsbourne,
Kent.
25.9.20

My dear Admiral,[2]

Your most unexpected – and most welcome – letter from Saldanha Bay[3] reached me in Deal, of all places! But this house is only 18 miles from there and we had run over for a week's change.

After I had finished reading I looked away to the eastward and had a particular feeling that it was good to get this "Well done" from a Flag Officer in sight of the historic anchorage where as a very young seaman I lay at anchor for the first time in 1878.[4] It was also the year when I heard first the

---

[1] A facetious or ironic version of 'chauffeur'.

[2] Admiral William Edmund Goodenough (1867–1945; knighted 1919), who began his career as a naval cadet in 1880, moved up through the ranks during service in North America, the West Indies, the Mediterranean, and South China waters. He became Captain of the naval training college at Dartmouth in 1905, but soon returned to active service. He served in the war, and in 1920 became Commander-in-Chief of the Africa station. In retirement he was President of the Royal Geographical Society (1930–3) and Chairman of the British Sailors' Society.

[3] A harbour on South Africa's south-west coast.

[4] The *Mavis* must have anchored in The Downs on her way to Lowestoft in June 1878.

honoured name you bear on the lips of men in the ships of the Australian wool fleet in which I began my deep-water life and where I got my first promotion. The universal affection and respect for the Commodore[1] is one of my earliest impressions and has remained a part of my sea-memories. While you had your broad pennant in the Southampton[2] I was more than glad to see history repeating itself like this, in home waters and at a crucial moment of Fate.

I have written all this to make it clear why, even apart from considerations personal to yourself, no word from you could be regarded as coming from a "perfect stranger" (your own words).

I am immensely pleased at your good opinion of the Rescue and very touched that you should have taken the trouble to tell me that. There are acts of kindness for which it is very difficult to thank a man. One does not know what to say.

That thing has been on the stocks for something like twenty years. I laid it aside the year my eldest boy was born and did not take it up again till he returned after the Armistice after 3 1/2 years on the French front. It struck me then that my time was running out and I wanted the deck cleared before going below. As to leaving any loose ends hanging over the side I couldn't bear the thought of it! For that reason I have been collecting all my occasional writings into a vol. which will appear next spring under the title of *Notes on Life and Letters*. I will send it out to you not for its interest but as a token of my warmest regard – which is yours hereditarily and personally. I don't know how small your "little ship" is but I can trust you to have the book stowed somewhere where it will not spoil her trim.

Believe me, my dear Admiral,

most sincerely and gratefully yours
Joseph Conrad.

To Lady Millais
Text MS Private collection; Unpublished

[letterhead: Oswalds]
26.9.20

My dear Lady Millais

One shrinks from worrying you with telegrams of inquiry but we are living here in a state of anxiety[3] which extends to yourself as well. It is many years

---

[1] The admiral's father, Commodore James Graham Goodenough, (1830–75) enjoyed a distinguished career, seeing service in the Americas, the Far East, and Australia.

[2] In 1910, William Goodenough was posted to HMS *Southampton*, where he flew his admiral's pennant; his father had commanded the previous ship of that name.

[3] About her son Sir John, who died on the 30th.

now since our appreciation of your friendly kindness has grown into deep regard and affection. But love even of the nearest and dearest can do but little. I feel dear Lady Millais that there is nothing to bear you through the hours of cruel suspense but your devoted courage I have watched admiringly for years and for which you must let me express here my most respectful sympathy and recognition.

Pardon me if I venture to enclose a form already addressed.[1] Perhaps one of the nurses would kindly send it off when an occasion offers to Hamstreet.

Believe me dear Lady Millais

ever Your most affectionate servant.

Joseph Conrad

To Captain David Bone
Text MS Sprott; Knowles

[letterhead: Oswalds]
28 Sept 1920

My dear Capt Bone.

Many thanks for your letter and the invitation it contains. If I ever do go to sea again it will be under your command – but I don't see any prospect at present to shuffle off this mortal coil[2] of beastly affairs literary and others which holds me fast to the earth.

I *don't* think much of the practice of seafaring as you illustrate it from your recent experience. I had some trouble of the sort in '88 in Adelaide with the Union of F & S which tried to hold my ship up – on general principles.[3] Asses.

I am pleased to hear you have an agreement with Dutton.[4] Everybody speaks well of that House. When the *Brassbounder* is republished do send me a copy.[5] I'd like to have it *from you*. Since we moved into this house I've been looking high and low for my copy of the 1st Eng^sh Edition which Edward

---

[1] I.e., a pre-addressed telegram form.
[2] From *Hamlet*: 'what dreams may come/When we have shuffled off this mortal coil' (3.2.66–7).
[3] Conrad's departure from Adelaide in 1889 as a passenger was untroubled. When the *Otago* sailed from Sydney on 7 August 1888, the city was gripped by maritime crisis, caused by the breakdown of negotiations on wages and crewing between the Federated Seamen's Union of Australasia and the Steamship Owners' Association.
[4] E. P. Dutton & Co., founded in 1858, were the American publishers of Dent's Everyman Library and Temple Classics series. Its English authors included Max Beerbohm, George Gissing, W. H. Hudson, and Arthur Symons.
[5] Bone's *The Brassbounder* was first published in 1910. At the time, Conrad told Garnett it was 'the most suburban thing (I mean spiritually) I've ever read' (*Letters*, 4, p. 380). The new edition was American, to be published by Dutton.

Garnett sent me years ago. Moves are the devil! Books and other things vanish somehow. All good luck and happiness to you and yours

Warmest regards

Yours

Joseph Conrad.

To F. N. Doubleday

Text MS Princeton; Unpublished

[letterhead: Oswalds]
1st Oct [1920][1]

Dear Mr Doubleday.

We will be delighted to see you here for lunch any day after next Monday. If you came by road You must leave town at 10 o'clock and proceed to Canterbury and from Cant^{ry} to the village of Bridge (on the Dover high road) (3 miles) where you had better inquire for Oswalds.

If by train then the best will be from Victoria 10.45 arr^{vg} Canterbury 12.46 where I'll meet you at the Station.

It will be a great pleasure to see you and your son[2] under [my] own roof. My wife sends her best regards.

Very faithfully yours

Joseph Conrad.

To J. B. Pinker

Text TS/MS Berg; Unpublished

[letterhead: Oswalds]
Oct. 6th. 1920.

Dearest J. B.

Your impatiently awaited letter arrived this morning. The origins of this misunderstanding are so remote that I of course could think of nothing else but its being some sort of incomprehensible hoax to annoy D[oubleday]. I thought it just as well to wire him too, disclaiming any interference, and assuring him that I didn't want to interfere in any material details of publication.

I am very glad you have now finally settled this matter to everybody's satisfaction I hope – and certainly to *my* completest satisfaction. I admit I was startled by your letter in so far that you seemed to believe me capable

---

[1] Letters to Pinker and Curle of the 9th confirm the year.

[2] The child of Doubleday's first marriage, Nelson Doubleday (1890–1949) entered publishing in the magazine trade, joining his father's firm as a junior partner in 1918. He became president in 1928, pioneering various modern sales techniques.

of a rather crazy action. On the other hand I was quite touched by the patience and good temper which, assuming your belief, seemed to me almost a miraculous feat of self-command.

This morning I had a shock of a different kind in a note from Evans telling me that poor Heinemann was dead.[1] I wonder what will become of the Bedford Street Home of Letters. S. S. is not the man to run it by himself, I fancy.[2] Whatever happens I suppose the prospects of the Limited Edition can not be affected in any way since it is already publicly announced that it has been fully subscribed for. It would be, however, a horrible thing if Fisher Unwin, for instance, were to take over the business. This notion flashed through my brain on the receipt of the news, but I dismissed it at once as too dreadful to contemplate.

Doubleday and his son announce their coming here for lunch on Saturday. Everything now being settled all we will have to do will be to receive them with impressive aimiability.* At any rate the ordeal will not be very long and need not be very trying.

I note what you say about signing the Lim: Ed: sheets and I presume that the lot I have now here may be cast into the fire without more ado. I will of course go on with the "One Day More" signatures, as I suppose that the number of these will not be altered, since it is a separate undertaking having nothing to do with the Collected Edition. There are about 150 sheets signed now.

I am enclosing here three bills for settlement. You may remember that the day you left Deal I asked you to transfer a further sum of £100 into my account at the bank. If you haven't done so yet please make it £150.

I am going on with the Prefaces to complete the set. The work doesn't come particularly easy somehow, but I suppose that for the purposes of copyright the finish doesn't matter very much, since I can always correct, alter, or even recast those things on the galley slips which will come in due time in the course of the next year.

We consider your visit next week as a fixed and unalterable thing but we are not so certain about the actual day. Walpole follows Doubleday on Sat. evening and goes on Monday, to be followed by Miss Mackellar,[3] who will go on Tuesday, also in the morning or in the early afternoon. Therefore the room for you will be ready for Tuesday night and you have only to wire your train. The Prefaces will be done by then and the course clear for the last lap of the cinema circus.

---

[1] He died on the 5th.
[2] Whatever his abilities, Heinemann's partner, S. S. Pawling, was in poor health.
[3] Dorothea Mackellar (1885–1967), Australian poet. For an earlier visit, see *Letters*, 5, pp. 50, 71.

Jessie has just told me of Williamsons death. I can imagine how you'll miss him after all those years of close friendship and the memory of work done in common.[1] All my sympathy.

Ever affec^ly Yours

J. Conrad.

To Captain J. G. Sutherland

Text MS Syracuse; Unpublished

[letterhead: Oswalds]

6.10.20

My dear Captain Sutherland[2]

Many thanks for the copy of *The Navy* with Your interesting article[3] and the photo of the ships quarter deck which we have paced together for so many hours.

It is for me a very great and delightful memory. The most pleasant part of it I owe to Your truly sailor-like kindness and hospitality. I am very sorry You are not in the picture.

Things here are not going on very well yet. We have been away for some time but my wife is laid up again with a fresh complication. As to me I haven't been able to do a stroke of work for nearly a year – what with mental worries and severe fits of gout. I am however feeling a little better now.

With kind regards

Yours sincerely

Joseph Conrad.

To Hugh Walpole

Text MS Texas; J-A, 2, 247

[letterhead: Oswalds]

7.10.20

My dear Hugh.

I left the "civilities" to Jessie who has no doubt written to you already. This is only to tell you that I have read the book[4] – which is a book – a

---

[1] C(harles) N(orris) Williamson (1859–1920) and his wife A(lice) M(uriel) (1869–1933) were among Pinker's most energetic and profitable authors. They specialised in motoring adventure and romance. Conrad thought their fiction 'rot' (*Letters*, 4, p. 44).

[2] Captain John Georgeson Sutherland (born 1871), received his master's certificate in 1897. He served in the Royal Navy during the war and was the captain of the Q-ship *Ready*, in which Conrad made a perilous ten-day voyage in November 1916. He capitalised on Conrad's fame by spinning out the experience into a short book, *At Sea with Joseph Conrad* (1922).

[3] 'At War in a Q Brigantine. When Mr Joseph Conrad went U-boat Chasing', *The Navy, Organ of the Naval League*, October 1920, pp. 140–2.

[4] *The Captives, A Novel in Four Parts*, just published.

creation – no small potatoes indeed – très chic; and if the truth must be told très fort even – considerable in purpose, successful in execution and deep in feeling – a genuine Walpole, this, with an unexpected note of maturity in design and composition; and holding the interest from page to page, which in itself is not a common quality. O! dear, no!

All I want to do here, really, is to shake hands with you over it in friendship and congratulation. More when we meet on Sat.

Ever Yours

J. Conrad

To J. B. Pinker

Text MS Berg; Unpublished

[letterhead: Oswalds]
9.10.20.

Dearest J. B.

We are very sorry to hear you are feeling out of sorts. Let us hope you'll be all right by Tuesday. We expect to hear from you on the morning of that day.

I have just finished the last preface.[1] D[ouble]day is due here in an hour or so. He will probably lose his way and be late. Poor Jessie is going to make an effort and come down to lunch.

Thanks for all the settlements and payments You've made for me.

Our love to Mrs Pinker, Yourself and all the family.

Ever Yours

J Conrad

To Richard Curle

Text MS Indiana; Curle 71 (in part)[2]

[letterhead: Oswalds]
9.10.20.
1 o'clock

My dear Richard

While awaiting the arrival of Doubleday ("with my son Nelson") who are coming to-day by road to lunch and may be here any moment, I begin this letter to you. And I am very sorry to confess that it is only my second.

I am my dear fellow treating you badly, very badly. But I am too old to change my spots[3] – and anyhow animals of my sort never do.

I have this morning (in fact about 10 minutes ago) finished my last preface (or Au'rs Note) for the volume of collected pieces. It will appear (1st Ed)

---

[1] To *Notes on Life and Letters*.   [2] Curle omits the postscript.
[3] Like the Biblical leopard (Jeremiah 13.23).

next spring. While revising the text You were very vividly with me – your friendship, your kindness, your personality and I missed more than ever your voice, your characteristic turn of conversation, the downrightness of your mind and the warm genui[ne]ness of your feelings. I arranged finally the order of the papers on the list in your own handwriting you made for me quite a long time ago. After some tentative shiftings the order remains practically as you wrote it down – with the addition of course of the 3 D Mail pieces which were not on your list and of the short article on my flight.[1]

We spent 3 weeks in Deal to give poor Jessie a change. After our return here (on the 21st Sept) she went on improving in her walking powers till a few days ago when she had to go to bed again with a new development of the old pereostitis. She is getting quite sick of these ups and downs. Still the pain has subsided since and she will attempt to-day to come down to lunch.

As to me I feel a depression of spirits against which I can and do react – up to now. My novel is hung up for the present. I am writing a cinema play based on Gaspar Ruiz – I mean *I*, myself, am doing it – and Laskers[2] C⁰ is interested in my efforts. It will be done next week – as to the rough draft, from which I shall dictate an extended scenario to Miss H[allowes]. Laskers "literary editor" (Heavens!) is in London.[3] He will read it first (and pay for the privilege) and if approved of the thing will go to the "Continuity Writer" (did you ever hear of such an animal?) while another payment will go into my pocket and make it bulge out. At least Pinker says so. He comes frequently over here and is actually (and effectively) assisting me in this performance which seems as futile and insecure as walking on a tight rope – and at bottom much less dignified.

The sensation of the moment in this household is that Norman McKinnel asked for the play and after reading it 'phoned to P's office asking about terms.

What happened afterwards is just at present "wropt in mystery."[4] But that, as you know, is Pinker's way. I am not worrying myself. In the States Belasco asked to see it – but he has *not* telephoned, I believe.

---

[1] Three book reviews for the *Daily Mail* published in July 1910 and 'Never Any More: A First and Last Flying Experience' (later 'Flight') published in June 1917.

[2] A survival from Victorian Oxford, the affectionate ending in '-ers' was still popular in college, school, and officers' mess. C. S. Lewis, for example, used to call J. R. R. Tolkien 'Tollers'. Perhaps Conrad learned the trick from Borys.

[3] Famous Players-Lasky Company was established in 1916 by the American producer Jesse L. Lasky, a founder of Hollywood cinema. The company had recently assigned Robert MacAlarney, formerly head of the scenario department in New York, to a permanent post in London (Famous Players Film Co. to Pinker, 11 August, TS Berg).

[4] A catch-phrase in the early twentieth century; the facetious pronunciation hints at an origin in the music halls.

Those are the news. Apart from that: Walpole has been here and inquired tenderly after you. He is very pleased with the reception of his new novel *The Captives*. It is a very good "Walpole", a little larger in conception and in treatment.

I wish to goodness *you* would write a novel! Edward was here for two nights and a day. Rather mellower – but not looking happy.

Doubleday and his son Nelson paid their visit. The usual sort of thing. He is apparently pleased with the prospects of my work in America and very confident as to its permanent (paying) value. I don't know how much all these speeches are worth. Obviously there is a sale; but the advance of Rescue on the Arrow (so far) is insignificant (if any) notwithstanding their high hopes. As to the Coll^{ed} Edition in the States it is now finally fixed at 750 sets – and through P's efforts a payment of $12,000 has been secured. Here the death of Heinemann makes no difference. You will be interested to hear that the whole Ed^{on} is subscribed. Print and paper are very good.

I trust nothing will delay your return next spring. John is to try for Tonbridge on the 15 Nov^{er}. If he passes he will go there on the 20 Jany. 21. I am still in hopes to arrange to take Jessie to Corsica for Fbr. Mch & Ap: Ajaccio is a good wintering place. *If* we are there when you pass through the Med^{rran} you must land in Marseilles and come over (one nights passage) to us for a week. But all my plans are doubtful and my hopes are faint. Poor Millais died – at last![1] Lady M. is heartbroken. Colvin is very, very shaky. You are much in our thoughts – never doubt that.

Ever affectionately Yours

Joseph Conrad.

P. S. Quinn paid up after groaning heavily. Wise has been here and was quite amusing. Not a bad little man.

To Jenny Doris Thorne

Text MS Duke; Unpublished

[letterhead: Oswalds]

15.10.20

Dear Mrs Thorne

I lived in hopes of finding a day – but now I have a swollen foot and must give up all thoughts of coming to town.

You must in the well of your inexhaustible mercy find a drop of forgiveness for me. I'll say no more except to remind you that the greater the sinner the greater the merit in forgiving him.

---

[1] On 30 September, of complications from tuberculosis.

I trust you will have a pleasant passage and find no plagues in the land on your arrival.[1] And pray don't think unkind thoughts of your very faithful and obedient servant

Joseph Conrad.

Please express to your husband my great regret on missing this occasion to make his acquaintance. My warm regards to your father.

To J. B. Pinker
Text MS Berg; Unpublished

[letterhead: Oswalds]
[mid to late October 1920][2]

Dearest J. B.

The document is what is wanted.[3] Pray have it engrossed and perhaps I had better come up to sign it at the Polish Legation where they would witness my signature – You perhaps consenting to come with me and be the other witness.

I am getting on fast as I can with the Film.

It is rather a job; but I am glad I decided on dictating it myself as the thing wanted rewording in many places.

The "foray" series of pictures (only three)[4] was fairly easy to do.

I am going to work late to-morrow by arrang[t] with Miss H[allowes].

Love from Jessie.

Ever Yours

J. Conrad.

PS I don't think N. Mackinnel* will want to fix about the play till the Grain of Mustard Seed shows signs of going off.[5] I fancy it is *his* production *by arrangement* with L. MacCarthy.[6]

---

[1] She was bound for Egypt, land of the biblical plagues.
[2] McKinnel's performances in *The Grain of Mustard Seed* and the completion of 'Gaspar the Strong Man' by month's end suggest the period.
[3] Transferring Polish translation rights to Aniela Zagórska.
[4] The visual sequences as opposed to the intervening captions: in this case, scenes of guerrilla warfare.
[5] H. M. Harwood's *The Grain of Mustard Seed*, starring McKinnel, played at the Kingsway Theatre from 11 October to 13 November after a run at the Ambassadors.
[6] Lila Emma ('Lillah') McCarthy, later Lady Keble (1875–1960), an actress notable for her interpretations of Shaw and Shakespeare.

Plate 1. Conrad by Powys Evans, *London Mercury*, December 1922

Plate 2. G. Jean-Aubry

Plate 3. Deck of the *Endymion*, painting by John Everett

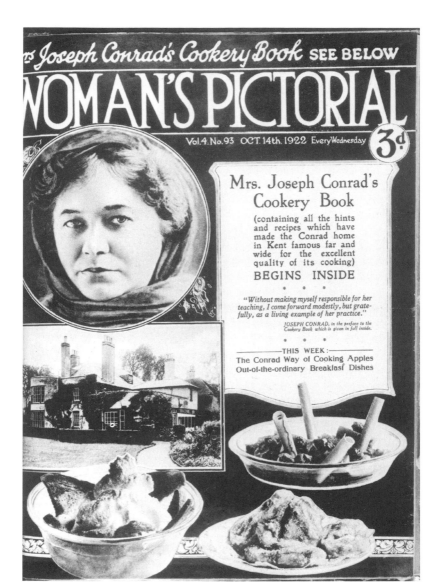

Plate 4. Jessie Conrad featured in the *Woman's Pictorial*, 14 October 1922

Plate 5. Conrad in rehearsal with Miriam Lewes and Russell Thorndike

Plate 6. Thomas J. Wise

Plate 7. Conrad with Aniela Zagórska, Oswalds

Plate 8. Conrad with J. B. Pinker, Reigate, c. 1921

To J. B. Pinker
Text MS Berg; Unpublished

[letterhead: Oswalds]
Sunday. [17 October 1920][1]

Dearest J. B.

Thanks very much for your letter. That scheme for the Prefaces with Heinemann is a great stroke of business evidently.[2] I no longer attempt to thank you for your unwearied planning and working on my behalf. Yes. 250 cop. will fetch something worth having. I will of course sign the copies.

Miss H[allowes] must have written to you about the batch of Am: pages received here through your office. They are obviously (shape-size) the signature-pages of the Ltd Edition. But the declared number (735) of sets does not agree with the terms (750 + presentation sets) settled finally with D[ouble]day. I refrain therefore from signing them – lest it should be a mere mistake and the pages have to be cancelled in the end. Could you get hold of young D'day? He may be in UK yet.

Ever Yours

J. Conrad

PS Pray settle this old acct for me.
PPS Half of Film text is done. I'll be going on with it steadily.

To Thomas J. Wise
Text MS BL Ashley 2953; Unpublished

[letterhead: Oswalds]
22.10.20

My dear M[r] Wise

You may of course insert the portrait.[3] As to The Black Mate the sooner it is forgotten the better.[4]

I'll have in a few days 3 more prefaces (first drafts) for you if you wish to have them to complete your set. There will be also a considerable lot of pp

---

[1] 'Gaspar the Strong Man' was completed on the 29th. At the rate Conrad was working, the 17th is the only likely Sunday after the visit from Doubleday, who was soon to depart for America.
[2] The collection of Author's Notes published as *Notes on My Books*. Doubleday brought out 250 copies in March, and Heinemann 250 more in May 1921.
[3] As the frontispiece to his Conrad bibliography.
[4] Hoping to win a prize offered for a story by a sailor, Conrad submitted 'The Black Mate' to *Tit-Bits* magazine in 1886; probably after much rewriting, a version appeared in the *London Magazine* in 1908 but did not come out in book form until the posthumous *Tales of Hearsay*. See Keith Carabine's article on the story in *The Conradian*, 13 (1988), 128–48.

of actual MS. work I am engaged on now – the scenario of a film-play –
Perhaps you may like to have that too.

But pray treat this as disclosed to you in confidence.

Yours in haste

J. Conrad.

To J. E. Hodgson

Text MS Bodley MS Eng. c. 4802; Unpublished

[letterhead: Oswalds]

24.10.20.

Dear Mr Hodgson.[1]

The publication is *The Fledgling* N° 1. which was edited by Macdonald
Hastings.[2]

The whole press, it seems, took notice of the prices fetched by *Chance* (1913)
and the copy of the *Nigger* at your latest sale.[3]

I am glad that Holland takes an interest in my work. I had no idea that it
did.

Yours faithfully

Joseph Conrad.

To Thomas J. Wise

Text MS BL Ashley 2953; Unpublished

[Oswalds]

Sunday. Oct. [24] 1920[4]

My dear Mr Wise.

Thanks for your letter and ch: for £30 which is quite right for the three
prefaces: to *Arrow of Gold*; to *Rescue*; to a vol of collected pieces which will
appear next spring under the title of *Notes on Life and Letters*.

Miss Hallowes will dispatch the lot to you to-morrow by reg: post.

The critical (very just) remark on G. Ruiz will be acted upon. Thanks.

---

[1] John Edmund Hodgson (1875–1952) was the director of the long-established London auction
house Hodgson & Co., a firm dealing in literary manuscripts and fine books; he was also a
historian of British aviation and aeronautics.

[2] Conrad's 'Never Any More: A First and Last Flying Experience' (later 'Flight') appeared
in the June 1917 issue of *The Fledgling: The Monthly Journal of the No. 2 Royal Flying Corps Cadet
Wing*. Basil Macdonald Hastings (1881–1928), playwright, journalist, essayist, and drama critic
dramatised *Victory* (1919).

[3] *The Times* of the 13th (p. 7) noted the prices reached at Hodgson & Co.'s sale the previous day.
Originally published at 6s., the books sold for £9 5s. and 10 gs., respectively.

[4] Postmarked 25 October.

The MS of the Film-play will be reserved for you together with the first T.S. copy containing all variations and corrections in my own hand.

I asked you not to mention to anybody that I had written such a thing because it may not after all be accepted – though it was written at the request of Laski* Film Players Co. – and I don't like to have a failure (should it turn out to be that) publicly known.

At any rate you'll have another unique piece: – Conrad as a Film Author.

I'll be very pleased to sign anything for you. But the copy of the book you advise did not reach me this morning.

Many thanks for you[r] kind inquiries. I am fairly well. My wife walks with crutches about the house. She sends you her thanks and kind regards.

Yours faithfully

Joseph Conrad

To J. B. Pinker
Text MS Berg; Unpublished

[letterhead: Oswalds]
29.10.20

Dearest J. B.

I am sending you this TS¹ to your home so that you should have something to amuse you on Sunday. Do please glance at this product of our joint toil. I don't think you'll find anything to object [to]. The alterations are merely verbal. The action remains as we have elaborated it together. Will you have a clean copy (or two) made? If however you want to show it to our Am^{can} Patron without loss of time you may let him [see] this copy (if you think it is advisable) but with the *severest* stipulation for its return as soon as read through. I *must* have it back when done with.

Mrs Bell has asked us to let her know when you are here. Her object in this I do not divine. Generally there is any amount of good will towards the house of Pinker, latent in Bourne House. Will you name the day R[alph] is coming to us. And won't you bring your boy to school yourself?

Love from Jessie and myself to Mrs Pinker, to yourself and to the Children of the House.

Ever Yours

J Conrad.

PS Thanks for everything done.

---

¹ Of 'Gaspar the Strong Man'.

To J. B. Pinker

Text MS Berg (incomplete); Unpublished

[Oswalds]

Sunday. 31.10.20.

Dearest J. B.

Great thanks for the Hall's* book.[1] It is a charming edition. The one I lost was quite different and nothing so fascinating as this in form.

I have read with care the D. P & C° letter and your notes thereon. I can not supplement the information you give. The transactions in which you had no part date such a long time back (and I had so little to say to them, as the publishers did what they liked) that they have by now escaped my recollection completely.

To J. B. Pinker

Text MS Berg; Unpublished

[Oswalds]

1 Nov. 20

My dearest Pinker.

You'll think I am making too much fuss – but since sending you my last I have heard that Col. Bell would be very glad (in case you should be here) if you would come with R[alph] yourself to see him sometime about six on Friday – the idea being that R. should begin work on Monday – this day week.

It looks as tho' he wanted to receive him from your hands. I fancy he wants you to hear what he has to say to R. It is *he* (not I) who is fussy a bit. His fixed idea is that he wants *help* and that R should give it to him.

[*Cancelled paragraph:*] Anyway R may have a couple of days longer at home. Suppose you both arrive on Thurs – for dinner? Or if it suits you better Friday *for lunch* – that is if with the reduced Rwy service[2] you can manage to catch the 10.45 from Vic.

Yours Ever

J Conrad.

---

[1] To the degree it has been reconstructed, Conrad's library offers three possibilities: Captain Basil Hall, *Extracts from a Journal written on the Coasts of Chili, Peru, and Mexico in the Years 1820, 1821, and 1822* (1824); Harry R. Hall, *Ancient History of the Near East, from the Earliest Times to the Battle of Salamis* (1913); and Kate M. Hall, *Notes on the Natural History of Common British Animals* (1913). Captain Hall's book seems the likeliest.

[2] On 25 October the National Union of Railwaymen decided to walk out in sympathy with the striking National Union of Miners. The strike ended on 4 November, with full services resuming on the 8th.

PS If our Film friend requires a few pp of *detailed* description – faces – dresses – scenery – I could of course furnish him with them, up to a certain point.

I am always ready to see him here if desired – or in town. "Anything for a quiet life!"[1]

PS Your wire received this moment. I let this letter go and take everything back except the Bell request.

To Thomas J. Wise

Text TS/MS BL Ashley 2953; J-A, 2, 249–50 (in part)[2]

[letterhead: Oswalds]
Nov. 1st. 1920.

My dear Mr Wise.

I have now finished working at the Film play and can tell you something of what that item will look like.

It consists: *First*, of a Manuscript composed of 175 leaves numbered in red pencil 1 to 168, and with seven more, interpolated in their proper place, and numbered 87A to 87G. Of these leaves the two first are written in black pencil, and there are eight others, about the middle of the MS, written in blue pencil. All the rest are in pen and ink; and the whole is written on two kinds of paper: thin from p 1 to p 109 incl., and thick from p 110 to the end.

This MS is the complete summary scenario of the Film Play entitled THE STRONG MAN, and is of course from beginning to end written in my own hand. It is in no sense a collection of notes, but a consecutive development of the story in a series of descriptions, just as the whole thing presented itself to me when I first began to think the subject out in its purely visual aspect. Such a line of composition being perfectly novel to me, I found it necessary to write it all down so as to have the whole thing embodied in a definite shape, before I could attempt to elaborate it into a detailed presentation for the reading of the Films' Literary Editor.

Second: from that MS I went on then to dictate a more detailed and final version into a typescript numbering 81 pages, of which every one contains slight modifications and corrections in pen and ink in my own handwriting. That TS has been marked "First Copy" and together with the MS described above gives the whole process of conception and composition of my first (and perhaps my last) Film Play. It is based on the story called "Gaspar Ruiz" (*Set of Six*, 1908).

---

[1] The title of Thomas Middleton and John Webster's comedy of 1621.
[2] Jean-Aubry stops at '(*Set of Six*, 1908)'.

I suggest you should pay me for the item – that is the MS and TS together – 100 gs.

I must tell you that from the "First Copy" two copies (T.S.) are being made, but those will be *clean copies* and will contain no corrections in pen and ink, unless of mere misprints, and these, if any, will not be corrected by me. I will keep one for a record in my possession, at any rate for a time, and the other copy, if accepted by the Literary Reader, who is now in England, will be sent off to the United States and put into the hands of the so-called Continuity Writer who will, so I am told, prepare a version for the use of the Producer; a version, I suppose, which will contain a minute description of dresses, landscapes, and so forth, as to which I have in my author's version given only general guiding suggestions.

The MS itself is now in my possession.

The TS is with my agent now for the making of the two clean copies of which I have spoken above. I have sent instructions for its careful preservation and prompt return to me. I suppose it will be a matter of a week.

I received yesterday the repr^{on} of the portrait[1] (excellent) and the Quinn letter which I return here. I have the cuttings of the newspaper in question.[2] I am dear Mr Wise, with kind regards from us both,

Always sincerely Yours

J. Conrad.

PS On second thoughts I will send you this ev^g (by reg^d post) the MS for your inspection, without waiting for the return of the "First Copy" (T.S.).

To Edward Garnett

Text MS Virginia; G. 298

[letterhead: Oswalds]

8.11.20

Dearest Edward.

I was laid up with very beastly gout when your letter arrived. It seems to me I heard something of that copy.[3] Perhaps Hodgson[4] has sent me the cat^{gue}?

---

[1] Conrad's photograph used as the frontispiece to Wise's *Bibliography*.

[2] See Conrad's letter to Quinn of 2 March, an extract from which appeared in the *New York Tribune* of 5 April 1920. Wise was gathering material for his Conrad bibliography.

[3] According to Garnett, a copy of *An Outcast of the Islands* that he had given to a physician.

[4] J. E. Hodgson, the dealer in rare books and manuscripts.

I wondered what it was really but did not hit on the "medical" solution.[1] I remember now the man very well.

The news of you thinking of a novel is great news. Do, my dearest Edward, do give it an honest trial and who knows! Perhaps it will grip you. As to you getting a hold on it to some purpose I have no doubt of it whatever. I accept the title provisionally (for purposes of reference only) because it is too literal – too explicit – too much of a definition. – You perceive I have sat at your feet, don't you?

But you may call it what you like even An Angel's Tears (an Angel would naturally weep over a fool)[2] and have my excited blessing in any case. Don't be afraid of being rough and of being exquisite. You are quite capable of blending both these strains. You are! And let "all thy words bear the accent of heroic truth"[3] properly seasoned by malice. But before everything switch off the critical current of your mind and work in darkness – the creative darkness which no ghost of responsibility will haunt.

All our loves

Ever Yours

J. Conrad

To G. Jean-Aubry
Text MS Yale; *L.fr.* 160–1

[letterhead: Oswalds]
8.11.20

Très cher.

Pardonnez de ne pas avoir écrit aussitôt le reçu de Votre bonne lettre. J'ai été au lit et très déprimé par une legère attaque de goutte.

Je me suis permis de faire une ou deux petites corrections of* texte français de la préface pour La Flêche en Or.[4] Mais en vérité je suis enchanté de la traduction. Vous avez rendu cela admirablement.

---

[1] The physician being Albert Edward Tebb (1863–1943)? In the early 1900s, he was family doctor to several literary and artistic families, including the Hueffers, Rothensteins, and Conrads; after the war, his finances became precarious. See Martin Bock, *Conrad and Psychological Medicine* (Lubbock: Texas Tech University Press, 2002), pp. 44–53, 213. In 1919, Conrad tried to help Tebb sell part of his art collection: *Letters*, 6, pp. 481–2.

[2] Cf. 'man, proud man . . . / Plays such fantastic tricks before high heaven / As makes the angels weep', Shakespeare, *Measure for Measure*, 2.2.117–19. Conrad quotes the line in *Lord Jim* (ch. 9). Garnett's novel came to naught.

[3] Not a quotation but a rendering of an idea in Marcus Aurelius' *Meditations*, III, 121. Conrad also cites it in 'A Familiar Preface' to *A Personal Record*.

[4] Published as *La Flêche d'or*.

Je ne sais pas si je réussirai a venir a Londres avant Votre départ. J'en doute fort. Si Vous trouvez un jour libre – ou même une soirée vous n'avez qu'a envoyer une [carte] pour dire Votre train. Je n'ose pas insister mon cher – mais Vous savez que Vous voir est toujours une joie pour moi et que tout le monde ici a une vraie affection pour Vous.

Aussitôt Votre article fini je vais me mettre a la traduction.[1] P[inker] est enchanté de l'idée.

A vous de coeur

J. Conrad

PS Madame Jessie s'en va-t'en guerre[2] – non, a Londres, Lundi prochain et d'après ce qu'elle m'en dit on ne verra qu'elle dans les rues de la Capitale pendant une semaine au moins. Quand a moi je reste ici – avec le jeune Pinker qui vient recommencer sa carrière agricole sous l'oeil bienveillant du Colonel Bell.

Translation

My dear friend.

Pray forgive me for not having written on receiving your good letter. I was laid up and very depressed by a slight attack of gout.

I made a correction or two to the French version of the Author's Note to *The Arrow of Gold*. But I am delighted with the translation. You pulled it off admirably.

I don't know if I'll manage to get to London before you leave. I rather doubt it. If you have a day free, or even an evening, you need only send a [note] indicating your train. I dare not insist, my dear, but you know that seeing you always makes me happy and that everybody here is genuinely fond of you.

As soon as your article is finished I will get down to the translation. P. is delighted with the idea.

Affectionately yours

J. Conrad

PS Mrs Jessie is off to the wars – no, in London, next Monday, and from what she tells me, there'll be eyes for no one but her in the streets of the capital for a week at least. As for myself, I am staying here – with young Pinker

---

[1] Conrad translated his 'Joseph Conrad's Confessions', which appeared in the *Fortnightly Review* in May 1921 (115, 782–90).

[2] A whimsical echo of the children's song about the Duke of Marlborough, 'Malbrouck s'en va-t'-en guerre'.

who is going to start his agricultural career again under the genial eye of
Colonel Bell.

To G. Jean-Aubry
Text MS Yale; Unpublished

[letterhead: Oswalds]
[8 November 1920][1]

Très cher
  C'est entendu. Le car sera a la station 12.45.
  Je me réjouis a l'idée d'une bonne causerie. Bien content que le Merimée
a produit son effet.

Tout à Vous

J. Conrad

Translation

My very dear friend
  Agreed. The motor-car will be at the station at 12.45.
  I rejoice at the prospect of a good chat. Very glad the Merimée piece has
had an impact.

Yours truly

J. Conrad

To J. B. Pinker
Text MS Berg; Unpublished

[Oswalds]
9.11.20

Dearest J. B.
  Please pay in £110 to my acct so that I may settle up with some people.
Under another envelope[2] Miss H[allowes] is sending In^me Tax & Sup. Tax
papers.
  The corr^d *clean type* will be posted to-night in still another envelope. (Film)
It may be that *your* copy is complete – but in the carbon copy I have, a lot of
red text has been left in blank! We want the man to get a good impression on
his first reading – don't we?
  All the sheets of *Ltd Ed* (760 + 5) – and of the *Preface book* (250 + 5) have
been signed, packed and posted from Canterbury P. O. direct to Garden
City. U.S.A. yesterday 6 p.m. (8th Nov).

[1] Date in Jean-Aubry's hand. If correct, Conrad presumably received a telegram from Aubry
  after writing his letter of the same date.
[2] The choice of preposition is a Gallicism.

There is *now* for me nothing more to sign except the 250 pages of the Eng^{sh} Book of Prefaces[1] when Hein[emann] has got them over for his edition.

What follows is not to worry you but to be answered at your leisure.

Seeing that now my signatures for his edition are secure and all the "Author's notes" delivered could you ask D. P. & C° to pay say $3,500 by a draft in favour of B[orys] Conrad on account of the agreed sum. He may charge a small interest up to the date of the first agreed payment, of course.

R[alph] was detained late by the Col yesterday studying books on lime. Very exciting. I think this thing will work.

Our love to you

Ever Yours

J. Conrad

To J. B. Pinker

Text MS Berg; Unpublished

[Oswalds]

Wednesday [10 November 1920][2]

Dearest J. B.

Please let B[orys] have £5. He's in town to see Dr Mac and get some things for me.

Many thanks for your kindness in sending the two books which have reached me this mor^{ng}.

Ever Yours

J. Conrad.

To R. D. Mackintosh

Text MS Alberta; Jellard

[letterhead: Oswalds]

11. Nov. 20

My dear Mackintosh.

Borys came home very much impressed with what he had seen in your place.[3] As to Borys's father and mother they would be more than delighted if you would give him a trial and see whether he can be any use to you at your works in Putney.

---

[1] *Notes on My Books*, for which Conrad signed the contract on 4 November (Hallowes).

[2] The letter to Mackintosh of the 11th fixes the date.

[3] Mackintosh's factory making wireless telegraphy equipment.

B says that you would like to talk things over with me. Will you then name a day on which I could come over. I would suggest that we meet in town and lunch together. Of my interest in what you may have to say you cannot doubt and I repeat that we would be very much gratified if you could give B something to do.

He has a great regard and I may say affection for you. His interest in your activities is very great. I know he would work for you better than for any other man – but as to his capacity I can say nothing as I have never had an opportunity to form an opinion.

Jessie has a very heavy cold and her visit to London is put off for a week – till the 21 inst. Is it too much to hope you can find time to run down here before then and stay the night. It will be a great pleasure for us both. Pray drop us a line. Our love to you

Yours ever

J Conrad

To Eric Pinker
Text MS Berg; Unpublished

[letterhead: Oswalds]
11. Nov.'20

My dear Eric.

Thanks for your letter. I know the magazine. The difficulty is that 4–5 thou. words is not my length. I don't think I ever wrote anything so short as that.[1] And then he doesn't say (in his letter to me) when he wants the thing delivered. However I suppose I must answer him myself. Perhaps you would write too and give him a hint that I am too busy (which is the truth) with things in hand to be able to make any promises. Our regards.

Yours

J. Conrad

To Hugh Dent
Text MS BL Egerton 3247, f. 11; Unpublished

[letterhead: Oswalds]
12.11.'20

My dear Mr Hugh.[2]

I am glad to have a word about the Chief. I was wondering how he was getting on. I do hope Bath will do him good!

---

[1] Anything fictional, that is; some of his essays are that short.

[2] Hugh Railton Dent (1874–1938), Dent's eldest son, spent his professional life in the family publishing house, J. M. Dent & Sons, joining it in 1909. He took over the running of the firm as his father entered his last years and became its head on 'The Chief's' death. Interested in classical music, 'Mr Hugh', as Conrad called him, also sang.

I shall be glad to meet Mr Ernest Rhys,[1] but I am not likely to be in town before this next Thursday week. Do you think he would care to run down here for the night (by 3 o'clock from Char +) or the day (by 10.45 Vic) in the course of next week. We would be very glad to see him here.

Mrs C sends her kindest regards (in a very hoarse voice). She has caught a beastly cold. Otherwise she is getting on and contemplates rushing to town (on the 21 of this month) in order to paint it red. I have nothing to do with this enterprise except that I've said I will pay for the paint.

Pray give our kindest regards to your wife and remember us to the Chief.

Yours sincerely

Joseph Conrad.

To Karola Zagórska
Text MS copy Yale;[2] Najder 264–5

[letterhead: Oswalds]
16.11.20.

Ma chère Karola[3]

Vous avez passé par des jours d'angoisse; heureusement votre carte pour Jessie qui vient d'arriver nous rassure. Je suis très content de savoir que vous êtes à la veille du départ pour l'Italie. Je vous prie ma chère enfant de me faire connaître votre adresse aussitôt que vous serez arrivée là-bas.

Oui, ma très chère, je sens que la vie et le travail en Italie vous feront du bien.[4] Si je trouve moyen d'amener Jessie dans le midi cet hiver on pourra peut-être se voir. Mais je ne sais pas encore si cela peut se faire. Enfin, nous verrons. Elle en a grande envie. Son état s'ameliore sensiblement – mais elle a été un moment menacée d'une bronchite – chose dont j'ai une peur atroce pour elle.

Je crois que Borys va s'établir sous peu à Londres où il trouvera une occupation avec un de mes amis qui a un considérable établissement pour la manufacture (expérimentale) d'appareils pour la télégraphie sans fil. Jean se présente la semaine prochaine à l'examen pour Tonbridge que est une "public-school" assez distinguée. J'espère qu'il passera. Quant à moi j'ai été

---

[1] A member of the Rhymer's Club, Ernest Rhys (1859–1946), a literary journalist involved in publishing, had founded Dent's Everyman Library in 1906.

[2] A transcription of the lost original, written in French.

[3] Karola Zagórska (*c.* 1885–1955), Aniela's sister, stayed at Oswalds from late February to late August 1920. The visit cemented Conrad's affectionate and active interest in her well-being and resulted in his paying her a regular allowance. A professional singer, she sometimes lived in Italy, and later in the United States where she sang in opera.

[4] She was threatened with tuberculosis and climate was thus a concern.

assez souffrant depuis trois semaines et j'ai dû même mettre au lit pour 3 jours. Je n'ai rien fait qui vaille depuis votre départ. Depuis le 10 sept. nous avons eu du beau temps mais dernièrement je n'ai pas pu en profiter car avec la goutte une toux atroce m'est venue et je n'osais pas sortir.

Dans le courant de la semaine prochaine je vais écrire à Angela et lui envoyer un document.[1] Pardonnez-moi ma chère de ne pas vous avoir écrit. J'ai beaucoup pensé à vous deux – mais je n'étais pas dans un très heureux état d'esprit et quand je suis comme cela il m'est impossible de toucher une plume. J'en ai horreur.

Jessie sends her love. Je vous embrasse toutes les deux de tout mon coeur.

Conrad.

Translation

My dear Karola

You have been through anguished days. Happily your note to Jessie, which just arrived, reassured us. I am very glad to hear that you are just about to leave for Italy. Pray let me have your address as soon as you get there, my dear child.

Yes, my dear, I feel life and work in Italy will do you good. If I find a way of taking Jessie to the South of France this winter, we might perhaps see each other. But I don't yet know if that will be possible. Anyway, we shall see. She would like it very much. Her health is noticeably improved, but at one point she was threatened with bronchitis – something I dread awfully for her.

I think Borys is going to set up in London soon, working for one of my friends who has a large establishment for the production (experimental) of wireless telegraphy equipment. Next week John sits the exam for Tonbridge, a rather distinguished 'public school'. I hope he will pass. As for myself, I haven't been well for three weeks and even had to take to bed for 3 days. I have done no work of any value since you left. Since September 10th we have had good weather, but I couldn't take advantage of it lately because a beastly cough came with the gout and I dared not go out.

In the course of next week I will to write to Angela and send her a document. Pray forgive me, my dear, for not writing to you. I have thought of both of you a great deal, but I wasn't in a very happy frame of mind and when I'm like that it is impossible to take up the pen. I have a horror of it.

Jessie sends her love. I kiss you both most affectionately.

Conrad.

---

[1] Transferring to her the Polish and Russian translation rights for Conrad's works.

To D. Appleton & Co.
Text MS Texas; Unpublished

[letterhead: Oswalds]
17.11.'20

Mr Joseph Conrad begs to thank Messrs D Appleton and Co for the copy of Mrs Wharton's book[1] they have been good enough to send him.

To Harriet Mary Capes
Text MS Yale; Unpublished

[letterhead: Oswalds]
17.11.'20

Dearest Harriet

You had my authorisation for the little book years ago and you knew what were my feelings on that matter then. No one else in the whole world would have had it – and to refuse *you* anything seems as unthinkable now as then.[2]

I've been gouty, seedy, crusty, moody, stupid, perverse, cynical and lame for the last few days. As to Mrs Jessie she had a cold lately but is now better and is preparing to go up on Monday to prance in town for a week or so. She's growing more active, restless, mischievious, independent débonnaire[3] outspoken, and generally Shakespearian, every day. Well! God be praised.

I don't think I will come up with her. I really don't feel well enough to face London, but I may go to spend 3–4 days with my friend J. B. Pinker in Surrey.

This year I have done no work worthy of the name – and I feel distinc[t]ly that I am *not* growing younger.

Love from all here. Always my dearest friend

your most affectionate and faithful
J. Conrad.

---

[1] Edith Wharton's *The Age of Innocence*, published in October.
[2] *Wisdom and Beauty from Conrad* selected by Miss Capes appeared in 1915. Conrad had given her permission the previous year (*Letters*, 5, p. 400). A reprint was now under discussion: see the letter to Eric Pinker of 19 November 1922.
[3] 'Mischievious': a facetious spelling by the late nineteenth century, but unremarkable in the seventeenth; 'débonnaire': although infrequent in English, the standard French spelling.

To J. B. Pinker
Text MS Berg; Unpublished

[letterhead: Oswalds]

17.11.'20

Dearest J. B.

Thank you for your letter from Burys Court. So far Max[1] has not given me an appointment but he is by his nature dilatory and I have no doubt I'll hear from him in a few days.

I am sending you here Aubry's article "englished" by J. Conrad; but for goodness sake keep this secret – don't let a whisper transpire! I have been most careful to disguise the Conradian style. It tried to creep in all the time. Please have two copies made (for, I hope, you'll try to place the thing in U.S. too) and send me back my own pages. It would be just as well if I looked through the 2 copies also, as misp[rin]*ts* are sure to creep in.—— Aubry has started on a lecturing tour (on Modern French Music) to Norway and Sweden. He came here to say goodbye. He has made up his mind to write a book (about the length of Curle's monograph) on J. C. to be ready about the end of the year. (?)[2] He will arrange for an English text (*not* a translation) and what he would like to know is whether you will handle it for him both in Eng? and in Am: His idea is to keep the French text back and give full priority to the Eng*sh*. Will you consider?—— I have still a swollen foot and have been feeling rotten. Jessie's cold is nearly gone. She will go to town on Monday. Suppose I turn up on Thursday? Would it suit you?—— And by the bye – can we get back the play (for Aubry to finish his translation) – say in a month's time? Thanks for the deed – and generally thanks for everything you do for me. I have only heard lately that Mrs C is making use of you as a courier to retain rooms in hotels for her and so on. Infernal cheek – but understand I wash my hands of the Lady and her impudence. I read with astonishment of your gaieties. Still, you were a small boy when I was a watch officer in the Southern seas and I must be hard on a youngster like you.

Ever Yours

J Conrad.

---

[1] Henry Maximilian ('Max') Beerbohm (1872–1956; knighted 1939), caricaturist, writer, and drama critic, made a caricature of Conrad before the year's end; see Conrad's letter to Harmsworth of 16 June 1921. Beerbohm's *A Christmas Garland* (1912) includes a memorable parody of Conrad's early manner.
[2] Nothing came of this project; Jean-Aubry's biography of Conrad did not appear till 1947.

To J. B. Pinker

Text MS Berg; J-A, 2, 250 (in part)[1]

[letterhead: Oswalds]
18.11.'20

Dearest J. B.

Thanks for your holograph received this morning. All this looks nice and hopeful and *is* cheering. I am absolutely at one with you as to giving McK[innel] all reasonable latitude. I am sorry that the S[ecret] A[gent] is to be 2[d] – not because I am impatient to see it on the boards but because the *previous* play's success (or failure), it seems to me, must be reflected in the judgment that will be pronounced on my first effort. I know how the minds of professional critics work. They live on comparisons, because that is the easiest method of appreciation. Whereas I hate them, even if made in my favour. This is a very private confidence which I impart to you who understand me now as well as I understand myself. That good friend Vernon's interest is also very gratifying to me. Tell him so please when occasion offers. I hope that he will be the producer and will be able to carry out *his* notions of the play's stage management, in which I have a great confidence.

So, after all, it is M[r] Verloc who appealed to McKinnel! So much the better; but I confess I thought it would have been Heat. I will even tell you (under the seal of secrecy) that I allowed myself to think how the part might have been written up more for him! You didn't think I was so full of McK – did you? Well I was! But I daresay you guessed how my heart was set on the play and my fancy taken up by the actor.

I am having a happy morning – but this is not a reason to take up your time with mere chatter. Jessie too is delighted and sends her love. She takes is* it all in a more calm way because, I believe, she is convinced that you can work miracles – in which case, of course, there is no reason to get excited – is there?

My foot is still swollen. Rhys (of Dent & Son) is coming this evening to talk over an article on J. C. which he is commissioned to write for an American Mag[ne].[2] I don't know which.

Ever affect[ly] yours

J. Conrad

---

[1] Jean-Aubry prints only the first paragraph.
[2] Rhys's 'An Interview with Joseph Conrad' appeared in *The Bookman* (New York) in December 1922 (56, 402–8). It is also available in Martin Ray. ed., *Joseph Conrad: Interviews and Recollections* (Macmillan, 1990), pp. 131–5.

To J. B. Pinker

Text MS Berg; Unpublished

[letterhead: Oswalds]
20.11.'20

Dearest J. B.

Herewith corr*ᵈ* copies of Aubry's article. I would be glad if you glance through it and tell me what you think. It's in some sort a sample [of] what his book on me is likely to be. Thanks for your promise to handle it eventually.

R[alph] has been working hard all day and looking contented in his evenings. I fancy he feels virtuous which is a very good thing for him.

By the time you look at this the Missus will be rolling towards town. If my beastly hoof is no worse you shall see me on Thursday.

I enclose Mac's letter. Unless I don't understand it looks as tho' he meant to associate permanently both the boys with his wireless enterprise. Anyway for B[orys] it will mean thorough training at first and management later.

I haven't seen Mac yet.

Our love to you both

Ever Yours

J Conrad

To Richard Curle

Text MS Indiana; Curle 72

[letterhead: Oswalds]
Monday. 22ᵈ Nov. 1920. 6. pm.

My dear Richard

We were much distressed be* the news of your illness. I am sorry you discovered the realism of my hospital scenes at your own cost.[1] Still there are worse places than tropical hospitals. I wonder if your cruise in the pilot-brig will set you up sufficiently for the trip up country. I am awaiting with anxiety your next letter if only a few words just to tell us how you are getting on.

Jessie is gone today to town for a week. This news will give you the measure of her improvement in general. In particular it means that she can walk about the house with both crutches with some facility and that she can get in and out of the car without too much trouble. My mind about her is much more at ease than it has been for the last 2 years and she herself is quite hopeful as to the future. Sir Robert will see her on Thursday in London and I will run up on that day to hear his verdict and then I'll proceed to Burys Court (Pinker) for the week end.

---

[1] Scenes such as those in *Lord Jim* (ch. 5) and *The Shadow-Line*.

We have had a most glorious dry weather since 1st Sepr. The last few days there was frost in the morning, all the slope of the Park being white till about 10 o'clock.

Did I tell you that I've finished all my Author's notes? I have even written the one for the Vol of *Life and Letters*. (next March). They are also to be pub^{d} in book form 250 cop. in Eng^{d} and as many in the US.[1] I will keep a copy for you. It will of course bring me a little money about £180 for the Eng^{sh} E^{d} and quite £200 for the US set. Every little bit counts. Money runs out like water! I am quite nervous. I *don't* get on with the novel.[2] The actual piece of news for this letter bears upon the play. (Secret Agent) Norman McKinnel has definitely accepted it.[3] He is now making his financial arrangements and intends to make it his *second* production. I would have preferred it to be the first. However! But the actor is good – he believes in the thing – he will no doubt put his back into the part (Mr Verloc) and so I have accepted these conditions. Nothing is signed yet tho'.

I have finished the film-play of G. Ruiz ("The Strong Man") – but as to its actual fate, Borys' prospects of entering a Wireless Manufacturing establishment (experimental work and inventions) and John's success in his entr^{ce} exam for Tonbridge these will be told you in my next.

I can't shake off the feeling of anxiety about you. I do hope it will occur to you to write soon. Mrs Iris[4] has been asking for news of you. Jessie is seeing her to-day. I can't tell you how delighted and excited I am at what you say about the post in London[5] which will enable you to settle in Eng^{d}. Can't you tell me what it is? I am a discreet person. All our loves.

Ever most affect^{ly} yours

Joseph Conrad.

To Thomas J. Wise

Text TS/MS Private collection;[6] Unpublished

[letterhead: Oswalds]

Nov. [1920][7]

Dear Mr Wise

Thank you very much for the interesting pamphlet you have been good enough to send me, which I have read with great interest.[8]

---

[1] *Notes on My Books*, published by Doubleday on 4 March and by Heinemann on 19 May 1921.
[2] *Suspense*.
[3] In the end he abandoned his plans, and the play was produced by J. Harry Benrimo.
[4] Iris Wedgwood, who had met Conrad through Curle. For a letter to her, see 7 July 1922.
[5] With the *Daily Mail*.   [6] Mounted on the back of a photograph.
[7] The month is legible, but the day is not. News of Curle's illness points to the end of the month.
[8] Wise produced fifteen Ashley Library pamphlets in 1920, including works by Charlotte Brontë, Swinburne, E. J. Trelawney, and Robert Browning.

My wife sends her kind regards. We had a letter from Curle who was ill with fever but is better now.

Yours sincerely,

Joseph Conrad

To J. B. Pinker
Text MS Berg; Unpublished

[Oswalds]

Tuesday. 5 pm. [23 November 1920][1]

Dearest J. B.

I've just heard from Jessie that Mac is coming to lunch with her (and to meet me) on Thursday. We would then talk over Borys's case exhaustively. B is immensely keen.

I will come up in the car – for I am still lame tho' improving every day. I shall try to be in your office about 12 o'clock and then shall go on to Dover St.[2] I've suggested to B to lunch out somewhere so that Mac can talk freely with Jessie and me.

If you care to run to Burys Court by road we could start at 3.30 (probably) from Dover St or I could call for you after the conference with Mac.

Anyway You and I will have plenty of time to talk this and some other matters over during the week-end.

I have made a move with the novel.

Ever Yours

J. Conrad

PS Please settle this for me

To Jessie Conrad
Text MS Yale; *JCLW* 51–2

[letterhead: Oswalds]

Tuesday 5.30 [23 November 1920][3]

Dearest Kitty.

Thanks for your wire. I had a good report of the journey from Long Charley.[4] Nevertheless on opening my eyes this morning and not feeling you in the next room I began to worry a little. I will be glad to get a few lines of your handwriting to-morrow morning.

[1] The letter to Mackintosh below fixes the date.
[2] I.e., to Brown's Hotel, Conrad's favourite during this period.
[3] *JCLW* places the letter in 1921. The preceding letter to Mackintosh fixes the date.
[4] Charles Roberts Vinten (born 1900), the Conrads' chauffeur, was 6ft 3in tall.

It was funny going upstairs to bed in the empty house last evening (11 o'clock). The Eaton Colonel[1] turned up about 7 and I asked him to share our dinner, which he did and then we had a game of chess. He's a bore.

Kitty! – I don't like you being out of the house, and that's a fact.

You are a dear, charming, precious, sweet delightful and ever-so-good girl to have arranged with Mac for Thursday (and for other reasons too). I suggest B[orys] should lunch out on that day and perhaps drop in later. Mac must be given full opportunity to say freely what he has to say. However you had better decide all that. I can always get in touch with Mac as to hard facts by letter. So exercise your tact and wisdom on the point and tell B what to do.

I've done a little work this morning and got through a lot of thinking. Foot is better – got Jaeger boots on both feet today.[2] But not to have you or even B or anything that is mine about is *not* nice. What *is* nice is to think that you may have a little good time. Last night I woke up sure I had heard you coughing. Asino boy.[3] I hope you will have the sense to tell me about the cough in the letter I expect to-morrow morning. Don't do crazy things please. Love to B[orys]. Many thousands kisses to yourself.

> Ever your most devoted in heart and mind
> Conrad.

PS. My regards to the Audrey-child.[4]
PPS You'll send John his chess board – won't you?

To R. D. Mackintosh

Text MS Alberta; Jellard

> [letterhead: Oswalds]
> 23.11.20

Dearest Mac.

I've just heard from Jessie that we are to meet at lunch at Brown's Hotel on Thursday.

We are most anxious that B[orys] should be with you and the boy himself is very keen. If you will give him an opening he will get enough from me to live on (modestly) while he's learning the technical part and till he becomes

[1] Lt-Colonel W. A. Eaton, who had served with the East Kents on the North-West Frontier of India and in Nigeria and South Africa.
[2] Boots made of the heavy but breathable fabric devised by Gustav Jaeger, who gave his name to the 'sanitary Woollen System'. Victims of gout, such as Conrad, found them more comfortable than leather.
[3] 'Asi no, boy' – pidgin Spanish for 'we can't have that'.
[4] Audrey (Etheldreda Maud Victoria) Seal, Jessie Conrad's nurse-companion, was in her thirties. When she married Charles Vinten in 1923, the certificate gave her age as thirty-six.

worth something to you. He has also £1000 of his own (not paid over yet) and the income from that say £50 will help him through.

I tell you this so that you should know how he stands as to means. I can't tell you how deeply touched I am by your friendship for us and your more than kind thought for our boys. A prospect of going to work with you will, I am sure, be a great incentive for John to work well in school.

Both of them have always had a very real affection for you.

Always my dear Mac affectionately Yours

Joseph Conrad.

To André Gide

Text MS Doucet; *NRF* 111–12; Putnam

[letterhead: Oswalds]

1.11 [30 November?]. 20[1]

Mon cher ami,[2]

Mille fois merci pour Votre bonne lettre et pour le petit volume[3] dont je vais couper les pages précieuses ce soir "dans le silence de mon cabinet"[4] et dans la paix de la maison ou tout le monde sera couché – "to sleep, perchance to dream".[5] Pour moi c'est l'heure pour les livres d'amis.

Ma femme s'imaginait que nous étions tombés en disgracc puisque Vous avez été en Angleterre sans venir nous voir.[6] Je l'ai rassuré de mon mieux et elle Vous envoie ses amitiés avec prière de ne pas recommencer. On m'a gâté cette femme completement. Elle a passé la semaine dernière a Londrcs pour célébrer son retour a la vie perpendiculaire. Tout le monde lui a fait fête de sorte qu'elle s'imagine être une personne de consequence et telle qui peut parler à André Gide d'une façon familière. Enfin mon cher après

---

[1] Jean-Aubry read '11' as 'II' and dated the letter 1 February. Conrad completed his Author's Notes only in autumn 1920, and Jessie Conrad's London visit began on 22 November. Vidan (1970–1), 533, n. 20, suggests 1 December, but Conrad's specific mention of December rather than 'this month' suggests that the month had not turned and '11' is thus given greater weight.

[2] Of all the literary friends of Conrad's later years, André-Paul-Guillaume Gide (1869–1951) was the most distinguished and most artistically remarkable. A born-again pagan and a recidivist puritan, his strengths lay in intimate autobiography and ironic fiction. Among his works are *Les Nourritures terrestres* (1897), *L'Immoraliste* (1902), *La Porte étroite* (1909), *Les Caves du Vatican* (1914), and *Les Faux-monnayeurs* (1926). He first met Conrad in July 1911, translated *Typhoon*, directed the other translations of his work into French, and dedicated *Voyage au Congo* (1928) to his memory.

[3] Gide's letter of 25 November (Stape and Knowles, pp. 165–6) and *La Symphonie Pastorale* (1919).

[4] A French (and English) commonplace at that time. For example: 'apportant, dans le silence de mon cabinet de travail, sa gaieté juvenile' (Maurice LeBlanc, *L'Arrestation d'Arsène Lupin*, 1907).

[5] *Hamlet* 3.1.65.   [6] Gide had been in England and Wales during the summer.

trois ans de souffrance, 3 operations majeures et trois incisions – elle marche, avec les bequilles encore mais avec la certitude de pouvoir les rejeter bientôt. C'est un retour a la vie pour elle – et a vrai dire pour moi aussi. Depuis 1917 j'ai vécu dans une espèce de cauchemar perpetuel dont je ne voyais pas la fin.

Je viens mon cher d'inscrire Votre nom chez Heinemann pour qu'ils Vous envoient un "set" de l'édition limitée (750 sets) de mes oeuvres en 18 vols. Ils commenceront a paraitre en Dec*re* je pense. De cette edition limitée anglaise (car il y en aura une en Amerique aussi) je me suis resérvé six "sets" dont trois pour ma famille et trois pour les amis – dont Vous êtes un. Les autres sont Edward Garnett – qui a accepté mon premier livre quand il lisait pour Fisher Unwin[1] (1895) et Sir Robert Jones l'ami et le chirurgien distingué qui a mené a bonne fin la guérison de ma femme.

Je suis très, mais très content de la traduction de Western Eyes.[2] Je vais écrire un petit mot a M. Neel pour le remercier.

Cette année ci, je n'ai rien fait que revoir et établir le texte definitif pour l'edition limitée et ecrire quelques petites préfaces. Ma santé n'est pas bonne mais j'y suis habitué. Croyez moi toujours mon cher Gide

Votre très devoué.

Joseph Conrad

Translation

My dear friend,

Many thanks indeed for your good letter and for the little book whose precious pages I will cut tonight 'in the silence of my study' in a peaceful house where everybody has gone to bed. 'To sleep, perchance to dream'. For me, that is the moment for friends' books.

My wife thought we had fallen out of favour since you came to England without coming to see us. I did my best to reassure her, and she sends you her regards along with a plea not to do it again. That woman has been thoroughly spoiled for me. She spent the past week in London to celebrate her return to perpendicular life. Everybody pampered her so she now thinks of herself as a person of consequence and thus someone on familiar terms with André Gide. Well, my dear, after three years of suffering, 3 major operations, and three incisions, she still walks on crutches but with the certainty of doing without them soon. It is a return to life for her – and, truth to say, for me as

---

[1] Garnett had worked as a reader for Unwin until the end of 1899.
[2] Philippe Neel's recently published translation, entitled *Sous les yeux d'occident*.

well. Since 1917, I have lived in a kind of unending nightmare whose end I couldn't see.

I have, my dear, just put down your name at Heinemann's so that they will send you a set of the limited edition (750 sets) of my work in 18 volumes. Heinemann will, I think, begin to publish in December. Out of the English limited edition (there will also be one in America) I have reserved six sets for myself, including three for my family and three for friends, among whom yourself. The others are Edward Garnett, who accepted my first book when he read for Fisher Unwin (1895), and Sir Robert Jones, the friend and distinguished surgeon who succeeded in bringing about my wife's recovery.

I am very, really very, pleased with the translation of *Western Eyes*. I am going to write Mr Neel a word of thanks.

During this year I have done nothing except revise and establish the definitive text of the limited edition and write some short prefaces. My health is not good but I'm used to that. Believe me always, my dear Gide,

Yours very devotedly

Joseph Conrad

To Elsie Hueffer

Text MS Yale; Unpublished

[letterhead: Oswalds]
29 [30?].11.20[1]

My dear Elsie[2]

I found your letter on my return home yesterday.[3]

We were under the impression that you did not care to keep up your relations with us any longer. You made it pretty clear as, since the spring of 1914 when my wife called on you last, you gave no sign of life of even of the most conventional "interest". Now, at the end of 1920, you say you want to resume relations as before. Without trying to discover your motives either then or now, we are convinced that no real regard or even mere superficial sympathy could possibly have had anything to do with them – either then or

---

[1] If Conrad returned to Oswalds on Monday, as he mentions to Pinker on the 30th, his date is wrong.

[2] Elizabeth ('Elsie') Hueffer (née Martindale, 1876–1949) married Ford Madox Ford in 1894. Her translations of Maupassant appeared in 1903, and she published fiction as Elizabeth Martindale. After the quarrels of 1909, the Conrads kept their distance from her. She was separated from Ford but refused to give him a divorce.

[3] From Burys Court, where he had been staying with Pinker.

now. Therefore you will not think it strange if I venture to suggest, with all deference, that things should be left as they are.

Yours obediently

Joseph Conrad.

To R. D. Mackintosh
Text MS Alberta; Jellard

[letterhead: Oswalds]
30.11.20.

My dear Mac.

Pray drop me a line to say whether I may *definitely* turn up in* the Bungalow on Sat: about noon and carry you off to lunch in town before we catch the train for here, where we hope you will be able to stay a full week-end.

We are all looking forward to your visit in* this our latest home. J. B. Pinker will be here too and I should like very much you two to know each other.

Ever affectly yours

Joseph Conrad.

To J. B. Pinker
Text MS Berg; Unpublished

[letterhead: Oswalds]
Tuesday. [30 November 1920][1]

Dearest J. B.

We arrived at 3.30 yesterday and glad enough to get out of the weather, which, at 30–35 miles p.h., was not really nice. We are settled down now, and the flurry being over we miss the warmth and spaciousness of Burys Court literally and figuratively speaking. Give my grateful love to our infinitely kind hostess. Jessie I believe is writing by this post. R[alph] after gathering patiently all the "many happy returns" thrown at this head this morning, went off to lunch with the shooters being invited thereto by the only Colonel.[2] Joy reigns in B'bourne the disease of the late lamented cow being not anthrax but some other dam' thing. Everybody is bucked and so am I for to tell you the truth I didn't like the boy being mixed up with such an infernal thing.

Upon consideration:- why should we not put off the Little The*re* exp[editi]on till next week, you of course coming here on Saturday next

---

[1] Dated by the excursion to Burys Court.   [2] His employer, Colonel Bell.

as arranged all the same. Mrs C says you wouldn't be shocked if I did not arrive (with Mac) till after your arrival. I must go and fetch Mac as otherwise I fear he will be "detained."

Just got the agreement of SA. and have done what you ask. Please pay £100 into my acct.

The D. P & C° parcel of proof[1] shall be attended-to immediately.

Ever affct[ly] yours

J. Conrad.

To [?]

Text MS Morgan; Unpublished

[letterhead: Oswalds]

1.12.20

My dear Sir,[2]

The photograph in question was taken by an amateur photographer of genius (I have a wonderful head of my wife taken by him too) who I fear is dead now – and his plates must have perished with him in the whirlwind of war.

The photograph was taken in the dining-room of the lady (a very distant relation of mine – also no longer in this world) with whom we were staying in Zakopane at the outbreak of the war.[3] The date is late Sep[t]. 1914. I don't look like that now. The years of war have counted double for many of us. Of course you may reproduce the portrait.

Your letter arrived this morning and this will be posted this afternoon, too late, I fear, for the Wed. packet. But it will catch the Saturday ship for certain.

Best wishes and regards

Yours

Joseph Conrad.

---

[1] For the collected edition? Pinker would not yet have had Russell Doubleday's letter of the 23rd (TS Berg) with the welcome news that, since the Regular and De Luxe editions were printed from the same plates, Conrad would only have to face one set of proofs.

[2] Unidentified: perhaps one of Doubleday's employees assembling pictures for the collected edition, or a magazine editor working against a deadline.

[3] Conrad's relative by marriage, Aniela Zagórska (née Unrug), who owned the *pension* Konstantynówka. The close-up photograph of Jessie and Borys Conrad reproduced in *Joseph Conrad As I Knew Him* and *My Father Joseph Conrad* probably dates from the same session.

To J. B. Pinker
Text MS Berg; Unpublished

[letterhead: Oswalds]

1.12.20.

Dearest friend

I have just wired to you. I am determined to get there to-morrow but the foot is very untrustworthy and I had better rush back home after the performance.[1]

You have a great talent for making life interesting, and it would be most ungrateful of me not to respond – as long as there is breath in the body – to all the surprises You may think fit to spring on me. This time even Jessie lost her stolidity for a time and yelled to me from her room: "You must go!!!" She sends her love

Ever Yours

J. C.

PS. Orchard returned me this cheque. I have sent him one of my own. Please pay in the amount to my acct instead.

To J. B. Pinker
Text MS Berg; Unpublished

[Oswalds]

Thursday [2 December 1920?][2]

My dear Pinker

Will you pay B[orys] his £8 for this month and also an extra fiver to pay his expenses of this trip to town for me?

He will tell you all the news.

Ever Yours

J. Conrad.

---

[1] From a matinée at the Little Theatre (the goal of the 'expedition' proposed on the 30th) of Jose Levy's London Grand Guignol Season: H. F. Maltyby's *What Did her Husband Say?* and Pierre Mille and Cilia de Vylars' *The Medium* featured Russell and Sybil Thorndike and Lewis Casson. For Conrad's motive in going, see the letter of 10 December.

[2] Catalogued as from December 1920. The request for Borys Conrad's allowance makes an early date likely. Conrad's visit to town on the 2nd, if it came off, seems, however, to be the visit referred to (see the previous letter), but he was also due up to see Mackintosh on the 4th (see the letter of 30 November). The 2nd may not be reliable since the requests, unless they were afterthoughts, could have been made in person.

To G. Jean-Aubry

Text MS Yale; *L.fr.* 161–2

[letterhead: Oswalds]
10.12.20.

Mon très cher.

Merci de vos deux cartes – et voulez-vous faire un besomanos (on peut dire cela – n'est-ce pas?) a Mme Alvar, de ma part, pour ses gracieux messages. Mes felicitations sur ses succès. Je suis heureux de vous savoir content de votre voyage et de votre reception dans les "regions boréales".

Pinker me prie de vous dire qu'il sera "très heureux (very glad) d'avoir votre livre (projété) sur J. C. confié a ses soins en Ang^{rre} et en Amerique".

Depuis la traduction de votre article[1] je n'ai rien fait qu'un drame pour Le Grand Guignol (anglais) 2 actes, 3 tableaux. ça se jouera en 40 minutes. Sujet: Laughing Anne (Because of the Dollars)[2] – Du reste cela c'est fait tout seul, pour ainsi dire, – et j'en suis tout ébahi encore.

Mrs C a passé une semaine a Londres a Browns Hotel – et pendant ce temps là Dover Street ne desemplissait pas.

Pendant ce temps aussi moi je vivais retiré a la campagne chez P[inker].

Au revoir cher. A bientôt. Envoyez-moi un petit mot dés votre retour

A vous de coeur

J. Conrad.

Translation

My very dear friend.

Thanks for your two notes and would you kindly kiss the hand (one can say that, can't one?) of Madame Alvar from me for her gracious messages. My congratulations on her successes. I am glad to hear you are pleased with your journey and reception in the 'Boreal regions'.

Pinker asks me to tell you that he will be 'very happy to have your (projected) book on J. C. confined to his care in England and America'.

---

[1] See the letter to Jean-Aubry of 8 November.

[2] Named in honour of Guignol, the rowdy star of French puppet plays, the original Théâtre du Grand Guignol opened in Paris in 1897 and soon became notorious for farces and melodramas featuring cuckoldry, madness, and sadistic terror. The Little Theatre's Guignol seasons, which ran until 1923, were a homage to the Parisian originals and caused much outrage. The London Underground banned its posters, and the censors at the Lord Chamberlain's office never tired of lopping the scripts. Double-bills were the norm, so the forty-minute running time of *Laughing Anne* was well suited to the needs of the house, as was the grotesque presence of the Man Without Hands.

Since translating your article I have done only a play for the Grand Guignol (English): 2 acts, 3 scenes. Acting time: 40 minutes. Subject: 'Laughing Anne' ('Because of the Dollars'). Moreover, that came of its own volition, so to speak, and I am still bowled over.

Mrs C spent a week in London at Brown's Hotel and during that time Dover Street was never empty.

During that time I lived in retirement in the country at P's.

Farewell, my dear. We shall see you soon. Drop us a line as soon as you return.

> Yours affectionately
>
> J. Conrad

To G. G. Frisbee

Text TS Haverford; Unpublished

> [letterhead: Oswalds]
> Dec. 13th. 1920.

Dear Mr Frisbee[1]

I cannot write to you in pen and ink because I am laid up.

Thank you very much for Mr Holliday's book,[2] which certainly has got a lot of good things in it and which I enjoyed greatly. You might point out to Captain Woodside that a cargo of pressed cotton bales doesn't shift. If he is a seaman in anything but name he will know that sort of cargo requires a certain amount of ballast; and the trouble with the "Narcissus" was that she had not enough ballast put into her. Not my fault, as I did not join her, coming overland from Madras to Bombay,[3] till the ground-tier was laid. His discrimination in the matter of my art is no better than his judgment of my seamanship, since it is obvious that I have done much better things than "Victory".

> Yours faithfully
>
> J Conrad.

---

[1] Tentatively identified as George Gordon Frisbee (1874–1949).

[2] Robert C(ortes) Holliday (1880–1947) was a popular belletrist. Several collections of his newspaper essays appeared around the time of this letter, among them *Walking-stick Papers* (1918), *Broome Street Straws* and *Peeps at People* (both 1919), and *Men and Books and Cities* (1920).

[3] In April 1884.

To W. T. H. Howe

Text MS Berg; Unpublished

[letterhead: Oswalds]

15.12.20

Dear Sir.¹

The impending amalgamation is most gratifying to my feelings of affectionate regard for each individual of that great mass of men, great in numbers, great in endurance and fidelity, great in achievement – and now knit together into one great Brotherhood-in-Arms.²

Words do not flow easily out of a full heart – and there are great facts which are best acknowledged in silence. But if you find anything *you* would like to print you are of course welcome to quote anything I have published.

Believe me very faithfully Yours

Joseph Conrad.

To R. D. Mackintosh

Text MS Indiana; Unpublished

Oswalds.

15.12.20.

My dear Mac.

Infinite thanks for your good letter and the medicine which has arrived safely.

The printed matter on the case does *not* say whether the "pituitary" is or is not included; but I suppose it is all right. I am taking 6 per day and propose keeping at it for 14 days.

B[orys] sends his love. Tammage³ being away he will stay on with us. In fact he will be busy getting the car ready for our long journey. It wants a few

---

¹ A publisher, William Thomas Hildrup Howe (1874–1939) headed the American Book Company of Cincinnati. He was also a noted collector of Americana, and early American glass, and eventually amassed one of the most distinguished rare book and manuscript collections in the USA. On his death, it was purchased by Albert A. Berg, from whom it eventually passed to the New York Public Library. He commissioned Theodore Spicer-Simson's medallion of Conrad.

² Plans to reorganise the US Army regulars, the National Guard, and reserves into a single effective force were afoot in 1920. Conrad's opening paragraph on this topic reads as if written for public consumption.

³ Apparently a friend of Borys, Tammage (or Tamage) had invested his savings in Mackintosh's company.

things done to it. B will come on the 2ᵈ Janʸ to you – and we shall come to town on the 20. John goes to Tonbridge on the 21st.

Love from everybody here.

Ever Yours

J Conrad

To Edward Garnett
Text MS Dartmouth; G. 299

[letterhead: Oswalds]
16 Dec. 1920

My dear Edward

I sent your name and address to Heinemann so that they should forward you direct your set of the Collᵉᵈ Edition, which, they say, is to begin to appear this month.[1]

It was nice and dear of you to go and see Jessie when she was in town. She was immensely pleased and told me that you were specially delightful that evening. She has a very strong sense of your personality – always had. Of course these things are obscure in her – yet the feeling is always perfectly genuine.

I have had the Cat: Nº 1. from Taviton Sᵗ. and am writing to ask for 2 or 3 items – and also to wish these young men[2] the best of luck.

I have been beastly invalidish these 2 months. I shall take Jessie out South in Jan. It may do me good too – but I doubt it. The Secret Agent (4 acts) has been taken by McKinnel. We shall see what comes of it. I have done nothing – can do nothing – don't want to do anything. One lives too long. Yet cutting one's throat would be too scandalous besides being unfair to other parties.

Xmas greetings.

Ever affectionately Yours

J. Conrad.

To André Gide
Text MS Doucet; Vidan 1970–1

[letterhead: Oswalds]
[mid-December 1920][3]

Mon cher Ami.

Je suis de Votre avis.[4] C'est très bien. Je me suis permis de corriger les *Verres à Bordeaux*.[5]

---

[1] The first volumes were just about to appear.
[2] David Garnett and Francis Birrell had set up a book shop at 19 Taviton Street, Gordon Square. See the letter of the 28th.
[3] Conrad's reply is to a letter from Gide of the 12th; see Stape and Knowles, pp. 165–6.
[4] About Philippe Neel's translation of *Under Western Eyes*.
[5] Claret glasses – a phrase that does not match anything in Conrad's novel.

Vers le 20 du mois prochain nous partons pour la Corse ou nous resterons
un mois ou deux. On dit beaucoup de bien du climat d'Ajaccio. J'espère
pouvoir travailler la-bas a mon roman du 1814. J'irai passer la nuit a l'ile
d'Elbe pour interroger l'ombre de Napoleon. Pensez Vous que Le Tondu[1]
m'accordera audience?

Nos meilleurs souhaits pour le bonheur et prospérité de tous ceux qui Vous
tiennent au coeur. Car enfin on n'est jamais heureux que dans les autres. Du
moins il me semble. –

Je Vous serre les deux mains et je suis toujours le Votre

J. Conrad.

Translation

My dear friend.

I agree with you. It is very good. I corrected *Verres à Bordeaux.*

Around the 20th of next month we are leaving for Corsica for a month
or two. Ajaccio's climate is well spoken of. I am hoping to work on my 1814
novel there. I shall spend a night on Elba to quiz Napoleon's ghost. Do you
think 'The Little Shaver' will grant me an audience?

Our best wishes for the happiness and prosperity of those dear to you.
Because in the end only others give one happiness. At least so it seems to
me. –

I give you a warm handshake and am ever yours

J. Conrad.

To William Rothenstein

Text MS Harvard; J-A, 2, 251 (in part); Rothenstein, 2, 370 (in part)[2]

[letterhead: Oswalds]

17.12.20.

Dearest Will.

Thanks ever so much for the admirable book of portraits.[3] Every one is
a revelation – especially of course those of the people one knows, if ever so
little. Of course I don't know many; but one has in all the sense of looking at
a final expression in art and psychology.

---

[1] Bestowed on him by his troops, Napoleon's affectionate nickname 'Le Petit Tondu' evokes a
newly shorn recruit.

[2] Jean-Aubry omits the last paragraph, Rothenstein the third and fifth paragraphs.

[3] *Twenty-Four Portraits, with Critical Appreciations by Various Hands.*

Thank you dear people for being good to Jessie when she was in town. I couldn't face the racket (!) of it. Perfectly ridiculous – but I can't help it. I don't know what to say to people when I do meet them. I came for a day, arriving late and leaving early.

I'll try to take Jessie south in Jany. She needs it, and it may do me good too – but I doubt it.

I have been writing a series of short prefaces for Heinemanns L^d. Ed: which will be published separately also in a 250 copies edition. I will send you a copy – not that the things are of any interest. I have done nothing for more than a year and feel as if I couldn't do anything. I'll try however to keep in the collar. One must.

My most affectionate wishes for the health and prosperity of you both and of your dear children – big and little.

Always yours

Joseph Conrad

To J. B. Pinker
Text MS Berg; Unpublished

[letterhead: Oswalds]

Monday [20 December 1920?][1]

6 pm.

My dear Pinker

The boys[2] are flying about somewhere (with a General) and the house is quiet. My troubles for the day are over – too.

Jessie says You would give us a long week-end out of Your holiday. If you do that You will be a fine fellow, a man of Sense and Sensibility, a great character and in short "a perfect Gentleman".

Oh! for really warm weather so that we could sit lazily outside and exchange sagacious remarks in drowsy tones!

I dare say I'll see you in town soon when you will give me no doubt some idea of your plans. Poor Ralph had a rough life of it here – but he will tell you all about it.

My love to you all

Yours ever

J Conrad.

---

[1] Ralph Pinker's stay at Oswalds and the upcoming holidays suggest the period. If Pinker's visit on Saturday the 4th came off (see the letters of 30 November), Monday the 6th would be precluded, whereas on the 13th Conrad claimed to be unable to write.

[2] Borys Conrad and Ralph Pinker.

To Catherine Willard
Text MS Colgate; Unpublished

[letterhead: Oswalds]
Wednesday [22 December 1920][1]

Dearest C.[2]

You are the nicest child!

Play finished.[3] Let us know your train on Sat as soon as you can.

Our united love to you both.

Yours

J. Conrad

To R. B. Cunninghame Graham
Text MS Dartmouth; J-A, 2, 251–2; Watts (1969) 190

[letterhead: Oswalds]
23.12.20

Très cher ami.

What to me – an old friend for whom your prose (with your poetry) and your friendship, have been an inherent part of daily existence for so many years – seems most wonderful in the Carthagena* book[4] is its inextinguishable vitality, the unchanged strength of feeling, steadfastness of sympathies and force of expression. I turned the pages with unfailing delight (only regretting that there were so few of them) recognising at every turn the eye, the voice, the hand of the Captive of Kintafi.[5] As to the soul You and I cher ami, are too honest to talk of what we know nothing about. Still, after all these years, I think I may venture to say to you this: that if there is such a thing, then Yours Don Roberto is a very fine one both in what it receives from the world and in what it gives to it. May you ride, firm as ever in the saddle, to the very

[1] The letter to Pinker of the 28th suggests the Wednesday in question.
[2] Born in Ohio, the actress Catherine Livingston Willard (1895?–1954; Mrs William Edwin Barry 1925–31; Mrs Ralph Bellamy 1931–45) spent her childhood in England, with her mother Grace Robinson Willard. After studies in England and France, she made her début at the Theatre Royal, Exeter, in 1915, and went on to play in Shakespeare at the Old Vic. Conrad recommended her to H. B. Irving for a role in his never-staged production of *Victory*. After returning to America, she was a leading lady on Broadway for twenty-five years. Her date of birth is uncertain: the *New York Times* obituary gives 1900, while theatrical directories give 1895.
[3] *Laughing Anne.*
[4] *Cartagena and The Banks of the Sinú*, a travel book about Colombia published this month.
[5] Graham himself, who in October 1897 had been held captive by a Berber chieftain, the Caid of Kintafi. He recounts the episode in *Mogreb-al-Acksa* (1898).

last moment, et la lance toujours en arrêt,[1] against The Enemy whom You have defied all your life![2]

He is a multitude[3] – for who can count the follies and meannesses of the suffering mankind? He is probably invincible. But what of it! Could I wish you a better fate?

Je vous embrasse

Yours

Joseph Conrad.

Veuillez presenter mes devoirs les plus fidèles et les plus respéctueux a Madame Votre Mère.[4]

Give my most affectionate good wishes to Mrs Dummett with my thanks for her letter.

To J. C. Squire

Text MS Lubbock; Rude (1983)

[letterhead: Oswalds]

23.12.20.

My dear Mr Squire[5]

You have probably heard from Pinker by now. The publication in the *Dial*[6] was without my knowledge, and I don't know at this moment which are the prefaces which got into print in that irregular way. I am really annoyed, but since they did get out in America I can not stand out against their publication in England.[7]

---

[1] 'And your lance ever ready'.

[2] Don Quixote's famous attack on the windmills and Graham's skill as a horseman provide the image, although there may also be a dash of Cyrano de Bergerac's last moments. In 1902, Graham had served as the model for William Strang's series of drawings of Don Quixote.

[3] Cf. the man possessed by 'an unclean spirit' who tells Jesus 'My name is Legion, for we are many' (Mark 5.9).

[4] 'Pray give my most faithful and respectful duty to your mother.'

[5] On going down from Cambridge, John Collings Squire (1884–1958; knighted 1933) went in for politics. His enthusiasms for sport and literature soon won out, however, and he became a 'Georgian' poet, essayist, anthologist, and captain of a side of cricketing bohemians. In 1917–18 he was acting editor of the *New Statesman*, and from 1919 to 1934 he edited the *London Mercury*, a magazine loved or loathed for its traditional tastes. Conrad's 'Stephen Crane: A Note without Dates' appeared in its first number.

[6] Of the prefaces to *An Outcast of the Islands*, *Lord Jim*, and *Nostromo* in the December issue.

[7] Under the title 'Five Prefaces' the March 1921 issue of the *London Mercury* featured the prefaces to *Victory*, *Chance*, *The Secret Agent*, *The Shadow-Line*, and *'Twixt Land and Sea*.

I am really sorry I have no short story for you. I feel most friendly towards the Mercury and I am flattered by your request.

Pray accept my best wishes and most friendly greetings

Joseph Conrad.

To Aniela Zagórska
Text MS copy in French Yale; Najder 265

Oswalds,
24.12.20.

My dear Aniela,

My thoughts are with you on Christmas Eve as I wish you good health and tranquillity for the coming year; how that may be obtained – God alone knows.

Mr Sliwiński[1] (I don't know if you know him) was here and told me about a Polish bookseller or publisher, who, on returning from England, was telling everybody that he had been to my home and arranged the publication of my books with me, etc. etc. I am very annoyed because I have never met any Polish publisher either at home or elsewhere. If anyone told you about this, believe nothing about it, and act according to my previous letter transferring to you copyright in my works for Poland and Russia. I will send you the official document in a fortnight.

I had news from Karola from Milan. I am going to write to her to-day.

Jessie and the boys embrace you warmly and send you their best regards.

Your devoted

Konrad.

To Hugh Walpole
Text MS Texas; J-A, 2, 252 (in part)[2]

[letterhead: Oswalds]
26.12.20.

Dearest Hugh.

I was very deeply touched by your letter and I am grateful to you for the impulse which prompted you to put your feelings (which are infinitely precious to me) into words so simple and so direct.

Your friendship is of course part of my reward for some years of honest toil which sought not the favour of men and yet without it would have been a waste of barren effort. And in so far I have perhaps deserved it. But for the

---

[1] Najder suggests the Polish historian Artur Sliwiński (1877 1952).
[2] Jean-Aubry omits the last paragraph's second sentence.

warmth of your personal[ity], for that genuine friendship which you have extended to all belonging to me thanks are due to a higher Power which having made us what we are has allowed us to come together. And this my dear Hugh I feel profoundly.

Jessie and the boys send you their affectionate greetings and good wishes. John goes to Tonbridge on the 21st Jan: and the present programme is for M^r & Mrs J. C. to start for the conquest of Corsica on the 23^d. The Ex[peditiona]^{ry} Force (composed of two women, two men and one motor car) will remain in the occupation of the country for about three months, after which it will return and the usual distribution of medals (with clasps) will take place. Later the Chief will sit down and count the cost. . . .

B[orys] will cross over and see us as far as Rouen (2 days) returning via Havre from there. He is joining Mackintosh wireless implements factory (in Mortlake) on the 2^d just to get his hand in at once and settle down in his diggings. Jessie is improving slowly (but surely) and I am no worse than usual – except for fits of depression not usual with me and very worrying to look back upon. We shall see each other in town I hope before very long. When do you return? Let us know.

Ever Yours

J. Conrad.

To David Garnett
Text MS Texas; Unpublished

[letterhead: Oswalds]
28.12.20

My dear David.[1]

Please send me N^o*433* and N^o*83*.[2]

I am afraid that as to the first I will be too late; in which case please credit me with the amount and I'll send you some other numbers.

Also N°468.[3]

---

[1] The son of Constance and Edward, David ('Bunny') Garnett (1892–1981) became the author of *Lady into Fox* (1923) and many other novels. Married to Virginia Woolf's niece, Angelica Bell, he moved in Bloomsbury circles in the 1920s and 1930s. His *Great Friends: Portraits of Seventeen Writers* (1979) recalls the era of his father's friendship with Conrad.

[2] Garnett and Birrell's *A Catalogue of Secondhand English & Foreign Books* [19 Taviton St, December 1920] identifies these as *Degas: Quatre vingt dix huit reproductions signées par Degas* (1914) and *The Log of a Jack Tar, or The Life of James Choyce, Master Mariner, now first published, with O'Brien's Captivity in France* (1891), ed. V. Lovett Cameron.

[3] *Personal Recollections of the late Duc de Broglie*, 4 vols. (1887).

My best wishes for your happiness and prosperity. I hope N° 19 Taviton
St will be a great success.

Yours sincerely

Joseph Conrad.

To J. B. Pinker
Text MS Berg; Unpublished

[letterhead: Oswalds]
28.12.20

Dearest J. B.

You have been free from my correspondence for a few days but now you
must understand that your vacation is over and that you will be worried now
about one thing and another till I am out of the country.

Though silent (for nearly a week) I have been with you all much in thought.
I don't know what fun your wife & daughter got out of this festive season –
but I was glad yesterday to see good hunting weather for poor Ralph whose
mind was so much exercised on that point for weeks together. Give them all
my love – and may the year about to open be without clouds individually
and jointly for all the Family.

I suppose it's not much use talking to You of serious matters till, aided
and abetted by Eric, you have had your new-year fling. Still I must remind
you that B[orys] will begin his London life on the 3ᵈ Jan – as he wants to
put a fortnights work at the factory before he comes down here to celebrate
his birthday and eventually see his parents across the Channel. I should like
him to have his first quarter (£75) paid in to his acct on that date. I'll pay his
expences* right up to the door of his new diggings and want him to start fair,
with nothing to grumble about.

We have had Catherine here and Aubry (who went away this morning).
The confounded oysters (don't laugh) at Everitts[1] lunch must have poisoned
Jessie who after 3 very listless days went to bed on Xmas eve and has lived on
sips of milk-and-soda ever since. She's better to-day! But henceforth when
You want to be generous to her it must *never* take the form of oysters.

The second serious matter is my meeting with McKinnel. I am really very
anxious to meet him before we go away. After all a "first play" does not
happen very often and you are not likely to be worried again in this way by
me. It is not altogether because of the part for Cath: tho' after much discussion

---

[1] S. A. Everitt of Doubleday, who was in England on business.

both Aubry and I are confirmed in our impression of her suitability. I hope you don't suspect any "frivolity" on my part there. I really feel as I *must* see the man (my old pen has gone to pieces)[1]

Further serious matters shall be unloaded on you – next year; and you may believe me when I say they'll make your abundant hair stand on end. Remember this is J. C.'s last fling. It has lasted some time but the end of it will come precisely on the 30[th] of April '21. Then You won't know me, I'll be so changed. But till then there is no use in grumbling.

Ever Yours

J. Conrad

To Agnes Ridgeway
Text MS Dartmouth; Unpublished

[letterhead: Oswalds]
28.12.24 [1920].[2]

My dear Agnes.[3]

As you may imagine we were much distressed at the unexp[ec]ted news of your breakdown.[4] We do hope you are improving in the sunshine and charming surroundings of Rapallo. It was very sweet and dear of you to write me the friendly letter about John. Indeed you and your husband have been very good to us in all this affair.

With John in Ferox Hall we will start on our southern journey with easy minds. Jessie's only regret is that she will not be able to see you this time. We will, as M[r] Ridgeway suggested, bring together the boy to Tonbridge on the 21st; and on the 23[d] we will leave home for Corsica. Our stay in Ajaccio will extend to two months probably. I want to breathe the air of [the] Western Mediterranean where my young life began – and I hope I will be able to do some work on my new novel. For the last year I have done nothing except correcting the text of my Collected Edition and writing prefaces for the same. I have also written a 4-act play which Norman McKinnel is to

---

[1] An erratic pen-stroke rather than a word follows 'man'.

[2] If the date were right, this would be a letter from beyond the grave rather than an announcement of the journey to Corsica in January 1921.

[3] Agnes Mary Warner Ridgeway (née Sanderson, 1875–1936) was Ted Sanderson's second-oldest sister. The affectionate enmity between Conrad and 'Miss Agnes' began around 1894, the time of his first visit to the boisterous household at Elstree. In 1908, she married the Revd Neville Vibart Ridgeway, and helped to make Ferox Hall at Tonbridge School an especially successful house for many boys, including Conrad's son John.

[4] Chronic ill-health forced her to seek out warm climates.

produce sometime within the next 12 months. A beggarly tale, truly! I am ashamed of my indolence.

Directly on our return home I'll bring Jessie to see you and tell you herself how delighted she is at having her boy in your home. Perhaps on that occasion you'll let me come into your drawing room to sit on the edge of the chair and speak only when spoken to. You know I was always timid and apprehensive in your presence ever since (don't you remember) you nearly ruined my first novel out of pure lightness of heart and just for the sake of the fun.[1] Tempi passati[2] my dear Agnes, tempi passati! very dear to my memory. Believe me always with the greatest regard and affection

Yours

Joseph Conrad.

May this New Year remain unclouded for You and all Yours.

To F. N. Doubleday

Text MS Princeton; Unpublished

[letterhead: Oswalds]
29.12.20.

My dear Mʳ Doubleday

Many thanks for the charmingly bound copy of Kipling and for the other books – especially the most interesting work of Ad. Sims[3] which I have read with the greatest appreciation both of the distinguished author's personality and of the unselfish devotion and loyalty to the Allied cause of the Great Service of which he writes. I don't mention the skill, dash and fearlessness, because when one speaks of the United States Navy these things are understood without saying.

Pardon this ugly-looking scrawl but my wrist is bad. Yet there are feelings which I cannot bring myself to convey by the impersonal agency of a typewriter. Pray accept for Yourself and those who are near and dear to you, for your associates in business and for the workers in the same my warmest wishes of health, prosperity and content for the New Year – together with

---

[1] The whole Sanderson family took a lively interest in *Almayer's Folly*.
[2] 'Bygone times'.
[3] Rudyard Kipling's *Letters of Travel, 1892–1913* and Rear-Admiral William Sowden Sims's *The Victory at Sea*, written with Burton J. Hendrick, both published by Doubleday in 1920.

the expression of my grateful sense of their thought, care and toil in the production of my books.

Believe me very cordially Yours
Joseph Conrad.

PS Mr Everitt came here and was very interesting and perfectly delightful. Pray remember me to him.

To J. B. Pinker

Text MS Berg; Unpublished

[Oswalds]
Wed^ay [29 December 1920][1]

Dearest J. B.

Please give B[orys] £10 as I have no ch- book here to give him money for various purchases.

Will you give him word when you propose to come down here for a day or two.

Jessie has retained appts[2] at Brown['s] hotel for Mond & Tuesday night.

Ever Yours
J. Conrad.

To Warrington Dawson

Text MS Duke; Randall 202–3

[letterhead: Oswalds]
30.12.20

Dearest Warrington

Infinite t[h]anks for sending me the text of the Inter^al Commission's findings in the famous North Sea Inquiry.[3] It is marvellous you should have remembered a wish uttered so many years ago.

---

[1] The letter to Mackintosh of the 31st fixes the date.
[2] A Gallicism: 'app[artement]s', meaning here a suite.
[3] An international commission convened in Paris to investigate an attack on Hull fishing trawlers by the Russian Baltic squadron on 21 October 1904. The incident, which killed some of the trawlermen and injured others and also damaged their ships, sparked public outrage in Britain. Conrad comments on it in a letter to *The Times*, 26 October 1904 (*Letters*, 3, pp. 173–5).

May you find your life easier your hopes brighter your courage and endurance better rewarded this year. All here send you their best and most sympathetic wishes.

We will be leaving on the 23 Jan for Corsica where we, that is Jessie and I, propose to stay for 2 months or so. John goes to Tonbridge School this term, and B[orys] will take up his work in London; so we will have no one with us but a nurse-comp[ani]on for Jessie.

Perhaps on our return journey we will be able to look you up.[1] But our outward route must be (for various reasons) through Rouen, Orleans and so on.

Just before your letter arrived Everitt (of D. P & Co) was here and we conversed in a most appreciative and hopeful spirit [of] your novel[2] they are going to publish shortly. I hope my dear fellow its merit will be recognised not only by fellow-spirits but by ordinary minds of the general public.

Ever affectionately Yours

J. Conrad

To George T. Keating
Text MS Yale; Unpublished

[letterhead: Oswalds]

30.12.20

My dear Mr Keating

My hand prevented me from writing you before my thanks for the magnificent binding of the *Shadow Line*. It is very much admired. But you must not overwhelm me with the splendour of your generosity. A friendly gift is welcome but I don't want to be made to feel as though I were being paid in an indirect way. I signed the pamphlets and books for your collection in a purely friendly spirit and as a most willing acknowledgment of your appreciation of my work. The copy you sent me will pass after me into the possession of my eldest son to whom the story is dedicated. The paper knife is very pleasant to my hand and is and will be in daily use.

May this coming year be one of prosperity, peace and content to you and all that are dear to you.

Believe me very sincerely Yours

Joseph Conrad.

---

[1] Dawson was living in Versailles.　　[2] *The Gift of Paul Clermont* (1921).

To Marguerite Poradowska

Text MS Yale; G. & S. 119; Rapin 202 and partial facsimile

[letterhead: Oswalds]
30 Dec. '20

Chère Tante et Amie.[1]

Nos meilleurs souhaits pour cette Nouvelle Année.

Nous partirons pour la Corse vers le 24 du mois prochain pour y passer 2 mois. On m'assure que le climat d'Ajaccio est excellent. Je veux debarasser Jessie de sa bronchite qui menace de devenir chronique. Après deux ans de souffrances, 3 operations (sans compter trois entailles) elle commence a marcher avec des béquilles. Naturellement tout mouvement lui est encore un peu difficile et voilà pourquoi j'ai decidé de ne pas nous arrêter a Paris. Nous ferons toute la route en auto par Havre Rouen Orleans Lyon a Marseille. Serez Vous là cet hiver? Je n'ose l'ésperer – mais ce serait une grande joie de pouvoir vous embrasser en passant.

Jean Alexandre reste [à] l'école et Borys a la fabrique d'appareils tele-graphiques sans fil ou il est entré en fonctions dernièrement. Nous aurons seulement une "nurse" avec nous.

Je viens de recevoir une lettre de Karola. Elle est a Milan depuis trois semaines. Je vous envoi[e] son addresse.* Je sais que Madzia[2] est guérie et qu'Angèle est en bonne santé et a un emploi il semble dans un bureau. Voilà tout ce que [je] peux Vous dire. Tout le monde ici Vous embrasse bien tendrement. Je suis toujours très chère Tante Margueritte* le Votre de coeur

J. Conrad

adresse. Mlle Karola Ostoja Zagórska

21. Via Libertà
au soins de Sign[re] Sternieri
Milan (Greco Milanese)

Translation

Dear Aunt and Friend.

Our best wishes for this New Year.

---

[1] Marguerite Poradowska (née Gachet, 1848–1937) was the widow of Conrad's distant cousin, and thus his 'Aunt' – but also his good friend in the 1890s, and the first novelist of his acquaintance. She lived in France, and her novels of French, Belgian, and Polish life were well known in their day. Often serialised in the prestigious *Revue des Deux Mondes* before book publication, they include *Yâga* (1887), *Demoiselle Micia* (1888–9), and *Marylka* (1895).

[2] Probably Magdalena Ołdakowska, the Zagórska sisters' niece by marriage.

We will leave for Corsica about the 24th of next month for 2 months there. I am assured that Ajaccio's climate is excellent. I want to rid Jessie of her bronchitis, which is threatening to become chronic. After two years of suffering and 3 operations (not counting 3 incisions) she is beginning to walk with crutches. All movement is still somewhat difficult of course, and that is why I have decided not to stop in Paris. We will make the entire journey by motor-car via Le Havre, Rouen, Orleans, Lyons to Marseilles. Will you be there this winter? I daren't hope so, but it would be a great happiness to be able to embrace you while passing through.

John Alexander stays at school and Borys at the wireless equipment factory where he recently began to work. We will have only a nurse with us.

I've just received a letter from Karola. She has been in Milan for three weeks. I am sending her address to you. I know that Madzia is better and that Angela is in good health and has a job, apparently in an office. That is all I can tell you. Love from everybody here. I am, my dear Aunt Marguerite, ever affectionately yours

J. Conrad

To R. D. Mackintosh

Text MS Hurrell; Unpublished

[letterhead: Oswalds]
31. Dec. '20

My dear Mac.

Just a line to send you wife and yourself our very best wishes of health and prosperity for the coming year.

Jessie will come to town (Brown's Hotel) on Monday for two days. On the same day Borys will take up his residence in Mortlake[1] and put in some days of work at the factory; but I am afraid I shall have to call on him to help us to get away. I am really not well enough to do all the running about myself. I'll also want him to cross over with us and see the car through the customhouse in Calais.

I don't think I will come to town with Jessie. There is an enormous lot of proofs and other matter for me to look through before I leave.[2]

All here send you their best love. John goes to Tonb^ge on the 21st.

Ever affect^ly Yours
Joseph Conrad.

---

[1] On the Thames, in South-West London.
[2] Including the proofs of *Notes on Life and Letters*, due out in February 1921.

PS Through poor Heinemann's death I failed to secure enough sets of the English Coll^{ed} Edition – and I couldn't buy one now if I tried ever so much. So I am afraid you will have to wait for an American set which I have reserved for you.

To J. B. Pinker
Text MS Berg; Unpublished

[Oswalds]
[1920?][1]

Dearest P.

Nothing done. Further delay is necessary.

Thanks for you letter   and [photo]graph

Ever Yours

J.C.

[1] Catalogued as 1920. The stationery has the same watermark as the letter of 26 January 1921. The handwriting suggests gout.

1921

To Major Gordon Gardiner

Text MS Harvard; Unpublished

[Oswalds]
Sunday [2 January 1921][1]

My dear Gardiner.

I find I have to come up on Wed^{ay}.

I'll call at 12 Q Ann[e]'s Gate a little before noon on the chance of seeing you.

It would be impossible to leave Eng^d without taking a look at you; but please do not let this note disturb your plans.

Jessie's love.

Ever yours

J Conrad

To J. B. Pinker

Text MS Berg; Unpublished

[letterhead: Oswalds]
Sunday. [2 January 1921][2]

Dearest J. B.

John has got in – by favour of course, and I would have preferred the other way.[3] He will have to join on the 21st Jan. M^r and Mrs J. C. will be thus at liberty to depart on the 22^d for the conquest of Corsica.

I have a bandaged hand, a sore heel, and a suspicious knee; but intend nevertheless to be as busy as a bee (a perfectly sound bee) for the next week. Borys having given me your message about Everitt I want to know (if you please) whether you can arrange any of our functions for Wed – or Thurs: I will come up on Wed: to haunt shipp^g offices and the RAC[4] touring dep^t – and if you can persuade Mrs Pinker to let me curl myself up in the hall (an outhouse would do) of Burys Court for the night of Wed^y I would be definitely obliged to you. I will have plenty of occupation for Thursday too – but a lunch can be fitted on either (or both) of these days.

---

[1] Conrad's approaching departure and his presence in London on Wednesday the 5th (see the letter to Garnett of the 6th) fix the date.

[2] The plans for London suggest the date.

[3] Gaining admission to Tonbridge by a strong performance in the Common Entrance Exam rather than by knowing a housemaster.

[4] The Royal Automobile, Conrad's favoured club at this period.

Letter to Levy[1] went by mistake to L[ittle] T[heatre] direct. It contains precisely the request that (if accepted) he will give me an opportunity to meet his company before my departure for the south.

Our love.

Ever Yours

J. Conrad

To Thomas J. Wise

Text MS BL Ashley 2940; *Listy* 396–7; Original unpublished

[letterhead: Oswalds]
3^d.1.21.

Dear Mr Wise.

While putting away my papers with a view to our approaching departure for France it occurred to me that you may like to have the option of the *MS* of the little play I have written lately (finished 16 Dec '20) with a view to the *Little Theatre* but which of course may be never performed for all I can tell.

The item consists of 53 pp of MS – complete, full, *first draft* from which was dictated a *first copy* (about 40 pp) TS much, scored, interlined and corrected in pen and ink on nearly every page.

The title is *Laughing Anne. Drama in Two Acts and Three Scenes*. It is calculated to play in about 50 minutes.

With this you would have *all* I have done in the years 1918, 1919 and 1920 including of course the new Author's Notes and in fact every line I have written for publication in these years.

Will you be willing to give me £100 for the item?

My best wishes for the opening year.

Yours faithfully

Joseph Conrad.

---

[1] Jose G. Levy (1884–1936), educated in Portsmouth and Lausanne, managed The Little Theatre until 1936 and ran its English Grand-Guignol seasons, featuring Sybil Thorndike and Lewis Casson, from 1920 to 1923. A noted translator of French drama, he championed its cause in Britain.

To J. B. Pinker
Text MS Berg; Unpublished

[letterhead: Brown's Hotel, London]
Wednesday. [5 January 1921][1]
7. pm

Dear J B.

I forgot before we parted to ask you to pay in £100 to my acct to settle here and pay some bills that are coming in

Yours

J. C.

To Captain David Bone
Text MS Sprott; Knowles

[letterhead: Oswalds]
6.1.21.

My dear Capt. Bone.

I am in a most difficult position. I have refused to do that very thing[2] for men whom I meet often, belonging to the literary side of my life, some of whom I respect and like. They accepted my refusal kindly on the ground of its being a reasoned rule of conduct which they could understand. I will confess to you frankly that I haven't the courage of breaking it now. It would give too much offence to friends and lay me open to persecution from strangers.

Everybody knows that in the 25 years of my literary life I wrote only 2 introductions. One to Edward Garnett's *Turgeniev** and another (10 years ago) to Mrs Ada Galsworthy's translation of some of Maupassant's tales.[3] These however were merely the appreciations of two great writers no longer amongst the living.

I venture my dear Captain to count on your indulgence and I hope You will accept in a friendly spirit my warmest thanks for the copy of *The Brassbounder*[4] which reached me two days ago.

Always sincerely Yours

Joseph Conrad.

---

[1] A combination of hotel letterhead and location in the Berg folders associates this note with the 'Wednesday' trip to London mentioned on [2 January].

[2] Bone had apparently requested a preface for the American reprinting of *The Brassbounder*, first published in 1910.

[3] Forewords to *Turgenev: A Study* (1917) and *Yvette and Other Stories* (1904), respectively, both reprinted in *Notes on Life and Letters*.

[4] An advance copy of Duckworth's February reprint.

To Edward Garnett

Text MS Bryn Mawr; G. 303

[letterhead: Oswalds]

6.1.21.

My dearest Edward.

I went to Pawling on Wed. morning about the ded^{on} of the Nigger.[1] Everybody in the office was appalled – but they took jolly good care to point out that Miss Hallowes and I had to bear our share of the guilt. Miss H is, in her own words, "frightfully upset" about it; and I won't tell you how bad I feel myself. However I have arranged with Pawling that 780 pages with the dedication should be printed at once and inserted into those sets that are not gone out yet. Those subs^{ers} who have already received their sets will have the dedication page sent to them with an explanatory letter. I must say that S. S.[2] apparently took the matter to heart and instructions to carry the thing out at once were given in my presence.

Miss Hallowes wants me to explain to you that the pre[li]m^s were sent to her at Windermere where she was spending her holiday and where she had no copy of *The Nigger* to compare them with.

I, of course, am wholly inexcusable. Pink. when told after his return from the theatre gave me a withering look. Jessie sends her love and hopes it will not affect our relations. I told her I hoped not – and anyhow I am

Ever Yours

Joseph Conrad.

To Thomas J. Wise

Text MS BL Ashley 2940; Unpublished

[letterhead: Oswalds]

6.1.21

My dear Mr Wise

Thanks for the cheque[3] which arrived during my absence from home.

Miss H[allowes] is preparing the MS & TS for dispatch to you by this evenings post. I will presently write the title page.

My wife thanks you for your kind references to her and joins me in kindest regards

Yours faithfully

Joseph Conrad.

---

[1] To Garnett, and missing from the volume in the Heinemann collected edition.
[2] Pawling.   [3] For the *Laughing Anne* manuscript.

To Lieutenant-Commander F. G. Cooper
Text MS Private collection; Unpublished

[letterhead: Oswalds]
11.1.21.

My dear Sir[1]

I am deeply touched by the sympathetic and charmingly expressed appreciation[2] of my work by a brother seaman.

In dealing with the men (and ships) of the Merchant Service, my companions and fellow-workers from the 19th to the 36th year of my life I have always aimed at truth – and truth alone – as far as I was able to see and feel it. The testimony to my fidelity which I receive at Your hands in the first inst^t of Your article in N.M. gives me the greatest possible satisfaction.

Pardon my delay in writing to you. I was overwhelmed by a mass of various matters requiring immediate attention. Will you in sign of forgiveness accept the little (cheap – alas!) copy of *Shadow Line*? I have nothing else at hand and I want to put myself right with You at once.

Believe me

very cordially Yours

Joseph Conrad

To J. B. Pinker
Text MS Berg; Unpublished

[letterhead: Oswalds]
11.1.21.

My dearest J. B.

I understand (from Ralph) that there are *2* quarters rent owing: *Sept.* and *Dec.*

As to the first I thought that it had been paid of course. As to the second I was under the same impression.

Your books of course will show.

---

[1] Frederic George Cooper (1876–1966) obtained seaman's certificates from the Board of Trade. He served in the war as a transport officer and was named Lieutenant Commander in 1915, leaving the service as Commander in 1921. His articles on Conrad, whom he met, appeared in the *Nautical Magazine* (1921), *Blue Peter* (1929), *Mariner's Mirror* (1940), and *Annual Dogwatch* (1953).

[2] In Cooper's 'Joseph Conrad: A Seaman's Tribute' in *Nautical Magazine: A Technical & Critical Journal for the Officers of the Mercantile Marine*. The four-part article began in January and concluded in April (105: 4–9, 97–101, 199–204, 328–32). It was reprinted in Cooper's *Yarns of the Seven Seas* (1927), pp. 44–73.

I fell into the habit of leaving everything to you so much that I did not send a reminder to the office. I am sorry. Will you see to it?

Au revoir on the 14th.

Ever Yours

J. Conrad

To Thomas J. Wise
Text MS BL Ashley 2953; Unpublished

[letterhead: Oswalds]

12.1.21.

Dear Mr Wise.

I don't know if Miss H[allowes] wrote to you on the subject – but we think that as you have secured that fine copy of A's. F.[1] you had better sent* it on here at once for me to sign. I can find time for *that*.

I am glad to hear you were interested in the short play.

Kindest regards

Yours

J Conrad.

PS I enclose your cheque returned from the bank. There seems to be some irregularity in the drawing.

To J. B. Pinker
Text MS Berg; Unpublished

[letterhead: Oswalds]

Thursday [13 January 1921][2]

Dearest J. B.

Please give the bearers (or bearer) of this £5.

They have come for John's specs.

See you to-morrow about 12.30

Ever yours

J. Conrad.

---

[1] The first edition of *Almayer's Folly*, published 29 April 1895.
[2] Assigned to '1/21' by an unknown hand. If the January dating is correct, the meeting in London would be that connected with Pinker's intended visit to Oswalds on the 14–16th.

To Lieutenant Commander F. G. Cooper

Text MS Melbourne; Unpublished

[letterhead: Oswalds]

16.1.21

Dear Capt Cooper

Thanks for your letter and the proof[1] you sent me. The facts are quite correct. Your surmise that M[r] George of the *A of G* is in a sense myself is just. When that adventure was over I came to England and served on the East Coast in a barquentine belonging to Lowestoft – "Skimmer of the Seas" 208 tons. I have my discharge from her as O[rdinary] S[eaman].

My old and very close friend M[r] J. B. Pinker (who has been for many years my literary agent) is staying the week end with us. I showed him the first inst[t] (and the proof of the second) of your article, which he appreciates very much. He suggests to me that if you were to send him the slips of the 2[d] & 3[d] inst (I have two copies of the Mag: and could furnish him the first) he would try to place your article in U.S. in some periodical. It is quite possible that some literary weekly might be disposed to print it as a "professional" appreciation of J. Conrad's work, which apart from being attractively written would give a particular point of view. Should you care for it, his address is Talbot House. Arundel S[t]. Strand. WC 2.

Kindest regards

Yours

J Conrad

To John Galsworthy

Text MS Forbes; Unpublished

[letterhead: Oswalds]

17.1.21

Dearest Jack.

I have directed Pawling to send your set of my Coll[d] Ed[on] here where I'll store the vols till your return. The revision of the text – nothing very considerable; mostly striking out words and a few phrases here and there – and the writing of very short prefaces (which I call Author's Notes) has taken up the best part of 1920. The rest was wasted in vain efforts at "concentration". I didn't manage to "concentrate" for the value of one cent (Am. currency).

Yesterday I read the first inst[t] of *To Let*[2] in a spirit of philistinish curiosity. Pray forgive me. I shall resist the temptation to munch the future slices. One

---

[1] Of his 'Joseph Conrad: A Seaman's Tribute' (see the letter of 11 January).

[2] In *Scribner's Magazine*. The serial ran from January to September.

misses all rhythm all continuity of composition and most of [the] colour effects. Yet my dear Jack its astonishing how good your slices are by their inherent quality of conception and style!

We are leaving on the 23ᵈ for Ajaccio for 3 months. It will no doubt be very good for Jessie. John goes to Tonbridge this week, for his first term. This makes him look thoughtful. B[orys] is in a factory for all sorts of wireless implements (experimental) in Mortlake. I mean he is going through the workshops with a view to promotion. He's very keen.

The most cheering thing is that Jessie does really walk (not creep) with one crutch still, it is true, but with every prospect of being able to throw it away before very long. I can't shake off my depression. Perhaps I will be able to do some work in Corsica. All the vendettas have been settled or have died out and it is very quiet there, I am told. On the other hand no golf courses have been laid out yet and no invasion from the dismal tribe with clubs is to be feared – for this year at least.

McKinnel has taken my play for production within this year. That man is clearly not afraid of frost. However I am glad that it is he – for he has some talent and is pleasant to deal with.

Rudo shows much charm in Awakening,[1] which harmonised with the charm of the text in a fascinating way. It is altogether a delightful book. – Pray give my dear love to Ada. We often think of you both making the best of Californian sky.[2] May it smile and smile on you – and never be a villain to either of you.

Ever affectionately Yours
Joseph Conrad.

To Edward Garnett
Text J-A, 2, 253–4; G. 304[3]

Oswalds
17.1.'21.

My dearest Edward,

We could not find the Crane article in any printed form (either U.K. or U.S.) and so we have dug out an old typescript.[4] I am awfully sorry for the

[1] The son of Galsworthy's brother-in-law, Rudolf Helmut Sauter (1895–1977) illustrated 'Awakening', a short story from *The Forsyte Saga* which Heinemann issued as a 63-page book in November 1920.
[2] Galsworthy replied from Arizona (Stape and Knowles, pp. 168–9).
[3] Text from Garnett.
[4] Now at Texas, a TS of 'Stephen Crane: A Note without Dates', a memoir published in the December 1919 issue of the *London Mercury*.

delay, I agree with your opinion of these "War pieces". Oh yes! They are good. And truly in all the work he left behind him there is nothing that could be dismissed as rubbish. For even the *Third Violet*[1] is merely a characteristic failure.

I am sending you also four Nos of *L. Mercury*.[2] I have selected them with some care, and in a spirit of scrupulous fairness.

Aubry and I have been talking you over lately here. You must have felt on that particular evening prolonged shudders as if an infinity of geese had been walking over your grave. (You know the popular saying?)[3] However we can't help our "effete intellects". Still I found in that Frenchman of Frenchmen more sympathetic understanding of you – the real you – than in any Islander I've ever met. Perhaps you don't know – but at that séance at Brown's[4] you were really Great. I am proud of having been discovered by *you* all these years ago.

Jessie sends her dear love. We start on Sunday.

Ever yours

Joseph Conrad

To J. B. Pinker
Text MS Berg; Unpublished

[letterhead: Oswalds]
Monday. [17 January 1921][5]

Dearest Pinker.

Directly I left you at the station horrid doubts assailed me as to the correctness of my time table for your trains. I hope to goodness you made your connection in Tonbridge all right and got home in decent time.

I have to pay my tailor and some other bills so please transfer £50 to my acct.

Yours ever

J. Conrad.

---

[1] Crane's *The Third Violet* (1897) is about an artist's courtship of a New York heiress. The 'War pieces' would be either Crane's reports from the Cuban battlefields of the Spanish-American War or the short stories that came out of his experiences such as 'The Price of the Harness'.
[2] The first and third numbers of the lavishly produced literary magazine edited by J. C. Squire featured work by Conrad.
[3] A Polish one: *Gęsprzeszta po moim grobie* (a goose walking over your grave).
[4] An evening at Brown's Hotel?
[5] Pinker's visit on the 14–16th (see the letter to Cooper of the 16th) and the mention of tailor's bills on the 22nd fix the date.

To Christopher Sandeman

Text J-A, 2, 253

Oswalds
17.1.'21.

My dear Sandeman,[1]

In a few days we depart for Corsica in search of "climate." Had it not been that I really must pull myself together and do some work, we would have tried a tour in Spain – and a small invasion of your sumptuous Hermitage.[2] But it must not be. Not this year at any rate. We are going to settle down for three months in Ajaccio and lead a dull, laborious and God-fearing existence.

Just at the end of last year McKinnel accepted a play of mine. Thus unexpectedly I shall find myself your confrère – car vous avez tâté des planches.[3] I foresee for it a "frost" modified – or tempered – by a certain amount of curiosity on the part of a small section of the public; with the conclusion on the part of the critics that "Conrad can't write a play." It is a pretty horrible thing too – but McKinnel is an artist and may prolong the agony for six weeks or so.

My wife sends her kindest regards and hopes very much to see you under our roof in the course of this year. We'll be back here at the end of April. My âge des folies is over, which would be satisfactory if it was not for a long (too long) fit of depression which I cannot shake off. Pray think kindly of me and believe in my unalterably affectionate regard.

To Aniela Zagórska

Text MS copy Yale;[4] Najder 265–6

Oswalds,
19.1.21.

My dear Aniela,

I am sending you the document endorsed by the Polish Consulate.

---

[1] Rather than follow the family tradition of marketing port and sherry, Christopher ('Kit') Sandeman (1882–1951) became a journalist, lecturer, and author. Opera, politics, poetry, history, and botany all fascinated him, and he also wrote and translated plays. Between the wars he led several expeditions to Peru and Brazil, rafting on the headwaters of the Amazon and the Huallaga, and collecting orchids for British herbaria.

[2] El Palacio, the family mansion in Jérez de la Frontera.

[3] 'Because you've tested the boards yourself'. Sandeman's plays *The Match-Breaker* (1912) and *Blind Fate* (1913) were produced at the Little Theatre. He co-wrote *The Widow's Mite* (1917), which had a long run at the Haymarket and co-translated José Echegaray's *The Cleansing Stain* (1917). Conrad's play is *The Secret Agent* rather than *Laughing Anne*.

[4] In French.

I received your letter. I embrace you warmly for all you say. How wonderful your English is! Jessie is going to write to you to-day. The day after to-morrow we leave for Corsica (Hôtel Continental, Ajaccio) for two or three months. I will try to work there because I have done nothing for a year. The boys send their dear love to you. Pray forgive the shortness of this letter but I'm very busy with our Corsican expedition.

Yours very affectionately

Konrad

To Lady Millais

Text MS Private collection; Unpublished

[letterhead: Oswalds]
20.I.'21.

Dear Lady Millais.

It is with a very full heart that I sit down to try and express to you my thanks for the memento of him for whom I most sincerely mourn,[1] and whose brave and lovable personality I shall remember tenderly all the days that are left to me on earth.

I was grateful to him for the liking he had for me and I am deeply grateful to you for the gift by which you are good enough to recognise my great regard and affection for him. My dear Lady Millais I can hardly bear to write about this!

I could not come with Jessie yesterday having been called to town unexpectedly by an early wire on a business which had to be attended to without delay. But I was very determined to come over to Leacon Hall[2] today, till I heard from Jessie that you would be from home on this and the two succeeding days.

Nothing but a fear to intrude on your grief has kept me away – and frankly my heart failed me too, at the thought of your admirable devotion to him and of his confiding and dependent love for you, which I have been privileged to see and at which I have looked for nearly ten years with a great and anxious sympathy.

Believe me always with the deepest regard your faithful friend and servant

Joseph Conrad.

---

[1] Her son John, who had died in September.   [2] Her home near Ashford.

To J. B. Pinker
Text MS Berg; Unpublished

[Oswalds]
20.I.21
3.20 pm.

Dear J. B.

Just got your wire "Passport through." – Thanks no end for your assistance. Sir, you are a White Man.[1]

That good fellow Eric (he's that) being with us I refrained from talking to you yesterday. Not that I have the slightest objection – in principle – to Eric knowing all there is to know – but I was not sure how you felt about it as to things between you and me.

1/ I saw yesterday the bank manager and the fact is that I drew £1700 since, say, May 1918. (I won't comment on this here. You know that I am not quite hopeless.) As the *present value* of the invest^{nt} (£3130 worth of 4% Gov^t Loan 1919) is but a trifle if (anything) over £2000 I am well up to the limit. However the manager said he would let me draw a few cheques more – £200 or so – on my mentionning* to him that I would ask you to pay in £300 in the course of the next six or seven weeks – either at once or in several amounts – to my account. Please do that as convenient as I would like to have something in case I should want to draw a cheque later on. In Corsica of course there will be no occasion.

1a/ At present I shall draw against this extension to settle some bills. Others perhaps to the amount of £150 I will send to you. I thought this arrangement would make it easier to deal with this situation which is not likely to occur again.

2/ In view of the depreciation the Gov^t 4% & 5% term-loans are liable to I think that when our friends the film-buyers (not Laskers) exercise their option (limit in March) perhaps it would be better to employ the money in reducing the overdraft simply – on which I pay 8% to the bank – instead of buying any kind of stock. Your wisdom will decide; but I think there is something in my view. You will tell me what you think when we see each other in 19 days from this.

---

[1] In the sense of 'a man of honourable character', the *OED* finds the origin of this phrase in American slang.

3/ Apart from the payments to be provided for under 1a/ there would be £30 to pay Ninnes for the first quarter of this year and a further similar sum for the quarter beginning in March. I have arranged this with him.

4/ I think that in regard to my long standing promise to B[orys] I would like to pay him interest 5% on the £1000 till we can pay him the amount. £12.10 a quarter will make a considerable difference to him. I want also to give him his fares (2^d cl. return unless he manages to get a season at a better rate) for coming down here for week-ends. I told him to let you know what it is to be. Please pay him his 1st quarter's interest too, as from 1st Jan^y.

5/ Miss H[allowes] will stay on in Canterbury till the sixth of Febr. to receive and attend to the revises of *Life & Letters* – the texts of S. Agent and Chance which are due any day from America (R[oman]^{ce} & In[herit]^{ors} will be ready for America to-morrow) and the proofs from Heinemann which are coming in every day and I imagine will continue to flow without interruption till the end. She will come here from time to time but I imagine she will work at her lodgings mostly. On the sixth she will go to stay with her relatives at Petersfield and await there my letter directing her to come to Ajaccio. I am determined to put in 60 days' work *at the least* out there. At the same time America will be directed to send (from 5th Febr.) the galleys to Ajaccio. H[einemann] too will be warned.

We hear that Don Roberto & Mrs Dummett intend to call on us in Corsica while you are there. Say 20th Febr. Sidney Colvin was delighted with you and Lady Colvin most grateful at the encouraging way you spoke to him of his work. Both these people were very anxious to meet the man who "has carried Conrad on his back" as poor C in his funnily grim way expressed it. Slightly sinister simile this when one recalls the tale of the Old man of the Sea, who was – not to mince matters – a curse to Sinbad.[1] I found poor Sidi (as we call him) actually at work on the printed text of his sketches[2] – you had bucked him up so!

My love to Your wife and Oenone and Eric.

Ever Yours

J. Conrad.

---

[1] The demonic figure who will not let go his stranglehold in the Fifth Voyage of 'The Tale of Sinbad the Sailor' in *The Thousand and One Nights*.
[2] *Memories and Notes of Persons and Places, 1852–1912*, for publication later in the year. Several chapters had appeared in periodicals.

To Richard Curle

Text MS Indiana; Curle 73

[letterhead: Oswalds]
22.I.21.

My very dear Richard.

Your letter was just in time to catch us before our departure to Corsica.

John has been deposited at Tonbridge and I do hope will be happy there. We are leaving (with the car) to morrow at 8.30 – for Calais Amiens, Rouen, Orleans Moulins, Valence Marseille – Ajaccio, and the weather is by no means promising.

Borys will take us as far as Rouen making a detour to Amiens [and] Albert[1] to see a little of the Somme front.

At Rouen he will leave us and go back to Mortlake where he has a berth with a wireless appliances M[anufacturin]g C^o directed by Dr Mackintosh – a very old friend of ours. B is very keen on this opening.

Jessie trots about – with one crutch – quite smartly. The only worry is a persistent pain area which we can't get rid of yet. She sends you her affec^{te} regards in which all here join.

We will be in Ajaccio (Hotel Continental) till the 20th Ap. for certain. Will you be able to push a point that way on your homeward journey?

I am glad you had such an interesting time and still more glad to know of your good health and spirits.

Au revoir cher – here or in Corsica.

Ever affec^{tly} Yours

Joseph Conrad

To J. B. Pinker

Text MS Berg; Unpublished

[letterhead: Oswalds]
22^d.1.2[1]
Sat. morn^g.

My dear Pinker

I can't come myself, with my gouty foot.

It seems R[oyal] A[utomobile] C[lub] was confident of getting the passport Monday. Pray see the head of the Pass^t dept and ask him for the favour of delivering it to You, *as my representative*, to day – to save me infinite trouble and expense.

---

[1] Borys had fought in the Albert sector in 1916 and 1917.

I demand the passport as a matter of right having duly filled the form. I can do no more. I am properly attested as a fit and proper person by my bank and I ask for the passport in the name by which I have been known under which I have paid taxes, signed contracts and legal documents for a 1/4 of century or more.[1]

It is also the name by which I am known in the Br^sh Emp. and on the continents of Europe & N^th America. At the same time it is common knowledge among educated people that J. Conrad has also another name. There is no secrecy about it. I have not and do not intend [to] divest myself of it for sentimental reasons. But I have lived legally and socially under the other for so long that I naturally wish to travel under it. I have as a matter of course signed the custom house papers with that name, obtained my letter of credit and retained my rooms. Another name on the passport would cause infinite complications and no end of worries.

Unless the passport is delivered pray claim in my name the return to you of my Nat[uralisati]on Certificate[2] and of the form *as filled*. I will refer the Matter to the Secretary of State without delay.

Yours

Joseph Conrad

To J. B. Pinker
Text MS Berg; Unpublished

[letterhead: Oswalds]
[22 January 1921][3]

Dearest J. B.

I have scrawled the other letter as suggestion for your action – and as your authority to act.

You are no end good to take all this trouble – especially as you are out of sorts. Your letter just to hand.

I don't know how to thank you.

Ever Yours

JC.

---

[1] I.e., Joseph Conrad rather than Józef Korzeniowski.   [2] Issued in August 1886.
[3] Dated by the previous letter.

To Sir Hugh Clifford
Text MS Clifford; Hunter (1985, 2)

[letterhead: Oswalds]
23.I.21

My dear Friend,[1]

Your good letter[2] just catches us at the moment of leaving home to go for a stay of 2–3 months in Corsica. We'll be in Ajaccio Hotel Continental. Perhaps you will drop us a line as you start for your leave.

Ad[miral] Goodenough's letter did give me an immense pleasure. I am so glad Lady Clifford[3] likes *The Rescue*. I won't say anything of you. You always had a soft spot for me and were prejudiced in your judgement of my scribbling.

Jessie sends her love. She really begins to walk, still with one crutch however. Pray give my best regard to Lady Clifford. Au revoir in the spring.

Ever affect[ly] yours

Joseph Conrad

To J. B. Pinker
Text MS Berg; Unpublished

[letterhead: Oswalds]
22 [23?]1–21[4]

My dear Pinker.

Many thanks for your most affective* action which has saved a lot of worry and vexation.

I have read your letter in a proper spirit. There is not much to say – and anyway this is not the place to say it – for myself.

---

[1] Born into an aristocratic West Country Roman Catholic family, the Cliffords of Ugbrooke, Hugh Charles Clifford (1866–1941; knighted 1909) went out to Singapore as a cadet in 1883 and spent his life as a colonial administrator. He was serving as British Resident in Pahang, Malaya, when he wrote one of the earliest general appreciations of Conrad's work. Later, he was appointed to the governorships of Labuan and North Borneo, the Gold Coast, Nigeria, Ceylon, and the Straits Settlements. He published many volumes of short stories and sketches, collaborated on a Malay dictionary with Frank Swettenham, and produced a Malay translation of the colonial penal code.
[2] Of 1 January from Lagos, Nigeria, where Clifford was posted (Stape and Knowles, pp. 167–8).
[3] Elizabeth Lydia Rosabelle (née Bonham, 1866–1945), a novelist and playwright who wrote, under the name of her first husband, as Mrs Henry de la Pasture.
[4] The two letters of the 22nd and the reference to an 'action which has saved a lot of worry and vexation' (presumably securing Conrad's passport) cast doubt on the date. In any case, this letter responds to Pinker's comments on the long letter of the 20th.

No my dearest J. B. I didn't know I drew £8000 in a little more than two years. As a matter of fact I didn't *know* either the incomings or the outgoings – and as usual in such cases I have no doubt over[e]stimated the first and under estimated the last. I certainly did give some thought to the matter. Of course into that expenditure there comes in a lot of things bought – the move into this house – the journey to Liv'pool – the London festivities and the Deal journey – items that are not of a recurrent nature. Still it is in the character of this human animal to be optimistic in the absence of any positive check. Well you have seen me through worse predicaments. Don't imagine I am talking lightheartedly. I feel anything but lighthearted.

There will be sent to you the tailors bill – bootmakers – and some small accts. In addition pray send C. Hayward & Son.[1] 34 New St. Ashford. Kent. £57. I *have* paid all licenses claimed = £35. and made other payments. It was no use thinking of giving up the Corsican journey. But I start in no high spirits on it. Still there is always time for reform and repentance.

My dear love to you all

Yours Ever

J. C.

To J. B. Pinker
Text MS Berg; Unpublished

Orleans.
26 Jan. '21

My dearest J. B.

I have already managed to fall one day behind my programme. We had an involuntary stoppage on the plain of Beauce between Chartres and Orleans. A great nuisance of course. But it was a wonderful experience to stand in the falling dusk on this plain with a horizon like a sea in perfect stillness and solitude.

We spent the night of yesterday in a little village wher[e] a café proprietor took us in fed and housed us. That too was an experience worth having as to the life of the people.

We arrived here this morning and leave to-morrow 9.30 for Bourges and Moulins. We shall be in Marseilles on Sunday p.m. instead of Sat evening.

---

[1] Garage proprietors.

But as the boat does not leave till Monday 4 pm. there is no reason to worry. –
We – and I particularly have been thinking a lot of you all. I hope all is well
with you.

Ever Yours

J. C.

Jessie's love.

To Thérèse Aubry
Text MS Yale; *L.fr.* 162–3

Orleans
27.1.21

Madame.[1]

Je suis sur que Vous voudrez bien me pardonner de ne pas avoir ecrit
auparavant. La petite communauté ambulante Vous remercie bien vivement
du cadeau que nous a été remis par Jean, et dont l'excellence a été on ne
peut plus appreciée.

Ma femme et moi fûmes très heureux de lui voir bien meilleure mine
que quand il était chez nous dernièrement. Il m'est difficile de Vous dire,
Madame, tout le plaisir que nous éprouvons a l'avoir avec nous.

Ma femme et moi nous Vous prions Madame d'accepter pour Vous même
et pour M. Votre mari l'expression de respectueuse amitié que, quoique per-
sonnellement inconnus, nous portons aux parents de notre chèr* et apprecié
ami.

Croyez moi Madame toujours Votre très devoué

Joseph Conrad.

Translation

Madam.

I am sure that you will forgive me for not having written to you before.
The little travelling community thanks you very much for the gift you sent
to us through Jean, the excellence of which could not be more appreciated.

My wife and I are very glad to see him on much better form than he was
when at our home recently. It is difficult to tell you, Madam, all the pleasure
we feel in having him with us.

My wife and I pray, Madam, that you accept both for yourself and your
husband the expression of our respectful friendship, which, though we do

[1] Thérèse Aubry (née Contant), the mother of Conrad's friend Jean-Aubry, lived in Rouen with
her husband Frédéric-Ferdinand Aubry.

not know one another personally, we extend to the parents of our dear and esteemed friend.

Believe me, Madam, always very devotedly yours

Joseph Conrad.

To J. B. Pinker

Text MS Berg; J-A, 2, 254 (in part)[1]

[letterhead: Splendide Hôtel, Marseilles]
Sunday,
30. Jan. 21,
9. pm.

Dearest J B

(This is a most horrid pen)

We arrived here at 5.30 after some more adventures but this time amongst the foothills where I lost the way trying for a short cut. But, we found a magnificent sunset over these wild and barren peaks. Then night set in and we had to lower the car as it were foot by foot under an amazingly starry sky, creeping down in perfect solitude into a sort of purple-black abyss which was in fact the Valley of the Rhone. Eventually we reached Montelimar at about 8 o'clock – all four (Vinten inc.)[2] frightfully thirsty with sheer excitement.

Great fun – to look back upon.

For some reason or other the French post refuses to accept parcels of Nougat for the U.K. I suspect it's some of our Custom house fun in the matter of sugar. However we take all Your rations to Corsica.[3]

Pray explain to Your Ladies to whom our love.

To-day skies cloudy but soft. Everything looks promising J. B! Throw care to the winds and come out south with punctuality and dispatch. To morrow I'll have to fly round about embarking my party and "matériel".[4]

Ever Yours

J. Conrad.

PS Love to E[ric] & R[alph]. We heard by wire that everybody at Oswalds was well.

---

[1] Jean-Aubry omits the postscript.
[2] The Conrads' chauffeur, Charles Vinten, and Audrey Seal, Mrs Conrad's nurse-companion, accompanied the Conrads to Corsica.
[3] A case of war-time restrictions not yet abolished. Nougat is the great delicacy of Montélimar.
[4] As if starting on a military expedition.

To Eric Pinker

Text MS Berg; J-A, 2, 254–5 (in part)[1]

G[d] Hotel d'Ajaccio & Cont[al]
5.2.21. Ajaccio.

My dear Eric.

I wired you yesterday a request to pay J. Burchett (my gardener) £5 per week. I did forget to ask J. B. in my last letter (in Engl[d]) to him. It contained a request to pay B[orys] interest at the rate of 5% on the £1000 I promised him a long time ago, which for th[e] current quarter will amount to £12.10. Also to pay for him either his railway fares (to Oswalds) as incurred or the amount of a season ticket.

Will you please see to it? I will of course mention these matters to J B when I see him here.

The weather is bad – and no mistake. Cold. Wet. Horrors. A lot of rather smart people are staying in this beastly hotel. Amongst others Col Hunter[2] the distinguished Polo player with a delicate wife and two stylish girls of whom one is his step-daughter. Also Cap[t] Abercrombie[3] the great authority on Corsica of which he is supposed to know more than any other man: history, topography, customs, habits (dirty rather), shooting, fishing, climbing – and everything else you can think of. I haven't cross-examined him yet. There are also a few mature wandering women and a small proportion of (rather better class) frumps. An atmosphere of intense good form pervades the place. Low tones – polite smiles – kind inquiries – small groups. The only disreputable looking person is the unavoidable Clergyman of the C[hurch] of E[ngland] who looks as tho' he must have had a few adventures in his time . . .

The exploring of Corsica will be no small undertaking – I can see. The confounded island is bigger than one thought, and wilder too.[4] My wife sends you her kindest regards.

Affect[ly] yours

J. Conrad.

---

[1] Jean-Aubry omits the first and second paragraphs and the last sentence of the third.
[2] Lieut Col Charles Finlayson Hunter (1880–1956), educated at Repton, had served with distinction during the war.
[3] Robert Alexander Abercromby of the Scots Guards.
[4] More than 3,300 square miles, not many of them flat.

To Eric Pinker
Text MS Berg; Unpublished

[Ajaccio]
13.2.21.

My dear Eric

I hear they sent you from home a cheque made to order of Mrs Conrad which I forgot to sign. (£9.*10.0*)

Pray send a cheque for the amount to Mrs J Conrad's account at
Lloyd's Bank. Ashford. Kent.

And oblige

Yours

J. Conrad.

To S. S. Pawling
Text MS Morgan; Unpublished

G^{d} Hotel d'Ajaccio
Ajaccio.
France.
23.2.21

Dear Mr Pawling,

In the matter of the set of the Ld Edition reserved for Mr Jean Aubry: – I was under the impression that the late Mr Heinemann wished to give it to him.

It is possible that he had not made it clear (before his death) to the office, and thus an acct has been sent to Aubry. Please let the cost of the set be charged to me as in the terms of our agreement.[1]

Kindest regards from my wife

Yours very sincerely

Joseph Conrad.

To G. Jean-Aubry
Text MS Yale; *L.fr.* 163–4

Ajaccio.
23.2.21

Tres chèr*.

Je viens d'écrire a Heinemann au sujet de l'edition. Puisque ce n'est pas le don de feu H. ce sera le mien.

---

[1] Notes on the letter read 'Credit Aubray* chge Conrad 1/2' and '1/2 Price to J. C 1/2 cost to org.'

Je croyais que ma femme vous a envoyé une C[arte]-P[ostale] ou même deux. Moi j'en ai donné une a l'employé de l'agent de R. A. C pour la mettre a la poste. Il a oublié de le faire il parait.

Pardonnez moi le long silence. Cette expedition n'est pas tout a fait le succès que nous ésperions. Enfin!

Je suis nerveux, exaspéré, ennuyé – et ainsi de suite. La famiglia del Signor P[inker] est ici. Miss Hallowes va arriver dans 7 jours. Nous n'avons pas fait d'excursions. Il fait assez froid dans l'après midi.[1] L'hotel est détéstable. Les Corses sont charmants (je veux dire le peuple), mais les montagnes me donnent sur les nerfs avec leur chemins qui tournent tournent[2] en corniche indéfiniment. On a envie de hurler.

Vous nous avez manqué beaucoup, mais beaucoup – après Lyon. Ma femme Vous fait toutes ses amitiés auquels Audrey joint ses best regards. Nous avons eu une petite panne entre Lyon et Montélimart* compensée par un magnifique coucher de soleil dans les montagnes ou j'ai perdu le chemin, de sorte que nous ne sommes arrivés a M^{art} qu'a 8^h du soir.

Par contre nous sommes arrivés a Marseille (Dimanche) avant 5^h. Dejeuner a Avignon – très bon.

Je Vous raconterai tout cela par le detail quand nous nous reverrons.

Je suis content de savoir que Vs avez passé les epreuves des deux livres. Je suis impatient de les lire. Le vol *En Marge* sera aussi le bienvenu. Tous nos souhaits pour Votre succès en Espagne.

Mme C. marche avec la canne seulement. Nous avons de bonnes nouvelles des garçons. Il n'y a que moi qui reste grincheux et déprimé. P[inker] envoit ses salutations. Nous ésperons que Vs voudrez traduire la petite pièce pour le Guignol, plus tard.

Je Vous embrasse mon cher Jean et je suis toujour[s] votre vieux

J Conrad

Translation

My dear friend.

I have just written to Heinemann's about the edition. Since it is not a gift from the late H., it will be my own.

I thought my wife had sent you a postcard or even two. *I* gave one to the employee of the R. A. C. agent to post. It seems he forgot to.

---

[1] Too cold, in other words, even for an afternoon drive.
[2] Dittography or a stylistic effect?

Pray forgive my long silence. This expedition isn't at all the success we'd hoped for. Oh, well!

I am restless, exasperated, bored, and so on. Signor P.'s family is here. Miss Hallowes arrives in a week. We have not gone on any excursions. The afternoons are quite cold. The hotel is beastly. The Corsicans are charming (I mean the people), but the mountains get on one's nerves with their everlasting hair-pin bends. One wants to scream.

We missed you very much, very much indeed, after Lyons. My wife sends friendly best wishes to which Audrey joins her best regards. We had a minor breakdown between Lyons and Montélimar made up for by a wonderful sunset in the mountains where I lost the way, with the result that we didn't arrive in Montélimar till eight in the evening.

On the other hand, we arrived in Marseilles (on Sunday) before 5 o'clock. Lunch at Avignon – very good.

I will tell you about all this in detail next time we meet.

I am very glad to hear you have finished the proofs for the two volumes. I am impatient to read them. The *Within the Tides* volume will also be welcome. All our wishes for your success in Spain.

Mrs C. is walking with just a stick. We have good news of the boys. I alone remain ill-tempered and depressed. P. sends his greetings. We hope you will want to translate the little Guignol play in due course.

I embrace you, my dear Jean, and remain ever your old

J Conrad

To Lillian M. Robins

Text MS Indiana; Unpublished

G^d Hotel d'Ajaccio.
Ajaccio.
23. Febr. 1921.

Dear Mrs Robins.[1]

I have this moment received your letter of the 7th inst. addressed to Miss Hallowes (who has not arrived here yet) and containing the "front matter" of the Life & Letters vol.

That is quite all right as far as form is concerned. The only exception I take is to the list of my works which I should like printed *not* in order of publication in book form.

J. C.[2]

---

[1] Lillian M. Robins was F. N. Doubleday's secretary.
[2] Here Conrad rearranges a printed alphabetical list as a numbered and roughly chronological one, adding the note 'order of Publication in book form J. C.'

To Karola Zagórska
Text MS copy Yale;[1] Najder 266–7

G^d Hôtel d'Ajaccio
Ajaccio.
6.3.21.

My dear,

I assure you that on the day we arrived here I gave a whole packet of postcards – among them one for you – to the hotel door-keeper to post. I don't understand how your card did not reach you. I confess that since then I have not written any letters, not only not to you but to no one except Borys about a matter concerning him.

I am quite ashamed of myself. But please forgive this sin – as well as all the others – of your Conrad who cherishes you. Just before leaving I caught an awful cough and for about ten days after we arrived here did not feel at all well – it was something similar to asthma. Add to that a depression that I am unable to get rid of. Je vous dis ça en confidence because with people and with my wife I put a good face on things.

Jessie is enjoying Corsica. She walks with a stick and looks well. But she, too, has become lazy and neglects her correspondence. She sends you her dear love and promises to write to you in a few days. The boys send us good news. B[orys] is working in London, and John is at Tonbridge at school where we sent him before leaving.

Pray drop me a line to say you've forgiven my long silence. That is enough for to-day. We will stay here for about a fortnight and then perhaps go to Bastia.

Always your affectionate
Konrad

To J. M. Dent & Sons, Ltd
Text Telegram UNC; Moore

[Ajaccio]
[8 March 1921][2]

Templarian London
Correct if possible page eighteen line eight first word[3] also on page one hundred sixty nine line fifteen print when instead of where

Conrad

---

[1] In French.
[2] Date-stamp. Despatched from Ajaccio at 11.25 a.m. and received at the West Strand P. O. at 5.20 p.m.
[3] The misprint 'perosnal' in Dent's *Notes on Life and Letters*.

To Edward Garnett

Text MS Sutton;[1] J-A, 2, 255–6; G. 305–7

G^d Hotel d'Ajaccio Corse
18.3.21.

Dearest Edward

I am a prey to remorse for not having thanked you yet for the marine prints you mentioned in your letter to the Audrey child. It's very dear of you to have thought of me in that particular way.

To read your letter was the greatest pleasure, for you know praise for you would count against the world. For that very reason blame from you causes me a great concern. It may be I failed to understand the Ascending Effort,[2] but I did not mean to treat Bourne disrespectfully. The thesis of the book is vitiated by the fact that poetry and religion having their source in an emotional state may act and react on each other worthily – whereas "Science" at its amplest (and profoundest) is only the exercise of a certain kind of imagination springing either from facts eminently prosaic or from tentative assumptions of the commonest kind of common-sense. And you will admit that Bourne's writing in its slightly grotesque heaviness made it very difficult to read the whole book in a spirit of impartiality – let alone benevolence. I agree with you about Tchehov, absolutely. But that great and wonderful man did not write his stories in praise of the Medical science.[3] Poetical genius must be nourished on knowledge – it can't have too much of it – but you will imagine easily what a poem in praise of knowledge would be like – even if an Archangel came down from Heaven on purpose to write it for our edification. Nevertheless I am sorry to have provoked your displeasure. But also pray reflect that I had only a column on the last page of the Daily Mail – and that it couldn't either help or hurt Bourne's book. As to myself I simply said (quite superficially) what I thought, and damaged myself in your opinion – which is punishment enough. Justice is satisfied.

I had no idea you had never read the Autocracy and War lucubration. How far all that is! I wish I had your M. Guardian article.[4] You are a dear

---

[1] Formerly in the now-dispersed Sutton collection, the original was not available for rechecking. In the second paragraph, 'Bourne's writing in its ... heaviness made' is a conjectural emendation. J-A reads 'Bourne, writing in his ... heaviness, made'; G. (and Karl) read 'Bourne, writing in its ... heaviness made'.

[2] *The Ascending Effort* by George Bourne (pseudonym of the author and wheelwright George Sturt, 1863–1927) was published in April 1910. Conrad's review for the *Daily Mail* was reprinted in *Notes on Life and Letters*.

[3] Though Anton Chekhov was a doctor.

[4] His review of *Notes on Life and Letters* in the *Manchester Guardian*, 15 March, p. 5, reprinted in the *Manchester Guardian Weekly*, 18 March, p. 214. For its gist, see the notes to the letter of [11 April].

to have made a fuss till they sent you the book; but you cannot doubt that a copy (of the first issue) has been reserved for you. I did not tell Dent to send it to you because I always inscribe your copies and was going to do so on our return from here – which by the bye will be at the end of April.

I am glad you like the "Maupassant". I was never satisfied with it but shall think better of it now. After all the things in that book – it is not my trade! There's not a single one (with the exception of the Censor)[1] that I haven't done unwillingly – against the grain.

I won't bore you with a relation of the Island of Corsica and its inhabitants. This outing is a success as far as Jessie is concerned. She sends her dear love to you. I am neither the better nor the worse for being here – in health, that is. I would perhaps [have] done some work if I had stayed at home. But God only knows! Head empty. Feelings as if dead – except the feeling of my unalterable affection for you.

Ever yours

J Conrad.

To R. D. Mackintosh

Text MS Alberta; Jellard

G^d Hotel Continental

Ajaccio

Corse.

19.3.21.

My dear Mac.

Many thanks for your good friendly letter. I don't remember exactly that my meeting with Simpson had that dramatic complexion Your letter gave to it. He has not written to me yet. Perhaps (like me) he is too lazy to write letters, and only thinks of writing them, (for days) without putting pen to paper. I shall act with prudence and discretion so as not to make an enemy of a professional critic.

I wonder what the D[aily] T[elegraph] article about my book was like to make B[orys] so very ill.[2] That boy can read a lot of rubbish without turning a hair. But you had perhaps better not show him any more newspaper articles since he seems to be so easily upset by them.

---

[1] 'The Censor of Plays: An Appreciation', written at Garnett's request in October 1907.
[2] Arthur Waugh favourably reviewed *Notes on Life and Letters* in the *Daily Telegraph* of 4 March, p. 15. Waugh's inoffensive prose offers no obvious cause for distress, but Borys's psyche was still fragile.

I can't tell how happy we both are made by what you write about that same delicate creature that can't digest a D. T. article. Pray my dear Mac never doubt our grateful sense of your kindness to our boys and Your friendship for us all.

B apart from his affection for You personally has a great fund of loyalty at the disposal of any work his heart may be engaged in. This is the case with the work you have put in his way. There is no doubt of his sticking to you as long as you have any use for him. We can see from his letters that he is perfectly happy where he is and most intensely interested both in the technical side and the business future of your Scientific appliances comp^y.

We intend to arrive home on the 30 Ap. after being driven through France by B. A great treat for his mother who sends her love and will be writing to You in a day or two.

Always most affectly Yours

Joseph Conrad

PS Your copy of Life & Letters in now at Oswalds awaiting the inscription.

To J. B. Pinker
Text MS Berg; Unpublished

[Ajaccio]

Sunday. [20? March 1921][1]

Dearest J. B.

Just a line this time to tell you that we returned from our expedition which had a certain charm and included the town of Cap Corse. I can not tell you how much you have been missed at the back of the car and also in front and in the monkey-house of the Bastia hotel and generally all the time and at every occasion of a charming or quaint sight of Corsican scenery or people.

I do hope (and everybody with me) that you are well – or at any rate better than you were when you left us. On Friday at dinner we drank to your happy return home trying to figure the scene to ourselves. Give our love to your

---

[1] On the 6th Conrad mentions plans to stay in Ajaccio for a fortnight before touring the island, but even given changes, a return to Ajaccio on or before the 13th seems too early. The letter promised for Tuesday (written, in fact, on Thursday) likewise supports the 20th as does the letter from Mackintosh to which Conrad replied on the 19th.

troops which I hope did not mutiny on the passage and did not get out of hand to loot the Paris shops.

Ever affect^{ly} yours

J. Conrad.

PS Found here a letter from Mac quite enthusiastic about B[orys] from every point of view. I'll write you on Tuesday.

To J. B. Pinker
Text MS Berg; Unpublished

G^d Hotel Ajaccio.
24.3.21.

My dear J. B.

As you know by now we regarded your wire as eminently satisfactory. I was writing to Mac in answer to his enthusiastic letter about B[orys] hinting that he had better keep him at work since he was so useful, but I cancelled that page as the matter is now settled on the boy's own initiative – which is much better in every way.

Mac expresses his hope that he will "stick to us". I think there can be no doubt of his sticking. B. has a fund of loyalty in him – loyalty to his work as well as to people. He likes Mac very much. M. says he is thinking of giving him a "position that will give him a personal interest in his work". I will know what this phrase means exactly when we get back.

The cough still tormenting me I have fixed our departure from here for the 5 April (Tuesday's boat: the *Numidia*). Another reason is that I have started on the novel and wanted to give myself 12 days more before the interruption. Also the weather will be better for rolling across France. This means arr: Mars^{lle} on the 6th – leaving M. on the 7th early morning – arriving Amiens (by the R[oyal] A[utomobile] C[lub] route all the way) on the 15th – I hope – for the night.

Here comes a wish I have formed and which I impart to you for your judgment. The 15 is a Friday. Perhaps by starting by the afternoon Paris train B having John with him could get to Amiens that night and on Sat and Sunday take us along the Flanders front passing Sund. night at Mont de Cats[1] – reaching Calais on Monday night and crossing over on Tuesday morning.

---

[1] Overlooking the site of the war's last German offensive.

So that he could be back at work on Wed^y morning. He can hardly have any business appointements* fixed for these days, already; at* as to attendance in the workshop he would only miss two days – no great matter. Of course if there is something special going on there he mustn't absent himself; but the fact is that unless this proposal is carried out I am not very likely to ever see the front and certainly Jessie never will. We are not likely to have the car over in France again, soon, if ever we have! Please dear J. B. feel the way and if it can be done let B. know of the plan – in fact show him this letter if you like.

I am writing this before the arrival of Your promised letter, but we assume that You and Mrs Pinker will have the kindness to have John at Burys Court when his holidays begin. Please give her, the Elf and Your two young Braves our united love.[1]

As to our return: I'll have two weeks to settle in this beastly hotel before our departure. The Customs made me pay 6 months tax on the car. I shall make a claim for the return of half of it through the R. A. C. agent in Marseille. But that will take time. I don't know exactly what my petrol bill will be as I want to go to Sartène[2] before leaving Corsica and Jessie must go out a little every day. I sent *1000* frs to B. & *1000* to Karola (pray complete her quarter). She has a hard enough life of it. (If you are uncertain of the address direct to

Consolato di Pologna p. la Signa Karola Zagórska
33 piazza Cajazzo.
Milan)

and I had to lend 500 frs to Miss Dickson who may pay back before we leave – but on the other hand may leave it till her arrival in England. (She got into trouble for quarrelling with a French Count – in Piana – and calling him a Boche! She must be mad. All Corsica is ringing with the story.)

Please send me 2.500 frs to Marseille c/o Basden Smith Esq. Roy. Auto. Club. 3 Rue Noailles. Dr[awn] to the L[ondon] C[ounty] W[estminster]. & Parr's Bank which has a branch in M.

I will answer Your letter by return. This day is the 25 anniversary of Mrs J. C. and me entering into the bonds of wedlock. I wonder what sort it would have been if J. B. P had not entered into our life?

Our dear love to you.

Yours ever

J. Conrad.

---

[1] Oenone, and Eric and Ralph Pinker.
[2] A mediaeval hill-town in the south of the island.

To J. B. Pinker

Text MS Berg; Unpublished

Ajaccio.

Easter Sunday [27 March 1921]

(This leaves to night via Ile Rousse[1])

Dear J. B.

On receipt of Your later news I made up my mind to leave here on Tuesday (29th) a week before the day mentionned* in my letter to you; but on account of the derrick of the *Corsica* being too small to lift the car I had to make up my mind to leave on Thurs: (31st) by the *Liamone* for Nice. There was the alternative of waiting here for the Saturday boat (which would have taken the car) and proceeding to Marseilles. But this means arriving in Mars: on Sunday – a day on which everything would be closed. Also as pursuant on my request to you I would have to call on the L. W. Parr's Bank on Monday, the start would have to be made late on that day I decided for Nice. The hotel expences* will be about the same running as staying and I am doing no good here. Too worried. I want to feel myself moving home to face whatever there is to face good, bad or indifferent.

I will arrive then at Nice on Friday (1st Ap) at 5 AM and hope to reach Marseille (168 miles) the same evening about 6.30. I will wire you to-morrow (to day P.O. closed) asking to request bank telegraph order to pay me to their branch at Mars: so that I can get the money on Sat. before noon. I'll start from M. after lunch and sleep at Avignon on Saturday (2[d] A). From there I am not very certain what route I will take – but it will be Versailles – Amiens – Calais at the northern end, but I will post a letter to B[orys] from Mars: and let him know by wire every day how we are progressing.

Anyway I can't be in Amiens before Friday (9th) and if the boys could meet us there for the week-end we could see something of the front on Sat & Sunday and cross over from Calais on Monday (13th) morning.[2] In that case I would send Vinten and Miss H[allowes] by rail from Amiens.

Or B & J[ohn] could come to Calais. From there in 24 hours we could see Ypres at least. Or if even that cannot be done I should like B to meet me at Calais to see me through there as I don't feel (now) as if I could rush about. Two days away could not affect his prospects.

Ask him please for the name of the hotel in Amiens (which I have forgotten) and also the name of one in Calais where we could go for the night, and

---

[1] The seaport on the north coast or a ship named after it?

[2] In fact, Friday the 8th and Monday the 11th.

wire them to me Hotel Louvre et Paix, Marseille. I reckon this scrawl will reach you on Thursday or early on Friday (1st) at latest in time for wires to get through to me on that day. Pardon all this long rigamarole.[1]

Ever Yours

J. Conrad.

To J. B. Pinker

Text MS Berg; Unpublished

Ajaccio.

Monday. [28 March 1921][2]

Dearest J B.

I sent you a letter yesterday which you would have read by this. It did not contain the thanks due to you for your support of and advice to Borys. As to that I wanted to write separately.

You must not imagine for a moment that we are (or ever were, even for a moment) cut up by the upsetting of the "family plans". I am only thankful that you were on the spot for the boy to come to you with his tale and ready to assist him. I can't but conclude that you think well of the proposed transaction. As to me it is in a sense more than I expected. I suppose You take the same view with me of the required investment (of £350) – that it is meant to qualify him for the seat at the board. It is natural to suppose that if Mac had *wanted* the mere amount he could have found it easily amongst his own connections. He is a man of transparent sincerity in all his actions and purposes. He really means to give a lift to the boy and has formed a good opinion of him. *That* is the most satisfactory thing to me.

As to you my warmest thanks are due to you for setting my mind at rest as to the condition being fulfilled.

We will leave here on Thurs: evening. It's no use staying on till the fifth as I intended at first. In fact I am sorry I didn't make a move a week after your departure.

I would love dear JB to get in contact with you even before my return is generally known. I will not be good for much till the situation is taken in hand.[3] Will you let me see you as soon as possible after my arrival home. The very next day if you like. I am only wondering how your health is for I

---

[1] Facetious spelling.

[2] The letter of the 27th matches Conrad's description of what he had written 'yesterday'.

[3] Conrad's finances were in disarray (see April's letters).

would hate to be a nuisance to you. Yet up to a certain point I must be – and I can't tell you how sorry I am for it.

Give our love to the Family

Ever Yours

J. Conrad.

I have done a lot of reading and have picked up some good stuff for the novel. From that point of view the journey has not been all loss. I enclose a press [?] cutting somebody sent me.[1]

To Edward Garnett
Text MS Indiana; G. 307–8

Oswalds
Monday. [11 April 1921][2]

Dearest Edward

We returned yesterday, and the first letter I write is to thank You with all the warmth of which I am capable for Your review in Guardian. Anything coming from You has a particular value and on this occasion you have been as generous to me as You have ever been from the earliest day of our acquaintance, with a deep understanding and clear eyed affection which makes it easy to accept – and indeed to cherish.[3]

Give David my and Jessie's very best and most friendly good wishes on the occasion of his "change of status".[4] I don't know how he may feel about it, but to me marriage still seems as great an adventure as tho' I myself had never been married. As to his proposed attitude toward a "cold and critical" world it is eminently praiseworthy in its independence and, apart from that, practically very sound. I, in my utter loneliness, was never faced by the problem of "friends". You were the only land one and I remember the charitable indulgence with which you received the news and the priceless simple kindness with which your wife and you received Jessie when I brought

---

[1] A review of *Notes on Life and Letters?*   [2] Garnett supplies the date.

[3] Conrad and Garnett first met in 1894. Garnett's review of *Notes on Life and Letters* (*Manchester Guardian*, 15 March, p. 5) is judicious rather than adulatory. Although he writes admiringly of 'Autocracy and War' and 'The Censor of Plays', his emphasis falls on the literary pieces. These, he argues, are the work of a 'born artist' rather than a 'born critic'. Thus, the piece on Henry James 'yields only the most ghostly impression of that master's literary kingdom'. 'When moved by sympathy of understanding', however, Conrad's 'critical appreciations are lucid, penetrating and comprehensive, as his luminous pages on Daudet, Maupassant, Anatole France, and Turgenev . . . attest, but his temperament does not readily imbue itself with the atmosphere or follow the curves of other men's works'.

[4] He married Rachel ('Ray') Marshall on 30 March.

her to the Cearne.[1] From the first you extended to her your characteristic generosity of acceptance of which she became aware early and has received with an admiring understanding of you[r] personality reached by God knows what mysterious intuitive process and therefore perfectly unshakeable – to the end of time.

I rejoice at the news of the American publication of Your critical articles in book form.[2] The prospect of Your activity dearest Edward arouses my excited interest. We must soon have a talk. There can be no question of me coming to town yet and I don't know how You may feel about running down here when the train service becomes normal again.[3] Drop us a line. I am anxious to know what You have exactly in your mind.

Our dear love to You.

Yours ever

J. Conrad

To G. Jean-Aubry
Text MS Yale; Unpublished

Oswalds
Lundi. [11 April 1921][4]

Mon très cher.

Pinker vient ici aujourd'hui pour un jour ou deux pour causer de mes affaires qui sont pour le moment fort embrouillées.

Donc choisissez un jour (après Mercredi) pour Votre visite – journée, ou passer la nuit, ou si Vous pouvez le prochain week-end. Nous desirons fort Vous voir avant Votre départ pour Paris.

Amitiés de la part de tout le monde. Je vous embrasse

Conrad

Translation

Monday.

My very dear friend.

Pinker is coming to-day for a day or two to talk over my affairs which are very muddled at the moment.

---

[1] The Garnetts' woodland house on the Kent/Surrey border. Their generous welcome there in March 1896 concealed misgivings about Conrad's impending marriage to Jessie George.
[2] Garnett's *Friday Nights*, accepted by Knopf, appeared in 1922.
[3] A miners' strike had caused a shortage of coal, disrupting services throughout April and May.
[4] Date from postmark.

So choose a day (after Wednesday) for your visit – for the day, or to stay the night or, if you can, next week-end. We should very much like to see you before you leave for Paris.

Friendly regards from everybody. I embrace you

Conrad

To E. L. and Helen Sanderson
Text MS Yale; Unpublished

[letterhead: Oswalds][1]
[mid- or late April? 1921][2]

Dearest Ted and Helen.[3]

Here is the thing of sheets and patches[4] – but you must have all my books as they come out.

Thank you my dear Ted for your letter. Give my love to all your children and a special message of "Good luck" to Ian.[5] I wish I had been able to run over and see you all and hear some of his Naval yarns.

The first 5 vols of my limited Edition (sorry it is U.S. one) will be reaching you shortly. —

Heinemann's sudden death deprived me of my allowance of the English ed^{on}. On his visit to me he made a note of my requirements but did not send it to his counting house before he died. I managed to get sets for my boys – and as to more I could not buy them in the market by now, even at a premium. It was subscribed twice over. Our dearest love to you all.

J. C.

---

[1] On a note-card with abbreviated letterhead.

[2] Contents provide clues for this placement: a date not long after Conrad's return from Corsica seems plausible, and the promise of only five volumes of the Doubleday collected edition, which appeared in January, argues against a date too late in the month since ten volumes were in print by then.

[3] Edward Lancelot ('Ted') Sanderson (1867–1939) travelled from Australia with John Galsworthy in the *Torrens* in 1893. On that voyage, Conrad, then serving as first mate, showed him a draft of *Almayer's Folly*. Sanderson, who had read Classics at King's College, Cambridge, taught at Elstree, his family's preparatory school in Hertfordshire. After service in the Boer War, he and his wife, Helen, remained in Africa, first in Johannesburg, then in Nairobi, where he served as town clerk. He returned to England in 1910 to become Elstree's headmaster.

Helen Mary Sanderson (née Watson, 1874–1967), who married Ted in 1898, was a Scotswoman full of moral and intellectual vigour. As 'Janet Allardyce', she contributed sketches of East African life to *Scribner's Magazine*.

[4] Playing on a number in Gilbert and Sullivan's *The Mikado* (1885), Act I: 'A wandering minstrel I – / A thing of shreds and patches', which itself makes fun of Hamlet's 'A king of threads and patches' (3.4.102). Conrad may refer to *Notes on Life and Letters*, which appeared in late February while he was abroad, or, less aptly, *Notes on My Books*, published in March.

[5] Ian Campbell MacDougall Sanderson (1900–79) trained as a naval cadet and joined the Royal Navy during the war, rising to become a commander before retiring in 1931. From 1935 to 1969 he was Headmaster of Elstree.

To J. B. Pinker
Text MS Berg; Unpublished

[letterhead: Oswalds]
19 Ap. '21

Dearest J B.

I send you herewith two statements A & B and beg you to give them a little time and patience. I believe you want me to realise the situation clearly and give my personal attention to my affairs. These 2 statements are my view of it at the present moment and as to the way of reckoning the future.

You will see I make a fresh start from the 13 April. What happened up to then is done with and no reckoning it up backwards can affect the future. I assure you of my sincere regret at having caused you some temporary worry and I believe some irritation also. It was quite natural but pray my dear friend remember that I had not a scrap of writing for 6 years to make me realise the pace in *black and white*; that I am not a careful person naturally. You cannot doubt that if I had been given a clear view of having doubled my expenditure between the years 1918–1919 I would not* have pulled myself together and prevented the doubling of it again between 1919–1920 – which is pretty near what in fact happened. To a man of your ability in judging character I need not protest that I am not a reckless spendthrift. So I won't. This moral aspect may be left aside and only the material result considered.

Believe [me] my dear it is not good for a man (even of much steadier character than mine) to have money falling on him in envelopes as if from heaven without ever a clear wiew* of the resources from which it flows and opportunity of comparing and checking. Especially if he's a man by nature not particularly given to counting pennies. And if you ask me: Why the devil didn't you ask for the information? I can only answer: For the same reason for which you refrained from imparting it to me. From delicacy. I thought you preferred it to be so. While you must have thought that it was better for me to be without it – for reasons which could not and were no other that* kind: for my peace of mind, for freedom in my work, for ease in my thoughts busy with creative effort. Of that I am certain. As certain as you are of the truth of what I say to you. With us two it can not be otherwise.

On one occasion in Ajaccio you said: of course if you prefer that I should pay everything into a bank . . . I interrupted you. There's nothing that I want less! Please read the two statements enclosed here and if my frame of mind commends itself to you you will tell me that you will still act as my banker: – that is, receive and hold all payments in your hands, give me your advice, finance me over any difficulties that may arise by advances against the moneys that may be coming due – in fact be what you always have been from the start a moral and material support – and at the same time instruct you[r] counting house to keep me informed frequently of incomings and outgoings and generally of my position in the way a pass-book informs a man as to the state of his account. This will do away with all occasions of worry. The other method has been tried. Ignorance I believe is never a check. Let us try knowledge, and there will be no irritating surprises. I ask you this not as a client but as a friend who is sure of your friendship. For if that is not a certain thing I wonder what is in this world? Try it at any rate for the next six months – and then if you find that troublesome for your office (which after all is not meant to be a bank) you will tell me so and see me safe before you cut me adrift to take care of myself like all your mere "clients" have to do.

Don't answer this, but give it your consideration and tell me what you think when we meet.

Ever affect^{ly} Yours

J Conrad.

PS I send this to your home but I have no objection to Eric being fully informed as to all my business – *if you think fit.*

Statement A

Oswalds,
Bishopsbourne,
Kent.
April 18th. 1921.[1]

View of immediate provision. To get a clear view of the situation we will start from *13th of April*, 1921, when I received your verbal assurance that "some money having come in" I was owing you nothing; but the amount that had come in was not mentioned, as I did not ask for it – the important matter, then, for me being only my position towards you as my banker so to speak – in contradistinction to the results of your activities as my literary agent.

The position then as resumed from the year 1914 (when I had the last statement of account) to above date was:-

To J. B. P. *indebted* nothing.

To various bills admittedly not complete or correctly ascertained, £562, as far as I could see then. This not including, so far, Hayward's bill and payments of £25 per quarter to Ninnes in future till extinction of his account against me.

---

[1] The statements are TS/MS and form part of the letter of the 19th.

To provide for these debts I proposed that the balance of net royalties on the English Limited Edition still owing to me and due for early payment, amounting in fact to £*894.9.0* (calculation enclosed) should be used; and this was agreed between us verbally.

The other payment due on an early date is the payment for *Notes on My Books*, Limited Edition of 250 copies, advertised to appear shortly.

At the royalty of 15/- per copy (English issue) it ought to bring in £187. gross, and £163 net. I am entitled to estimate that the American edition will bring at least the same amount net, making together £326.10. net. This will cover the £300 advanced for Borys's shares: the balance of £26 to go to what we may call the "Debt Covering Fund" of £894 (as stated above) making it altogether £920 to meet liabilities as shown on the note of "accounts due" which was handed to you (amounting to £562) and also any further claims which may come in – but which, I believe, will not exceed the "debt covering fund," including eventually Haywards bill now due for settlement.

J. C.

From our conversations here on the 12 & 13 April I have the impression that your financing me for the above purpose against the moneys soon coming due is a settled matter. I honestly believe that the sums specified above will cover the claims.

Statement B.

Statement for the Future

Starting from April 13th, 1921, as the day on which we reckoned up my outstanding liabilities and agreed as to the resources to be utilised for meeting the same (Statement A) the expenditure for the next year and the means to meet it present themselves to me as follows:-

1° For the means the only document I have to go upon is the statement given me by you estimating the yearly income from books already written (yearly royalties on book[s] old and new up to and inclusive of *Notes on Life and Letters*) at £4264. I accept this estimate in full as the basis of the budget for the next twelve months on your verbal assurance that I may do so safely.

2° Apart from that amount the only incoming moneys that I am positively aware of for the year 1921–2 (for I have known nothing since 1914 either of my incomings or of my outgoings except as I estimated them in my mind) is the 15% royalty payment for the U.S. Limited Edition of 735 Sets at (I think) $100 per set or £25 per set: £*18375* for the *whole* – and (deducting 20% commission) leaving me a net royalty (at 15% of price) of £2190 roughly, and not taking now into consideration Hueffer's proportion, half royalties on two volumes, which will have to be deducted.

Approximately then the moneys to look forward to, say for a twelve month, are (1) £4264 (estimated income) and (2) the U.S. Limited Edition royalties of £2207 (also estimated, as I do not know if any payment on that account has already been made to you by Doubleday and expended to make us "all square" on April 13th).

Therefore in charges and maintenance of my household as against the est^{ed} income of £4264 we have:-

Year's Maintenance of Household		Charges yearly.	
House rent & garden	£500	Borys	200
Jessie's cheques		John	180
(£14 every 7 days)	728	Karola	120
Light & car	400 (est^d)	Mrs George	50
Wages: Vinten and two women	247		—
Miss H. sal: & living	250		£550
Audrey	126		
Serv. ins^{ce} & local taxes (land)	50 (est)		
	—		
	£2301	£2301	
		550	
		—	
		£2851	*expenditure*
		4264	est. income from roy^{ties} books old and new
		—	
Balance	£1413		

which may or may not be wholly absorbed by the income-tax. I have also a doubt in my mind whether the est^{ed} income as stated is net or gross. If the last then the balance will certainly *not* be sufficient to cover taxation. And in *any case* there is nothing for contingencies – pocket money books, clothing, travelling, entertaining or anything in the way of club subscription and such like disburs[e]ments.

Remaining in this house under such conditions would be out of [the] question if it were not for the U.S. Ld Edition royalties, of the amount of which I am not positively certain for the reasons you know. Pray dear J. B. direct the office to let me know how that matter stands precisely. If the amount turns out somewhere about £1.800 I propose to appropriate £1000 to income and leave the balance in reserve to meet a possible deficiency in the esti^{ed} income (one never knows), or some utterly unexpected call. A thousand for contingencies may seem a large sum; but you will note that (assuming the balance (£1413) of est^d inc^{me} to vanish in taxation) my whole expenditure (maint^{ce} charges – and contingencies) including that 1000 will be only £3851 *for the year*.

Under these conditions I would be inclined to stay here for six months longer as an experiment and to see meantime how things are going to shape themselves as to the new book, the prospects of our film-play and as regards the staging and fortunes of the Secret Agent. There will be also the payment for the film-rights of Rescue to come in as those will have to take up their option definitely in a month or two I think. This I believe is fixed by agreement at £1100. (Also to be held in reserve to help out the income if need should arise).

J. C.

English Lim^d Edition[1]

750 sets. 18 vol p. set. Roy^{ty} 3/- per vol	=	
	40 500 shgs less 20%	= £2025 Gross 405^2
	nett Roy.	£1620.

---

[1] Text from the TS. A heavily corrected MS draft in Conrad's hand accompanies this calculation.

to deduct 5% on roy^ties on 4 works in three vols

to Fisher Unwin	=	£16.17.0

5% Methuen on roy^ties
   on six works in

	six vol	33.14.0

to publishers on royties	50.11.0	
on 9 vols}		
leaves nett Roy		£1569.90

to deduct 1/2 roy^ties on two vols to F. M. Hueffer = 112.10.0

leaves as my proportion of _____
nett roy^ties

                          £1456.19.0.

But 5 vols having been issued and presumably paid for and expended before 13 April '21 the nett balance to come to me deducting the £562.10 roy. on 5 vols is *£894.9.0*

To J. B. Pinker

Text MS postcard Berg; Unpublished

Oswalds. B'bourne
20.4.'21.

Dear J. B.

    Thanks for wire. It's understood that I come *in car* to see McKinnel with you.[2] Pray instruct office to have 5 £ notes for me.

Yours

J. C.

---

[1] According to Hallowes, Pinker's share in the proceeds from the collected edition.

[2] As the next three letters show, Pinker and Conrad went to see him play the lead in his own production of Rudolf Besier and May Edginton's *The Ninth Earl*, which closed on the 23rd. Pinker did not however join Conrad in his meeting with McKinnel on Sunday night or early Monday morning.

P.S. Car will have to go back and V[inten] must run light-engine[1] on Friday. B[orys] being in town all the morning tomorrow I write him to be at the club about 12.45 and lunch with us.

To Jessie Conrad
Text MS Yale; *JCLW* 47

[Burys Court, Leigh, Surrey]
Friday. [22 April 1921][2]

Dearest Girl

All well here and I hope You are as chirpy as circumstances and You[r] poor knee will allow.

Saw B[orys] at lunch yesterday. Play rotten. McKinnel very good.

B *may* come down on Sat: Not certain.

Can you send me the car here on Sunday to arrive in the evening and take me up to town on Monday early.

I shall try to see Jack who is back. I want also to have a look at the Mortlake establishment if all that can be managed in one day.

I will wire you for my medicine which was left behind.

Am going with J. B. for a drive in 10 minutes, and the conference with American[s] will take place after lunch to-day.

Give my love to boy John and to the child Audrey

A great hug and kisses on Your dear face.

Your very own

J. C.

To Jessie Conrad
Text MS Yale; *JCLW* 49

[Burys Court, Leigh, Surrey]
Sat. 10. AM. [23 April 1921][3]

Darling Girl

Thanks for your letter. I have now 2 bottles of medicine – but I have no gout; I am only looking out for it in case it should come.

---

[1] Minus passengers, like a railway engine running without carriages or wagons. Vinten was to ferry Conrad and Pinker from the theatre to Burys Court on Thursday evening and drive by himself to Oswalds the following day. He would come back for Conrad on Sunday evening.

[2] *JCLW* dates this as '1919 or early part of 1920', but the reference to 'the Mortlake establishment' where Borys was then working, points to the spring of 1921. With its plans to see McKinnel and instructions for the chauffeur, the postcard of 20 April dates the episode precisely.

[3] Dating turns on the previous letter, with its reference to overlooked medicine, and is confirmed by the story of lunch with the film-people.

I'll wire you on Monday about middle day. I intend to see B[orys] at Barnes – and if possible Jack[1] or perhaps the Colvins. In any case I won't get back before dinner.

I expect a wire from You in the course of today to tell me the car is coming for me tomorrow (Sunday) evening here.

The Americans came yesterday determined to reject the film-play[2] – as I perceived from the first. Being pretty sure of it I gave them a few home truths in my best style. J. B. was immensely amused. I will tell you all about it when I get back.

I have to write to McKinnel (thank him for the seats) before we go out for a drive so I cut this short. I am with you in my thought[s] every minute my dearest. I am somehow under the impression that you had something on your mind when I left you. My dear Kit there is nothing (*that I know*) for you, to worry about.

Lots of love and hugs from your ever most devoted

J. C.

To J. B. Pinker

Text MS Berg; Unpublished

Oswalds.
Tuesday. [26 April 1921][3]

My dear J. B.

Herewith report of my activities yesterday:

– I saw McKinnel as arranged. He had with him a *partner* in his theatrical venture, and the author of the comedy which is to succeed the *Ninth Earl* on Wednesday next.[4] His name has escaped me. I opened at once the subject of doubling the parts.

MacK.* at once raised all the objections which we have foreseen, as: – damaging to the artistic value of the play – critics agreeing that McK is

---

[1] Galsworthy.

[2] 'Gaspar the Strong Man', Robert MacAlarney, Lasky's man in London, put his objections in writing on the 23rd, telling Pinker that the script 'would be weak commercially' (Gene M. Moore, 'Conrad's "Film-play" *Gaspar the Strong Man*', in Gene M. Moore, ed., *Conrad on Film* (Cambridge University Press, 1997), p. 41).

[3] The events described or anticipated in the two preceding letters and the postcard of the 20th settle the date.

[4] *The Ninth Earl* was followed by Ernest Cecil's *A Matter of Fact*; it actually opened the following day rather than 'Wednesday next'; once again McKinnel both produced and took the lead. The original plan had been to meet McKinnel on the 25th. Unless the meeting was switched to Sunday evening (to suit the needs of an actor-manager in the throes of dress and technical rehearsals), it took place early enough on Monday morning for Conrad to have time on his hands before going out to Mortlake, hence the visit to Dent.

descending to tricks – the thing in itself *not* popular with theatre-goers really – likely to arouse more antagonism than curiosity – the difficulty of producing two different voices unless one is made squeaky or foreign in pronunciation, peculiarities *not* advisable in a strong drama – the similarity of the two men in age and appearance taxing the actor's powers of differ[e]ntiating them too much, almost beyond the possibility of success; if one were old and the other young it would be easier – the danger of creating an interest *extraneous* to the dramatic power of the play on which he bases all his hopes of profound and successful effect on the public.

My conclusions are that practically his objections are in the main sound. That the risks are considerable and in his already recognised position as actor not worth taking. He is afraid of his personality "coming through" in both men – and I am not prepared to say he is wrong in this.

What is eminently satisfactory is his increased comprehension and interest in the play. He must have read it many times for he knows it backwards and forwards in (to me) a most surprising way. His partner too seems to have got hold of all its points. McK's great trouble is an actress for Mrs Verloc. I assure you I was not even thin[k]ing of Katherine[1] when he asked me "What about that young lady?" The upshot of the discussion which *he* started was that I should find out when Kath: is free from Ben Greet[2] and arrange then for her visit here over a Sunday.[3] The difficulty was to get McK here tho' he was very willing to come. Finally I said: What if I sent my car to bring you on Sund. morning and take you back in the evng? He said he would like it very much. This I suggest should be put under the head of business expences.*

---

[1] I.e., Catherine Willard.

[2] (Philip Barling) 'Ben' Greet (1857–1936; knighted 1929), actor-manager especially known for his interest in the Elizabethan classics and a leading director at the Old Vic. Catherine Willard was working with the Vic's touring company. Later in the year, she returned to the USA and began to appear on Broadway.

[3] The following extracts from a note to Catherine Willard dated 29 April 1921 and written on Oswalds stationery appear in Christie's, New York, sale catalogue, 8 December 1985, no. 150. The location of the MS is unknown. The reference to seeing McKinnel 'last week' provides some reason for thinking that Conrad might have seen him on the Sunday night rather than the Monday morning.

My dear Katherine*
Just a word to tell you I saw McK last week. He asked about you. His difficulty is very great and his difficulty may be yet your chance! We arranged that you should come for some weekend here. I would then send my car up to bring Mack for Sunday lunch here . . . He has accepted this plan. Therefore ma chère let me know when you return and name a week-end convenient to you. We shall then see whether Mack can come . . . I hope his blessed comedy will be a success. We don't want to deal with a disappointed man. You would have to be here on Sat . . . so that you and I would talk Mack and the play over, à fond[.]

He has an old actress for Mrs V's Mother. He knows where to lay his hands on a boy. Mr Vladimir, and Ass^t Comm^er the Professor are provided for. But the principal parts will be a hard nut to crack.

I went to Dent in the morning not having anything to do and H[ugh] D[ent] showed me a letter from F. U[nwin] which means that unless he has the publ^ing of it he will not enter into the scheme of a uniform edit^on – at least so it struck me. From there I went to see Evans[1] and was assured that the mistake in binding *The Nigger* has been rectified. I was also shown the Acme Lib: ed^on of the above and of the complete Typhoon. I told him the paper was beastly, which he could not deny; but he said that the cost of prod^on was 1/9 per copy.[2] I was also shown a copy of the 250 Ed: of *N. on my Books*. These are all here and they have only to stick the labels on the backs. I selected the red lettered. The little book looks all right. In the afternoon I was at the Surrey Man^g Com^p. and stayed nearly two hours talking with Ward Miller[3] who was there. The place is small but full of activity. We shall see how it develops. It all rests on orders in the next 6 months. I had no time to see the Colvins or the tailor. I'll have to come up again I fear.

Ever Yours

J. Conrad.

PS. Please pay into my acct the first month's £100 as I have no money at all. If you pay £95 as from the 15th Ap. that will make the hundred with the 5 I had from you already.

PSS I will call on you this week to arrange for manner of payment of different items from income you have fixed at 4.200 for next year ending I take it on Ap 15 1922.

To Clement K. Shorter

Text MS BL Ashley B. 502; Unpublished

[letterhead: Oswalds]
27. Ap 21.

Dear Shorter.

Thanks for your friendly note. I sent it on to Pinker but am afraid that my novel is in too embryonic a stage to be fit for anything by July.

---

[1] C. S. Evans, at Heinemann's.

[2] Of a book selling for half-a-crown (two shillings and sixpence).

[3] Ward-Miller was one of the principal investors in Surrey Scientific Apparatus, the company started by Dr Mackintosh, and managed the technical side of the business.

I'll have to shut myself up with it for the next 3 months to make some progress. So a visit to your country home can not be an early event. As to the signatures – if you send your copies I will do that at once if you like.

Believe me

Sincerely yours

Joseph Conrad

To J. B. Pinker

Text TS/MS Berg; Unpublished

Oswalds,
Bishopsbourne,
Kent.
May 1st. 1921.

Dearest J. B.

Herewith I send you John's school account being the first term under our new arrangement which your office will pay. As it stands it is more in its proportion than its allocated sum of £180 per year. The next two, however, will be smaller and will bring the total within the sum allowed for that purpose. If there is anything above it it will be my own affair.

Thank you very much for the receipted bills received this week, including Hayward's bill, but not including Taylor's, the optician,[1] the receipt for which may have been sent back to you instead of direct here. As I mentioned to you the last time we met there is only one disputed bill from the buried past which has not been sent to you; and this is simply because the people have not written yet in answer to my communication since our return home.

I do not know whether you have paid in yet the sum to complete my first month's allowance up to the sum of £209.15.0. When you complete it I point out again that I have had already £11 from it, of which £6 for myself and £5 for the gardeners' wages I had from you when we went together to the theatre. Therefore the sum to my account for the first month, from the 15th April to the 15th May would be only £198.15.0, of which I know (by your advice) £95 has been already paid in. You will make it clear to the Manager that the monthly sums are to be put to my current account and no part of them to be used for reduction of overdraft. I may mention that Jessie's fortnightly cheque didn't come this week, yet.

---

[1] J. & H. Taylor of 19 Red Lion St, London EC1.

I had a pleasant afternoon with Jack and Ada after leaving you, and from there went to see the Colvins, whom I found both better than I expected. I am glad those two visits are off my chest and I do hope I will be able to shut myself in now to some purpose; for indeed all my worries, more or less of my own making, are off my mind now.

The next interlude will be, I suppose, McKinnel's visit here to see C. W[illard]. The date of this will of course depend on Mc.K. To tell you the truth I would really like you to be here too, but this house fills up so quickly that with C. W. in the spare-room, there may be some doubt as to putting you up comfortably; for you, of course, would have to come for a full weekend. However, that weekend B[orys] would come only for the day, driving McK. down in the morning and taking him up on Sunday night, so his room would be available.

However, we will return to this subject later on.

I had a short talk with R[alph] before he left here on Friday. You are by now in possession of all the facts so I need not say anything here.

Ever Yours
J Conrad.

To John and Ada Galsworthy
Text MS Forbes; J-A, 2, 256–7 (in part)[1]

Oswalds.
10 May 21

Dearest Jack and Ada

I don't believe your heads are swelled. I believe you are pulling my leg – but anyhow I am pleased that you like your set to be N° 1.[2] But could it have been any other? . . .

Anyhow dearest Jack you have written me a letter of the dearest kind. Yes – talk. But could we talk? Could we recapture the fine (tho by no means careless) rapture of the early days? A sense of unreality creeps over all things – I am speaking for myself – which a life of industrious – say – stock-broking would not have left behind . . . perhaps!

John left for school last Friday and I am still missing him horribly. I can't get my teeth into the novel – I am altogether in the dark as to what it is about – I am depressed and exasperated at the same time and I only wish I could say to myself that I don't care. But I do care. A horrid state. Don't

---

[1] Jean-Aubry omits the postscript.
[2] Other sets of the Heinemann collected edition went to Garnett, Gide, Pinker, Sir Robert Jones, and Colonel James Lithgow.

forget me in Your prayers You who have never strayed beyond the precincts of the Temple.[1]

Ever Yours

J. C.

Our dearest love to You both.

To J. B. Pinker
Text TS/MS Berg; Unpublished

Oswalds,
Bishopsbourne,
Kent.
May 10th. 1921.

My dear J. B.

I forward you the enclosed communication from "Great Thoughts" which I suppose cannot be made use of.[2]

In regard to the Limited Edition in England, which Evans seems to have hinted to you was delayed by us here. That simply is not true. Their proofs always came to them before the American set could reach Garden City and the Garden City has put out ten volumes now. This proves clearly that we here are not guilty of any delay. As a matter of fact when Miss Hallowes left for Corsica on the 24th Feb. Hein[n] had six completed volumes in hand – that is one more than the second instalment – and since that time they have had four more up to date, not counting half "The Rescue" which is at present in their hands. I think that instead of casting aspersions Evans had better send on some more proofs here, as none has reached this house since our return just a month ago. Nothing has come so far from America either, except "Within the Tides" which has gone back to Doubleday directly it was corrected, and must be in their possession now.

Apart from the accidental mislaying of "Within the Tides" proof (which did not affect Heinemann in the least) no hitch whatever occurred with the American copy, and we have a letter of thanks from Mrs Robins to that effect.

We want now proofs from Evans of the following works – "The Arrow of Gold" and "Notes on Life and Letters", not counting the half of The Rescue proof which is in Miss H.'s trunk and has been delayed in transit. But that delay cannot by any possibility have affected or affect in the future the

---

[1] A doubly ironic play on the legal and religious associations of 'Temple': before turning to literature, Galsworthy had read for the bar as a fellow of an Inn of Court (Lincoln's Inn, however, not the Inner or the Middle Temple); having little faith in the transcendental, he placed his hopes in the social gospel and indeed strayed beyond the bounds of religious orthodoxy.

[2] Letter to Conrad of 9 May from the magazine *Great Thoughts* (TS Berg).

Limited Edition unfavourably, because before they reach The Rescue they have at least to publish ten other volumes.

The proofs we want from America are the following – "Victory", "The Arrow of Gold", "Rescue", and "Notes on Life and Letters", and I imagine they will be coming over very soon. I own I am very anxious for this job to be done with. If Heinemann and Doubleday had been feeding us properly for the last month it would have been done by now. This is the absolute truth of the case.

After you departed yesterday I made a good start with the novel. Your Palgrave[1] left for your home last evening. Our love to You

Yours ever

J. Conrad.

To J. B. Pinker

Text MS Berg; Unpublished

Oswalds.

10/5/21

Dear J. B.

Will you please see whether those demands[2] relating to the year 1919 (2^d half) and 1920–1 have been paid by the office already? They are both anterior to Jan 1921 and it seems to me that they must have been sent to me before and as was my practice then sent on to you for settlement.

Of course if they have *not* been paid I am prepared to pay them now as under our new arrangement. Only I don't want to pay twice.

Ever Yours

J. Conrad

PS Pray return encl^s

To J. B. Pinker

Text MS Berg; Unpublished

Oswalds

12.5.21

2.30 pm.

My dear J. B.

I have had a letter from Karola who has an opportunity to go with some friends for a stay in Lucca (anti-rheumatic baths) of a month or so. She

---

[1] Sir Francis Palgrave's popular and often reprinted *The Golden Treasury of Best Songs and Lyrical Poems in the English Language* (1861).
[2] Probably from the Inland Revenue.

asks me whether I could not send her the next three months allowance a fortnight earlier. In this connection I must remind you for the guidance of your Paymaster-General that Karola's payments fall on the 1st Dec–1st Mch–1st June and 1st Sept. This arises from the fact that we sent her the first £30 in Nov last year on her arrival in Italy. When she left here (in June '20 I think)[1] I gave her enough money to see her through her visit to Poland and to cover her journey to Milan where the first instalment of her yearly allowance was sent her, as above.

Will you please my dear J. B. when You pay in my monthly allowance on the *15th inst* deduct £30 and send it at once to *Karola Zagorska c/o Consolato di Polonia 33 Piazza Cujazzo Milan* and pay to my acct her allowance (for June-July-Aug*st*) when it falls due on the *1st of June*. Like this the order of payments made by the office won't be disturbed; but pray call W.'s[2] attention to Karola's dates as above.

Pardon all the trouble I am always giving you with a lot of small matters – but that will soon cease when we get into running-order, here.

I am well underway with the novel and have got up to 1500 w. done this morning. I am off for a drive this afternoon. Jessie sends her dear love.

Ever Yours

J. Conrad

PS M[a]cM[illans] have sent the book. Many thanks.

To Eric Pinker
Text TS Berg; Unpublished

Oswalds,
Bishopsbourne,
Kent.
May 14th. 1921.

My dear Eric,

Thank you very much for your letter and your promise to send the draft to Karola to-day. So that there should be no mistake about it I repeat here that this is to cover the months of June, July and August. The next payment to K. will fall due on the 1st of September.

Thanks for paying in my monthly allowance on the 15th, and if you don't mind and it's not a thing to complicate the book-keeping we will keep to that date right through now, as far as my portion is concerned. Mrs J. C. of course is paid every fortnight and Audrey every month.

---

[1] In August, in fact.
[2] W. C. Wicken? Presumably a relation of James Wicken, to whom Conrad wrote in 1913 and 1916, and the guardian of Pinker's cash.

I am disabled in my right hand and generally feeling beastly seedy. However it is nothing new with me and will doubtless pass away in due course.

Best regards

Yours

J. Conrad

To J. B. Pinker
Text TS/MS Berg; Unpublished

Oswalds,
Bishopsbourne,
Kent.
May 21st. 1921.

My dear J. B.

Thanks for your letter of the 18th, enclosing N[innes]'s bill, which is being checked now by Mrs C. and will be put into the envelope before this letter is posted.

I will deal now with the postscript of your letter stating that Heinemann "has debited you with £14.8.8., the cost of four sets of the first five of the Collected Edition" and asking me whether it is right.

My answer is that I don't know about the amount, but as an *item* it certainly is *not* right.

The position is this: Under my agreement I was entitled to six sets, of which I instructed the office to send (and go on sending as the books appear) one to Sir R. Jones, one to Edward Garnett, to their respective addresses, and four to me here. And this has been done both in respect to the first five and the second five vols, which I have here. I suppose Sir Robert and Edward have had their second five already, since mine, four in number, arrived last week. On that there is no charge whatever to be made – they are in the agreement. Further what happened is this: 1° Directly the publication had begun it occurred to me that I ought absolutely to send a set to André Gide, who has been sending me his books and has the general direction of the translation of all my works into French. I wrote then to Mr Pawling at once asking him whether he could manage to spare a set to send to Andre Gide direct from the office. Mr Pawling's answer was that it would be all right and I have heard since by a letter from Gide that he received the first five vols. I have no doubt that the second five have either gone or are going in due course. I was under the impression that that set has been found for him as an extra out of the thirty "presentation" sets which have been printed for that particular purpose. But if my impression was wrong I have no objection to pay for it.

2° There is also a set which is being sent to Jean Aubry from Heinemann's office, which also may be the subject of a claim on me. The story of it is as follows: when the late Mr Heinemann was here to settle the details of the Edition I mentioned that Aubry was one of the men to whom I would want to give a set. To this Mr Heinemann said: "Oh, I will send him one." As he knew Aubry very well and was very much in touch with him on many literary subjects I found nothing extraordinary in that; and then we agreed that six sets would be enough for me, as it stands embodied in the agreement. I didn't trouble my head about Aubry any more but while we were in Corsica I had a letter from Aubry telling me that the firm of Wm. Heinemann had sent him an account for the first five vols. I was certainly surprised, but under the circumstances I could do nothing but write to Mr Pawling telling him that I would be responsible for that set (on terms set forth in our agreement) and Mr Pawling acknowledged the receipt of that letter.

You will see therefore that I can be made responsible *at the most* for two sets and no more. Because the one which is being sent to Garnett and the one being sent to Sir Robert Jones (direct from the office) are part of the six sets secured to me by the agreement which you hold.

I enclose you here Mr Pawling's letter offering to pay for half the set for Aubry. This is the whole story. What I repudiate here and which is clear from my statement is that I cannot be made responsible for four sets. They seem to be trying to debit me with that number, which is a mistake. The gist of the matter lies in this: that the sets sent to Garnett and Jones come out of my six, whereas the Gide and the Aubry sets do not fall into that category. And as to these I won't say much, except that I thought that the publishing house would find a set for Gide, who, anyhow, is a distinguished-enough man of letters to have one presented to him in that way; and as to Aubry that Mr Heinemann's intention not having been made perfectly clear the publisher and I would share the cost.

I go into this matter, dear J. B. fully because I know that as things stand every pound coming in is of great importance. Indeed, if I had ordered four sets I would have certainly warned you of that prodigality, for the deduction would have been important, and you ought to have been warned that such deduction had to be made from the anticipated sum. But as you see, I was under the impression that I was liable only for *half* the cost of *one* set (I suppose at "trade price" as my agreement stipulates that). However, it isn't a matter to fight about much. If my view as to Gide's and Aubry's sets is not acceptable and Hein: will insist on making those deductions in full, then I may mention to you that I have reserved two sets out of my six for myself, but, strictly speaking, I could do with one only and the second could be sold to make up in a certain measure for the deduction. I don't mean to say that I would be glad to do so, but I tell you that I am ready to do so, if necessary.

Our thoughts were with all of you on Thursday last, but there was a silly muddle about sending a congrats telegram – Jessie thinking I said I would see to that, while I was under the impression that she would do so. As the Campbells[1] were here the subject was not mentioned again till six o'clock – and it was too late then. We are very sorry.

Love to you all.

Ever yours

J Conrad

To J. B. Pinker
Text TS/MS Berg; Unpublished

Oswalds,
Bishopsbourne,
Kent.
May 24th. 1921.

Dearest J B.

Thanks for your letter relating to the Film agreement. I think that what you have done was the wisest under the circumstances as of course thing may improve in three months' time. I have a suspicion however that at the end of that term they may still not be prepared to take up the option.[2] Slumps have a way of lasting longer than booms. In that case I would submit for your consideration whether it would not be better to let the thing lapse in order to obtain complete liberty of action in case of something else offering in another direction; while as far as *they* are concerned should things improve there would be nothing to prevent them approaching us again. I have seen lately paragraphs about film producing activities, both in England and Holland, but I have a sort of feeling that the bottom is about to fall out of that business. Whether the crisis will eventuate in a change of methods or technique or even in an altered view of what the character of film-plays should be, nobody can tell; but that there will be a change of some sort in the fundamentals of the whole film business, I have no doubt.

I am glad McK[innel] is going to produce Jack's play[3] rather than mine just now. Thank you very much for sending me the text, which I have looked

---

[1] Dr Kenneth Campbell, an ophthalmic surgeon, had returned to civilian life after war service in the Royal Army Medical Corps. He and his wife divided their time between London and a country house in Kent. For his attention to Conrad's health, see *Letters*, 5, p. 438.

[2] On film rights for *The Rescue*, or on 'Gaspar the Strong Man'?

[3] *The Family Man* opened at the Comedy Theatre on 2 June and ran until 16 July.

over with considerable interest. There are several rather considerable typing mistakes in that copy, which I will correct and return to you for handing back to McK. I hope our friend will manage to tide over the present depression and will be able to give The Secret Agent a chance on a rising tide.

I return you Col. B[ell]'s letter. I imagine you will be coming down soon – that is, directly Eric returns to business life. I must tell you for your information that Kinkie[1] is coming down with her paint-box on the 1st (June) and will stay over the week-end, in all probability – I mean the first week-end in June. On the second week-end Walpole has an option and I have an idea that he will take it up. As you know the capacity of this house as well as I do you will regulate your movements in accordance with this information. I presume that when Eric is back you would be at liberty to come any day in the week; and from the point of view of meeting the Colonel that would be rather better. The man is apt to fly off somewhere about Friday, I have noticed. When you have fixed the thing in your mind pray let us know.

I have had heartrending letters from old Dent and young Dent, and have received all the copies they could scrape together (five in number)[2] including the two they had reserved for themselves. I don't know what to do with these last, I have a good mind to send them back and freeze to the three others. On the other hand I don't want to do anything that would look like condonation. It is a vexing business altogether. As to the issue of The Rescue, which seems to have been done for reviewing purposes, you needn't apply the thumbscrew to them now; for it is hardly worth while. The thing is done and it can't be undone. It has got into Wise's Bibliography[3] and there it is. The only thing is to ask them not to do it again, but be content to send the usual advance copies for review like my other publishers have always done and as it is their plain duty to do in good time – without creating any special issues which always arouse some sort of suspicion. I will drop a line (I suppose I must) to Dent, acknowledging the copies and asking him never to do anything of the sort in the future. There is nothing more to be done since we can't call in that silly issue which is scattered now all over the world – and be damned to it!

By the by, in this connection, have you got my copy of the Second Edition of Wise's Bibliography? I have a dim notion that you took it away as

---

[1] Alice Sarah Kinkead, an artist whom the Conrads and Pinker met in Corsica. See the letter to her of 30 June.

[2] Of a special limited issue of *Notes on Life and Letters* for reviewers and friends of the Dents. Conrad kept the five copies and later sold them through Wise (see the letter of 4 October).

[3] An edition of forty review copies appeared on 4 June 1920, three weeks before regular publication.

documentary evidence to batter old Dent about with. Anyway I can't find it here, either upstairs or downstairs and I have looked everywhere for it.

And since we are on the subject of books and copies and all that botheration tell me whether you have D[oubleday]'s second set of five of Limited Am^{an} Edition? I know that the box of the *first* five was left in the office when we unpacked the first big case, but I think that when we unpacked the second all the little boxes were taken away.

B[orys] was here this week-end and we had a long talk about the business. In consequence of orders coming in they are going practically to double the number of their workmen. At the last Board meeting B. had his way and got authorised to expend £300 on advertising. He had one advertisement in trade papers which brought him eleven letters within 48 hours and ever since two or three a day, which he considers extremely satisfactory. There is plant enough to accommodate the additional numbers of workmen at once in the downstairs workshop, and upstairs there is another room where all the shafting is in place though not the actual benches. He talked to me with great sense and acuteness. He seems to have a very good grip of the business side of the thing and has generally the complete backing of Ward-Miller with whom apparently they concoct plans for development within practical limits. He assured me that there is room on the present premises to do three times the work they are doing now and when that is not sufficient there is a possibility of obtaining premises on the other side of the road. The only trouble is the man Jefferies next door (the second-hand bookseller) who has 500 shares and for some reason opposes every move, being apparently frightened of the future, and imagining that he has got the whip hand because he thinks that they would have to go to him to enlarge the workshop if they wanted to do so. Last time I was there I had a good look at the man and listened patiently to his silly chatter. I carried away a very unfavourable impression and formed then an idea that he was not a very desirable person to have in the Company, being unreasonably timid and mistrustful. I think that he would sell his shares now and go out of it altogether, but it may very well be, as Borys pointed out to me, that in another three months when development has been effected in the teeth of his opposition he would want to hold. Since B. came in Mac. leaves all things to him and as far as Jefferies is concerned has a neutral attitude, though of course at Board meetings he backs up Ward-Miller and B's schemes. Mac and his brother have the most money in it. Ward-Miller has a thousand, B. three hundred and Tamage[1] two, which I believe are all his savings. B. of course said nothing to me but I can see that

---

[1] Conrad usually spells the name Tammage.

he would like immensely to have Jeffries out of it, replacing him himself, or perhaps inducing Ward-Miller to increase his holding. Of course I said nothing either; and there is time yet. But it is a fact that I did promise him the money more than two years ago and this would be a legitimate opportunity to make use of it if he had it. Thus my sins come home to roost. I am rather wretched about it. Of course to a certain extent this is a chancey thing, but after all everything of that kind is a chancey thing, and the chance here seems quite good and may give B a footing for life in a different sense than a thousand invested in an old-established business could give him. However what can't be, can't be, but I am rather cast down at not being able to keep my promise.

The novel is moving on and I am now doing the last chapter of Part One, feeling an increased confidence that the thing will be pulled off with some success.

Ralph is very busy both in the farming and impressario* business. Yesterday after working hard all day he went off to rehearse his troupe and coming home late talked of his plans to me. I wont tell you of them because you would be frightened at their magnitude. You know, he seems really to have a talent for organisation in the entertainment line. Originally it was B and he who started it, but B has been out of it for months and its R's driving power and ideas that made the thing the success it is. The situation with the Col. is quiescent. Mrs C sends her love. A[udrey] is away on leave till to-night. Mrs C has gone off to see her mother to day.

Ever Yours

J. Conrad.

P.S. I am sending you a copy of Tales of Unrest – not inscribed yet as you may not like it since it had to be doctored. Just have a look at it.

To J. B. Pinker
Text MS Berg; Unpublished

Oswalds.

25.5.21

Dearest J B.

My attention has been called by the person most interested to the payment of Jessie's allowance. If you look up the statement of expenditure you will see that we agreed that she should have £2 per day reckoning the year as 364 days. Therefore the amount standing against her name in the statement I sent you is £728 per year. A sum which falls within the total amount of the agreed income.

By the payment (fortnightly) of £28 every 1st and every 15th of each month she does not get what is put down against her name and what she is entitled to. For the two pay^{ts} amount only to £56 per month and in the twelve-months (full year) only to £672 instead of the £728 allot[t]ed to her out of the income – (as per my statement sent to you last April).

What she ought to get is £60. per month in two pay^{ts} of £30. (whether the month is 30 or 31 days). Like this she will get in the 12 months (full year) 720 per year which is really *less* by £8 that* the amount which stands now against her name out of the guaranteed income, and which must be made up to her by an extra pay^t at the end of the financial year.

As this is no extra call but only a matter of payment of an allot[t]ed sum no remarks on my part are necessary. But I think that £2 per day is not too much for feeding 7 people (3 of us & 4 serv^{ts}) keep up the linen and meet various small expences.* Please then my dear fellow when you send her the next fortnight on the 1st of June make it £30 as is due and henceforth that sum every fortnight. As the financial year (as between you and me) begins on 15 Ap. please add to that a ch for £6 to make up the deficiency of her allowance for 1/2 Ap. and whole May as is only just and proper. Sorry to trouble you with all these matters. I ought to have pointed it out before.

Our love to you

Yours ever

J. Conrad

To Thomas J. Wise
Text MS Leeds; Unpublished

[letterhead: Oswalds]
25.5.21.

Dear Mr Wise

Thanks for your sympathy. I am a little better in myself and the right wrist is nearly well.

I am thus ready to sign the copies of which you speak as soon as they arrive.

Would you do me the kindness of posting me the 3^d Act ("first copy") of the Secret Agent.

MacKinnel's* copy has got typing mistakes which I want to correct and they dropped a whole line there which I cannot remember.

I will return the act at once by registered post.

Miss H[allowes] will do the typing corrections (small and great) on McK's copy so that there should be no copy with my handwriting except the two in your possession ("First Draft" & "First Copy").

With kindest regards

Yours

J. Conrad.

To Conrad Hope

Text MS Wright;[1] Unpublished

[letterhead: Oswalds]
27.5.21.

My dear Conrad[2]

I am sending you by post (in two parcels) the first ten vols of the Sun-Dial Edition of my works inscribed to your wife and yourself.[3]

The other eight volumes will appear in the course of this year and will be sent to you as they reach me here.

We were delighted to have a good report of you[r] book[4] from Borys on our return from abroad.

My wife joins me in dear love to you both.

Believe me most affectionately

J. Conrad

To J. B. Pinker

Text MS Berg; Unpublished

[letterhead: Oswalds]
Friday. [27 May 1921][5]

Dearest J. B.

I had your letter for which thanks.

We must run over the new road in the car some time before the date of the journey. I had an idea that the other way was no good from the driving point of view.

[1] The original was not available for rechecking.

[2] Conrad Hope (1890–1963), named in honour of Conrad, was the youngest of the four children of G. F. W. Hope, Conrad's first friend in England. A motor engineer, he was the director of Candor Motors in Colchester.

[3] (Stella Dorothea) Vera Hope (*c.* 1899–1972). Other Doubleday sets went to Borys's comrade-in-arms D. R. Bevan, Hugh Clifford, Richard Curle, Dr Mackintosh, the Ridgeways, and the Sandersons.

[4] Untraced and presumably never published.

[5] Miss Kinkead's forthcoming visit (see the letter of the 24th) fixes the date.

The road from Tonb^dge to Ashford is quite fair as to gradients and has a good macadam surface. We must run over it when you come down here.

Jessie had already (on the 26th) her £28 which she did not expect till the 1st for that was how her allowance was coming since our return – on fixed dates. Hence her protest to me. Of course if she is to get her £28 every 14 days it would be quite all right. But that would make a shifting date all along for the office. Therefore my suggestion [is] to make it £30 – every 15th & 1st (= to £720 per year) so as to simplify matters.

Miss K[inkead] will come on Wed: 1st for, it seems, a week. But Jessie suggests that you should come on Monday 6th (if Eric is back by then) flirt with Kinkie and survey the picture. Think it over dear J. B.

Ever Yours

J. C.

PS *That would mean you having B's room.*

To J. B. Pinker
Text MS Berg;[1] Unpublished

[letterhead: Oswalds]
Monday.
30 5 21

Dearest J B.

Our letters crossed. Of course 26 cheques per year make it perfectly right for Jessie.

We are awaiting your acceptance of our proposal for Monday-scheme.

There will be about 20 thous: words by the time you arrive. You may see them – but as to reading them . . . I don't know.

I have done no corre^ons and dont intend to revise till part II is done. I have of course begun it.

Our love

Yours

J. C.

Enclosed is Income Tax form.

---

[1] Postscript in Miss Hallowes's hand.

To John Galsworthy
Text MS Forbes; Unpublished

[letterhead: Oswalds]
4.6.21

Dearest Jack.

My congratulations on the success of the Family Man.[1] May his "shadow (not only) never grow less"[2] but steadily increase, covering triumphantly the Town and the Country and the Plains of America even to the remote Pacific. And I have an idea (from the notices) that it will do that – at which I rejoice.

My dearest fellow I can not overcome my distaste for Howe's scheme.[3] I have no liking for [the] medallionist's art. As reproduced by photogravure on shiny paper it produces on me a most disagreeable impression. The proposal to smash the thing is really the limit of fatuousness. Why smash it? Why not give it to me? (Not that I would want it but on the ground of merest decency). If Mr Sr[4] likes the idea that's his own affair; but for myself I must say that to be asked to sit (as a party to fabricating a rarity) only to have the reproduction of my living countenance (ex hypothesi[5] a fine piece of art) smashed with a hammer – seems to me simply outrageous.

I write to you this with a swollen hand which prevented me from writing sooner. I haven't been very well lately. I have done some work tho' – but my grasp on it is very precarious – at any rate I feel it to be so. Jessie's operated limb gives her a good deal of pain I am sorry to say. Still she is able to move about and her general health is good. She sends her dear love in which I join to you both.

Ever Yours

J. Conrad

---

1 *A Family Man*, Galsworthy's latest play.
2 Originally an Arabic blessing and often combined with others such as 'May you live a thousand years.' For a variation on the idea, see the letter to Eric Pinker of 20 October 1922.
3 The New York publisher and collector of books and manuscripts W. T. H. Howe, who was acquainted with Galsworthy, had apparently seen him during his recent visit to America. He had proposed casting medallions of eminent writers for publication, the medallions to be destroyed after use. Galsworthy's letter to Conrad of 20 May 1921 (Stape 2000) urges Conrad's participation.
4 Theodore Spicer-Simson (1871–1959), French-born American sculptor and painter, who was to make the medallions.
5 'Assuming it to be'.

To Sir Sidney Colvin

Text MS Fitzwilliam; Unpublished

[letterhead: Oswalds]
Tuesday [7 June 1921?][1]

My dear Colvin.

We will be more than delighted to see you here this week end. Please let us know the train. I am now more or less fit for human society, but I've had a horrid time of it with the gout since our return. I long for a talk with you. Our kindest regards to Lady Colvin and yourself.

Pardon this scrawl.

Yours always

J. Conrad

To John Galsworthy

Text TS/MS Forbes; Galsworthy 11–13 (in part); J-A, 2, 257–9

[letterhead: Oswalds]
June 8th. 1921.

Dearest Jack

I have just had your letter[2] and I admit I was a little surprised that McKinnel should have bothered you with my play, which, if he has any doubt about, need not be performed at all. I assure you quite honestly that though I wouldn't be indifferent to its fate if it were staged I will not be at all concerned if he doesn't stage it for some reason or other. I have no great confidence in the art of actors as a body. As far as I can judge it is as much conventionalised as it ever was in the palmy days of Italian comedy;[3] and as to what the present-day men may make of my play fills me with more dread than curiosity.

I am sure you will believe me, my dear Jack, when I tell you that all the remarks you made on it have been very vividly in my mind while I was putting down on paper line after line. The only question that presented itself to me was as to their weight as against other and more intimate considerations.

My general attitude finally was this: that considering that very likely I will never write another play, that I can't have any pretension to dramatic gifts

---

[1] Complaints about gout on 25 May and 4 June tend to confirm the holder's placement in June 1921. Of possible Tuesdays, the first is the most likely: Curle was invited for the weekend of the 17–19th, and later in the month Jessie Conrad was in poor health.

[2] Of the 6th (Stape 2000).

[3] In the *commedia dell'arte*, actors performed *lazzi* – standard knockabout routines.

though I have my own idea as to the artistic reproductions of life, that the rules of any art contain in their summarised expression as much error as truth and also a certain admixture of completely unreasonable prejudice (as for instance in the art of painting the not quite 100 year old pronouncement of a famous connois[s]eur that "a picture to be good should be brown like an old fiddle"[1]) – I could allow free play to my temperament, attending only to the plain sense and clear connection of the story which, as a matter of fact, I had ready to my hand, with all its implications (more or less wide) arising not from a conflict of motives or passions but simply from various points of view. I resolved in short to write a Conrad play, not straining stage conditions unduly for the sake of originality but stretching them out to my conception for the sake of that freedom (possibly in wrong directions) by which no art is ever injured. The critics and the public will take jolly good care that it doesn't get too much of it.

This, my dear Jack, is the general answer to what you have said. Strictly speaking it has no value except in so far that it is rooted in human nature fortified by some reflection. As to the particular points I am in a manner too much at one with you to try to controvert what you say. Indeed I have often felt that not only the Third but the Second Act could come out altogether. After all: why the Professor? Why the Assistant Commissioner? Even Inspector Heat himself would be sufficiently characterised by his appearance in the Third Act, if it were not for the actual subject of the play. What the subject of The Secret Agent is I am not ready to state in a few words, not because I myself don't know it but because it is of the sort that does not lend itself to exact definition. All I can say is that the subject is *not* the murder of Mr Verloc by his wife and what subsequently happens to her. It is all a matter of feeling, without which the existence of Mrs Verloc's mother as a personage in the play could not be very well justified. For after all what is that old woman doing there? She too could be eliminated; and also Mr Vladimir? Indeed I was tempted, or I might have been tempted, to begin the play with the three delightful anarchs sitting in the parlour round the fire and Mr Verloc explaining to them the circumstances which force him to throw a bomb at some building or other, discussing ways and means, and ending the effective scene by taking Stevie by the scruff of the neck, "Come along, youngster, you carry the bomb", and Comrade Ossipon blowing a kiss as they all go out at

---

[1] Accustomed to well-smoked Renaissance paintings, Sir George Howland Beaumont (1753–1827), patron of Wordsworth and Constable, collector, and landscape painter, claimed that 'a good picture, like a good fiddle, should be brown'. Taking a fiddle and setting it on the lawn of Sir George's house, Constable begged to differ. One source of this story is C. R. Leslie's often-reprinted *Memoirs of the Life of John Constable* (1843).

the door to Mrs Verloc who stands horrorstruck in the middle of the stage. Curtain. From there one could go, direct, without changing a word to the Third Scene of the Fourth Act and on to the end, obtaining a rather pretty Guignol play,[1] with no particular trouble.

All this is perfectly direct and certainly would not lag by the way, but it would miss altogether the subject of the play, which in its nature, I mean the play, is purely illustrative. It is because of that nature that I have let it spread itself into scenes which from the point of action alone may, and obviously do, appear superfluous and detached from the subject. Whereas to my feeling they are all closely to the point.

I admit that I wrote the play to be acted but at the same time I will tell you frankly that I look with no pleasurable anticipation to seeing it on the stage. The mere thought of what a perfectly well-meaning actor may make in the way of conventionalised villain of my Professor which I assure you is quite a serious attempt to illustrate a mental and emotional state which had its weight in the affairs of this world,[2] gives me a little shudder.

I can't hope to convince you dearest Jack since to your practical remarks the only answer I can make is: feeling. I hope you won't get too bored by all this type. I had to dictate as I can't use my pen very long. I have however a matter which makes me very unhappy which I must tell you of. You can't imagine my disgust with myself and my consternation when I discovered that the article I wrote on you (on the occasion of M of P)[3] has got left out of the Life & Letters vol. What can I do but confess to you that I had forgotten all about it. Indeed I had forgotten the Henry James, Books and a lot of others. They had to put the texts under my eyes to convince me! When P[inker] asked me about you lately I said "No – I never wrote anything. Galsworthy wrote an appreciation of my work[4] which I have, but I never wrote about him." Of course they sent me a typed copy of the article in the Outlook – and as soon as I glanced at it a lot of actual phrases rushed into my memory. My dear this is not to be explained – except by a lamentable decay of mental faculties which I did not suppose to be advanced so far as that.

Dent printed 9000 copies of the vol. Another edition won't be needed for the next two years (if ever). But we are not too late for the Coll[ed] Editions of

---

[1] In the bloodcurdling style of Grand Guignol theatre.

[2] Cf. Conrad's provocative opinion of 'les extrêmes anarchistes' in a letter to Cunninghame Graham of 1899 (*Letters*, 2, p. 159).

[3] A review of *The Man of Property* entitled 'A Middle-Class Family' (later 'John Galsworthy') in the *Outlook* of 31 March 1906.

[4] 'Joseph Conrad: A Disquisition' in the *Fortnightly Review* of April 1908.

which Life & Letters will be the 18th vol. I have sent a typed copy to America and another to Hein[emann][1] with the intimation that it *must* go in. For the moment I can do no more – except to bite my thumbs with vexation that this thing should have happened. Yet truly I am not very proud of what I wrote. Neither you nor the book get half your due in that article. Still it was the best I could get at that time from the depths of my admiration.

In the matter of the medallion: since you say definitely that I *ought* to have it done all my doubts as to the propriety of the act must vanish. I'll drop Simpson* a line – that is if he can and is willing to come down. I dread the ordeal all the same.

What with one thing and another I dont feel very happy and can only hope my face won't reflect too faithfully the state of feelings. My bodily sensations are wretched too – but we will try to brazen it out before the artist.

Our dear love to you both

Ever Yours

Joseph Conrad.

PS I am sending you a copy of the vol all the same.[2] You must have all my first editions.

To Richard Curle
Text MS Indiana; Curle 74

[letterhead: Oswalds]
9.6.'21

Dear Richard.

Our love and welcome to you.[3] Yes. Certainly next week will do. Will you come on Friday 17*th* for lunch. Car will meet you.

9.15 am from Vic gets Cant*ry* 11.20 and the next good train is 3 pm from Char + gets to C at 5.4.

Pray drop us a line.

Ever Yours

J. Conrad

---

[1] Although a proof dated 16 June 1921 has survived in a typesetting for Heinemann's collected edition (Indiana), this article did not appear in book form until *Last Essays*.

[2] Acknowledged in Galsworthy's letter to Conrad of 12 June (Stape 2000).

[3] On his return from nearly a year in the Far East.

To Bruno Winawer

Text MS draft (partial), TS copy Yale; *Głos* (108); Najder 267–8[1]

[letterhead: Oswalds]
10.6.21.[2]

Dear Sir.[3]

Thank you very much for sending me the comedy. I found it interesting and (pourquoi pas le dire)[4] greatly entertaining, which however did not prevent me from taking your work quite seriously.

As far as a translation is concerned I have no connections in the world where these things get done. Therefore for the time being I can think of nobody, and it seems to me that if I looked for someone (which would be rather difficult as I seldom go to London) it would be difficult to find someone suitable.

I am very busy at the moment, but I hope to be more free in some three weeks and will then see what can be done.

Translation, however, isn't everything. What you probably have in mind is placing the play with a London theatre. I must explain that although I have a fairly wide reputation it is strictly confined to my own work. Personally I have no influence in the publishing or theatrical world. I don't know a single actor or actress, director, or capitalist entrepreneur, nor, in fact, do I have anything to do with the theatre. I must furthermore add that I have never met my publishers either socially or in business. All my affairs are in the hands of Mr. J. B. Pinker, my literary agent and friend of twenty years' standing, who acts on my behalf and sends me contracts to sign.

That is the position. Your comedy appeals to me so I will try to do all I can, but please do not count on me. In any event I shall write to you in three weeks' time.

Pray accept my friendly regards

Yours sincerely

Joseph Conrad.

---

[1] Translation from Najder with minor alterations.

[2] Date from MS draft. Winawer's copy gives the 12th, which is possibly a transcription error; on the other hand, Conrad may have begun writing on the 10th, finishing on the 12th.

[3] Polish short-story writer and dramatist Bruno Winawer (1883–1944) sent his play *Księga Hioba* (*The Book of Job*) to Conrad in the hope that he would find an English translator for it. Conrad himself took up the challenge and produced a translation that was hawked about to London producers without success. Winawer, in turn, translated Conrad's dramatisation of *The Secret Agent* into Polish with Aniela Zagórska.

[4] 'And why not say so'.

To J. B. Pinker

Text MS Berg; Unpublished

[letterhead: Oswalds]
Tuesday. [14 June 1921][1]

Dearest J B.

Will you have the enclosed typed[x] with what speed you can get out of the typing establishment. Also please read this *first act*. I will send the other two along as they get done. Don't suppose I am neglecting my proper work. Every morning sees[?] its task done (aver[ge] 600w.). The other is extra – and I must say it has given me some amusement – and even more, a renewed assurance in the handling of the language. For it was not easy to do. Far from it!

I shall have to consult you as to the future disposal of it both as a wise friend and as a sagacious manager of my work.

Lots of considerations occur to me.

Our love to you

Ever Yours

J. Conrad

x) One copy

PS There's no list of Persons or any directions but you will get the hang of everything as you read.

To Lord Northcliffe

Text MS Harmsworth; Unpublished

[letterhead: Oswalds]
16.6.21

My dear Lord

Ever so many thanks for your letter. We were wondering how your health was after your trip abroad.

The caricature when it comes – even if of the most atrocious kind – would be received affectionately as a gift from you. I have heard however that

---

[1] Since only the first act of *The Book of Job* is ready, the most likely Tuesday after the letter to Winawer of the 10th would be the 14th. Conrad finished his translation on the 25th (date on TS).

Max has treated me not unkindly.[1] I did not go to his exhibition.[2] Since we returned from Corsica I have been nowhere.

My wife's walking powers have much improved but she is not yet quite free from pain. She begs to be remembered to you with warm regards. She thinks it would be very delightful if on one of your journeys this way you would pull up at Oswalds' door. John before going back to Tonbridge for his second term asked me to remember you with love. Borys is at work in London and very happily experimenting and fabricating all sorts of wireless implements under Ward Miller.

Believe us in our greatest regard

Always yours

Joseph Conrad

To Thomas J. Wise

Text MS BL Ashley 2953; Unpublished

[letterhead: Oswalds]
21.6.'21

Dear Mr Wise.

I have been lately doing some work of for me unusual character. I have translated from the polish a three act comedy with a view of course of having it produced in London. But that of course is all in the future. The first draft is being typed clean (one copy only) for my further correction as is usual with all my work. (1st copy)

Please tell me whether you would like to have the MS (first original draft partly pen partly type). It consists of about 90 pp. (mixed) and some additional pen and ink pp perhaps 3. of directions and description.

I have had lately some inquiries about any MS of mine; but of course you must have your say first. Should you want this MS I would ask you to pay me a 100 for 1st Orig^{al} draft and the 1st Copy (when it is done with). Should you think that sum too much pray let me know.

I have asked our friend Curle to take this letter with him as in that way it'll reach you sooner than by post.

---

[1] Max Beerbohm's caricature, entitled 'Somewhere in the Pacific', done in late 1920, features Conrad on an empty beach contemplating a snake crawling through a skull and saying 'Quelle charmante plage! On se fait l'illusion qu'ici on pourrait être toujours presque gai!' ['What a charming beach! It gives the illusion that one could always be almost cheerful here!']. It was published in Beerbohm's *A Survey* (1921).

[2] At the Leicester Galleries, Leicester Square, in May.

I was glad to hear you were looking well. We must see each other soon. My wife sends her kind regards. I am sorry to say some fresh trouble is developing in her limb, and I am somewhat depressed by the prospect of more surgeons more doctors, more anxiety.

Believe me with friendly regards

Yours

J Conrad

To J. B. Pinker
Text MS Berg; Unpublished

[letterhead: Oswalds]
Thursday. [23 June 1921][1]

Dearest J. B.

Do if you can put this out at once to be typed (one copy).

Of course it is my own original that I am in a hurry to get back.

I would like to have your opinion of the whole as soon as you feel like giving it to me.

Our love

Yours

J. C.

To J. B. Pinker
Text MS Berg; J-A, 2, 260

[letterhead: Oswalds]
27.6.21

Dearest J. B.

The clearest result of my interview with McK[innel] is – that he himself *never* noticed the superfluity of the 3^d act. It is Jack who called his attention to it. He told me this in so many words; a strange confession to make if that act is a "blemish" on the play. I set forth my own theory of relief to gloom, of ampleness – to which he listened intelligently. His attitude is by no means obstinate. What seduced him was the advantage of shortening the play and the possibility of dispensing with an actress (the G^t Lady) very difficult to find.

He is really a very nice fellow. He confessed to me that his partners tho' most interested in the play were somewhat afraid of it. That is excusable. They are all determined to produce it but they want to do it under the best possible conditions. The idea of staging it at once has been given up. Autumn

---

[1] Mention of the entire play makes the 16th too early, while haste to have the original returned seems to disallow the 30th.

or early spring are the only times in which to attempt to give the public that treat. In this I agree with him. He has in reserve a light comedy – an Italian thing – to replace Jack's play.[1] The audience was very thin. The thing has no *body* in it. It's mere stage production. Of course it's far from contemptible. But it's neither farce nor comedy nor drama. Its atmosphere is uncertain. It is Jack with all his skill, his talent and his manner but robbed of all earnestness (the underlying righteousness of passion) which give weight and body to his theatrical art. McK himself was simply admirable.[2] I regretted you were not there with me in the old box. McK was a delight to watch but the play left an impression of a fairy tale. Yet it was not "light".

I was with McK. for an hour. He *is* a nice fellow. I reproached him with showing the play and he was quite genuinely surprised and concerned at the view we (you & I) took of it. It was quite touching. In the end before leaving I swore him to secrecy and imparted him the news of *the* Comedy.[3] The upshot is that I have sent it to his *private* address (he'll read it today). I hope you will not be annoyed with me. It was an impulse – and he is really an artist. Of his discretion I am certain. Moreover I did not tell him I was the translator. On the title page M^r X is the translator. I am going on with the novel and am pretty full of it. No other news whatever.

Yrs ever

J. Conrad

To E. L. Sanderson
Text MS Yale; Unpublished

[letterhead: Oswalds]
27.6.21.

My dearest Ted.

Pardon my inexcusable delay in answering your letter re Chesson.[4]

I am sorry you have been worried. I am not inclined to give any information to anybody connected with Unwins office. All I wanted to say about it I've said in the Personal Record.

I've had a lot of people here some who were welcome and others who were simply worrying. My work is in arrears. My spirits not exalted. My body full

[1] Galsworthy's *The Family Man* was now nearing the end of its run.
[2] In the role of John Builder.   [3] *The Book of Job*.
[4] Wilfrid Hugh Chesson (1870–1952), a reader at T. Fisher Unwin's, had recommended publishing *Almayer's Folly*. Sanderson, who met Conrad aboard the *Torrens*, had read the novel in MS. Evidently, Chesson had been assigned to dig out background for the publisher's advertisements.

of twinges. I am my dearest Ted simply tired of thinking on purpose and away from reality – as a daily task.

I was truly sorry for poor Ian and his parents. But dear Ted *why* May should have contained the *brightest* week of his life. Have I missed the Gazette of his promotion – or something of that kind. Or is it the May week in Camb^ge[1] that you mean? Give him my sympathy and my love.

My love goes to all of You – such a vain word it seems from a sinner like me. But you all must charitably believe in it.

Returning to that bothersome Chesson. He isn't a bad fellow and if you feel like telling him something please do so. But all that is Unwin's dodge to exploit the book[2] which is his (for £20 down) and from which he must have made many hundreds of pounds.

I am tied up to the desk – the price of the Corsican journey.

Jessie had a return of periostitis and is as it were half-laid up. We had a plan to rush your defences one afternoon this very week but it's all off. She mustn't go into a car for months perhaps. She sends her dear love.

Ever yours

Joseph Conrad.

To G. Jean-Aubry
Text MS Yale; Unpublished

[letterhead: Oswalds]
28.6.21

Très cher Jean.

C'est entendu. Vous arrivez par le train de 4^h.20 (Victoria).

Je vais envoyer le vieux Sneller[3] a la station. C'est un gros avec des moustaches cirées en pointes comme un general Russe du temps d'Alexandre II.[4]

Toutes nos amitiés

le votre

Conrad.

Votre train arrive 6.32 Cant^y East.

---

[1] An annual series of social events held, despite their name, in June.
[2] *Almayer's Folly*, whose copyright and French translation rights Conrad had sold to Unwin outright (*Letters*, 1, p. 180). The sale was to cause much rancour.
[3] The local taxidriver.   [4] Tsar from 1855 to 1881.

Translation

My very dear Jean.
    Agreed. You arrive by the 4.20 train (Victoria).
    I am sending old Sneller to the station. He's a big fellow with a moustache waxed in points like a Russian general of Alexander II's time.
    With all our regards

                                                                 Yours

                                                                           Conrad

Your train arrives at Cant^y East at 6.32.

To A. S. Kinkead
Text MS Indiana; Unpublished

                                                    [letterhead: Oswalds]
                                                             30.6.21

Dear Miss Kinkead[1]
    You were very good to take so much thought and trouble over the frame (Louis XV). Will you please direct the dealer to send me his acct covering also the cost of slip and framing, direct here.
    Our car is being severely overhauled and won't be ready for action for another week at least; when, I hope, its first service will be to fetch you and Mrs C (properly framed) down here.[2] We are all impatience to see you both arriving pleased with each other. It will be a charming sight.
    Will you now tell me the amount of the cheque which I should send you?
    With love from my wife, myself and indeed the household
    I am always Your most faithful friend and Servant

                                                            Joseph Conrad

---

[1] A portraitist, landscape painter, and goldsmith, Alice Sarah Kinkead (1871–1926) was born in Tuam, County Galway. She studied painting in Dublin, Paris, and London in the 1890s, and exhibitions of her work were held in Ireland and Scotland as well as in London, Liverpool, and Paris beginning in 1897. She met the Conrads during their Corsican sojourn, and painted portraits of both of them. Conrad provided a foreword to the exhibition catalogue of her Corsican and Irish landscape paintings held at the United Arts Gallery, London, in late 1921.
[2] She had just finished a portrait of Jessie Conrad.

To Thomas J. Wise
Text MS BL Ashley 2953; Unpublished

[letterhead: Oswalds]

1.7.21

Dear Mr Wise.

Herewith the "first draft" of the translated play. The "first copy" will be sent as soon as the clean copies are made.

I ought to have thanked you for your letter myself but the house was full of guests staying for a few days and I could not have a moment to myself.

You know that I was always ready to sign books for you in the past and I'll be always at your disposal in that way in the future whenever you want it done.

I'll no doubt be able to manage a call on you when I am up in town next time. It was impossible last week. I came up for the specific purpose to see McK[innel] in Galsw$^{thy's}$ play[1] and had to catch the 6.15 to be home in good time. My wife joins me in kindest regards. She is very sensible to your interest in her wretched trouble.

Believe me sincerely yours

J Conrad

To J. B. Pinker
Text TS/MS Berg; Unpublished

Oswalds,
Bishopsbourne,
Kent.
July 4th. 1921

Dearest J. B.

I asked Borys, who was here for the weekend, to 'phone you this morning my thanks for your Friday's wire and I repeat them here most heartily. We hope to see you here before long, in fact in the course of this week perhaps, as you will like probably to give your invitation to Mrs Bell yourself and settle the date for the proposed drive.[2] Upon the whole I think that would be the best course.

B. was I won't say depressed but extremely uneasy and anxious about the situation of the S[urrey] S[cientific] A[pparatus] Co. He talked to me a long time about it, expatiating on the dilatoriness and want of nerve and, as he said, "of kick" in everybody connected with the concern. He was most

---

[1] *The Family Man.*

[2] To the Kent County Cricket Ground in Pinker's four-in-hand mail-coach. For a picture of the coach and an entertaining account of the expedition, see John Conrad, pp. 178–86.

hurt and angry at them dropping the offer of a contract for a supply of mirolite wheels[1] which has been actually put into his hands for disposal by Major Hunt (an officer whom he knew in France)[2] and which, B. said, would have been worth £4000 a year. Even if he said, "Suppose I exaggerate, it was well worth immediate attention and some trouble which nobody would take." B. has very proper ideas about it all, because he said that being in the position he is with the S.S.A. Co. he meant the commission of that order, though obtained by him, to go to the Company; and he remarked very justly that a commission like that was worth having for a business needing every profit it could make. That thing fell through simply because the Mirolite secretary took absolutely no notice of the offer for a fortnight and when urged to do something wrote a letter which put Major Hunt off altogether. This is only one of the latter instances of neglect of opportunities of which there were many, both on the part of the Mirolite and the S.S.A. Co. B was also afraid that the S.S.A. CO. would lose the contract for the medical instruments of which I have been talking to you, one of the conditions of which was that two of them should be executed by next Friday for show purposes. He said with great indignation that this would be the limit, and complained quite naturally that it was very vexing and disheartening to see how he was wasting his interest amongst his friends, while he had to look on at the steady deterioration of the Company's financial position which is now in such a state that no wages have been paid within the last two months except to the two workmen who are being kept on still. Only three days ago or so when Julian Orde[3] asked B whether his Company would be open to take in the radio-news of the Carpentier fight[4] on their apparatus, the Board would not take it up on the ground that Warde* Miller would have no time to tune up the instrument for long-distance receiving. And when B offered to do so himself with Tam[m]age and stay late to receive it, he was told it wasn't worth while. Julian Orde had offered a fee of £30 for this job and Borys's view is that under the circumstances £30 was quite worth having, especially as it was all clear profit, and cost the Company nothing. The only person who backs him up at the Board is Warde* Miller but he is

---

[1] A rustproof hub too light for modern cars, but still in use for racing bicycles. Mirolite or miralite is an aluminium alloy.
[2] William Morgan Hunt, a major in the Royal Artillery.
[3] Julian Walter Orde (1861–1929; knighthood 1919), the Secretary of the Automobile Club 1903–20, keenly promoted racing and was a leader in the development of modern motoring.
[4] The French boxer Georges Carpentier unsuccessfully challenged Jack Dempsey for the World Light-Heavyweight Championship on 2 July in New York.

not always at the meetings, being manager of the Radio Company and his time being taken up with that mostly. He often comes to the works of the S.S.A. in the lunch hour bringing a sandwich with him and puts in an hour or an hour and a half's work there in the middle of the day; and he and B. work in the evening between six and nine at testing and experimenting; but the business side is quite hopeless, for Mac and his brother are wrapt up in the deaf-apparatus which they seem to imagine will make a fortune for them all at once. But granted even that it could do that, how is it going to do it if the manufacturing Company comes to an end for want of funds? I can't tell you here everything I have heard in the way of facts and very sensible, I fancy, remarks B made to me on them, but if we were to meet I would be able to give you a better idea. B wants you to understand the position as it is now, and take the right view of his efforts to get something else to do in case of his present job failing him completely; because, as he says, he needs a salary to live on and if they can't pay it to him he will have to take up something else. Last week he was introduced to Sir Robert A. Hadfield,[1] a most distinguished person, and I suppose the greatest engineer that England has; but B is quite aware that his lack of scientific qualifications puts him at a tremendous disadvantage. He is going to see Hadfield this week, the man having been very amiable to him and having told him to do so, but B is afraid that he will offer him something which he will not be competent to take, simply on account of his lack of training, which is not his fault, as you know. Of course the Chairman of *Hadfield's Limited* who employ over 6000 men (and of many other undertakings) could find some place for him. I advised B however to be very frank about it and to tell the man that he is only fit for some inferior position either in workshops or anything else, which he would be ready to take. Pray don't believe that either he or I are pleased at what has happened. On the contrary B is quite cut up at the necessity of looking for something else, but things look as if he had to do something of the kind, for, as he says himself, he couldn't go back to doing nothing now. He very sincerely wishes for nothing better than to stay with the S.S.A. Co. almost at any cost, but he could not conceal from me a certain feeling of hopelessness about the prospects of the concern – even if the industrial situation improved generally – in view of the nerveless management or rather lack of management from which it suffers, that grossly incompetent and ignorant creature Jefferies being apparently in charge of it. B left us last night

---

[1] Robert Abbott Hadfield (1858–1940; knighted 1908, Baronet 1917), engineer and inventor, metallurgist, and industrialist.

as usual telling me that three weeks are bound to decide the matter anyway. I must say that I feel bitterly disappointed and somewhat depressed about this development.

I am sending you here the play which McK. returned with the enclosed letter, which to me seems a strangely stupid sort of thing. I let you be the judge. Will you have two copies made and return me the copy I send you, which, being a personally corrected copy must go to Wise under the terms of my understanding with him. Aubry who was here for the weekend read the play on Saturday and considers it very good indeed and even appearing better the more it is looked into. He being a literary person pointed out that it shows distinct signs of Shaw's influence in its general conception and of Arthur Schnitzler in its construction.[1] He pointed out to me too its tactfulness in dealing with situations which could be easily made not so much shocking as unpleasant to an audience. In all this I agree, and also in Aubry's opinion that the times are now very difficult and that it is not easy to think of a suitable theatre to offer it to. You, however, are the man to face those difficulties. I communicate to you A.'s suggestion that perhaps Everyman's Theatre would offer the best chances,[2] merely for what it may be worth in your opinion. I myself confess to knowing nothing about it except in the matter of my feeling, which is this: that Everyman is a sort of theatre from which nothing much in the way of profit can be expected. But there too you are "the man who knows". My other feeling is that the thing is good enough to be given every chance of material success, deserved, I fancy, by its scenic qualities.

The MS of the novel is growing and I really do think that, unless something unfavourable steps in, you may be able to handle it in the autumn as you thought you would like to do – I mean even to begin the serial about that time. But days do go by with frightful rapidity; *that* I must admit!

Now, I want to communicate to you a few figures which have come in my way. In the American "World's Work" for *July 1921*, which was sent to me by Doubleday, there is my portrait, wearing a pained smile, and a distinct

---

[1] The plays of Irish dramatist and critic George Bernard Shaw (1856–1950) tackled political and realistic subjects, overturning theatrical conventions. *Heartbreak House*, his most recent play (1920), was among his most sombre. The Austrian playwright Arthur Schnitzler (1862–1931) specialised in psychological dramas dissecting bourgeois life. These playwrights shared with Conrad an ironic sense that even the task of staging *The Secret Agent* could not entirely suppress.

[2] Built as a drill hall, the Everyman in Holly Bush Vale, Hampstead, eventually became a much-loved repertory cinema. From 1919 to 1923 it was a theatre, known for its willingness to take chances on plays too controversial or difficult for the West End. Its survival depended on both the quality of its repertoire and its policy of paying actors no more than £5 a week.

statement that the sales of Conrad in '21 (June) have reached 300,000 copies.[1] In the same number in an article on Authors and Best Sellers there is also another statement: that in 1920 the sales of the books of Joseph Conrad amounted to 36 times what they did in 1911.[2]

I looked up at once the tabular Statement which you brought me from America, from which I see that that last statement (as far as yearly sales are concerned) is quite correct. The sales of 1920 alone *were* about thirty-six times as much as those of 1911 alone. Therefore I conclude that the other statement giving my sales (total) up to date as 300,000 in all, is correct too. I looked into the matter further and see that from the tabular statement the total of Conrad's sales in *Feb. 1920* reached in round figures 218,000 copies; from which it follows that the sales from Feb. 1920 to, say, April 1921 amounted to 82,000 copies of which 50,000 must go to the sale of "The Rescue" on the strength of the same article. I am inclined to think that this shows the true state of affairs; and as you may not have seen the number of The World's Work, I send the intelligence to you for your information.

The man Spicer-Simson, the medal-maker, is not to be kept out of this any longer. Both the Galsworthys have been worrying my head off about the sittings and even for the sake of peace and quietness I must let him come. So I named Thursday next, when he will take lots of photographs to carry off with him to Paris and from those execute the medallion roughly. On his way to America, sometime in August, he will come again for a day and finish the work from the living model. This was the best I could do for myself, and I thank my stars it isn't worse.

The only real worry is poor Jessie. That pain is certainly increasing and spreading over a larger area. Reid has been twice to see her and will call again to-morrow. I'll have a talk with him then and drop you a line. That wretched thing is like a nightmare on one.

Our love to you

Yours ever

Joseph Conrad.

PS I have now *one* Am^can copy of *Notes on My Books* and *one* English copy. The Am: binding is much the nicest.

---

[1] In fact, the June issue. The caption under Conrad's half-page photograph reads: 'This year the Conrad sales total about 300,000 copies. "The Rescue" alone sold about 50,000 copies. A recent chart indicated that sales of Conrad in 1920 were thirty-six times greater than they were in 1911' (p. 189). The photograph accompanies Arthur B. Maurice's 'Authors and "Best Sellers"' (pp. 185–99). The magazine was published by Doubleday, Page.
[2] Virtually a word-for-word quotation (p. 185.)

To J. B. Pinker
Text TS/MS Berg; Unpublished

Oswalds,
Bishopsbourne,
Kent.
July 6th. 1921.

Dearest J. B.

I have been considering Mais'[1] letter and I have even gone so far as to check the passages he wants to quote; and apparently he wants to quote a lot. As to my opinion of the man it coincides exactly with your own and I have not the slightest sympathy either with his creative work or his critical outpourings. On the other hand one can't call him a fraud.

Upon the whole my feeling is that if one could decently refuse, that would be the thing to do. I really don't see why I should display benevolence towards the Metropolitan Review and their infernal Board of Directors whose motives in getting out that book may be frightfully high-minded, democratic and philanthropic and all the rest of it, but are based no doubt on the vulgar idea of profit on outlay.[2] It is obviously their idea, and Mais is to be the hack. If it were to help a brother-scribbler I would not be so hostile to the notion. As it is I hope that you will harden your heart, and I leave it at that.

We take it as understood that you arrive here next Saturday by the train due in Canterbury West at 5.4. Unless we hear to the contrary, this is the train the car will meet – that is if it is put together by that time. V[inten] has begun assembling it this morning and hopes to be done by Friday evening. The overhaul has been very thorough and when it has had another new tyre it will be quite fit to play tender to the coach during the cricket-week.[3]

Our love to you all

Ever Yours

J. Conrad

---

[1] S(tuart) P(etre) B(rodie) Mais (1885–1975), essayist, journalist, and critic.

[2] There was no such journal as the *Metropolitan Review* at the time. Since the book in question was probably Mais's *An English Course for Everybody* (Grant Richards, 1921), Conrad may be referring to a civic organisation. According to *An English Course*, 'You read Conrad because he happens to be the finest writer of English alive. Never has a nation received quite so high a compliment as that which we have received from this Pole. He is difficult to read: his method is quite uncannily cumbersome. He seems unable to say anything at first hand, but once overcome the seemingly unnecessary obstacles which he sets up and you will arrive at some very definite statement about life of inestimable value' (p. 45).

[3] Pinker's mail-coach was to arrive on the 29th; he and his family planned to stay for the entire week, a highlight of the cricket season.

I enclose a demand for land tax which I fancy is Bell's affair. Will you tell me? enc^d Mais' letter

To A. S. Kinkead
Text MS Indiana; Unpublished

[letterhead: Oswalds]
7. July. '21

Dear Miss Kinkead.

Thanks for your good letter. I most certainly intend you to travel (with your masterpiece) down here by car. As far as I can tell the car will be ready for the road about Tuesday next.

Would you like to come Sat. next and have your Sunday prayers with us?[1]

Out of regard for JB's feelings (which are touchy and childlike) we could not possibly remove the gold frame as yet from the Corsican picture.

Pray consider the common weaknesses of humanity with a charitable eye.

Walpole is abroad already I believe.

All our loves to you.

Yours always

Joseph Conrad

To Ada Galsworthy
Text MS Forbes; Unpublished

[letterhead: Oswalds]
8. July. 21[2]

Dearest Ada.

No end of thanks for Your dear letter.

S[picer]-S[imson] was here yesterday, took some photographs and started on the plasticine. From what I have seen I feel already the thing will be a success.[3] S-S is coming again on Thursday next. We got on very well together, I think. His impression may be different, however; but I hope not as I like the man.

---

[1] One suspects an irony.
[2] Below the telegraphic address, Conrad wrote 'Aug: 1?', perhaps a date for the visit to town mentioned in the letter.
[3] The medallion appears in Spicer-Simson and Sherman's *Men of Letters of the British Isles: Portrait Medallions from the Life* (New York, 1924), p. 38.

Poor Jessie is again crippled and in constant pain. Her coming up to town is at present out of the question. She would dearly love seeing You and dear Jack, but what with the grind of the journey and regard for Your time and many engagements one hardly dares suggest a visit here.

I may have to come up for a day and then I will take my chance of finding You at home.

Our dearest love to You both.

Ever Yours

J. Conrad

To A. P. Hatton

Text TS Black; Unpublished

[letterhead: Oswalds]

July. 14th. 1921.

Dear Sir,[1]

In reference to your letter of the 7th, I really don't think there are any stories that would be suitable for the "British Legion", both on account of length and subject, which have no direct connection with the aims and ideas it is your paper's mission to propagate. I have no didactic purpose in my writings, as for instance Mr Kipling has.[2]

As a recognition of your patriotic purpose and a sign of most sincere goodwill, I am sending you a copy of my latest published work.[3] When you find leisure to look through it you may find amongst the papers composing it and especially those entitled "Tradition" and "Confidence" paragraphs and passages which you may perhaps like to print either separately or combined together, as an expression of views or sentiments which you may well believe are identical with yours and which you are at liberty to use in the way you think best. At any rate I hope you will give the volume a place on your shelves and believe me

Very faithfully Yours

Joseph Conrad.

---

[1] A. P. Hatton edited the *British Legion*, the Legion's weekly magazine, from July to October 1921. Founded in June 1921 by an amalgamation of four veterans' organisations, the Legion campaigned for the welfare of ex-servicemen and women, lobbying for housing, jobs, medical care, equitable pension rights, and seeking to avoid another war.

[2] The magazine had reprinted Kipling's poem 'The Return' on 8 July.

[3] *Notes on Life and Letters*. Hatton chose 'Tradition' for the issue of 12 August.

To J. B. Pinker
Text MS Berg; Unpublished

[letterhead: Oswalds]
[14 July 1921][1]

Dearest J B

Herewith letter to Mc.[2] B[orys] has just let me know that he is going to begin work tomorrow by request.[3] He explains that for to-night and Friday night he got a room at the club.[4] On Sat night he will be here when I shall know more. He will leave here on Sund: night and if necessary take advantage of Barton's offer to stay with him[5] for a day or two.

Pray censor or otherwise control the letter to M[c].

Jessie sends her love and thanks for all You have done for me, in these damned circumstances.

I'll have to write you at length soon. Sir R Jones is coming tomorrow and the car goes at 7 am to fetch him from Seddlescombe.[6]

Ever Yours

J. C.

To J. B. Pinker
Text TS Berg; Unpublished

Oswalds,
Bishopsbourne,
Kent.
Tuesday July 18th. [18 or 19 July 1921][7]

Dearest J. B.

I will engage rooms for Samson at Bridge at one of the inns early next week. As to Culverwell,[8] he had better, as you suggest, come here with Vinton* on his return trip and Mrs Burchett[9] will provide for him on that day, as during my absence from home Jessie will be alone with Audrey in the house till late

---

[1] The next letter fixes the Thursday and Friday mentioned.
[2] Mackintosh, as the letter of the [19th] makes clear. Pinker helped Borys and his father deal with the collapse of Mackintosh's company, which brought the loss of a friendship, a job, and a substantial amount of money.
[3] Borys had accepted a job with Autoveyors, Ltd, 'automobile engineers and light car specialists', of 84 Victoria St, SW1. The company was founded by three ex-officers who had served together in France.
[4] The Royal Automobile.
[5] B. C. Barton had also been a junior officer in the Royal Army Service Corps.
[6] Where the Watsons, Sir Robert's daughter and son-in-law, spent part of each year.
[7] Tuesday was the 19th.
[8] Pinker's butler; Samson also worked at Burys Court. Bridge is near Canterbury.
[9] The wife of Jack Burchett, one of the gardeners.

on the 28th, when the cook, I believe, will join. C. will then have, as it were, a day off, unless he likes to come over and have a look at the things in the house; and he could begin to be helpful on the 29th for the first dinner of the Pinker family in Oswalds. As to the lunches on the Ground I believe the best thing would be – as there will be always the party from Bourne,[1] number uncertain – not to provide them from home. I intend to make arrangements with either the County Hotel or the Fleur de Lys to get them ready during the week, for the number of people that are coming for each day's match. Or perhaps there may be a marquee on the spot where we might make arrangements. The difficulty about providing the lunches from here is this:- as Jessie says she is not used to catering, has no room to keep provisions in this hot weather, and what's worse she says she wouldn't be able to look to things herself. This electricity treatment which is to begin to-morrow will certainly cause her pain during application and therefore disable her more or less. Apart from that she would have to keep quiet for an hour or two after it so that the middle of the day, as it were, will be taken up by it. I am afraid that those lunches won't be tip-top, for Canterbury is not up to much, but they will serve, and at any rate this arrangement will ease Jessie's mind, who is very anxious about the adequate performance of her duties. At any rate I intend to use all my powers of persuasion and fascination to get those Canterbury people to turn out decent things, whatever they may be. I will go to work next Monday and fix everything up; this week being devoted to work, exclusively and without interruption.

Jessie also with many apologies and regrets wants me to tell you that you mustn't count on her to join the party in Ashford to lunch. It's no use expecting miracles from the treatment and she is afraid it won't make her fit for doing about 35 miles in the car on that day, at any rate without paying for it with severe suffering which she wishes to avoid while her honoured guests are here.

Borys has been here for Sunday. He has got himself a room in a house of flats within two minutes walk of his place of business. He hopes to be able to come for the Sunday of the cricket week and the following Bank Holiday,[2] unless something unexpected turns up and he is required in London, which is not very likely.

You remember the account of uncertain amount which has been kept in suspense. It is Rayner's bill,[3] the amount of which of £146 we are not in a

---

[1] The Bells and their entourage.   [2] The first Monday in August.
[3] Dr Edwin Cromwell Rayner, a recent arrival from London, was now in practice with Clifford Hackney, for many years the Conrad family doctor, at 7 High St, Hythe.

position to dispute. However, I am sending you the solicitor's letter and I trust that some arrangement to at any rate spread the payments can be made with him. I hoped I could contribute and have this hope still, but I don't think I could do it this month. I could contribute a little in August perhaps, and more in September. Meantime perhaps you will communicate with him and see what he says.

As you have not said anything about my letter to Mac. I presume you have sent it, either altered or unaltered. I imagine it will be possible to get something, if not all, back again; but of course as things stand it is difficult to be sure of that or anything else.

Jessie joins me in love to you all.

Ever Yours

J. Conrad.

To J. B. Pinker
Text MS Berg; Unpublished

[Oswalds]
Tuesday. [19 or 20 July 1921][1]

Dearest J. B.

I wrote you yesterday on many things.

Thanks for agreement which I return duly signed.[2] I suppose Conard[3] is gone bust?

Thanks also for you[r] letter to Barton. James Lithgow[4] sent an extremely strong testimonial in the form of a letter to B[orys] by return of post.

Good old Jimmy.

Jack and Ada "asked for leave" to motor down here on Bank Holiday. That need not interfere with our arrangements except that I will stay at home that day to give them lunch. We don't like to put them off as the visit is specially on Jessie's account.

---

[1] The day after the letter 'on many things', whose given day and date do not match. Hallowes notes the signing of two agreements on the 19th.
[2] With William Collins & Co. for an edition of *The Rescue* for the Continent and North Africa, signed on the 19th. This might also explain the reference to Conard.
[3] The well-known Parisian publisher of, among others, Flaubert.
[4] Lithgow (1883–1952; 1st Baronet of Ormsary 1925) was chairman of Lithgow's, one of the great Clydeside shipyards. Borys Conrad had served under him in France; see Borys Conrad, *My Father: Joseph Conrad* (Calder & Boyars, 1970), pp. 125–7. Wounded in action and invalided out of the army, Lithgow then served as the Admiralty's Director of Merchant Shipbuilding until 1919.

This heat is growing alarming. If it continues the horses will have a hard job.[1] Would you think of altering the hours to *very early* morning and late afternoon?

Ever Yours

J. Conrad.

To J. B. Pinker

Text MS Berg; Unpublished

[Oswalds]

[20 or 21 July 1921][2]

Dearest J. B.

Thanks for your letter with the D[oubled]ay agreement[3] which I return.

John and I will arrive next Wed: at about 5 oclock. If then Vinten with Culverwell start at 6 they will be here at 9 pm at latest when Mrs Burchett will be ready to receive him.

I am working all the morning and gasping most of the afternoon.

Our love

Yours ever

J. Conrad

First electric application yesterday was done leaving no particular increase of pain.

To J. B. Pinker

Text MS Berg; Unpublished

[letterhead: Oswalds]

Thursday 20 [or 21].7.'21[4]

Dearest J. B.

A p-c from the Surrey Scientific Apparatus C° has arrived this evening here addressed to Borys and signed by Tammage saying that *"A meeting of Directors will take place on Friday evening at 8.30 pm"*.

I am sending it on to him – but I don't understand the object. He is not a director as far as I know and I am under the impression that he has been formally dismissed by one of the directors who has paid him his salary up to date.

What is the meaning of this convocation? Is he to take any notice of it?

One would not like to give them the slightest opening for any unexpected move.

---

[1] On the drive from Burys Court to Oswalds.

[2] Jessie Conrad's electrical treatment began on the 19th or 20th.

[3] For a volume containing the dramatic version of *The Secret Agent* and *One Day More*, signed on the 19th.

[4] Once again, day and date do not match.

I don't want to have your head worried off with this affair but I have taken the liberty to tell B to ring you up if he should have any doubt as to the proper course to take.

Pray tell me about Edwards and the two other men. Has R[alph] got lodgings for them? If so I would arrange for their meals (morning and evening) at the Inn in Bridge. If not then I will arrange for lodgings too.

Ever Yours

J Conrad

To Richard Curle
Text MS Indiana; Curle 75

[letterhead: Oswalds]
27.7.'21

Dear Dick.

What has become of you? Drop us a line to say you are well.
Am leaving for P's today and shall be back on Friday evening.
Our love

Yours

J. Conrad.

To G. Jean-Aubry
Text MS Yale; Unpublished

[letterhead: Oswalds]
27.7.21

Cher Jean.

Je pars ce matin, pour Burys Court (Pinker) d'ou je reviendrai en mail-coach Vendredi soir.

Envoyez nous un petit mot pour nous dire que Vous allez bien. Je suis un peu inquiet.

Affectueusement le votre

J. Conrad.

Translation

Dear Jean.

I leave for Burys Court (Pinker's) this morning whence I return by mail-coach on Friday evening.

Drop us a line to say you are well. I am a little uneasy.

Yours affectionately

J. Conrad

To G. Jean-Aubry
Text MS Yale; Unpublished

[letterhead: Oswalds]
1st Aug '21

Très cher.

Voulez [-vous] venir for weekend Samedi prochain quoique La Famille Pinker sera ici?

On pourra Vous loger chez Borys qui sera absent.

Ecrivez nous un petit mot.

Our love

Yours

J. C.

Translation

My dear friend.

Would you like to come for the week-end next Saturday even though the Pinker family will be here?

We could put you up in Borys's room since he'll be away.

Drop us a line.

Our love

Yours

J. C.

To Richard Curle
Text MS Indiana; Curle 76

[letterhead: Oswalds]
Tuesday 1st [2]. Aug. 1921[1]

Dearest Dick

Most sorry we can't have you this weekend. The whole Pinker family are staying here till the 8th. Could you come on the 10th till the 12th evening?

Pray drop us a line.

Our love

Yours

J. C.

---

[1] Again, the day is more likely to be correct than the date.

To André Gide
Text MS Doucet; *L.fr.* 165–6

[letterhead: Oswalds]
5 Août 21

Très cher Gide,

Votre lettre du 22 vient d'arriver,[1] et je vous envoi[e] ce petit mot tout de suite pour Vous remercier de tout mon coeur de Votre inalterable amitié qui parait dans toutes les lignes de Votre séduisante écriture.

Je suis heureux d'apprendre que vous avez l'intention de revoir, personell-ment, la traduction de *Lord Jim*. Oui, M. Néel est un traducteur excellent et Vous avez bien fait de lui confier Votre "livre préferé". Je suis profondement touché de Votre intention d'écrire une étude sur mon oeuvre.[2] Ma recon-naissance vous en est acquise – mais je comprends très bien que Vous pouvez être empêché de la faire.

Nous sommes désolés du mauvais état de la santé de Mme Votre femme.[3] Notre sympathie va vers Elle et Vous car tous les deux nous savons ce que c'est. Ma femme me prie de la rappeller affectueusement a Votre souvenir. Nous avions l'espoir de Vous voir chez nous cette année. D'après ce que Vous dites de Votre travail et de Vos projets je crains qu'il ne faut plus y penser?

C'est une grande nouvelle pour moi, celle de Votre projet d'un long roman! Justement il y a quelques jours j'ai relu les Caves de* Vatican, toujours avec le même interêt mais avec une admiration qui croit a chaque nouvelle lecture.[4] C'est vraiment merveilleux l'infinité des choses que vous avez mis dans ce livre ou la main est si legère et la pensée si profonde.

Borys mon ainé e[s]t a Londres ou il a trouvé un emploi dans son gout – le negoce des automobiles; une maison fondé[e] par 3 officiers qui ont fait campagne ensemble en France. John est au collège de Tonbridge et fait des bonnes études. Il se rappelle très bien de Vous comme le bienfaiteur qui lui a donné son premier Meccano.[5]

Ma pauvre femme souffre encore beaucoup de son genou. Ca n'en finit pas. Quand* à moi je travaille mal et je me fatigue très vite. Le voyage en

---

[1] See Stape and Knowles, pp. 180–1.   [2] Nothing came of this project.
[3] Madeleine Gide (née Rondeaux, 1867–1938) suffered from chronic ill-health.
[4] Conrad first read *Les Caves du Vatican* in 1914; he wrote Gide two letters about it, but the second, dispatched from war-time Cracow, went astray (*Letters*, 5, pp. 331, 494). The novel's fifth part has an epigraph from *Lord Jim*.
[5] The perforated metal pieces in a Meccano set can be bolted together to make all sorts of models. (In the USA, such kits are known as erector sets.) Father and son loved playing with Gide's gift, and Conrad was soon buying more elaborate versions. See John Conrad, p. 36, and *Letters*, 5, p. 591.

Corse a été très agréable. J'ai eu depuis un fort accès de goutte qui m'a laissé
deprimé et maussade.

Croyez-moi mon cher Gide toujours à Vous de coeur.

Joseph Conrad.

Translation

My very dear Gide,

Your letter of the 22nd has just arrived, and I send this word immediately
to thank you with all my heart for the unaltering friendship that appears in
every line of your seductive handwriting.

I am happy to hear that you plan to revise the translation of *Lord Jim*
yourself. Of course, Monsieur Neel is a fine translator, and you did well to
assign him your 'favourite book'. I am profoundly touched by your intention
to write a study of my work. I am already grateful for this but understand
very well that you may be prevented from doing it.

We are sorry to hear of your wife's poor health. Our sympathy goes out
to her and you because we both know what that is like. My wife asks to
be affectionately remembered to you. We hoped to see you here this year.
According to what you say of your work and plans I fear we must no longer
think of it?

What great news for me your idea of a long novel is. A few days ago, in fact,
I re-read *Les Caves du Vatican*, with the same interest but with an admiration
that grows on each new reading. The infinity of things you put into that book,
where the hand is so light and the thought so deep, is truly marvellous.

Borys, my elder son, is now in London where he has found a job to his
liking in a motor business set up by three officers who fought together in
France. John is at school in Tonbridge and is doing well in his work. He
remembers you very well as the benefactor who gave him his first Meccano
set.

My poor wife is still suffering a good deal from her knee. That is never-
ending. As to myself, I work badly and tire very easily. The sojourn in Corsica
was quite pleasant. Since returning I had a bad attack of gout that left me
depressed and ill-tempered.

Believe me, my dear Gide, always affectionately yours

Joseph Conrad.

To Bruno Winawer

Text TS copy Yale;[1] J-A, 2, 261 (in part);[2] *Głos* (108); Winawer ix-xii; Najder 268–70

> Oswalds,
> Bishopsbourne,
> Kent.
> Aug. 10th. 1921.

Dear Mr. Winawer,

I am writing to you in English this time, as I am confident that you know the language well and it is easier for me to dictate.

I must begin by thanking you for the little book of satirical pieces[3] which I read with great enjoyment and in that sympathetic mood which your work arouses in me. As a matter of fact I like all the pieces, both as point of view and as expression.

Now as to the play. As I anticipated I have not been able to find a translator. I did not even know very well how to begin to look for one. Of course there are translating and typewriting offices where they would translate from any language, but to deliver your play to that fate was not to be thought of. Therefore I took the matter in hand myself notwithstanding the arrears of my own work in the way of preparing my Collected Edition, of which ten volumes have appeared by now and the fact that I have [a] long novel in hand which causes me much labour and worry.

The work now is finished and I am sending you a copy by registered post. I don't for a moment suppose that you will be pleased with the translation. No author is ever pleased with a translation[4]of his work. That cannot be expected. The first reading will no doubt exasperate you, but I am confident that after a time you will discover an amount of fidelity to your thought and even your expression which you could not have been able to find in any other translation more accurately verbal. You will notice no doubt that it is strictly idiomatic and you may take it from me that the idioms are absolutely correct and employed in strict accordance with your artistic intention. My guiding idea was to make the work acceptable to a theatrical audience. In one or

---

[1] Typing errors not reproduced or signalled. A missing postscript, which Winawer summarises in a manuscript note, requested him to keep this matter confidential and not to ask for other translations.

[2] Jean-Aubry goes as far as 'appreciative' in the fifth paragraph.

[3] *Groteski* (1921).

[4] On its virtues, errors, and concessions to the understanding of a British audience, see Grażyna Branny, 'Bruno Winawer's *The Book of Job*: Conrad's Only Translation', *The Conradian*, 27, no. 1 (2002), 1–23.

two places you will discover a certain shortening of speeches, but nothing
material has been missed. I have also summarised rather than translated
the preliminary descriptive matter, leaving just enough to guide the English
actors. In one or two places I have altered the phrasing so as to make the
thought more accessible to the English or American public, and I have taken
the liberty to invent names for certain characters, in order to make them
acceptable to the ears of the audience.

    This being done I showed the play to several people capable of judging,
not one of them being a dramatic author but any of them being possible as
an intelligent member of the theatrical public. All the opinions [were] very
favourable and indeed, I may say, very appreciative. Then I had down here
my agent, Mr. J. B. Pinker, and we discussed the matter thoroughly. Personally
he was very pleased. From a business point of view he said that the difficulty
of getting it accepted would be great, but once accepted a success would be
quite possible. He declared himself ready to take the matter in hand, both
in America [and here], not only on the ground that it is my translation but
on the merits of the play itself. There are two courses now open before you.
First: with the copy I am sending you may personally approach anybody
here or in America by whatever means you can command. And in that case
I can only wish you luck and beg you to submit the English text simply as
a translation without mentioning my name. It is quite good enough to pass
on its own merits. That is one alternative and in that case there can be no
question of any financial transaction between you and me. I was very glad
to do the translation for you, as a friendly act, and here is an end of it. The
second alternative is that you should put the play in the hands of Mr. Pinker
as a translation by Joseph Conrad, in which case the net proceeds, whatever
they may be, would have to be divided as follows: 50% for you, 40% for
me and 10% for Mr. Pinker, which is his usual charge for all the business he
does for me and his other clients, such as A. Bennett, John Galsworthy and
many others. In other words: we divide the proceeds but I pay the whole
of the agent's commission; both our names appearing on the bills and in
the advertisements. This seems to me a fair arrangement. Before you decide
you must thoroughly understand that the chances are very much against
us, and that the placing of the play and (even if placed) its financial success
are very doubtful indeed. Pray keep that well in mind. The success of a
play, both with managers and the public, is mostly a matter of luck and in
this particular case the foreignness of the play is bound to be an adverse
element. I hope therefore you will not build any hopes on it and that you
will regard the transaction as something in the nature of taking a lottery
ticket.

However should you select the second alternative you will have to write a letter, either in French or English, addressed to J. B. Pinker, Esqre., Talbot House, Arundel Street, London, W.C. 2, empowering him to act on your behalf on conditions specified in this letter. This will be sufficient, and I do not think that a formal agreement as between you two is necessary, and as to me, of course Mr. Pinker will act under the general power he has to treat on my behalf for all my work whatever kind it may be.

Yours faithfully

Joseph Conrad

Bruno Winawer, Esq. Warsaw

To J. B. Pinker
Text MS Berg; Unpublished

[Oswalds]
Wed^y [10 August 1921][1]

Dear J. B.

Will you post the letter to B. Winawer if you approve of the terms in which it is written.

I think my proposal meets the justice of the case.

Ever Yours

J Conrad.

To J. B. Pinker
Text MS Berg; Unpublished

[Oswalds]
Friday [12 August 1921][2]

Dearest J. B.

Herewith the *Times* affair.[3] I send you a letter already typed (except the figures which I suggest should be 52.10.0.) which you may have filled in and the lot forwarded – *if* you *quite* approve.

---

[1] The same date as the draft letter to Winawer.
[2] The first Friday after the Pinkers' visit.
[3] I.e., the following letter inquiring about payment for 'Heroes of the Straits', the piece collected in *Last Essays* as 'The Dover Patrol'. It appeared in *The Times* on 27 July, p. 11. During the war, the sailors and airmen of the Dover Patrol kept German vessels out of the Straits of Dover and guarded Allied convoys. On occasion they took their mission into enemy territory, as in the daring raid on Zeebrugge and Ostend in 1918.

If not perhaps you will write as my agent as your view prompts you. It's an unpleasant development. Thank your wife and daughter for the letters. We were glad to hear you came home feeling fresh and well.

Ever Yours

J. C.

Your wire this moment to hand.[1] I will do my damnedest of course but the prospect of anybody seeing it makes me nervous. I suppose I'll hear by letter the exact day you want the stuff for post. The difficulty would be to have it clean-typed as I cannot be parted altogether from my text. I must have by me what I have written.

I have been seedy with a swollen knee ever since Tuesday night. Better this morning.

JC.

1 pm.

To the Day Editor, *The Times*
Text TS Berg; Unpublished

[letterhead: Oswalds]
[12] August, 1921.[2]

Dear Sir.

I return you the enclosed documents. I am not in the habit of sending printed bills for my work, and why the "Times" should make out a bill for me without as much as asking me what my terms are passes my understanding. If it is not a mistake it is mere impertinence.

I am not a "Times" employee, neither have I asked the "Times" to print any article by me. Writing for the press is not my occupation and it is not to my taste. As you thought it proper to ask me by wire for an article without mentioning the price, you will be good enough (if you wish to pay at all) to send me a cheque for £   which I will acknowledge by letter in the usual way.

Yours faithfully

Joseph Conrad.

The Day Editor,
The Times.

---

[1] As subsequent letters reveal, a request for a sample of *Suspense* to circulate in the hope of securing serialisation.
[2] The date of the cover letter to Pinker.

To J. B. Pinker

Text MS Berg; Unpublished

[Oswalds]
Saturday. [13 August 1921][1]

Dear J. B.

I have both your letters the typed and the written, which reached me only this morning. Many thanks.

I am going on with the text and only regret that the action is not more engaged. However I like to think that the writing is interesting enough to impress the Cosmop[an][2] favourably. I will push on as fast as I can without trying to reach finality in my corrections. There will be a further opportunity for revision on the "serial" text. I will be sending you the pages as they are ready, so that clean-typing can go on parallel with the corrections. Pray dear J. B. see that my "first draft" is returned to me integrally. Pardon me being so fussy about it.

We are delighted to hear that from all your points of view the "Journey to Kent" was a success. That being so there is nothing to spoil its charming memory for us. The team looked simply lovely on leaving Ashford. It was something to remember! You were much missed. Our love to You all.

Being gouty and in pain The Times proceeding irritated me exceedingly – the damned printed acct form as much as the rest. You must decide on the course to take: whether to send the letter at all and if so what amount is to be filled in in the vacant space; or whether it would not be better for you to take the correspondence in hand yourself. I had my misgivings but this is too bad.

I must go back to my corrections.

Ever affect[ly] yours

J. Conrad.

I anticipate they will answer, "of course we meant it only as a nominal fee, supposing that M[r] C would wish to participate in the good work of the Memorial to the Patrol".

– But if so it ought to have been done in another form with an appreciative letter to that effect not as if paying a reporter in regular employment and in the way of business, without a word of thanks.

– You see my point?

---

[1] Allusions to the coaching expedition and the letter to *The Times* give the date.
[2] In 1918, the *Cosmopolitan Magazine* had shown interest in US serial rights to *The Rescue*, but Conrad had been in no hurry to accede to their request for a synopsis and a romantic ending (*Letters*, 6, pp. 338–40).

To J. B. Pinker

Text MS Berg; Unpublished

[Oswalds]
Sunday 6pm [14 August 1921][1]

Dearest J. B.

To save time I am sending you by Borys Chap. III of P[t] I corrected.

Chap. III will take some more grinding. Meantime the III may be typed.
I will send you more corr[d] copy monday even[g].

Ever Yours

J. C.

To Ford Madox Ford

Text MS Yale; Unpublished

[letterhead: Oswalds]
Agst *15*[th] [1921][2]

Dear Hueffer[3]

The matter of the inclusion of Romance (which is a fact) I must refer to J.
Pinker who arranged the whole thing. I fancy he must have consulted you as
your participation in the royalties on *that* vol was taken into account.

I don't see why you should not include collb[ve] work in the Coll[ed] Edition
of your works – in any case. In fact I dont see what else either of us could
do.[4]

Can you give me an idea how much you think I owe you as I can't tell
what did or did not reach your hand.

Pardon this scrap of paper.

Yours

J. C.

---

[1] The dates of this and the next letter depend upon the previous one.

[2] Work on the collected edition gives the year.

[3] In his novels and memoirs, Ford Madox Ford (1873–1939) created some of the best English
fiction of the twentieth century. He was also a poet and an inspired editor. His collaborations
with Conrad included *The Inheritors* (1901), *Romance* (1903), and 'The Nature of a Crime'
(*English Review*, April–May 1909). Conrad and Ford quarrelled in 1909; by the end of 1911
a rapprochement had begun, hastened by Ford's admiring essay in the *English Review*, but
the friendship never regained its earlier closeness. In the present letter, as elsewhere, Conrad
ignores the change of surname from Hueffer to Ford, which occurred in 1919.

[4] *Romance* and *The Inheritors* did appear in the collected editions, but Ford came to feel that his role
in these collaborations was inadequately signalled. The lack of consultation also continued to
annoy him. See Saunders, 2, p. 142.

To J. B. Pinker

Text MS Berg; Unpublished

[Oswalds]

Monday. 6pm. [15 August 1921?][1]

Dearest J B.

This moment I got a letter from F. M. H[ueffer] who asks me whether I pub^d Rom^{ce} in my coll^{ed} Edition – as he has "not been consulted." Or at least does not *remember* being consulted.

I think he wants to touch the roy^{ies}.

Anyway he complains of want of money.

Perhaps it would be just as well to settle with him?

He asks me to keep his letters private – but in this matter I must refer to you.

Yours

J. C.

To J. B. Pinker

Text MS Berg; Unpublished

[Oswalds]

[15 or 16? August 1921][2]

Dearest J. B.

Herewith another instalment of corrected text.

As you may see these were no fools of corrections to make. I can't possibly finish to-day; but by to-morrow (evening post) the balance will be ready. So the copy may be completed on Thursday for Friday's packet – if there is one on Friday.

A page (54) in the returned batch is missing. It went out from here all right as I checked the pages myself before sending them off. No doubt it will turn up either in your office or at the typewriting establishment. My great concern is lest those people should have missed copying it for the Cosmo^{an}.

Many thanks for your masterly treatment of the Times incident. I am much comforted by the noble solution.

In haste

Ever Yours

J. Conrad

---

[1] Dated by the letter to Ford.

[2] The Sunday letter's promise of more copy on 'monday' and the resolution of 'the *Times* incident' suggest its placement. If Conrad wanted the clean typescript 'completed on Thursday', Tuesday the 16th would be the latest possible date.

To G. Jean-Aubry
Text MS Yale; Unpublished

[Oswalds]
[17 August 1921]¹

Très cher.

Mais certainement! Nous Vous attendrons donc Mardi par le train qui arrive Can^ry East 6.18

Votre devoué,

J. C.

Translation

My very dear friend.

Of course! We shall wait for you then on Tuesday by the train arriving at Canterbury East at 6.18.

Yours devotedly,

J. C.

To F. N. Doubleday
Text MS Princeton; Unpublished

[letterhead: Oswalds]
21.8.'21

Dear Mr Doubleday.

I congratulate you heartily on being able (in the judgement of all competent men) to look back at 25 years of work in your selected calling with the consciousness of having done much good in your generation. I join to this my earnest wish that your work m[a]y long continue adding to the prestige and honour of the House you have founded the lustre of further successes and of augmented influence.

I am touched by your associating my name with your personal feelings about your own achievement. Nothing would please me more than to have the novel published in 1922. And I really do not see why it should not come to pass according to your friendly wish. The novel though not very much advanced yet, has already a body and is progressing steadily and may be ready for the spring season.

Believe me dear Mr Doubleday always yours with most friendly regard

Joseph Conrad.

¹ Date in Jean-Aubry's hand.

To [?]
Text MS Lubbock; Unpublished

[letterhead: Oswalds]
21.8.'21

My very dear Sir.[1]

I read your letter with the warmest appreciation – as you may believe. You must forgive me not answering you before. Now with this paper before me I can't find anything to say but a word of thanks. It is really very difficult to convey ones mingled sensations of pride and humility to a man who tells one that his literary life has been influenced by one's work.

On reading further I came on the word *affection* for which it is easier to be simply grateful, without misgivings. And as I reached the part in which you speak of the "steadying and inspiring influence" I thought to myself that a letter like this was a fine reward for any worker to win as he nears the end of his appointed course.

Most of all I must thank you for the kind thought of writing to me in this spirit of kindness, acceptance and spiritual comradeship.

Pray accept a most cordial shake of the hand from your profoundly grateful

Joseph Conrad.

To Aniela Zagórska
Text MS copy Yale; Najder 270–1

Oswalds,
21.8.21.

My dear Angela,

I write in English because it is easier for me today. I ought to have told you long ago how deeply touched I was by your gifts to Jessie and myself on the occasion of our silver wedding.[2] My dear, I think you ought not have deprived yourself of these mementos of the past. But you may be sure that at least with us they shall be cherished not only as coming from you two but also for the sake of your loved dead, to whom we too lay the claim of memory and affection.

I am truly glad at your news of the contract with a good publishing house; and still more glad that you, personally, are taking the translation in hand. I of course consent in advance to *all* changes and modifications you may find necessary to make in the course of your work. *Almayer's Daughter* may be a very good title especially in point of view of the public.

---

[1] An unidentified author.   [2] Celebrated on 24 March.

A few days ago we had a letter from Karola. The treatment seems to have done her good. I am fairly well. Jessie is still in pain but improving slowly. We all here send you our dear love.

Ever your faithful

Conrad.

I am sending you Notes on Life & Letters by tomorrow's post. Many thanks for the books & newspapers. I shall remind Jessie about the photos. Je vous embrasse.

To J. B. Pinker

Text MS Berg; Unpublished

[Oswalds]

Monday. [22? August 1921][1]

Dearest J. B.

Thanks for returned draft and 1st copy of the Novel.[2]

The 1st copy would have to be corrected for press because of the mistakes of typing very few in truth but some of them making nonsense.

As a matter of fact the batch You sent me has been already corrected by Miss H[allowes]. So when the Am: set is returned mine will be ready to send to them by "return of post".

Directly we get 50–60 pp more I will revise them and copy may be sent out to US. so that they have a big batch when they begin printing in Nov – that is if they still want to do so.

I have heard nothing as yet from The Times. Should they send ch^{que} to you please pay £90 to my acct. If I get it I will send you £10 – which either way, will make us all square on the transaction.

Everitt[3] announces his visit for an hour or so for Thursday next. So be it!

All is comparatively well here. My gout's over – up to a point. Hope you all are well. B[orys] seems "placed" this time. R[alph] seems happier since your visit.

Ever Yours

J. C.

Thanks for copy of trans^{d} play. I understand you have another. *Is that so?*

---

[1] Just before the 24th, when Conrad was able to send Pinker the cheque from *The Times*.

[2] I.e., a supposedly clean copy of *Suspense*, Part One.

[3] Of Doubleday's, then in England on business.

To J. B. Pinker
Text MS Berg; Unpublished

[Oswalds]
Tuesday. [23 August 1921][1]

Dear J B.

I am glad you thought the sample effective. I hoped it might be.

I can't think of the title and may not be able to hit on one till Nov^er^. They *must not* begin before. It would be most unsafe. Will you impress that on them definitely. We don't want any fiasco. It must be understood that Nov^er^ would be the earliest date and that even in that case notice will be given a month beforehand. Use all your authority to prevent them playing us a trick. I mistrust these people.

———————

Certainly. We'll let Morley have the extracts from *Pers^al^ Rec^d^* for his school book.[2]

———————

This moment enclosed wire from Winawer delivered.
Trans[lati]on at back

Ever Yours

J. C.

To J. B. Pinker
Text MS Berg; Unpublished

[Oswalds]
Wednesday
24.8.21

Dear J B.

Herewith Times cheque. As You warned me not to sign away the copyright I send you the blamed thing which on endorsement makes me do that.

I don't know whether it would be correct to run the pen through the line, simply. But You will know what to do and either will return me the cheque for endors[e]ment or get them to send me another.

---

[1] The reference to the 'sample' of *Suspense* suggests the Tuesday in question.
[2] Christopher Darlington Morley (1890–1957), a prolific and influential American man of letters and a great admirer of Conrad, wrote essays, poetry, and novels. He reprinted all but the last four paragraphs of 'A Familiar Preface' to *A Personal Record* in his anthology *Modern Essays* (1921), an abridgement of which was issued as *Modern Essays for Schools* in 1922.

Do you dear JB think this short thing of sufficient importance to stick out for its copyright? Or is it a matter of general principle.

Ever Yours

J. C.

To J. B. Pinker
Text MS Berg; Unpublished

[Oswalds]
[late August 1921][1]

Dearest J B.

I return the play[2] which is a very very poor sort of thing.

The first Act (2 sc) embodies (literally almost) the first third of the book – no great trick as the scenes with Haldin and the General had only to be transcribed in the form of stage copy. The other two thirds of the novel are supposed to be contained in the 2^d Act – which I can't even call bad. It is just nothing at all. No intelligence no characterisation no interest either in the situation or in the persons.

I tell you all this so that you should know that I did really consider the work. But to the man You may say truthfully that C. does not want this novel to be dramatised by anyone, as he has the intention of doing it himself at some time or other.

I am looking forward to your visit next week. We had some people here in a sort of procession which if it did not help me with my work did not actually stop all progress.

E. G[arnett] saw the novel & made critical remarks on matters of detail but declared himself delighted with the whole.

We expect to see you here next Friday. Au revoir then.

Ever Yours

J. C.

To Frederick O'Brien
Text MS Stanford; Unpublished

[letterhead: Oswalds]
30 Augst '21

Dear Sir[3]

Let me thank you warmly for the two magnificent and interesting vols about the South-Sea Isles which you have been good enough to send me.

---

[1] The letter to Garnett of 2 September, written after his visit to Oswalds, suggests placement.

[2] A dramatisation of *Under Western Eyes*; see the letter of 6 September to David Bone.

[3] The American journalist and travel writer Frederick O'Brien (1869–1932) covered the Russo-Japanese War for the *New York Herald*. His later adventures in the Pacific led to the books acknowledged here: *White Shadows in the South Seas* (1919), a bestseller about the Marquesas, and *Mystic Isles of the South Seas* (1921) about Tahiti, where he met Gauguin.

One envies you your opportunities and the artistic use you have made of them. Believe me

Yours gratefully

Joseph Conrad.

F. O'Brien, Esqre

To Richard Curle

Text MS Indiana; Curle 77

[Oswalds]
31 Aug^st 21

Dear Dick.

The week-end after this next one will not do. But any day after Tuesday the 13th you will be welcome for a night's stay – or if not then the week-end of 17th (Sept.).

Pray drop us a line.

I am trying desperately to get on with the novel and feel rather worried about it.

I am glad of your good news. Jessie joins me in love to you

Yours

J Conrad

To Edward Garnett

Text MS Colgate; G. 308–9

[Oswalds]
2. Sepr. 21

Dearest Edward.

Many thanks for the MS and your good and enlightening letter.[1] All your remarks carry absolute conviction and will have to be carried out as occasion offers. The first page of Chapter 1st must be rewritten obviously before the serial begins. Thanks for pointing out the two anachronisms of speech.[2] Those are the most difficult to guard against but the easiest to correct, luckily.

It was good to take contact with Your mind and your unerring judgement. It was a great tonic to a solitary man. I am going on with the thing more confidently, now that you have seen it and found it has some quality.

---

[1] Of 31 August about *Suspense* (Stape and Knowles, p. 183).
[2] On the typescript (Berg), Garnett objected to 'great vital force', which Conrad changed to 'moving force', and to 'It's awful', which he altered to 'I am awed' (*Suspense*, pp. 38, 54).

I have just read through the Zeromski novel you mean: *History of a Sin*.[1] Honestly I don't think it will do for translation. The international murdereress* episodes take but a little space after all. The whole thing is disagreeable and often incomprehensible in comment and psychology. Often it is gratuitously ferocious. You know I am not squeamish.

The other work the great historical machine is called *Ashes* (Popioły).[2] Both of course have a certain greatness – the greatness of a wild landscape – and both take too much for granted in the way of receptivity and tolerance.

Our dear love to You.

Ever Yours

J Conrad.

To J. B. Pinker
Text MS Berg; Unpublished

[Oswalds]
Monday.
5.9.21

Dearest J B.

I have had nothing from the Times yet. Perhaps they have made the cheque to you?[3]

Should you get it please advise me as I would like to settle some accts which this money has got to pay.

Ever Yours

J. Conrad

To Captain David Bone
Text MS Sprott; Knowles

[letterhead: Oswalds]
6.9.21

My dear Captain Bone

Many thanks for the charming copy of the *Brassbounder*.[4] It is as fresh and attractive as ever to read and I am still under the charm of this sincere and fascinating record of things that have now passed away for ever.

---

[1] Stefan Żeromski (1864–1925), Polish novelist and short-story writer whom Conrad had met in Zakopane in 1914. The novel mentioned, *Dzieje grzechu*, had appeared in 1908; its sexual frankness caused a scandal.

[2] Published in 1904, this novel tells the story of the Poles who fought across Europe in the Napoleonic armies and their disillusioned return home.

[3] Part of the prolonged saga about payment for 'The Dover Patrol'. Conrad had received a cheque in late August and sent it to Pinker, but evidently another had to be drawn.

[4] The recent issue by Dutton of New York. Conrad had declined to write a preface for it in January. A brass-bounder was a midshipman or, in merchant ships, a privileged apprentice distinguished by his braid and buttons.

The stage version of the *Western Eyes* has reached me through Pinker. I am very sorry that Mʳ K.[1] should have taken this trouble. Of all my novels this, especially, is the one I do not want anybody to touch. If there is ever any adaptation it will be done by myself.

I have read with interest your preface to this new edition and I have liked it very much in every way – as a seaman and as a writer, and as a man who shares your feelings and ideas and has for you a great personal regard.[2]

Believe me always very sincerely yours

Joseph Conrad.

To J. B. Pinker
Text MS Berg; Unpublished

[Oswalds]
6.9.21

Dearest J B.

Herewith cheque from which You'll see that The Times has paid-up.

– I've had a very enthusiastic letter from Winawer about the translation. He tells me he has already written to you accepting the terms as presented to his consideration (50% author, 40% translator and 10% commission) but with the variant as follows: 45% for W. 45% for C. 10% for J. B.

When you answer him You may let him have his way. You and I'll have another arrangement, for if you manage to plant *that* thing on a manager You will have earned more than 10%. It's your character and the position you have made for yourself that will do it. We'll talk when we meet.

Yours

J. C.

To Tadeusz Marynowski
Text MS Zagayski; Janta (1957) with facsimile; Najder 271–2[3]

[letterhead: Oswalds]
8. September. 1921.

Dear Sir.[4]

Thank you very much for your letter informing me of the illness of my cousin Miss Karola Zagórska.

---

[1] S. Karrakis, a Russo-American. He also received Conrad's refusal in person at Oswalds; see his 'Joseph Conrad at Home in England', *Poland*, April 1924, 225–8, 247–8.

[2] Bone's preface, written on a North Atlantic crossing, dwells on a favourite Conradian topic: the contrast between the mechanical efficiency of the modern ocean liner and the skill, daring, and endurance demanded by the old sailing ships such as the barque whose voyage around Cape Horn figures in his mainly autobiographical novel.

[3] Translation from Najder with minor alterations.

[4] A career civil servant, Tadeusz Marynowski (1892–1949) served as Polish consul in Milan from 1919 to 1923. He later held consular posts in Buffalo and Prague and was Consul-General in New York from 1947 to 1949, returning to Warsaw shortly before his death.

My health does not allow me to make the journey to Mil[an], and it would also interrupt my work, which is my sole source of income.

I trust that you will wish to exercise your care in a larger than a purely official way when trying to organise a tolerable life for the invalid. It is, therefore, only a question of finances.

The situation is as follows: last year before she left us, I assured her of an allowance of £120 (pounds sterling) annually for three years – that is £10 per month, payable quarterly. I know that this is not a lot, but she assured me she could manage. The current quarter's allowance was paid to her at the beginning of July (£30). The next quarter's is due in October.

At the moment this is what can be done: in the course of next week (probably on Monday) I will send her £20†[1] with a letter in which I will explain that because of my concern about her health I am sending her an additional £20 to enable her to make herself more comfortable, etc. and that I intend to raise her allowance from £30 to £50 per quarter until her health definitely improves. In this way your intervention in this matter will remain undisclosed, and I trust you will be kind enough to inform me if £200 a year is adequate to ensure a more or less tolerable life for Miss Zagórska in her present state of health. We shall see what happens later.

In any case, I take the liberty of asking you, in case of need, to advance Miss Zagórska any sum necessary, informing me by wire or letter so that I could repay you immediately. Once again thank you for your letter, and I remain with great respect

Your devoted servant
Joseph Conrad.

† for the current quarter July-September.

To Richard Curle

Text MS Indiana; Curle 78

[letterhead: Oswalds]
12.9.'21.

My dear Curle.

In fixing Your visit for this next week-end I had forgotten that my very old friend Hope's[2] visit was booked for that date.

That being so would You prefer to come down here for a couple of nights in the course of this week?

If so please let us know by a p-c as soon as possible.

[1] Conrad then wrote '(c/o)' but crossed it out.   [2] G. F. W. Hope.

Otherwise we can put you up for the week-end but it would be in the Nursery wing.

Yours affect^{ly}

J. Conrad.

To J. B. Pinker

Text MS Berg; Unpublished

[Oswalds]
Monday. [12 September 1921]¹

Dearest J. B.

Herewith John's acct. He goes to Tonbridge on Friday next.

Goulden² in Cant^{ry} will give an estimate and submit samples of paper and type when he has seen to copy to be set up.³ If you send me the play I'll show it to him and explain what we want done. I'll then direct him to send you estimate and samples for your decision.

Would you please ask Methuen by phone to send me a copy of *Europe and Beyond* by J. A. R. Marriott.⁴ 6/-. It will save me writing to them.

Ever Yours

J. C.

To Arthur Symons

Text MS Virginia; Hunter (1985, 3)

[letterhead: Oswalds]
12 [13?].9.'21⁵

My dear Symons.

I am awfully sorry but I have an abominable cough which will prevent me from taking a motor run as far as Wittersham⁶ for some time to come. I havent been from home for more than a month. I have been told to be careful – and I suppose I must; for any longer interruption of my work would be a very serious matter to me.

---

¹ John returned to Tonbridge on the 16th; see the letter to Goodburn of that date.

² H. G. R. Goulden ('Gontran', 1884–1970), who since 1908 had been in partnership with his father, H. J. Goulden, a Canterbury bookseller and stationer.

³ I.e., when he has worked through the typescript, assessing length, costs, and difficulties. The work in question is the dramatisation of *The Secret Agent*. Between them, Conrad and Pinker solicited at least two other bids, one in London, one in Kent: see the letter of the 30th.

⁴ *Europe and Beyond, A Preliminary Survey of World-Politics in the Last Half-Century, 1870–1920.*

⁵ The envelope was postmarked on the 13th at 10 p.m.   ⁶ Roughly thirty miles away.

I am concerned to hear of your difficulties with Brentano and Doubleday.[1] But there are other publishers in America and in Europe. Of course the conduct of these firms seems to me unjustifiable but I don't see what could be done if you have no written agreements with them. Jessie joins me in my friendly regards to You both.

Yours

J. Conrad.

To Harold Goodburn

Text MS Hawkins; Unpublished

[letterhead: Oswalds]
16.9.'21.

Dear Mr Goodburn.

Will you kindly let me know the amount of John's tuition fee. If I did not stop the car yesterday morning on meeting you it was only because I was in a hurry to get home where I had somebody waiting for me on a rather urgent matter. John begs me to give you his love. He leaves for school this afternoon.

Believe me

very sincerely Yours

Joseph Conrad.

To J. B. Pinker

Text MS Berg; Unpublished

[Oswalds]
Tuesday. [20 or 27 September 1921][2]

Dear J. B.

Thanks for your letter on the various subjects.

I don't think it would be appropriate for Jessie to write to Mac[kintosh] on that matter. The whole affair is a matter of right and a woman's letter unless written in a very firm tone would sound like an appeal "ad misericordiam"[3] for which there is no occasion, strictly speaking. Besides he's quite capable of answering her by a mere letter of recriminations of which she has seen enough as it is.

---

[1] Doubleday had rejected *Notes and Impressions*, a compilation of previously published work, sent at Conrad's suggestion, and Brentano's declined *Wanderings* after considering it for two years; the latter stayed unpublished till 1931.

[2] This letter could fit on either side of the 24th, when Conrad nudged Pinker to choose a printer for *The Secret Agent* and wrote at length about Borys's financial plight, caused in part by the collapse of Mackintosh's firm. By the 30th, Pinker had agreed to write to Mackintosh himself.

[3] 'To pity'.

I quite understand that You may be unwilling to press him, since owing to my own desire of not tying him up strictly You are not in a position to do so in definite terms. I could write of course and am ready to do so after further advice from You.

I am going on steadily with the novel – and it is quite possible that there may be 300 typed pages ready by end Oct*er*. But on the other hand the book will be long. It will be!

Ever Yours

J. C.

I'll be glad to hear who is to print the Play as soon as it's fixed.

To Bruno Winawer
Text TS copy Yale; *Głos* (108); Najder 272–3[1]

Oswalds,
Bishopsbourne,
Kent.
20.9.21.

Dear Sir.

I am pleased to learn that you liked my translation. My error in connexion with Okólnik[2] is amusing; but you know what – we could leave it like that. During the war, and even after, the English public heard a lot about various government 'Circulars A/W 5087A' so it will be accepted at face value as something relating to a gentleman with two names and of doubtful nationality.

Qu'en pensez-Vous?[3]

Pinker was here at the end of last week. He has two copies of Job – one for England and the other for the United States, and you can rest assured that everything possible will be done to put the play on stage. But it is a doubtful matter. Generally speaking, circumstances are not favourable. My dramatised version of the novel "The Secret Agent" has been wandering around the world for the last fifteen months. Recently Norman McKinnel paid £50 for the privilege of keeping it for consideration for a further six months. But I feel that nothing will come of it.

That is the situation. One can't count on success.

Bien à Vous

J. Conrad.

---

[1] Translation from Najder with minor alterations.
[2] The name of a Warsaw street in which one of the characters lives and, in Polish, a circular.
[3] 'What do you think about it?'

To J. B. Pinker

Text MS Indiana; Unpublished

[Oswalds]
24.9.'21.

Dearest J. B.

I half-hoped to hear from you about the printing of the play, as Gouldens told me on Monday they would send you the estimate early this week with two specimen pages. I havent been near their place since. The specimen they showed me, (Act I) one page of text, seemed to me very adequate for what we want to do with it.

I have had a talk with B[orys] as to his position in the situation he holds now. He has been now three months (or nearly) there and apart from the general feeling that he is getting on well with everybody, he has been told in so many words that his work is satisfactory; so that his staying on after the show[1] is no longer in doubt with a rise of salary, since he has been till now admittedly on trial at a provisional rate of pay – as I have been given clearly to understand by the two partners early in July, in the course of the interview I had with them at that time.

As I told you before he should like to have his quarter's allowance (due on the 25 inst I think) paid to him monthly. Say £12 p month. [H]e has the same amount from the Autoveyors. It works out £6 per week and he stated to me his expenses as: for his room in Half-moon St. with bath, electric light, gas ring, breakfast and light supper £4.10. on an average. Obviously he could go into cheaper lodgings say 3.10 with dinner. But from the nature of his work he is often late and the landladies make no reduction generally and the idea of a boarding house is distasteful to him. To get something under £3 he would have to go to the suburbs. Anyhow I don't think that the sum is extravagant as things are now – and considering the conveniences. But it leaves him only £1.10. for his lunches and cigarettes. He has of course incurred no further indebt[ed]ness but he feels uncomfortable and straitened never having even one pound in reserve. It is awkward too as for instance when he is told suddenly to go away in a car, when he must first go to the cashier and get his journey money if it is only a few shillings – and on such like occasions. I quite see the point of his not liking to appear hard up to that extent. I propose therefore to restore to him for the next two quarters (to Mch 1922) the fifty pounds p.y. which were deducted when he left the Surrey C⁰ and found this new berth for himself.

---

[1] The annual Motor Show, held in early November.

Will you please then pay him the next quarter at the old rate (200 p.y.) that is £16.13 p. month instead of the twelve – since he asks to be paid by the month.

The premises of the Surrey C° are to let I hear. I do hope we will get the 300 back but it must be a long time. B's debts as stated by him in July amount to £283.10. Could you arrange to pay the pressing ones (say roughly £150). The rest he says can wait and he hopes, quite soberly, to be in a position to help to pay them in the course of next year. Please let me have your answer on this point as the boy is being dunned and is a bit worried.

All here send their love.

Ever Yours

J Conrad.

To Edward Garnett
Text MS Sutton;[1] G. 309–10

[Oswalds]
Monday. [26 September 1921][2]

Dearest Edward.

I have warned our friend Pinker that you will be writing to him in the matter of the publication in vol form of certain selected critical articles of yours;[3] of which some would belong to the collection about to be pub^shed in the US and other specially reserved by you for the English edition. I hope I have not misrepresented your intention.

J. B. Pinker declares himself ready and anxious to make the best possible arrangement for this. I don't suppose you have changed your mind, but in any case please let Pink know what you want done – or not done.

Love from us all here.

Ever yours

J Conrad

To Hugh Dent
Text MS Berg; Unpublished

[letterhead: Oswalds]
29.9.'21

My dear Mr Hugh

Many thanks for the Hudson book.[4] I have no doubt that it is delightful but I cannot look into it for a day or two yet.

---

[1] Formerly in the Sutton collection, the text was not available for rechecking.
[2] Garnett supplies the date.
[3] *Friday Nights*, published on both sides of the Atlantic in 1922.
[4] An advance copy of W. H. Hudson's *A Traveller in Little Things*, published by Dent in October.

The serialising of the next book (I haven't a title yet!) will begin this year I think. I am not *unhappy* about it but I confess to feeling worried about its slow progress. In composition of that kind "making up for lost time" is a dangerous business.

My wife joins me in kindest regards to The Chief, to your wife and to yourself.

Yours sincerely

J. Conrad.

I'll call the very next time I am in town – prob[ab]ly next month.

To J. B. Pinker

Text TS/MS Berg; Unpublished

Oswalds,
Bishopsbourne,
Kent.
Sept, 30th. 1921.

My dear J. B.

I have been more or less tormented by gout since the beginning of the week, and to-day I am properly laid up; but I hope it will be no more than for twenty-four hours.

Thank you, my dear J. B. for your hospitable reminders as to Bury's Court. I don't know whether I can let Jessie go to London before the 15th of next month, as those expeditions have got to be financed by me. When she moves on the Capital I also will have to leave here as she wants to give leave to the whole lower deck for three days. It was then that I propose to quarter myself on you and your wife's kindness in your Palazzo near Reigate for at least three days, if I may be permitted. You will understand why I would dispense with that interruption when I tell you that to complete the 300 pages which I want to have ready by the end of October (300 in all) I have yet about 90 to write; that is about three a day of new stuff, not counting the time necessary for revision and correcting of the text, which would require close sitting for a considerable part of each day. Still the interruption needn't be fatal and the temptation of a visit to you is very great. So far the gout has not stopped work, though it may have slowed it down a little.

I have had a touching letter from Karola, full of gratitude, both for me and Jessie for our forethought and assistance. There is no doubt that she did need it. Things don't seem to be well with her, though she doesn't seem aware of her real condition and writes very optimistically as to the future. Apparently she had some heart symptoms, which she mentions slightingly;

but it is a pretty serious thing in a person suffering from kidney trouble. The Consul also wrote just to tell me that the augmentation is sufficient to make her situation tolerable and promising to extend his friendly care to her in case of any sudden developments.

The departure between the two printing estimates is surprisingly wide.[1] I hope Goulden had made a mistake (as you suggested to him) in the figures, because I like his specimen-work – but I doubt it. Does the estimate of the London people include the proper binding of the pages?

I note that you have decided to write to Mac yourself. My offer to do so was made in perfect good faith, but since you take it upon yourself I will confess that I like it much better. Of course I would not have written without sending you a draft first. I feel that I have been guilty of optimism in my view of the transaction. I am naturally inclined to make the best of people without mental reservations. It is not exactly a weakness for my mind sees as a rule all the unpleasant possibilities. But I put them aside nevertheless from a sort of secret loyalty.

Our love to you and all at Burys Court where I am sending this.

I won't send you any new pages till about 13th–14th next. I am now at 209th.

Ever Yours

J Conrad

To J. B. Pinker
Text MS Berg;[2] Unpublished

[Oswalds]
Tuesday. [4 October 1921][3]

Dearest J B.

I found this on getting home and wonder if Vance[4] has not already turned up and, in fact, is *the* man. There is no reason to discourage the writer of this letter so I'll send her a few notes.

Shall write you this even^g.

Ever Yrs

J. C.

---

[1] *The Kentish Observer* quoted £12 for fifty copies, a figure that did not include paper, folding, or binding; Gouldens' figure was £37.5.0 (Goulden papers).
[2] On the verso of a letter from Mary Austin to Conrad, dated 21 September, New York. The postscript is on the accompanying envelope.
[3] The same day as the next letter, which tells Pinker what has happened to the '155 pp.'.
[4] Arthur Turner Vance (1872–1930), American journalist and editor. His *Pictorial Review*, a women's magazine, had a circulation of 2,500,000; the serial of *The Rover* began there in September 1923.

Am catching train with the 155 pp. that are ready.

Ever Yrs

JC.

Letter from Mrs Austin[1] inside this

To J. B. Pinker
Text TS Berg; Unpublished

Oswalds,
Bishopsbourne,
Kent.
Oct. 4th. 1921.

Dearest J. B.

I thought I was doing well by sending the MS by rail. Vinten took it to Canterbury East this morning, but as I did not know that the railway did not undertake special delivery I could not very well warn him to hold back the MS in that case. He sent it off of course, but had the sense to telephone to B[orys] to let you know it had been dispatched. I daresay you have sent a messenger boy to fetch it from Victoria, but I am sorry I gave you the trouble. My intention was good.

You will have seen by this Mrs Austin's letter. When it comes to publicity anybody's voluntary help may be accepted and in the case of Mrs A. she is much less noxious than she looks and talks; and that air of a very superior scarecrow she has doesn't come through the print. Moreover if she has no public Vance's Women's Pictorial certainly has; and anyway we can't stop her any more than we could stop that other awful thing – an earthquake![2]

My scheme doesn't seem to work in practice and therefore I may have to call upon your kindness next week, but I have by no means given up the hope of being able to contribute at least in part to the amount before anything comes in from Mac. B[orys] admits that he had spoken to you of "deduction"

---

[1] Mary Austin (née Hunter, 1868–1934), American nature writer, literary journalist, and feminist. Her article on Conrad, 'A Sermon in One Man', had appeared in *Harper's Weekly*, 16 May 1914, p. 20.

[2] Austin's letter, written from New York, bristles with ideas for placing and publicising Conrad's work in the USA. She herself had already sold a proposal for 'an essay on the three Major English Prophets, Hardy, Conrad and Shaw.' To intrigue the reading public, who 'are so anxious to do what they ought that they are grateful for being told', she would need 'personal material. Why should you mind? What I propose is that you turn this over to Mrs Conrad and your able secretary and let them put together everything they can think of about you and your work, the way you do it and all that has happened to you on account of it. Then if it bothers you to read these things in print – I know it does, because I am often bother[e]d that way myself – why, just don't read them' (21 September, Stape and Knowles, pp. 184–5).

(if that is the word he used) but his meaning was that it should be taken from what Mac. returns, not from his monthly allowance, since he was already feeling the pinch of which he spoke to me the same weekend. His address is, 8 Half Moon Street, W. 1, or C/o Autoveyors, 84 Victoria St. S.W.1.

A man called Adams[1] bought from some bookseller the Preface I wrote for Jessie's Cookery-book.[2] I think I ought to have had them before they came on the market, as in my ignorance I had told the man that there was nothing he could obtain except the well known set of booklets. Naturally he wrote to me saying that obviously I didn't know what was being done and that he was very glad to give me the first news. Will you please instruct the office to send six copies here.

As to the projected printing of the Play, please reserve me ten copies out of the 50, as I will want two for Poland and two for France and four for England (presentation) including Walpole and Garnett. The other two I will keep myself. I wish I could exclude all sounds and sights from my life and devote myself for the next 25 days to that novel which has not even a name. The sun, the wind, the little birds, the electric pump, everything seems to get in the way. It's like trying to fight off a cloud of gnats. One does it though, but it's damn fatiguing.

Ever Yours.

Joseph Conrad.

To Thomas J. Wise
Text TS/MS BL Ashley A. 469; Unpublished

[letterhead: Oswalds]
Oct. 4th. 1921.

Dear Mʳ Wise

A parcel containing the five Privately Printed Vols. of "Life and Letters"[3] will be dispatched to you by the same mail as this letter.

---

[1] E(lbridge) L(apham) Adams? An American bookman and lawyer, Adams (1866–1934) had become acquainted with Conrad in 1916.

[2] The Preface appeared by itself as a four-page pamphlet in 1921 under the title *Simple Cooking Precepts for a Little House*. The edition was of 100 copies. Conrad wrote this piece in 1907 in the hope that Alston Rivers might publish Jessie Conrad's collection of 130 recipes (*Letters*, 3, p. 410). By the time it went to Doubleday in 1921, the total had reached 190; see the letter to Pinker of 14 November.

[3] Copies of the special run of *Notes on Life and Letters*, about which Conrad had bitterly complained in May.

That parcel contains also the paper-covered copy of "Some Reminiscences" which you said you would like to have.[1] I have inscribed it and have also made a few notes on the subject of its changed title.[2]

The two editions as far as I have received them, that is 25 vols, in all, will be dispatched to you by rail either to-morrow or the next day.

Thank you very much for the very friendly part you have undertaken to play in this matter of business which I could not have very well managed by myself.[3]

I promise myself the pleasure before very long of another call on you and another view of your treasures. It is very likely we shall be in town for three days very early in November.

Sincerely yours

Joseph Conrad

To the Hon. Bertrand Russell

Text MS McMaster; Wright

[letterhead: Oswalds]
5.10.'21

My dear Russell.[4]

We are delighted at the news[5] in your letter and beg you both to accept the assurance of our warmest sympathy and of all possible good wishes.

Your letter arrived only this morning. We are rather further from you than you thought.[6] This place is about 3 miles from Canterbury where I would meet any train if you intend to come by rail. I suggest next week as Cockerell is coming to-morrow for the night and H Walpole has announced his visit for Saturday – and I would prefer to have you to myself on this occasion.

---

[1] The American 1908 copyright issue of the first section (in perhaps as few as six copies), got up by Paul R. Reynolds of New York at Pinker's request.

[2] The first American trade edition appeared as *A Personal Record*. Later English editions used this rather than the serial title 'Some Reminiscences'.

[3] Selling the privately printed copies of *Notes on Life and Letters*.

[4] The Hon. Bertrand Arthur William Russell (1872–1970; 3rd Earl Russell, 1931) met Conrad through Lady Ottoline Morrell in 1913. A lecturer at Trinity College, Cambridge, he had written *Principles of Mathematics* (1903) and the three volumes of *Principia Mathematica* (with Alfred North Whitehead, 1910–13). He felt an intense admiration for Conrad and his work and named his son after him. His pacifism during the war resulted in the loss of his fellowship and a prison sentence; his willingness to take unpopular stands on moral and political questions persisted for the rest of his life. His later books included *The Analysis of Mind* (1921), *The ABC of Relativity* (1925), *Marriage and Morals* (1929), *A History of Western Philosophy* (1945), and his *Autobiography* (1967–9).

[5] Of the forthcoming birth of a child.

[6] The Russells were in Winchelsea, Sussex, from August to October.

I don't know where, from what, you gathered that you could ever be unwelcome under our roof. Our last conversation was in the Strand and surely then I did not give you that impression. My conscience is so clear about it that I can't even begin to get angry with you for your misapprehension.[1]

If you don't elect to come this week then any day after next Monday you will find us at home. You can catch in Ashford a train that gets to Can^y at 12.17. Pray drop us a line. Our united warm regards to you both.

Yours

Joseph Conrad

To Max J. Herzberg
Text MS Virginia; Herzberg (in part)

[letterhead: Oswalds]
Oct. 10th. 1921.

Dear Mr Herzberg.[2]

I really don't know the names of literary men that Crane had met in England besides Hueffer, to whom you have written, and Harold Frederic who died many years ago.[3]

As to the erection of the Memorial Tablet to the memory of my old and unforgotten friend I associate myself with all my heart and with all the strength of my old affection with the tribute of the citizens of Newark to the genius of their fellow townsman who did not live long enough to reap the reward of his honest toil in the field of letters. After twenty years of fidelity to his memory both my wife and myself feel immensely grateful to the originators of the Memorial and to all the inhabitants of Newark who have contributed to that most worthy object.

Believe me, dear Sir with friendly regards

Yours very faithfully

Joseph Conrad.

Max J. Herzberg, Esqre

[1] Perhaps Russell suspected that his pacifism would estrange him from Conrad.
[2] Max John Herzberg (1886–1958), an American secondary school teacher and anthologist, championed Crane's work as president of the Stephen Crane Association.
[3] An American novelist and journalist, Frederic (1856–98) served a stint as London correspondent for the *New York Times*. He is best known for his novel *The Damnation of Theron Ware* (1896). Conrad and he were acquainted, and Frederic reviewed *The Nigger of the 'Narcissus'*. Among others who had known Crane were Henry James, who had died in 1916, Ford, and H. G. Wells, who was very much alive but no longer on close terms with Conrad. Conrad felt Crane's death in 1900 deeply, and his essays on him contributed to the revival of his literary reputation, first in Britain, then in the USA.

To A. S. Kinkead

Text TS Texas; Unpublished

[letterhead: Oswalds]
Oct. 10th. 1921.

Dear Miss Kinkead.

I am sorry for the delay in answering your good letter. A beastly fit of gout is responsible for it, and also accounts for this reply being type-written.

You mustn't be offended with me if I do not answer categorically the series of questions Miss Somerville[1] has put to me through you; as if Macdonald Hastings were a servant requiring a character for employment. I lunched with him once at the Garrick Club with the late H. B. Irving,[2] at whose instigation the adaptation of "Victory" for the stage was made by him. He also once came to my house in the country; but I did not discuss the matter of adaptation with him at all, still less did I collaborate with him; neither did I discuss the business side of the arrangement. That was done and a careful agreement drawn up by J. B. Pinker. H. B. Irving not being ready to take up the adaptation when it was done it was eventually produced by Marie Lohr[3] in the spring of 1919, under an agreement drawn also by Mr Pinker acting both for Macdonald and myself. The play was extensively noticed and criticised by the whole press, metropolitan and provincial. I did not either touch Macdonald Hastings' text or attend rehearsals or see the play on the stage. I had absolutely nothing to do with the adaptation.[4] The reasons why I consented to it are neither here nor there. It ran for about eleven weeks to full houses and was then withdrawn and went on a tour of the provinces; all this strictly under the terms of the agreement between J. B. Pinker[X] and Marie Lohr.

[X] acting for JC & M. H.

---

[1] The Irish writer Edith Oenone Somerville (1858–1949) was a friend of Miss Kinkead's. She and her cousin Violet Florence Martin (1862–1915) published novels such as *The Real Charlotte* (1894) and stories such as the three *Irish R[esident] M[agistrate]* collections under the names E. O. Somerville and Martin Ross. Somerville was a spiritualist who felt that the collaboration endured even after Ross's death.

[2] Henry Brodribb Irving (1870–1919), like his famous father, Sir Henry, was an actor-manager. He considered staging Hastings's adaptation of *Victory*.

[3] Australian-born Marie Löhr (1890–1975), a manager and leading lady of the London stage, débuted in 1901 and gave her last performances in 1966. She also enjoyed an extensive career in film.

[4] In fact, he made numerous and detailed suggestions about the staging and dialogue (see *Letters*, 5, pp. 635–6, 642–4, 652–7, 658–9, and the prompt copy, Gene M. Moore and Allan H. Simmons, eds., *Documents*, pp. 87–176).

All these are matters of common knowledge since the notices of provincial performances have appeared as late as the early part of this year. Not a step in all this affair was taken without consultation with J. B. Pinker, who is also the agent of Miss Somerville and I think that she could do no better than consult him in the matter. She knows, I suppose, as well as I do that his agency is no mere manuscript-posting but a position of confidence and trust, which can be depended upon. He knows much more about M. Hastings than I do and is much better able to say whether the proposed connection will be of advantage from various points of view, to Miss S.

In an affair like this there is much more than meets the eye. It is by no means so simple as it looks, but in any case Macdonald Hastings is not an obscure person. He is the author of several plays which have all been performed and which are all published as far as I know. Perhaps Miss S. had better have a look at them. When the proposition was first made to me I simply wrote to Pinker and asked him to send me all Hastings had done. Whatever may have been the discretion of my final decision I may say for Miss Somerville's information that from the material point of view I had no reason to be dissatisfied.

As to your own request[1] it puts me in a state of immense trepidation. I have never seen the foreword of a picture catalogue. I don't know how the thing looks or ought to look; and my fundamental ignorance of the art of painting frightens me more than I can say. I don't know where you got your idea of my enthusiasm for Corsica. The truth of the matter is that I like Corsica incomparably more in your pictures than in nature and I am quite willing to state that in print, but perhaps that wouldn't do. As to Ireland I don't know it at all. I feel utterly unfit to write anything of the kind. The fact of the matter is that I am not a literary man apt by temperament and practice to put his emotions and opinions upon anything under heaven on a piece of paper – especially in the matter of art. All I care for is creative work; and how much it costs me to get *that* out of myself God alone knows, for I could not explain it to any mortal man. However I will send you something, merely as a tribute of affection and appreciation, but you must clearly understand that you are at perfect liberty to throw it into the waste-paper basket and that such a proceeding will not affect the deep regard with which I will always be

Your most faithful friend and Servant

Joseph Conrad

PS Jessie is writing to you to-day I think.

---

[1] To write an introductory note for the catalogue of her forthcoming exhibition of Corsican and Irish landscapes at the United Arts Gallery.

To Richard Curle

Text MS Indiana; Curle 79

[Oswalds]
Wed[ay]
12.10.21

Dear Richard.

Will you come on Sat for lunch and week end. It was impossible to find out before what were Jessies plans.

Hope you are bright and chirpy. M[r] J. H. W.[1] has been a brick in that business you know of.[2] I have had £56 for the lot and he sent me [the] cheque already.

Yours ever

J Conrad.

Drop us a line.

To J. B. Pinker

Text MS Berg; Unpublished

[Oswalds]
12. Oct. 21.

Dearest J B.

Many thanks for Chq[u] (83-10-0) advanced by you for a special purpose which I received today.

I am improved and grinding very hard. Miss S[omerville] had to come to London on acct of her brother's sudden death at Knellers Hall last Sunday.[3] This I hear from Kinkie for whom I am trying to do something.

I'll drop you a line very soon – on various matters.

Ever aff[tly] yours

J. Conrad.

---

[1] An error for T. J. W. (Thomas J. Wise).
[2] The sale of the privately printed copies of *Notes on Life and Letters* (see the letter to Wise of the 4th).
[3] Actually it was her brother-in-law (and cousin) Sir Egerton Bushe Coghill, Bart, a keen amateur painter and singer. He died on 9 October while on a visit to Kneller Hall, Twickenham, the Army's school of music, where Miss Somerville's brother Cameron had been head until 1919.

To Sydney Cockerell
Text MS Rosenbach; Unpublished

[letterhead: Oswalds]
14. Oct '21

My dear Mr Cockerell.

Ever so many thanks for sending me the copy of the Shadow-Line. The truth of the matter is that Borys to whom I hinted that I could get a 1st Edition had absolutely no feeling about it. An edition means absolutely nothing to him – as long as he has some copy. The actual volume I sent him was the one he cared for. That being gone he appreciates the second copy I gave him with the inscription reminding him of the other he had lost.[1] He has no 1st edition of any other of my books so that no set is spoiled by his loss.

Under these circumstances I really do not like to keep the copy you have sent for a specific purpose – tho' I am very touched by your kind thought and appreciate immensely the friendliness of the act. Pray let me send it back to you or I would feel I am detaining it under false pretences. Pardon this scrap of paper[2] and the hurried scrawl. Always very cordially

Yours

Joseph Conrad

I hope you have tried to express to Mrs Cockerell[3] my admiration of her work. The thing dwells with me. Our regards.

To J. B. Pinker
Text MS Berg; Unpublished

[Oswalds]
Sat. AM. [15 October 1921][4]

Dearest J. B.

If you see no objection I should like to let Harriet & Melrose[5] to get their "hearts' desire", so that H should get her roy^{ies}.

I remember giving a reluctant consent – it must have been 2 years ago.

Ever Yours

J. C.

---

[1] When he was gassed and wounded in October 1918?
[2] A half-sheet of letterhead.
[3] Florence Kate Cockerell (née Kingsford, 1892–1949) was an illustrator.
[4] Plans elaborated in the letter of the 18th suggest the date. The luncheon with Doubleday came off on the 28th.
[5] Andrew Melrose (1860–1928), a Scotsman, established his publishing house c. 1910 after working in the Sunday School Union publication department. In 1913, Conrad was a judge for his prize novel competition. He put out a new edition of Harriet Capes's *Wisdom and Beauty from Conrad* in 1922, and the present letter must concern permissions.

F. N. D. asked me to come up for lunch next week. I excused myself. I have a beastly cough and a swollen foot. I told him that we will be in town early in Nov.

Then we can both (I mean you an[d] I) lunch with the Effendi.[1]

To H. J. Goulden, Ltd
Text MS Goulden;[2] Unpublished

Oswalds
Bishopsbourne
Kent.
Oct: 17th 1921.

Dear Sirs,[3]

I return herewith revised proof of Act I of "The Secret Agent". Please note corrections on pages 2, 3, 8, 11, 12, 13, 14, 15, 16, 19, 21, and pull off.[4]

Yours faithfully,
Joseph Conrad. pp. L.H.

To J. B. Pinker
Text MS Berg; Unpublished

[Oswalds]
Monday. 6. pm. [17 October 1921][5]

Dearest J. B.

Not having heard from You I shall post my answer to Kinkie in an hour's time.

I got down[6] on Sat. afternoon feeling rotten – but am better to-day. So is Ralph who had a go of neuralgia for 3 days but looks himself again since this morning.

B[orys] had a severe bout of his old trouble last Tuesday. Cook[7] (I think you know him) took him in a car to his diggings[8] and called in a doctor who

---

[1] A title of great respect in the old Ottoman Empire, and a nickname Kipling invented for Doubleday, playing on his initials.

[2] In Miss Hallowes's hand and signed by her for Conrad.

[3] H. J. Goulden, Ltd, of 40, High Street, Canterbury, booksellers and stationers, continued a family business begun in 1840. Its early history, in addition to printing and bookbinding, involved proprietorship of various newspapers in Kent, including the *Kentish Gazette* (until 1905). Conrad dealt with the firm for the private printing of a few of his works, and it apparently also supplied his stationery.

[4] 'Go ahead with the printing.'   [5] The arrival of Act 1 proofs fixes the date.

[6] Downstairs.   [7] One of the three ex-officers who directed Autoveyors.

[8] 'Digs' or lodgings.

lives at N° 12. B was only one day away from business but he did not look at all well yesterday as he left in the evening.

The doc: advised him to be treated by injections (extract of various glands – which you told me a couple of years ago now did some permanent good to your wife) and offering him an introduction to a specialist – if he liked – with a reduced fee. B. trusts the man but asked my advice. I advised him to try – a matter of 3 months at most. What makes him awfully anxious to be fit is the definite announcement that after the show[1] (which Cook and he will attend) he will be put in charge of the workshop, the man now there going to the depot (for Surrey and Sussex) in the country. His salary is 500 – but B unmarried and a newcomer cannot expect that. It will not be less however than 350/ to begin with. – I told him to ease his mind that his pressing debt (the exact amount is £83.10) will be paid by me on Friday this week at the latest. So if you will as you kindly offered send me that amount I'll see that it gets to the right spot. But the transaction had nothing usurious about it and the man seems a decent sort of person of the name of J. Granger.[2] Proof of play *Act One* reached me today – is corrected and goes back to Goulden this evening. Our dear love.

Ever Yours

J. C.

To J. B. Pinker
Text TS Berg; Unpublished

Oswalds,
Bishopsbourne,
Kent.
Oct. 18th. 1921.

Dearest J. B.

Thanks for your letter.

I have at the present moment a swollen wrist and a tender knee; but in view of Doubleday's infatuation for me perhaps you wouldn't mind shifting around your suggested arrangement of you coming here to hold my hand. Next Saturday is impossible as the lower deck has got a general leave to attend Ford's wedding.[3] How would it be if Jessie came up on that London visit next week instead of waiting till November? In which case perhaps you could arrange for both of us to lunch with D. together on Thursday or Friday

---

[1] The annual Motor Show.
[2] John Grainger (or Goldstein), financial agent, 11 Duke St, SW1; see also the letter to Hammond Clark & Daman of 25 July 1922.
[3] Louis Ford was one of the Conrads' gardeners.

and afterwards let me take shelter at Burys Court, if Mrs Mary approves, probably till Sunday, but at any rate for no longer than two or three months. I would bring with me some MS for correction as it will be an exceptional opportunity to sit with it in your glass-study. I wish to goodness mine was like that. Pray give your opinion on this suggestion please.

I have sent to Kinkie yesterday the Foreword, about 300 w. and stipulated for six free copies of the Catalogue, this being a formed habit now. However nothing can prevent us from going to the Exhibition and stealing a few handfuls more.

Goulden has this moment sent proof of Act 2. and is now pulling off Act 1. I expect the whole thing will be ready before the next eclipse of the moon comes round.[1]

I have settled that business of B[orys]'s in which you helped me and am now in possession of all the documents in the case. Love to you three.

Ever Yours

J. Conrad.

To J. B. Pinker
Text TS Berg; Unpublished

Oswalds,
Bishopsbourne,
Kent.
Oct. 19th. 1921.

My dear J. B.

Thank you very much for the advice about the money and the letter about Nash's proposal.

I certainly think those are not bad terms for the scheme. As the royalty would be 2 1/2d, he would have to sell 10,000 copies to cover the advance of £100. This is what I may call an honourable proposal and if it can be accepted under the terms of our old agreements I would be very pleased to sign.

I assume here that the vol. will consist of "Youth" and H. of D. as per Nash's amended proposal.[2] I can have no objection to that. It's a very good combination. "The End of the Tether" could, strictly speaking, make a volume by itself later, should Nash want to do it.

Yours ever

J. Conrad.

---

[1] A partial lunar eclipse, visible in the United Kingdom, occurred on the night of 16–17 October.

[2] In the end, Eveleigh Nash and Grayson printed *Tales of Unrest* (see the letter of 30 March 1922). In 1912, Nash had published *Some Reminiscences*.

To Major Gordon Gardiner
Text MS Harvard; Unpublished

[letterhead: Oswalds]

22.10.21.

My dear Gardiner.

I am touched by the thought and trouble you have taken for my instruction and amusement. That last is certain because what I have already seen of Berenson (the Leonardo)[1] has roused my curiosity extremely. As to "instruction" it has already begun: I had somehow got the notion that Berenson was a noxious old Jew – and now I know better! I know it positively. I am also très flatté, inwardly, by the discovery that I not only can get the hang of but even assimilate sympathetically what Old B has to say.[2] Who would have thought it!

What more your friendship could have done for my *mental* happiness I can't imagine. You have done there a stroke of genius.

As to my moral state that of course is beyond human help. – You would be a perfect friend if your health did not cause tender concern to those whose warmest affection you have and command whether far or near. I trust you will stand the change to autumn better than I have done – for I am seedy without interruption. It's becoming monotonous.

With love from us both

Ever Your[3]

J. Conrad

To Bruno Winawer
Text TS copy Yale;[4] J-A, 2, 262–3; *Glos* (108); Najder 273–4

Oswalds,

Bishopsbourne,

Kent.

Oct. 23rd. 1921.

My Dear Sir,

Thanks for your last letter in which you show your interest in the adaptation of my novel "The Secret Agent" for the stage, which has been done by myself in Four Acts, of which the Second is in 2 Scenes and the Fourth in three, I

---

[1] Bernard Berenson (1865–1959) began *The Study and Criticism of Italian Art* (1901) with a chapter on Leonardo da Vinci. Berenson's monographs on the painters of Florence, Siena, Umbria, and the Veneto had made him the most influential critic, connoisseur, and art historian of his time.

[2] In, possibly, *The Study and Criticism of Italian Art* (1916), which figured in Conrad's library.

[3] As on some other occasions, the 'your' may be deliberate rather than a truncated 'yours'.

[4] Typing errors not reproduced or signalled.

am sorry to say. By Scenes I mean here what in French is called Tableaux.[1] It was impossible to avoid that, at any rate for me, but one of our most clever producers (Metteur en scène) assured me that it could be managed without much difficulty. However, the play has been hung up for more than a year now, McKinnel, one of our new actor-managers, having had an option on it for some time. But apparently he was afraid of beginning his career with it. He made three failures with other plays, and I imagine that his funds are now exhausted, and that he will never produce it now. His option terminates at the end of this year. This has been a very bad time for theatres and the improvement is not very marked yet.

I am sorry to have no news to give you about our joint undertaking. One copy is in America by now and the other is here of course, but I have not asked Pinker what precisely he is doing and he has volunteered no statement; therefore I beg you to arm yourself with patience and dismiss for the moment all optimistic thoughts, as I have done. You may however be assured that no opportunity will be neglected and no opening left untried. You may also be certain that my own play will not be allowed to get in the way. The two things are very different; and, frankly, I don't care very much whether the "Secret Agent" gets on the stage or not. I have lost all interest in it by now and when McKinnel's option expires it will be put into a drawer.

I am, however, having 30 copies[2] of it privately printed for distribution amongst friends, and I will send you one as soon as they are ready. But as to your most kind and flattering proposal to translate it for the Polish stage I must first explain to you the whole situation.

More than a year ago I made over all my copyrights, for translation in Polish and Russian, to my cousin, Miss Angela Zagórska, whose address is: 5 ul. Wilcza, Warsaw. Therefore I must refer you to her for all arrangements, literary and others, connected with the translation and production of that play in Poland. The property of all translation rights in Poland and Russia has been made over to her by a legal instrument and she may dispose of them as she thinks fit. All I can venture to say here is that nothing could please me more than to have the Secret Agent translated by you and to express an earnest hope that you two will come to a definite understanding on the matter of staging it in Poland.

Would you care to get in communication with her, tell her confidentially of our recent relations and of course show her this letter? I don't think I will

---

[1] In this tradition, a new scene begins each time a character enters or exits.
[2] Apparently a mistranscription for fifty copies, although as many as sixty may, in fact, have been pulled.

warn her beforehand that she may hear from you because I do not know
how you may look at the situation.

She has written to me lately to say she is very anxious to see The Secret
Agent in its stage form. Therefore I will send her a copy by the same post by
which I will send you yours.

Thanks very much for your friendly promise to send me your new fantastic
play "FF Rays".[1] I am looking forward impatiently to its arrival. A fantastic
play is a dangerous thing, generally speaking: and I am very curious to see
what you have made of it. My warmest wishes for its success with the Cracow
public.

With kindest regards

very cordially Yours

J. Conrad.

To J. B. Pinker
Text MS Berg; Unpublished

[Oswalds]
Tuesday. ev^g [25 October 1921][2]

My dear J. B.

S. S. P[awling] wants to lunch me on Thursday at the Bath Club. I wish
to goodness he had the sense to ask you; but I don't suppose he can have
anything to say.

We will arrive at Dover S^{t3} about 12.30. I think I'll come in the car too. I
feel seedy and wretched but I must try to pull myself together. At 3.30 or so
Lady Colvin will come to see Jessie and I *must* be there. Then Kinkie about
5 and Don Roberto a little after. I don't see how I can get away to see you in
the afternoon and I don't know how you may feel about looking us up. But
I'll try to escape from S. S. P. before 3 and perhaps you will cross over from
your club before going back to the office?

In any case I will, if I may be with you about noon on Friday.

Ever Yours

J. Conrad

I have revised Acts II & III of the SA.

---

[1] *Promeienie FF*, then on stage, was not published until 1926, so a typescript must be at issue here.
[2] Assigned in the Berg Collection to '10/21'. The London sojourn fixes the date: the Conrads
were in town on the 27th and 28th and then at Burys Court, arriving home on the 31st.
[3] I.e. at Brown's Hotel.

To Harold Waldo

Text TS Private collection; Unpublished

[letterhead: Oswalds]

Oct. 25th. 1921.

Dear M[r] Waldo.[1]

I want to thank you at once for the book[2] you have been good enough to send me. It is of course of the greatest interest and secures my personal sympathy by the kindly attitude of the author towards the people he treats of, and by the poignancy of the action.

The technique of course has interested me too. It is characteristic of a large part of American literature of fiction. I have met it before and at one time and another I have given serious consideration to the nature of its methods and its artistic effect. I have no academic prejudices. I am open to new impressions, and, whether these are welcome or not to my temperament, I am in the habit of thinking over their nature and try to account to myself for the result obtained. But constitutionally I am not a critic. I have really too much respect for an artist's personality to sit in judgment on what may often be the outcome of sheer inspiration, and certainly always is, in the main, the outcome of a temperament. Least of all would I dare to pose for an authority or try to be a teacher in matters which should lie strictly between the artist and his literary conscience, or even only his literary impulse. But since you say that you like my work (which means that there are somewhere and somehow basic similarities in our temperaments) I would submit to your consideration a thought, the result of many meditations on our common art. And it is this: that no matter how rapid the action and the swiftness of impressions inherent in the conception of a given piece of fiction, there should be for the fulness of effect (and for depth of truth too) a certain leisureliness of style, something on which the mind (as distinguished from the emotions) of the reader should be able to rest; a sort of solid ground on which he can follow the writer through the changing scenes of the story. Otherwise, no matter how much telling detail you present there will be an effect of the story being too much summarised; and as much of its truth lost in the reading, as the perception of a beautiful, tragic, romantic, smiling or savage landscape is lost when seen through the window of a train moving at the rate of sixty miles an hour.

I am saying all this, not as a fellow-craftsman, but just as a reader of average intelligence and average sensibilities. We must not forget that those phrases that have a complete set of connotations in the mind of the writer

---

[1] Harold Waldo, an American, was the author of *Stash of the Marsh Country* (1921) and of *The Magic Midland* (1923), both published by George H. Doran of New York.

[2] His first novel, *Stash of the Marsh Country*, published in June. The book recounts the experiences of a Polish boy in the Great Lakes region.

come, as it were, as strangers to the reader, who, as he reads, will not attach *all* those connotations to them, and perhaps will attach even altogether different connotations, unless he is kept straight by the stylistic development, by what I may call the steadiness and the continuity of the literary outline.

I don't know whether I express myself clearly but I have a feeling that I can trust your mind and your sympathy (or else I would have never written all this) and I also beg you to believe that all this disquisition is but a proof of the regard in which I hold your work and of my friendly sentiments towards the writer.

Believe me very sincerely

Yours

Joseph Conrad.

To Major Gordon Gardiner
Text MS Harvard; Unpublished

[letterhead: Oswalds]
31. Oct 21

Très chèr*.

Just a scrawl to catch post.

No such notion or *shadow* of it ever entered my head! It could not enter anybodys head who knows you. How could it? Be reasonable O! Man.

How dear of You to send those photo[gra]phs. Blessings on You[r] head and love from the House.

Ever Yours

J. Conrad.

Pinker thinks much of the scheme and is going to write to U. S.[1]

We returned home 1/2 hour ago.[2]

To J. B. Pinker
Text MS Berg; Unpublished

[letterhead: Oswalds]
31. Oct '21

Dearest J. B.

Herewith letter to our American new-friend. If approved please send it on.

---

[1] The nature of the scheme is unclear.
[2] From London and Burys Court; see the letters to Mary Pinker and to Curle of 4 November and [5 November], respectively.

I found here a letter from Gardiner bearing on the very point which had occurred to us last night. Please read it through, however annoying his handwriting may be to you.

It is a sincere thing.

I answer[ed] him denying all suspicion of his motives on behalf of us both. The fact however of this thing having a potentiality of material advantages does remain.

We had a prosperous run. The household sends its collective love

Ever Yours

J. Conrad.

Please drop us a line about Mrs Mary.

To the Editor of the *London Mercury*
Text *London Mercury*, December 1921, p. 187

[Oswalds]
[November 1921]

[This letter appeared under the heading 'The Loss of the *Dalgonar*' in the December 1921 number of the *London Mercury*. Conrad comments on an article published in the October issue. Given that journals appeared at the end of the month previous to publication date, the letter must have been written before the 25th, but there are no other clues as to its placement. The text appeared in *Last Essays*, and will be reprinted in the Cambridge Edition of that volume.]

To Sir Sidney Colvin
Text Lucas 307–8

[Oswalds]
1st Nov. 1921.

My very dear Colvin

The reading of *Memories and Notes*[1] has been one continuous delight. As you know, I have been privileged to see some of these papers even in typescript – and some in their serial form.[2] But the quality of their interest and freshness is of the kind that does not perish in the reading and re-reading. I feel much honoured by my presentation copy bearing corrections in the text in your own handwriting.

---

[1] *Memories and Notes of Persons and Places, 1852–1912* had just appeared.
[2] The first chapter, on Colvin's boyhood, had appeared in *London Mercury*, 3 (April 1921), 606–17.

These detached pages have a singularly charming oneness of atmosphere – a touching serenity in their clear light, and a classical simplicity of suggestive lines in portraiture and landscape which is most satisfying to one's tastes and one's emotions. My warmest and most loving congratulations on the effectiveness of your memory and the sureness of every vital touch. Dearest love to Lady Colvin (who ought to be pleased with the marvellous glow of the dedicatory preface)[1] and to you from us both.

Ever yours,

Joseph Conrad

To John Galsworthy

Text MS Forbes; Marrot 508–9

[Oswalds]

1st Nov. 21

Dearest Jack

I was just about to sit down to write to you when your letter arrived with the PEN circular.[2] I'll do as directed. I have also noted the Chairman's leniency[3] in the matter of attendance at dinners. Indeed my dearest Jack I would very seldom find anybody I know there – by which my natural shyness would be increased by 1000% and probably cause my death from acute embar[r]assment.

I think that The Press has said – with a surprisingly sympathetic under-standing – everything which could be said in praise of To Let.[4] I can't describe sufficiently the glow of inward joy with which I went through the pages crowning triumphantly the Forsythe* Cycle. It is a great achievement in conception, in the whole and in the detail – where the serenity of your humane genius shines with an enchanting light. It is a great performance my dear Jack – so great that without for a moment stepping out of the scheme it escapes from the particular into the universal by the sheer force of its inner life.

I don't suppose you will do me [the] injury of suspecting that I have missed things. Honestly I don't think I did – though I admit that the narrative has carried me along in a most irresistible way. But there were more readings than one, and the quality of the execution is so fine as to keep one's receptivity *constantly* on the alert – and of how many great novels can this be said?

---

[1] A five-page letter 'To My Wife'.   [2] Of the 30th (Stape 2000).
[3] Galsworthy himself was the first president of PEN.
[4] The novel had appeared in book form in September.

The very day the Watsons[1] were here an attack of gout came on and laid me up (more or less) for over a week. There has been another since. I have now a sort of astmathic* cough which depresses me exceedingly. On the other hand Jessie is progressing in a most satisfactory manner.

With our dear love to you both

Ever yours

J. Conrad

To the Hon. Bertrand Russell
Text MS McMaster; Russell 144

[letterhead: Oswalds]
2 Nov '21

My dear Russell

We were glad to hear that your wife[2] feels none the worse for the exertions and agitations of the move. Please give her our love and assure her that she is frequently in our thoughts.

As to yourself I have been dwelling with you mentally for several days between the covers of your book[3] – an habitation of great charm and most fascinatingly furnished; not to speak of the wonderful quality of light that reigns in there. Also all the windows (I am trying to write in images) are, one feels, standing wide open. Nothing less stuffy – of the Mansions of the Mind – could be conceived! I am sorry for the philosophers (p 212 – end) who (like the rest of us) cannot have their cake and eat it.[4] There's no exactitude in the vision or in the words. I have a notion that we are condemned in all things to the a-peu-près,[5] which no scientific passion for weighing and measuring will ever do away with.

---

[1] Sir Robert Jones's daughter Hilda Watson and her husband Frederick (1885–1935); he edited the *Cripple's Journal*, and wrote boys' adventure stories, books about fox-hunting, and his father-in-law's biography, *The Life of Sir Robert Jones* (1934). Galsworthy's letter to Conrad of 30 October (Stape 2000) identifies the Watsons in question.

[2] Dora Winifred Russell (née Black, 1894–1986), Russell's second wife, whom he had married this year (marriage dissolved 1935), was a journalist, writer on women's issues, and autobiographer. With Russell, she co-authored *The Prospects of Industrial Civilization* (1923). In November 1921, she was pregnant and suffering from toothache. The Russells had returned to London from a sojourn in Kent (see the letter of 5 October).

[3] *The Analysis of Mind*, published in June, and presented to Conrad by Russell during a recent visit to Oswalds.

[4] In fact, pp. 213–30, comprising Lecture XI on 'General Ideas and Thoughts'.

[5] 'The nearly so' or 'the approximation'.

It is very possible that I havent understood your pages – but the good try I have had was a delightful experience. I suppose you are enough of a philosopher not to have expected more from a common mortal.

I don't believe that Charles I was executed (pp 245–246 et seq) but there is not enough paper left here to explain why.[1] Next time perhaps. For I certainly intend to meet you amongst your Chinoiseries[2] at the very earliest fitting time.

Always afft^{ly} Yours

J. Conrad

To J. B. Pinker
Text MS Berg; Unpublished

[letterhead: Oswalds]
Friday. [4 November 1921][3]

Dearest J B.

Ralph will tell you all about *my* cold no doubt.

I hope You are really getting on.

When we are recovered all round I hope to see you here. I have been pressing Gouldens to hurry-up with the S[ecret] A[gent].

Our love.

Ever affec^{tly} yours

J. Conrad.

To Mary Pinker
Text MS Yale; Unpublished

[letterhead: Oswalds]
4. Nov. '21

Dear Mrs Pinker

Receive the thanks due to you and the Vice-Hostess from the invading barbarians of the Oswalds tribe.

We were most distressed by the news of the visitation afflicting Burys Court in the person of its Chief and the Vice-Hostess herself. However, her letter was cheerful in tone and the intelligence of you being in charge of J. B's case gives us a favourable impression of the future.

---

[1] A playful response to an example in Lecture XII on 'Belief': 'I believe that Great Britain is an island, that whales are mammals, that Charles I was executed' (p. 245).
[2] Collected on his recent visit to China.
[3] Printing of *The Secret Agent*, completed by mid-month, the state of Conrad's health (the letter to Galsworthy of the 1st) and of Pinker's (the letter of the 4th) suggest the placement. By the 7th Pinker was apparently better.

Mrs J. C. is laid up (since yesterday) with what looks like a severe cold. I hear her coughing now. She sends her love to You all in which I join.

Believe me always Your most affectionate friend and Servant

Joseph Conrad.

To Richard Curle
Text MS Indiana; Curle 80 (in part)[1]

[letterhead: Oswalds]
Saturday. [5 November 1921][2]

My dear Curle

I hoped to get back from Burys Court to town last Monday and then see you. But I felt pretty bad in the morning and so went on with Jessie home in the car. Ever since I've been lame in the left hand and generally in the dumps.

I've been thinking of you a lot tho'. During Jessies stay in London there was a lot of people all the time in the rooms. As I remained only the Thursday evg and the Friday morning I had to be in attendance. My absence would have been too marked. On Friday I lunched with Doubleday and left town at 4. It was an awful grind. Your silence (after the first intimation) since you left here makes me wonder if all is well – in Scotland and elsewhere.

Ever Yours

J Conrad.

Jessie just tells me th[a]t Mrs Iris[3] told her (on Sat) that you had lumbago. If I had known I would have gone back to town on Monday anyhow – you may believe me. Give me a word of news.

To J. B. Pinker
Text TS/MS Berg; Unpublished

Oswalds,
Bishopsbourne,
Kent.
Nov. 7th. 1921.

Dearest J. B.

Will you please, if at all possible, send me a copy (of the two made, from my First Draft) of the novel. If you remember I sent you mine some time ago to show to Mr Vance.[4] It would be a great help to have a copy by me as my First Draft does not lend itself to further revision.

---

[1] Curle omits the third paragraph.   [2] Curle's date, confirmed by Conrad's activities.
[3] Wedgwood.   [4] See the letter of [4 October].

I suppose, my dear J. B., that it is thoroughly understood in the office that those first copies that have been made were only for convenience and are subject to further correction before copies *for the printers* are made from them. The lot that was sent to America was only to give serialisers an idea of the stuff; and the copy Mr Vance had lately is of course in the same case, being identical with what has been sent to America.

I presume that my letter to the American lawyer about Film has been passed and forwarded.

Could you spare me a copy of "The Book of Job"? Unless you have an objection to its being shown to anybody; as what I want it for is to let our friend G. Gardiner have a look at it. My idea is that he may be of some use. But if you don't like the idea, or even have the faintest feeling against trying to make use of him in the matter, then do not send it. I wish to make it clear that I do not know that he can be of any use, and, indeed, have nothing positive in my mind. The notion occurred to me on a general consideration of his extensive relations amongst all sorts of people. If you remember the conversation we had at your house, about a possible connection with Winawer in the future, you will understand why I am anxious that the play should have a chance to get through somehow or other.

Ralph told me that you will be in town to-day. I hope you are feeling quite fit for the office – but I've my doubts yet. I send this however in the belief that you will not let my correspondence worry you. I have started work again and hope to get some sort of pace on now.

Ever affct^{ly} yours

J. Conrad.

To J. B. Pinker
Text MS Berg; Unpublished

[letterhead: Oswalds]
9 Nov. 21.

Dearest J. B.

The copy of novel received. Many thanks.

I have been working at the American slips of play-volume.[1]

There was a considerable lot to do in the way of corrections and typographical rearrangement; and as I read and considered these things it struck me that some day someone will perhaps discover that this vol of two plays resumes and exhibits my fundamental mental characteristics better perhaps than the whole series of the novels.

---

[1] In the end Doubleday's plan to publish *One Day More* and *The Secret Agent*, contracted in July 1921 (Hallowes), was cancelled; see also the letter of 28 March 1922.

It is truly "concentrated Conrad". But having discovered no reason to be ashamed of what it shows I yielded to the impulse of inserting in the pre[li]ms sent me for revision a page with a dedication to you – just *one* line as for special friends like Gals. & C. Graham, with no phrases[1] at all. If you don't like the idea there will be time to stop it by next weeks mail.

I imagine there would be no difficulty of arranging for an English ed. which, if the dedication is to stand, I would like to see out. But not otherwise.

Our love

Ever Yours

J. Conrad

To Thomas J. Wise
Text MS BL Ashley 2941; Unpublished

[letterhead: Oswalds]
9. Nov '21

My dear M[r] Wise

Would you mind lending me for a few days the First Copy of the play *Book of Job* as I have no clean copy of my own.

In haste for post

Very sincerely yours

Joseph Conrad.

To H. G. R. Goulden
Text MS Goulden;[2] Unpublished

[letterhead: Oswalds]
Nov: 11th 1921.

Dear Sir,

I return herewith the corrected proof of Act Four of the "Secret Agent". Kindly note small corrections on pages 50, 51, 57, 66, 69.

Yours faithfully,

Joseph Conrad.
pp. L.H.

[1] A Gallicism: *sans phrases* – 'with no fine phrases' or 'without any fuss'. For more on this expression, see the notes to the letter to Henry Arthur Jones of 7 November 1922.
[2] In Miss Hallowes's hand and signed by her for Conrad.

To J. B. Pinker

Text MS Berg; Unpublished

[letterhead: Oswalds]
11 Nov. 21

Dearest J B.

I am glad that the idea of that particular dedication commends itself to you. It is perfectly true that the S Agent in its dramatic form owes its existence to your encouragement.

I hear from Goulden that the 50 copies will be ready by Friday next.

I'll instruct him to send me 10 – and the other 40 to your office with the account.

Your personal copy will be amongst my ten – and I will send it to your home.

Glad to hear you feel equal to the celebrations.

Suppose you come down here when you recover from them – next week.

Love to everybody

Ever Yours

J Conrad

To Richard Curle

Text MS Indiana; Curle 81 (in part)[1]

[letterhead: Oswalds]
12. Nov. '21

Dearest Richard.

Pardon the delay in answering your last which made me feel a bit unhappy about you. The very fact that I understand your feelings thoroughly makes it difficult to write. You may feel sure of my understanding and sympathy – but no words can be of any help in an unhappiness so intimate;[2] and my thoughts if I were to set them out in their confused state would not be of any use to you. This is not a matter for action. It is a question of sheer endurance – a call not on your wisdom (in which I believe) but of your character – in which I have the greatest confidence. But that is comfort for me – not for you. As to the Edinburgh affair I hope it will go through without a hitch.

In the matter of the preface[3] I have thought it over and I regret not to be able to tell you more than that I'll see what I can do. I am very doubtful – not of my wish but of my ability. I won't talk to you now of my mental state.

---

[1] Curle omits the last sentence of the first paragraph.
[2] Marital difficulties? Curle was divorced in 1922.
[3] To *Into the East: Notes on Burma and Malaya*, published in 1923 with a preface by Conrad.

Send the MS anyhow. I may find a way to squeeze something out of myself. If affection alone could do it you would not have to wait long.

Jessie sends her love and I am always most affectionately

Yours

Joseph Conrad.

To J. B. Pinker
Text TS Berg; Unpublished

Oswalds,
Bishopsbourne,
Kent.
Nov. 14th. 1921.

Dear J B.

Herewith the completed, corrected and arranged text of the famous Cookery Book,[1] which the author has asked me to send to you with such remarks as I wish to make.

First of all then I would suggest that there should be only one copy made of this, which after some additional slight touches (probably) is destined for the printer. I imagine the procedure will be that Doubledays will set up and send galley slips here; from which after correction Heinemann will be able to set up on this side. Therefore I don't see the use of having two copies; but of course if I am wrong you will direct things to be done in the manner you want them. I would also with all due modesty suggest that the book should be got up inexpensively but with a certain elegance and in a manner not suggesting a Cookery Book, but rather, say, a volume of a new poet's verse, or a small volume of Essays, or something of that sort; so that it could perchance be left in a drawing-room without blatantly asserting itself as a thing of the kitchen. A more practical suggestion is that there should be at least two ribbon markers in it – one red and one blue.

The text sent to you here consists of 120 pages and includes apart from the general matter just 190 recipes, I think quite a sufficient number for what is professedly a Handbook and, really, not meant for professionals at all. It isn't meant to compete with the more extensive works which would naturally be consulted in the library (of the Little House).

The Preface[2] and the preliminary pages are not included, as the Preface is quite correct and the pre[li]ms I have not thought out yet. We will type

---

[1] Jessie Conrad's *A Handbook of Cookery for a Small House* was duly forwarded to Doubleday but did not appear until 1923 to allow for its US serialisation in the *Delineator*.

[2] By Conrad himself. It was later collected in *Last Essays*.

them here, either in one set or two, according to your decision, and join them to the clean text, if you will kindly send it here for a day or two after it is done. I will also make a skeleton of a Table of Contents for the printer to be completed when the book is set up.

Ever Yours

J. Conrad

To H. G. R. Goulden
Text MS Goulden;[1] Unpublished

[letterhead: Oswalds]
Nov: 16th 1921.

Dear Sir,

You will have received my telegram today,[2] with instructions to cut the pages at the top.

Will you kindly send 40 copies to M' Pinker, and the remainder (including the extra copies) to me.

Yours faithfully,

Joseph Conrad.
pp. L.H.

To William Rothenstein
Text TS Harvard; Unpublished

[letterhead: Oswalds]
Nov. 17. 1921.

My dear Will.

I must dictate this letter because I am disabled in my hand and could not use the pen for any length of time.

It is indeed good news to hear that you could find time to come down to us during the Christmas vacation. I won't tell you much about myself now. There are things not easy to write about and even to an old friendship wearisome to read. I can only thank you for keeping me in mind, notwithstanding appearances, and leave the rest to your sympathetic understanding.

---

[1] In Miss Hallowes's hand and signed by her for Conrad.
[2] The text of the telegram (Goulden papers), sent at 10.58 a.m. on 16 November from Bishops-bourne, reads: 'All correct please proceed pages should be cut letter follows'.

But as to Everett's pictures[1] the difficulty would be to find words to express the deep nature of the feelings which they awakened in me. Those things are, properly speaking, marvellous, in truth, in sentiment, and in rendering. What an accurate and imaginative vision! I who for twenty years or more have lived with those things, have been moved almost to tears by his work as by a poignant memory. And it isn't as if only one or two or three of those pictures were so great. All of them get home absolutely; even the three little studies of the hull; which are little only in size but positively great in truth, and as moving to me as some great sculptor's drawings of the human form.

I could go on for pages like this without ever managing to express to you adequately the effect produced on me by those photographs. In a more special way they appeal to me because I have been always alive to the shadow-effects of the sails. Some of those paintings might be considered studies of sail shadows. But this is particularising; since with the same truth one may say that all the aspects of the sea are in it too; all impressive by the inherent greatness of the bare truth and the vastness he manages to put, as it were, in the mere corner of the frame.

I can't go on speaking of each one in particular. The furling-the-topgallantsail picture is simply admirable right down to the deck and right away to the horizon – but I must not let myself go to talk about them or else this letter would extend to a volume.

And talking about a volume. I showed those tremendous things to J. B. Pinker who is now on a visit here, and directly he had looked at them he was moved to exclaim: What a combination it would be with the text of the "Mirror of the Sea" in a special limited edition! My enthusiasm for the idea is practically unbounded. The only thing would be how Mr Everett may look at it. My point of view has nothing to do with the usual conception of illustrations. The feeling I have towards the combination would be more that of collaboration, the art of Everett so to speak treating of the same subject of which my prose treats in terms of not only his own art but of his own conception and knowledge of the sea: that is, the use of these actual things that Mr Everitt* has already painted. The whole thing reduces itself to a matter of selection. I write all this to you because you say that Mr Everett is your old friend, but as his address is on the envelope in which I am going to return the pictures to him I have asked Mr Pinker to write to him direct and

---

[1] John Everett (1876–1949), marine and landscape painter, photographer and engraver. See the letter to him of 26 November. The photographs and reproductions of paintings and drawings that Conrad saw were the fruit of Everett's voyage under sail from Bristol to Sabine, Texas, in 1920 as third mate in the *Birkdale* – the last barque to fly the Red Ensign (the flag of the British Merchant Navy).

ascertain how he feels about it, before he takes any steps towards planning and negotiating such a publication.[1]

I don't write to E myself but I have no doubt you will communicate the essence of this letter to him and convey to him the assurance of my truly affectionate admiration and regard.

After two years of considerable suffering and three operations Jessie has regained her power of walking and, as she says herself, is like a person born again. Our love to you and Alice and all the children. Remember me specially to John,[2] whom I know better than all the others. Borys is now, to state it baldly, in the motor trade, but he cherishes with undiminished affection the water colours of his toys you made for him when he was five years old. Our John is at Tonbridge and is a lanky person of a certain individuality. I won't say more just now but perhaps in a few days I will be able to write to you in pen and ink.

Ever Yours affection[ate]ly

Joseph Conrad.

To Richard Curle

Text MS Indiana; Curle 82

[letterhead: Oswalds]

Friday. [18 November 1921][3]

Dear Dick

Can You and do You care to come down tomorrow by train arriving Cant^ry 5.4 or 6.18 to dine and stay over Sunday?

Please wire

Yours

J. C.

To the Hon. Bertrand Russell

Text MS McMaster; Russell 145

[letterhead: Oswalds]

18 Nov. '21.

My dear Russell.

Jessie must have sent yesterday our congratulations and words of welcome to the "comparative stranger"[4] who has come to stay with you (and take charge of his household as you will soon discover).

---

[1] Although under discussion for some time, the project was aborted.

[2] John Knewstub Maurice Rothenstein (1901–97; knighted 1952), the future art historian and director of the Tate Gallery.

[3] Curle supplies the date.

[4] John Conrad Russell (died 1987; 4th Earl Russell 1970) was born on the 16th.

Yes! Paternity is a great experience of which the least that can be said is that it is eminently worth having – if only for the deepened sense of fellowship with all men it gives one. It is the only experience perhaps whose universality does not make it common but invests it with a sort of grandeur on that very account. My affection goes out to you both, to him who is without speech and thought as yet and to you who have spoken to men profoundly with effect and authority about the nature of the mind. For your relations to each other will have its poignant moments arising out of the very love and loyalty binding you to each other.

Of all the incredible things that come to pass this – that there should be one day a Russell bearing mine for one of his names is surely the most marvellous.[1] Not even my horoscope could have disclosed that for I verily believe that all the sensible stars would have refused to combine in that extravagant manner over my cradle. However it *has* come to pass (to the surprise of the Universe) and all I can say is that I am profoundly touched – more than I can express – that I should have been present to your mind in that way and at such a time.

Please kiss your wife's hand for me and tell her that in the obscure bewildered masculine way (which is not quite unintelligent however) I take part in her gladness. Since your delightful visit here she was much in our thoughts – and I will confess we felt very optimistic. She has justified it fully and it is a great joy to think of her with two men in the house. She will have her hands full presently. I can only hope that John Conrad has been born with a disposition towards indulgence which he will consistently exercise towards his parents. I don't think that I can wish you anything better and so with my dear love to all three of you I am always Yours

Joseph Conrad.

I am dreadfully offended at you associating me with some undesirable acquaintance of yours who obviously should not have been allowed inside the B[ritish] Museum reading-room.[2] I wish you to understand that my attitude towards [the] King Charles question[3] is not phantastic but philosophical and I shall try to make it clear to you later when you will be more in a state to follow my reasoning closely. Judging from my own experience I imagine that it's no use talking to you seriously just now.

[1] On or about the 16th, Russell had written to Conrad: 'I wish, with your permission, to call my son John Conrad. My father was called John, my grandfather was called John, and my great-grandfather was called John; and Conrad is a name in which I see merits', *The Autobiography of Bertrand Russell, 1914–1944* (1968), p. 209.
[2] According to Russell, the interloper 'did not agree that Julius Caesar is dead, and when I asked why, replied: "Because I am Julius Caesar"'.
[3] See the letter to Russell of 2 November.

To Hugh Walpole
Text TS/MS Texas; Unpublished

[letterhead: Oswalds]
Nov. 18th. 1921.

My dear Hugh

I ought to have written to you before, but either I could not collect my thoughts sufficiently having been pretty seedy and physically worried for quite a long time, or in the intervals had to concentrate on other matters much belated in their progress. And even at this moment I sit with my hand in a sling and feeling by no means alert physically. But I have been able to think a little and I hope you will not mind the mechanical process of this letter. I am not well enough to use the pen for any length of time.

And first of all my tender thanks for the copy of the limited edition,[1] the get up of which pleases me by the harmonious sobriety of its aspect and by the interior grace of its pages. I handled it with reverence. The reading of it was a[n] absorbing experience. The meditation which came later confirmed the sense of the work's value, which I feel to be considerable. Its atmosphere is extremely fascinating (which of course means the clear atmosphere in which the author wrote), its interest very real (which means the state of mind of the reader), its detail amusing by its exactitude and manner of presentation; its ending though (perhaps on purpose) not conclusive has an episodic finality which leaves our sympathies satisfied in a way which is particularly attractive; and the whole picture, even to the framing, is very Walpolean (which means that the design, the colouring, the perspective and the very grouping have an individual quality to which I, together with a large portion of the world, am easily responsive).

It is a great tribute to your gift, dear Hugh, that when I read you it is always like a member of the public, (I suppose the more intelligent part of it) but as a matter of fact reacting emotionally, that is directly to your appeal and not to any suggested reflections of my own. But as of course your work when finished is not the sort of thing that is thrown away, the ensuing meditation over it must be to a certain extent analytical; for you and I, my dear Hugh, are both "of a trade" and therefore (isn't there a proverb to that effect?) cannot always agree.[2]

It is not however here a matter of disagreement, it is but a train of thought which has suggested itself and which I will mention to you not at all in the

---

[1] Of *The Young Enchanted: A Romantic Story*, published this month.
[2] The idea dates to antiquity, but the allusion is to John Gay's formulation in 'The Rat-catcher and Cats', in *Fables* (1727–38): 'In ev'ry age and clime we see / Two of a trade can never agree.'

hope that it may receive your assent but as a proof of the intimate interest in your temperamental and creative individuality – or shall I say entity? The trouble is the Danish girl-part, and it is of the same nature as the glimpse of motive that was given one in "The Secret City"[1] towards the end of the book – the suggestion of something deeper and larger which had not been made use of. In "The Secret City" it was in the region of psychology, a state of feeling not brought into line; here it is just a matter of fact (in itself) but which ought to have affected the psychology of H. T.[2] more or less all through the book. And it is a considerable fact, on which you yourself rather insist – I mean the meeting and the pursuit of Christina, with the peculiar circumstances of her existence and with all the implication of her sudden, instantaneous, attractiveness to H. T. Yet, my dear Hugh, it apparently has no influence, or at any rate that influence is not indicated, either on the whole of H. T.'s psychology or on the whole march of the story which strictly speaking is *his* story running parallel with the story of Millie; the two having for trait d'union[3] the existence of the excellent Peter, who in himself is quite justified, I hasten to say. The whole treatment of the Christina part is too episodic. I mean to say that H. T. is suddenly as if blown by a gust of wind in her direction and then returns and goes on in his own line as if nothing had happened, apparently unaffected in thought or emotion till the next gust comes. That is how it strikes me. Of course you may answer that I am obviously blind in one eye and deficient in certain brain-cells not to have perceived that H. T. is actually affected and influenced by the existence of Christina and the peculiar circumstances of her life. And it may be so. But frankly, and without vanity, I think that I am not more defective in vision or in brain-cells than ninety-nine per cent of your readers. Therefore my objection will still stand in point of artistic effect.

Each of the Christina episodes leaves behind a curious sense of baffled expectation which does not lie in a faulty conception of them, but, I verily believe, in the summariness of the treatment. I don't mean lack of vigour. Vigour of treatment and summariness of presentation can exist together. H. T.'s life, in that slice of it which is presented to us so vividly, interestingly and with such telling detail, does not seem to be influenced in the slightest degree by the "magicality" of Christina. He seems to forget her and her charming mother completely after every contact. He goes about his work and goes away to the country without apparently giving them a single thought – till the next gust comes and drives him in their direction. His contacts with

---

[1] *The Secret City: A Novel in Three Parts* (1919).
[2] Henry Trenchard, the main character.   [3] 'Connection'.

them might belong to a series of recurrent consecutive dreams. And I don't mean to say that they are like dreams to him – but that this is to a certain extent the effect on the reader.

I have asked myself once or twice since finishing the book whether that was not the result of something inherent in the mere phrasing. It is exactly the same as in the other portions of the narrative dealing with H. T.'s and Millie's experiences with men and women of another sort. I will own to you, my dear Hugh, that I am very interested in my own impressions derived from that part of the book and I would like immensely to talk with you about them and especially to hear what you would have to say if we ever came to grips over that affair – the Christina affair which might have been made mystic altogether but to my mind remains simply unsubstantial in its effect as a thing of real life.

Thanks for the invitation my dear Hugh – but really I am not fit for general human intercourse just now, and I don't want to appear in the company in the character of "poor Walpole's undesirable acquaintance". Our dear love to You.

Ever Yours

J. Conrad.

To Thomas J. Wise
Text MS BL Ashley A. 4789; Unpublished

[letterhead: Oswalds]
18 Nov. '21.

My dear Mr Wise

Many thanks for the cheque for £100 which makes you the owner of the "Mediterranean Novel" MS as soon as it [is] finished – together with the "first copy" of the same when that is done with for printing purposes.

I will send you of course a holograph of title page as soon as I decide upon the title.

Enclosed here the Play (Secret Agent) privately printed. There are 50 copies in existence. Also the catalogue of Miss Kinkead['s] exhibition of Corsican and Irish landscapes on account of the foreword by me. Kindest regards from us both

Yours

J. Conrad

To J. B. Pinker
Text MS Berg;[1] Unpublished

> Oswalds
> Bishopsbourne
> Kent.
> *21.11'21.*

Dearest J. B.

Here's the Cookery Handbook with all the prems, Contents and Preface, OK for the printers.

Will you suggest to D[oubled]ay to send proofs in galleys in case of small alterations.[2]

Our love

> Yours
>
> J. C.

To J. B. Pinker
Text MS Berg; Unpublished

> [letterhead: Oswalds]
> 22 Nov. '21

My Dearest J B.

I send you here an amended title-page[3] as the one with the MS says nothing about the preface.

You won't mind the reminding you that poor Karola's quarter begins with the 1st Dec. You will send her the extra £20 (50 instead of 30) and deduct the amount from *my* cash payment on Dec[er] 15 (£10) on Jan '22 (another 10), as we have done during the last quarter.

I suppose you have found in the office the batch of 40 copies of the play from Goulden. I of course have had my lot, nominally 10 but actually 13, as there were 3 extra copies printed which, I suppose, are covered by the agreed price. But the edition may be called as of 50 of which 40 for sale.[4] I've sent out already a few, and the funniest thing is that both Wise & Dick wrote saying that "it looks very handsome". And I who prided myself on having produced something "real ugly"!

Borys was here last weekend. The question now is whether he is going to take charge of the Depot and repairing shop. (Cook still wants him in the

---

[1] Address in Miss Hallowes's hand.
[2] Conrad received proofs in February 1922.   [3] For the cookery book.
[4] Goulden's records show that on the 18th they sent fifty-five copies to Conrad, a figure repeated in Hallowes. Later correspondence with dealers and collectors indicates that the firm itself disposed of five copies and suggests that sixty may have been printed.

sale-room.) If he does the conditions would be a free hand, fixed salary and perc^{ge} on profits. The department has been in existence about 18 months and shows a loss in that time of £500. It is admitted that it was very badly managed by the man (a partner) who is now leaving it to take the Sussex agency branch. B thinks that he can *stop* the loss in the first year. The thing will be decided I believe this week.

Ever Yours

J. Conrad.

To Richard Curle
Text MS Indiana; Curle 83

[Oswalds]

23.11.'21

Dear Dick

Certainly – come for next week end arr^{g} on Sat at 12.44. The car will meet – unless something unexpected prevents.

Could you look up Gordon Gardiner 12 Queen Ann[e]'s Gate – in our name, so to speak. He has been rather seedy – but should he be able bring him along if you can. You would not mind giving him up the best spare room.

Of course this is only a suggestion.

Drop us a line

Our love

Yours

J. Conrad.

To Thomas J. Wise
Text MS BL Ashley A. 4789; Unpublished

[letterhead: Oswalds]

23 Nov. '21

Dear Mr Wise.

Thanks for the cheque.

Herewith the copy of play for Mr Spoor,[1] together with the 1st Copy of B of Job which I return with many thanks.

Would you tell me as an expert whether I may hope to sell say 35 copies[2] (there will be only that number for sale) in bulk to a bookseller at £5 a piece?

---

[1] John A. Spoor (1851–1926), Chairman of the Board, Chicago Junction Railway Co. and Union Stock Yard and Transit Co., amassed a major collection of books and manuscripts, with a concentration on English nineteenth-century poetry and essays. In touch with English dealers and bibliophiles, he purchased various Conrad items from Wise.

[2] Of the dramatic version of *The Secret Agent* (see the letter to Eric Pinker of 25 March 1922).

I want to know for my guidance in instructing P.
Kind regards

Yours

J Conrad.

To J. B. Pinker

Text MS Berg; Unpublished

[letterhead: Oswalds]
[26? November 1921][1]

Dear J B.

I am truly glad Everett likes the idea of joint publication – his pictures and my Mirror.

Would you get a copy from Meth: (crown 8vo) and if you judge fit present it to him when he calls on you. For if we are to have a personal interview (which is also left to your judgment) it would be well if he had read the book before we sit down together amicably to make a selection – 12 or 18 big ones let me say. The little studies (in dock) of the hull must also be included. They are admirable in feeling. He probably has many more than we have seen. The three I am thinking of are all of the same ship at slightly different angles. Then the anchors. In one of his bigger paintings he has a wonderful one (part of) lashed down. I imagine he must have some drawings of a forecastle-head as at sea. Would do for my "Emblems" section. If that man has not *seen* an anchor then nobody has seen an anchor. The question of reproduction is a very solemn one – I leave it to your piety.

Thanks for all you say. I have just paid a doctors bill for £62.8.0 and have felt the "nip" severely. I ought to have been prepared better. However but for Jessies portrait[2] and the new suit I had (God only knows why) in the summer it would have been all right. But I've had some other nips too – pump dynamos and other things about the house and the London visit – which made things crack all round me. Very stupid all this on my part. So I will be very glad. Will you please hold for a moment till I ascertain what reasonable expectations can be had as to the disposal of the 35 copies.

In connection with this I am sending you a set of Wise proofs which can be made use of (for business purposes). Also I could send you one copy out of my lot, and there is a good typed copy here. That would give us 3 copies for chucking around where they may do good. (The typed copy *is* a *good* one.) I enclose it here anyhow. Of course I have no objection to keeping back the

---

[1] The letter to Everett of the 26th suggests either that date or a day or so before it.

[2] By A. S. Kinkead. It was then on view in her show at the United Arts Gallery.

5 if you think necessary in addition to the above. Of course they would look valuable and may please the other parties.

I am sending you also *one* clean copy of the *B[ook] of Job*. (of the two I received yesterday.) If I remember rightly you had no copy of that for England. There was only the one in America.

Ever Yours

J. Conrad.

Had a note from Northcliffe (Borneo). Just friendly with his regards to my "sweet lady". Thereupon Jessie assumed the Daisy Ashford smile[1] – but she is not unduly puffed up and sends you her love all the same.

To John Everett
Text TS Private collection; Unpublished

[letterhead: Oswalds]

Nov. 26th. 1921.

Dear Mr Everett.[2]

I have asked J. B. Pinker to send you a copy of "The Mirror of the Sea" and have heard from him to-day that you intend to call on him shortly. Therefore I conclude that the book commends itself to you for the association of your art with my prose. It will give me the greatest possible pleasure.

The scheme presents itself to me distinctly as association. In my mind it has nothing to do with illustration so-called. It would be simply your vision of the sea and ships and mine between the covers of the same book.

I don't know how many pictures you may have apart from those photographs dear Rothenstein sent to me for my delectation and which I returned to your address direct. I have been profoundly moved by your beautiful, inspired renderings of the realities we both know, and I only wish it were possible to include them all in the book; but we will have to take account of

---

[1] One of the great successes of the 1919 literary season was *The Young Visiters* by Daisy Ashford. This was the work of a nine-year-old girl with a fondness for romantic stories and a gift for creative misspelling, submitted to the public by her older self, Mrs George Norman (1881–1972). Chatto & Windus published it with a preface by J. M. Barrie, widely but falsely suspected of being the real author. Conrad alludes to the frontispiece of Mrs Norman as a girl. Barrie says of it: 'it has an air of careless power; there is a complacency about it that by the severe might perhaps be called smugness. It needs no effort for that face to knock off a masterpiece.'

[2] (Herbert Barnard) John Everett (1876–1949), marine and landscape painter and engraver, studied at the Slade School of Art and was a friend of Augustus John and William Orpen, who lodged in his mother's house. Conrad, who came to know Everett's drawings through Will Rothenstein, was keenly interested in publishing an edition of *The Mirror of the Sea* illustrated with them, but the project fell through. Everett sold none of his marine work, bequeathing all of it to the National Maritime Museum. For an example of his work, see Plate 3.

the limitations of size and cost of production: matters which I, for my part, must leave to J. B. Pinker in consultation with you. I will only say here that whatever engagement he enters into in my name will be agreed to by me. The necessary negociations with Methuens who hold the copyright must be left to him.

All this being settled a selection will have to be made. But apart from the full page reproductions I would suggest that use should be made also of small drawings for head and tail pieces for the different sections: such as your admirable studies of hulls, or of a ship's interior, nooks of the deck and even single pieces such as anchors, capstans and so on. At sea more than anywhere there is a soul in things. They have an emphatic character of their own which you more than any other man have seen with a penetrating vision. I am certain you could give a particular character to a pair of mooring-bits.[1]

I trust that as soon as the business side is arranged with Methuen we will be able to meet and talk the matter over. I am sorry to say I am not always in a fit state to come up to town, but I hope we may have the great pleasure of seeing you here before long and then we will settle the details.

Believe me very faithfully Yours

Joseph Conrad.

To J. B. Pinker
Text TS/MS Berg; Unpublished

Oswalds,
Bishopsbourne,
Kent.
Nov. 28th. 1921.

Dearest J B

In the matter of the privately printed collection, going by what I hear from R. C[urle] (who was here for the weekend), I would be quite satisfied to sell at the rate of £5 a copy, whatever number you will dispose of with due regard to our possible requirements. It occurs to me however that there is sure to be a request for signatures. I will of course sign as many as you may arrange for, either now or at some future time – if you decide to get rid of them gradually. I would even have no objection to sign them all (since I have done that thing already for Jessie's lot).

This morning I received one copy of the 3/6 edition of A[rrow] of G[old] from Fisher Unwin. Binding quite good in its way, but the paper looks very inferior.

---

[1] Timber or metal posts to secure an anchor cable.

Borys arrived late on Saturday and went away on Sunday. Last Wednesday he was asked suddenly whether he would take charge at once of the Autoveyor's depot and workshop, without waiting to know the exact terms which will be fixed at a Board meeting this week. He thought it best to say he would, providing that his position vis a vis of Ketley was made perfectly clear and that he would have a free hand as promised. These conditions were acceded to, Ketley being told in his presence that his reign was over. Borys went over and took charge at one o'clock that day. He suggested however that since he is taking over an establishment which has shown a loss for the last twenty months the commission to him should be paid on the turnover, not on the profits, which he told the directors he could not be certain to show on the first year's working. That was agreed to, also, verbally by the directors, Barton and Cook. The only points that were not mentioned were the actual amounts of salary and percentage which the meeting will fix in the course of this week. He thought, I think justly, that he couldn't very well raise that point. After all, he said to me, it's bound to be an improvement on the present situation; and even should the terms be disappointing to a certain extent he could always propose to have them reconsidered later on, after showing what he could do. It occurred to me that if there is a formal agreement he may be bound to them for a certain time; but I didn't say anything, as it may not be the case, and, whatever may happen, the position is the one which he was very anxious to get. On taking charge on Wednesday he began by closing the place to clear up the mess, as he expressed it, which, he says, the store-keeper, the mechanic and himself have managed to do by working late every day. It will be open in the usual way this morning and he assured me that he is very confident to have no loss on the next year's working. He also told me he would like to see you either Thursday or Friday of this week.

You will have seen McKinnel's letter by this.[1] I acknowledged it to him with an expression of regret and no more and so the chapter is closed; but I don't think the tale is. You will no doubt go on with it and I am curious to see how it will end.

Our love to you

Yours ever

J. Conrad.

I dropped a few lines to Everett to the effect that whatever you may arrange with him will be binding on me – and expressing generally my high appreciation of his work.

---

[1] He evidently told Conrad that he was abandoning his plans to stage *The Secret Agent*.

To J. B. Pinker
Text MS Berg; Unpublished

[Oswalds]
Monday. [28 November? 1921][1]

Dearest J. B.

The typed letter is so written to be shown to the parties who will have the thing in hand.

R[alph] says you are looking well. Jessie told me that you cannot just yet give us a date for your visit here. I advise you that G. Gardiner (unless ill) may turn up for the next week end. Hope this won't stop you tho'. Only we would like to know beforehand on acct of bedroom arrangements.

Our love

Ever yours

J. C.

To J. B. Pinker
Text MS Berg; Unpublished

[Oswalds]
[28 November? 1921][2]

Dear J B.

Herewith the letter. I quite understand what's happened or at least I think I do.

Ever Yours

J. C.

To William Rothenstein
Text MS Indiana; Unpublished

[letterhead: Oswalds]
28.11.21.

Cher Maître.[3]

Many thanks for your letter with the copies of the "Catalog" (new spelling).[4]

---

[1] Catalogued with the November 1921 letters. Conrad wrote to Pinker on the 7th, 14th, and 21st, although more than one communication on those dates is possible. Mention of Gardiner's health on the 23rd, however, suggests either the 21st or 28th; support for the latter is offered by the letter to Pinker of 1 December, which mentions a date for the proposed visit.

[2] Catalogued with the November 1921 letters. An enclosure with the previous letter?

[3] This letter is about Rothenstein's current show at the Alpine Club Gallery.

[4] Observing the principles of the Simplified Spelling Society, founded in 1908.

I did wish, and I hoped, to be able to run up. But it is no use. I can't shake off the trouble and I feel as seedy as ever.

Our love to you all

Yours ever

J. Conrad

To John Livingston Lowes

Text TS/MS Harvard; Lowes 564–5 (in part)

[letterhead: Oswalds]
Nov. 29th. 1921.

Dear Mr Lowes.[1]

You ask whether the tale the summary of which you sent me is one of the usual sailors' yarns. That it certainly is not. The so-called sailors's yarn proper is never concerned with the supernatural.[2] A sailors' folk lore is to me an inconceivable thing. The only legend that is authentic of which I ever heard and which is referred currently in sailors' talk (or at any rate before the sailors became mere deckhands of mechanically propelled vessels) is the tale of the Flying Dutchman,[3] of the historical origin of which I know nothing, except that it must have arisen after the discovery of the Cape of Storms. That the phantom ship should be a Dutchman and not a Portuguese is a curious fact testifying to the preponderance of Dutch shipping on the Southern tracks.

The narrative of the Norwegian sailor can not be judged on the sort of thing you have sent me, which is a bare statement.[4] The manner of telling alone would reveal whether the tale had the nature of a legend or was merely

---

[1] John Livingston Lowes (1867–1945), educated at Harvard, Oxford, and in Germany, taught at various American universities before becoming Professor of English at Harvard where he taught from 1918 to 1939. A specialist in poetry, he was particularly interested in Chaucer and the Romantics, his best-known book being *The Road to Xanadu* (1927), a study of the sources of Coleridge's *The Rime of the Ancient Mariner*.

[2] Five of Conrad's own fictions, *The Nigger of the 'Narcissus'*, 'The Inn of the Two Witches', 'The Brute', 'The Black Mate', and *The Shadow-Line* connect the maritime with the supernatural. *Nostromo* and 'Karain' also bear uncanny traces, and some interpreters would add 'The Secret Sharer' to the list.

[3] An old legend given currency by Edward Fitz-Ball's nautical drama *The Flying Dutchman* (1827), Frederick Marryat's novel *The Phantom Ship* (1839), and Richard Wagner's operatic version, *Der fliegende Hollander* (1843).

[4] The Norwegian sailor's tale, recounted to a German ship's boy, concerned a voyage in 1915 off Argentina, the killing of an albatross, and the death of the crew. See Lowes's *The Road to Xanadu* (1927), p. 563.

a patchwork. There would be characteristic touches and turns of phrase which would give a particular physiognomy and a genuine atmosphere. In such cases bare facts are nothing. The manner of wrecking, through a nip of ice floes, would point to a whaler's legend. There is a true realistic touch in the body of the albatross not being found, for that is what most likely would have happened if a bird were shot over an expanse of hummocky ice. But the albatross being there at all is absurd, since albatrosses keep to open water on the northern limits of anything resembling field ice. In a genuine whaler's story the bird would certainly be some kind of gull, which breed far south. The instance of a ship, (I think a sealing schooner) being found frozen-in with all the crew dead on board is genuine enough and is sometimes mentioned amongst sailors.

The rest doesn't seem to me genuine. Of course I don't know what legends may be current amongst Norwegian sailors but the whole thing with the man *nailed* to the mast and the apparently unrelated circumstance of a *priest* being on board the boat, with the vague touch of spirituality it connotes, seems to me a shore fabrication and may appertain to some old legend current on some Northern coast.

Believe me very faithfully

Yours

Joseph Conrad.

Dear old Coleridge invented the Albatross of that tale.[1] There can be no doubt of that. The indifference of the animated corpses to the living people resembles the indifference of the secular ghosts in the overgrown ship in E. A. Poe's impressive version of the Flying Dutchman ("MS Found in a Bottle").[2] A very fine piece of work – about as fine as anything of that kind can be – and so authentic in detail that it might have been told by a sailor of a sombre and poetical genius in the invention of the phantastic.

---

[1]   *The Rime of the Ancient Mariner* (1798).
[2]   The narrator of Poe's tale, first published in 1831, is a rationalist swept up in the uncanny and sublime. On a voyage through the Malay Archipelago, he experiences an eerie calm followed by a deadly storm and a collision with a titanic ship into whose rigging he is thrown. He is invisible to the aged crew, who are bent on sailing their vessel (bearing a strong resemblance to the *Flying Dutchman*) ever southward. At last they reach an enormous whirlpool at the South Pole, where everything save the MS in the bottle founders. Poe balances the sublimity with a precise deployment of maritime language.

To Karola Zagórska
Text MS copy Yale;[1] Najder 275

Oswalds,
29.XI.21.

My dear Karolcia,

I have been rather seedy this autumn. What bothers me most is the difficulty I have working – whole days with nothing done! One needs courage to look into the future calmly. I would like to know, my dear, if your health is improving. Have you received the book (*Notes on Life & Letters*) that was sent c/o the consulate?

I am sending you *Arrow of Gold* in the new cheap edition[2] which is none the less very attractive; and *Youth* – small-size edition – on bad paper but the print is quite good.[3] *Typhoon* is out of print at the moment.

With us nothing has changed. Borys is working in London and likes his job very much. John is at school; he is working at his best and is liked by everybody. He has a formidable appetite which, however, does not make him put on weight. Jessie is taking a good deal of exercise but it is impossible for her to claim to be slim. One of my hands (the left) is in a sling, but it doesn't matter since for the last week my work has gone well. That is all for the moment, my dear.

Ever yours affectionately

Konrad.

To Warrington Dawson
Text MS Duke; Randall 204–5

[letterhead: Oswalds]
30 Nov. 21

Mon très cher.

Now I have absorbed it I send you my thanks for the gift of Paul Clermont.[4] It is a very charming and touching performance which one likes more the deeper one gets into it. The development of the boy is done with masterly simplicity as to means. The war part is certainly very fine and deeply moving in its economy of sentiment and charm of expression. Indeed the whole my dearest Dawson is beautifully written. The descriptions of the country are

---

[1] In French.   [2] Unwin's first edition was sold at 8s, its recent reissue at 3s 6d.
[3] Presumably the 2s Popular Edition issued in June 1919.
[4] *The Gift of Paul Clermont* (1921), a novel drawing on Dawson's experiences in war-time France when serving as an aide to the US ambassador. Paul Clermont, a young Frenchman who dies in battle, is close friends with an American, Henry Aubret.

bien senties.[1] And what is wonderful in a book with so many people in it, every single character comes off as a creation. They live.

My congratulations. I won't go into details now; but France has in you a wonderful friend – that is one strong general impression amongst others. The fact of the dedication to Joffre[2] pleased me very much.

I exist wearily, work with difficulty and am not having a good time – so to speak. The bright spot is Jessie's recovery after years of trouble. We talk of you often and think of you always with affection and sympathy.

Believe [me] my dear friend ever Yours

Joseph Conrad.

Jessie's dear love.

To J. B. Pinker
Text TS/MS Berg; Unpublished

Oswalds,

Bishopsbourne,

Kent.

Dec. 1st. 1921.

Dearest J. B.

Dealing with the most important part of your letter first – we will be delighted to see you here on the 9th or any day you may fix. I haven't been out much since you saw me last, and at the present time I have my left hand still tied up. As long as that lasts I will be feeling seedy and shrink from travelling.

I have read Kommer's[3] commentary and I neither agree nor disagree with it. From a certain point of view of course he is right; and it is very obvious that the work has stirred up his imagination. I have not elaborated the anarchist part of Act I because what is there is quite enough for my purpose, which is to make clear Winnie Verloc's story. This play in my mind is not an exposé of anarchism, or a study of it, but simply a tale on the stage. Primarily – any way. For the same reason the first scene of Act II. (Ossipon – Professor) is what it is. It elucidates the situation created by the accident of the bomb and that is enough for my purpose. It amuses me to notice that Kommer doesn't

---

[1] 'Well-felt' or 'well-perceived'.
[2] Joseph-Jacques-Césaire Joffre (1852–1931), French Chief of Staff who achieved victory at the Marne, and Commander-in-Chief of the French army in 1915–16.
[3] An American theatrical agent.

find the Third Act superfluous, and wants apparently some more put into it, which would be the only way of bringing in another scene with Assist. Com. and Heat. Generally what he says is far from being stupid, but practically it amounts to a rejection and we will have to leave it at that. For even if I were to tinker at it in accordance with his ideas he would still require a performance in England.

I haven't heard from Borys this week. He must be very busy and I conclude that the fixing of terms has not taken place up till yesterday, anyhow. I am afraid I didn't report him quite correctly. He asked me whether he might venture to go and see you one day this week, about Thursday or Friday, and I assured him that you would always be willing to see him when he called; in which I see I did right.

Of course the great news of your letter is the advance with F. U[nwin] and I will be glad indeed to hear the story.[1] I suppose the man will have to be bribed in some way or other. But though I appreciate immensely your wish to refer the state of the negotiation to me, you know, my dear J. B., that I am not very likely to raise objections of a purely sentimental order. Of course I will be very glad to tell you what I think about it. But the man who bore the brunt of the fray will have to decide the conditions of peace.

I have had a very nice letter from Everett. He seems to be an artist very much wrapped up in his work and feeling deeply about it. Those men however are often very impracticable* in matters of business; though I have no reason to think you will find Everett so. It's merely a general remark. He seems to have twenty or more of the big paintings and a portfolio full of small drawings from which a selection could be made. He offers to have the rest of the paintings photographed and to bring them and the portfolio here for my inspection. He seems very much taken up with the idea, and so, in truth, am I; but I know that there is much to be done, and that *you* only can do, before it becomes embodied.

Thanks for the cheque for £175. As I have directed Goulden to send the acct to you will you please tell me what the agreed amount is so that I can send you my cheque for it as yours is clearly in full (35 cop. at £5 each).

I have looked again at Kommer's letter. The best and really the only answer to it is that the play was written for an English audience.

Our love to you

Ever Yours

J. Conrad.

---

[1] The plan to bring out Conrad's first books in a popular edition? Dent took over this project.

To Ford Madox Ford

Text MS Yale; Unpublished

[letterhead: Oswalds]
6. Dec 21.

My dear Ford.

I regret the delay; but I have been too horribly seedy for weeks to investigate the matter to any purpose. So for the present I will not say anything more about it. Have you no document connected with it? Thinking hard about it I fancy I may owe you still something.[1] At any rate I enclose here £20. I have done no paying work so to speak for the last 2 years and this is all which in any case I could do at once. I wont go into any explanations why it is so – which I suppose you would not demand from me.

I have got to keep indoors just now but later perhaps we could arrange a meeting in town.

Yours

J Conrad

Please if you want to acknowledge this to address (in type) to Miss Hallowes here.

To R. B. Cunninghame Graham

Text MS Dartmouth; J-A, 2, 263 (in part);[2] Watts (1969) 191–2

[letterhead: Oswalds]
6. Dec 21

Très cher ami

I ought to have written to you long before this to thank you for the letter[3] you sent me from Scotland. You must forgive me for not telling you at once how deeply I felt every word of it. It would not have been an easy task and I do not know that I can do it at all.

Ever since I saw you in London I have been seedy and often in pain; which I would not mind much but for the depression (consequent on the inability to work seriously) – which I can not somehow shake off. Your letter so full

---

[1] Buying livestock for his small farm, where he lived with Stella Bowen, and trying to deal with the financial aftermath of his long liaison with Violet Hunt, Ford was short of money. Neither Ford nor Conrad ever seemed able to work out how much the latter owed the former, but some of the debts seemed to go back either to the period of leasing Pent Farm (1898–1907) or to the early days of the *English Review* (1908).

[2] Jean-Aubry omits the postscript.   [3] Of 13 November (Stape and Knowles, pp. 188–9).

of friendship and appreciation was a great moral tonic. I am glad that those two early works had kept enough of their quality to bring me such a letter from you.[1] Their existence is just as old as our friendship;[2] and I can assure you that I never wrote a book since without many mental references to you of whom alone almost amongst my readers I always thought that *He* will understand.

You have been one of my moral supports through my writing life; and this latest letter I had from you made me happy in a particular way. To write it was a true friend's thought.

Yours with the greatest affection

J Conrad

PS. Jessie sends her love and begs you to give her love to Mrs Dummett in which I humbly associate myself

To Holbrook Jackson
Text MS Lubbock; Unpublished

[letterhead: Oswalds]

8. Dec 21.

Dear Mr Holbrook Jackson[3]

Very many thanks for Your little journal containing Your fine essay addressed if I may say so, to me.[4]

It is very delightful to be remembered like this. The little To-Day looks a very charming thing. My best wishes for Your success, health and happiness.

Believe me

Yours

J. Conrad.

---

[1] On a cold November day in the west of Scotland, Graham had been gripped by a rereading of *Almayer's Folly* and *An Outcast of the Islands*. He told Conrad: 'If good wine gets better with years, so have these two books.'

[2] Their friendship began in August 1897, when Graham sent Conrad a letter praising 'An Outpost of Progress'; see *Letters*, 1, pp. 369–70.

[3] Editor, literary journalist, and bibliophile (George Henry) Holbrook Jackson (1874–1948) was particularly involved with *T. P.'s Weekly* (where *Nostromo* first appeared) and edited *To-day*. As well as verse and essays, he wrote studies of the 1890s, of Edward Fitzgerald, and Bernard Shaw, and published a biography of William Morris.

[4] 'Ships and the Sea', *To-Day*, 8, no. 48 (December 1921), 219–22, dedicated to Conrad. Jackson often mentioned Conrad in *To-Day*, and in 1919 (5, no. 26, 43–9) devoted an article to him.

To J. B. Pinker
Text MS Berg; Unpublished

[letterhead: Oswalds]
9. Dec. 1921

Dearest J. B.

We are sorry to hear of you being laid-up. My impulse was to come over but first I did not know how you would feel about a visitor.

Do let us know how you are getting on.

I wonder whether you heard yet from the man whose letter I enclose.

Our dear love to You and the Family

Ever Yours

J. C.

To Bruno Winawer
Text TS copy Yale; *Głos* (108); Najder 275–6[1]

Oswalds,
Bishopsbourne,
Kent.
9. Dec. 21

My dear Sir.

Many thanks for the Monomachia.[2] I like the way it is illustrated. C'est tout-à-fait bien.[3] The pattern-scheme of these little pictures, their colour and details are most interesting and entertaining. I am glad to have this attractive Polish publication; moreover, the quality of the paper and typography are faultless.

Your favourable opinion of my play pleased me a lot. No doubt, Vous y mettez beaucoup d'indulgence[4] but I cannot really quarrel with you about it. Pray accept a cordial handshake – sans phrases.[5]

The division of labour between Aniela and yourself[6] strikes me as an excellent idea. Most likely the first performance will take place on the Polish stage as just a week ago Norman McKinnel returned the MS. to me. I have asked Pinker to put it into a drawer for the time being. I am sorry not to have anything to say about our business.[7]

---

[1] Translation from Najder with minor alterations.
[2] A mock-heroic poem by Bishop Ignacy Krasicki (1735–1801), reprinted in 1921 with illustrations by Zofia Stryjeńska.
[3] 'It's altogether well done.'   [4] 'You are very indulgent towards it'.
[5] 'Without further ado'.   [6] On translating the stage version of *The Secret Agent*.
[7] Placing *The Book of Job*.

My best wishes to you for Christmas, for the new year and for many years to come.

Bien à Vous

J. Conrad.

To Thomas J. Wise
Text MS BL Ashley 2953; Unpublished

[letterhead: Oswalds]
13.12.21.

Dear Mr Wise.

I have signed the two books you have sent me. As I have written something in other 1st Ed^{on} copies which you have acquired previously I had some difficulty in finding what I could say in these without repeating myself. I've done my best. But from the nature of things they can not have the same interest. It is a pity that the "best state" copies can not now have the most material notes.

If you want me to write something in all the other copies you have bought lately perhaps it would be just as well to reproduce simply the notes written in your earlier acquired copies of the same works. If you send me more please say what you think of this suggestion. You must have now a double set.

I had a letter from R. Curle lately in which he mentions that you want to print "The Black Mate" in booklet form.[1] I suppose you have the text of it in some form. I haven't. Neither do I remember where that thing was serialised.[2] Would you be prepared to print (on the condition you mention) 30 cop. and let me have 8 of them?

Believe me yours faithfully

Joseph Conrad.

To Aniela Zagórska
Text MS copy Yale;[3] Najder 276–7

Oswalds,
14.12.21.

My dear Aniela

I read with pleasure your letter which reached me two days ago. You can imagine how glad I am that you like my play. I am relieved that the translation of Almayer has already been decided on. I am sure your translation is excellent. J'ai beaucoup de confiance dans votre tempérament et le tour

---

[1] Wise issued the story in 1922 as a privately printed pamphlet limited to fifty copies. It was printed by the Dunedin Press, Edinburgh.
[2] The *London Magazine* in April 1908.   [3] In French.

particulier de votre esprit m'est infiniment sympathique.[1] And I have always felt you understood me. The clearest proof of it was the good letter you sent me after reading "Notes on Life and Letters." It is difficult for me to express how happy it made me.

We still haven't thanked you for your portrait. What sort of people we are – simply shocking! C'est un très beau dessin – vision d'un artiste;[2] but the resemblance is not striking. In my memory you look different. Perhaps after looking at it longer I will understand better what Kamieński wanted to express. Allow me to kiss you on both cheeks for this gift which is none the less precious.

I am very pleased you liked Mr Winawer. I was unsure how your meeting would turn out. I was afraid something might not be to your liking. Men don't always resemble their work. The project of a joint translation pleases me a good deal. Pray, my dear, remember me to Mr Żeromski and give him my deepest respect and affection. C'est un Maître! And the impression his personality made has not disappeared from my memory.[3] At times I see and hear him.

We send you best wishes of the season.

Very affectionately yours

Konrad.

To Ford Madox Ford

Text MS Yale; Keating 358

[Oswalds]
15. Dec 21

My dear Ford

Thanks for your letter and enclosure.

The novel I am writing (very slowly) now has nothing to do with the Restoration[4] – or anything so reasonable as that. The date is Jan. Febr. 1815, but all the action takes place in Genoa and thereabouts and does not touch upon affairs in France except in the most distant way. It ends with Nap[oleon]'s departure from Elba.

---

[1] 'I have a good deal of confidence in your temperament and the individual cast of your mind is wholly sympathetic to me.'
[2] 'It is a very fine drawing – the vision of an artist'.
[3] They had met during the Conrads' visit to Poland in 1914. For Conrad's reservations about his work, see the letter to Garnett of 2 September.
[4] That is, the restoration of the monarchy in France after the Revolution.

We can't possibly clash.[1]

I am not surprised at you turning Cincin[n]atus.[2] You had always a love for Mother Earth. The first time I set eyes on you was in your potato-patch. Tempi passati![3]

Yours

J. Conrad.

To J. B. Pinker

Text MS Berg; Unpublished

[letterhead: Oswalds]
15.12.21

Dearest J. B.

Somehow or other I gathered from R[alph] the impression that you were well enough to be in town all the week. It's quite a shock to hear you are still imprisoned. If you don't mend soon I will have to come and prescribe for you. My dear I am quite anxious to see you but really directly I put my nose out of doors I get a most dreadful cough (no doubt of a gouty nature) and a swollen joint. I get so tired with it or of it – I don't know which – that I can't work. And just now I want to go on. So I won't risk a run this week, and perhaps the next I'll feel more fit.

Our dear love to all your house

Ever Yours

J. C.

To Richard Curle

Text MS Indiana; Curle 84

[Oswalds]
16.12.21

Dear Richard.

Perhaps I misdirected the short note I wrote some days ago proposing You should come to us on Saturday 24th for dinner an[d] stay till Wedy morning.

---

[1] Ford's Napoleonic interests led to *A Little Less than Gods* (1928).

[2] In September 1920, Ford had taken up residence at Cooper's Cottage, Bedham, Sussex, a 300-year-old house on ten acres, and hoped to make money from selling pedigree pigs, eggs, garden produce, and firewood. Lucius Quinctius Cincinnatus (*c.* 519 BC), a farmer turned general and politician, returned to his farm after saving Rome.

[3] 'Times gone by!' They met at Grace's Cottage, Limpsfield, Surrey, in autumn 1898. Conrad mistook Ford, who liked to dress in rustic smock and gaiters, for the gardener. See Saunders, 1, pp. 99, 101, and Ford Madox Ford, *Return to Yesterday* (Gollancz, 1931), p. 52.

Jessie however wants You to come on Sat for *lunch* and I have wired You to-day to that effect. This confirms it. So we shall expect you then. Should the car not be there (par force majeure) You must take a taxi. But I'll try to get it there in time.

Au revoir.

Ever Yours

J. Conrad

To E. L. Sanderson

Text MS Yale; Unpublished

[letterhead: Oswalds]
16.12.21.

Dearest Ted.

Thank you for your dear good letter. The promise of a visit from Helen & you is the best thing in it.

Send me my dear fellow your address (to be) in Rye. Now you dear People are coming so near no wild horses should keep us apart – though a lame car might.

May all the blessings of peace and content descend on you and all yours. Our dear love to you all

Ever Yours

Joseph Conrad.

To J. B. Pinker

Text TS Berg; Unpublished

Oswalds,
Bishopsbourne,
Kent.
Dec. 19th. 1921.

Dearest J. B.

I was delighted to get the holograph statement of your improved condition. Therefore I won't disclose the nature of the prescription which I would have made for you, lest you should think that it is worse than the disease. I do hope however that you will be careful not to start for the U.S. in February unless you feel really pre-war fit.

On the point of copy. You shall certainly have "The Rover" to take with you, and I will tell you frankly now that I will try to make that tale as long as possible, within the long short-story limits, for the practical reason that by itself it may fill up the volume of short stories up to the proper market capacity. Of course, I wouldn't spoil it for that object.

Thirty thousand words would of course approach the short serial size, that is, six instal. of five thou. each. More of course it will not be; but since I am now committed to finish it right off I am afraid I will not be able to add very much to the text (as written up to now) of the long novel.[1]

I wanted to answer you on those two points at once, but as to talking them over we will do that, together with other things, when I come to Burys Court, as you kindly ask me to do next Saturday week.

John is coming home to-morrow and on Wednesday we are going to the Watsons, where Sir Robert will be staying.[2] Dr Reid is sending him a report about Jessie. Everything is not well there and it's only Bobbie who can say distinctly whether anything more can be done.

Our dear love to you all

Ever Yours

J. Conrad.

To J. B. Pinker

Text MS Berg; Unpublished

[letterhead: Oswalds]
Tuesday. [20 December 1921][3]

Dear J B.

Eric on sending me the month's balance did not deduct anything for the extra £20 sent to Karola. I was going to send him £10 this month; but if you don't mind it would be more convenient for me if the deductions were made in *Jan & Febr*ʸ so that on each of these months you will send me £199.15. instead of 209.15.0

The worst is that like a dam' fool I forgot to write to Eric – so he must be wondering what sort of lunacy I am suffering from. Pray explain to him with proper apologies.

Yours Ever

J. Conrad

---

[1] *Suspense*, now laid aside for *The Rover*, begun in October as a short story.
[2] In Seddlescombe, Sussex.
[3] If payment to Karola Zagórska was made as arranged on the 15th (see 22 November), this is the likely Tuesday.

To Thomas J. Wise

Text MS BL Ashley 2953; Unpublished

[Oswalds]
20.12.21.

My dear Mr Wise.

You have all my sympathy in the loss of an old friend throwing such a dark shadow on this season of good wishes.

Pray be assured of mine for Mrs Wise and yourself, of the warmest kind.

I note all you are good enough to say in your letter. I am of course quite ready to inscribe all the copies you may feel inclined to send me.

The matter of the Black Mate may stand over till you are at liberty to consider it. Curle is coming here for the week-end.

My wife joins me in Xmas greetings and regards.

Yours

J. Conrad.

To Edward Garnett

Text MS Indiana; G. 310–11

[letterhead: Oswalds]
22.12.21

Dearest Edward.

Many thanks for your letter,[1] which moved me deeply with the sense of your affection continued for so many years.

I am grieved to learn that you have not had your copy of *Notes on L & L.* Miss H[allowes] waved in my face a list of names where your name stands first with a cross against it and the letter (E) after it – meaning an English ed. copy sent! There must be a special devil with a mission to make trouble between us. As you know the Jewish God (under whom You and I were born) is not always direct in his methods. It would have been simpler to put hatred into our hearts without all that low intriguing. But I always suspected him of being a Futile Person.

I haven't a copy at this moment in the house – but you shall have one before the year is out. Your suspicion of Pawling is not justified I think. I believe he really meant to have that dedication page put in.[2] He had also reminders – because I know that *I* did mean it. And now it is done!

---

[1] Of 17 December (Stape and Knowles, pp. 189–90).
[2] See the letter to Garnett of 6 January 1921.

Our best wishes my dear Edward. In this world where the seasons of curses and congratulations are still ruled by the Jewish God it is not prudent to be more precise – at least for us incorrigible Gentiles.

But I commend you to The Merciful, The Compassionate[1] – the same whom I would like to look on me at times. Of course I know He can't do much. Still . . .

Give my best regards to your wife and my congratulations on the triumphant achievement of Dost:[2] and my season's greetings to David.

Ever affect^{ly} yours

J. Conrad

To J. B. Pinker
Text MS Berg; Unpublished

[Oswalds]
Tuesday.
27.12.21.

Dearest J B.

We drank your wine to your health on Xmas eve. Many thanks for the treat.

I have been coughing my life half out these last 5 days. I feel utterly exhausted. Altogether this was not a lucky time. We went on Wednesday last to see Sir Robert and had a beastly mishap – the cog of the middle gear being smashed and the lay-shaft[3] bent. Had to hire to get back. Our car however limped home late after us. B[orys] effected temporary repairs and is taking her to town himself to-day to put in new gear and new shaft. All this spells ruin. You may all the same expect me in your office on Friday when I shall put myself into your hands to be taken to Burys Court – haven of refuge – till Monday, if I may.

I think Jessie will deposit me at your office door about 3–3.30.

My love to You all

Yours

J. C.

---

[1] The Koranic invocation that also ends *Almayer's Folly*.
[2] Constance Garnett's translations of Dostoevsky, now published by Heinemann in twelve volumes as *The Works of Fyodor Dostoevsky*.
[3] The secondary shaft in the gear-box.

To Michael Holland

Text MS Private collection; Unpublished

Oswalds
Bishopsbourne
Kent.
28.12.21.

My dear Holland

Many thanks for the book which has given me the greatest pleasure. I have always had a great admiration for Sir Alfred[1] whose verse and prose appeal strongly to my mind and feelings.

Anxious as we are to see you all in your Sussex home I do not think we could run over just yet. I can't shake off my cough and Jessie too has got to be careful how she exposes herself to the weather. Borys has asked me to thank you warmly for your invitation but he has just taken the management of the Autoveyors C° service depot, is enlarging and altering it and has to work late on Saturday and be early on the spot on Monday. When he has set the thing going he will have a little more leisure.

With our love to you all

Ever Yours

J. Conrad

---

[1] Alfred Comyn Lyall (1835–1911; knighted 1881), a civil servant in India, wrote on history, India, and literature. He also produced biographies of Warren Hastings and the Marquis of Dufferin and Ava, a critical study of Tennyson, who was a personal friend, and *Verses Written in India* (1889).

1922

To G. Jean-Aubry

Text MS Yale; *L.fr.* 166–7[1]

[letterhead: Oswalds]

3. Jan 22

Très cher ami.

Nous sommes rentrés hier ma femme de Londres et moi de Burys Court.

Nous sommes véritablement désolés de ne pas Vous voir chez nous, tout-de-suite, ce week-end même. Mais que voulez Vous? Le gros Walpole c'est* invité il y a un mois!

Pouvez Vous venir pour le w-end suivant?

Ma santé ne vas* pas trop. Jessie n'a pas trop bonne mine aussi. Mais B[orys] va bien et a pris la gérance du "service depot" des Autoveyors; et Jean a apporté un excellent certificat de l'école.

Je garde les autres nouvelles pour Votre visite. Mon très cher je suis ébloui par la nouvelle de l'article international![2] Votre amitié est toujours en éveil toujours agissante. Elle s'est donné pour tâche de me faire un[e] belle fin de vie littéraire.

Je vous embrasse bien tendrement.

Vôtre

Conrad.

Jessies and John's love and wishes for a happy new year in which I join.

Translation

My very dear friend.

We got back yesterday – my wife from London, myself from Burys Court.

We are truly sorry not to see you here right away – this week-end even. But what can one do? That stout Walpole invited himself a month ago!

Could you come down for the following week-end?

My health isn't very good. And Jessie doesn't look well either. But B is doing well and has taken over managing the Autoveyors' service depot, and John has brought back an excellent school report.

I keep other news for your visit. My dear, the news of the international article overwhelms me! Your friendship is always alert and active. It has assigned itself the task of giving a fine conclusion to my literary life.

I embrace you most tenderly.

Yours

Conrad

---

[1] Jean-Aubry omits the postscript.   [2] See the letter to Pinker of the 4th.

To J. B. Pinker

Text MS Berg; Unpublished

[Oswalds]
Tuesday 3^{d}. Jan '22

Dearest J. B.

I enclose you here a letter from Cecil Roberts[1] which will speak for itself. I found it on my arrival home.

I will only acknowledge it to him in a friendly way this evening. As he says: "in a few weeks", perhaps *The Rover* could be placed in Eng^{d} as he suggests in the character of a Short Serial. You could hitch up before leaving[2] (and complete on your return) with those people. That is if you think it worth while.

You would oblige me infinitely if you would advance me now £33 (or say 35) of my next monthly balance. It is to pay rates[3] now overdue. The money for it was eaten up by the car-repairs which I had to pay cash for as I had all the materials at trade price. That would reduce the net 15th Jany payment from £199–15 to £164.15.

Of course I have still a balance but after sending the rate-cheque to night I wont have quite enough left for current wages, or any small disbursements.

Our love to you

Ever Yrs

J. C.

To Cecil Roberts

Text MS Churchill; Unpublished

[letterhead: Oswalds]
3. Jan '22

My dear Mr Roberts.[4]

I am sorry to hear you had a bad time with your health; but it was a great pleasure to be told of the remarkable success of your play.[5] May health and prosperity attend you through long years.

---

[1] Of the 2nd (Stape and Knowles, p. 191), expressing an interest in serialising *The Rover* in the *Westminster Gazette*. For Roberts, see the next letter.

[2] For New York on business towards the end of the month.

[3] Local taxes levied on householders.

[4] (Edric) Cecil (Mornington) Roberts (1892–1976) was a best-selling novelist, acclaimed playwright, and cosmopolitan *bon vivant*. Among his books were *Pilgrim Cottage* (1933) and *Victoria Four Thirty* (1937). During the First World War, he was a correspondent with the Dover Patrol, the RAF, and the Allied armies in France while doubling as literary editor of the *Liverpool Post*. Between 1920 and 1925, he edited the *Nottingham Journal*. His introduction to Conrad had come through Grace Willard.

[5] His *A Tale of Young Lovers: A Tragedy in Four Acts* had recently opened.

I have forwarded your letter to Mr Pinker. You will hear from him before long I am sure. I can say nothing as I don't know what has been done.

With kind regards from us both believe me

sincerely Yrs

J. Conrad.

To J. B. Pinker

Text MS Berg; Unpublished

[letterhead: Oswalds]
4. Jan 22

Dearest J. B.

Herewith the completed document for the insurance.

Enclosed also envelope containing some papers relating do* B[orys]'s connection with the Surrey Scient^ic C°. I dont know whether you have seen him yet – but if not I put here for your consideration that it is not a fresh transgression but an affair for which he had been lectured more than once and that what he asked for is after all a natural wish to close that chapter. For the rest I associate myself with all you have or will say for it would not do for him that father gets somebody else to say things which he would not say himself to him.

– Aubry writes me (from 11A G^t Marlboro' St. c/o J. N. Chester) that he has arranged for an article on me by him, to be published simultaneously in Spain Switzer^d Sweden. Norway and France.[1] He does not give me the date or any other details. He will be here on a visit the week end after this. Do you think it advisable to try to get the article for the US at least if not for UK too? I could say something to him if I hear from you what you think.

Our love

Ever Yours

J. C.

To J. B. Pinker

Text MS Berg; Unpublished

[Oswalds]
[7 or 8? January 1922][2]

Dearest J. B.

Perhaps R[alph] told you I was laid up again since Thursday ev^g.

---

[1] Nothing of this sort appeared in 1922.

[2] The letter of the 9th indicates that Pinker already knew of Conrad's ill-health, and thus the Thursday referred to must be the 5th. A letter on the 6th would refer to that day as 'yesterday', and hence the 7th or 8th are the only plausible dates.

Thanks ever so much for your letter. I am somewhat better. I shall have a day to-morrow with the latest pp of the novel[1] and send it to the office.

You will have altogether to take with you 239 pp of which the last eighty-two are "first draft" and will have to be typed clean the "first draft" being sent back to me – as otherwise I will have no text at all.

To J. B. Pinker
Text TS/MS Berg; Unpublished

Oswalds,
Bishopsbourne,
Kent.
Jan. 9th. 1922.

Dearest J B.

Will you please look at the enclosed Land Tax demand and tell me whether I am supposed to pay it or the ineffable Colonel.[2]

I am sending you here John's term account for settlement in due course. He rejoins the school on the 20th.

There also is his account for clothing last year, which I will ask you to pay direct to Varlet,[3] as the sum we have set out for John in the budget will cover that too.

I am heartily ashamed of myself lying in bed like this. I've had a rotten time made worse by the wordy consequences on* enforced idleness.

Jessie has just told me that you can manage to give us a day here before your departure; I am much comforted to hear that. Pray come soon. I intend to get up to-morrow and get myself fit to receive you.

Ever affec^ly Yours

J. C.

To Harold Goodburn
Text MS Moser (incomplete);[4] Unpublished

[Oswalds]
17.1.22

Dear Mr Goodburn.

Herewith the cheque with many thanks for giving your time to the boy.

I am so sorry I did not see you the last time you were here. I was

---

[1] *Suspense.*   [2] Colonel Bell.
[3] Charles Varlet, an Ashford tailor.   [4] Second page missing.

To J. B. Pinker

Text MS Berg; Unpublished

[Oswalds]

17. Jan '22

Dearest J B.

I send you the booklet[1] corrected by myself; but I am also sending you a correct type-written text to be used eventually for book form. The booklet is for your collection. I will do the same for *Prince Roman* presently and then when you come back you will let me have for a few days your copy of *The Tale* for correction.[2]

To-day I really feel more like myself again. Thanks for the cheque – advised to-day. I'll go on now with The Rover and try to make something of it.

Ever Yours

J. Conrad.

To J. B. Pinker

Text TS/MS Berg; J-A, 2, 264 (in part)[3]

Oswalds,

Bishopsbourne,

Kent.

Jan. 19th. 1922.

Dearest J. B.

Thank you very much for your good letter of this morning. I have had a bad night, I can't get rid of that spasmodic sort of cough, though I have been taking drugs and attending Fox's instructions most scrupulously. I think it is no use deluding myself any longer with the notion of being able to run up and see you in town before you depart for the States. I don't think it would be prudent on my part; the more so that I am upon the whole feeling somewhat better and can work a little. I am also comparatively free from gouty symptoms and I think I ought to nurse those good dispositions for every reason, practical and sentimental.

I would suggest you should leave to me the procuring of the "Black Mate" text. I can do that through Wise while you are away. I am surprised at the length of the thing. My feeling about it is that there will be nothing

---

[1] 'The Warrior's Soul', printed as a pamphlet in 1920. The copy is inscribed 'to J. B. P. affect[ly] from J. C. corrected in 1922' (Yale). The TS mentioned is now at Lubbock.

[2] Like the others, for a collection of short stories, in the end posthumously published as *Tales of Hearsay*.

[3] Jean-Aubry prints only the first two paragraphs.

actually disgraceful in its inclusion in my collected editions (for that is what its publication in book form would ultimately mean) but it would complicate my literary history in a sort of futile way. I don't remember whether I told you that I wrote that thing in '86 for a prize competition, started I think by Tit Bits.[1] It is an extraneous phenomenon. My literary life began privately in 1890 and publicly in 1895 with "Almayer's Folly", which is regarded generally as my very first piece of writing. However, the history of "The Black Mate," its origins etc. etc., need not be proclaimed on housetops, and "Almayer's Folly" may keep its place as my first serious work. Therefore I agree to your proposal, with the proviso that should "The Rover" turn out a longer piece of work than we anticipate, we will try to do without the "Black Mate". This on the assumption that the new volume of stories must be 60,000 words *at the very least*.

I can't tell you how wretched and cast down I am at the interruption of my work which has done away with the possibility of you taking the story with you to US.[2] It can't be done now even if I were able to do 1000w a day for the next 8 days – which really I could not be capable of doing. I noticed (after writing to you) that you have not deducted the £35 you advanced me before the 15 Jan. I am very grateful since I must settle now the Oct^er rate which is being asked for with threats. (1/2 year Oct to Mch). What with one thing and another I don't seem to have a good grip on the situation and things are as it were springing on me right and left. It makes me quite nervous. Could you my dear JB in your kindness arrange with our bank an overdraft of £100 for me. I won't use it unless I am absolutely obliged. There will be however Jessie's treatment bill which may be big (but that is finished now I think) and something will have to be done with the lighting plant. B[orys]'s estimate is £40 labour included. The alternative would be going back to lamps – but then there is the electric drain pump to work by some other means. Jessie has offered to send Audrey away but I don't want to do that yet.

Aubry was here. The article for four countries is settled but he thinks it would have too much of a continental point of view to be suitable for Am: & Eng. readers without certain alterations which he will do. Then I may translate it myself. My dear love to you all.

Ever Yours

J. Conrad

[1] Keith Carabine traces the story's complex textual history in '"The Black Mate": June–July 1886; January 1908', *The Conradian*, 13.2 (1988), 128–48.
[2] Conrad still expected to complete *The Rover* as a long short story. Most of his novels from *Lord Jim* onwards had a similar history.

To J. B. Pinker
Text MS Berg; Unpublished

[Oswalds]
Tuesday. 24.1.22

Dearest J B

I return the F. U[nwin] agreement[1] which I have studied and investigated with incredulous eyes as though it had been something more in the nature of a miracle than a mere legal instrument. Apart from you who would have thought (only 3 months ago) that such a thing would ever come to pass? A great coup, that! My most affectionate thanks my dear friend for this crowning stone of the edifice on which you have worked for so many years.

I note what you say about any eventual Reminiscences. I must tell you however that as long as the "novel" vein lasts I would not take up deliberately the other thing.[2]

I am still in bed. Simply giving what recuperative power I possess its chance. I think it good policy. But its a dreary business and I'll get up to-morrow and get hold of things downstairs.

I hope Ralph has not caught anything in this fluey house – (damn it! It's the very nest of it). Or is it some business development that keeps him at home?

I am sending you all the pp. pinned in batches.[3] Those that are to be copied are marked in *red* pencil to that effect. They are "first draft" and ought to be returned to me. The earlier batches (up to p. 158) are first copy and you have I think already a set. In that case please send mine back to me. I mean *only* if you *don't want* that lot, yourself.

I hope you are feeling fit, and look at the prospect with composure. I have made no note of the ships name. Please mention it when you write.

Yes. Let Bell have his little way with the insur*ce*.

I am writing by candlelight and in a constrained position, so I will end here with love to you and everybody.

Ever Yours

J. Conrad

I shall not fail to send title of Short Stories to Eric for transmission to F. U.

---

[1] For a collection of stories and two new novels. The agreement, signed on this date, is summarised in Hallowes.
[2] Conrad had considered extending *A Personal Record* to include more Polish reminiscences. See, for instance, *Letters*, 5, p. 20.
[3] Of *Suspense*, which Pinker was taking to New York in order to place the serial.

To Mr Miller

Text TS Private collection; Unpublished

[letterhead: Oswalds]
Jan. 26th. 1922.

Dear Mr Miller[1]

It was very good of you to send me the assurance of the British Fund's efficient distribution. If the result is what you say (and I have not the slightest doubt of it) then it is an unequalled triumph of personal character and devotion in the cause of humanity on the part of all the workers on the spot; even if we keep in view the fact that the men responsible for the present state of Russia are anxious, for reasons which we all know, not to hurt the emotional susceptibilities of public opinion in this country.[2]

Believe me very faithfully yours
Joseph Conrad.

To Eric Pinker

Text MS Berg; Unpublished

[letterhead: Oswalds]
26.1.22

My dear Eric.

I wrote to Father about McFee's article, and I send it to you with the idea that you *may* find a moment in which you could show it to him. I am interested too by the portrait which is *from no photograph* and seems to me good.[3] What do you think?

---

[1] Mr Miller evidently worked for a British charity sending food and other aid to Russia, where crop failure, war, and revolution had caused a devastating famine. One of the charities, the Russian Relief Fund, an offshoot of the Imperial War Relief Fund, had launched an appeal on 6 January.

[2] The Soviet leadership, in other words, alert to the power of propaganda, did not want to seem responsible for conditions in Russia. Working-class men and women in some parts of Britain, notably the South Wales coalfields and the 'Red Clyde', were showing enthusiasm for the new regime and a willingness to blame Russia's woes on reactionary forces, including the British and American governments, which had sent troops to back the Whites against the Reds in the civil war. Like the majority of his fellow countrymen, however, Conrad feared that such sympathies might lubricate a British revolution engineered by Moscow.

[3] 'Great Tales of a Great Victorian', *New York Times*, Literary Section, 1 January 1922, pp. 1 and 22, was a review of the 'soberly magnificent' Sun-Dial Edition of Conrad's works. In his novels, essays, and stories, William McFee (1881–1966) drew on his experiences as a ship's engineer in the Royal Navy and the United States Merchant Marine. Conrad inspired his life as a writer. In 1942, McFee edited the handsomely produced and illustrated *A Conrad Argosy* for Doubleday; he also wrote introductions to several Doubleday editions of the novels. The illustration Conrad liked was a portrait drawing in high romantic style, set against a background of tumultuous seas.

Please send the thing back to me as I wish to preserve it on account of that portrait. Kindest regards

Yours

J. Conrad

To Edward Garnett
Text G. 311–12

Oswalds
27.1.22.

Dearest Edward,

I've been in bed for about 3 weeks and this is the first time I am using a pen for God knows how long.

Thanks my dearest fellow for the Chehov vol.[1] He is too delightful for words. Very great work. Very great.

Do tell your wife of my admiration that grows and grows with every page of her translations I read. The renderings in this vol have impressed me extremely.

Jessie sends her love.

Ever yours

J. Conrad

To Aniela Zagórska
Text Ruch; Najder 277–8[2]

Oswalds,
Bishopsbourne,
Kent.
27th January 1922.

My dear Anielka,

The reason for my not writing to you was that for about a month I have been in bed with influenza complicated by an attack of gout. C'était charmant. Just to-day I came down to my study, where everything somehow looks strange and uninviting.

Thank you for all your letters; vous m'avez réchauffé le coeur;[3] and thank you, my dearest, for all the books you have presented me with, in particular

---

[1] An advance copy of Chekhov's *The Cook's Wedding and Other Stories*, translated by Constance Garnett, due to appear in February.
[2] Translation from Najder with minor alterations. [3] 'You have warmed my heart'.

for Fredro,[1] qui m'a donné un plaisir extrême à lire et à regarder les images.[2] You are very good to me, Anielka dear, and I am grateful to you for it although I behave comme un brute.

Nevertheless you must forgive me. I couldn't work properly the whole of last year – couldn't even concentrate my thoughts without a great effort. This makes me worried and fretful. Je ne suis pas très heureux ma chère.[3]

There is only one complete edition of my works. Edition de luxe – 750 in England and 750 in America. It was sold out before publication. The price for the 18 volumes was £20 sterling. I see now in various catalogues that it is difficult to get for £30. The author had six sets (18 vols. each). Of these I kept two sets – one for each of the boys – the remaining were sent as 'politesses' to various persons to whom they were owed. That is why, my dear, I could not send you one. C'était tout simplement impossible.[4] However, I can now tell you that this very morning I signed a contract for the publication of a uniform edition,[5] unlimited, of all works, pour le grand public. I shall send one to you as soon as it starts to come out! But it may possibly take a year's time. Voilà, that is all for to-day.

                                                    Always yours most faithfully
                                                                           Konrad.

To Clarence E. Andrews
Text TS Ohio; Unpublished

                                                              [letterhead: Oswalds]
                                                                Feb. 6th. 1922.[6]

Dear M[r] Andrews.[7]

I must confess that your professorial career of lectures and research does not seem to me safe from that particular Devil whose mission is to lead people into strange places where they have no business. Your conception of a settled life, consisting as to one-third of roaming and as to the rest of reading about wanderers, is calculated to fill a well-wisher with anxiety; and as I see that you lay, without the slightest ambiguity, the guilt at my door – why, I think that

---

[1] *Trzy po trzy* (1844–6), an autobiographical work by Aleksander Fredro, a writer of comedies, in Henryk Mościcki's 1917 edition.
[2] 'Which has been an extreme pleasure to read and to look at'.
[3] 'I'm not very happy, my dear.'   [4] 'That was simply impossible.'   [5] With Dent.
[6] Conrad's handwritten telegram direction 'Bridge' appears over 'Bishopsbourne' but the date is secure; see the letter to Jean-Aubry of the 10th.
[7] Clarence Edward Andrews (1883–1932), a professor of literature at Ohio State University, specialised in verse, writing books on the seventeenth-century playwright Richard Brome, on Romantic and Victorian poetry, and the poetry of the 1890s.

the least you can do is to dedicate your book on the Forbidden Atlas[1] to me. I am glad to see you have seen the propriety of doing so and I can assure you that I accept your offer in the same friendly spirit which has prompted you to make it. Considering however the load you have laid on my conscience I think you ought in addition to send me an inscribed copy at the earliest possible moment.

I haven't read anything about Morocco for years, except the sort of futile bits one finds in newspapers; nothing in fact since the first edition of Cunninghame Graham's Mogreb-el-Acksa.[2] And that is ancient history by now. Very ancient! So your book will find my curiosity whetted and my mind eagerly receptive. My best wishes for its success.

Believe me very cordially Yours

Joseph Conrad.

To Eric Pinker
Text TS Berg; Unpublished

Oswalds,
Bishopsbourne,
Kent.
Feb. 6th. 1922

My dear Eric

I have received this morning the receipt for Super-tax[3] for which thanks. I am sorry to say that I have been again laid up for more than a week with a relapse of that beastly flu complicated with gout. Great fun! To-day is the first day I can think connectedly and it occurs to me that just before J. B. left he passed on to me Fisher Unwin's request for a title of the forthcoming volume of short stories, which is the first book he is to get under the latest agreement. Titles are a beastly nuisance, especially for short story vols, and I haven't hit upon anything yet. While I was lying on my back with the temp. about 102 I think I found about 50 titles, but I don't think any of them would have done, and, anyhow, I have forgotten them now. Should F. U. write to you about it please just say that Conrad is keeping the matter in mind and that he will send something before long.

I saw the ship's arrival up to time and I trust our travellers haven't had to land in the middle of a blizzard or an earthquake or some other convulsion

---

[1] *Old Morocco and The Forbidden Atlas* appeared later in the year, dedicated to Conrad.
[2] *Mogreb-el-Acksa; A Journey in Morocco* (1898), which includes a narrative of Graham's imprisonment in the Atlas Mountains.
[3] An extra tax levied on high incomes.

or conflagration – you know those things that happen in America. When, or if, you write this week please send them both[1] my love.

Kindest regards

Yrs

Joseph Conrad.

To G. Jean-Aubry
Text MS Yale; *L.fr.* 167–8

[letterhead: Oswalds]

7. Fevr. 1922

Très cher.

J'ai été alité pendant 10 jours. Je me suis levé samedi soir car H. Walpole allait arriver pour diner. Je suis mieux, mais je n'ai pas confiance.

Je suis content de savoir que Votre traduction d' "En Marge" a interessé tant de monde. Ce livre m'est particulièrement cher a cause de notre amitié.

Je ne reponds pas a Vos questions parceque nous éspérons que Vous pourrez venir nous voir Samedi prochain pour le week-end. Envoyez nous un petit mot.

Je n'ai rien fait tout ce mois de Janvier. J'ai travaillé un peu aujourd hui, mais je ne suis guère en train.

Je viens de recevoir une lettre de H. de Regnier[2] que je Vous envois ici. Le bon Neel e[s]t ci-inclus aussi.

Je Vous embrasse

Tout à Vous

J. Conrad

Translation

My dear friend.

I was confined to bed for ten days. I got up on Saturday evening because H. Walpole was coming to dinner. I am better but lack confidence.

I am glad to hear that your translation of *Within the Tides* interested so many people. I am particularly fond of that book because of our friendship.

I don't answer your questions because we hope you will come to see us next Saturday for the week-end. Drop us a line.

---

[1] Pinker's daughter Oenone accompanied him.

[2] Henri-François-Joseph de Régnier (1864–1936) was a Symbolist poet, novelist, critic, and member of the Académie Française. 'The Planter of Malata' is indebted to his work; see Yves Hervouet, *The French Face of Joseph Conrad* (Cambridge University Press, 1990), pp. 248, 277, n. 17. His letter of 6 February thanks Conrad for a copy of *The Arrow of Gold*, passed on by Jean-Aubry, and expresses the hope of a meeting that summer (Stape and Knowles, p. 192).

I wrote nothing during the whole of January. I have worked a bit to-day but am hardly on form.

I just received a letter from H. de Regnier which I am sending with this. One from that good fellow Neel is also enclosed.

I embrace you.

Yours truly

J. Conrad

To Ada Galsworthy
Text J-A, 2, 265

Oswalds,
Bishopsbourne,
Kent.
9th Feb. '22.

Dearest Ada,

Your wire was a great grief. We hope dear Jack's cold has no relation to any sort of 'flu. I was laid up for nearly a month with some form of it and I felt the disappointment of your cancelled visit with the peculiar invalid's acuteness of emotion. For if you had come you would have inaugurated, so to speak, my first coming downstairs after what seemed to be ages.

As I know that dear Jack's colds are no amateurish interludes pray drop us a word how he is getting on. I suppose he was producing "Justice" himself and that adds to his anxiety.[1] Theatres, I think, are most dangerous places. – I don't mean morally but as microbe menageries. I suppose a complete collection could be found in any theatre. But perhaps I take a jaundiced view! I am generally fractious yet and depressed.

I have done no work to speak of for months, – such is the dreadful truth which I conceal from as many people as possible.

Our dearest love to you both.

To Eric Pinker
Text J-A, 2, 265–6[2]

Canterbury
11 A.M. Feb. 10, 1922.

Dear Eric,

I am not fit to come up to-day to see you as I was most anxious to do in my concern for you all in this bereavement[3] which I too feel more deeply

---

[1] The play, which premiered in 1910, was being revived at the Court Theatre from 7 to 25 February. Galsworthy was not the producer.

[2] Jean-Aubry reports that this was the text of a telegram.

[3] J. B. Pinker died in New York on 8 February.

than anyone outside his family can do. Twenty years' friendship and for most of that time in the constant interchange of the most intimate thoughts and feelings created a bond as strong as the nearest relationship. But you know enough to understand the depth of our grief here and our sense of irreparable loss. There are no words of comfort for such a blow. I can only assure you of my affectionate friendship. Our anxious thoughts are with you all. But to think of poor Oenone is harrowing. Please keep us informed. If you feel you would like to talk with me and can bear the idea of coming to this house, where he was loved and honoured as if it were his own, pray do so as early or as late as you like and you could be back home in town by noon to-morrow. I hope to be able to come up on Monday prepared to stay the night so as to see you at your own time after business hours.

With our love

To G. Jean-Aubry
Text MS Yale; Unpublished

[Oswalds]
Vendredi. 6. pm. [10 February 1922][1]

Mon cher.

Avez vous [reçu] ma lettre expédié[e] le six courant.[2]

Pas un mot de Vous! Pouvez Vous venir pour le week end. Si oui telegraphiez de bonne heure aussitôt ceci lu – pour que le car puisse venir a la gare a temps.

Adresse teleg^{que} après un h est
Conrad. Oswalds.
Bridge

La mort de P[inker] a été un rude coup. Vingt années d'intimité toute particulièr[e] ça crée un lien.

Tout à Vous

J. C.

Translation

Friday. 6 pm.

My dear friend.

Did you get my letter sent on the sixth instant?

No word from you! Could you come for the week-end? If yes, telegraph as soon as you read this so that the car might come to the station on time.

---

[1] Jean-Aubry's date, confirmed by contents.   [2] In fact, of the 7th.

Telegraphic address after 1 pm
    Conrad. Oswalds.
       Bridge
P's death has been a real blow. Twenty years of a quite special intimacy creates a bond.

Yours truly

J. C.

To Hugh Walpole

Text MS Texas; Unpublished

[letterhead: Oswalds]
10 Feby 22

My dearest Hugh.

It is very much like You to write at once as you have written, and indeed tho' not surprised I am deeply touched by your sympathetic understanding of my actual feelings as to P's death.

Gradually since 1914 an intimacy developed between us in a strange way. He seemed to think that he had earned the right of laying his innermost thoughts and feelings before me. A peculiar but in its way a touching assertion of the right of good service and – no other word will do – of devotion.

The notice in the Times is perfectly true. He had a pride in his work and in his power to help people in ways that from a cold business point of view could not be justified to common prudence.[1]

As to the new situation created by his death it may be for me a little awkward for a time. In any case it must be a loss for no one would be able to conduct my affairs as he did. But my affairs too are nearing their end – in a manner of speaking. But I feel that we all in this house have lost a personality that counted in our lives for stability and support.

Our dear love to You.

Ever Yours

J. Conrad.

I shall be probably in town on Monday for the night.

---

[1] The 'Appreciation' in *The Times* (10 February, late edition, p. 9) is introduced by the formulaic 'a correspondent writes', the correspondent being Walpole. He singles out Pinker's generosity: 'It was his kindliness of heart that brought him his final success; his judgment and decision were good, his knowledge of men was wonderful, but it was his personal sympathy with, and liking for, individuals that made him the exceptional human being he was.' Among these individuals were 'two of the greatest literary geniuses of his time – the late Henry James and Joseph Conrad … For 30 years [*sic*] he staked all his faith and trust in the world-wide recognition of Conrad's genius.' The working relationship with Pinker actually began in September 1900.

To G. Jean-Aubry
Text MS Yale; Unpublished

[Oswalds]
11.2.22

Cher ami
    Entendu! Car will meet 12.42 on Wednesday.
    Our love
                                    Yours
                                            J Conrad.

To Douglas Sladen
Text MS Richmond; Unpublished

[letterhead: Oswalds]
11.2.22

My dear Sir.[1]
    Thanks for the invitation card[2] you have been good enough to send me.
    I have just got up after a very complicated sort of 'flu' and coming up to
town will be out of the question for me this month. I regret it very much.
                                    Yours faithfully
                                            Joseph Conrad

To Bruno Winawer
Text TS copy Yale;[3] *Głos* (108); Najder 278–9

Oswalds,
Bishopsbourne,
Kent.
Feb. 12th. 1922.

Cher Monsieur,
    Je vous remercie de votre très intéressante lettre. Votre idée de partager la
scène en deux au 4me acte me plait beaucoup.[4]
    Voulez vous avoir la bonté de donner à Madame Retinger[5] mes sentiments
de la plus respectueuse amitié.

---

[1] After reading History at Oxford, Douglas Brooke Wheelton Sladen (1856–1947) went on to
    hold the first chair of History at the University of Sydney. An avid traveller, he published a
    number of books on Australia, Japan, Italy, Egypt, and Persia.
[2] To the 22 February meeting of the 'After Dinner Club', founded by Sladen to introduce 'new
    blood into literary society'. A special guest was invited to each gathering.
[3] Typing errors not reproduced or signalled.
[4] For more on the split stage, see the letter to Wade of 4 April.
[5] A note on the text by Winawer indicates he had roughed out a translation of *The Secret
    Agent* dramatisation with her, but Aniela Zagórska was also apparently involved (see the letter
    of 14 December 1921).

J'ai eu la douleur de perdre mon vieil ami J. B. Pinker, mort à New York il y a cinq jours après une très courte maladie. C'est une grande douleur pour moi. Notre amitié datait de 22 ans. Il était plus jeune que moi de 6 ans. Je suis comme assommé par ce coup du destin.

Ceci n'avance pas nos affaires. Il devait s'occuper là-bas a placer la comedie. Son fils qui prend la suite n'a ni l'experience ni la position influente de son père. Enfin! Nous verrons.

Voulez vous passer la nouvelle à ma cousine Angèle. Je n'ai pas le coeur à écrire des lettres.

Pardonnez moi cette courte note.

> Tout à Vous
>
> Jph. Conrad.

Translation

Dear Sir,

Thank you for your very interesting letter. Your idea of dividing the stage in two in Act 4 pleases me a good deal.

Would you be so kind as to give Mrs Retinger my friendly and most respectful regards?

I have suffered the painful loss of my old friend J. B. Pinker, who died in New York five days ago after a very short illness. It is a great grief to me. Our friendship dated back twenty-two years. He was six years younger than I. I feel knocked down by this blow of fate.

It does not help our affairs. He was going to try to place the comedy over there. His son, who is taking over, has neither his father's experience nor his influence. Enfin! We shall see.

Would you kindly pass this news on to my cousin Aniela? I'm in no mood to write letters.

Pray forgive this short note.

> Yours ever
>
> Jph. Conrad.

To F. N. Doubleday

Text TS/MS Princeton; J-A, 2, 266–7

> [letterhead: Oswalds]
> Feb. 19th. 1922.

Dear Mʳ Doubleday

I need not tell you how profoundly I feel the loss of J. B. Pinker, my friend of twenty years' standing, whose devotion to my interests and whose affection borne towards myself and all belonging to me were the greatest moral and material support through nearly all my writing life.

During the years of the war our intimacy had become very close. For the last two years he was very frequently staying in our house and I learned more and more to appreciate in him qualities which were not perhaps obvious to the world which looked upon him mainly as a successful man. It is certain that the value of my connection with him can not be wholly or truly expressed in terms of money.

My sense of loss, very acute now, will always abide with me, whatever alleviation time may bring to the present distress of my feelings. Eric Pinker, who understood well the extent of my affection for his father, came down here two days after the news reached the family. He spent a few hours with me in my study and seemed to derive some comfort from that visit. We did not talk business on that occasion except in so far that I asked him to continue to look after my affairs since it was his resolve to go on with the business if he could be certain of the support of the majority of his father's clients. I gather from many letters I have received that this will be the case. I have known Eric since he was seven years old, and as J. B. Pinker and I often talked our children over I know pretty well his character and abilities. I have the most favourable opinion of them and have always liked him personally.

I do not know that there are any negotiations left pending between you and J. B. P. The last agreement I signed was for the volume of plays[1] and nothing, I suppose, has arisen since then. Eric, though not a partner, seems to have been altogether in his father's confidence and, apparently, is aware of everything that has been done; but in any case I feel that my affairs in America need give me no concern since your invariable kindness, forethought and interest expressed so often in word and deed assure me that they are in the hands of a friend.

This profound conviction, dear Mr Doubleday, is a source of comfort to me; for it is not "agreements" but the certainty of friendly appreciation in those closely associated with his work that give confidence and support to a writer.

With our kindest regards

Sincerely Yours

Joseph Conrad.

---

[1] *One Day More* and *The Secret Agent*. The agreement dates from 19 July 1921 (Hallowes).

To Eric Pinker
Text MS Berg; Unpublished

[letterhead: Oswalds]
21.2.22

My dear Eric.

I had to-day (in the morning) an acknowledgment from Methuen of one of those circular letters to publishers[1] which I sent you to post at your convenience.

I suppose you dispatched them all and that the situation now has cleared up.

Sir R. Jones wired asking my wife to come up to London to be examined. We intend accordingly to come up on Thursday and you shall hear from me in the course of that day.

I trust that B[orys] who took 2 letters to you on Sunday evening to post in town has not kept them in his pocket. It's hardly likely however.

Would it be possible to arrange a visit to Everett's studio on Friday? I'll keep all the afternoon free from 2 o'clock. But pray don't pay any attention to this suggestion if your hands are full, as they must be. I am not impatient. You'll never find me impatient. But as I *have* to come up now I thought I would mention that transaction.

Affect^{ly} Yrs

J Conrad.

To Lord Northcliffe
Text MS Private collection; P. & H. 834 (in part)

[letterhead: Oswalds]
[*c*. 21 February 1922][2]

My dear Lord.

I had a scruple in adding even a small scrap of paper to occupy your time directly after your return. I venture it now just to tell you that you have been welcomed back in spirit in this house, after your Progress which we have

---

[1] Presumably to inform them that Conrad would remain a Pinker client, but if so, one was not sent to Dent (see the letter of [2 March]).

[2] Northcliffe's return to Europe from a world tour begun in 1921 fixes the month while Conrad's plans to be in London on Thursday the 23rd (mentioned in the previous letter) suggest the date.

been following, with the rest of the world.[1] The greatest *joy* was the report of your Marseilles speech[2] because that one gave us positive assurance of your improved health, conveyed as it were in your own voice. The greatest *interest* for me at least, was the Australian part of your significant pilgrimage. I knew Australia first in its "cut-the-painter" stage which was short. Then came "Australia for White men", [the] cry so inconsequently associated with the anti-immigration attitude for so many years. I hope that your serious words inspired by the wisest patriotism and a deep sense of political future will put an end to this selfish folly once for all.[3]

Pardon this long screed; but I must add that I have read all you have given us to read, finding in every line that directness of feeling and that simplicity of utterance which are a delight to a troubled spirit. For you have a "style parlé" of marvellous perfection and altogether your own. A triumph of personality. I fancied I could hear your very voice.

My wife sends you her love. I am sorry to say I will have to bring her up on Thursday to the same old Brown's Hotel for the same old anxious time of being looked at by Sir R. Jones – a dear and unwearied friend. Things are not right with her knee. She is again very much crippled and in considerable pain. The boys beg to be remembered to you.

Believe me my dear Lord always affectionately Yours

Joseph Conrad.

---

[1] In *The Times*, which covered his reception and speeches throughout his tour.

[2] On arriving in Marseilles on 18 February, Northcliffe delivered a speech in French (written by H. Wickham Stead) in reply to an official committee of welcome. He called for 'a close union between France and England', which would make a 'rallying-point' for the whole of Europe, insisting that 'we should never forget we are Europeans; that the reconstruction of Europe can be undertaken, in the first place, only by Europe herself; and that we shall have the effective support of the United States only in the degree that we are able to compose our differences and find in accord the solution of our own problems' (*The Times*, 20 February, p. 12).

[3] Older than the country itself, the 'White Australia Policy' originated in Queensland and Victoria, where, as early as the 1870s, thirty years before Federation, laws banned immigration from Asia and the Pacific Islands. Over the next decade, most of the other Australian colonies followed suit. Most members of the labour movement strongly supported these prohibitions, and, in the post-war slump, their hostility extended to British migrants. Meanwhile jobs in Britain were also hard to find, and the Northcliffe press, including *The Times* and *Daily Mail*, was promoting emigration to the Empire's white-settler countries. Australia was prominent among them. Northcliffe's chief purpose in going there was to talk the federal government into accepting more Britons. Facing a hostile audience of union organisers in Melbourne, he 'spoke on the very unpopular topics of immigration and the difficulty of maintaing a "white" Australia without immigration ... They could not exclude both British and Orientals from a continent equal in size to the United States. They must expect it to be called a dog-in-the-manger country if they deliberately allowed it to remain empty by the exclusion of immigrants' (*The Times*, 28 September 1921, p. 10).

To Lillian M. Robins
Text MS Indiana; Unpublished

[letterhead: Oswalds]
22.2.'22

Dear Mrs Robins.

Herewith proofs of the Cookery book[1] with my thanks for your letter received with them, I fear, some ten days ago already.

Miss H[allowes] and I have attended as well as we could to the remarks of the proof-reader in the matter of names and materials not known in America, such for instance as *"crumb* of the loaf" for the soft part of bread, and a few others. Will you please ask the Reader to cast his eye over the slips before they go back to the printers?

A recipe had to be shifted bodily from one slip to another. Otherwise the corrections are not heavy and for the most part, dealing with the queries of the proof-reader.

The composition of the title-page, I see differs entirely from my suggestion as embodied in the title page of the TS. I enclose it with the proof but leave the decision to the publishers.

The word Recipes should be printed by itself in suitable type on the page following the end of General Remarks. The sections of that part of the book should begin each on a new page. I have marked all this on the slips, I hope, clearly enough.

I am, dear Mrs Robins very faithfully Yours
Joseph Conrad

To Karola Zagórska
Text MS copy Yale;[2] Najder 279

Oswalds,
22.II.1922

My dear Karola,

I was laid up in bed for a whole month – with influenza and gout – and even now I still don't feel well. Meanwhile Jessie got suspicious pains in her leg and another operation looks essential. We are going to London to-morrow for a few days so that Sir Robert Jones can see her and decide.

---

[1] For the Doubleday edition of Jessie Conrad's *A Handbook of Cookery for a Small House*, due in May. To accommodate serialisation in the *Delineator*, its appearance was delayed until February 1923.
[2] In French.

Mr Pinker, my agent and friend (did you meet him?), died suddenly in New York a fortnight ago. And so after twenty years all my affairs have fallen on my head. Mr P's son will take over his business – but it won't be the same.

We embrace you all most warmly.

Yours affectionately

Konrad.

PS For more than a year now I've had no peace of mind and couldn't work properly. You understand what that means. Recently I've begun to feel a slight relaxation. Perhaps it will pass? The boys are well. Pray think of me.

To [?]

Text MS Private collection; Unpublished

[letterhead: Oswalds]
23. Febr 1922

My dear Sir.[1]

My warmest thanks for your interesting letter. Your appreciation of my work has moved me by its tone of real friendliness and understanding. I am grateful to you for all you have said and still more for the kind impulse which prompted you to address me with words of the kind that is* treasured by a writer.

But to answer your question is not so easy – it may be even impossible. In one sense I could confess truly that I don't know why my books are what they are. I've *felt* them that way. But such an answer to mean anything would require to be commented [upon] analytically – a sort of thing I would not care to write and you would not care to read.

I came nearest to *defining* (not expressing[2]) my attitude to life in my prefaces. They (and every other page of my work) are absolutely sincere. I stand disclosed in them whole, with my innermost thoughts. They must speak for me for I myself can say no more. You can't call upon an artist to be *explicit*. It is not his province. His appeal is to mankind's sympathies which no argument and explanation can secure. Nobody can charge me with intentional gloom or lack of belief in mankind – and that is enough.

Pardon this rather disconnected scrawl. I have a gouty wrist.

Believe me, with grateful regards very sincerely Yours
Joseph Conrad.

---

[1] He remains unidentified.   [2] This phrase was an afterthought.

To Jean Fayard
Text L.fr. 168

Oswalds
24.2.22

Cher Monsieur,[1]
Mes remerciements pour le livre.[2]
J'ai goûté un très vif plaisir à le lire. Le sujet, la manière de le traiter, la finesse des aperçus et surtout le style "parlé" qui semble "impersonel" et qui est cependant très distingué – tout ça m'a plu extrêmement.

Permettez moi de vous féliciter sur ces pages si bienvenues et surtout, Cher Monsieur et Confrère, pardonnez moi la "crudité" (si cela peut se dire) de cette appréciation que j'écris à la hate pour ne pas manquer le courrier. (Et avec une main enflée par la goutte.)

Believe me very cordially yours

Translation

Dear Sir,
Thank you for the book.
Reading it gave me very great pleasure. The subject, the manner of treatment, the delicacy of insight, and especially the 'spoken' style that seems 'impersonal' but which is none the less very distinguished – all that pleased me immensely.

Allow me to congratulate you on these most welcome pages, and, moreover, dear Sir and colleague, forgive me the 'crudity' (if it might be called that) of this appreciation, which I write in haste so as not to miss the post. (And with a hand swollen by gout.)

Believe me very cordially yours

---

[1] The novelist and short-story writer Jean Fayard (1902–78), the grandson of the very successful French publisher, Arthème Fayard, had read English at Oxford. In 1931, his novel *Mal d'amour* was awarded the Prix Goncourt.
[2] *Oxford et Margaret* (1922), a novel about a young Parisian studying literature in England. It recounts his friendships, impressions of university life, and unhappy romantic entanglement with an English girl. In 1924, Fayard published *Deux ans à Oxford*.

To Richard Curle

Text MS Indiana; Curle 85

[letterhead: Oswalds]

Sat: 5 pm. [25 February 1922][1]

My dear Curle

So sorry I forgot to ask Miss H[allowes] to drop you a line of my safe arrival last night. I was 1/2 a day in bed just to rest. I have dictated a memo to Eric of which I send a carbon for you to see. Pray return. I think it is all right.

Au revoir soon. Our love

Yours

J. Conrad

To Hugh Walpole

Text MS Keswick; Unpublished

Oswalds

Bishopsbourne

Kent

Monday. [February 1922?][2]

Dearest Hugh

We are no end sorry to hear of you laid-up.

You dear – your answer is absolutely good enough and you must believe that I felt what you meant too.

It's a matter of phrasing after all – of tonality; and I would not have said anything more here if you had not given so to speak authority to speak in and out of season.

Yours ever Paternally

J. Conrad

---

[1] Curle dates this note only as February. The memo, possibly about Conrad's business affairs in the wake of Pinker's death, suggests a date late in the month, a surmise supported by the letter to Zagórska of the 22nd, which places Conrad in London on the 23rd.

[2] Only an approximate placement. The intimate tone and Walpole's absence in America from September 1919 to April 1920 set a limit, but lack of evidence disallows more precision. Rupert Hart-Davis's *Hugh Walpole: A Biography* (1952) records that at this time 'A slight chill caused Hugh to spend a happy day in bed, looking through the Abbotsford letters and reading Scott's *Journal*' (p. 219).

To Eric Pinker
Text MS Berg; Unpublished

[letterhead: Oswalds]
3 [2].3.22.
Thursday.[1]

My dear Eric.

Will you tell me whether this £50 for Carola Zagorska have been sent to Milan c/o Consolato di Polonia or any other address?

I have settled down to work and feel happier in consequence. How are things going with You? Dent wrote me "presuming" that M[r] E. Pinker is to take charge of my affairs". I told him it was so. Enclosed letter from D[ouble]day which please return.

Yrs

J Conrad.

To Mary Pinker
Text MS Yale; Unpublished

[letterhead: Oswalds]
2. Mch. '22.

Dear Mrs Pinker.

This is only to send you our love and to beg you to give it from both of us to Oenone. She has been constantly in our thoughts but I did not want yet to write to either of You dear ladies – not being able to express all my thoughts which are still oppressed and confused by my heavy sense of loss. But I have just had a letter from Doubleday (Everitt) telling me that the dear child was suffering from a cold just before leaving America. Could you give us news of You both or ask Ralph to write for You? A line would do.

With love to you all I am dear Mrs Pinker always

Your most affectionately faithful
Joseph Conrad.

To [?]
Text MS Indiana; Unpublished

[letterhead: Oswalds]
7.3.22

Dear Sir.[2]

Your mate is not the same man as mine. The Chief Officer of the Loch Etive (in 1879–80) was M[r] Purdie who was deaf and did get washed overboard

---

[1] Assuming the day to be more reliable than the date.
[2] He remains unidentified.

in a gale off the Horn.[1] But he was not then serving on board the Loch Etive. I never heard the name of the ship.

Strange coincidence of initial letters, of the bodily defect and ultimate fate, in our two mates!

I do not think that Mr Purdie was a native of Stornoway;[2] but he certainly served out of Glasgow like your Mr Pope.

Believe me

Sincerely Yrs

Joseph Conrad

To Eric Pinker
Text TS/MS Berg; Unpublished

Oswalds,
Bishopsbourne.
Kent.
March 8th. 1922

My dear Eric.

Your first business communication has been put away in my archives, the first I hope of a long and profitable series.

I agree with your view of our position as regards Pawling in relation to the "Typhoon" volume. I am therefore prepared to sign an agreement in that sense – that is, 5% on the school edition and 10% on the copies sold to the public in a different binding.

Even if circumstances were different this first of your transactions on my behalf should not have been made an occasion of a squabble with a publisher.

I forward you here a letter just received from Everitt, which is a nice letter in every way and will no doubt interest you. It strikes me that perhaps they would like to see it at home, and, if you think so, please forward it to your mother on its way back to me.

I believe that the references to the character of your father's relations with Doubleday are quite genuine. That he had a great influence over F. N. D. there could be no doubt for anybody who had observed them for an hour together. I don't think that anything could arise to disturb the particular atmosphere of his relation with Doubleday as long as with the utmost friend-liness you preserve a firm attitude on the ground won by your father by his extraordinarily patient and tenacious diplomacy. I remember the time when

---

[1] Glasgow-born William Purdu (1853–86) served with Conrad in the *Loch Etive* in 1880–1 (not 1879–80). He was drowned when serving as first mate in the *Charles Connell*. On his deafness and the trouble it caused, see also *Documents*, p. 36.

[2] The chief town on the Isle of Lewis, Outer Hebrides.

the atmosphere was quite different.[1] But those are things easier to talk over than to write about.

I don't know whether you would care to come here to lunch on Sunday by the quick train that leaves Vic. at 10.45 and arrives at 12.24. You could at a pinch be back in town at 7.15, and it would give you four clear hours here. If your wife would give us the pleasure to come with you I would get a closed car to meet the train.

This, my dear Eric, can not be called an invitation. It is but a suggestion. It would give us both great pleasure if acted on, and I certainly would like to see you. But of course the journey is a grind, and the weather may be bad, and, after all, the things to be talked over are not of immediate and urgent importance.

Our kindest regards with thanks from my wife for your friendly inquiries. Nothing new yet as to her future.

Always Yrs

Joseph Conrad.

To Eric Pinker
Text MS Berg; Unpublished

[letterhead: Oswalds]
9.3.22

My dear Eric.

I think it only fair to let you know that D[ick] Curle is coming here on Sat. and will stay over Sunday.

I had forgotten that we had promised to give him his birthday-dinner this year. As his birthday is on Sat: he has announced his arrival for Friday ev[g] as of right.

I don't know that this need be an objection. We could have our talk all the same, entre-nous. And I don't know that a meeting between you and C need cause awkwardness of any kind. For myself I still think that the move is worth trying. (I am thinking of *you only* in this). An exchange of ideas – without even mentioning the business itself – may give you an insight into his fitness – or otherwise.

Pray drop us a line.

Afft[ly] Yrs

J. Conrad.

---

[1] As in 1916, when Conrad proposed delaying the collected edition until after the war. See *Letters*, 5, pp. 613, 619–20, 632–3.

To G. Jean-Aubry

Text MS Yale; Unpublished

[letterhead: Oswalds]
Dimanche [12 March 1922][1]

Cher Ami.

Je Vous envois ce petit mot pour dire que les affaires vont assez bien, pour le moment.

Comment allez Vous. Envoyez nous de Vos nouvelles.

A Vous de coeur

J. C.

Translation

Sunday

Dear Friend.

Just a word to say that things are going quite well at the moment.

How are you? Send us your news.

Yours affectionately

J. C.

To Eric Pinker

Text MS Berg; Unpublished

[letterhead: Oswalds]
Sunday. [12 March 1922][2]

Dear Eric.

Thanks for yours. We shall be glad to see you on Sat next for lunch. 10.45 from Vic arrives Canterbury 12.30.

The locality of The Rover is the south coast of France between, say, Toulon and Cannes.

Yours

J. C.

---

[1] Postmarked 13 March.

[2] Placement must come after Conrad's letter of the 9th. Whatever the business at hand, literary or financial, Pinker apparently did not wish to share his visit with Curle and suggested the next weekend instead.

To Eric Pinker
Text MS Berg; Unpublished

[Oswalds]
[12 to 16 March 1922]¹

Dear Eric.

I don't think this is to be entertained anyhow.² But will you give your consideration to the position we would be in relation to F. Unwin should a serious proposal as to A's Folly ever come our way.

Yrs

J. C.

Car will meet 12.30 on Saturday.

To G. Jean-Aubry
Text MS Yale; Unpublished

[letterhead: Oswalds]
Jeudi. [16 March 1922]³

Très cher.

Merci de votre bonne lettre. Nous regrettons de ne pouvoir vous prier de venir ici avant ce Dimanche prochain pour lunch – si cela vous convient. Mais peut-être Vous aimeriez mieux remettre Votre visite au Dim*che* après pour un "week end" plus long.

Il me tarde de Vous voir tout de même. Envoyez nous un petit mot.

Our love to you

Ever Yours

J. Conrad

Translation

Thursday.

My dear friend.

Thank you for your good letter. We are sorry not to be able to ask you to come here before next Sunday for lunch – if that suits you. But perhaps you would prefer to put your visit off to the Sunday after for a longer week-end.

---

¹ Possibly enclosed with the previous letter, but in any case plans for Pinker's upcoming visit suggest placement.
² Conrad wrote this note on the verso of a letter from Laura Hinkley, dated 28 February from Mount Vernon, Iowa, requesting permission to dramatise *Almayer's Folly*.
³ Date from postmark.

In any event, I'm eager to see you. Drop us a line.
Our love to you

Ever Yours

J. Conrad

To Thomas J. Wise
Text MS BL Ashley A. 2948; Unpublished

[letterhead: Oswalds]
16.3.22

Dear Mr Wise

Thank you for the books[1] which arrived this morning. Your copy and that of Mr Spoor[2] are going back duly inscribed, this evening.

There are two painful misprints (substituted words) in the text which play havoc with the sense. Otherwise the little book looks very neat and pleasant. I expected to see a pamphlet.[3]

My wife sends her kind regards.

Yrs

J. Conrad

To Philippe Neel
Text TS copy Neel;[4] *L.fr.* 168–9; Putnam

Oswalds
March 18th. 1922

Cher Monsieur Neel,[5]

Merci de votre aimable lettre[6] que je viens de recevoir.

Je vois bien la difficulté. Evidemment Victoire est un nom de femme. Mais à ceux que vous proposez il y a des objections, car:

Un drame dans les Iles

---

[1] Copies of *The Black Mate*, which Wise had had printed by the Dunedin Press, Edinburgh.
[2] The Chicago bibliophile.   [3] Clothbound, the text came to 80 pages.
[4] The missing greeting and final paragraph are from Jean-Aubry.
[5] A Parisian physician, Philippe Neel (1882–1941) had a keen interest in contemporary English writing and in addition to Conrad translated Thomas Hardy and Henry James. His Conrad translations, commissioned by André Gide, included *Lord Jim*, *Nostromo*, *Under Western Eyes*, and *Victory* (the latter with Isabelle Rivière). Conrad professed himself well content with the quality of Neel's work.
[6] Of 15 March, printed in Putnam.

est un peu trop roman pour "Petit Journal";

                         Dans les Iles
pourrait être le titre du'un livre écrit par un touriste, et

                         Un Aventurier
ne s'applique pas bien à Heyst qui surement n'a ni l'ame ni la mentalite d'un aventurier dans le sens propre du mot. Ce titre a le desavantage aussi de mettre Heyst au premier plan; tandis que j'ai mis le mot Victory en tete de mon livre pour faire ressortir le drame obscur et la mort triomphante de Lena.

Evidemment je tiens à mon titre – mais je n'insiste pas. Il me semble cependant que le vrai équivalent (en traduction) de *Victory* serait *La Victoire*.[1]

Pensez-vous que ce titre est impossible? Il y a bien eu *La Curée, La Débacle*.[2] L'article definitif ne gate rien. Je pense que la* public acceptera La Victoire.

Veuillez, cher Monsieur, consulter Gide et lui faire mille amitiés de ma part. Je suis heureux de savoir que vous êtes content de votre traduction de "Lord Jim."[3] Je me fais fête de voir "Lord Jim" en français, car j'ai beaucoup de confiance en le traducteur des "Yeux d'Occident." Veuillez croire à mes sentiments les plus amicaux.

                                                              J. C.

Translation

Dear Mr Neel,

Thanks for your good letter, just received.

I see the difficulty clearly. Of course, 'victoire' is a woman's name, but there are objections to your suggestions:

                    A Drama of the Islands
is rather too novel-ish for the *Petit Journal*.

                         In the Islands
could be a book written by a tourist, and

                         An Adventurer
doesn't suit Heyst, who certainly has neither the spirit nor the mentality of an adventurer in the proper sense of that word. That title also has the disadvantage of placing Heyst in the foreground whereas I called my book *Victory* in order to throw into relief the inner drama and Lena's triumphant death.

---

[1] The translation appeared under the title *Une Victoire*. It was published in *Le Temps* between 4 April and 11 June; the book form came out in 1923.
[2] Novels by Zola, published in 1871 and 1892.   [3] Published in 1924.

Of course I hold to my title but don't insist. I think that the real equivalent in translating *Victory* would be *La Victoire*.

Do you think that's an impossible title? There has been *La Curée* and *La Débâcle*. The definite article does not spoil anything. I think the public will accept *La Victoire*.

Pray, dear Sir, consult Gide and give him my very best wishes. I am glad to hear that you are pleased with your translation of *Lord Jim*. I very much look forward to seeing it in French because I have great confidence in the translator of *Under Western Eyes*. Pray accept my most friendly regards.

J. C.

To Richard Curle
Text MS Indiana; Curle 86

[Oswalds]
Monday. [20 March 1922][1]
6 pm.

Dear Dick

This letter came in the afternoon. Seeing my name on the envelope I opened it before I noticed that it was addressed to you. Sorry.

I have been working hard ever since you left the house, dictating in the morning correcting all the rest of the time.

Ever Yours

J. C.

PS I will be coming by train on Thursday Vic 11.28. Therefore if you happen into the R[oyal] A[utomobile] C[lub] you may find [me] there about noon.

To Richard Curle
Text MS Indiana; Curle 87

[letterhead: Oswalds]
22.3.'22

Dear Dick

Sir W. R.[2] not coming up to-morrow. I shall try to transact some business with Eric in the morning.

Ever so many thanks for the admirable memorandum.[3] I shall of course be guided by it.

---

[1] Curle's date, confirmed by the next letter.
[2] His identity is moot. Curle sees these initials as an error for Sir R[alph] W[edgwood], but he had not yet been knighted.
[3] About Conrad's finances and investments?

I intend to lunch at the R[oyal] A[utomobile] C[lub] about 1.15 and remain there till you turn up.

But it *may* be possible that I should have to go see E. P[inker] again in the afternoon. However its unlikely.

I hope to get off by the 4.20.

Ever yours

J. C.

To Eric Pinker

Text MS Berg; Unpublished

[letterhead: Oswalds]
Wednesday. [22 March 1922].[1]

Dear Eric.

As I must be in town tomorrow (Thursday) I write to ask you for 1/2 an hour of your time.

Would you to save time have the Rescue (serial Land & Water) agreement got out and also that relating to the film rights (4 novels) entered on early in 1919.[2]

I will turn up about noon; but if you are busy then please leave word when it will be convenient for you to see me – any hour till 3 pm. which will be the latest as I hope to be able to get off home by the 4.20.

Thanks for acct received to-day.

Affc^{ly} yrs

J Conrad

To Eric Pinker

Text MS Berg; Unpublished

[letterhead: Oswalds]
23.3.22
6.40.

Dear Eric

I scrawl this in a hurry to catch post. Could you let B[orys] have the letters that passed between your father and Mac just *before* the money was paid. B asked me to speak to you about that but I forgot.

Affct^{ly} yrs

J. C.

---

[1] The previous letter and that of the 25th fix the date.
[2] Conrad signed the film contract in June 1919 (*Letters*, 6, pp. 434–6).

To Eric Pinker

Text TS/MS Berg; Unpublished

Oswalds,
Bishopsbourne,
Kent.
March 25th. 1922.

My dear Eric

In respect of certain matters touched on in our conversation last Thursday, amongst which there was the question of the copies of the play for which I received from your father on Dec. 1st. of last year a cheque for £175. You will easily ascertain whether I have been debited in my general account with that amount at about that time. If I have not been debited, which would mean that father paid me, as it were, out of his own pocket for them, then that transaction was in a sense private and those copies are your absolute property as against the sum paid. I must tell you that this £175 I received from your father by a cheque sent to me here and not paid into my account at the bank. Therefore it may very well be that the money came out of dear J. B.'s pocket.

On the other hand if you find a debit against me for that sum then it would mean that father paid it out of the general fund of my professional income which was in his hands. In that case, my dear Eric, I think it would be just as well that you should negociate the sale with Maggs[1] and credit me with the proceeds. I can see very well your point in disposing gradually of them to collectors at high prices, which those copies will certainly reach. But that, without exaggeration, may take years; and, after all, selling 'collectors' items' is neither your business nor mine, and we have neither the experience nor the connections. In all purely trade matters of that kind a middleman is a necessary evil. I see by J. B.'s letter that Maggs was prepared to give £5 a copy for 35 copies; and that was the basis on which father sent me the cheque. Maggs will no doubt be prepared to give that much now; and that amount (assuming that the whole transaction was on my account) would be useful to have now, with Mrs C's treatment expenses hanging over my head. If Maggs wants some of those copies signed I will do five or ten of them, and for such copies I think we could ask a pound more apiece.

---

[1] Maggs Bros Ltd, the well-known dealers in manuscripts and rare books, established in the 1850s.

I had a communication from Curle who had lunch with the Daily Mail man and settled with him about an article about J. C.[1] As to the prospects of serialising anything in the Daily Mail, C. tells me that, without opening the matter plainly to him but talking generally of the D. M.'s feuilleton,[2] it appears that those things are written to a cut and dried pattern and that there would be no opening for anything by me there. C. however calls my attention to the fact that "The Times" weekly edition for abroad and the colonies runs a feuilleton too and that this might be a better opening. It certainly might be, as I am on friendly terms with Lord N[orthcliffe] and as a matter of fact I could approach him personally. However nothing whatever must be done that could in any way interfere with your own negociations in the U.S. Perhaps then, after the U.S. is fixed, I could approach Lord N. myself with the proposal, leaving of course the completion of the business to you. *I hope you will understand that this suggestion is not meant to trammel the freedom of your action in any way*. If you can conclude in England as well as in U.S. you must do so without hesitation and I will be satisfied with whatever you do.

With regard to Everett I suppose the sooner we see him after his return the better. When you arrange for the meeting will you please secure for me the choice of two dates. Will Everett be paid money down for the right of reproduction or will he have a royalty too? I have no doubt you will give some of your thought to the question of the price at which the book[3] will have to be published. I suppose a thousand copies would be pretty sure to be sold out at £2.2. But while negociating with Pawling you had better decide without further reference to me. Of course the principal business in that quarter is the Uniform Popular Edition; for looking at the statement of accounts that has been made I can't help feeling that there is more money in England for my work than we are now getting from the various publishers.

I was no end sorry having missed Oenone & R[alph] here. I was told they were dear children, and their visit was a great pleasure to Mrs C. She asked R naturally (I never told her of our conversation) what his plans were and he said he was going into the business with you. Does it mean that he would come in at once?

---

[1] Curle's 'Conrad at Home', *Daily Mail*, 7 April, p. 8.
[2] A feuilleton is a newspaper insert devoted to fiction or essays; in Conrad's day, they were more common in France and Germany than in Britain.
[3] The long-projected but never-published edition of *The Mirror of the Sea* with John Everett's illustrations.

My quarter's rent is due to-day. Will you send a cheque to Col Matthew Bell (£62.10.0) as against the incoming moneys.

Affctly Yrs

J. Conrad.

To Sydney Cockerell
Text MS Indiana; Unpublished

[letterhead: Oswalds]
28.3.22

Dear Mr Cockerell.

I am sorry I could not write to you before.

If your vacation programme brings you at all this way perhaps you will let me know on what day we may expect the great pleasure of seeing you here.

The book[1] you sent me was a great pleasure to me. Some of the ships I knew personally. In two of them I served at the beginning and the end of my sea life.[2]

I am sending You the latest priv^{ly} prin^{ed} booklet.[3] The story in it is of no account, and I do [not] intend to include it in any collection of my tales. But it has been serialised a few years ago in some magazine.[4]

With our kindest regards to Your wife and Yourself

Always Yours

Joseph Conrad

To [?]
Text MS Private; Unpublished

[letterhead: Oswalds]
28.3.22

My dear Sir.[5]

I am sorry I have no copy to send you.

There is no other edition of the play. But before long D. P & Co will publish in the Deep Sea edition a vol containing my plays – The Secret Agent and One day More.[6] The date of that publication is not arranged yet however.

Believe me faithfully Yours

Joseph Conrad

---

[1] Basil Lubbock's *The Colonial Clippers* (1921).
[2] Mentioning Conrad's service in them, Lubbock discusses the *Loch Etive* and the *Torrens* and also provides photographs.
[3] Wise's privately printed *The Black Mate*.   [4] In the *London Magazine* in April 1908.
[5] Unidentified.   [6] See the letter to Doubleday of 19 February.

To Warrington Dawson

Text MS Duke; Randall 205–6

[letterhead: Oswalds]

29.3.22

My dear Warrington

I write a few words at once to thank You for Your dedication[1] which touches me by its generous expressions. But it would have been a more intimate and a closer communion if You had merely written "To my friend" above my name as only from one craftsman to another cou[ld][2] be done.

My dear, I am sorry at what you say of the late Pinker. That he should have in any way damaged your prospects is deplorable. But I do not feel remorse in the matter; for if You remember the only time we talked on the subject (outside the road-gate of Capel) my advice to you was *not* to go to him. A year or more later I heard from him that he was acting for You.[3]

I do not believe that any publisher would have a particular confidence in my judgment. What exactly would You like me to do.

Jessies love.

Affecly Yours

J. Conrad

To Eric Pinker

Text TS Berg; Unpublished

Oswalds

Bishopsbourne

Kent

March 29th. 1922

Private & Conf^{al}

My dear Eric.

I enclose here a letter from Doubleday which I received this morning. As you will see it is kind in tone and, I have no doubt, sincere in sentiment. You will notice the firm's anxiety (which was evident also in Everitt's letter) to have no intermediary in the shape of an American agent between you and themselves, especially as far as my affairs are concerned.

---

[1] Of *The Pyramid* (1922) to Conrad as 'the Prophet of Two Continents Who Looks With True Vision on the World Yet Keeps His Faith And with Wise Words Strengthens Faith in Others'.

[2] Randall reads 'can', but the word looks more like an unfinished 'could'.

[3] For the relevant correspondence, which suggests a more complicated story, see Randall, pp. 155–6, 170–3, and his introduction, pp. 54–5.

Of course I do not know precisely how J. B. transacted my business with D. P. & Co. You would probably wish to follow his precedent. It seems to me however from some letters he showed me and generally from the trend of our talks that he dealt with them direct. Personally I think that would be the best method. It is a fact that I have confidence in D. P. & Co. and, without making too much of it, have a belief in their declarations of goodwill and interest in my work. That they have been putting forward plans and schemes relating to my books before your father I know for a fact; and also that he never accepted them without much preliminary discussion, mainly of the terms they offered. And he generally had his way.

I suppose you will agree with me that the best policy would be to keep on good terms with D. P. & Co. who certainly have already a stake in the prosperity of my work. D. you will observe, promises another letter which I will communicate to you directly it arrives. There is a mysterious phrase about some additional things he could tell which arouses my curiosity. In acknowledging his letter I will encourage him to say all he has in his mind.

Affctly Yrs

J. Conrad

To Eric Pinker
Text TS Berg; Unpublished

Oswalds,
Bishopsbourne,
Kent.
March 30th. 1922.

My dear Eric.

I certainly think that what you propose to do is quite adequate, but paying good money for nothing is the most exasperating thing in the world.

Certainly, my dear Eric, it would be best to accept Nash's offer and let that old bandit F. U[nwin] have his share of the plunder, which he doesn't deserve.[1]

---

[1] In August 1922, Nash and Grayson reprinted *Tales of Unrest* (originally published by Unwin) in Nash's Famous Fiction Library.

Enclosed here you will find a cheque for £36 covering the money for which I suppose Borys has called. Pardon me worrying but that was the quickest way in which I could convey it to him.

Yrs

J. Conrad.

To F. N. Doubleday

Text TS Princeton; Unpublished

[letterhead: Oswalds]
March 31st. 1922.

My dear Mr Doubleday

Thank you for your very kind and interesting letter from the Bahamas,[1] and the portrait of the Sea Scamp which seems a very charming schooner.

As to the main subject matter of your letter I have always felt exactly in the same way – that the communication with us should be as direct as possible. I think that it was the practice of J. B. Pinker to negotiate directly with you, at any rate about my work, and Eric Pinker will continue to do so because of his own inclination and also because it is my own wish. So we are all in agreement. I have felt now for a long time that the natural home of my work in America is the Garden City.[2]

I wonder how the notion got about of dealing through an American agent. The thought had never entered my head, so I could not have been speaking in that sense to anybody. I can assure you that Eric Pinker has never thought of it either. I wonder if the rumour has not originated in the brain of some literary agent himself, for I believe that J. B. P. had an agent (whose name I never heard) in the U.S., though I always understood that he never had anything to do with my work.[3]

I have always felt that our relations have been very confidential and my feeling certainly was against the intrusion of any stranger. But all the same, when you have leisure to write to me I should like to hear all your reasons, not as a matter of practical importance but simply for information on a matter of which I ought to be fully informed as a sort of sentim[ent]al satisfaction.

Always Yours faithfully

Joseph Conrad

---

[1] From his winter retreat on New Providence Island.
[2] On Long Island, the home of Doubleday's Country Life Press.
[3] Pinker had long relied on Paul R. Reynolds of New York to place Conrad's occasional writings but not his books.

To Eric Pinker
Text TS Berg; Unpublished

Oswalds
Bishopsbourne
Kent.
April 1st. 1922.

My dear Eric
    I send you a letter I have received to-day from Allan Wade. Will you please
tell me whether in view of the paragraph marked with red pencil you want
me to send him a copy to show to his theatrical friend. I don't like to do
it without first communicating with you, as I don't know what your plans
may be or what the situation is with regard to these plays – my own and the
translated one.[1]

Yours

Joseph Conrad

To Eric Pinker
Text MS Berg; Unpublished

[Oswalds]
[early April? 1922][2]

Dear E
    What do you think of this. It seems to me he wants too many.[3] What sort
of vol is he going to make up with all these others too. A folio? Suppose when
you write to D. P & Co you ask their opinion, and, as your judgment prompts
you let them decide. I personally don't care very much for it. The money
can't amount to anything in a publication of that kind.

Yrs

J. C.

---

[1] *The Secret Agent* and *The Book of Job*. For Allan Wade, see the letter to him of 4 April.
[2] Written on the verso of a letter from Joseph J. Reilly, dated 22 March 1922, Ware, Massachusetts.
[3] Reilly (1881–1951) wanted to reprint 'An Outpost of Progress', 'Karain', 'The Lagoon', 'Amy
     Foster', and 'To-morrow' in a short-story collection to be published by Ginn & Co. of Boston.
     He had already written on Conrad for the *Catholic World*, and his essay 'The Shorter Stories
     of Joseph Conrad' appears in *Of Books and Men* (New York: Messer, 1942), pp. 79–92.

To Edmund Candler
Text TS/MS Morgan; Candler xxxix–xl

> Oswalds,
> Bishopsbourne,
> Kent.
> April 3rd. 1922.

My dear Candler,[1]

I send a dictated letter because I am laid up and can't use a pen.

It's good to feel you nearer England and established in that angle of the Bay of Biscay which on a map looks like the corner of a butterfly net for catching the airy Atlantic gales. Luckily I believe they don't blow home there, or else no inhabitant could keep his hair on – I don't mean cap, which could always be attached by a cable – I mean hair, which, meteorologically speaking, no amount of pomatum could keep on anybody's scalp.

Naturally directly I read your letter I looked round for a Bradshaw.[2] It was instinctive. The first impulse was to get a ticket and proceed to inspect your establishment. But my travelling days I am afraid are over. I am never really well for ten days together and I dare not trust myself from home even as far as London. When I have to go there I try always to get back for the night.

"Abdication" arrived four or five days ago. How short that book is and how much you have managed to put into it! As you may imagine, I read it at once. It is an admirable performance and if it suffers at all in contrast with "Siri Ram" it [is] simply because of the inferior personality of the principal personage, (I mean inherent[+]) and of the change in mental and political atmosphere that has come over the spirit of that dream. The execution is as admirable as the other. Every inhabitant of Hindustan, (including the whites) is done in a masterly way. As to the aim, the effect, and the impression, I assure you, my dear Candler, that there is no man who could have done more.[3]

[+] inferiority, not inferiority of execution)

[1] Novelist, traveller, a war correspondent and journalist in the Middle East and Tibet, and autobiographer, Edmund Candler (1874–1926) left England for India in 1896 in search of romance, living there until 1914. After 1906 he was Principal of Patiala College, where E. M. Forster met him during his first journey to the subcontinent. Candler's health, undermined by his experience in Asia, forced a return to Europe where he lived out his final years in the French Basque country.

[2] The comprehensive railway timetable.

[3] Constable published Candler's *Abdication* in March. His *Siri Ram, Revolutionist: A Transcript from Life, 1907–1910* had appeared in 1914. Conrad owned a presentation copy, dated November 1918. For his immediate response to *Siri Ram*, see *Letters*, 6, p. 303. The title character is a militant Indian student who is gaoled for publishing an incendiary article; when released, he assassinates a judge. *Abdication*, also rooted in Candler's experiences in India, tells the story

The reception by the press was very good as far as I have seen and heard. The "Times" article,[1] curiously stodgy, though of course immensely appreciative on every ground except that of literary achievement which doesn't seem to have been perceived by the reviewer; but after all, they have given you a special column and one mustn't be too hard on them.

I hope, my dear friend, that all you and yours will find peace of mind and comfort of body which make up the sum of daily happiness – that minimum which makes life tolerable. Am I right in believing that the summer temperatures are very pleasant where you live? I don't remember now. I hardly remember the features of the land. The last time I stood on Irun bridge (not a railway bridge) was in '76, I think;[2] and when I think of it I am surprised at being still on this revolving stage. The part I have been playing on it has grown intensely wearisome – I mean the part that I have been, so to speak, acting daily for twenty-six years. The run seems too long, the part has grown unreal – out of date.

My wife sends her most friendly regards. We often talk of you in this house which you have never seen. And yet you haunt it! A phenomenon not of spiritism but of affectionate memory.

Ever yours

J Conrad

of Brian Riley, a newspaper editor who loses patience with 'the impressions of the Imperial-minded, which run in channels none too broad at any time' (p. 2). Persuaded by his Indian friends, Riley becomes 'as impatient for Swaraj as a Nationalist' (p. 206). At the end of the book, inspired by Gandhi, he becomes a revered healer of eye diseases in the Himalayas and decries 'Race-hatred... and our gospel of efficiency' (p. 277).

[1] 'India's Discontents', *Times Literary Supplement*, 30 March, p. 204.
[2] Road and rail bridges across the Bidasoa river link Irún in Spain with Hendaye in France. As the only evidence that Conrad visited the Basque country, this memory is intriguing, especially because the date given is 1876, the year in which the Third Carlist War ended. Estella, the last Carlist stronghold, fell on 19 February, and on the 28th, Don Carlos, pretender to the Spanish throne, crossed the road bridge into exile. From 23 December 1875 to 10 July 1876, Conrad was in Marseilles between voyages to the Antilles (and as this letter suggests perhaps went to Spain). The Basque provinces of Spain were the Carlist heartland. It is also the homeland of Rita in *The Arrow of Gold* and of Rita, Theresa, and their uncle the priest in the unfinished novel *The Sisters*. A dense cloud of uncertainty envelops Conrad's activities in the Carlist cause, which may have extended to gun-running (*Letters*, 6, p. 451, n.1), but 1876 and the Basque country offer as likely a setting as 1877 and the coast of Catalonia – the time and place given in 'The *Tremolino*' (*The Mirror of the Sea*). Conrad may, of course, have been active in both areas, but Cervoni's *balancelle* was not ideally suited for the Bay of Biscay.

To G. Jean-Aubry
Text TS Yale; Unpublished

[letterhead: Oswalds]
April. 3rd. 1922.

Très cher.

Thank you for your letter. It finds me in a state of mental anxiety (most discouraging) as I have been laid up again in great pain and worry for four days.

To-day I am better physically; but I don't suppose for a moment I can resume my work yet. Perhaps to-morrow. The days do pass and they cannot be recalled.

I will take steps to find for you "The Tale"[1] since you want to go on with that. I have no copy here and I really don't know where to find one, but Miss Hallowes will write to Pinker by this evening's post. Meantime she will send you "Prince Roman" which I personally don't think is a very good thing for translation – I mean for 'effect' and as a representative piece of work, which it doesn't seem to me to be.

Pardonnez cette courte note.

A Vous de coeur

J. C.

To Allan Wade
Text TS/MS Leeds; J-A, 2, 267–9

[letterhead: Oswalds]
April 4th. 1922.

My dear Wade[2]

Thank you for your good letter which I have read with great interest. All your remarks are well grounded, especially as to the 4 Scenes of the last Act. In Warsaw, where I believe this play is going to be performed before long, the notion is to have the stage divided by a partition showing the shop and the parlour, with some modifications in disposing of the furniture; as for instance Mr Verloc not being visible to the audience as he lies dead on the sofa, and things like that. There are also other changes in the Polish version of which

---

[1] Jean-Aubry's translation, 'L'Histoire', appeared in *La Revue de Genève*, 6 (March 1923), 320–39.

[2] Allan Wade (1881–1955), actor, director, bibliophile, and scholar, made his stage début in 1904 and worked for Harley Granville-Barker from 1906 to 1915. A producer for the Stage Society, he was a founder of the Phoenix Society in 1919. He translated plays by Jean Giraudoux and Jean Cocteau. His large library of Modernist writers included Conrad. He edited Henry James's dramatic criticism (1948), published a bibliography of W. B. Yeats (1951), and edited Yeats's letters (1954).

I have only heard by letter. I should like very much to see it. I think I will write to the very clever adapter and ask him to send me a copy.

This play has been criticised by several people. McKinnel had it for a year, but as you know his management was a succession of failures and he obviously lacked courage to put this play on. I am certain it could not have been worse than it was for him. On the other hand he might have had a success of curiosity; which would have been better than the series of three dead failures with which he began his management.

The telescoping of the First Act cannot of course be denied, but I ask myself whether it is deadly? I should not like to touch that because it was difficult to do and I do not see any other way of explaining the situation. I wonder whether the public would bother their heads about the time Winnie has been away. As to the visit of the three anarchists, well, yes, it may appear to be what you say, but I ask myself whether it is not justified by the fact that it establishes the psychology of the whole play absolutely. I admit I don't know how things look on the stage. On the other hand, after a certain amount of reflection on these matters it seems to me that it mainly depends on the manner. Almost anything can be got down people's throats on the stage.

The Third Act, which is Lady Mabel's Drawingroom, I put there to give relief; and, though I don't know very well how to defend it, yet I stick to it after much meditation. It is a matter of feeling; and, after all, apart from its freeing the atmosphere a little from the general horror of this damned thing, it is a drawingroom scene which cannot be said to suffer from banality; and it seems to me that it is not altogether outside the action.

Reverting for a moment to the 'telescoped' effect of the First Act, I wonder if it could not be lessened by, for instance, letting the anarchists come in and establish themselves (as their habit was) round Mr Verloc's fireplace and then, after they had talked for a while, letting Winnie return with her brother. After she has gone up stairs taking her brother with her, the conversation would be brought round on the lines that produced that effect on the boy. I don't think there would be any difficulty about that, but I must tell you that the play since I fabricated it has become so real to me that I cannot imagine any change in it without it appearing a most shocking thing.

Of course the only distinctive quality of this play is the fact that it is excessively Conradian. It may have a succès de curiosité, which of course can never be very paying but may, at any rate, prevent a dead loss.

I am delighted to see that you like the Second Act. I suppose you mean both Scenes with two personages in each. From the letter I had from Warsaw I see that my adapter, an experienced craftsman, managed to cram the essence of the Second Scene in some way or other into the Third Act. How he did it God only knows. I cannot imagine it myself and I do not feel at all easy in my mind about it. However, what happens there is not my affair at all. Neither does their division of the stage in the last Act appeal very much to my sense of the fitness of things. That sort of thing is associated in my mind with farces. I can see the difficulty of the changes and I was worried about it before I began to write the Fourth Act. It was however Vernon, who was then associated with Vedrenne, who encouraged me by telling me not to worry, and that he would manage it all right.

I have got my wife to lend me her copy of the play to show to your friend, who, I suppose, is a man we can trust! It is the only copy I have in the house.

Early last year I translated a Polish play which the author had sent me in book form,[1] and which had some success over there. I do not like to add to your occupations but I wonder whether you would mind looking at it and telling me what you think of it and whether it is at all possible on a West European or American stage? But if you are busy or do not want to bother your head about it you may send it back to me.

But I would consider it a great favour if your wife would cast her eye over it. It is a comedy not devoid of ideas which are presented lightly and with a certain 'esprit'. Will you present my request to Mrs Wade avec mes hommages les plus respectueux.[2]

My wife joins me in kindest regards to you both.

Always my dear Wade Yours

J. Conrad.

PS I am addressing you from bed where the gout has kept [me] four days now.

To Richard Curle
Text MS Indiana; Curle 88

[Oswalds]

[5 April 1922][3]

My dear Curle

a/[4] You may just as well say, which is a truth, that I do read bi[o]graphy and memoirs. History has a fascination for me. Naval, military political.

---

[1] Winawer's *The Book of Job*, translated not 'early last year' but in June 1921.
[2] 'With my most respectful duty'. Claudine Wade was French.
[3] Curle supplies the date.
[4] Letters 'a' and 'b' indicate deletions by Conrad on proofs, preserved with this letter, of Curle's 'Conrad at Home', *Daily Mail*, 7 April, p. 8. Letter 'a' refers to the following deletion: 'For instance, favourite books of his are Wallace's "Malay Archipelago," Darwin's "Voyage of a Naturalist," Whymper's "High Andes," the sea yarns of Cooper and Marryat and the novels of Dickens.'

b/[1] Will that never be taken for granted? Do give it a rest in print.

I am interested even in party politics the develop[t] of institutions and opinions, and emotions of mankind in the mass. I feel deeply what happens in the world – a genuine sentiment qualified by irony – something like that.

Am laid up and in pain.

Ever Yrs

J. C.

To G. Jean-Aubry
Text MS Yale; *L.fr.* 170

[Oswalds]
7. Ap. '22

Cher ami.

Voilà The Tale. Il faudra me renvoyez le t-script car c'est le seul exemplaire que possède Pinker.

Merci du N° du Temps. La traduction[2] n'est pas mal. J'ai vu aussi l'article de Henriot.[3] Enfin.

Je suis encore au lit.

Tout est arrêté!

C'est a en devenir fou – mais je me retiens.

Je Vs embrasse

Votre

J. C.

Translation

My dear friend.

"The Tale" is enclosed. You will have to return the t-script to me since it's the only copy Pinker has.

Thank you for the issue of *Le Temps*. The translation isn't bad. I also saw Henriot's article. Oh, well.

I am still in bed.

---

[1] Letter 'b' refers to the following deletion: 'By choice and sympathy he is an Englishman and though English is not his native language he has frequently told me he could have written his books in no other. Altogether he is a man of whom England may well be proud.'

[2] Of *Victory*: the serial had just begun in *Le Temps*.

[3] Émile Henriot (1889–1961), French critic and literary historian, whose introductory note accompanied the translation.

Everything has come to a halt!
It's enough to drive one mad – but I hold on.
I embrace you

Yours

J. C.

To Eric Pinker
Text TS Berg; Unpublished

Oswalds,
Bishopsbourne,
Kent.
April 8th. [1922]¹

Dearest Eric

Here is Allan Wade's second letter² which you will read attentively espe-cially as concerns Mr Campbell and Mr Campbell's client. All those things will be much clearer to you than to me who have never heard of Mr Campbell. Is he a theatrical agent?³

Of course if he takes a hand in this he will require a commission, but you know, my dear Eric, that the position is such that no chance of a few pounds should be missed. I would propose that if anything eventuates from it, this man's commission which of course you will arrange on, I suppose, some customary basis, should be deducted from the proceeds which we would share as by previous arrangement. This, I mean to apply both to my play and to my translation.

When it comes to negotiations I hope you will part with as few rights as possible to the American, unless indeed your opinion is that it will be better for us to get hold of what offers rather than to take our chance of making separate bargains, but in any case, dear Eric, I should like you to reserve the European and Continental rights absolutely to ourselves. I am sorry to say I am dictating this still from bed. No use making a mystery of it. I have had a pretty rough time. But are we downhearted . . . ?⁴

NO!

Always Yours

J Conrad.

---

¹ The reference to Wade gives the year.   ² Of 7 April (MS Berg).
³ James Lawrence Campbell, of Albion Rd, South Hampstead, was indeed a theatrical agent.
⁴ Written in 1914, Arthur Boyton's song of this name became one of the war's most famous. At the end of each verse, Boyton would sing 'Are we downhearted?' and the chorus, usually joined by the audience, would answer with a raucous 'No!' Beyond the music halls, the words became a catch-phrase.

To Allan Wade

Text TS Leeds; J-A, 2, 269–71

[letterhead: Oswalds]
April 9th. 1922.

My dear Wade

Thank you very much for your letter of the 7th. I feel compunctious at taking up so much of your time and your thought. It is indeed very kind and friendly of you to take so much interest in the fate of those two plays.

Your commendation of my dialogue flatters me exceedingly, the more so that the effect you approve is the outcome of great care and of a very determined purpose to approach colloquial conversation as much as possible. To learn from you that I have been successful is a great comfort. As a matter of fact I think that even in my novels the dialogue is never very literary, unless the thing becomes unavoidable or is justified in some other way. The doubt however in my mind was always whether my dialogue however dramatic in form responds to the "requirements of the stage" – which at times appear to me as a great and august mystery, and at others vanish, as it were, before my meditations, into thin air.

Your care of my wife's copy has touched her very much. I don't think it would have been endangered, but even had it been mislaid or lost by some mischance I could have, I daresay, replaced it. Why I sent the printed copy is because I mistrust the correctness of the typed text; and as a matter of fact the play reads better in print.

I am glad, however, that you got in touch with Eric Pinker who is carrying on his father's business and has all my confidence. I had a note from him saying that no negotiations in which he has been engaged in America, are advanced enough to be the slightest obstacle to any proposal that could be made by Mr Campbell or any of Mr Campbell's clients. Pray address him direct on any matters of fact which you may want to know, since whatever is arranged he will have to come in at the end as representing me on the business side.

Of course it is a great comfort to see you take that friendly attitude towards the author. The mere notion of having to snip, readjust, fit in and alter that stuff already cut out and put together after much anxious thought is enough to make me shudder. This sensitiveness however may be simply the result of my physical state which is not good. I am dictating this in bed.

Still, the dreadful material difficulties of the 4th Act are always present to my mind. And yet Vernon who, so to speak, hung over me while I was writing that act did make very light of them apparently. Whenever he came down to see me at Spring Grove he used to draw little sketches with a bit of pencil on a scrap of paper and the whole thing seemed much easier than cutting bread and butter for afternoon tea.

I hope the repeated reading of The Secret Agent won't disgust you too much. I simply can't look at the thing any more. As to the comedy (with the absurd title) for which I have an inexplicable fondness as if it were my own, Mrs Wade's criticism is perfectly just. The Third Act is certainly the worst of the three, at any rate in the reading. I always felt that. Having undertaken the job to translate it you may imagine I know the blessed thing backwards. But on reflection there are things that do not look hopeless on the stage. There are good scenes, using the word scene in the French sense.[1] The dismay of that precious gang may be made very funny; then the scene between Herup and the policeman, if it is acted properly, has good elements of comedy that may get over the footlights all right; and at the end when Herup seeing all those people staring at him forgets himself and in his workman's clothes begins to address them as if he were lecturing some students, has got a certain value. His exit too with the remark of old Kurdys that this strange person (who holds in his hands all their reputations) wouldn't take a tip is extremely good. My opinion is that this is the Act which will require most acting, the most careful adjustment of effects and a most accurate judgment of what I may call tempo, since there are certain delicate shades which may be lost by acceleration. It certainly won't play itself; whereas the Third Act, as to which I share your opinion absolutely is comparatively simple if the actors can only be induced not to accentuate the farcical characteristics towards the end. As the play has been left in my hands by Winawer to do the best I can with it I will tell you at once that I am very much of your way of thinking as to trying whether the Stage Society will take it up.[2] It's very good of you to propose to act in that matter. I confess I should like this thing to get out behind the footlights, especially if there is a chance of it being taken by Mr Campbell's American. Otherwise a performance by the Stage Society has always struck me as a sort of cheerful funeral ceremony, or at any rate as a certificate of unfitness to live as far as the large public is concerned. As to the identity of "Mr X."[3] I shouldn't like it to be proclaimed from housetops, but it need not be made a mystery of. Do you think the disclosure would help the chances of

---

[1] In the French tradition, a new scene begins whenever an actor enters or leaves the stage.

[2] Founded in 1899, the Stage Society mounted small-scale professional productions of valuable but uncommercial plays such as Conrad's *One Day More*, performed in 1905. As a private organisation, the Society enjoyed two advantages: it could put on Sunday performances when theatres were normally date, and it could mount productions without submitting scripts to the Lord Chamberlain's deputy, the Examiner of Plays, who could insist upon cuts or ban a play entirely.

[3] Conrad himself as translator.

the play? What I would like is that when it gets as far as the bill stage[1] Mr X. should remain, while at the same time everybody would know who Mr X. is. It would fit the spirit of comedy that 'All London' should know it – which would still leave about five million people in the dark.

Pray note, my dear Wade, that the whole thing is one single trap for the easy-going, unharrowed, after-dinner sentiment. With perhaps, the sole exception of the wife, who is not made odious, every single person is sympathetic – the sympathetic burglar-sharper, the sympathetic professor-workman, the precious Tola, down to that ass Klotz and the music hall-ditty writer with his German alias who is simply fair game. And yet I feel that the acceptance, let alone the success, of that thing will hang on a hair:[2] the creation of a responsive mood in the audience. On the other hand if the hair holds it may give the play a real good chance.

Give your wife my dutiful regards and thanks for reading the play.

Always affectl[y] Yours

Joseph Conrad.

To G. Jean-Aubry
Text MS Yale; Unpublished

[Oswalds]
[10 April 1922][3]

Cher Jean.

Merci de Votre lettre et du magnifique vol.[4]

Voulez Vous venir ici Samedi pour lunch jusqu'a Mardi.

Je me suis levé aujourd hui. Nous serons tous heureux de Vous voir.

Envoyez moi un petit mot

Tout à Vous

J. C.

Translation

Dear Jean.

Thank you for your letter and the superb volume.

Would you like to come here from lunch Saturday until Tuesday?

---

[1] The stage of distributing play-bills around London.
[2] Like the sword hung above Damocles' head by Dionysius, tyrant of Syracuse.
[3] Jean-Aubry supplies the date.
[4] *La Vie et l'oeuvre d'après les lettres et les documents inédits d'Eugène Boudin*, a biography of the French painter, Louis-Eugène Boudin (1824–98), a precursor of the Impressionists.

I got up to-day. We shall all be very glad to see you.
Drop me a line.

Yours truly

J. C.

To Eric Pinker
Text MS Berg; Unpublished

[letterhead: Oswalds]

11.4.22

My dear Eric

I've crawled downstairs yesterday, and this damned push is over without breaking up.

I send you this note mainly to tell you that Somerset House[1] have sent me ch. 15.4.6 in reduction of supertax – which I have paid into my acct.

Your office has acted in that matter so you ought to know.

Did I thank you for statement of my debits? I have received it a few days ago.

Ever Yours

J. C.

To G. Jean-Aubry
Text MS Yale; Unpublished

[Oswalds]

Mercredi [12 April 1922][2]

Mon très cher.

On vous attend ici Samedi prochain. Quel train prenez vous?

J'ai lu votre biographie de Boudin.

C'est très interéssant et très sympathique.

Je vous embrasse

Votre

Conrad

Translation

Wednesday

My very dear friend,

We expect you here next Saturday. What train will you take?

I read your biography of Boudin.

---

[1] Headquarters of the Inland Revenue.   [2] Jean-Aubry supplies the date.

It is very interesting and very likeable.
I embrace you.

Yours

Conrad

To Eric Pinker
Text MS Berg; Unpublished

[letterhead: Oswalds]
12.4.22

My dear Eric.

I take it that as arranged verbally You will provide for the service of the month beginning on the 15. prox^{mo}.[1]

You will get a large batch of the Rover for clean copy on Tuesday next.

Of course the end will be delayed somewhat by my having been laid up again. The pain was too severe to let me work.

Affct^{ly} yours

J. Conrad.

To Bruno Winawer
Text TS copy Yale; *Głos* (114); Najder 279–80[2]

Oswalds,
Bishopsbourne,
Kent.
12.4.22.

Dear Sir.

I apologise for the delay in replying to your letter of 14 March. I have been very ill. I found your letter most interesting. Tout ce que Vous avez fait est bien fait.[3] However, I must admit to feeling curious as to how it was all done. Would you please send me a copy (typescript) of the text? As to our affairs, I cannot get a definite answer from America, and it seems to me it would be best to offer our patient Job to the London Stage Society.

During the London season the Stage Society produces two or three plays pour l'élite de l'intelligence et de la société.[4] They give three performances of each and pay nothing, but that is the way to get known as theatre managers attend the performances. I am not a member of the Stage Society, but I have friends there. I wrote to the Secretary the day before yesterday. I am only afraid that their programme for the 1922 season is already fixed. We shall see.

---

[1] Service on an outstanding balance?   [2] Translation from Nadjer with minor alterations.
[3] 'Everything you've done has been done well.'   [4] 'The intellectual and social élite'.

In any case c'est une distinction to be played by the S. S., and it might lead to a contract. At the moment there is an American in London (I can't remember his name) who is an agent for several theatres. Perhaps something could be done through him.

Pardon my scrawl. Pray be so kind as to tell Miss A. Zagórska that you had news from me and that I shall write to her soon.

Faites mes amitiés je Vous prie à Żeromski pour qui j'ai une vraie affection.[1]

Tout à Vous

J. Conrad.

To Aniela Zagórska

Text MS copy Yale;[2] Najder 280–1

Oswalds,
19.4.22.

My dear Aniela.

I am replying to you immediately though I think you ought to have received Jessie's letter by now.

I was in bed for a fortnight and am now beginning to work again. My finances are a bit shaky. Pinker was an optimist. I spent too much during the past two years and will now have to suffer for it. Enfin. I had nothing to congratulate myself about, and that's why I didn't write. I answered Mr Winawer's letter and asked him to give you my news.

Jessie is on the whole well but still in pain. The treatment was not very successful. Borys is working in London, and John is on holiday. We embrace you very warmly.

Forgive me for not writing for so long. I am still not feeling completely well and after half a day's work feel awfully tired.

Ever affectionately yours

Konrad.

To Eric Pinker

Text MS Berg; Unpublished

[Oswalds]
24.4.22

My dear Eric.

Herewith Chaps. 4. 5. 6 of the Rover. I am going on with him and there will be no reason for either of us to be ashamed of the thing when its done.

Is F. N. D[oubleday] expected over here?

---

[1] 'Pray give my regards to Żeromski of whom I am genuinely fond.'   [2] In French.

I am nearly recovered but I mean to take no chances; so I don't propose yet to come up for Everett. If there is hurry, well, you and Pawling perhaps would be good enough to make a selection. Just now I don't want to do anything but write. It's slow enough at best – God knows!

I will send you in a day or two John's school *acct*. He goes back on the 5th. prox.

R. C[urle] has been given a post on the Dy Mail – £750 – not bad, considering. But these positions are not very secure as you know. He will be sending you an article on me (of which I will say nothing here) written for The *Blue Peter Mag*. which he would like you to place in U.S.[1]

Yrs affect[ly]

J. Conrad.

To Richard Curle

Text TS/MS Indiana; Curle 89

Oswalds,
Bishopsbourne,
Kent.
April 24th. 1922.

My dear Richard.

I did ask Jessie to express to you my intense satisfaction at your having obtained that post on the Daily Mail. If it will leave you time enough to do your own work I certainly think that the salary is not at all bad to begin with. May every possible success attend your work in the journalistic sphere. I shall be immensely interested to know what precisely you will have to do and whether you will be able to find some intimate satisfaction in your daily task.

I have this morning received the article for the Blue Peter. I think I have given you already to understand the nature of my feelings. Indeed I spoke to you very openly expressing my fundamental objection to the character you wished to give to it. I do not for a moment expect that what I am going to say here will convince you or influence you in the least. And indeed I have neither the wish nor the right to assert my position. I will only point out to you that my feelings in that matter are at least as legitimate as your own. It

---

[1] Curle's 'Joseph Conrad in the East' for the September–October number. *The Blue Peter: The Magazine of the Sea, Travel and Adventure* was named after the blue and white flag flown when a ship is about to sail.

is a strange fate that everything that I have, of set artistic purpose, laboured to leave indefinite, suggestive, in the penumbra of initial inspiration, should have that light turned on to it and its insignificance (as compared with I might say without megalomania the ampleness of my conceptions) exposed for any fool to comment upon or even for average minds to be disappointed with. Didn't it ever occur to you, my dear Curle, that I knew what I was doing in leaving the facts of my life and even my tales in the background. Explicitness, my dear fellow, is fatal to the glamour of all artistic work, robbing it of all suggestiveness, destroying all illusion. You seem to believe in literalness and explicitness, in facts and also in expression. Yet nothing is more clear than the utter insignificance of explicit statement and also its power to call attention away from things that matter in the region of art.

There, however, I am afraid we will never agree. Your praise of my work allied to your analysis of its origins (which really are not its origins at all, as you know perfectly well) sounds exaggerated by the mere force of contrast. I wouldn't talk like this if I did not attach a very great value to everything you write about me and did not believe in its wide influence. It isn't a matter of literary criticism at all if I venture to point out to you that the dogmatic, ex-cathedra tone that you have adopted in your article positively frightens me. As you tell me that you have a copy of the article by you I'll venture to make a few alterations, more to let you see what is in my mind than with any hope of convincing you. I will only remark to you, my dear, that it is generally known that you are my intimate friend, that the text carries an air of authority and that a lot of dam-fools will ascribe to me the initiative and sanction of all the views and facts expressed. And one really could not blame them if they thought and said that I must have wanted all those facts disclosed.

All those are my personal feelings. You won't wonder at them if I call your attention to the fact that in "Youth", in which East or West are of no importance whatever, I kept the name of the Port of landing out of the record of "poeticised" sensations. The paragraph you quote of the East meeting the narrator is all right in itself; whereas directly it's connected with Mintok[1] it becomes nothing at all. Mintok is a damned hole without any beach and without any glamour and in relation to the par: is not in tone. Therefore the par: when pinned to a particular spot must appear diminished – a fake. And yet it is true!

---

[1] I.e., Muntok, a port town near Bangka Strait off Sumatra, the refuge the *Palestine*'s crew reached after she sank.

However those are all private feelings. I think too that the impression of gloom, oppression, and tragedy, is too much emphasised. You know, my dear, I have suffered from such judgments in the early days; but now the point of view, even in America, has swung in another direction; and truly I don't believe myself that my tales are gloomy, or even very tragic, that is not with a pessimistic intention. Anyway that reputation, whether justified or not, has deprived me of innumerable readers and I can only regret that you have found it necessary to make it as it were the ground-tone of your laudatory article.

One more suggestion. Perhaps you may find it possible to shorten to a certain extent the quotations which are of course admirably selected. I think that for "Blue Peter" there would be too much text; in America it would of course not matter.

I have written lately to Eric telling him about your post, at the end of my letter, and just mentioning that you will be probably sending him an article on me which you would wish him to place in the U.S.

I have been again laid up, but I attempt to scrawl a little more. It is to ask you to consider the modifications I have suggested to your article P^t I. After all your thought remains untouched and they are not much in themselves.

I absolutely object to being called a "*tragedian*". The thing is shocking.

Ever yours

J. Conrad.

Jessie sends her love.

To Eric Pinker
Text TS Berg; Unpublished

Oswalds Bishopsbourne.
April 25th. 1922

My dear Eric

Doubledays have presented me with a copy of that book[1] some time ago and as a matter of fact I told Pawling that they had. He must have forgotten.

No, decidedly I can't do that thing. Not even as a matter of business. A few words for a friend's work are another matter but even that I feel always most unwilling to do. I haven't got the knack of it and am too old a dog now

---

[1] Perhaps Warrington Dawson's *Paul Clermont*, published by Doubleday in 1921, and taken up by Heinemann? Given his reservations about Dawson's work, it is likely that Conrad would not want to write more than 'A few words' about it.

to learn new tricks. Pray put this into the language of common civility for
Pawling.

As I have already a copy of the book I think it only fair to return this one
which I have not even opened.

Always affet^ly Yours

J. C.

To Michael Holland

Text TS Private collection; Unpublished

[letterhead: Oswalds]
April 26th. 1922.

My dear Holland

I return to you Mr Lewis' letter. I thought it best to write to him direct to
say that I did not want "Lord Jim" adapted for the stage, if indeed such a
thing were possible. But I don't think that it is possible. The story is in itself
nothing, it is composed of detached episodes, and such value as it may have
depends purely on its literary quality which of course can not be transferred
to the boards of a theatre.

Since the beginning of the year I have been laid up twice for many days
and now I am laid up again for the third time. This is the reason why I dictate
this letter.

It is very good of you to remind us of your invitation, which indeed we have
not forgotten. I am desperately in arrears with my work and getting quite
unhappy about it. My wife too is expecting another visit from the surgeon.
Under those circumstances it is impossible to say when we will be able to get
away from home.

Our love to you all big and little

Ever sincerely Yours
Joseph Conrad.

To Eric Pinker

Text MS Berg; Unpublished

[letterhead: Oswalds]
27.4.22

My dear Eric.

Thanks for your letter and the typed copies of IV. V. VI. of The Rover. I
am going now steadily. I only wish I could be as quick as your typing people.

I enclose John's acct.

He is going to school on the 5. prox.

I have heard of Sieroszewski[1] but not *from* him as far as I can remember. I could do nothing with his MS. I daresay the work is clever enough but if you think you can do nothing with the prisoner story you had better return both to him.

Where is he anyhow? In Eng^d or in Pol^d?

———————

I understood from A Wade that there was an American looking out for plays here. Probably Campbell's client. If you are in touch and think it worth while to offer the civility of a personal interview you may bring him here.

It's just a suggestion. The matter is important enough for a small sacrifice of that sort.

———————

When I get a good lot of The R[over] ready we shall try to arrange for a visit to Burys Ct as your mother has so kindly proposed – returning via London when you could perhaps fix a day with Everett's masterpieces.

Affec^ly Yrs

J. Conrad

To Richard Curle
Text MS Indiana; Curle 90

[Oswalds]
Sat. 10. AM. [29 April 1922][2]

Dearest Dick

I was just going to write to you that I was perfectly satisfied when your second letter arrived and has troubled me greatly. Why scrap a valuable piece of work?

I respect your labours too much to remain unmoved by your proposal. You have, I fear, my dear fellow thought too much of what I have written. I am in the habit to be unreserved with you as to my feelings and opinions – but I can never feel *hostile* towards anything you do. I respect your point of view even if I do not totally agree. It is after all a question of more or less expediency.

[1] Wacław Sieroszewski (1858–1945), a Polish novelist, poet, and ethnographer whose work reflected his eighteen years of exile in Siberia. During the First World War, he fought in the Polish Legion.
[2] Curle supplies the date.

Suppression would lie on my conscience – unless you have arrived at some personal conviction about it. My alterations could not have disgusted you to that extent. In p[art] I I have run my pen through 2 statements of fact – of quite minor importance and slightly altered the wording in one or two cases. Also made a few verbal changes. In p' II apart from some slight verbal changes – not interfering with the spirit of your argument – I struck out the phrase in which the word *tragedian* occurs. It is a repetition but you have no idea with what force it comes to the ordinary reader! You have called me a poet more than once before and the word tragedy (or tragic) occurs also at least twice before. You are supposed to be the man who knows more about me than anybody else. Don't forget my dear that as a *selling* author my position is by no means assured in the U.S. yet; and the average mind shrinks from tragic issues.

I had to write this before settling down to my dictating.[1]

Yours with great affection

J. Conrad

To Captain J. G. Sutherland

Text Sutherland 9–10

[Oswalds]
[May? 1922][2]

Dear Captain Sutherland,[3]

When you first told me of your intention to publish a little book about the cruise of the "Ready" in October-November 1916, and asked me if I had any objection, I told you that it was not in my power to raise an effective objection, but that in any case the recollection of your kindness during those days when we were shipmates in the North Sea would have prevented me from putting as much as a formal protest in your way. Having taken that attitude, and the book being now ready for publication, I am glad of this opportunity of testifying to my regard for you, for Lieutenant Osborne, R.N.R.,[4] and for the naval and civilian crews of H[is] M[ajesty's] Brigantine "Ready,"

---

[1] Of *The Rover*.

[2] Conrad writes here as if some time has passed since proofs of Sutherland's *At Sea with Joseph Conrad* arrived. He was 'laid up and not in a condition to read anything' in early April (see the letters of the 3rd), but as his letter to Garnett of 24 May notes, Conrad had taken to his bed on three other occasions since December. In any case, as Sutherland was able to use the present letter as the Foreword to his book, which appeared in June, a date far into May seems unlikely.

[3] Captain John Georgeson Sutherland (born 1871), received his master's certificate in 1897. He served in the Royal Navy during the war and was the captain of the Q-ship *Ready*, in which Conrad made a ten-day voyage in November 1916.

[4] Henry Osborne was the *Ready*'s first lieutenant.

not forgetting Mr Moodie, the sailing master, whose sterling worth we all appreciated so much both as a seaman and as a shipmate.[1]

I have no doubt that your memories are accurate, but as these are exclusively concerned with my person I am at liberty, without giving offence, to confess that I don't think they were worth preserving in print. But that is your affair. What this experience meant to me in its outward sensations and deeper feelings must remain my private possession. I talked to very few persons about it. I certainly never imagined that any account of that cruise would come before the public.

When the proofs of the little book, which you were good enough to send me, arrived here, I was laid up and not in a condition to read anything. Afterwards I refrained on purpose. After all, these are your own recollections, in which you have insisted on giving me a prominent position, and the fitness of them had to be left to your own judgment and to your own expression.

Joseph Conrad.

To Richard Curle

Text MS Indiana; Curle 91 (in part)[2]

[Oswalds]
2 May '22

My dear Richard

I have just got your letter. If you do not object to my alterations then publish the article in the form in which you have first conceived it. And if you could work into it (since it is written for the man in the street) something about my work having the quality of interest – as the m-in-the-s understands it – the interest of surprise, of story etc you will be rendering me a great service. I still suffer from the reputation of being a gloomy depressing author.

I have had a very unsatisfactory letter from D[oubleday] P[age] & C⁰. On the other hand I have been able to do some work.

I showed your letter to Jessie who sends you her warm sympathy and suggests you should come down on Sat for the week end if you can manage it. How do you feel about it my dear fellow?

Drop us a line.

Affct^ly Yrs ·

J. C.

---

[1] Captain W. Moodie, a Shetlander, had 'charmed' Conrad (Sutherland, p. 25).
[2] Curle omits the second paragraph.

To Eric Pinker
Text TS/MS Berg; Unpublished

Oswalds
Bishopsbourne
Kent.
May 2nd. 1922.

My dear Eric.

I send you here the letter received this morning from Doubleday.[1] It may be called a thoroughly unsatisfactory letter, both in its facts and in its implications.

The tone of the very first paragraph doesn't please me.[2] However that is a matter of no importance.

The par marked A is unsatisfactory as to facts,[3] which can not be helped in view of the general economical position, I may say, of the world. We can only regret them. The advertisements to which he alludes consist of two leaflets which I forward to you too with my own remarks on the back. The matter of "subscription and mail sales" in the U.S. has been mentioned to me some time ago by your father. In 1920 I think. As far as I remember dear J. B. was inclined to let them have their way as to terms, but I don't remember what those terms were, though that too was mentioned I believe.

The paragraphs B and C are thoroughly unsatisfactory in another way;[4] for that scheme is certainly of very great importance to us and was so regarded

---

[1] Of 30 April (TS copy Berg). Not marked with the letters of the alphabet to which Conrad refers (the original having been returned to him), the points of reference can be reconstructed from his comments.

[2] Doubleday wrote: 'I am glad to be able to forget the rumor about an American representative of Mr. Pinker Jr. in so far as it reassures old friends, at least, and probably the idea never had any foundation in fact.'

[3] Doubleday wrote: 'The first was a set to be sold by subscription and mail in the US – a field in which we have disposed of millions of books – and the matter of accepting a royalty which would make the plan possible. Pinker met our needs entirely for this plan. Unhappily, this branch of the business has had a tremendous sinking spell ... So for the present we are able to make little or no progress along these lines. But the general sale has held up well as with other books, which does not satisfy us and we hope to remedy it. The enclosed advertisement indicates one of our plans for pushing the whole Conrad property. This page appears in many places.'

[4] Doubleday wrote: 'The second scheme was the whole idea of printing a uniform set from the revised plates to be marketed in Great Britain through Heinemann. Pawling has been ill, as you know, and overwhelmed with pressing matters, and has only, I judge, but lately been able to bring the idea to a focus. Unfortunately the terms suggested by young Pinker are impossible. If accepted, it would mean a loss, not profit, from the first volume, and leave no adequate amount for promotion expenses – and without liberal and continuous expenditure and active work, I personally feel that the plan could not be made the kind of a success which you and Heinemann would be proud of.'

by J. B. who considered it as the crowning stone of his efforts on my behalf. "Impossible" is a big word to throw at one in a negotiation. The argument on which it is based (beginning with the words "If accepted") is the sort of thing that makes one angry from the suspicion that one is being taken for something soft. Does Doubleday really mean to begin a publication of an edition like that with one single volume and expect it to pay for all the initial expenses? Fancy poor old "Almayer's Folly" having to get up on its hind legs and hold up the whole business of "promotion", of the "liberal and continuous expenditure", and "active work" (whatever that may mean!). Who the devil would expect one volume to do all that? Whereas beginning with a batch of four at least these together could bring in something for the publicity of the other seventeen (not including Hueffer's coll[aborations] or nineteen including Hueffer's coll.). I may be wrong in what I say, but if I am wrong then Doubleday is still more so. One really can't take that sort of argumentation seriously.

The related par. C[1] reads as if Doubleday had taken a leaf from Lloyd George's book. But L. G. as far as I remember used to offer people ninepence for fourpence,[2] whereas Doubleday seems to be offering me ninepence for one shilling – which I presume is about what you have in your mind as a minimum royalty.

As to finding new readers, your father's opinion was that there were already in England new readers for my old books in an accessible edition, as my success was really made with the latest generation which often had a difficulty, amongst my scattered publishers, to find the book it wanted. Of that I had personal experience having received a good many letters of enquiry from all parts of England and Scotland. It is possible that father was unduly optimistic, but that really was not his characteristic; and the way Dent's reprints of four old books[3] had been sold seemed to point to that conclusion. As to D's talk of "small editions" and "selling in detail" I really don't know what it exactly

---

[1] Doubleday wrote: 'This plan is quite different from selling a new book of yours for which there is a ready market; it involves taking old books which have been on the market for years and finding new readers. My own judgment is that it would be impossible to do this and pay more than 9d. per copy royalty, and these were about the figures I had in mind when I talked of the subject with Mr. Pinker when I was in London last fall. My argument was that whatever books we succeeded in selling in this new edition would be additional to the sales which go on now; the books would have to be prepared in small editions, and sold in detail, so to speak.'

[2] See the letter of 26 May 1920.

[3] *Lord Jim, Nostromo, Youth* (all 1917) and *A Personal Record* (1919).

means. The principle of this transaction I take it was the keeping up of a stock of books for a, probably variable, but more or less continuous demand.

What is most unsatisfactory is the evidence that the English business has to got to be treated of in America. I remember, when the Heinemann partnership first came to light,[1] expressing my fear of something of the kind happening, to your father. And now it has come and we will have to make the best of it, which needn't be so bad; but there is no doubt that D. has a position of advantage. I foresaw something of the kind when I observed Doubleday making an infernal fuss about the new plates for the limited edition. Perhaps you don't know, or perhaps you do, that he went to every one of my publishers then, and tried to form an alliance on purpose to force those damned plates down their throats. He made himself a perfect nuisance to old Heinemann and was very badly received by F. U[nwin] whose back he set up to that extent that it took poor father two years hard work to get it down again. I must tell you, dear Eric, that father would always let me air my views and would discuss them with me because he by no means thought me a fool in practical affairs. Of course I never pretended to a knowledge of details or of methods. But of these he was a master.

What I dislike most, really, is the short par. D,[2] the tone of which doesn't please me at all. All this part about the "plan being abandoned" of "some other publisher" and going "over stale tales" displeases me mightily. It has not been put in there without an intention. There is no denying the fact that to a certain extent the man has got the whip-hand and no doubt knows it, as, evidently, he has the plates. What other publisher could we go to? Where is the man who would believe in my work to the extent of setting up twenty-one vols? Doubleday really can not believe that either you or I would want to drop the plan. That is why, my dear Eric, I dislike those few lines which there was not the slightest necessity for him to write.

Now I will confess to you that I am not surprised at this development. I did not confide to you my anticipations because I didn't think that it was advisable for me to worry your head with what I thought; and also because I was certain that you would recognise the situation as soon as it arose. Having received this letter from D. I would have come to you with it to talk it over had I been fit; and I can hardly send it to you without any comment.

---

[1] Doubleday purchased a controlling interest in the company after Heinemann's death.
[2] Doubleday wrote: 'I made up specimens of the kind of books I had in mind – two "dummies" will show you the idea (sent by mail). However, I fear that the plan has been abandoned, or has been taken up with some other publisher, so possibly I am only going over stale tales.'

I will say nothing more now, because this morning my wife had a letter from your mother renewing her invitation for Wed. next week, which I think we will be able to accept; in which case my dear Eric, I would see you on Thursday week, when we will be able to exchange our impressions. But please make no arrangement with Everett for that date as yet. The reason I ask you not to do so is that Sir R. Jones must see my wife and has asked her whether she expects to be in London soon. She is therefore writing to him that she hopes to be there on that particular Thursday; and if Sir Robert says he will see her, then, of course, I am bound to be there too. She is getting more and more crippled and this is a serious anxiety.

I will be sending you Rover VII in a day or two.

Affect^{ly} Yrs

J. Conrad

PS My remarks on prop[agan]da leaflets are on the back of one of them. If you think of sending to D. P & C° you must guard against them being reproduced as "Conrad says" or in an interview form. I think these are legitimate suggestions for any other man's judgment as to whether they are true or useful.

Please return me FND letter when read. (I am not going to write to him yet.)

To Eric Pinker
Text MS Berg; Unpublished

[Oswalds]
Monday. [8 May 1922][1]

My dear Eric

The stars seem propitious for the visit to B[urys] Court. We shall go on to town on Thur^{day} and I write this that you may if you can (and [it] is convenient to you) arrange for the Everett business any time on Thurs: afternoon.

Sir R Jones can not see my wife till Friday 10.30 AM so I will be with you on Thurs^{day} noon and free for the rest of the day.

Yours

J. C.

---

[1] The previous and following letters fix the date.

To C. F. Tebbutt

Text MS Neville; J-A, 2, 271

[letterhead: Oswalds]

9.5.22

Dear Sir.[1]

In truth I think the story is rather simple than subtle. A thing like that can not go on for ever; and Rita[2] with her greater maturity, greater experience of the world and in her perfect sincerity in the face of the given situation sees it clearly.

A connection of that kind would have spelt ruin for a young fellow of 19 without fortune or position. Or *any* young fellow, for the matter of that. Had R been merely sensual and selfish she could have kept George chained to her by his passion. Rita is what she is; but whatever she is she is honest as the day. By going away beyond his reach she gives him the supreme proof of her love, stronger than mere passion, stronger than the fear of her own and of his suffering. That is all there is to it.

Yrs.

J. Conrad

To Richard Curle

Text MS Indiana; Curle 92

[Oswalds]

Wed. 10.5.22

Dearest Dick.

We will be in London on Thursday for the night.

Could you meet me at the R[oyal] A[utomobile] C[lub] at say *11.45*. At 12.45 I will have to go to Pinker's office and all my afternoon will be taken up with worrying negociations.

Article received.

We start for Burys Court in an hour, and will spend the night there.

If you can not be at RAC as above please, dear R, send me a *wire* there.

Ever Yours

J. C.

---

[1] (Charles Frederick) 'Fred' Tebbutt (1900–1986) wrote a number of books about Huntingdonshire, including *Huntingdonshire Folklore* (1952) and *St Neots: The History of a Huntingdonshire Town* (1978). From 1935 until his retirement in the 1960s, he was involved in running the family firm of C. G. Tebbutt, Ltd, lumber merchants, whose history he wrote. In later years, he became a member of the Sussex Archaeological Society. Elected a Fellow of the Society of Antiquaries, he was also awarded an OBE.

[2] Heroine of *The Arrow of Gold*.

To G. Jean-Aubry

Text MS Yale;[1] Unpublished

[Oswalds]
[10? May 1922][2]

Mon très cher.

Je Vs envoie ceci. Voulez Vs dire a Pinker s'il peut marcher.

Mille amitiés de la part de la maison

Votre

J. C.

Translation

My very dear friend.

I am sending this on to you. Would you tell Pinker if he can proceed?

Many friendly regards from everybody here

Yours

J. C.

To Eric Pinker

Text MS Berg; Unpublished

[letterhead: Oswalds]
10.5.22

My dear Eric

Thanks for your letter. I will be delighted to lunch with you on Thursday. I proposed noon as I did not know whether you had not some engagement. But if we are to lunch together I will come a little later – before one – and, I am afraid, take up a lot of your afternoon. If need be could you arrange for us to get hold of Pawling *after* we [have] had our talk?

I want to put my point of view before you on the general policy rather than on the terms of the pending negociation.

I hope the Everett visit will come off and be conclusive.

We start for Burys Court at 2 o'clock.

Yours

J. C.

---

[1] Jotted on a letter from Eric Pinker to Conrad of 3 May. Pinker had written: 'I have another application for the Spanish rights in all your works. Will you, please, let me know how the matter stands with M. Aubry?'

[2] Jean-Aubry noted on the MS that he received this on the 11th.

To Eric Pinker
Text TS Berg; Unpublished

> Oswalds.
> Bishopsbourne.
> May 14th. 1922

My dear Eric

Thank you very much for your note about Curle's article about me. I think that from the point of view of publicity it will do good if it gets published in the right place. That is why I venture to suggest that a newspaper as medium would be more effective than a magazine – and of course nothing high-brow.

I wish to remind the office that Karola's quarter[1] will be due on the 20th of this month.

I have got hold of my work again, though, to tell you the truth, I have got a swollen wrist which I have picked up in the course of my late travels.

> Affect[ly] Yours
> J. Conrad.

To Eric Pinker
Text TS Berg; Unpublished

> Oswalds,
> Bishopsbourne,
> Kent.
> May 16th. 1922

Dear Eric

Thank you very much for your letter of this morning advising me of the payment into my bank.

I had this morning a letter from Pawling telling me he is going himself to Everett's studio. I am glad that this affair is moving. P. has asked my wife to write to the Delineator[2] a personal request to consent to the publication of the Cookery Book in October.[3] She has done that.

I enclose here a communication from the Washington Treasury which the office ought to have as the care of my Income Tax is in your hands. The cheque for $110.26 I have paid into my account.

> Affct[ly] Yrs
> J. C.

---

[1] Her quarterly allowance.
[2] The popular American womens' magazine was to serialise Jessie Conrad's cookery book from August 1922 to January 1923.
[3] The book appeared in February 1923.

To The Registrar of Oxford University

Text TS draft Texas (damaged); Unpublished

[letterhead: Oswalds]
May 19th. 1922.

The Registrar of the University of Oxford.
Sir,[1]

With the deepest appreciation of the resolution of the Hebdomadal Council,[2] conveyed in your communication to me, I beg to be allowed to decline, with all possible deference, the distinction of an honorary degree.

In obeying thus the promptings of a strong personal feeling, which remains closely associated with the highest sense of the proffered honour, I venture to hope that you will be good enough to lay before the Council my sentiments of profound respect and [. . .]

To Captain David Bone

Text TS Yale; Unpublished

[letterhead: Oswalds]
May 24th. 1922.

Dear Cap[t] Bone.

I am sorry I can not write myself[3] in answer to your letter which I read feeling in sympathy with your point of view, though I must admit that I did not consider the question from that particular standpoint.

After all, personal feelings, what appertains to the inner man, have their own claims which must be recognised. There is nothing reprehensible in an individual acting to please himself in matters that do not affect the happiness or the comfort of other human creatures. This distinction was offered not to the seaman but to the literary man; and it is only from that point of view and in relation to my own sense of the fitness of things that I have looked at it. My two lives are absolutely disconnected; the second began after the first was definitely ended.[4] The generation with which I have worked is off the seas now. The few men I have met went to sea after I had left it. The first man is not dead in me, and will not die till I cease to breathe, but my day at sea has a long time ago come to an end, and it would be mere presumption in me

---

[1] Charles Leudersdorf (1853–1924), a mathematician, was the current Registrar.

[2] Oxford University's governing body is so called on account of its weekly meetings.

[3] In his own hand rather than dictated to his secretary: cf. the following letter to Garnett. Although gout often forced him to ignore it, Conrad was punctilious of the convention that typing should be reserved for business letters.

[4] Conrad began to write before, but was not published until after, he had left the sea.

to take myself even for a moment as a representative man of the Merchant Service of to-day.

I have here put my view against your argument,[1] but the matter can not really be discussed since I have already declined other proposals of that kind.

With kindest regards

Yours most sincerely

Joseph Conrad.

To Edward Garnett

Text TS/MS Colgate; G. 312–13

[letterhead: Oswalds]
May 24th. 1922.

Dear Edward

I am extremely disgusted at not being able to write to you myself, but I must thank you for the volume[2] which has just arrived – the pure light of the past cutting across with a tender, softer ray the first-class illuminative arrangements under which we live to-day. What I have felt and thought is more suitable for talk, warm and many coloured, than for the cold blue tint of the typewriter. Let me only say at once that the American papers have fascinated me by the illuminative quality of the statement of the whole case and by the particular insight in the appreciation of the men.[3]

I am trying to get through a sort of long short story (the title of which is The Rover) so as to complete a volume this year. I have done no work that matters for the last eighteen months and I have not looked at the novel[4] since December last. But then since December last I have been laid up four times without ever being given a chance to recover my tone and grapple with my work. For the last week though my right hand has been tied up I have been able to work with a certain sense of mastery over my subject.

---

[1] That he write a preface for Bone's *The Lookoutman* (1923)? Or that he take a public stand on some maritime cause?

[2] Garnett's *Friday Nights: Literary Criticism and Appreciations*. It includes his essay 'Mr Joseph Conrad'. Among the other Britons he treats at length are a former protégé, D. H. Lawrence, and a perennial enthusiasm, C. M. Doughty.

[3] True to his conviction that the English-speaking world is a literary continuum, Garnett also discusses American poetry and fiction, devoting separate essays to Robert Frost and Stephen Crane. Like Conrad and Wells, Garnett held to his admiration for Crane even when he had been almost forgotten in his own country, and Garnett was one of the first critics on either side of the Atlantic to recognise Frost's promise. Few American reviews of *Friday Nights* had yet appeared, the most notable so far being Galsworthy's piece in the *New York Times* of 14 May.

[4] *Suspense.*

We must certainly arrange to meet soon and it ought to [be] here, my dear Edward, because as soon as I get away from home I seem to go to pieces mentally and physically. Except for not running about naked I have become a complete savage and look upon all mankind with hostility – I mean the mankind in the street: exactly like a Masai warrior perambulating the bush.

I will make you a signal about joining company for a few days directly The Rover has ceased to rove – and be damned to him. You have no idea how that fellow and a lot of other crazy creatures that got into my head have also got on my nerves. I have never known anything like this before. I have been infinitely depressed about a piece of work, but never so exasperated with anything I have had to do.

We are sorry to hear of your wife having had a bad time.[1] Give her our love and sympathy

Ever Yours

J Conrad

To the Hon. Bertrand Russell
Text TS McMaster; Wright

[letterhead: Oswalds]
May 24th. 1922.

Dearest Russell.

I must at last acknowledge your wife's and your letters and the photographs of the boy, by typewriter since that wrist of mine will not improve. To write anything adequate under such circumstances is out of the question; but I can anyhow say hastily here that I am extremely proud to be associated by an honourable ceremonial bond with such a charming, delightful and promising individual.

Do please, my dear Russell, give my duty to your wife, my thanks for her most delightful letter, my regrets at not being able to answer it as yet. But I hope however that next week will bring a change and that I will be able to regain by then my control over my hand and over my thoughts.

This is the fourth time since New Year's Day that I have been laid up surrounded by odds and ends of my work from which I don't seem to get a chance of making anything at all.

Our warmest regards to you both

Ever Yours

J. Conrad.

---

[1] She was suffering from 'rheumatic gout': Richard Garnett, *Constance Garnett: A Heroic Life* (Sinclair-Stevenson, 1991), pp. 316–17.

To Richard Curle

Text MS Indiana; Curle 93

[Oswalds]
Thursday [25 May 1922][1]
6. pm.

Dearest Dick

Come along for lunch tho' I fear we wont be able to meet *that* train.

The 6.18 pm we could meet.

Your proof[2] has just arrived.

I've been working a bit lately and will not "cut the vein" on account of Your visit, but there will be plenty of time for talks.

Ever Yours

J. C.

To G. Jean-Aubry

Text MS Yale; *L.fr.* 170

[letterhead: Oswalds]
27.5.22

Mon très cher

Je [ne] vous ai pas écrit car je ne pouvais pas manier la plume. Ceci est ma première lettre depuis 15 jours.

J'ai reçu avec joie le vol La Musique et les Nations hier. J'ai lu Debussy tout de suite avec le plus grand plaisir.[3] Que je suis content d'avoir un Volume de Vous!

Ecrivez-nous. Et venez nous voir aussitôt que Vs aurez le temps.

Je Vs embrasse de tout mon coeur

Votre

Conrad

Translation

My very dear friend

I have not written to you because I've been unable to hold a pen. This is my first letter in a fortnight.

---

[1] Curle supplies the date.   [2] Of 'Joseph Conrad in the East' (see the letters of late April).

[3] As its title suggests, *La Musique et les nations*, published simultaneously in London and Paris, traces the influence of national idioms and nationalist ideas on European music. It has chapters on Spain (Albéniz, Granados, Falla), Italy (Malipiero), Britain (Elgar, Vaughan Williams, Bax, Bliss, Goossens, Lord Berners), Liszt, Chopin, and Debussy. Most of these pieces are revisions of articles written for *Le Correspondant*, the *Musical Times*, or Jean-Aubry's own magazine, *The Chesterian*.

I was very happy to receive *La Musique et les nations* yesterday. I read the Debussy immediately and with the greatest pleasure. How very glad I am to have a book of yours!

Write to us. And come to see us as soon as you have the time.

I embrace you very affectionately

Yours

Conrad

To Eric Pinker

Text MS Lubbock; Rude (1987)

[letterhead: Oswalds]

30.5.22

Dearest Eric.

I ought to have sent you the VII & VIII of The Rover a long time ago. Here they are for "clean copy" typing.

IX & X are finished but not revised. XI is begun. The XII will finish the job.[1]

I have my dear fellow worked well. If I had been able to work like that in April the thing would have been done long ago. I can't however pick up the lost time. That's impossible. Still I expect to be done by the 10th prox. I am feeling better than I have felt I may say for years. If I could only be sure of 12 months like that!

I had the enc^d which I have acknowledged. I did not know the West[minst]^{er} Gaz: was interested.[2]

Affecly Yours

J. Conrad.

To Cecil Roberts

Text MS Churchill; Unpublished

[letterhead: Oswalds]

30.5.22.

Dear Mr Roberts.

Let me thank you warmly for the dedication of your play.[3] It is a great pleasure for me to be remembered by you in that way. I hope you will send me a copy. I should like to have it from you.

---

[1] In the end, the novel expanded to sixteen chapters.

[2] In serialising *The Rover*. See Cecil Roberts's letter to Conrad of 25 May (Stape and Knowles, p. 193).

[3] *A Tale of Young Lovers: A Tragedy in Four Acts*, just published by Heinemann. This tragedy is in verse.

I've no doubt P[inker] has answered you on that subject of my story. I did not know that there had been any negociations with the West[minst]^er Gazette.

I expect I will have finished it by the 10th June.

My wife joins me in very kind regards

Very sincerely Yours

Joseph Conrad.

To Eric Pinker

Text MS Berg; Unpublished

[Oswalds]

Thursday. [1 or 8 June 1922][1]

My dear Eric.

Thanks for Your letter. I *was* pleased with the B'man article but did not connect Swinnerton with it.[2]

Chap X went up this morning, and I enclose here the Am^an inc^me tax form for you to deal with. Such communications may just as well be opened in the office tho' addressed there only c/o for me.

One question: I suppose that all our Ins^ce policies fire and All Round one on goods furniture etc and also the House Ins^ce (under the terms of my agreement) are in order? Father used to look after all this for me.

I am going on at my best gait. It isn't like greased lightning you know. But what a relief it is to feel the whole thing there in one's hand with only one or two more squeezes to get everything that there is in it.

Affct^ly Yours

in haste

J Conrad.

---

[1] The completion of Chapter 10 gives the general parameters. On 30 May, Chapter 11 was in its early stages, and Chapters 9 and 10 awaited revision; progress on the novel rules out later Thursdays in the month.

[2] 'The Londoner' was a regular column in the New York version of the *Bookman* signed by 'Simon Pure', the pseudonym of Frank Swinnerton. (For Swinnerton, see the letters of 11 November and [mid-November?].) Part of the May column (which is dated 1 March) honours the memory of J. B. Pinker (55, pp. 274–5). After recalling the encouragement he gave to authors young and old, Swinnerton describes his way with publishers: 'Pinker did not let the publisher become sentimental. His "yes" had extraordinary potence as an interjection. It was quiet, expressionless, and it pulled the publisher up short. It held all the significances of assent, deprecation, sarcasm, and baffling incomprehensibility. It is quite likely that some publishers were rather afraid of Pinker in his lifetime.' Swinnerton rounds off by hailing Eric as a successor who has inherited many of his father's qualities. Meanwhile, the May issue of the London *Bookman* printed the results of a competition to name 'the most effective phrase or sentence ending any English novel or play'. The winners, a woman from Wales and a man from Lancashire, argued for the final sentence of *The Rescue*.

To Warrington Dawson

Text TS Duke; Randall 206–8

Oswalds,
Bishopsbourne,
Kent.
June 2nd. 1922.

My dear Dawson.

I dictate this letter because I really don't know when I will be able to write in pen and ink, my right wrist having been bad for a long time now and showing no signs of serious improvement.

Neither will I be very long in what I have got to say now. I find it very difficult to express myself to the typewriter. Shortly then, my dear Dawson, I have given the fullest and most friendly consideration to the letter you have written me. Facts as the proverb says are stubborn things.[1] I now find from repeated attempts that the form of writing consisting in literary appreciation of other men's work, implying analysis and an exposition of ethical and aesthetic values on which all criticism and even a mere panegyric must be based, is not in my way. And the deeper my untutored feelings are affected the less I am able to put them in a form that would influence peoples minds. If you have looked at my volume of collected papers,[2] on the side of 'letters', you will see how few they are and how utterly useless anything I could write would be to give a start to a literary reputation. Whatever I say I can only talk about myself; not because I am a megalomaniac but because I am not sufficiently cultured to talk with authority to the public about other men. Whenever I have attempted it the effort has been out of all proportion to this miserable result. I won't enlarge further on the state of affairs which is generally known. I dislike writing, I don't believe in my own wisdom, and I shrink from putting forth my opinions to the general public. I am like that. I cannot help it. It is temperamental; and it is closely associated with the unliterary complexion of my mind. The only thing that ever qualified me to take a pen in hand is the possession of a certain creative gift. And even in that I am not secure. It has never been a source of gratification to me; on the contrary, it has brought me many hours of unhappiness in the doubts and heart searchings it has forced me into at every step.

---

[1] From Alain-René Le Sage's *Histoire de Gil Blas de Santillane* (1715–35), Bk 1, ch. 1, as rendered in Tobias Smollett's 1749 translation.

[2] *Notes on Life and Letters.*

The above confession is strictly entre nous. To be conscious of one's own deficiencies is not a crime, though I admit it is a great hindrance to the carrying out of many good intentions. In that sense it may be called a weakness – but enough of this.

On the other hand, my dear Dawson, whenever it has happened to me to address my friends intimately and personally on the subject of their work I have always written with perfect sincerity of feeling, however inadequately expressed; and to what I have written in private I will of course stand to in public. Therefore my dearest fellow if you think that the publication (whole or in extracts) of what I have said to you in the open intimacy of our friendship may be of any use I would be glad if you would deal with it to the best advantage.

Now specifically as to "The Rock".[1] I have read about half of the MS and I can say here at once that it has from the first engaged my interest, both by treatment and expression. The descriptive parts are first-rate. The two scenes between Vera and Errington on board and during the shooting trip are very good. As to the book's chance of success it is impossible for me to say anything; the more so that I have not finished it yet; but it is all very characteristic, very 'Dawsonian', and is penetrated through and through by your characteristic earnestness of emotion. As to criticism of details my dear Dawson, I don't suppose you want it; and in any case I would offer it with great diffidence if I were to offer it at all. For in those matters I am not, by any means, sure myself. This mainly for the reason that having a pronounced temperament and a sort of personality in my writing which has not been acquired but was inborn (and therefore is very masterful) I know that I would be prejudiced in many ways by the mere fact of being what I am.

Pardon all the delays in my correspondence, my dear friend. I have been laid up four times since New Year's Day. I have been unable to finish anything for the last two years; which is for me a cause of serious worry. When I have a chance of a few days' work I absorb myself in it in a sort of desperation, and then feel too tired to put two consecutive thoughts together.

Jessie (who is still very crippled) sends her love

Ever affect^{ly} Yours

J Conrad.

---

[1] A novel planned in 1909, and begun in 1914 but interrupted by the war. Dawson resumed work in August 1920 and finished it in January 1922.

To G. Jean-Aubry

Text MS Yale; Unpublished

[Oswalds]
2.6.'22

Très cher

Merci de votre bonne lettre. On sera heureux de vous voir le week end prochain.

Je vous embrasse de tout mon coeur

Votre

Joseph.

Translation

My dear friend

Thank you for your good letter. We will be glad to see you next week-end. I embrace you very affectionately

Yours

To Eric Pinker

Text MS Berg; Unpublished

[Oswalds]
Monday. [12 June 1922][1]

My dear Eric

I have been hindered in my work for a couple of days. Also Miss H[allowes] had to have a little break during my holidays. The end of the story is however a matter of days. I dont send you the XI tho' it is ready. I may want to look at it again.

I am afraid I am a source of vexation to you. But I am not conscious of having lost any time except what was unavoidable.

The thing itself has got bigger as it were (I don't mean longer) and can't be dashed off. Still I am sorry at having failed to keep to the promised date. I repeat it is a matter of very few days – of *any* day almost.

Affect[ly] Yours

J. C.

PS Please send my agreement with Bell for the house as I want [to] ascertain a point. If it is not in the office Withers[2] must have it.

---

[1] Chapter 11 had been begun by 30 May. Given the pace of work, the 19th would be too late; by the 27th, Conrad had finished the fifteenth and last chapter.
[2] Withers, Bensons, Currie, Williams & Co., solicitors, established in 1896.

To G. Jean-Aubry
Text MS Yale; *L.fr.* 171

[Oswalds]
13.6.22

Très cher ami.

Nous Vous attendons pour la fin-de-semaine prochaine. J'espère que Votre santé c'est* ameliorée depuis Votre dernière lettre.

L'écriture de Votre livre La M[usique] et les N[ations] fait mes délices. Je veux dire a part le sujet qui naturellement m'a interessé beaucoup comme information et comme points de vue.

J'ai le volume la-haut et chaque soir j'ai une demi-heure avec J-A. C'est la seconde lecture, vous comprenez.

Je Vous embrasse

Tout à Vous

J. C.

Translation

My very dear friend.

We look forward to seeing you next week-end. I hope your health has improved since your last letter.

The writing in your *La Musique et les nations* delights me. I mean apart from the subject, which naturally interested me a great deal both as to its information and point of view.

I have the book upstairs and spend a half-hour with J-A every night. It's my second reading, you know.

I embrace you.

Yours truly

J. C.

To Sir Richard Rees
Text TS/MS UCL; Unpublished

[letterhead: Oswalds]
June 13th. 1922.

Dear Sir Richard[1]

As a matter of fact I am extremely busy, or I would have asked you to come down here at once and spend the night. What I propose is that I should let

---

[1] Richard Lodowick Edward Montagu Rees (1900–70; 2nd Baronet, 1922), writer and painter, edited the *Adelphi* from 1930 to 1936, wrote books on George Orwell (1961) and Simone Weil (1966), translated Weil's notebooks and essays, and edited a selection of J. Middleton Murry's writings (1960).

you know directly I have finished a particular piece of work that is worrying me now and suggest a day for a visit here. Should you happen to be abroad or in any way prevented you could write to put it off to a time more convenient to you.

I will, however, point out to you at once that the way in which you intend to direct your life is not so simple as it may appear.[1] You are moved by an altruistic impulse which one cannot but respect; yet the question presents itself whether you are practically fitted for systematising and organising your efforts. Your letter does not make very clear what it is exactly you have in view and what you intend to bring to the working classes for their improvement and assistance.

You tell me that lately you have been able to be sincere with yourself, and so I will venture to be sincere with you in asking whether it is your general wisdom, or practical sagacity, or some kind of experience you want to impart to them. Or is it only of material assistance that you are thinking? That, of course, is a matter of sheer organisation. Its moral benefits, unless in the lowest strata, are questionable. But there are many people able to give you excellent advice how to proceed in that sort of work, whether with men or with boys.

You must not forget that the working classes have their own wisdom, their own experience, and their own sense of the fitness of things. But whatever may be your precise intention I would recommend a long and earnest meditation before you take any decisive step. There is no need to 'give up' anything until you have tested to a certain extent your capacity for sustained effort in the direction of which you think.

Pardon these unconnected and unnecessary remarks. They will appear to you no doubt very stupid and conventional. Pray take them merely as the evidence of my sympathy and regard

Your[s] faithfully

Joseph Conrad.

---

[1] Rees explains his youthful dilemma thus: 'In 1922 I was suffering the first pangs of what I would later have described as a social conscience, and some instinct prompted me to write to Conrad for advice. With characteristic generosity to an unknown correspondent, he replied with a helpful suggestion, of which I made no intelligent use, and with some general reflections, which at the time had a rather damping effect, as was probably intended': *For Love or Money: Studies in Personality and Essence* (Secker & Warburg, 1960), p. 126.

To Charles Chassé
Text TS Berg; J-A, 2, 271–2

[letterhead: Oswalds]
June 21st. 1922.

My dear Sir,[1]

I hoped to have answered your letter before but my hand remains disabled and so I must dictate these few lines in English.

The passages and articles relating to Poland I ever wrote* are all to be found in the "Record" and in the "Notes on Life and Letters", so I suppose you have seen them all except one short story which appeared years ago in the "Cambridge and Oxford Magazine"[2] but not yet in any collection in book form. My intimate friend M. Jean-Aubry, the well-known critic of art and letters and a much appreciated lecturer in many countries, has been on a visit to us yesterday. I mentioned to him your letter and he told me that when last in Paris he had seen the secretary of the Revue "Pologne" and that they had accepted from him his translation of that short story of which the title is "Prince Roman".[3] M. Aubry has translated much of my work already and is engaged in doing more for the complete edition which is now being published by the Nouvelle Revue Française.

In answer to the direct question I have to say that the peasants who sacked the house of my grand-uncle, Captain Nicholas Bobrowski, were Ukrainians, that is the Ruthenians of the Southern Provinces of the old Republic.[4]

---

[1] Charles Chassé (1883–1965), a French writer on modern art, was particularly interested in the work of Gauguin and the Fauvists. He directed the Paris School of New York University, and in 1922 published *Les Sources d'Ubu roi* on Alfred Jarry's iconoclastic play.

[2] 'Prince Roman', in the *Oxford and Cambridge Review*, October 1911.

[3] Either the editor of *La Pologne politique, economique, littéraire et artistique*, a Parisian monthly mostly devoted to items of current interest, changed his mind or a misunderstanding is at issue: no such translation appeared.

[4] During the Polish insurrection of 1863, Orthodox peasants raided the house of Mikołaj Bobrowski (1782–1864), a veteran of the Napoleonic Wars. Conrad describes the incident in *A Personal Record*, pp. 57–63, drawing on his uncle Tadeusz Bobrowski's *Memoirs*; the relevant passage appears in Zdzisław Najder, *Conrad under Familial Eyes* (Cambridge University Press, 1983), pp. 73–4. The 'Old Republic' of Poland came to an end in 1697, when the Elector of Saxony re-established a monarchy. The terms 'Ruthenian' and 'Ukrainian' reflect a whole history of ethnic conquest and contention involving *inter alia*, Poland, Austria, and Russia. Ukraine was independent from early 1918 to late 1922, when it was absorbed into the USSR, but faced separatist revolt in the western provinces and a war with Poland (1918–20); after that, the Ukrainians allied themselves with the Poles against the Bolsheviks.

Believe me, my dear Sir, with the kindest regards,

Very sincerely yours,

J. C.

Joseph Conrad.[1]

M. Charles Chassé.

To Eric Pinker

Text MS Berg; Unpublished

[Oswalds]

27.6.22

My dear Eric.

The text of the Rover is to-day finished. The revision will take some doing and may not be finished till the end of next week.

Fifteen chapters.

As to the actual length in words. It will be dam' close on 70,000. That's so my dear fellow. It is now more but the revision will reduce it no doubt. The great point will be not to let Dent lay a claim to it as a "novel" (in terms of his agreement). Likewise F. U[nwin] must not be allowed to publish it without the other 3 stories. Is that so?[2]

Pray think it over. I will be coming to town on Monday next with Mrs C who is really on the mend and must have a week's change after a most painful treatment. Of course I can revise in town. In fact the change of "millieu"* may do me good.

I have just heard from F. N. D[oubleday]. Thanks for keeping him away for indeed I could not afford to be interrupted. I'll confess to you that I have been laid up for 5 days, last week. Work went on however but of course not so well. I am all right now.

---

[1] Holograph initials followed by the typed name.

[2] Disputes over the point at which a long story became a novel apt for solo publication had often affected Conrad's relations with his publishers. Sometimes a work's brevity was the issue, as when Dent was reluctant to publish *The Shadow-Line* on its own; sometimes the problem was contractual, as in the protracted wrangle with Methuen about whether *The Secret Agent* should count towards the total of novels Conrad had agreed to supply. Here both issues were at stake. In the end, Fisher Unwin won the right to publish, and did so without extra stories.

I am very sorry for poor S. S. From FND's letter it looks like a knock out. He uses the words "desperately ill" and hints that in the best case S. S. would not be fit for business for more than a year.[1]

Pardon this incoherent [s]crawl. I have a couple of par[agraph]s to dictate yet – and then I shall be "desperately" busy with that revision.

But what a weight off my chest.

Affect^ly Yours

J. C.

PS Thanks for your letter and the MS (Rover X) received to-day

To R. B. Cunninghame Graham
Text MS Dartmouth; Watts (1969) 192

[letterhead: Oswalds]
28.6.22

Dear Don Roberto.

I would have written to you before about my delight in The Conquest of Granada[2] if it had not been for the beastly swollen wrist which prevented me holding the pen. G[onzalo] J[iménez de] Q[uesada] is the most sympathetic of them all, no doubt about it; and you give a fine portrait of him. The display of perseverance and endurance is marvellous and worthy of admiration tho' as an edifying instance it fails, for reasons I need not point out to you. You make the most of it in a way that is touching in the earnestness of its sympathy and the sober force of its language. A fine performance in which I seem to detect an under-note of wistfulness. But then, très cher ami, I believe that you have missed by a mere hairsbreadth of 400 years being a conquistador yourself.

We are looking forward eagerly to your visit on Sunday with Mrs Dummett to whom pray give my duty.

Ever most affectionately Yours
J Conrad.

[1] S. S. Pawling, of Heinemann's, died in December 1922.
[2] *The Conquest of Granada, being the Life of Gonzalo Jimenez de Quesada*, published in June. The territory conquered was New Granada (now Colombia).

To Richard Curle

Text MS Indiana; Curle 94

[Oswalds]
Thursday. 29.6.22

My dear Dick.

I expect to be in London next week (Mond or Tues^d) with the finished (but not quite revised) Rover. You may imagine in what mental state I am. The whole thing came on me at the last as through a broken dam. A month of constant tension of thought.

Could hardly bear to speak to anybody – let alone write.

I feel I've to thank you for the sympathetic note on With Conrad at Sea – that preposterous bosh. I am very grateful.[1]

No more now. I am still at work and under the strain

Ever Yours

J. C.

Jessie's love.

To Eric Pinker

Text TS Berg and Leeds; J-A, 2, 272–3 (in part)[2]

Oswalds,
Bishopsbourne,
Kent.
30/6/22

My dear Eric.

I write according to promise but it's mainly to thank you for sparing me a very disagreeable time, for Vernon wired to me this morning that after hearing what you had to say as to my views he found it unnecessary to come and see me. I am really very much obliged to you, my dear Eric, for

---

[1] Not for a letter of condolence on being the subject of Sutherland's *At Sea with Joseph Conrad*, but for a brief notice in the *Daily Mail*: 'Book about Conrad', 28 June, p. 7. Curle distinguishes clearly between victim and narrator: 'Even without the letter from Mr Conrad to the author, which is printed as a Foreword, it would be obvious that such a book, full as it is of reminiscence of a full and trivial nature would not be to the taste of so modest a man as Joseph Conrad, but the letter, friendly as it is, does not leave the matter in doubt.'

[2] The page at the Berg ends with 'a play like the S[ecret] A[gent] can not be'; the other page is at Leeds. Jean-Aubry omits the section from 'All this' to the end of the third paragraph.

I must say that though determined to assert my complete freedom and the absence of any obligation, I did not look forward with any pleasure to the interview.

Vernon then being out of the way I have given a most careful and anxious consideration to the Calthrop[1] proposal and I see many reasons against it. First of all to deal with mere superstitions: McKinnel is not a lucky man and the Aldwych is an unlucky theatre, whether it is because it is the furthest east or because somebody has cast a spell on it, I don't know.[2]

And now to talk sense. My fear is that the play may sink unhonoured and unsung, which morally speaking would be a great disaster for me. I have put to you verbally the considerations that make me fear such an inglorious event. In July and August the principal critics will be replaced probably by their understudies in the press. The Conrad public will be away from town too; and not only the Conrad public but the most intelligent part of play-goers who, at any rate, have heard of me as a novelist of long standing and some reputation and, being theatre-goers, would be interested enough to see what I had done in that medium. I have reason to think, from correspondence and other sources, that my name, if not my work, is known in a good many spheres. The play in itself is not inept – that is, it does not contain the seeds of an obvious failure. It is not a mere exercise in intellect, or in style, or in delicate subtlety, or in over-refined sentiment, as poor Henry James' were who never dealt with a situation but only with the atmosphere of it.[3] On the other hand in its innermost quality it is as Conradian as anything I ever have written; therefore I may hope for a succès de curiosité: say an existence of six to eight weeks, which would satisfy me if associated with a certain amount of recognition as expressed in varied criticism and discussion. (I may of course be the most deluded of mortals in that respect but that is how I feel.) A money success I never dreamt of. For that of course it would be necessary for the same people to come over and over again, and this for a play like the S[ecret] A[gent] can not be expected; unless indeed there was some marvellous acting,

[1] From Donald Calthrop (1881–1940), a theatrical manager and producer who also acted on stage and screen.

[2] Unlike its near neighbour the Adelphi, the Aldwych (opened in 1905) did not have a sinister reputation. Apart from the more serious interlude described below, it was known for musical comedies, farces, and revues.

[3] Productions of Henry James's plays fared badly. The dramatisation of *The American* (1890) had an uninspiring run in Lancashire followed by another in London. On the first night of *Guy Domville* (1895), the audience booed the playwright. His theatrical pieces replaced the cabinet dramas of nineteenth-century poets as stock examples of what can happen when even a brilliant author strays into the wrong field.

on the part of some principals, which would fascinate people. All this reduces itself then to the hope of just a little money and the advantage of fairly wide interest. But by coming on in August (surely they would want three weeks to learn and rehearse the play, get into its spirit in a way) we risk certainly to miss both; and if we miss it then we may practically consider it as missed for ever. Even the mere play-going suburbs will be empty. There is also nothing in my name to break the bad luck of the Aldwych, which, since the Beecham Opera episode in its history,[1] had never I verily believe, had a full house. Barrie could do it but I don't think any other living man could; and even Barrie would be handicapped by the season of the year.[2]

A minor but vexing consideration (don't laugh) occurs to me that my personal friends, say twenty to thirty people, who had read the play and would certainly have liked to see it on the stage, would miss their only chance by being out of town. It's all very fine for those fellows who have perhaps a dozen plays in their little bag, but this one is my all and I really think that if it comes out it must be given every possible chance.

I have written to you at such great length because, my dear Eric, I don't want you to think I am captious or merely capricious, or even funky.[3] Indeed I hate to raise all these objections to something which you are arranging for me. But there is also this: a succès de curiosité, well marked and discussed, would not make an attempt in the U.S. impossible; whereas a failure in the dead season would close that field to us completely. But of course all those circumstances I have put before you may be appreciated differently. However we shall see each other in a few days and you will then give me your opinion.

Always affectionately Yours

J. Conrad.

---

[1] Thomas Beecham (1879–1961; 2nd Baronet, 1916) conducted and managed highly successful summer and autumn opera seasons in 1916 at the Aldwych; in 1920, however, a suit by Diaghilev caused the opera company's cessation, and for years Beecham was preoccupied with bankruptcy proceedings against the Covent Garden Estate, of which the Aldwych was a part. See Alan Jefferson, *Sir Thomas Beecham: A Centenary Tribute* (MacDonald & Jane's, 1979), pp. 151–6.

[2] J. M. Barrie (1860–1937) had written several plays, but Conrad was thinking of the hugely successful *Peter Pan*, revived every Christmas season.

[3] 'Scared', a colloquialism dating to the early nineteenth century.

To Richard Curle
Text MS Indiana; Curle 95

[Oswalds]
Sunday [2 July 1922][1]
5.30

My dear Dick.

We are coming up on Tuesday, for a week or so. Can not give you the name of hotel, but it will *not* be Brown's. May phone you on Tuesday or rather ask B[orys] to do so for he will know on Monday.

Our love to You

J. Conrad.

To R. B. Cunninghame Graham
Text MS Dartmouth; Watts (1969) 193–4

[letterhead: Oswalds][2]
7.7.22

Très cher Ami.

We will be delighted to lunch with Mrs Dummett and you at Claridge's on Sunday. 1.15.

I can't tell how grateful I am for your kind wise and patient attitude to B[orys].

I hope I received the shock with becoming fortitude. One does not want to quarrel with one's son as long as one still keeps some belief in him. It is a crippling affair for me. One could get the money by extra work but in this affair the element of time is important. A thing like that must be settled as quick as possible by some arrangement of the sort that kind of citizen is used to.[3]

Jessies love.

Ever Yours

J. Conrad

---

[1] Curle supplies the date.
[2] Although on Oswalds stationery, this letter was composed in London, as were the following ones. The Conrads returned home on the afternoon of the 12th.
[3] See the letter to Curle of the 25th.

To Iris Wedgwood

Text MS Private collection; Unpublished

[letterhead: Oswalds]
7.7.22
Friday.

Dear Mrs Wedgwood

We will be delighted to lunch with You to-morrow at one and bring our child Borys with us, since You are good enough to include him in the invitation.

It will be a great pleasure to see the general[1] for whom as You know we all have a great affection.

Jessie sends her love.

Always Your most faithful Servant
Joseph Conrad

To Eric Pinker

Text MS Berg; Unpublished

[letterhead: Oswalds]
11th 7.22 Tuesday. 9.45.

My dear Eric

I am going to work with Miss H[allowes] at 10 as arranged and have no one to send to bank; so will you please obtain for me cash against the enclosed ch for £60.0.0 which ought to be enough to buy me out of captivity in this confounded place.[2]

Apologies for the trouble. As long as I have the cash by one it will suit me. You could send it by Mess[eng][er] boy perhaps. Give a word of verbal answer to Vinten who will deliver this at your door.

The MS pages you saw yesterday require a good deal of correction so I'll perhaps take the whole lot home. I won't keep more than absolutely necessary.

A lot of people came yesterday afternoon so I could not work except for a couple of hours after dinner.

Yours affect[ly]

J. Conrad.

---

[1] A brigadier-general during the war, Ralph Wedgwood had returned to civilian life and was not usually addressed by rank. See the letter to him of 28 July.
[2] His hotel.

To Eric Pinker

Text MS Berg; Unpublished

[letterhead: Oswalds]

Tuesday 6.30 [Wednesday, 12 July 1922][1]

My dear Eric.

Arriving safely I found this rep[ly] p[ai]d wire.

As I am sure You know who Macassey is[2] you will perhaps make an appt for me any day *next* week here, or next Monday between three and four at the R[oyal] A[utomobile] C[lub].

This *only* if in your judgment the interview may be of advantage from the publicity point of view, or ought to be granted as a matter of courtesy.

If not pray excuse me.

Thanks!

Yrs in haste

JC

PS I can't remember who Macassey is exactly. U.S. of course?

To Eric Pinker

Text TS Berg; Unpublished

Oswalds
Bishopsbourne
Kent.
13/7/22

My dear Eric.

I am sorry that I am twenty-four hours late with Chapters XI & XII, but yesterday afternoon I was really too tired to finish in time for post. With those Chaps. XI & XII you can now proceed with the typing of final copy in three sets. For you have in your possession Chaps. XIII & XIV of the MS and the XV & XVI are lying now before me scattered all over the table, undergoing the process of revision. I shall either hand them over to you personally on Monday or send them by post if anything prevents me from coming up to town as I propose to do.

Now the thing is finished my misgivings have left me. The story will make a good volume. Perhaps a remarkable one.

---

[1] The telegram referred to is date-stamped Bridge, 11 July, 8 p.m. (Berg) and places Conrad's return to Oswalds. Given the hour of receipt, his 'Tuesday' should be 'Wednesday'.

[2] Apparently an American editor. His wire asked: 'Will you give one of our reviewers an article or interview any topic you please reminiscence possibly'. The telegraph clerk wrote 'your reviewers', which Conrad emended to '(our)?', adding his initials.

I enclose here the signed agreement for the Dutch translations,[1] the terms of which are distinctly good. I really don't know how to advise the Dutch publishers as to the order of publication. The chronological would be the simplest. On the other hand there may be reasons connected with the chances of the sale which would make it advisable to make a selection. They must decide themselves, for I can form no opinion as to what book might please most the public of the Netherlands.

Sorry to give you trouble about Macassey. I know I wrote to him in 1920, probably in answer to a letter of his which has not been preserved and on an occasion which I can not remember now. Miss H[allowes] thinks that it was to thank him for a nice article about one of my later books, or upon my work as a whole; but what his paper was, and what his position was on it, neither of us can remember. He seems to be the editor of something weekly or monthly, I think. I am laying myself out to make friends in the U.S. or else I would not have troubled you.

In re pamphlets. Many thanks for specimens. In case I accept the estimate from that source I should certainly select the type shown on the largest page, but with a larger margin and not of the demy-octavo size. I must give you the correct estimate of the number of words in which I have made a mistake when talking to you last. The Galsworthy article contains about 2160 words, and the Dover Patrol about 2200 words. You see then that the two pamphlets will be very much of a size. A simple wrapper of, say, yellow rough paper (not glazed) would be all I require, with the title, my name, and the usual "printed for the author" with date at bottom.

Always my dear Eric

Affectionately Yours

Joseph Conrad

To [?]

Text TS Rendell;[2] Unpublished

[letterhead: Oswalds]
July 19th. 1922.

Dear Sir[3]

My literary plans are really impossible to talk about much, for reasons purely psychological. I [. . .] mean to say that that psycholog [. . .] but, such as it is [. . .].

---

[1] With Elsevier of Amsterdam to publish Dutch translations in serial and book forms, signed on 3 July (Hallowes).
[2] Original unavailable: text based on a poor photocopy.   [3] Unidentified.

[. . .] tell you that I have just finished a novel, not of immense length, called "The Rover," about which I am unwilling to speak at large as I have written the last words only two days ago. It strikes me that those who read will see it for themselves – another reason not to enlarge on it now – and as for those that don't read Conrad I don't see why I should offer them any information. I do not say this in a spirit of resentment but because I do not like to be intrusive.

I will, however, disclose the mystery so far as to say that Lord Nelson has a speaking part of about 100 words in it, though the novel is by no means a sea novel in the usual sense of the words, being concerned mainly with people ashore where there is a psychological situation forming the basis of the tale. The scene is the South of France.

Apart from this finished novel which will be published in the early spring of next year, there is another, half written, of proportions which may be called either noble or monstrous, in which Napoleon 1st will have a speaking part of about twenty-two words. If I were to say more I would be disclosing secrets, therefore I stop here.

Yours faithfully

Joseph Conrad.

To Redfern Mason
Text TS Berkeley; Unpublished

[letterhead: Oswalds]
July 19th. 1922.

Dear Mr Mason.[1]

Pardon my delay. I was finishing a novel – the first one for two years – and I had to sit very close the last few days, and then take up directly the revision of the text for America, as it is not always that I have a proof from there.

Thank you very much for your friendly letter. Of course I shall be very glad to see you but I am afraid you will find me a great bore because I feel absolutely empty and stupid just now. Will you suggest a day next week?

By your mention of the "Iliad" and the "Divina Commedia" you have not only covered me with blushes but made me feel very small indeed.

---

[1] (James) Redfern Mason (died 1941) was for many years music critic for the *San Francisco Examiner*. In that role, he became an advocate for new music, especially Schoenberg's. Another passion was politics: he wrote *Rebel Ireland* (1923) and once ran for mayor on the United Labor ticket. His wife, Grace Sartwell Mason, wrote fiction and travelled to Europe as special correspondent for the *Ladies' Home Journal*.

The train to come down here by is the 10-40 from Victoria arriving at Canterbury at 12-29, where the car will meet you. You can return by the 5-4 train in time to dine in London.

Yours sincerely

Joseph Conrad

To Eric Pinker
Text TS Berg; Unpublished

[Oswalds]
July 19th. 1922.
6. p.m.

Your letter with the clean copies of Chapters XV & XVI arrived this afternoon. The other chapters are ready and I hope to send you at least two complete sets to-morrow in time for them to reach you Friday morning so that you catch the American mail this week with the balance for Hearst.[1]

May success crown your efforts!

I will be writing to you on various matters to-morrow.

Affect[ly] Yours

J. C.

To Cecil Roberts
Text TS/MS Churchill; Unpublished

[letterhead: Oswalds]
July 19th. 1922.

My dear Cecil Roberts

I wonder what you think of my long silence after the receipt of your play?[2] I was just finishing a novel and put off looking at the play deliberately. I confess it without shame, because you will clearly understand the psychological motive of that delay.

Neither will I write to you at length now, but let me at once congratulate you affectionately on the charm and skill and beauty that is in your work. I am very grateful to you for dedicating it to me. Do not be surprised at receiving a letter of admiration from my wife who has been very much fascinated by your verse and by the dramatic story it tells.

I have to do the revising on my text for U.S. to catch the next mail.

Affectionately Yours

Joseph Conrad.

---

[1] The Hearst Magazines Syndicate considered but in the end did not serialise *The Rover*.
[2] *A Tale of Young Lovers: A Tragedy in Four Acts.* Conrad had asked for a copy on 30 May, and no doubt Roberts promptly sent him one.

To Bruno Winawer

Text TS copy Yale;[1] *Głos* (114); Najder 281

Oswalds,
Bishopsbourne,
Kent.
July. 19th. 1922.

My dear Sir,

I dictate these few words to thank you most heartily for your letters and especially for your little tale[2] which I have read with absolute delight and appreciation of every point, and greatest sympathy with the mind which conceived it and the literary gift which guided the pen.

During the last few weeks I have been finishing a novel and was too absorbed to write to anybody. You must therefore pardon my long silence.

This moment I received your letter telling me that the S[ecret] A[gent] will be performed in Warsaw.[3] I have been made very happy by hearing this. I hope, my dear Sir, you understand that any part I may have in the proceeds of the royalties has been made over to Miss Angela Zagórska who has the property of my works in Poland and Russia, by a document duly executed here.

I must stop now because I am correcting the MS of the novel to go at once to America and the time in which to do it is very short.

J. Conrad.

To Eric Pinker

Text MS Berg;[4] Unpublished

[Oswalds]
20.7.22

Dearest Eric.

Herewith I send you *two* sets of XI. XII. XIII. XIV. XV. XVI completing two final *copies of* the Rover.

The third set of the above I will post to you on Sat: next.

One of the sets here is corr^d by me the other transp^{d5} by Miss H[allowes]. If the part I-X which you sent to the U.S. was the one corr^d by me then please send over the XI-XVI incl also corr^d by me. If not then please complete the US by sending the balance of XI-XVI transposed by Miss H.

---

[1] Typing errors not reproduced or signalled.
[2] A recently published novella, *Ślepa latarka* (*Dark Lantern*).
[3] The Teatr Polski did announce the production but later cancelled it.
[4] A cancelled draft on letterhead stationery is at Yale.   [5] 'Transp[ose]d', i.e., fair copied?

Included also in this package I send you a letter embodying our verbal agreement for your consideration and approval.

Very affct Yours

J. Conrad.

To Walter Tittle
Text MS Texas; Unpublished

[letterhead: Oswalds]
20.7.22

My dear M[r] Tittle.[1]

Would you be inclined to come down here on Sunday next?

Train from Vic: 10.40 will bring you here for lunch. Car will meet you in Canterbury for which please take your ticket.

Yours truly

J. Conrad.

To Thomas J. Wise
Text MS BL Ashley 2953; Unpublished

[letterhead: Oswalds]
20.7.22.

Dear M[r] Wise.

I understood from our friend Curle that you would like to have a look at the MS of my story *The Rover* which I began last Oct[er] and finished on the 16th of this month.

I call the item a MS but it is of course First Draft.[2] You will however see that it contains a remarkable amount of writing apart from about twelve MS pages. The whole number of pages is four hundred (including the MS pp).

Will you please look through it and see whether you would care to give for it £150? (All the cancelled pp are included).

As a record of actual literary composition I think it is curious certainly. But that is a matter of opinion.

---

[1] The American illustrator and portraitist Walter Ernest Tittle (1883–1966) produced two oil paintings, two lithographs, and a dry-point etching of Conrad after their meeting in July 1922. Tittle helped persuade Conrad to go to America in 1923 and met him on his arrival in New York. He maintained friendly contact with Jessie Conrad after Conrad's death and wrote several reminiscences of him. See, e.g., Martin Ray, ed., *Joseph Conrad: Interviews and Reflections* (Macmillan, 1990), pp. 153–63.
[2] In Conrad's current usage, dictated typescript.

I must tell you that of the 3 clean copies taken of it one has been corrected (minor corrections) by me and two by Miss Hallowes. The copy corr^d by me has been sent to the U.S. for serialisation purposes and I fear will be destroyed in the process, as the US. magazines never send me a proof.

If how[ev]er I can save it (by writing to US a special request) I will hand it over to you. That how[ev]er can not be counted upon.

If you agree to my price I will be glad to give you the MS of a preface which I intend to write for Curle's book of travels,[1] immediately.

In a month's time or so I intend to take up my long novel the First Draft of which is your property, and part of which is in your possession already.

My wife joins me in kindest regards.

Believe me faithfully yours

Joseph Conrad

To Sir Richard Rees

Text MS UCL; Unpublished

[letterhead: Oswalds]

22.7.22

Dear Sir Richard

I have just finished a piece of work. The revision will take some 10 – 15 days more. You understand that I am doing this for a living, not for my own satisfaction – or else I would not let the work stand in the way of our meeting.

I will drop you a line directly I have this job off my shoulders. Meantime pray write to Major Gordon Gardiner 12 Queen Anne's Gate. S.W. I have taken him into my confidence as to your communication to me. Please don't mistrust my discretion and arrange to meet him. He's quite prepared. His heart is full of devotion and his mind of knowledge in the matter.[2] His experience is unrivalled in a particular way. He is a man for whom I have a very great affection and esteem. You may open your mind to him safely. Later I hope to bring you together again here. In haste

Yours

Joseph Conrad

---

[1] *Into the East: Notes on Burma and Malaya* (Macmillan, 1923).

[2] Gardiner devoted much of his time to visiting prisoners, and wrote a book about his experiences, published posthumously in 1938. Thus he would be a helpful contact for a well-to-do young man in search of a calling.

To Major Gordon Gardiner

Text MS Harvard; Unpublished

[letterhead: Oswalds]

22.7.22.

My very dear friend.

I've just finished the piece of work I was at. Am flattened out.

No end of thanks for your kindly disposition toward Rees (who is Sir Richard now). I have written to him giving him your Q A's Gate address. I thought it would be better. Herewith the two letters I had from him for your information and judgment. I think he is in earnest but at sea. Show him the land if you think he's worth saving. He may be! Chi lo sa?[1]

A cool request – you may think. But mon très cher I am unworthy even if I did know the ropes. When oh! When! shall we see you here.

Our love

Yours

J. Conrad.

To Thomas J. Wise

Text MS BL Ashley B. 498; Unpublished

[letterhead: Oswalds]

22.7.'22

Dear Mr Wise

We have been extremely sorry to hear of the bad time you have had with your severe cold. We do hope your stay in Seaford will put you right in every way.

I send you here the title-page as requested. I also inclose some cancelled pages which we have found after the MS was dispatched to you. I think they are worth preserving. The opening of XI was first scribbled in pen and ink as you see. The duplicate of the last page of the story is perfectly authentic. It was re-typed by Miss H[allowes] the same day – within the hour when I finished correcting the page you have already – as we thought that no copyist could find his way in it.

Now I think you will have every scrap of paper connected with the com-position of The Rover.

My wife joins me in kindest regards

Yours sincerely

Joseph Conrad.

---

[1] 'Who knows?'

PS I perceive I haven't thanked you for the cheque enclosed in your letter so I do it now

To Richard Curle
Text MS Indiana; Curle 96 (in part)¹

[Oswalds]
24.7.22.

My dear Curle.
Thanks for your friendly letter. The solicitors had my ch. for £250 to-day, to settle that awkward car business. I am feeling still a little sick at heart for that will not be the end of it.

B[orys] was here this week end. He showed me several communications from both sides of [the] Daimler business (The Hire D C⁰ London & The Daimlers Coventry)² from which one can not but suppose that they mean to give him at once some sort of job. Firms don't write letters for a joke or simply to kill time.

I have begun your Preface. Done about 400 w. It will be finished this week for you to see. 2000 w. minimum. I suppose that will do?

Let me know at once how I am to address Wedgwood.³ General – or what – on envelope and inside.

Love from us both

Yrs

J. Conrad.

To Richard Curle
Text MS Indiana; Unpublished

[Oswalds]
25.7.22

My dear Dick
I enclose you here the communication received from HC & D⁴ with copy of B[orys]'s letter to them.⁺ What B said to the moneylenders when pushed for money is understandable.

⁺ and the answer I am sending them by tonights post.

---

¹ Curle omits the first paragraph's second and third sentences.
² Gottlieb Daimler started Daimler Motoren Gesellschaft, the original German company, in 1890. Its British offshoot was the Daimler Motor Syndicate, Ltd, established in 1893; in 1896, the Daimler Motor Co. produced the first British-made cars at its Coventry plant.
³ See the letter of the 28th.   ⁴ Hammond Clark & Daman (see the next letter).

But the last paragraph of his letter is a lie directed against me. Why? For what object? Is he mad or am I? Do *you* believe that I said to him several times that I had £1000 invested in US for him and his brother?

I feel rather heartbroken. Will you meet me at Victoria 11.28 tomorrow (Wed:)? If you can't send me phone mes^ge to R[oyal] A[utomobile] C[lub] where I shall proceed on arrival. I know now what it is to be thoroughly unhappy.

Ever Yours

J. C.

To Messrs Hammond Clark & Daman
Text TS carbon Indiana; Unpublished

[Oswalds]
July 25th. 1922.

Messrs: Hammond Clark & Daman[1]

I am in receipt of your letter of yesterday's date.

I quite see that this puts a different complexion on the whole case and to tell you the truth I am quite shocked to learn that he has made those representations to those moneylenders, giving them thereby a false impression.

The true facts are like this.

Primo: He knew very well that the allowance I made him and that I make him now was not from money invested either in America or elsewhere, the true fact being that I have no money invested anywhere, either in this or any other country and am living on the proceeds of my pen, that is from the copyright royalties on my past books and on the payments I receive from those I am writing now.

Secundo: As to the thousand pounds of which he speaks for himself and his brother, it is simply the expression of what I would have liked to do, and at one time thought I would be able to do. The story is this. Some time about 1919 some American dealers in cinema subjects acquired the right of a couple of novels of mine and had an option for more which they were bound to exercise in 1920, and I thought that that would enable me to give my eldest son a thousand with a view perhaps of acquiring a share in some small business or other.[2] However that option was not exercised and lapsed and I

---

[1] Hammond Clark & Daman, 11 Great St Helens, Bishopsgate, was a partnership started by Frederick Hammond Clark (1846–1921), a barrister and former colonial administrator, and Gerard William Daman, who was admitted as a solicitor in 1919.

[2] In his correspondence, Conrad mentions the £1,000 as a sum promised to his elder son when circumstances allowed. It is unclear whether Borys knew that the money coming from Pinker's office was interest on a principal that did not yet exist. See the letters to J. B. Pinker of 20 January and Eric Pinker of 5 February 1921.

have had no further proposals from the cinema people. I was in the habit at that time of talking to him openly of my affairs, which I rather regret now and which I certainly would not have done if I had known he was already then involved in those debts, which was of course the case. Had he then had the candour to state the true facts of the case to me I could have remedied it then more easily than I can now. But this by the way.

I spoke of all this matter to my friend and literary agent, the late Mr J. B. Pinker, who told me that I certainly was not in a position to do that at once and thought that I had better not do it even if I could unless there was a definite opening and told me that if I liked I could to satisfy my conscience pay the interest on it till I was in a position to help him with some little capital. Some months afterwards an opportunity offered for him to invest £300 in a concern[1] which offered him the berth of assistant manager. Not long afterwards he parted from those people on bad terms and so far they have not yet paid back his investment. At that time also he confessed to an indebtedness to the amount of about £280 which Mr Pinker and I settled (the Grainger[2] cheques you hold are part of it) both of us being then under the impression that we had cleared him completely. I remember when handing him the £300 for investment that I said "Understand well that if I am in a position to do anything in the way of cash down for you and John this £300 would be deducted from the £1000 of which I spoke to you." But I wish to affirm that all this talk about the £1000 was always conditional and never amounted to anything which would justify the statement which he has made to those people. I write this to you at once in order that you may have the facts as I see them before you for consideration, but I intend to come up to town to-morrow and hope you will be able to give me an appointment at any time from noon. If you will be kind enough to telephone in the course of the morning a message for Mr Joseph Conrad to the R. Automobile Club I will find it there on my arrival.

I have written this letter with a view to clear the ground for the consultation for which I ask. I will probably bring Mr Richard Curle with me, if you have no objection, and if you think that we had better have my son in attendance please say so in your message to the Club.

S[incerely] Yrs

J Conrad

---

[1] Mackintosh's Surrey Scientific Apparatus Co.
[2] John Grainger, the money-lender or 'financial agent'; see the letter to Pinker of [17 October 1921].

To Eric Pinker
Text MS Berg; Unpublished

[letterhead: Oswalds]
25.7.22.

My dear Eric

I am glad to have your letter and that you think my letter covers the ground accurately.

As to the enclosure which I return here: I think that on the mere grounds of publicity we must give our consent, providing D. P. & C° agree.

If you are of the same mind please forward my consent in gracious terms.

In haste

Yours

J. C.

To Eric Pinker
Text TS/MS Berg; Unpublished

Oswalds
Bishopsbourne
Kent.
July 26th. 1922.

My dear Eric.

Thanks for your two communications received today, together with the specimens of print and covers for the intended pamphlets.[1]

I am forwarding you here the balance of the third *final* copy Chapter XI to XVI, which completes your three sets one of which is in the U.S. by now.

If of the two in your possession you have the one corrected in my own hand, pray keep it for use in England, as that may give me a chance to recover it when the printers have done with it, and I would very much like to have it, if possible.

In the same big envelope with the copy, dispatched to you last Thursday, there was a private letter to you relating to our conversation on the matter of finance. It seems to me that it embodies correctly the conclusions we arrived at; but you will understand that I am prepared to modify it in the sense of your suggestions if you have to make any. Perhaps you may not find it precise enough in its terms. It seemed to me that I have really put everything material into it and that the meaning was pretty clear.

[1] See the letter to Pinker of the 13th.

Goulden, the printer in Canterbury who did the "Secret Agent", has reminded me lately that I promised him that if I printed any more pamphlets I would give him a chance to compete. As it is true I will ask him also to send me his estimate. Thank you very much for sending me the specimens which I will hold for a little while. What I had in mind for the forthcoming pamphlets was something of a similar appearance as the set of ten bearing the imprint of "Orlestone" "published by the author" which are smaller than demy-octavo and have only thin coloured paper wrappers. I will take a little time to consider what will be best, and also see what Goulden can produce.

Yesterday I sat for a very successful sketch of my head in lithographic pencil by W Tittle an American artist working for Scribners & Century here. He's very talented and has already done a lot of big-wigs here.[1]

Affect^ly Yours

J. Conrad.

To Samuel C. Chew
Text TS Bryn Mawr; Unpublished

[letterhead: Oswalds]
July 27th. 1922.

My dear Sir.[2]

We will be delighted to see your wife with you here. Friday, the 4th Aug. is the earliest convenient day.

The 10.40 a.m. Victoria, arrives at Canterbury at 12.24, where I will meet you. You could return to town by the 5.17.

I never for a moment suspected you of interviewing propensities. I will indeed be very glad of a talk with you but whether you will find it "inspiring" is another question. I have just finished a piece of work and am feeling extremely dull and empty. You had better be prepared for the worst.

With kind regards

Yours faithfully

Joseph Conrad.

---

[1] Among them were Arnold Bennett, G. K. Chesterton, and Walter de la Mare.

[2] Samuel Claggett Chew (1888–1960), an American university teacher, specialised in Romantic poetry and late nineteenth-century literature. Most of his career was spent as a professor of English at Bryn Mawr College, Pennsylvania. He won first prize in the *Saturday Review* contest to provide an ending to *Suspense*.

To George Herbert Clarke

Text TS Queen's; Unpublished

[letterhead: Oswalds]
July 27th. 1922.

Dear M[r] Clarke[1]

Thank you very much for the charming and appreciative pamphlet[2] which you have written about me. I am very much touched and pleased by its general tone and by its conclusion.[3]

Would you care to come down here next Sunday week, Aug. 6th? If you leave by the 10.40, Victoria, I will meet you in Canterbury at 12.24. There is an up train at five which will get you back to town in time for dinner. Pray drop us a line in the course of the next few days.

With kind regards

faithfully Yours

Joseph Conrad.

To Ralph Wedgwood

Text MS Private collection; Unpublished

[letterhead: Oswalds]
28.7.22

Dear M[r] Wedgwood[4]

Let me thank you with all my heart for your consent to act as trustee and executor under my will together with Curle.

---

[1] American-born George Herbert Clarke (1873–1953) was educated in Canada and taught in various American universities before taking up a professorship at Queen's University in Ontario where he served as head of the Department of English from 1925 until his retirement in 1943. The *Sewanee Review*, which he edited from 1920 to 1925, featured his essay on Conrad in July 1922. He reviewed *The Rover* and *Suspense* for the same journal.

[2] An offprint of Clarke's essay 'Joseph Conrad and his Art', *Sewanee Review*, 30, 258–76.

[3] The conclusion reads: 'I do not understand the mystery of cosmos, implies Conrad; it is too large, too various, too arbitrary for me, but I do know that it is so fashioned as to make possible the ways and aspirations of good men and women who, despite all their sufferings, learn to grow in goodness. And so I know that the centre of cosmos is in some way, however remotely, responsible for the determination of such men and women to pitch their lives high. Courage, Fortitude, Fidelity are Conrad's words. They are enough.'

[4] Ralph Lewis Wedgwood (1874–1956; knighted 1924, baronetcy 1942) came from a celebrated family of potters but devoted his career to railway administration. On going down from Cambridge, he went to work for the dock and traffic departments of the North Eastern Railway; between 1923 and 1939, as Chairman and Chief General Manager of its successor, the LNER, he was a powerful advocate for innovative design. During the war, he had taken charge of docks and military railways in France, rising to the rank of Brigadier-General. He had literary and musical tastes, and his cousin Ralph Vaughan Williams dedicated several pieces to him. Ralph and Iris Wedgwood were the dedicatees of *Within the Tides*.

This act of friendly kindness, for which I confess I would not have ventured to ask without Richard's encouragement, takes a great load off my mind. And for this relief, which I really needed, I am indebted to you more than I can say. My wife sends her grateful regards and love to all, in which I join.

Believe me always faithfully Yours

Joseph Conrad

To Eric Pinker
Text TS Berg; Unpublished

[Oswalds]
July 30th. 1922.

My dear Eric

I return you the Texas letter.[1] There is no end to those requests, the last one (a few days ago) to which I assented being from Michigan the furthest north of the U.S.; while this one of course is from very nearly the furthest south. On the principle I mentioned to you before of creating readers for my work in the coming generation we ought to assent to this one too; but in any case we must refer to Doubleday Page, of whose permission the Texas letter does not speak at all. Perhaps you would suggest to D. P & C° to decide and communicate with the man either one way or the other.

I will be in town on Wednesday, which is the day of cheap return tickets, and should like very much to have a talk with you before you start on your little holiday.

I won't treat of it in writing, its beastly enough, but I will be able to put it before you in a very few words. Perhaps you wouldn't mind dropping me a line by an early post on Tuesday naming the time most suitable to you. If posted about four it is sure to reach me in the morning before I leave the house for the station.

Very Affec^ly Yours

J. Conrad.

To F. N. Doubleday
Text MS Princeton; Unpublished

[letterhead: Oswalds]
3.8.'22

Dear Mr Doubleday

It gives me great pleasure both as to my publisher and my friend to tell you that the novel at which I was engaged when you were over here has been

---

[1] Of 5 July from Leonidas Warren Payne (TS carbon Texas) about reprint rights.

finished – and, I think, successfully. The serial publication will be out of the way, I hope, in time for its publication in book-form in the spring. In fact I have very little doubt about that.

I regretted very much not having been able to see you. But under the sad circumstances of your visit[1] you had your hands very full, I imagine; and as to myself I was really very much absorbed in my work, wishing to take advantage of every hour in a period of comparative good health. I had a very bad time in that respect for the last 18 months. I have however every reason to hope that the improvement is permanent. I shall turn my energies now to the finishing of the "Mediterranean novel" which is half-written and, with a little luck, will be finished early next year.

My wife joins me in best regards to Mrs Doubleday[2] and yourself.

Believe me always faithfully yours

Joseph Conrad

Pray give my friendly greetings to Mr & Mrs Everitt[3] and remember me to all my good friends in Garden City.

To Clement K. Shorter
Text MS BL Ashley B. 504; Unpublished

[letterhead: Oswalds]

5.8.22

Dear Mʳ Shorter.

You may print any letter of mine you have in your possession.

Yours faithfully

J. Conrad.

To Eric Pinker
Text MS Berg; Unpublished

[letterhead: Oswalds]

6.8.'22

My dear Eric.

I will be coming up on Tuesday, to conclude the arrangements in the matter you know of, and will call at your office about noon. I have asked

---

[1] Related to Pawling's failing health and its consequences for managing Heinemann?
[2] Florence Doubleday (née Van Wyck, 1866–1946) married Doubleday in 1918; she was active in civic, political, and cultural affairs.
[3] Mrs Everitt had drawn the map for the end-papers of the first Doubleday edition of *Victory*.

Withers to phone a message for me to say if it would be convenient for me
to come over and sign my will at his office.[1]
Ray Long advertised in last Times' Lit. Supp^t the appoint[men]^t of M^r
Frazier Hunt as editorial represen^{ve} of the Hearst Mags.[2]

Affect^{ly} Yrs

J. Conrad.

To John Galsworthy
Text MS Forbes; J-A, 2, 273–4 (in part)[3]

[letterhead: Oswalds]

7.8.22

Dearest Jack.

I am disgusted with myself but I assure you that while I was finishing the
novel (begun last Oct^{er}) I was not in a state to tackle the simplest letter. I
don't know that I am much better mentally now, but at any rate the novel is
finished even to the last word of the revision. It's gone out of the house; and
its like waking up out of a nightmare of endless effort to get out of a bog. I
was laid up 5 times between the New Year day and the end of June!

For the last two days I have been reading the Saga which makes a wonderful
volume.[4] The consistency of inspiration, the unfailing mastery of execution,
the variety of shades and episodes have impressed me tremendously. It's a
great art-achievement in which every part is worthy of the whole in a great
creative unity of purpose.

How fresh the M[an] of P[roperty] reads![5] For that book I have a special
affection. I had not read it for a couple of years, or more and I was fascinated
by the constant felicity of presentation: portraits, groups scenes. The lines
stand traced for all time; as to the details filling in that great conception they
are, all through the Saga, a source of delight to a craftsman. The preface is
"magistrale"[6] in its conciseness. Could not have been better.

The reading of these pages has been a source of great comfort in a time
when I did want to be taken out of myself. It was like stepping out of an arid
desert into an enchanted valley. Ever since finishing the Rescue (2 years or

---

[1] For Conrad's will, see Hans van Marle's transcription in *Documents*, pp. 247–51.
[2] *Times Literary Supplement*, 3 August, p. 502. Long was editor-in-chief of the International Magazine Company of New York.
[3] Jean-Aubry omits the postscript.
[4] *The Forsyte Saga*, comprising *The Man of Property* (1906), *In Chancery* (1920), and *To Let* (1921), had
recently appeared as an omnibus volume.
[5] Conrad reviewed the novel for the *Outlook* in March 1906; the review appears in *Last Essays*.
[6] 'Masterly' or 'magisterial'.

more ago) I have had, in one way or another, a pretty bad time. The reaction from the war, anxiety about Jessie, the growing sense of my own deficiencies, and even, lately, a special sort of worry, of which I do not want to speak on paper, have combined to make anything but a bed of roses for my ageing bones. My very soul is aching all over. My fault of course.

   Our dear love to you both

                                   Ever Yours

                                          J. Conrad.

Are you leaving town soon? May I come up for a couple of hours to see you both on some day convenient to you?

To G. Jean-Aubry
Text MS Yale; *L. fr.* 171–2

                                   [letterhead: Oswalds]
                                          9.8.22.

Mon très cher Jean.

   J'étais bien content de voir votre écriture. Votre affection m'est très pre-cieuse et en ce moment-ci, m'est d'un grand reconfort. Je viens d'arranger cette lourde affaire de B[orys], mais je reste sous le coup d'une amère déception – une espèce de fatigue morale ag[g]ravée par le doute, qui sub-siste, sur l'avenir. Je ne parle pas de l'embarras materiel que ça m'a causé, qui est serieux; c'est plutôt l'atmosphere de toute cette affaire qui m'opprime. Enfin! Je suis peut être injuste pour lui. On verra.

   Je suis très heureux de savoir que mon pauvre Nègre[1] a plu a Mme Votre Mère. Dites-le lui je Vous prie – avec mes hommages respectueux.

   Le Forban est en ce moment en Amérique, mais j'aurai une copie complète avant Votre retour. Il n'est pas encore placé là-bas mais j'ai bon éspoir* que Hearst[2] le prendra. Hearst paye bien.

   Je suis touché de Votre fidelité a Nostromo. Je me demande ce que Neel fera de ce livre.[3] J'ai un peu peur, je Vous avoue.

   Je suis bien faché, mon très cher, que le vieux La Fontaine[4] se montre récalcitrant. Du reste je n'ai jamais cru que c'était un personnage facile a

---

[1] Robert d'Humières's translation, *Le Nègre du Narcisse*, appeared in 1910.
[2] The largest newspaper empire in the USA, the Hearst Syndicate, owned by William Randolph Hearst (1863–1951), transformed American journalism.
[3] Philippe Neel's translation appeared in *Le Quotidien* (Paris) from 1 to 13 October 1924, and was published as a book the same year.
[4] None of Jean-Aubry's books has anything about Jean la Fontaine (1621–95), author of verse fables close to the heart of the French literary canon.

faire; mais je suis sur que vous finirez par nous donner quelque chose qui sera très bien.

Je me fais fête d'avance de lire avec Vous la IIème et IIIème parties de La Flêche d'Or. Je ne puis Vous dire combien je Vous suis réconnaissant de la peine que Vous Vous donnez avec mes traductions.

J'ai eu ici 3 ou 4 Américains – professeurs de college et universités.[1] C'était un peu fatiguant. Catherine[2] nous a quitté hier après le week-end.

Voilà près du* deux ans que je ne me suis si bien porté; mais j'ai un continuel sentiment d'angoisse dont je ne peux pas me debarrasser.

Jessie sends her love.

A Vous de coeur
Joseph Conrad.

Translation

My very dear Jean.

I was very glad to see your handwriting. Your affection is very precious to me and at this particular moment a great comfort. I have just settled that serious business of B's but remain under the blow of a bitter disappointment – a kind of moral fatigue aggravated by a lingering doubt about the future. I won't mention the financial trouble it caused me, which was significant; it's rather the feel of the whole thing that weighs on me. Well! perhaps I'm being unfair to him. We shall see.

I am very happy to hear that my poor *Nigger* pleased your mother. Pray do tell her that, and give her my respectful duty.

The Rover is in America at the moment, but I shall have a complete copy before you get back. It has not been placed there yet, but I have good hopes that Hearst will take it. Hearst pays well.

Your fidelity to *Nostromo* touches me. I wonder what Neel will make of that book. I confess I'm somewhat fearful.

I am quite put out, my dear, that old La Fontaine is proving recalcitrant. Moreover, I never believed that he would be an easy character to do, but I'm confident you will produce something really good in the end.

I rejoice at the thought of reading the Second and Third Parts of *The Arrow of Gold* with you. I can't tell you how grateful I am for the trouble you are taking over my translations.

Three or four Americans were here – college and university teachers. It was rather tiring. Catherine left us yesterday after staying the week-end.

---

[1] See the letters of 27 July.   [2] Willard.

I've not felt as well as this for two years, but I have a constant feeling of anxiety that I can't shake off.

Jessie sends her love.

Yours affectionately

Joseph Conrad

To Eric Pinker

Text MS Berg; Unpublished

[letterhead: Oswalds]

9.8.22

My dear Eric.

I can't let this day pass without telling you how much I appreciated your friendly and sympathetic attitude towards me in my trouble.

It has added tenfold to the value of the practical assistance you have extended to me. Indeed you have been very good.

My warmest thanks.

Affect^ly Yours

Joseph Conrad

To Eric Pinker

Text MS Berg; Unpublished

[Oswalds]

10.8.'22. 3. pm.

My dear Eric

This is the wire just received from Borys.

The salary he mentions is subject to 15% deduction. He was informed of that by the manager of the Trading Dep^t Daimlers a fortnight ago during his first interview with him in London. He told him that this deduction applied to whole of Daimlers' staff (on account of the trade depression) during the year 1922.

He got this job quite by himself. It may be *the* turning point.

Affec^ly Yrs

J. Conrad.

To Eric Pinker
Text MS Berg; Unpublished

[Oswalds]

10.8.22.

6.30.

My dear Eric.

As the evening post brought no letter from you I send this to ask whether you have arranged yet with the bank to guarantee up to 500£ overdraft.

Of this I may need 300 by monday to settle finally with the money lenders. I don't like to draw unless I know that all is in order. I also have now nothing in my current acct as I used the balance to make up the £243.17.0 to be paid today.

As I have mentionned* before I think I ought to assign to you formally my royalties (£50 per vol) (as security for your guarantee) on the first 12 vols of the uniform edition to be published by Dent. Gouldens are going to take in hand the booklets next week,[1] the proceeds of which (say 200) will be applied to the reduction of the above overdraft as soon as realised.

Always Yrs

Joseph Conrad.

Please wire me the words: *all right* in the course of the day.

To Eric Pinker
Text MS Berg; Unpublished

[letterhead: Oswalds]

12.8.22.

My dear Eric.

Thanks for your letter received to-day. I am glad to hear that Evans[2] apprehends no difficulty on the part of D. P. & Cº.

I agree with you as to making things easy for Dent. I return you here the agreement[3] duly signed.

It is of course regrettable that Hearst's manager declined *The Rover*. I had no doubt that you had more than one string to your bow, and I am not in the least depressed by the incident. In this connection, may I ask you to send me *One* set of the t-written copy of R. just for a week. Garnett is coming to stay with us and he is sure to clamour to see it.

---

[1] See the letter of 13 July.   [2] C. S. Evans, at Heinemann.
[3] Not that for the Uniform Edition (see the letter of 12 October).

Carola's allowance will be due on the 1st Sept. I have had a letter from her asking for it to be sent earlier as she wants to start on a visit to Poland about the 18 inst. Could you sent* it on the 16th inst? addressed to Miss *C. Zagorska pensione Calosso. 17 Viale Monforte Milan.* If this should be inconvenient you may deduct the sum from my month's money (on the 15th) and then pay it to *me* at the proper time.

I hope to be able to settle down quietly to the consideration of the big novel now. When do you leave on your holiday? The weather seems to be going to pieces again I am sorry to see.

Thanks once more.

Always affct^{ly} Yours

Joseph Conrad.

To W. C. Wicken
Text MS Berg; Unpublished

[letterhead: Oswalds]

14.8.22

Dear Mr Wicken.[1]

Thanks for your letter and the copy of The Rover received to-day. I note that you are going to send a draft to Miss Zagorska before the exact date when her allowance falls due.

I do not know whether you have the knowledge of a certain undertaking not to make any claims or molest either my wife or myself made to the late Mr J. B. Pinker and signed by a Mrs Hearson. She persists in trying to see my wife, and this is the last letter she wrote to her. It is excessively annoying.

Mr Eric is aware of the undertaking which his father has told me he communicated to him before going to the U.S. Could a letter be written to her by the firm reminding her of her written promise? My wife has of course written already declining all sort of communication personal or by letter. This may not however stop her whereas a letter from the office may. Of course if you do not wish to do that in Mr Eric's absence I will understand the position.

Kind regards

Yours faithfully

J Conrad

---

[1] W. C. Wicken, Pinker's office manager. Among his duties was handling the firm's day-to-day finances.

To W. C. Wicken

Text MS Berg; Unpublished

[letterhead: Oswalds]

15.8.22.

Dear Mr Wicken.

I made a good many corrections in the copy of R[over] which you sent me. I should like to transpose them on to the other copy (in your office). If you were to send it to me I could do it in a day and send both back by return of post.

Of course if you think you may suddenly need it the matter is of no *vital* importance. I only thought it would be nice to have two perfect copies.

Yours faithfully

J. Conrad

To Borys Conrad

Text MS Yale; Unpublished

[Oswalds]

16.8.22

My dear boy[1]

I was glad to get your letter.

Enclosed ch £5 – I crossed it as I dont like to post uncrossed cheques. I have no doubt the office will cash it. I have been in town to-day and attended to the starting of the Mac business.[2]

I am very tired and not very cheerful. Poor mother has been in considerable pain since yesterday's injection. Dear love from us three.

The best of luck to you.

Your ever affect^{te} Father

J. C.

---

[1] The elder of Conrad's sons, Alfred Borys Conrad (1898–1978) was educated in a training-ship and later worked in the motor industry. Gassed and shell-shocked during the war, he suffered from poor health and emotional problems thereafter. His occasionally irresponsible behaviour, his entanglement in debt, and his marriage without Conrad's knowledge strained relations with his father.

[2] The winding up of Mackintosh's company.

To T. E. Lawrence

Text Lawrence 26 and facsimile; H. & M.[1]

[letterhead: Oswalds]
18.8.22

My dear M[r] Lawrence.[2]

I too have been looking for the crown 8vo edition for you.[3] It is out of print and I have been unable to obtain even a second hand copy. I hope you did not think I had forgotten.[4] I was on the point of writing to you.

Next year I trust there will be a new edition[5] (ill[d]) of a decent size and I shall reserve for you a copy out of my own lot.

I corrected an absurd misprint on p 217.[6] I know there are two or three more but I was unable to find them.

Yours

J. Conrad.

To Samuel C. Chew

Text MS Bryn Mawr; Unpublished

[letterhead: Oswalds]
20.8.'22

My dear Sir.

We have been much shocked by the news You give us of Your wife who has conquered all our hearts here. Please convey her the assurance of our heartfelt sympathy, which is of course extended to you in the fullest measure in the anxiety from which you must have suffered.

---

[1] Text from the facsimile.

[2] Popularly known as 'Lawrence of Arabia', Thomas Edward Lawrence (né Shaw, 1888–1935) read History at Oxford, writing his thesis on Crusader castles. From 1910 to 1914 he worked on archaeological digs in the Euphrates Valley. During the First World War, he fought alongside Arabs in revolt against Turkish rule and co-ordinated their efforts with those of the British army and navy. Reports by the American journalist Lowell Thomas of Lawrence's role in the sabotage of the Hedjaz railway, the capture of Akaba after a bold desert traverse, and the advance on Damascus made him a celebrity in the English-speaking world. He admired Conrad's work. At the time of his visit to Oswalds in July 1920, Lawrence was reconstructing *The Seven Pillars of Wisdom* (1926) from his recollection of a draft stolen from him the previous year. Lawrence continued to support Arab hopes after the war and was bitterly disappointed by the Allies' reluctance to foster national independence beyond the boundaries of Europe.

[3] *The Mirror of the Sea.* Methuen's first edition (1906) and the Popular Edition (November 1915) were both crown octavo. Conrad probably tried to find a copy of the latter.

[4] Lawrence had visited Oswalds on 18 July 1920.

[5] The proposed edition with John Everett's drawings.

[6] In the copy sent, 'Signed for T. E. Lawrence with the greatest regard by Joseph Conrad 1922', Conrad corrected 'musicians' to 'magicians' and deleted a comma after 'exiles'.

I have already taken steps by wire (funny phrase isn't it?) to get the kind of portrait Your wife did me the honour to ask for. Though your letter is reassuring pray drop us a postcard with further news. You will perhaps be good enough to give me Your wife's christian name for the inscription.

With our united warm regards to you both believe me always

Yrs

J. Conrad.

To Edward Garnett

Text J-A, 2, 274–5; G. 313–14[1]

[Oswalds]
22.8.'22

Dearest Edward,

I had no doubt you would feel deeply Hudson's death.[2]

I was never intimate with him but I always thought of him with real affection. The secret of his charm both as a man and as a writer remains impenetrable to me. A little uncanny. Yet there was nothing more *real* in letters – nothing less tainted with the conventions of art; I mean the most legitimate. He was a nature-production himself and had something of its fascinating mysteriousness. Something unique is gone out of the world. Yes my dear Edward we will miss him – you of course more than I. But then I am much older than you and begin to feel resigned.

Do my dear fellow. Come down next Thursday 31st – isn't it? On the 30 I must lunch with Galsworthy whom I have not seen for ages. – Strange fellows these Harmsworths![3] It is as if they had found Aladdin's lamp.[4] Strangest still to think that I had been more intimate with N. than with Hudson. Funny world this.

Ever yours

J. C.

---

[1] Text from Garnett.

[2] W(illiam) H(enry) Hudson (born 1841), novelist, naturalist, and ornithologist had died on the 18th. On the 21st, Garnett had written to Conrad: 'Hudson's death is a heavy blow. I loved him as a unique & precious personality, much as I love you' (Stape and Knowles, p. 194). Hudson, a reclusive man, saw little of Conrad, but many of the writers in Conrad's circle, including Garnett, Ford, and Cunninghame Graham looked on Hudson as a great master of English prose.

[3] Alfred Harmsworth, Lord Northcliffe, had died on the 14th. His brother, Harold, Lord Rothermere, was also a newspaper magnate.

[4] In the story in *The Thousand and One Nights*, Aladdin, the son of a poor widow, finds a magic lantern containing a genie able to grant his wishes, and he becomes prosperous and powerful. Rising from poverty, the Harmsworths acquired enough power to make or break governments.

To W. C. Wicken

Text MS Berg; Unpublished

[letterhead: Oswalds]
22.8.'22

Dear Mr Wicken

I return the D. P & C° agreement duly signed[1] and the pre[li]ms of the new edition of *Under Western Eyes*. I would certainly like to have all the books mentioned in the list.

I trust you have had news of Mr and Mrs Eric having a good time on their tour.

Yours faithfully

J. C.

To Richard Curle

Text MS Indiana; Curle 97

[Oswalds]
23.8.22

My dear Dick

I am thinking of coming to town tomorrow and perhaps you will meet me at the train (11.30) – that is if you do not get a wire early saying I am unable. I feel however pretty well so far and want to have a talk with you on one or two matters of importance.

Jessie's love

Yours

J. C.

Should you be engaged phone me a message at the R[oyal] A[utomobile] C[lub] in the course of the morning.

To R. B. Cunninghame Graham

Text MS NLS; Watts (1969), 194

[letterhead: Oswalds]
25.8.'22.

Très cher ami.

Pardon me for not answering your letter before. I knew you would feel Hudson's death deeply.[2] I was not an intimate with him but I had a real affection for that unique personality of his with its, to me, somewhat mysterious fascination. If there was ever a "Child of Nature" it was he; and he never grew

---

[1] The agreement for *The Rover*, which Conrad signed on 21 August (Hallowes).
[2] They had been close friends. Hudson's birth and upbringing in Argentina and Graham's own experiences there strengthened their affinity.

older except, of course, in his body. You and I will miss that mortal envelope, but the rare spirit it contained will speak to the coming generations which may appreciate his truth and his charm perhaps better than the men of his own time.

Strangely enough I was more intimate with that other dead Northcliffe. How quickly that power was snuffed out! Strange lot, these Harmsworths – it is as though they had found Aladdin's Lamp. But N. himself was absolutely genuine. He had given me one or two glimpses of his inner man which impressed me: And he was most friendly to us all. After all that fortune was not made by sweating the worker or robbing the widow and the orphan.

Our love to you dear Don Roberto.

Ever Yours

J. Conrad

Borys got a post with the Daimler Co. in Coventry. Went to work about 10 days ago.

To Rhoda Symons
Text MS Private collection; Unpublished

[Oswalds]
31.8.22

Dear Mrs Symons.[1]

Thanks for your letter with cheque for £80.

I was just about to write to you and send the license, when your man arrived. I'll hand it to him then together with the car.

I do hope you will find the car as sympathetic and pleasant to drive as we have done.

With our united regards to you both,

Yours sincerely

Joseph Conrad.

To Eric Pinker
Text MS Berg; Unpublished

[Oswalds]
2.9.22

My dear Eric

This is just a word of greeting on your return.

---

[1] Rhoda Symons (née Bowser, 1874–1936) met Arthur Symons in 1898, when she was a violin student at the Royal Academy of Music. Even then she wanted a theatrical career, but did not have her first professional part until 1912. In the same year she understudied Paulina in Harley Granville-Barker's production of *The Winter's Tale*. Over the next ten years she appeared in some dozen plays.

We were sorry to hear from R[alph] of you having been laid up in Glasgow – of all places in the world! We trust that apart from that you both had a good time and that your wife has benefitted by this tête-a-tête excursion, in health and spirits.

I will (unless I hear from you to the contrary) turn up in the office at about one o'clock on Wednesday next; unless indeed you would lunch with me, in which case we could meet at the R[oyal] A[utomobile] C[lub] 1.15. Our united regards to you both

Affect^{ly} yrs

J. Conrad

To Eric Pinker

Text MS Berg; Unpublished

[letterhead: Oswalds]
Wed^{y} 6.9.22[1]

My dear Eric.

I have seen Dent and settled with him the colour (dark crimson) the size (demy 8vo) the type of the uniform edition. Also that *every* work is to form a separate vol. (23 so far)

JMD does not wish to have the Am. plates.[2] I am very pleased with the dummy he had ready to show me. The books will look value for money, in my opinion. The gold lettering of titles on back (round) is also looking well. Pages to be cut. Top not gilt but polished in a good shade of colour, sort of greeny brown.

Perhaps you could some time step in and make them show you the thing. I would like to know what You think.

I told JMD that I will send him the correct text.

I hope my dear Eric that you will soon recover your "tone".

Always Y^{r} affec^{te}

J. Conrad

---

[1] Misfiled under September 1921, thanks to an ink blot on the final '2'.
[2] In the end he took them, and Dent's Uniform Edition is thus a reprint of Doubleday's 'Sun-Dial' Edition.

To Robert Garnett

Text MS NYPL; Unpublished

[letterhead: Oswalds]

7.9.22

My dear Garnett.[1]

I was very glad to get your note.

To-morrow we have a[n] old friend coming. On Sat Curle and Walpole are coming. W will leave on Monday, and next day my wife and I start (with the boy John) on a visit to L'pool[2] – of all places in the world! So I can't manage to be in town before the 20th, much as I want to see you again since Curle has told me of your invariable friendly sentiments towards me.

I read with the greatest interest your communications to the *Times* in* the Dumas-Maquet affair.[3] All this story was quite new to me.

Always affect^{ly} Yours

Joseph Conrad

To Eric Pinker

Text MS Berg; Unpublished

[letterhead: Oswalds]

10.9.22

My dear Eric

From things I have heard here and there it strikes me that perhaps we could get a chance with the play by going diplomatically to Basil Dean.[4]

I have heard from a good source that he is a man of intelligence. At the same time I've heard that he is more interested in stage effects than in plays themselves. Still! On the other hand it is a fact that he had been running four successes lately and ought to have plenty of money. He may not be averse from trying a not *very* costly experiment, after all, and containing a promise of a "success of curiosity". I understand also that he is not tied to any actor or actress and could select his cast with complete freedom.

---

[1] Robert Singleton Garnett (1866–1932), Edward's elder brother, was a senior partner in the law firm of Darley, Cumberland. During Conrad's breach with Pinker in 1910, he handled the writer's literary, as well as legal, interests, as he had for Ford Madox Ford and D. H. Lawrence. A keen book collector, he was an authority on Alexandre Dumas *père*.

[2] To see Sir Robert and Lady Jones.

[3] 'The Maquet-Dumas Case', *Times Literary Supplement*, 22 June, p. 412, and 'Dumas and Maquet', 20 July, p. 476, about the trials in 1856 and 1858 on charges brought against Alexandre Dumas by Auguste Maquet, his principal collaborator on such historical romances as *Les Trois Mousquetaires* and *Le Comte de Monte- Cristo*. A historian and would-be playwright, Maquet supplied Dumas with much of his background information.

[4] Basil Dean (1888–1978), actor, dramatist, theatrical impresario, and in the 1930s a pioneer of British talking-pictures.

This notion having occurred to me I impart it to you for what it is worth – tho' probably you may already have considered such a move with a fuller knowledge than mine could be.

I hope my dear you are improving

Always yrs

J. Conrad.

To Eric Pinker
Text MS Berg; Unpublished

[letterhead: Oswalds]

11.9.22

My dear Eric.

Will you kindly send me cash against the enclosed cheque in five pound notes. I do not trust the bank to do it in time. We are leaving on Thursday 10 AM for L'pool by the direct train from Dover.

We will be in London on Tuesday most likely for a day on our way back. I trust You are getting on.

Affectio[n]^{ly} Always Yours

J. Conrad.

Have you ever tried to place the film scenario[1] father & I concocted in '20? Or any of the unsold stories?

To J. M. Dent & Sons, Ltd
Text TS carbon Indiana;[2] Unpublished

[Oswalds]

Sept. 12th. 1922.

Messrs. Dent & Son.

London.

In the matter of the plates.

I bring to your recollection that I told you of Mr Doubleday's offer and that you said then to me that you did not want to use them. The plates Mr Doubleday offers to you now are the plates of the American Edition de Luxe (750 sets). His offer is perfectly straightforward and genuine. It is the English Edition de Luxe, arranged for in the lifetime of the late Mr Wm. Heinemann, the type of which has been distributed. Mr Doubleday had nothing to do with the English Edition de Luxe, though both were published at the same time. The American was printed from plates, which Mr Doubleday is offering to

---

[1] I.e., *Gaspar the Strong Man*, based on 'Gaspar Ruiz'.
[2] On the verso of the letter to Garnett of the same date.

you now, for use in printing your uniform edition. There is nothing dishonest in that. On the contrary I think it is rather a friendly act considering that Mr Doubleday has been refused the opportunity to publish the Uniform Edition which J. M. Dent & Son are going to produce.

If you recollect we have settled upon the type in which your Edition is to be printed; but if you like to accept Doubleday's offer of plates I have no objection to make.

To J. M. Dent & Sons, Ltd

Text TS carbon Indiana;[1] J-A, 2, 275; G. 314–15

[Oswalds]

[12 September 1922][2]

To J. M. Dent & Son

I have your letter, for which thanks.

As regards the article on Hudson suggested by Dr Smyth, of the *Times Book Review*,[3] I am the last person to write an "authoritative" paper on W. H. H. I don't suppose I have met Hudson ten times in my life, though when we did meet he was always extremely kind and friendly to me. It is six or seven years, or perhaps more, since I saw Hudson last. We never corresponded on any subject of general interest, and I have not a scrap of his writing in my possession.

The person eminently fitted to write an authoritative article is, of course, Edward Garnett, Hudson's friend for more than twenty years, one of his earliest appreciators long before the public, or for that matter the publishers, recognised the high quality of Hudson's work which he did his utmost to make known to the world. They saw each other frequently and, I believe, corresponded regularly.[4] I do not suppose there is another man who has such a profound knowledge of Hudson's work as Edward Garnett. I understand that E. G. is planning a study of Hudson which would be exactly the thing for the Times Book Review and for your own purposes[5] in the way of "authority" and sympathy. You could do no better than suggest Garnett to your friends in America for the work which I absolutely decline to undertake.

P. S. – E. Garnett's address is 19, Pond Place, Chelsea, S.W.

---

[1] The postscript, missing from the original, is from Jean-Aubry.
[2] The following note to Garnett fixes the date.
[3] Austin Edward Arthur Watt Smyth (1877–1949), Librarian of the House of Commons, contributed to the *Times Literary Supplement*.
[4] The Nonesuch Press published 153 of Hudson's letters to Garnett in 1923, with Garnett's notes and introduction.
[5] Of publicity? Dent was one of Hudson's publishers in his later years.

To Edward Garnett

Text MS Indiana; G. 314

[Oswalds]

[12 September 1922][1]

My dearest Edward.

This is copy of letter I wrote to Dent. It speaks for itself.

Ever Yours

J. C.

To Eric Pinker

Text TS/MS Berg; Unpublished

[letterhead: Oswalds]

Sept. 12th. 1922.

My dear Eric

I had this morning a letter from Ernest Dawson,[2] from whom you will hear soon no doubt. E. D. (whom your father knew and liked) is a Burmah official who used to write quite good stuff (not fiction) about the East, for Blackwood, some ten or more years ago. For the last two years he has retired and has been travelling about in Italy. He will ask you to try to place some of his sketches written lately. I have not seen them. I hope you will see your way to do something for that excellent fellow who at one time had the gift of writing amusingly. I only hope he hasn't lost it.

Affect[ly] Yrs

J. Conrad

I enclose E D. letter which I've answered

To Major Ernest Dawson

Text MS postcard Yale; Unpublished

[Oswalds]

[12 September 1922][3]

Dearest Ernest.

Address *J. B. Pinker and Son* (the son's name is Eric) *Talbot House Arundel Street. Strand WC.2.* I've dropped him a line. Our love

Ever yrs

J. C.

---

[1] Date from postmark.   [2] Of 11 September (Stape and Knowles, p. 195).
[3] Date from postmark.

To Eric Pinker
Text MS Berg; Unpublished

[Oswalds]
12.9.22

My dear Eric

Thanks for taking the trouble of answering my letter suggesting B. Deane.*
I heard of him some time ago – but what struck me lately was his running
Loyalties in two theatres simultaneously – and also having a hand in the
production of East of Suez.¹ I thought he was going to spread himself all
over the place.

Do you think that Sybil Thorndyke*² would do for Mrs Verloc? I imagine
she could make the people run to see her in the last long scene. But that
character requires more flesh and bone (I mean it literally) than she can give.

Always Yours

J. C.

To Richard Curle
Text Curle 98

[Liverpool]
Sept. 18. Monday. [1922]

My dear R. C.

We will be at the Curzon Hotel about five tomorrow (Tuesday).

I have been feeling far from bright all these days. Otherwise it was a good
time.

Yours,

J. C.

To G. Jean-Aubry
Text MS Yale; *L.fr.* 173–4

[letterhead: Oswalds]
22.9.22

Très cher ami.

J'etais absent quand Votre lettre est arrivée. Jessie et moi (avec Jean) etions
en visite a Liverpool chez Sir Robert qui nous avait offert de faire un petit
tour de 3 jours en North-Wales. Le temps etait mauvais mais la nouveauté
du pays et le mouvement ont fait plaisir a ma femme. Jean s'est bien amusé.³

---

¹ Plays by Galsworthy and W. Somerset Maugham, respectively.
² (Agnes) Sybil Thorndike (1882–1976; DBE 1931) was celebrated for both comic and tragic
  roles, and particularly associated with Shakespeare and Shaw. Later, she had a career in film.
³ He describes the tour in John Conrad, pp. 192–4.

Moi j'ai toussé affreusement. La vérité est que ma santé n'est pas bonne quoique je n'ai pas souffert de la goutte depuis du moins 3 mois. J'ai pensé a Vous beaucoup. Si je n'ai pas écrit c'est que je n'avais rien de bon a dire. Hearst a refusé *The Rover*, "not suitable for serial publication". Je n'ai pas ecrit l'article pour le *Times*. Je n'avais ni l'envie ni le sujet pour cela; et a présant* que Lord N[orthcliffe] est mort je n'aurai pas grande chance pour être imprimé. En verité je n'ai rien fait depuis le mois de Juillet. J'ai vécu – et c'est bien assez.[1]

Borys a une assez bonne situation avec la *Daimler C⁰*.[2] Il a trouvé cela lui même par les connaissances qu'il a fait au Club. Il est en ce moment station[n]é a Manchester. Il a meilleure mine. Nous sommes allés le voir là pendant notre visite a Sir R. Jones. Jean a bien travaillé a l'école. Il y est retourné hier. La maison semble vide. Je vais me mettre a travailler a mon long roman, qui me semble bien mauvais, a la lecture. Mais il faut bien le finir.

Je vois mon très cher que Votre Lafontaine vous donne bien du mal. Je suis bien curieux de le voir.

La traduction anglaise de *Du Coté de chez Swann* vient de paraître. L'auteur (Moncrieff)[3] me l'a envoyée. Nous verrons! Oui très cher il faut venir nous voir aussitôt Votre retour. C'est vrai – "Je me languis après Vous" comme on dit dans le Midi.

Jessie sends her love.

A vous de coeur

J. Conrad

Translation

My very dear friend.

I was away when your letter arrived. Jessie and I were in Liverpool (with John) visiting Sir Robert, who offered to take us on a three-day tour of North Wales. The weather was bad, but my wife was pleased with the novelty of the countryside and with travelling. John amused himself a good deal. As for myself, I had a frightful cough. The truth is I am not in good health though I have not had an attack of gout for at least three months.

---

[1] Abbé Sieyès (1748–1836), a veteran of the Jacobin Terror, epitomised his sinuous political career with the words 'J'ai vécu' – 'I have lived' (i.e., 'I survived').
[2] He was employed in the company's newly opened Sales Office.
[3] See the letters to him of December 1922.

I thought of you a good deal. If I haven't written it is because I had nothing good to say. Hearst rejected *The Rover* – 'not suitable for serial publication'. I did not write the article for *The Times*. I had no desire to and no subject for it and now that Lord N. is dead, I have no great chance of getting published. To tell the truth, I've done nothing since July. I have lived, and that is quite enough.

Borys has a fairly good position with the *Daimler Cº*. He found it himself through some acquaintances he made at the Club. At the moment he is stationed in Manchester. He looks better. We went to see him there during our visit to Sir R. Jones. John has been diligent at school. He went back yesterday and the house seems empty. I am going to get down to work on my long novel, which, on reading, seems quite bad. But it must indeed be finished.

I see, my dear, that your La Fontaine gives you rather a good deal of trouble. I'm quite curious to see it.

The English translation of *Du côté de chez Swann* has just been published. The author (Moncrieff) sent it to me. We shall see! Yes, dear friend, you must come to see us as soon as you return. It's true – 'I'm languishing for you' as they say in the South of France.

Jessie sends her love.

Yours affectionately

J. Conrad

To Harold Goodburn
Text MS Berg; Unpublished

[letterhead: Oswalds]

23.9.22

Dear Mʳ Goodburn.

Herewith the cheque.

John went off yesterday in a hopeful spirit. He asked me to remember him to you when I wrote.

I hope he will do well this term.

Our kindest regards to Mrs Goodburn and yourself.

Sincerely Yours

Joseph Conrad

To Edward Bok
Text TS Indiana; Unpublished

[letterhead: Oswalds]
Sept. 24th. 1922.

Dear Mʳ Bok.¹

Your kind and appreciative letter has caused me great pleasure. Pray convey to your household my deeply grateful sense of their sympathetic attitude towards my work. Mrs Nornabell,² who has charmed us all here, was the first to tell me of your kindly feelings towards my work and I was very glad to hear of it.

You are quite right in assuming that Mrs Nornabell has talked of you to me; and, from what she said, I understand easily that all your co-workers can not but have the feelings of esteem and affection for their Chief. My hearty thanks for the promise of the book³ which I shall await with impatience.

Believe me my dear Sir, with great regard,

Yours very faithfully

Joseph Conrad

To Eric Pinker
Text TS Berg;⁴ Unpublished

[letterhead: Oswalds]
24 Sept. 1922

My dear Eric

I am very sorry to cause a bother to the office but I must let you know that the American Treasury demand-note which was sent on to me has been mislaid, or, I had better say plainly, lost. We can't find it anywhere here. It has reached me (being forwarded on) in Liverpool. I just had a glance at it,

---

¹ Born in the Netherlands, the American editor, author, and philanthropist Edward William Bok (1863–1930) worked in the advertising department of Charles Scribner's Sons before becoming the editor of the *Ladies' Home Journal*, a position he held for thirty years. For a time he simultaneously directed the Bok Syndicate Press, which sold the work of prominent writers. The author of numerous articles and books, he also published an autobiography. In Philadelphia, Bok donated generously to the arts, especially music.
² Catherine Nornabell (née Van Dyke, *c.* 1888–1953) contributed to the *Ladies' Home Journal*, with particular attention to war-time Europe, and was the author of *A Letter from Pontius Pilate's Wife* (1929). Her husband, Major Harry Nornabell, was a friend of Bok.
³ *The Americanization of Edward Bok: The Autobiography of a Dutch Boy Fifty Years After* (1923).
⁴ Postscript in Miss Hallowes's hand.

from which I saw that the Treasury claims something like 105 or 110 dollars from me on account of Income Tax. I then put it away, as I thought safely, in my writing-case, intending to send it back to you on my return here. But, as I have said, I can't find it now either in the case or in any pocket of my garments. We have been two days hunting for it here and I think I ought to tell you now, we simply cannot find it, whatever may have happened to it. As I remember there was a notification on it that undue delay in satisfying the demand carries with it a penalty of 5% per month added, or something of that kind, perhaps you will be kind enough to communicate with the U.S. Treasury and explain the matter. I think it would be easier for the office to do that than for me as you must have had communications with the Department in the usual course of business you transact with the U.S. for other authors.

I can't tell you how sorry I am at being the cause of this complication.

I may mention on this occasion that on her return here last Friday, Miss H[allowes] has told me that she saw Sybil Thorndike in "Jane Clegg"[1] and was very much impressed by her acting in that quiet and poignant part. Miss H. is strongly of the opinion that S. T. would be an admirable Mrs Verloc if the part appealed to her at all. Miss H. thinks that even in the matter of physique S. T. could give herself a substantial enough presence for the part. As to the rest of the cast Clare Greet[2] would make an excellent Mrs Verloc's Mother and Leslie Faber[3] Inspector Heat. As to Lewis Casson[4] I think myself, as far as I remember him, that he would make a very good Assistant Commissioner.

Of course there would be many other parts to fill.[5] That play of mine contains a confounded lot of parts which all would want to be *acted* in the fullest sense of the word in order to make the whole thing go. But I have also the notion that there are a good many actors about who only want a chance to show they can act, a little out of the beaten track.

Always affect^ly Yours

J. Conrad

P. S. The M.S. of "The Rover", Chapters 1–10 arrived safely.

---

[1] The revival of St John Ervine's *Jane Clegg, A Play in Three Acts*, first produced in 1914.
[2] Clare Greet (1871–1939). In the 1920s and '30s her many film appearances included Alfred Hitchcock's *Sabotage* (1936), based on *The Secret Agent*.
[3] Leslie Faber (1879–1929), who débuted in 1898, played many supporting roles in the West End and on tour in America. He was a prisoner-of-war during the First World War.
[4] Lewis Thomas Casson (1875–1969; knighted 1945), stage and screen actor and director, and Sybil Thorndike's husband.
[5] None of the actors mentioned had roles in the eventual production.

To Fernand Divoire

Text TS draft Yale; *L.fr.* 174–5

[letterhead: Oswalds]
Sept. 25th. 1922.

Cher Monsieur,[1]

Non. Je n'ai pas vu le no. du Mercure[2] contenant le document cryptographique dont vous parlez. Je ne me suis jamais interressé* a la controverse Baconienne; car qu'est ce que ça peut nous faire qui a ecrit les oeuvres de Shakespeare? J'ai connu dans le temps une espece d'hermite (il vivait dans une hutte en planches au milieu d'un petit bois) qui voulait absolument que l'oeuvre de Shakespeare fut ecrite par un etre surnaturel a qui il donnait un nom que je ne me rappelle plus. Comme il semblait tenir beaucoup a cette theorie-la je lui dit que je voulait* bien, mais qu'au fond ca m'etait bien égal. La dessus il me dit que j'etait* un imbecile. Telle fut la fin de nos relations.

Comme il me serait penible d'etre pris pour un imbecile par un certain nombre des lecteurs de l'Intransigeant je serais heureux, cher Monsieur, si vous vouliez bien regarder cette communication comme confidentielle.

Translation

Dear Sir,

No, I have not seen the issue of the *Mercure* containing the cryptographic document you speak of. The Bacon controversy has never interested me because what does it matter to us who wrote Shakespeare's works? I once knew a kind of hermit (he lived in a wooden hut in a small wood) who affirmed absolutely that Shakespeare's works were written by a supernatural being to whom he gave a name I no longer remember. As he seemed greatly attached to this theory, I told him I wished him well but that in the end I was wholly indifferent to the question. Straightaway he told me I was an idiot. Thus ended our relations.

As it would be painful to me to be considered an idiot by some of the *Intransigeant*'s readers, I should be glad, my dear Sir, if you would treat this communication as confidential.

[1] Belgian-born French literary journalist and editor Fernand-Jacques-Paul Divoire (1883–1951) was associated with the journals *L'Intransigeant* and *Le Temps*. Among his enthusiasms were music, dance, and the occult.

[2] The issues of 1 and 15 September of *Le Mercure de France*, which aired the Shakespeare-Bacon controversy, caused some stir on the Continent. Conrad's response is to a circular letter of 22 September soliciting opinions.

To Eric Pinker

Text MS Berg; Unpublished

[letterhead: Oswalds]
26.9.'22

Dearest Eric.

The time approaches for giving notice to Bell. I am half-unwilling to leave this house, but this is mostly the dread of the move, I think. Will you send me my agreement for Oswalds which I think is either in the office or at Withers. I have got hold of the novel, but of course at first it's bound to go slow.

I have a receipt for Johns school fees. Thanks.

Affectionately Yours

J. Conrad.

To Richard Curle

Text MS Indiana; Curle 99

[letterhead: Oswalds]
1ˢᵗ Oct. 22

Dearest Dick.

I can't let the new month begin without asking how you are. In truth all at once I have become quite anxious about You. Do please drop us a line; a comprehensive line to tell us shortly of your "public" and "private" activities.

Are you going to invest in the Dy Mail stock?[1]

How is your health

a. physical
b. mental
c. moral – by which I mean the degree of depression or exaltation from which you may suffer.

We thought you may have proposed yourself for this week end.

Lady Millais came to lunch on Friday and asked about you.

I have been doing nothing but thinking – absorbing myself in constant meditation – over *the* Novel. It's almost there! Almost to be grasped. Almost ready to flow over on the paper – but not quite yet. I am fighting off depression. A word from you would help. Our love

Ever Yours

J. Conrad.

I've given a year's notice to Bell!! Am scared now.

---

[1] The sale of stock was announced on 27 September.

To Eric Pinker
Text TS/MS Berg;[1] J-A, 2, 276–7

[letterhead: Oswalds]
Oct. 8th. 1922.

My dear Eric

This is only to tell you that the more I think of our interview with B[enrimo] the more I feel pleased with it – looking, of course, at B. as the producer of the play. He has talked intelligently and I do not think that he will act foolishly as it sometimes happens. I assume that nothing is likely to turn up to interfere with the completion of the business side of this affair. Will you, my dear Eric, ask Unwin to send me two copies of the "Arrow". As B. has already a copy of the "Agent" and I promised him a book I will send him one of the "Arrows", from the author.

I don't know, my dear, whether it ever struck you that there is a very possible play in the "Arrow". I don't mean a play that could be cut out of the text as it stands in the book, but made of the tale itself and especially out of its atmosphere. I think if it ever came to it I could convey it into the writing and I am damned if I don't think that that man, whom you don't like, is not quite capable to put it on stage. Personally I feel that if that thing could be done at all I would sign an agreement with the Devil himself for the chance; and think the experiment worth trying. It's a fact that a woman like Rita has never been put on the stage, and there are many facts in her story which are merely indicated in the book (and some that are not in it at all) which could be used for purposes of the action. I can almost see it all in seven scenes distributed amongst 3 acts.... It is possible, of course, that I am labouring under a delusion. But I think you know me well enough not to be frightened by those confidences. Anyway you may take it that I am not likely to drop serious work to indulge in delusions. I got into this train of thought simply because you have brought me in contact with a man, who, apparently, seems to understand my conception of stagecraft – at any rate in this instance.

Then, pursuing the same train of thought a little further, there is the drama contained in the "Western Eyes" of which as a matter of fact I have the first and last act in my head very definitely indeed, and very different from the ideas of professional adaptors. I have heard one or two of that tribe talking to me of what they would do, and it seemed to me very asinine talk. There is a fascination in doing a thing like that over again in another medium; that is, if one were certain of intelligent interpretation. And if later people were suddenly to begin to say "Here is Conrad, been writing those blessed tales and now after thinking of some of them over for fifteen years he attempts

---

[1] Postscript in Miss Hallowes's hand.

to show us how they ought to be told on the stage" – well, my career as a whole is exceptional enough to have that evolution in it, too, recognised as a manifestation of creative art.

I hope you are getting on in setting your camp in the London wilderness.[1]

Affectionately Yours

J. Conrad.

M[r] Conrad asks if you could kindly get him a photograph of Miriam Lewis*[2] & send it to him.

To J. Harry Benrimo
Text MS NLS 7175/2; Unpublished

[letterhead: Oswalds]

12–10-'22

Book sent separately
Dear M[r] Benrimo.[3]

This copy of *The Arrow* is not for Your immediate reading. Some time next year when on Your holiday You may find time to look at it. I only wanted You to have a signed copy of something of mine; and as You have already *The S[ecret] A[gent]* I selected this book written 12 years after the other, but the material of which belongs to the days of my early youth – when on the very t[h]reshold of active life.

Eric Pinker has communicated to me Your note to him which contains such friendly references to myself. They have given me great pleasure. I assure You that I look forward to our association with great curiosity and let me add with complete confidence.

It would be a great pleasure to us both if You could come down here next Sunday. It is rather short notice. But if You can manage to catch the 10.40 AM Victoria to *Canterbury* (arr. 12.24) I will meet you with the car there, if You will drop us a postcard to that effect. You could be back in town 7.13 pm.

Kind regards.

Yours faithfully

Joseph Conrad

---

[1] He had recently abandoned rural Surrey for Hans Place, Chelsea.

[2] Russian born, Miriam Lewes came to Britain at the age of five. She specialised in 'exotic' parts – Eastern European, Mediterranean, and Jewish. She had recently come back to the London stage after two successful seasons in Chicago and New York. Her next role, after Winnie Verloc, would be Jocasta in the Martin-Harvey production of *Oedipus Rex*.

[3] Born in San Francisco, Joseph Henry ('Harry') Benrimo (1874–1942) pursued an acting career in New York before appearing on the London stage in 1897. The author of popular plays, he was also a stage director and producer, mainly in America.

To Eric Pinker
Text TS/MS Berg; Unpublished

[letterhead: Oswalds]
Oct. 12th. 1922.

My dear Eric

I return to you the Agreement duly signed,[1] and I imagine that all the ways are smooth now for the eventual success of the Uniform Edition. I take it that F. U[nwin] has definitely declined to take a sum down for his share of the royalties on his books.

I have had my two copies of the "Arrow of Gold." Thanks.

I am going to send one to Benrimo, as I told you I would, since he has already got the "Secret Agent". I am extremely pleased to know that the business is concluded and that the play is certain to get on the boards. I discover in myself, rather to my surprise, an extreme interest in the production and I am awaiting with something approaching impatience a summons from Benrimo to come and see the result of his preliminary work. Pray be prepared to come along with me when the hour strikes, for I can not imagine myself going there without your escort and support.

You have understood me perfectly. All those theatrical ideas are perfectly harmless. They can not possibly stand in the way of what I will always consider my proper work which is the writing of prose – in the shape, as it happens, of novels.

I confess that I would be glad to have news of how things are going on when you hear anything about it.

By the by, do you think it feasible and advisable to have the play published by itself in pamphlet book form, as Galsworthy does with his about the time when they appear on the stage? The performance may cause a demand for the text.

Jessie sends her kindest regards. She is immensely pleased with the start given her by the Womans Pictorial.[2]

Ever affec^{ly} yrs

Joseph Conrad.

---

[1] For Dent's collected edition. The terms are summarised in Hallowes, where the date of signature is 9 October.

[2] The weekly *Woman's Pictorial* serialised her cookery book. The serial began on 14 October as the leading feature, accompanied by photographs of the Conrads and their house (see Plate 4). Each instalment was also illustrated with pictures of Jessie Conrad's recipes as prepared at the Peter Pan Tearooms, 40 Shaftesbury Avenue, whose menu offered a selection of her dishes.

To John Drinkwater
Text MS Yale; Unpublished

[letterhead: Oswalds]
13.10.'22

My dear Mr Drinkwater[1]
You need not have reminded me of the two occasions we were in touch. They were not forgotten. I was always very grateful to you for giving One day More a chance.[2]
I was very pleased to be asked to sign the little book[3] for you. It's done with sc[r]upulous fidelity to facts.
Cordial congratulations on past and present successes.

Believe me Yours

J Conrad

To J. Harry Benrimo
Text TS/MS Private collection; Unpublished

[letterhead: Oswalds]
Oct. 14th. 1922.

Dear Mr Benrimo.
Thanks for your letter. Very good of you to write at length. As you may imagine I was extremely interested in the contents and am looking forward eagerly to meeting Mr Nettlefold,[4] yourself and the company on Wednesday. Your encouraging opinion of the play – as to its 'coming over' and the parts standing out – does away with my greatest anxiety. As far as experience goes I have worked in the dark or at any rate only by the light of nature. I have in my time meditated upon the stage, I hope with some intelligence; but meditation alone is very apt to lead a man astray. All the other things you say about the cast are very comforting too, not the least of them being the intelligent boy for Stevie.

Yes, Vladimir and the Professor will be the very devil to find. It will take a man of intelligence and temperament to pull off the scene of cynical bullying with Verloc. It borders on extravaganza and yet must never be allowed to

---

[1] Poet, dramatist, and critic, John Drinkwater (1882–1937) was a founding member of the Pilgrim Players and later managed the Birmingham Repertory Theatre. Conrad professed to admire his poetry.
[2] Drinkwater had produced the play at the Birmingham Rep. in March 1918 (see *Letters*, 6, p. 189, and Stape and Knowles, p. 128).
[3] The allusion to 'facts' suggests that the 'little book' was one of the pamphlets, perhaps *The Dover Patrol*.
[4] Arthur Nettlefold (1870–1944), a theatrical manager, co-produced *The Secret Agent* with Benrimo.

become in the remotest degree farcical. I have a notion that, on the mere text, the audience may be moved to laugh here and there, but it should be without forgetting the grim earnestness of its purpose. The starting point of the drama is in it. There must be no hint of 'Oxford' in the man. Polished continental society man, yes. That type is Russian in its underlying savagery and outward man-of-the-world aspect. In physique I make him in the book a round faced, clean shaven with rosy gills, sort of man, who talks wittily to women; the real nature to come out only in the hard eyes.

The Professor will be still more difficult to find, I fear, with his miserable physique and the suggestion of desperate self-confidence. He is the very soul of revengeful anarchy. The first scene of Act Two, where he and Ossipon (so to speak) unfold the tale to the public, fills me with apprehension. I may say without vanity that the dialogue, in itself, is good; as characterisation at any rate. But then, you see, I have never *heard* it. We have there anarchism in a nutshell but it seems to me, as I sit here, impossible for any average public to get hold of the facts. Yet the facts it conveys, one of them being the conclusion as to Verloc's death, are of great importance. At the same time that fact is false! But I must not think too much about it or I will think myself into a fright. I am convinced Russell Thorndike[1] will soon get hold of Ossipon and make a creation of it. My idea of him is outwardly, a bush of fair hair, blue serge suit, blue cap with peak. The psychology is as plain as a pikestaff, but the part is one of the longest in the play and of the utmost importance. The hanger-on on anarchy.

I certainly could not offer you a suggestion as to the filling of the parts you mention. There are also Michaelis and Yundt, of whom you do not speak. The mild humanitarian and the venomous windbag of anarchy. Michaelis's part has a certain importance too.

I have no doubts whatever about Miss Lewes in the part of Winnie. That part is not a star part in the conventional sense since it does not hold the stage all the time, but all the play hangs on her. It is as it were Winnie's life story. Whether, in its passive obscurity and deep-seated passion, it is tragic, or only horrible, I myself can not say. But I hope, in no selfish mood, that she will find in creating Winnie Verloc a triumph for her art.

Thinking it all over (after reading your letter) in a more confident mood I feel that there may be a success there; not an emotional success but a success of curiosity great enough to prevent the loyal efforts of the artists and of the sympathetic producer being utterly wasted.

---

[1] Russell Thorndike (1885–1972), stage and screen actor, producer, and novelist, was Sybil's brother.

So sorry you could not come. Perhaps you will be able to spare us a Sunday before long. Please give my compliments to Miss Lewis*. Will you tell me on a p-card where the Ivy Rest*[1] is exactly.

Believe in my most friendly sentiments

Yours

Joseph Conrad.

To G. Jean-Aubry
Text MS Yale; *L.fr.* 175–6

[Oswalds]

le[?] Dimanche [15 October 1922][2]

Cher Jean.

Merci de votre bonne lettre. On vous attendra Samedi prochain. Tachez donc d'arriver de bonne heure – pour le lunch.

Je suis on ne peut plus intéressé dans Vos nouvelles. Quel travailleur Vs faites mon cher!

Je ne sais pas si je Vs apprends quelque chose en Vs disant que la première du Secret Agent aura lieu en Nov[re]. – Ambassadors Theatre.

Je déjeune avec Nettlefold & Benrimo – "the producer" – Merc[di] prochain avant la première repetition. Je serai au R[oyal] A[utomobile] C[lub] entre 12 et 12.45 avant de joindre ces gens là; et mon intention est de prendre la fuite aussitot l'affaire finie. J'ai une toux qui malmène fort de temps en temps.

Miriam Lewis* sera Mme Verloc. Elle a le physique et on la dit intelligente.

Si Mme Alvar est de retour presentez lui je Vs en prie mes hommages et apprenez lui la grande nouvelle.

Borys est a Manchester. On est très content de lui et lui est très content de tout le monde. Jean est a Tonbridge. He has been doing well.

Jessie sends her love

Ever Yours

J. Conrad

Translation

Sunday

Dear Jean.

Thanks for your good letter. We shall expect you next Saturday. Do try to arrive early – for lunch.

Your news couldn't interest me more. What a worker you are, my dear!

---

[1] The 'theatrical' restaurant, then located at 1 West Street, Soho.
[2] Date from postmark.

I don't know if I am telling you something in saying that the première of *The Secret Agent* will take place in November – at the Ambassadors Theatre.

I am lunching with Nettlefold and Benrimo, the producer, next Wednesday before the first rehearsal. I will be at the RAC between 12 and 12.45 before joining those people, and I intend to get away as soon as the business is done with. I have a cough that torments me a good deal from time to time.

Miriam Lewis* will play Mrs Verloc. She has the looks and is said to be intelligent.

If Mme Alvar has returned, pray give her my regards and tell her the great news.

Borys is in Manchester. They are very pleased with him, and he is very pleased with everybody. John is at Tonbridge. He has been doing well.

Jessie sends her love

Ever Yours

J. Conrad

To Eric Pinker
Text MS Berg; Unpublished

[Oswalds]
Sunday 15.10.22

My dear Eric

Thanks for the money paid in and your two letters with the 1/2 year's acct. (It runs from 20th Mch '22).

I would not let myself grow despondent, for despondency will not put things right. As a matter of fact I do not feel that way. One may feel a bit anxious, as to – for instance – not getting on quite as well with one's work as one expected. One hardly ever does – but in a position like this one feels it more. And it would be a poor return for your kind letter to show any despondency. I assume You have not given up the attempt to serialize The Rover – unless You have decided that it would be better policy to let it be published very early next year. This is a matter with which you alone are competent to deal. Pity that the Med^{an} Novel is not more advanced. But it is a considerable piece of work which can not be hurried on recklessly; and I know you would not want me to do that.

I agree completely with your view of the negotiation with F. U[nwin]. The glimpse you give me of your plans for the future is very interesting – and indeed most important. Quite unexpected too, I must say. I will be more than ready to listen when you are ready to tell me all about it.

The issue of the play in a small vol was only a suggestion. I attach no importance to it. It has simply occurred to me that a few pence could have been made that way. What I had in my mind was Methuen getting it out. I had some time ago a friendly letter from M.

I had a letter from Benrimo who has got, it seems, a move on. He invited me to lunch on Wed^y next with Nettlefold and R. Thorndike. I have accepted. I am not clear whether there will be a rough rehearsal afterwards. It looks like it. (I am sending you the letter). If it is so then perhaps you could (if you can spare the time) 'phone B to say you heard from me and that I would like you to be present. I could not very well mention you in my answer to B as it was an invitation to lunch *not* to the theatre. And then my dear fellow I could not tell what engagements you may have for that day. It would be nice to have you there but please do not let me interfere with your arrangements merely on account of my own comfort and pleasure.

If you get in touch with B perhaps you could suggest to him somebody for the part of Mr Vlad^{ir} and also for the Professor. Thanks for the photos of M. Lewis.* As far as appearance goes she will do. I will be at the R[oyal] A[utomobile] C[lub] on Wed: noon, if you have occasion to phone me a message there.

Always Affect^{ly} Yours

J. Conrad

How do we stand for US rights?

To Richard Curle
Text MS Indiana; Curle 100

[Oswalds]
Monday. [16 October 1922][1]

Dearest Dick.

I snatch this bit of paper to thank you hurriedly for Your very welcome letter with the good news about the agreement.[2] I think you have reason to be satisfied. The McM. imprint has some value in itself.

I was in town last Wed: saw poor Hope[3] and had a long talk, then rushed home. I did not write to you because we were to meet at noon and we had none too much time till 4 pm to exchange our news.

---

[1] Curle's date, confirmed by contents.
[2] With Macmillan, for publishing *Into the East* (1923).
[3] One of Conrad's earliest English friends and (with his wife) the dedicatee of *Lord Jim*, G(eorge) F(ountaine) W(eare) Hope (1854–1930) had been in business. He was now an invalid, living in Colchester .

Am coming next We^d to lunch with Nettlefold, Benrimo & R Thorndike of the Ambassadors Theatre. Afterwards we will go to a rough rehearsal.

Would love to get a sight of you at noon in R[oyal] A[utomobile] C[lub] where I shall be till 1/4 to One. After rehearsal I will go home probably by the 6.12 Can[non] S^t.

Jessie's love.

Ever Yrs

J. Conrad

Myriam* Lewis* is to act Mrs Verloc.

To Ford Madox Ford
Text TS/MS Yale; Unpublished

[letterhead: Oswalds]
Oct. 16th. 1922.

Dear Ford.

I am sorry I haven't answered your letter before. It slipped somehow out of sight and I must confess that it slipped out of my memory too. Pray forgive me. As to the matter of it, it was a very long time ago and all I remember is that the claim was satisfied by the repolishing of the table and replacing the carpet by another one of the same size and character.[1] Jessie's recollection agrees with mine.

I am sorry, as I gather it from the last sentence of your letter, that your health is not good.

Yrs

J. Conrad

To Walter Tittle
Text TS Texas; Unpublished

[letterhead: Oswalds]
Oct. 16th. 1922.

Dear Mr Tittle.

We were away when your card arrived and after that I was not well. This is my excuse for the delay in thanking you. I was in London after the 7th but I was so overwhelmed by affairs of all sorts that I could not find time for a visit to the Leicester Galleries.[2] I hope that next time I run up I will have better luck, and, perhaps, we could arrange to meet; but my time just now is

---

[1] Furniture and fittings damaged by the fire at Pent Farm in June 1902 (*Letters*, 2, pp. 413, 428–31).
[2] To see his portrait, and others, in Tittle's current show.

so taken up with one thing and another that I will make no suggestion now. Besides, I have not been very well lately, and that, too, has handicapped me in my activities and my movements.

I trust you are flourishing in health and refreshed in mind after your tour in Italy. Are you going to stay in this country long and are you heavily engaged? Would you be willing to take a run down here some Sunday? In that case you have only to drop us a card on Friday. If it is the next you will find here my French friend, Mr Aubry, whom you met during your visit to make my portrait. Meantime I am sending you a signed copy of "The Arrow of Gold", which is one of my later novels.

My wife joins me in kind regards

Yours sincerely

J. Conrad

To J. Harry Benrimo
Text TS/MS Berg; Unpublished

[letterhead: Oswalds]
Oct. 19th. 1922.

Dear Mr Benrimo.

You must know that I am a man of lasting impressions. All my work, which is based on my own life's experience, is founded on that capacity. You will understand me then, when I say that the more I go in my mind over yesterday's impressions the more pleased and confident I feel. Will you give my regards to all my interpreters in Act One. The remarks I made to them yesterday bore merely on the "nuances" in the conception of their parts. I have been turning them over in my mind too, and I don't think they were of the kind to unsettle them. The only person with whom I did not speak at all was you; the master-mind holding the general conception of the whole as a theatrical creation, and therefore the actual and close partner of the man who had created all those things on paper. Other things just then claimed your attention and as a matter of fact I would not have been fit to talk to you at the time.

After coming home I had a steady think over my first *visual* experience of the play. The fruit of this meditation bearing mainly on what we may call "stage business" I am imparting to you now in the form of suggestions, which you may or may not accept, for the moulding of the action into its final shape. And first, a general remark. Could not my stage directions (which are very ample) be exactly followed in so far that the Mother should sit on the couch and the other two keep on their feet throughout the first part of Act one. In writing I attached particular importance to Winnie, as it were, filling the stage. I want the actual, physical Winnie to be in the eye of the audience all the time from head to foot.

I also care very much for the effect after the cue: – "... you are very lucky". Winnie then should lean back against the table while she talks with her Mother (nine replicas[1]) and stares straight at the audience; intention being to give the first hint that things are not what they seem and that there may be tragic possibilities in the woman.

I have looked carefully through all my directions as to attitudes and expression and I honestly believe that with the words attached they make for each actor concerned a psychological personality of a very definite kind, if not, perhaps, of the conventional kind. I don't think that in those directions there is anything inherently difficult to carry out. Of course I have made them as concise as possible on purpose.

The boy Stevie is quite good, except that his general expression is too bright for the part. He must really at times try to look half-witted. I notice he is dark; therefore, in the last Act, a few words will have to be changed in the scene between Winnie and Insp. Heat. In the play Stevie is nearly twenty years old. It's only his mind that had stopped growing. For that part too I notice that all my directions are very precise and clear.

It is the same for Mr Verloc.[2] I noticed that he shook hands with the Mother, which he doesn't do in my text. In the text he only says a few words gloomily, being too much absorbed in his own trouble to care whether she goes or stays. His first entrance is a very important event. When he is left alone, and his gloomy trouble forces him to mutter to himself, my directions ought really to be followed exactly; for I try, in them, to establish the character. Then directly afterwards when Mr Vladimir bangs the counter in the shop outside, Verloc shouts "Coming", not "Come in" as I think Mr West said, and doesn't move; being so to speak, appalled at Mr Vladimir turning up. I am so precise about those things for the reason that they belong to the first impressions Verloc gives to the audience.

Mr Vladimir's (when you have obtained him) characteristic personal note should be a sort of jeering insolence, the insolence of a superior; by which Mr Verloc from time to time is goaded into attempts at the sullen insolence of an inferior.

Yundt and Michaelis seem to have absorbed the spirit of my directions perfectly. Amazingly good, both of them; and I am sure Michaelis will be "a creation" in the Drawing-room Scene.

---

[1] A Gallicism deriving from *replique* ('cue').
[2] Played by Henry St Barbe-West (1880–1935).

Thorndike has got hold of Ossipon. With a little swagger, just a little, he will be perfect. Whenever he deals with the boy and during the anarchistic talk with the other two he is flawless. If he could only convey somehow a hint of a "sham" in his little passage with Winnie he would be flawless all through. Of course that is important because in the last Act his falseness will have to be accentuated – being part of the situation.

Pardon this long screed, but I felt I must convey to you the whole of my impressions at once so that, should they commend themselves to you, you could try my suggestions prompted by my intimate feeling of the play during the rehearsal. I hope you won't think I am making myself a nuisance from mere vanity.

It is not that at all. What I wish is an individual, personal, success for every one concerned and for a general effect that would be memorable. My vision here and there may be fresh. And I don't feel shy of putting my views before a man of such distinguished achievement and unrivalled experience as yourself because I feel that for that very reason You will receive them in a friendly spirit and with perfect comprehension.

Believe me

Yours

Joseph Conrad.

To Richard Curle

Text MS Indiana; J-A 2, 278; Curle 101[1]

[letterhead: Oswalds]
[19 October 1922][2]

Dearest Dick.

Herewith the pamphs.[3]

I wired you today: "Next Thursday".[4]

I do not think that it would be feasible to arrange the visit to the theatre afterwards.

I saw only Act One yesterday. They went through the motions with their parts in their hands. It *was* promising. M. Lewis* will do. The boy playing Stevie[5] is excellent!

---

[1] Curle leaves out the first paragraph.

[2] Jean-Aubry places this in October, Curle in October or November. The rehearsal on the 18th fixes the date.

[3] The same sent this month to Wise, Shorter, Quinn, and Keating.

[4] 26 October: the date of the next rehearsal and of Conrad's next visit to town (see the letter to Pinker of the 28th). This telegram corrected the date given to Curle on [16 October].

[5] The role was taken by Freddie Peisley (1904–76), who continued acting into the 1930s and was in the 1939 revival of W. H. Auden and Christopher Isherwood's *The Ascent of F6* at the Old Vic.

What was most pleasant was the atmosphere of belief in the play and the evident anxiety to do their best for it.

I am looking forward very much to the lunch.[1] You know how I prize women's appreciation which, for a man not specialising in sentiment, is about the greatest reward one's sincerity can obtain.

Yours always

J. Conrad

Suppose we lunch at one? I will have to leave you at 2.30. so as not to keep those people waiting. We could *meet* at 12.30.

To Thomas J. Wise
Text MS BL Ashley A. 2950; Unpublished

[letterhead: Oswalds]
19/10/22

Dear Mr Wise.

Herewith 2 copies each of my booklets on J. Galsworthy and The Dover Patrol.

I have signed one of each.

I trust Mrs Wise and yourself are in good health.

My wife joins me in kind regards

Yours sincerely

J. Conrad.

To Eric Pinker
Text MS Berg; Unpublished

[Oswalds]
20.10.22

Dear Eric

Herewith the Benrimo agreement duly signed.[2] I have no remarks to offer but I wish to offer you my congratulations for spotting this particular bird and bringing him down; and my thanks for all your efforts in the "good cause". May both our shadows grow bigger from its success.

Affc^{ly} Yrs

J. C.

I understand now your distaste. All the same the atmosphere of "belief in the play" was encouraging.

---

[1] With Iris Wedgwood or with one or more of Curle's other women friends? On [31 October?] Conrad asked Mrs Wedgwood's forgiveness for an 'intrusion' at the Club, but no intrusion seems on the agenda here.

[2] Extracts in Hallowes confirm the 20th as the date of signing.

To J. Harry Benrimo
Text TS Yale; Unpublished

[letterhead: Oswalds]
Oct. 21st. 1922.

Dear Mr Benrimo.

The only copy I have here is the set of corrected proofs which are covered with pen and ink emendations. You will disregard these altogether.

All the cutting down of speeches, according to your request, will be done *with red pencil.*

Any remarks I may wish to make on the subject of cutting down will be made *in blue pencil.*

All you have then to take notice of are the red and blue marks. The pages you need to look at will have their corners turned down.

I have carried out your request to the utmost limit, striking out every word that seemed to me superfluous; but I think that everything that has been left ought to stand. A play, of course, must be first and foremost a play; but these scenes contain also a stage exposition of the anarchist doctrine and of the police point of view. And that has a certain value which must not be destroyed by too much cutting down. I hope that you will feel that I have carried out your request in a spirit of loyal collaboration.

Regards.

Yours

J. C.

PS Please preserve the pages and return to me when we meet next Thursday.

To Sydney Cockerell
Text MS Morgan; Unpublished

[letterhead: Oswalds]
22.10.22

Dear Mr Cockerell.

I will sign with all my heart.[1]

I am only sorry to hear of Doughty's plight.

I return the draft.

My wife joins me in warm regards to Mrs Cock[e]rell and yourself.

Yours

J. Conrad

---

[1] The petition for a Civil List pension for C(harles) M(ontagu) Doughty (1843–1926), prose writer and poet best known for *Travels in Arabia Deserta* (1888). In straitened circumstances, he was awarded a Civil List pension in 1922; he resigned it the next year on coming into an inheritance.

To [?]
Text MS Lubbock; Unpublished

[letterhead: Oswalds]
22.10.'22

Rev. and Dear Sir.[1]

Thanks for your letter. I regret to say that I never visited the county of Caithness.

My only connection with Wick is that I served once in a ship registered in that port tho' she had never been within 400 miles of it.[2]

Believe me with the greatest regard very faithfull[y] yours

Joseph Conrad

To the Hon. Bertrand Russell
Text TS/MS McMaster; Russell 161–3

[letterhead: Oswalds]
Oct. 23d.[22–23]. 1922.[3]

My dear Russell.

When your book[4] arrived we were away for a few days. Perhaps "les convenances" demanded that I should have acknowledged the receipt at once. But I preferred to read it before I wrote. Unluckily a very unpleasant affair was sprung on me and absorbed all my thinking energies for a fortnight. I simply did not attempt to open the book till all the worry and flurry was over, and I could give it two clear days.

I have always liked the Chinese, even those that tried to kill me (and some other people) in the yard of a private house in Chantabun,[5] even (but not so much) the fellow who stole all my money one night in Ban[g]kok,[6] but brushed and folded my clothes neatly for me to dress in the morning, before vanishing into the depths of Siam.[7] I also received many kindnesses at the hands of various Chinese. This with the addition of an evening's conversation with the secretary of His Excellency Tseng[8] on the verandah of an hotel and

---

[1] Unidentified.

[2] The *Duke of Sutherland*, registered at Wick and owned by David Louttit of that town in far northern Scotland.

[3] Conrad writes 'this letter was begun yesterday', the day before the leader appeared in *The Times*.

[4] *The Problem of China*, published by Allen & Unwin in September.

[5] Present-day Chonburi, a town on the Gulf of Siam (now Gulf of Thailand).

[6] In his letters as in his fiction, Conrad used the nineteenth-century Polish spelling.

[7] The theft is dramatised in 'Falk'. Siam was named Thailand in 1939.

[8] In 'Falk', a character so named, a Commissioner, stays at Schomberg's hotel in Bangkok.

a perfunctory study of a poem, "The Heathen Chinee",[1] is all I know about Chinese. But after reading your extremely interesting view of the Chinese Problem I take a gloomy view of the future of their country. He who does not see the truth of your deductions can only be he who does not want to see. They strike a chill into one's soul especially when you deal with the American element. That would indeed be a dreadful fate for China or any other country.[2] I feel your book the more because the only ray of hope you allow is the advent of international socialism, the sort of thing to which I cannot attach any sort of definite meaning. I have never been able to find in any man's book or any man's talk anything convincing enough to stand up for a moment against my deep-seated sense of fatality governing this man-inhabited world. After all it is but a system, not very recondite and not very plausible. As a mere reverie it is not of a very high order and wears a strange resemblance to a hungry man's dream of a gorgeous feast guarded by a lot of beadles in cocked hats. But I know you wouldn't expect me to put faith in *any* system. The only remedy for Chinamen and for the rest of us is the change of hearts, but looking at the history of the last 2000 years there is not much reason to expect that thing, even if man has taken to flying – a great "uplift", no doubt, but no great change. He doesn't fly like an eagle; he flies like a beetle. And you must have noticed how ugly, ridiculous and fatuous is the flight of a beetle.

---

[1] Bret Harte's popular poem 'Plain Language from Truthful James' (1870), commonly called 'The Heathen Chinee', is about a card game in which the participants cheat, and the out-smarted cardsharpers blame everything on 'the ways that are dark' and 'tricks that are vain' of Ah Sin and his compatriots. See *Letters*, 2, p. 320. Apropos of 'tricks that are vain', Russell writes: 'I am convinced that in a game of mutual deception an Englishman or American can beat a Chinese nine times out of ten. But as many comparatively poor Chinese have dealings with rich white men, the game is often played on one side' (p. 199).

[2] 'American public opinion is in favour of peace, and at the same time profoundly persuaded that America is wise and virtuous while all other Powers are foolish and wicked. The pessimistic half of this opinion I do not desire to dispute, but the optimistic half is more open to question. Apart from peace, American public opinion believes in commerce and industry, Protestant morality, athletics, hygiene, and hypocrisy, which may be taken as the main ingredients of American and English Kultur ... Gladstonian England was more of a moral force than the England of the present day; and America is more of a moral force at this moment than any other Power (except Russia). But the development from Gladstone's moral fervour to the cynical imperialism of his successors is one which we can now see to be inevitable; and a similar development is bound to take place in the United States. Therefore, when we wish to estimate the desirability of extending the influence of the United States, we have to take account of this almost certain future loss of idealism. Nor is idealism in itself always an unmixed blessing to its victims. It is apt to be incompatible with tolerance, with the practice of live-and-let-live, which alone can make the world endurable for its less pugnacious and energetic inhabitants' (pp. 160–1).

Your chapter on Chinese character is the sort of marvellous achievement that one would expect from you. It may not be complete. That I don't know. But as it stands, in its light touch and profound insight, it seems to me flawless. I have no difficulty in accepting it, because I do believe in amenity allied to barbarism, in compassion co-existing with complete brutality, and in essential rectitude underlying the most obvious corruption.[1] And on this last point I would offer for your reflection that we ought not to attach too much importance to that trait of character – just because it is *not* a trait of character! At any rate no more than in other races of mankind. Chinese corruption is, I suspect, institutional; a mere method of paying salaries. Of course it was very dangerous. And in that respect the Imperial Edicts recommending honesty failed to affect the agents of the Government. But Chinese, essentially, are creatures of Edicts and in every other sphere their characteristic is, I should say, scrupulous honesty.

There is another suggestion of yours which terrifies me, and arouses my compassion for the Chinese, even more than the prospect of an Americanised China. It is your idea of some sort of selected council, the strongly disciplined society arriving at decisions, etc etc. (p 244).[2] If a constitution proclaimed in the light of day, with at least a chance of being understood by the people, is not to be relied on, then what trust could one put in a self-appointed and probably secret association (which from the nature of things must be above the law) to commend or condemn individuals or institutions? As it is unthinkable that you should be a slave to formulas or a victim of self-delusion, it is with the greatest diffidence that I raise my protest against your contrivance which must par "la force des choses"[3] and by the very manner of its inception become but an association of mere swelled-heads of the most dangerous kind. There is not enough honour, virtue and selflessness *in the world* to make any such

---

[1] 'The Chinese Character', pp. 199–213. According to Russell, 'New arrivals are struck by obvious evils: the beggars, the terrible poverty, the prevalence of disease, the anarchy and corruption in politics ... But, to compensate for these evils, [the Chinese] have retained, as industrial nations have not, the capacity for civilized enjoyment, for leisure and laughter, for pleasure in sunshine and philosophical discourse' (p. 200). He also observes that 'The Chinese, from the highest to the lowest, have an imperturbable quiet dignity, which is usually not destroyed even by an European education. They are not self-assertive, either individually or nationally; their pride is too profound for self-assertion. They admit China's military weakness in comparison with foreign Powers, but they do not consider efficiency in homicide the most important quality in a man or nation' (p. 202).

[2] 'It will be necessary for the genuinely progressive people throughout the country to unite in a strongly disciplined society, arriving at collective decisions and enforcing support of those decisions upon all its members.' The Platonic turn of Russell's argument in the chapter on 'The Chinese Outlook' goes against the grain of his earlier admiration for 'a degree of individual liberty which has been wholly lost in the rest of the world' (p. 204).

[3] 'From the force of things', or 'from the nature of things' – one of Conrad's favourite expressions.

council other than the greatest danger to every kind of moral, mental and political independence. It would become a centre of delation, intrigue and jealousy of the most debased kind. No freedom of thought, no peace of heart, no genius, no virtue, no individuality trying to raise its head above the subservient mass, would be safe before the domination of such a council and the unavoidable demoralisation of the instruments of its power. For, I must suppose that you mean it to have power and to have agents to exercise that power – or else it would become as little substantial as if composed of angels of whom ten thousand can sit on the point of a needle.[1] But I wouldn't trust a society of that kind even if composed of angels... More! I would not, my dear friend, (to address you in Salvation Army style) trust that society if Bertrand Russell himself were, after 40 days of meditation and fasting, to undertake the selection of the members. After saying this I may just as well resume my wonted calm; for, indeed, I could not think of any stronger way of expressing my utter dislike and mistrust of such an expedient for working out the salvation of China.

I see in this morning's "Times" (this letter was begun yesterday) a leader on your "Problem of China"[2] which I hope will comfort and sustain you in the face of my savage attack. I meant it to be deadly; but I perceive that on account of my age and infirmities there was never any need for you to fly the country or ask for police protection. You will no doubt be glad to hear that my body is disabled by a racking cough and my enterprising spirit irretrievably tamed by an unaccountable depression. Thus are the impious stricken, and things of the order that "passeth understanding" brought home to one![3] ... But I will not treat you to a meditation on my depression. That way madness lies.[4]

Your – truly Christian in its mansuetude – note has just reached me. I admire your capacity for forgiving sinners, and I am warmed by the glow of your friendliness. But I protest against your credulity in the matter of newspaper par[agraph]s. I did not know I was to stay in town to attend rehearsals. Which is the rag that decreed it – I wonder? The fact is I came

---

[1] The question of how many angels can sit, dance, or otherwise dispose themselves on the point of a needle was a favourite of Renaissance satirists and Protestant controversialists out to discredit straw theologians from the Mediaeval Schools.

[2] 'The Peace of Cathay', *The Times*, 23 October, p. 11.

[3] The biblical quotation (from Philippians 4.7) and the reference to 'forgiving sinners' in the next paragraph pay jocular homage to the sceptical author of 'A Free Man's Worship', an essay Conrad much admired. The playfulness continues as Conrad, young Conrad Russell's godfather, hails the parents as 'Compère' and 'Commère', linked to him by what are traditionally religious bonds as well as intimate terms of affection.

[4] *King Lear*, 3.4.21.

up for just 4 hours and 20 min. last Wednesday; and that I may have to pay another visit to the theatre (the whole thing is like an absurd dream) one day this week. You can not doubt mon Compère that I *do* want to see the child whose advent has brought about this intimate relation between us. But I shrink from staying the night in town. In fact I am afraid of it. This is no joke. Neither is it a fact that I would shout on housetops. I am confiding it to you as a sad truth. However this cannot last; and before long I'll make a special trip to see you all on an agreed day. Meantime my love to him – special and exclusive. Please give my duty to your wife as politeness dictates, and – as my true feelings demand – remember me most affectionately to ma très honorée Commère. And pray go on cultivating forgiveness towards this insignificant and unworthy person who dares to subscribe himself

Always Yours

Joseph Conrad.

To Clarence E. Andrews
Text MS Ohio; Unpublished

[letterhead: Oswalds]

23. Oct '22

My dear Mr Andrews.

It was a pleasure to get your letter. But is was a shock too. For I was convinced I had written to you (via Doran).[1] However after referring the matter to Miss Hallowes my secretary, who is just back from her holiday, I got no comfort but only a scandalised stare at there being a doubt about it; – the sort of "That man is perfectly hopeless" look which simply crushed me.

I hasten therefore to tell you without a moments delay what I did mean to write, (or have perhaps written) that the book[2] in its human zest for impressions, in its pervading sympathy for strange mankind, its acuity of observation bearing on character and on facts and the light but sensitive touch preserved in its style, has given me a very real pleasure, and an augmented sense of the honour you have done me by your dedication: – for all of which my renewed thanks!

This is what I meant to say. If that other letter turns up (but, maybe, there is no such thing) you will see that neither the lapse of 2 months nor the fact of re-reading has altered my original judgment "by first impression".

---

[1] The New York publishing house founded by George H. Doran in 1908; it merged with Doubleday in 1927.
[2] Andrews's *Old Morocco and the Forbidden Atlas*.

So sorry you have had an illness which has done away with your plan of visiting the Eastern Med*an*. I wish you luck next time and all along in your wanderings which your mind turns so charmingly into literature.

Sincerely Yours

J. Conrad.

To R. H. Fitz-Herbert

Text TS/MS Turnbull (damaged);[1] Unpublished

[letterhead: Oswalds]
Oct. 23th*. 1922.

Dear Mr Fitz-Herbert.[2]

Many thanks for sending me the extremely interesting account and photos of the two wrecks on your coast.[3]

In the case of the *Rona* it shows the disastrous effect of a mind in a state of doubt and indecision. I am very sorry for the Chief Officer.[4] In my sea life I too have been Chief Officer for some time, and in the Straits of Macassar, I remember, in [1885][5] steaming along a badly charted coast in a ship [that] always made her courses, as far as our experience [of her went] on a track we knew perfectly well, she played us the [tr]ick of getting inside a ledge of reefs, which, on th[at] course, she ought to have cleared by a mile and a half. However, I was just in time to snatch at the telegraph handle and we got out of a perfect tangle of rocks without touching anything.^X Indeed I am very sorry for the Captain of the *Rona* too; but, frankly, I cannot find it in my heart to quarrel with the findings of the Court which seems to me to have been very fair and sympathetic.

The contribution of the Hawke's Bay Branch on the Naval Actions of May and June is, as far as I know, historically complete.[6] The spirit of the Navy

---

[1] Words illegible because of damage to the original are supplied in square brackets from Fitz-Herbert's copy of this letter in his 'Notebooks 1921–1934', ff. 176–8 (MS Turnbull).

[2] Reynold Hall Fitz-Herbert (1890–*c.* 1937), a New Zealander from the Hawkes Bay region of the North Island, was interested in maritime affairs and shipping. He composed an unpublished work entitled 'A Ship-Lover's History of New Zealand'. He also privately published a pamphlet on the Battle of Jutland.

[3] The *Wiltshire*, approaching Auckland from Newcastle, ran aground in a storm off Great Barrier Island on 31 May 1922; the *Rona*, approaching Auckland from Fiji, went aground on Flat Rock in Hauraki Gulf on 26 June. The *Wiltshire* broke up after her crew was rescued; the *Rona*'s crew was also brought to safety, and, although damaged, the ship was salvaged.

[4] Who was ordered to steer for Flat Rock Lighthouse. The light was deceptively close, however, and the ship at her full speed of 10 knots crashed into rocks before she could turn.

[5] An error, whether Conrad's or Fitz-Herbert's, for 1888. Conrad served in the *Vidar*, the ship in question, during 1887–8.

[6] Fitz-Herbert's 'Notebooks' record that in addition to newspaper illustrations of the wrecks he had sent articles he had written for the monthly journal of the Hawke's Bay Navy League.

League as regards taxation is extremely sound, but to be quite frank with you I do not think any sort of danger from the quarter you mention is likely to arise for many years to come.[1]

Pray accept the expression of my friendly sentiments and transmit as occasions arise the feeling of affectionate gratitude which I share with the inhabitants of Great Britain towards New Zealanders for their accomplished manliness (that word includes everything) displayed in a time of mortal danger to our common existence and ideals.

Sincerely Yours

Joseph Conrad

[X] I must add the situation was disclosed at break of day after a night of rain-squalls and blinding lightning. No room to turn. The engines were working full astern when the capt came on deck. Neither of us said a word till at the end of 10 min when the capt observed "She will do now". Then he ordered me to steam her East 3 miles and then resume the usual course. For the 3 mos I was with him we never alluded to the incident.

To Robert B. Matier

Text TS NYU; Unpublished

[letterhead: Oswalds]

Oct. 23rd. 1922.

Dear Sir[2]

I regret I have delayed so long in thanking you for your most interesting relation of the voyage of the junk Amoy.[3]

It was quite a feat. I am sorry for poor "Bobbie" who was "too much seasick" and I hope he will never be so any more as long as he lives.

If you have occasion please give my regards and congratulations to Captain and Mrs Waard on their successful passage. I hope for Mrs Waard's sake and also for Bobbie's that Captain Waard doesn't think of doing the same thing to the westward.

Yours faithfully

Joseph Conrad.

Robert B. Matier, Esq.

---

[1] The Navy League saw Japan as a naval threat, and advocated greater investment in ships and sailors.

[2] Born in Ireland in 1885, Robert B. Matier had settled in the United States.

[3] The 23-ton, three-masted Chinese junk *Amoy*, under her owner Captain George Waard, a Dutch-Canadian, sailed from Amoy on 17 May 1922, with Waard's wife, Chang Yee, their son Robert (apparently the letter's Bobbie), and two Chinese 'boys'. They proceeded to New York via Shanghai, Vancouver, Victoria, Seattle, San Francisco, and the Panama Canal, arriving on 2 June 1924. See the *New York Times*, 3 March 1924, p. 21, and 8 June 1924, sect. 8, p. 7, for reports. Matier could have recounted only the voyage's earlier part.

To Thomas J. Wise

Text MS BL Ashley A. 2951; Unpublished

[letterhead: Oswalds]

[23 October 1922][1]

Dear Mr Wise

So sorry you have been suffering from your throat. It is such a depressing thing. I hope you have shaken it off for good now. Pray drop us a line in a day or two.

The issue for sale is 60 cop. of each,[2] of which Messrs. Maggs are going to keep 2 copies of each which I have signed for them. I myself have kept 15 of each to distribute mainly to friends who are not collectors – tho' R. C[urle] had two and Quinn one of each sent to them. Of course the copies sent to you come from my private lot of 15.

With regards

faithfully yours

J. C.

Mrs C thanks you for your kind references to her health. She is getting on slowly.

To F. N. Doubleday

Text TS Princeton; Unpublished

[letterhead: Oswalds]

Oct. 24th. 1922.

Dear Mr Doubleday.

I had no idea you were coming over here so soon till I learned of your arrival in the "Times" late last week.

This accounts in a measure for my finding myself tied up with one sort of engagement or other for the next few days.

The translation of all my works into French under A. Gide's direction is proceeding apace and I am glad to say meets with a pronounced success. The Revue de Paris which is about to serialise "Nostromo" has asked me to do some cutting down of the text.[3] I am going to have a couple of days with one of my translators who is coming down here for the purpose. On Friday we must lunch twenty miles from here with an old friend. On Saturday I must go to see my boy John at Tonbridge School and make the acquaintance of the new Headmaster.[4]

---

[1] Date from postmark.   [2] See the letter to Wise of the 19th.
[3] Nothing came of this. Philippe Neel's translation appeared in *Le Quotidien*, 1–13 October 1924.
[4] H. N. P. Sloman, M[ilitary] C[ross].

I regret to confess that I have not been able to do so much to the big novel as I wanted to do; but when you return from your sun-bath in the country of the Moors nothing will be allowed to stand in the way of our meeting. My wife (who sends her kind regards) promises to have then the pleasure of calling on Mrs Doubleday.

I am delighted and encouraged to hear that you think so well of "The Rover", and are eager to put it before the public. To be altogether frank with you I, too, am longing, in a way, to have it out in book form. But the material aspect of serialisation is important to me. I wish it were not. But it is! However, by the time you return to London we will have seen the situation more clearly and will be enabled to decide together on the course to be pursued in order to give that little book a good chance.

I am sorry that Mrs Doubleday and yourself won't be amongst my friends who intend to muster in force for the first performance of my play on the 2nd of November. Personally I build no hopes whatever on it. The whole thing is too ruthlessly presented to please. For myself I am simply very interested in this novel experience.

Pray give my most respectful regards to Mrs Doubleday, and believe me always

Your very grateful and faithful
Joseph Conrad.

To Philippe Neel
Text L.fr. 176–8; Putnam

[Oswalds]
Oct. 24th. 1922

Mon cher Monsieur,

Votre bonne lettre[1] arriva ici au moment que je finissais de lire votre magnifique traduction de "Lord Jim".[2] Il y a des années que je n'ai pas vu le texte anglais; donc j'ai lu votre traduction comme si c'était un ouvrage français. Et je me disais: "Ah, c'est très bien ça!... Tiens c'est remarquable." ... "Quelle belle langue" et ainsi de suite, d'exclamation en exclamation d'étonnement et de plaisir. Le petit mouvement de fierté que j'ai eu, à un moment donné, quand tout à coup, je me suis dit que, après tout, c'était moi qui avais écrit ces choses-là, c'est bien à vous que je le dois! Il est très difficile de vous exprimer tout ce que je ressens. Tenons nous en donc à une forte poignée de main.

La question des coupures pour la R[evue] de P[aris] a pour moi une certaine gravité surtout parce que, en France, il y a l'habitude pour la critique

[1] Of the 22nd, printed in Putnam.
[2] Recently published by the Nouvelle Revue Française.

de s'occuper des oeuvres qui paraissent en "serial". Ici, au contraire, il est de la plus stricte convention de les ignorer complètement. De sorte qu'ici je ne vois pas même les épreuves. Il me serait indifférent si l'on imprimait une ligne sur trois, au hasard, ou même commençant par la fin. La R[evue] de P[aris] voudra-t-elle consentir à mettre une petite note pour avertir la critique plutôt que les lecteurs. Surtout s'il s'agit de rien de moins que de supprimer la moitié du livre. Ça me semble beaucoup. En vérité, l'idée ne me sourit pas de tout. Mais je ne peux ni ne veux refuser mon consentement. Au contraire: je vous prie formellement de vous occuper de ce travail, et je me déclare d'avance satisfait de ce que vous jugerez nécessaire de faire.

Et cependant c'est mon plus grand effort créateur! Toute cette "matière à prose", entièrement inventée, me tient plus au coeur, et même à l'âme que si elle avait été vécue. Ah! si je pouvais faire une fugue à Paris pour deux jours seulement, nous pourrions arranger cela en quatre heures de travail sans nous éreinter. Mais c'est impossible. J'ai une toux abominable, et puis une pièce en répétition, ce qui me rend bien plus malade. Je vois bien les deux manières de s'y prendre, dont vous parlez. Le choix est difficile. Mais si la réduction demandée doit s'étendre sur toute l'oeuvre, vous pourrez peut-être vous servir de deux. Du reste, cher Monsieur, je suis sûr que de cette tâche d'ouvrier vous saurez faire une oeuvre d'artiste.

Jean Aubry a passé deux jours chez nous. Nous avons parlé beaucoup de vous. Il était plein de louanges de "Lord Jim". Comme il quittait la maison, l'exemplaire que vous avez eu la bonté de m'envoyer arriva par la poste. Merci mille fois, cher Monsieur.

Je ne sais pas ce que j'ai. Depuis que j'ai fini en Juillet mon roman "The Rover", je n'ai pas fait ligne qui vaille. Je suis là, indécis, sans direction, comme un navire dont l'équipage se serait sauvé a terre en laissant toutes les vergues en pagaye.

Faites mes amitiés à la Revue de Paris. Je suis très sensible d'y paraître d'abord avec "l'Ame du Guerrier"[1] et puis avec *Nostromo*. Quelle sacrée machine! Je l'entendais craquer tout en écrivant – et cependant – elle se tient bien debout, n'est-ce pas?

Croyez à mon affectuese reconnaissance.

Bien à vous

Translation

My dear Sir,

Your good letter arrived here the very moment I was finishing reading your excellent translation of *Lord Jim*. I have not seen the English text for years

---

[1] Jean-Aubry's translation was to appear in the 1 November issue.

and therefore read your translation as if it were a French work. And I said to myself: '*That* is good! . . . That is remarkable . . . ' 'How well written!' and so on, going from exclamation to exclamation of astonishment and pleasure. The stir of pride I felt for a moment (all of a sudden I said to myself, after all, *I* wrote those things) I owe to you! It is very difficult to tell you everything I feel. Let's exchange a very cordial handshake.

The matter of cuts in the *R. de P.* has a certain importance for me because in France critics usually pay attention to work appearing in serials. Here, to the contrary, the strictest convention is to ignore them completely. So much so that here I don't even see proofs. I couldn't care if they printed one line out of three, at random, or even began with the ending. Would the *R. de P.* agree to print a short note to warn the critics rather than its readers? Especially if it's a matter of suppressing half the book. That seems rather a lot. To tell the truth, the idea does not make me happy. But I can not and do not want to my refuse my consent. On the contrary, I formally request you to undertake the job and declare myself satisfied in advance with whatever you judge necessary.

It is my greatest creative effort, after all! All that 'stuff of prose', entirely made up, is closer to my heart, even to my soul than if it had actually happened. If I could only dash over to Paris for a couple of days, four hours' of work would settle the matter without breaking our backs. But that is impossible. I have a very nasty cough as well as a play in rehearsal, which makes me sicker still. I see clearly the two methods of doing it that you speak of. The choice is difficult. But if the required cuts must extend over the whole work, you can perhaps use both methods. Moreover, dear Sir, I am confident that you will know how to make a work of art out of this workaday task.

Jean Aubry spent two days with us. We spoke of you a good deal. He was full of praise for *Lord Jim*. As he was leaving the house, the copy you kindly sent to me arrived in the post. Many thanks indeed, dear Sir.

I don't know what the matter is. Since I finished my novel *The Rover* in July I've not written one line that is worth anything. I am uncertain and directionless, like a ship whose crew has gone to land leaving all her sails in disarray.

Pray give my regards to *La Revue de Paris*. I am very proud to appear in it first with 'The Warrior's Soul' and then with *Nostromo*. What a blessed machine *that* is! I heard it cracking while I was writing it – but it none the less holds up pretty well, doesn't it?

Pray believe in my affectionate gratitude.

Yours truly

To the Editor, *The Oswestrian*[1]
Text MS Karl;[2] TS copy Yale; *Oswestrian*

[letterhead: Oswalds]
25 Oct '22.

Dear Sir.

I was away from home for a few days when your letter arrived.[3] Hence the delay in acknowledging it.

As you may imagine I never knew Col. Fred Burnaby.[4]

In those years I was at sea; and it was on my return from a voyage to the East Indies that I saw in the first paper (it was the old *Standard*[5]) I picked up on coming ashore the news of his death.[6]

He was a loveable personality and, I am glad to say, an appreciated one. His professional ability was fully recognised and his fine character made him fit for the high position which he would have reached had he lived. I suppose you know that Lord Wolseley,[7] a good judge of men, intended him to take command of the Metemneh column in succession to Sir H. Steward[8] should the latter be wounded or killed. Sir H. Steward was killed in reaching the Nile but Burnaby was no longer there to take his place. The road to this highest distinction lay open before him when he was struck down at Abu-Klea.

Pray accept with my best wishes for the prosperity of your school-magazinne*, my best thanks for your friendly and interesting letter.

With my love to the School-Masters and Boys, I am

Sincerely yours

Joseph Conrad.

---

[1] The magazine of Oswestry School, a day and boarding school for boys, founded in 1406/7 in the market-town of Oswestry, Shropshire. Possibly Conrad visited the school in mid-September, when the Conrads and the Joneses went on a motor-tour of North Wales and the Borders (*John Conrad*, p. 194); the Jones's daughter and son-in-law, the Watsons, lived part of the year in the nearby Tanat Valley.

[2] Present whereabouts unknown.

[3] According to the headnote in *The Oswestrian*, its editor had requested Conrad to write a few lines about Colonel Burnaby.

[4] Frederick Gustavus Burnaby (1842–85), soldier and journalist, attended Oswestry 1857–62. In 'Youth', Marlow's reading includes the popular *Ride to Khiva* (1876), Burnaby's narrative of a mission to Afghanistan.

[5] Then a London morning rather than an evening paper.

[6] He died of a spear wound to the neck on 17 January 1885 at Abu Klea, in the Sudan.

[7] Garnet Joseph Wolseley (1833–1913; 1st Viscount 1885), soldier and writer, led the Egyptian campaign of 1885.

[8] Herbert Stewart (1843–85; knighted 1884) repelled the Arab attack at Abu Klea but died from his wounds a few days later.

To Clement K. Shorter

Text MS Berg; Unpublished

[letterhead: Oswalds]

25. Oct '22

Dear Mr Shorter.

Herewith the Gals^{thy} pamph:. I was going to send it to you in a day or two. What is unfortunate is that I have sent the Dover Patrol to so many sailors of sorts that I have no copy left – except one. I happened to sign by mistake two copies for Ad. Sir Roger Bacon.[1] On discovery I scratched out the insc^{on} to the Admiral and intended to keep that copy for myself. But if you care to have it (with your name inserted above the scratched place) I will send it to you.

This is the best I can do.

Pray let me know.

Meantime to make up for my oversight in not keeping a copy of D. P. for you I send you 2 Galsworthys, *one* not signed in the hope it may be useful in the way of exchange.

Kindest regards

Yours faithfully

Joseph Conrad

I am sorry I have none of the other pamphs you mention.

To J. Harry Benrimo

Text TS Indiana; J-A, 2, 277–8

[letterhead: Oswalds]

Oct. 27th. 1922.

Dear Mr Benrimo

I hope you got my letter sent by rail this morning in good time. I asked Pinker to collect it at the station and send it on to you at once.

I confess to you I am very frightened at the Professor.[2] I trust you have put into him some conception of his part. It can not be denied that *not a single one* of my directions as to tone and expression has been, I won't say carried out, but even so much as indicated by him, during that rehearsal. I know that you have formed a right conception of the part. The question is whether you will

---

[1] Admiral Sir Reginald Hugh Bacon (1863–1947; knighted 1916) commanded the Dover Patrol 1915–18 and was its historian.

[2] The role was created by G. Clifton Boyne (1874–1945), who debuted in 1892 and spent a long career as a touring actor, chiefly in the provinces and Empire.

be able to perform the miracle of making him see it between this and the first performance.

Inspector Heat[1] is very young and physically too tall and not heavy enough. His very voice is young. For goodness sake put a heavy moustache on him or something, and make him bear himself like a man of forty-five at least. He must have a certain stolidity and conviction. Pray think of the last scene of the last Act when he becomes a symbolic figure, as it were, when facing the Professor; and later when he has got to hold the middle of the stage in silence, contemplating in sombre thoughtfulness the crazy Mrs Verloc crouching on the floor while the crowd murmurs outside. There is a *"tableau"* there which must not fail because it is on that impression the audience will leave the theatre.

When rehearsing the last Act in the scene between Heat and Mrs Verloc the following corrections should be made. Instead of Heat saying with a (low whistle) "Exactly. And your brother now, what's he like? A thick-set dark chap" – he ought to say as follows:

Heat. (low whistle) Exactly. And your brother now, what's he like? A thick-set, *fair* chap?
And Winnie should say:
W. (with fervour) Oh no, that must be the thief. Stevie's slight and *dark*.

Will your charming secretary see that the copies of their parts are altered accordingly?[2]

Will you please tell Miss Lewes that she has got into the character of Winnie in the First Act very well; only beg her from me to keep all emotional inflections out of her voice altogether, when addressing either her Mother or Verloc. She is a woman who has schooled herself into the part of Verloc's wife for the sake of Stevie. Her emotion only breaks out after she has been driven to despair and murder; when she may put as much emotional force into her acting as she can; which will be then more effective.

Best regards

Yours

J. C.

---

[1] Jevan Brandon-Thomas (1898–1977) had débuted in his father's farce *Charley's Aunt*. He wrote some light comedies, and in the 1930s managed theatres in Edinburgh, Glasgow, and London. He was later an overseas announcer for the BBC.
[2] Evidently this did not happen. The reviewer in *The Referee* notes that Stevie 'is represented as dark whereas fair hair was discovered – a little matter that needs adjustment' (5 November, p. 7; see Hand).

To Edward Garnett

Text MS Indiana; G. 315–16 (in part)[1]

[letterhead: Oswalds]
27.10.'22

Dearest Edward.

Many thanks for D.'s little tale.[2] It's the most successful thing of the kind I have ever seen. There is somehow a slight flavour of 18 cen^t manner of diction which is quite fascinating.[3] The earnest flow of the narrative has not a single uncertain note. And, considering how many occasions there were to go wrong, I am impressed either by the wonderful genuineness of his imagination, or his surprising mastery over it. The whole psychology – man and beast – is, I should say, flawless in essence and exposition. Altogether an accomplished piece of work, touchingly amusing and without a single mistake (that *I* can see) in style, tone or conception. My most friendly congratulations to David, on this little piece so thoroughly "done". Nothing of the "amateur" there. Every page holds.

So sorry dearest E you had such [a] bad time with your veins. Mine have never played me such a trick – yet. Would you care old friend to see the first night of the "Secret Agent" next Thursday? I won't be there but I'll send you a stall? But I wont do it unless you send me word. I can't conceive anybody *wanting* to go to a theatre. Jessie's dear love.

Ever Yours

J. Conrad.

To G. Jean-Aubry

Text MS Yale; *L.fr.* 178–9 (in part)

[letterhead: Oswalds]
27.10.22

Mon très cher.

Faites mes remerci[e]ments et mes excuses a Mme Alvar. Je veux rester tranquille chez moi le Mardi. Je serai a Londres Lundi, je pense pour une repetition. Puis Mercredi vers 4 heures nous arriverons tous a Londres (Curzon Hotel). La répétition definitive aura lieu le soir.

Voulez Vous y venir avec moi?

---

[1] Garnett omits the second paragraph.
[2] David Garnett's *Lady into Fox*, published this month and sent to Conrad on the 26th (see Stape and Knowles, p. 195).
[3] In his reply to this letter, Garnett wrote of his son's book, 'Of course he must share the praise with his master, Defoe. He has soaked himself in Defoe' (Stape and Knowles, p. 196).

Je suis profondement deprimé. Ces gens ne pourront jamais comprendre la pièce – ni même l'apprendre convenablement – avant Jeudi.

Pardonnez moi mon très cher si je ne viens pas a la conference.[1] Je ne suis guère en état d'esprit (et de corps aussi) pour cela, a cause d'une extraordinaire irritation mentale dont je souffre a propos de cette maudite pièce.

Je Vous embrasse

à Vous

J. Conrad

Veuillez expliquer a Mme Alvar avec mes hommages.

Translation

My very dear friend.

Pray give my thanks and make my excuses to Madame Alvar. I want to stay quietly at home on Tuesday. I will be in London on Monday, I think, for a rehearsal. Then on Wednesday at about 4 o'clock we all arrive in London (Curzon Hotel). The dress rehearsal will take place that evening.

Would you like to go to it with me?

I am deeply depressed. Those people will never be able to understand the play – or even learn it passably – before Thursday.

Forgive me, my very dear fellow, if I don't come to the lecture. I'm hardly in a fit state of mind (or body) for it, owing to the unusual mental irritability I'm suffering from because of that accursed play.

I embrace you.

Yours

J. Conrad

Pray explain to Madame Alvar along with my duty to her.

To John Quinn
Text MS NYPL; Unpublished

[letterhead: Oswalds]
27.10.'22

My dear Mr Quinn

I beg you to accept these two pamph^s the text of which has never appeared in book-form.

---

[1] Jean-Aubry had invited the French poet Paul Valéry to England to lecture to invited audiences. He did so on 30 and 31 October, and lunched at Oswalds on 5 November.

I am afraid incorrigible sinfulness in the matter of correspondence has given You a wrong impression as to my feelings.[1] Pray believe me they are as cordial and full of regard for You as ever. As I am too old to amend my horrid ways, I hope You will continue me Your indulgence and think of me as kindly as You used to do.

Always faithfully Yours
Joseph Conrad

To George T. Keating
Text MS Yale; Unpublished

[letterhead: Oswalds]
28.10 '22

Dear M[r] Keating.

Here are two pamphs for your Conrad collec[on] by which I feel much honored. I have inscribed them as I think you prefer them inscribed. Neither text has ever been pub[d] in book form and probably never will be.[2]

I think my wife is writing by this mail to Mrs Keating.

Pray give her my duty, and believe me a most sincere well-wisher to you and all yours.

Regards.

Yours
Joseph Conrad

To Eric Pinker
Text TS/MS Berg; Unpublished

[letterhead: Oswalds]
Oct. 28th. 1922.

My dear Eric.

I think you are under a misapprehension when you say it is only a question now to drill the actors and fit in the play technically to the stage. I have seen the actors only twice and the first time they were reading their parts from the copy and the second time, last Thursday, they didn't know their words; while Miss Lewis,* for one, had her copy in her hand most of the time. As to the last

---

[1] In his letter to Conrad of 17 July (TS carbon NYPL), Quinn had written: 'Some cloud has seemed to come between you and me during this last year or two, but what caused it has been obscure – a minor mystery to me … A long time ago you wrote of dedicating a book to me. Let me say in the fullest sincerity that I now do not want you to have the slightest feeling that you are in any degree committed, by what you once wrote, to any such thing; nor do I expect it. You will, I feel sure, credit me with complete sincerity and utter lack of any feeling on that score. I cannot put it more strongly than that.'

[2] They appeared posthumously in *Last Essays*.

Act, which is certainly the principal in my play, all the prepared drama being then unfolded to the audience, I have *not seen* it at all. Those are mere facts about which there can be no dispute. I don't mean to say I was dissatisfied with what I saw (which was about what I expected) but the fact is B[enrimo] told me that he was going to rehearse twice every day, beginning on Monday. If he told you that he was going to rehearse only in the evening then I take a very serious view of the thing; because it would stand thus:- Friday, one rehearsal, Saturday and Sunday no rehearsals; and from Monday till the first performance, at any rate, there would be only four. It is quite possible that Benrimo after obtaining those photographs for the purpose of his publicity [1] doesn't want to see me any more, though, God knows, I addressed very few remarks to the actors and very few to Benrimo himself. I consented to that fooling out of regard for the people who took the play, and I perceive that I made an ass of myself by doing so. I don't mind so much making an ass of myself; the greatest and wisest of mankind have done that on more than one occasion, probably, in their lives. But I don't like to be made to look like a fool which is quite a different thing. I didn't realise at the moment, being quite unexpectedly beset by a crowd of people that had nothing to do with the play, that by my being made to hold the book in my hand I allowed it to be put on record that I had something to do with the production of that play. No doubt papers are rags and the public forgets what is in them. That's so. But it will remember just long enough to make it extremely unpleasant for me should there turn up anything absurd, which the author ought not to have let pass. Having been put into this position absolutely against my wish, as you know, I can't be eliminated; at any rate not with my consent. That this attitude of mine is justified and cannot be disputed there can be no question. For instance, looking over the Third Act last Friday I discovered that there is a line in Mrs Verloc['s] part, which in my judgment (and I really am not an idiot) may make the public laugh, though it is not intended to do so. A giggle from some fool in the audience may start others and be fatal to the effect of the situation (I won't enlarge here but if I were to show you, you would see at once what I mean). Well, I want to hear that line spoken on the stage. This is not unreasonable. There may be others – in fact I am certain that on account of the physique of the actor playing Inspector Heat there is a line which ought to be altered at rehearsal; a thing I alone ought to do, because I know what to put in its place. In the same way, on account of the boy being dark instead of fair, a few words had to be altered in the text. I called attention to that during the rehearsal myself, on Thursday.

[1] A photograph of Conrad reading the play with Amy Brandon-Thomas ('Lady Mabel') appeared in *The Times* on 27 October, p. 16. See also Plate 5.

I am writing like this to you, my dear Eric, though you will understand perfectly well that I am not addressing *you*, personally, and I state all this calmly without any irritation or undue anxiety, I assure you; but with a perfectly reasonable desire to give the best chance possible to the play. All this is perfectly consonant with great confidence in B[enrimo]. The fact of the matter is that I must see the Third Act and for that purpose I am ready to come on Tuesday to town and come to the theatre in the evening. I will also attend the dress rehearsal, to which I will bring my friend Aubry, for the reason you know.[1] I have been put forward and I can't be shunted off now. Moreover I have the right on my side.

I am sure you will know how to put all this to the parties concerned strongly, without straining the situation. Please drop me a line by early post.

Always aff^{tly} yours

J. Conrad

To R. L. Mégroz
Text TS Rosenbach; Unpublished

[letterhead: Oswalds]
Oct. 30th. 1922.

Dear Mr Mégroz.[2]

I greatly appreciate the interest, you say, is taken by the teachers in my personality.[3] At the same time, strictly "entre nous", I don't understand it very well. A politician, a successful man of action, may be better and, as a human being more interesting than his work. But a man expressing himself in imaginative literature can never really be worth more than what he gives to the world: his, as it were, disembodied personality; for the simple reason that the flesh is weak (as it has been observed before)[4] and moreover may be encumbered by unlovely and even contemptible material characteristics. The thought also as formulated in speech may be affected by the passing little incidents of the day, and cannot have the value either in truth or sincerity of the meditated page.

I don't think that a man who in thirty years has produced twenty-four volumes which are neither philosophy nor sociology, nor anything practical, improving, enlightening or even revealing (except a certain gift for writing

---

[1] His interest in doing a translation.
[2] Rodolphe-Louis Mégroz (1891–1968), English literary journalist of French and East Anglian ancestry, was an anthologist (especially of poetry), essayist, and biographer. He published *A Talk with Joseph Conrad* (1926) and *Joseph Conrad's Mind and Method* (1931).
[3] Mégroz's request for an interview resulted in 'Talks with Famous Writers: VI. Joseph Conrad', *Teacher's World*, 15 November, 367–8.
[4] Matthew 26.41 and Mark 14.38.

prose) can have much to say that would be worth hearing. The above rather obscure thoughts, so very badly expressed, are not a preliminary to a refusal. On the contrary I will be glad to meet you, for our feelings have nothing to do with what we are pleased to imagine our wisdom. I am going up to town to-morrow evening, but the nearest date I can suggest would be Thursday, the 2nd. And as to the time let us say four o'clock at the Curzon Hotel, Curzon Street. I will be in the lounge downstairs, which is generally empty at that hour. We will get into a corner and have a cup of tea. But if the idea doesn't please you pray drop me a line. Some other opportunity may offer before long.

I am,

sincerely Yours

Joseph Conrad

To E. L. Sanderson
Text MS Yale; Unpublished

[letterhead: Oswalds]
30 Oct '22

Dearest Ted.

I was in Ferox Hall[1] last Saturday and, after pouring (by command) my naïve impressions of the stage into Agnes ears, I got her (without difficulty) onto another subject; a subject in its reality and in its grip on my ageing heart infinitely removed from all the strutting shams that walk this earth. In listening to the excellent account of you all and about your doings I felt my heart grow light while at the same time the sense of my villainous unworthiness oppressed me heavily. But no more of that except that I will just mention that some actually saintly men have had the same experience – and that I being an ordinary sinner must be even more charitably judged.

Give my love to Helen the presiding genius of good fortune, to your two girls of whom A. told me many touching and charming things, and to Ian when you write. A. told me that his health was quite good now and that he was still at Camb^{ge}. A. said you worked too much, perhaps too anxiously? The Greeks (I don't mean Venizelos)[2] are very far away from me now; but I seem to remember they cultivated restraint, a perfect measure, an excellent moderation in all the arts including the art of living. I wouldn't be impertinent: – but why not apply that exalted and almost divine rule to the

[1] John Conrad's house at Tonbridge School. It was under the aegis of Ted Sanderson's brother-in-law and sister, Neville and Agnes Ridgeway.
[2] Eleutherios Venizelos (1864–1936), Greek statesman and Prime Minister (1910–15), an acquaintance of Conrad.

life of an Englishman of the 20th Centy – the heir of classical culture,[1] a man
moreover round whom so many precious affections are centred? I won't
mention his[2] (not wishing to be impertinent); I will only ask you to give him
my love old now but untarnished by time and never dimmed, even for a
moment, in all these years.

Ever Yours

Joseph Conrad.

To Allan Wade
Text TS/MS Leeds; Unpublished

[letterhead: Oswalds]
Oct. 30th. 1922.

My dear Wade.

I was about to write to you when your letter to my wife arrived and was
given me to read. Let me, first of all, express my concern at you both having
been victims of colds and coughs, and especially at the news of Mrs Wade
being far from well. Pray thank her very affectionately from me for her
message – as far as it relates to myself. Jessie is writing to-day, I think. I do
hope the Italian troubles[3] will subside enough (one can hardly hope for more
just now) to allow Mrs Wade to get her two months in Italy and derive all
possible benefit from them. Italy is very delightful; but I am sorry for the
reason of her having to go there, and, in this matter, let me offer to you both
my most sympathetic condolences.

I can't quite make up my mind to thank you for your share in pushing that
play on to the boards. My feelings are in a state of most agonising confusion.
I ought to have thanked you a fortnight ago when it would have presented
no difficulty. To-day at 1.30 pm I wish to goodness it had remained in the
safe obscurity of print – private print. But as I don't know whether at 4 pm
I will be crawling on the floor or walking on air, and this letter is already
begun, I think that upon the whole I will thank you. Anyhow I am certain
that in the course of twenty-four hours there will be moments when I shall
feel sincerely grateful to you. But, speaking seriously, I build no hopes on the
play. Its very nature is against its being a success from a worldly point of view.

---

[1] Sanderson had read Classics at King's College, Cambridge.
[2] A word is missing here – either 'identity' or 'name'.
[3] Benito Mussolini's National Fascist party engineered a mainly bloodless coup, clearing the
way for Mussolini to become Prime Minister on the 30th. There was some civil unrest in the
major cities as well as in the provinces, including the theatrical March on Rome.

My gratitude will be always due to your friendly help and interest in getting for me that new and instructive experience.

Benrimo is épatant. I never saw anything of the sort before and when I am talking with him I have often the sensation that he is a person in a tale. An air of unreality, weird unreality, envelopes the words, the ideas and the arguments we exchange, the familiar words of the play, the figures of the people, clings to the very walls, permeates the darkness of the fantastic cavern which I can by no means imagine will ever contain anything so real as an audience of men and women – I mean real, not makebelieve – so that I can't get rid of the feeling that presently I will wake up with a start and find myself in bed with a light by my side and listening to the silence of the night.

I must however say that the American characteristic you warn me against has not been to the fore. The cutting down of about twenty lines altogether was completely in accord with my own judgment and was done by myself. But I must confess that I have only seen the first two Acts (the 3rd we have incorporated with the 2nd so that the play is in 3 Acts now) twice, in a state of word-imperfection and general confusion which you may imagine. And yet I am not dissatisfied; but I will say that I think that a bare three weeks is not sufficient preparation for a play which contains not a single character that could be brought under the usual convention of acting without losing its significance. This makes me uneasy. What makes me still more uneasy is Benrimo's attempt, very indirect but very real nevertheless, to get rid of me for the future under various most friendly pretences. However I cannot let myself be dismissed airily like that; the more so that I have not seen at all the 3rd Act yet (the last). And as the whole drama is unfolded in it and it is really *the* vital Act I must certainly have my say on points that may arise. I presume it is my bare right. I intend also to see the dress rehearsal which takes place on Wednesday night.

It's very dear of you, busy as you are, to promise to see us – for I intend to be there when you call on my wife. Only the sense of decency (not dignity) restrained me from flying for comfort and support to a man so full of work as you are. Indeed I would have not written even all this had it not been for your friendly letter to Jessie.

My love to you both

very much Yrs

Joseph Conrad

This entre-nous trois – or four incl^{ing} *my* wife.

To Iris Wedgwood

Text MS Private collection; Unpublished

[cancelled: letterhead: Oswalds]
Curzon Hotel
Tuesday. [31 October? 1922][1]

Dear Mrs Wedgwood

Pray accept my most penitent apologies. When we asked Dick to escort you to the theatre my wife proposed to write to you at once. It's I (sinner that I am!) who said that this was *my* show and that I would write to you myself. It was last week and – well, I throw myself on Your mercy!

I assure you that you are the only person that we even thought of asking to come. And We hope that You will drop in for half an hour after the theatre to share Jessie's supper that I and her son are giving her here – being also the only friend (except Dick – but he is an institution) we have asked. Eric Pinker (who has been most devoted in this trying time) may also come in.

Unless you make me happy by coming I will think I am unforgiven.

Most remorsefully always your faithful servant
Joseph Conrad.

RC. told me that I[2] are lunching at the Club. Pardon this intrusion.

To Edward Garnett

Text MS Free; G. 316–17

[letterhead: Oswalds]
Tuesday. [Thursday, 2 November 1922][3]

Dearest Edward

I hope Jessie explained clearly yesterday.[4]

Herewith 2 upp circles for tomorrow.

I don't know whether they will be of any use to you.

---

[1] Dated by Conrad's movements: he attended a rehearsal on the 26th, but since he sent Benrimo a letter from the country on the morning of the 27th, he is unlikely to have stayed the night. According to letters of the 28th (to Pinker) and 30th (to Mégroz), he planned to watch a rehearsal of Act 3 on the evening of the 31st, a Tuesday.

[2] A slip for 'you'? In that case, Conrad's 'intrusion' may have been to address this letter to her at the Club; alternatively, Curle perhaps asked Conrad at the last minute to join him for lunch with Mrs Wedgwood, in which case, 'I' is a slip either for 'we' or for 'he and I'.

[3] Date from postmark, confirmed by the final paragraph. Misled by Conrad's 'Tuesday', Garnett gives 31 October.

[4] Garnett had written to Conrad on 30 October asking for '*two humbler seats* – which don't necessitate the horrors of evening dress!'(Stape and Knowles, p. 196). Jessie Conrad's letter of 1 November (MS Texas), written at Conrad's direction, explained that since the house was full Conrad could offer one stall ticket not the two Garnett wanted for himself and his companion Nellie Heath, but the situation obviously changed.

another from which, ultimately, the English Ed. could be set, so as to have the text in both countries exactly alike.

Ever affect^{ly} Yrs

J. Conrad

⁺P. S. Typescript just arrived. Many thanks.

To Eric Pinker
Text MS Berg; Unpublished

[Oswalds]

[late November 1922?][1]

My dearest E.

I quite see the inner meaning of your letter and the answer is meant to be shown, if you like. I expect all your support.

My dear, no man having the slightest sense of his value and, I may say, position would allow himself to be dismissed in such airy fashion.

Ever Yrs

JC

Sorry to worry you – but just consider! . . .

To Bruno Winawer
Text TS copy Yale;[2] J-A, 2, 287–8 (in part);[3] *Głos* (114); Najder 282–3

Oswalds,
Bishopsbourne,
Kent.
Nov. 23rd. 1922.

My dear Sir,

Please excuse my writing in English but my hand is painful and I am compelled to dictate – doing so in Polish would mean spelling it out letter by letter.

Thank you very much for your letter received three days ago and for the newspaper page which came by to-day's post.

---

[1] Catalogued as from November. Possibly related to the Melrose affair (see the letter of the 19th)?

[2] Typing errors not reproduced or signalled. The greeting, first paragraph, farewell, and signature, not in the Yale copy, are from Najder, who reconstructs them from quotations in Polish in a letter from Winawer to Jean-Aubry of 23 October 1924 (Yale).

[3] Jean-Aubry omits the first paragraph.

The thing has been marvellously vulgarised. I don't know whether to laugh or to swear. Of course it is not the actors fault – it's their destiny. They can no more help themselves than the immortal Gods can. And I too am the victim of my weakness in suffering these ridiculous agonies.

Are we to see you tomorrow? (Friday)

Ever Yours

J Conrad

To Henry Arthur Jones

Text MS Duke; J-A, 2, 278–9; Jones 344–5

[letterhead: Hotel Curzon, London]

3. Nov '22

Cher Maître – à nous tous.[1]

Let me thank you with all possible warmth for your kind note of welcome to the "youngest" dramatist.

This kindness so characteristic of you has touched me deeply; it brought vividly to my mind the day when dear Henry James presented me to you at the Reform Club, the friendliness of your words of appreciation which I was so proud to hear, and the grip of your hand.

If I deserve this word of welcome at all it is perhaps by this: – that I can assure you that this work, undertaken of course from impulse, is the product of earnest meditation – even in its defects – and not of airy self-confidence.

Let me subscribe myself with real gratitude

Affectionately Yours

Joseph Conrad

Will you give my affectionate thanks to Mrs Thorne for her precious autograph. It is so much like her delightful self.

---

[1] After a brief career in business Henry ('Harry') Arthur Jones (1851–1929) became a popular and prolific playwright whose work was regularly performed on the late-Victorian and Edwardian stage as well as in America. The author of music-hall sketches and a theatrical manager, he wrote *Patriotism and Popular Education* (1919) and engaged in lively controversies with Bernard Shaw and H. G. Wells.

To J. Harry Benrimo
Text MS[1]; Unpublished

Oswalds
6. Nov. 22

Dear Mr Benrimo.

I felt so much better on Sunday that I asked Eric Pinker to try to get in touch with you on the 'phone. I hoped you might be induced to give me the pleasure of lunching with me. As P failed I started for home at eleven o'clock with my wife, in the car.

She has asked me to convey to you her thanks for your great courtesy in seating her on her arrival. She was immensely impressed by the way the play had been "pushed together" and "brought forward" on its third performance. The lighting scheme she found on this occasion at the same time more subtle and more helpful for the better visualising of the facial expressions, so important for the full effect of certain scenes. Miss Royter[2] she found "the very thing" this time. L[ady] Mabel[3] too put on a fascinating finish on her performance. She expressed herself with great warmth on the growing "mastery of character" as displayed by Mr West, the increased substantiality (if I may say so of R. T[horndike]'s Ossipon and the enormous improvement in the "assurance" of the Professor. As to Miss Lewis* she expected great things from her from the first as Winnie and her expectations are in the way of being surpassed. The girl who was with my wife[4] told me that the way Miss Lewis* said the three words "I am satisfied" was a perfect revelation of what Winnie's married life had been. No mean triumph if you consider that the person was just the average playgoer. Perhaps Miss Lewis* would like to know that an eminent surgeon (Sir Robert Jones) was profoundly impressed with the truth of her psychological change from the frozen woman to terror, despair and madness. He complimented me on the truth – but he said that she had made it physiologically visible and that it was "great art" on her part.

I have seen the press-cuttings this morning.[5] Most of what they say I said to myself while at work and the rest seemed to me rather silly. However I have got my verdict. Nothing can change it. But the rest is in your hands: The

---

[1] Text from Frederick R. Karl's transcription; present whereabouts of MS unknown.
[2] Ellie Royter played Winnie's mother.
[3] The play's version of the novel's 'lady patroness'. The role was created by Amy Brandon-Thomas (1890–1974), whose brother played Inspector Heat. Like her brother's, her early career was dominated by *Charley's Aunt*, but she escaped it, going on to work with great managers and directors like Forbes Robinson and Beerbohm Tree.
[4] Her nurse-companion Audrey Seal?
[5] Hand reprints the twenty-four reviews that appeared between 3 and 5 November.

Producer and the artists; and as the devotion to your art and the hard creative toil will be yours so yours will be the credit of making something out of a piece of work which, at any rate, no critic has dared to call futile. I send you all my affectionate regards and best wishes for a personal success – one and all.

But before I step finally out of the thing in which my part is ended let me entreat you my dear Mʳ Benrimo to restore the Professor in the last scene. I ask you this as man to man and as an artist speaking to another artist. The *whole* of the play was written *up to these* 3 or four replicas: Verloc's wife? – No a madwoman . . . and so on to Winnie's last words "Blood and dirt" and the inspector's final significant phrase: "*She* has named it!" The retention of these few lines can't ruin the play's prospects. And they are mine. A man has his feelings. I am not made of wood. Moreover my dear Sir you are not presenting a Guignol horror but something which has a larger meaning.[1] If the public gives you a chance my last word to you is: "fight the ship under that flag."[2]

Cordially yrs

J. C.

To Eric Pinker
Text MS Berg; Unpublished

[letterhead: Oswalds]
Nov. 6th. 1922

My dear Eric

I have seen now all the press-cuttings. Some of the objections I have made to myself even while working and discussed with both your Father and Vernon. The rest is merely silly. I had a letter from H. A. Jones; a long screed of encouragement in which he quotes M. Arnold: "Even on the stage intellect will tell".[3] H. A. J. hopes that it may in this case. Garnett too is pleased.

I have written my final letter to Benrimo. I have had *my* verdict. I take it and step out. The glory and credit (if the thing goes on) will be B[enrimo]'s and the actors. I've sent them all my compᵗˢ and warm wishes, in the friendliest manner. Just as I feel about the whole thing.

Don't you think the book form of the play could be launched. Or is it too late in the year? If Meth: have started selling the book in the theatre they ought in fairness [to] publish the play.

Affecˡʸ Yrs

J. Conrad

---

[1] For the Guignolesque quality of Russell Thorndike's performance, which struck some reviewers, see Hand, p. 2.
[2] In naval speech, to 'fight a ship' is to take her into battle.
[3] Untraced in Matthew Arnold or elsewhere.

To Ada and John Galsworthy

Text MS Forbes; Galsworthy 14–15 (in part); J-A, 2, 282–3 (in part)[1]

[letterhead: Oswalds]

Tuesday [7 November 1922][2]

Dearest Ada and Jack

After leaving the theatre at 1.20 AM on Thurs: (after the rehearsal) I have not been near the place, and I don't know why the telegrams and letters of the day were not sent to me till last night's post. They might have been given to Jessie who with a large, agreeable grin assured me that she had *the* evening of her life. So, at any rate, one person enjoyed it.

Thanks for your wire of good wishes. I was certain of them, but directly Benrimo got hold of the thing I became so scared that I had not the heart to write. My spirit became like unto that of the field-mouse palpitating in its hole, though my body (and a considerable proportion of my native irritability) went up twice to town. By contrast, now it is all over, my state may be described as that of serene joy, only marred by remorse at the injustice of my past thoughts towards the actors who had a lot of characters, certainly not of a "stock" kind, thrown at their heads just 20 days before the first performance. Now like a man touched by grace I think of them with actual tenderness and almost with affection.

On Friday afternoon I made large cuts, pages, and 1/2 pages besides phrases here and there (the strangest thing is that I urged these very cuts to be made only to meet with loud protests! The mentality of theatre people is very curious); and last night I wrote my last letter to Benrimo with a message to the interpreters – which I hope they will believe.

The disagreeable part of this business is to see wasted the hard work of people who depend on it for their livelihood – and for whom success would mean assured employment and ease of mind. One feels guilty somehow. On Sat: Jessie went again (she loves the theatre) to see the effect of the cuts. Her report was that it all went better. It's of no importance now. Edward wrote to her. He is very pleased. I had a letter from H. A. Jones of the friendliest kind. Years ago when lunching with H. James at the Reform Club I was introduced to him.

---

[1] Besides the usual omission of farewell and postscript, Jean-Aubry cuts from 'but directly' in the second paragraph to 'By contrast', resuming with 'now it is all over'.

[2] Jean-Aubry places this between the letters of the 11th and 20th, but the Tuesday in question must fall between the play's opening on the 2nd and its closing on the 11th.

Now my tongue is untied I could write pages to you but I think I had better make "a cut" here. Why should you be bored twice with that?
With all love

Ever Yours

J. Conrad

All these days I was racked by an awful cough and am glad to be home.

To Edward Garnett
Text MS Leeds; G. 317 (in part)[1]

[letterhead: Oswalds]
7.11. '22

Dearest Edward.

It was very good of you to write to Jessie.

I did not ask you to give me your opinion just because it was for me the only one that mattered. Your subtlety (if not your affection) will understand what I mean.[2] I am much re-assured by what you say. You evidently think it an honest piece of work not altogether written in the dark – and certainly not from mere vanity – just to show. All you say of the acting is Gospel truth. Yes! I was unjust to the professor.

On Friday I made large cuts – the same I wanted to make 3 weeks ago but was not permitted. Funny mentality, that of Stage people.

Our love to you

Ever Yours

J. C.

How is your leg?[3]

---

[1] Garnett omits the postscript.
[2] Garnett's own plays, such as *The Feud* and *The Trial of Joan of Arc*, had also met with critical bafflement. For Conrad's reactions to them, see *Letters*, 4, pp. 218–19, 421–2.
[3] See his letters to Conrad of 26 and 28 October (Stape and Knowles, pp. 195–6); he was suffering from varicose veins.

To F. Tennyson Jesse
Text MS Berg; Unpublished

[letterhead: Oswalds]
7. Nov. '22

Dear Miss Tennyson Jesse.[1]

I am profoundly touched by your message from the nursing home. I hope you will reassure me by a few words as to the progress of your convalescence. Your note reached me only this morning. Why it was not given to my wife who was in the theatre on the first night and again on Sat – I don't know. For myself, after the dress rehearsal (which ended at 1.20 AM on Thursday) I did not go near the place. What would have been the good? I was also suffering from a cough which would have made me a nuisance to everybody – including the actors.

I feel remorseful when I think of their wasted work and loyal effort to get into their parts – of which not one was of the "stock" variety – or even remotely allied to the usual types of mankind generally represented on the stage.

As to myself my true vocation is to be a dramatic critic. I know it! Because the fact is that I anticipated *all* that was written in the press with an accuracy that on reflection appals me. Even to the "inspissated gloom" which was produced by Walkley[2] – of all people! That is: "thickened by the evaporation of moisture". What sort of gloom is that? Did ABW cry – did anybody cry? That *would* have been a triumph!

Believe me your very grateful and affec^te Servant

Joseph Conrad

---

[1] F(ryniwyd) Tennyson Jesse (née Wynifried Margaret Jesse, 1889–1955), a prolific writer, was fascinated by criminal trials, whose transcripts she edited for publication. Her best-known novels are *The Lacquer Lady* (1929), set in nineteenth-century Burma, and *A Pin to See the Peepshow* (1934), a fictional rendering of the trial and execution of Edith Thompson and her lover Frederick Bywaters for the fatal stabbing of Mr Thompson in October 1922. The thoughts of the condemned woman, whom Jesse treats with considerable sympathy, echo Winnie Verloc's after she has knifed Adolf. A dramatist in her own right, Jesse collaborated with her husband, Harold Marsh Harwood, on a number of plays produced during the war and in the 1920s.

[2] Arthur Bingham Walkley (1855–1926), *The Times* drama critic, wrote: 'We left the "inspissated gloom" of the theatre with a certain relief, and minded to read the novel again' (4 November, p. 8; see Hand). Walkley's phrase occurs in James Boswell's *The Life of Dr Johnson, LL.D.* (1791), during a conversation from 1769: 'In the description of Night in "Macbeth," the beetle and the bat detract from the general idea of darkness – inspissated gloom' (ed. Alexander Napier, 1892, 2, 94). If not a commonplace, the phrase had some currency: cf. 'The sturdy English soul . . . in inspissated gloom, hardened': John Galsworthy, *In Chancery* (Heinemann, 1920), Pt. 2, Ch. 5.

To Henry Arthur Jones
Text MS Duke; J-A, 2, 279–80; Jones 345–6

[letterhead: Oswalds]
7.11.'22

My very dear Sir

As you see one of my very few virtues is the virtue of obedience. It was very comforting to read your words of appreciation, where appreciation could be given. Of course I felt at times the play doomed even before the first night of which I had a report from my wife – who however was hopeful. But even a play written by an angel could not have stood up against the weight of a unanimous press. The most piously disposed would have been scared off. There is something awe-inspiring in a hostile cry from many throats in unison on a single note. Let this then be "la mort sans phrases".[1] I ought to have said *condemnatory* rather than hostile, for of course there was no hostility. Rather the reverse. I was very sensible of that while wading through the press-cuttings – a thing I have not done for many years. What however is really painful in this affair is the thought of loyal work wasted, of men and women devoted to their art and to whom the success of the play would have meant so much more that* it could have meant to myself.

Voilà. One doesn't think till too late – and then comes remorse, a decent thing, in so far that it is much less comfortable than callousness, but otherwise of no great account. So I am not boasting; I am just telling you in a spirit of repentance and for the good of my soul. A sort of "confession après la mort".[2] That situation though pregnant with grim irony could not be presented on any stage. It would be misunderstood and would ruin the play.

It is most kind of You to ask me to dine. Just now I am really not well and, like Mr Verloc, "want to be looked after". It has nothing to do with the grimness of the situation. I was feeling far from well even before the play was accepted. May I write to you when I feel fit to come up? And I hope we may have Mrs Thorne for company. I am afraid I have shocked and disgusted her on Friday by my manners and speeches which fell far short of that serene amenity which marks the behaviour of a vrai homme du monde[3] and, strangely enough, the faces of hairdressers dummies. Perhaps because both are strangers to remorse. My humble apologies and my repentant love to her.

I am dear Sir Your ever grateful and affectionate
Joseph Conrad

---

[1] 'Death – with no fine phrases': spoken when voting to execute Louis XVI, these words have been attributed to both Danton and the Abbé Sieyès. Cf. 'Amy Foster': 'It was death without any sort of fuss' (p. 122).
[2] 'Posthumous confession'.   [3] 'Real man of the world'.

To Agnes Ridgeway
Text MS Leeds; Unpublished

[letterhead: Oswalds]
7. Nov. '22

My dear Agnes.

The Ferox Hall wire only reached me this morning by post. Why it was not given to my wife who went to the first night I don't know. My warmest thanks for thinking of me on that evening, while I sat in the Curzon crouching over our bedroom-fire and racked by a cough. For *that* was *my* part on the first night. At 9.30 Borys managed to get away from the Daimler Depot somewhere near Vauxhall Bridge and came like a good child to keep me company. At 10.45 he left me to fetch his mother and saw the greatest part of the last act standing darkly at the back of the box with his over-coat collar turned up, looking no doubt like a mysterious anarchist in the midst of the brilliant gathering. I understand the house was resplendent. Mrs C confessed to me with an agreeable grin that she had *the* evening of her life, having never seen anything like that before and being sure of never seeing it again. The crowd around her box the compliments, the courtly respects ofBenrimo, the speeches on the stage after the last courtain* – a perfect Function, as the Spaniards say.¹

I must say I anticipated all the press said with an accuracy that borders on the miraculous. However that's all over. There is just a chance that the play may survive. To-day is the first matinée.

But all this is of no importance now. Miriam Lewis* did wonders. Of course they all felt at sea with parts for which there was no precedent on the stage – and only 20 days of study!

My dear love in which Jessie joins to you both.

Your affcte friend & servant
J. Conrad

To John Drinkwater
Text MS Yale; Unpublished

[letterhead: Oswalds]
8. Nov. 22

My dear Mʳ Drinkwater.

I consider myself highly privileged by the possession of an inscribed copy of the limited edition of the Preludes;² and thanking you for the beauty and

---

¹ The earliest example in the *OED* of 'function' as a grand social event dates from 1858 and is spelled in the Spanish way, without a 't'.
² *Preludes, 1921–1922*. The copy was of the trade edition, published in October (see the letter to Drinkwater of 13 December).

music therein contained I am especially grateful for the kind thought which prompted you to send them to me in this form.

My heart which never knew how to sing, and can no longer hope for an inspiring dawn, is quite willing yet to linger over the –
    . . . wash of sunlit dew shaken in song.[1]
for a few years longer.

Sincerely Yours

Joseph Conrad

To Philippe Neel
Text L.fr. 179–80; Putnam

[Oswalds]

Nov. 8th 1922.

Cher Monsieur,

1. Je ne suis pas allé en Corse pour le *Rover*.[2] Je ne suis pas allé en Corse pour aucun roman. Le roman "The Rover" est situé sur la côte sud de France, pas loin de Toulon, vis à vis du Cap Cicié. *The Rover himself* est Français, comme du reste la plupart des personnages dans cette histoire.

2. Non, cher Monsieur. Je ne peux pas vous indiquer aucun point particulier dans mon oeuvre ou dans ma vie; excepté peut-être que je suis heureux d'avoir commencé ma vie de marin en France et dans la Méditerranée avec les souvenirs inoubliables qu'elle m'a laissés.

3. Je regrette que Jean Aubry n'est pas en Angleterre. Je pense qu'il sera à Paris demain ou après-demain. Peut-être pourrez-vous vous aboucher avec lui par la N[ouvelle] R[evue] F[rançaise].

4. Je vous prie, cher Monsieur, de vous servir de toutes les citations que vous voulez faire, tant dans mes livres que dans notre correspondance. Amitiés.

Bien à vous.

Ma pièce est tombée. Elle a été exécutée par la presse avec tous les égards, et même respects imaginables, mais avec une fermeté tout-à-fait "Vieille Rome".
Translation

Dear Sir,

1. I did not go to Corsica for *The Rover*. I did not go to Corsica for any novel. The novel *The Rover* is set on the south coast of France, not far from Toulon,

---

[1] From 'Prelude', the collection's first sonnet.
[2] Conrad responds to a letter from Neel of the 6th, printed in Putnam.

towards Cape Cicié. The Rover himself, like most of the story's characters, is French.

2. No, dear Sir. I can't single out for you any point in my work or life except perhaps that I am glad to have begun my sea-life in France and the Mediterranean with the unforgettable memories that that has left me.

3. I am afraid that Jean Aubry is not in England. I think he will be in Paris to-morrow or the day after. Perhaps you can confer with him about the N[ouvelle] R[evue] F[rançaise].

4. Pray, dear Sir, make use of any quotation you wish either from my books or our correspondence.

With friendly regards

Yours sincerely

My play failed. The press put it to death with all conceivable respect and consideration but with an altogether 'Old Roman' resolve.

To Eric Pinker
Text TS/MS Berg; Unpublished

[letterhead: Oswalds]
Nov. 8th. 1922.

Dearest Eric.

Your wire last night did not surprise me. Neither did it cast me down. This morning a fresh batch of press-cuttings came in, mostly Sunday papers, of which the Lloyds was unreservedly admirative, the Referee intelligent, and the others generally less crushing than the dailies.[1] The whole collection is very interesting. As a *man* who has his own feelings, I certainly cannot complain – as a playwright (several papers made a distinction between the playwright and the dramatist) all I can say is that we expected a stir and we have certainly got it; only of the wrong kind. I perceive that even the settings came under criticism; at least seven papers objecting to Benrimo's flickers of darkness. My own preference would have been for the old-fashioned curtain. However all this is of no importance now. I have got only to thank you for your part of tireless good friend which you filled in a manner I am not likely ever to forget.

---

[1] The reviewer for *Lloyd's Sunday News* called the play 'a masterpiece of action', praised the acting, and called the piece 'an astonishingly fine play' (5 November, p. 8), whilst S. R. Littlewood in the *Referee* (5 November, p. 7) compared the play unfavourably with the novel and generally found the acting good if not exceptional. See Hand for both reviews in full.

I am returning you here the Canadian agreement[1] duly signed, and I hope to let you have Unwin's advertising matter by the first post on Friday.

Very affect^{ly} Yours

J. Conrad.

Do the rights revert to me? I don't know how the agreement is affected by failure. And do please render the deceased dramatist the last friend's services of getting back the pages of the play which are with B[enrimo] now.

To Aniela Zagórska
Text MS copy Yale;[2] Najder 282

Oswalds,

8.11.22.

My dear Aniela,

Pray forgive me for dictating this letter. My hand is in pain, and you know English perfectly. I returned from London very tired. It is easier for me to dictate.

As you will know by the telegram I am sending you to-day, the play has failed notwithstanding a good first night; nearly the whole of the press giving an unfavourable verdict on the ground of defective stagecraft and absence of concentration of effect as a whole. All this in a very friendly and respectful manner.

How it will affect the prospect of the play being produced in Warsaw I can not tell. I shouldn't be surprised if it stopped it altogether. I would understand it though I would be very sorry.

Please tell Mr. Winawer that of course that will affect the prospect of his play unfavourably. The Dramatic Society[3] has been considering it for the last three weeks, but there is very little chance of them taking it up now. I regret it very much. I hoped that even a half-success for the Agent would have helped to place the Book of Job.

Please, my dear, drop me a line about things in general. I am sending you, at Karola's request, a copy of *Victory*. Jessie and the boys tenderly embrace both of you.

Ever affectionately yours

Konrad.

---

[1] With the Ryerson Press, Toronto, for *The Rover* (1923), signed on the 7th (Hallowes).
[2] Beginning in French, in English from 'As you will know' to 'Victory'.
[3] I.e., the Stage Society.

To J. Harry Benrimo
Text MS Brown; Unpublished

[letterhead: Oswalds]
9. Nov: 22

My dear Mr Benrimo.

Thank you for your letter and for kind offer of a box. The beastly cough which kept me out of the theatre on Sat^y is most exhausting and will prevent me coming up to town to my great and sincere regret.

I am most grateful to my interpreters for their good feeling towards an author who has failed to give them that success which their loyal exertions, and their devotion to their art, deserved.

As to Yourself dear Mr Benrimo a cordial shake of the hand is but a poor reward for Your belief in the play, for the untiring energy, the thought, the artistic skill and personal effort You have put forth to make the production a success.

Believe me with regards and every good wish
Yours very gratefully
Joseph Conrad

To Eric Pinker
Text MS Berg; Unpublished

[Oswalds]
9. Nov. '22

My dear Eric

Herewith matter for F. U[nwin]'s list – some of it fit, I think, for the jacket if it is not to be of the "picture" kind.[1]

I had a request yesterday from the Evg: Stand^d for a few words which I have phoned them mainly expressing my concern with all the loyal workers connected with the production.[2] Quite discreet.

I thought that a dry refusal would look as though I were disgruntled which is *not* the case; I had also a long wire of sympathy from *The Referee* signed by Robert Donald asking me for some comment or else permission to print a few lines of the text. I gave the permission, as I like R. D. whom I knew during the war-years.[3]

---

[1] Publicity for *The Rover*, which would not appear in Britain for another thirteen months.
[2] 'I think no playwright has ever been executed with such consideration and friendliness, so that I don't even feel guilty. The only painful part of it is the loss of the hard work of everyone concerned being wasted', *Evening Standard*, 8 November 1922, p. 9.
[3] The *Referee*, a Sunday paper specialising in sporting and theatrical news, ran a sympathetic piece about the play's failure on 12 November (p. 3). The writer (probably Donald) cites

To day somebody from the Sunday Express called to know "Why I chose to write melodrama?" Refused to see. It's really too much that after screeching with the rest (the reading of these newspaper-cuttings was exactly like being in a parrot-house) they should want to peck at my eyes.[1]

I am truly sorry for Benrimo who has written me a heart-broken letter, but very nice withal. That is the point on which I do feel a bit sore – all those people! They were not given a chance to find their feet. And they needed it in a play like this – not of the current pattern, with not a single stock-character to lean on. I don't cavil, yet I think that another week's rehearsals may have staved off the smash – tho' it would not have made a success. But it might have made a mark. Poor B is very angry – but I am neither more nor less angry than a traveller who has spent a night in a Spanish inn.[2]

Ever Yours

J. Conrad.

To Thomas J. Wise
Text MS Yale; Wise 48 (in part)

[Oswalds]
[9? November 1922][3]

Dear M[r] Wise

It occurred to me that you may like to have the MS of this unique specimen of J. C. writing his own advertis[e]ment. It shows also how difficult to do I found it.

The other p. is "first copy".

F. U[nwin] asked me if I would not prefer to write a note myself for his descriptive spring list of new books – rather than let it be done by his "publicity man". – And this is the result.

You can always burn it if you consider it unworthy.

Benrimo's complaints about reviewers: 'We kept a record – a very careful record. The representative of the paper which gave us the least considered notice did not arrive till 8.55. Overture at 8 and the curtain at 8.10. Another critic did not arrive till 10.20. Another did not take his seat till after the rise of the curtain ... Others did not come at all.' The article concludes by saying that *The Secret Agent* 'is a work of power and imagination, treating of real human beings whose psychology is acutely understood by the author, and its literary merits are infinitely above the average drama seen in our theatres. It should at least have been heard with close attention and respect.'

[1] A. Beverley Baxter, managing editor of the *Sunday Express*, characterised *The Secret Agent* as 'an actionless and unmoving drama' and printed his review of this and two other plays under the heading 'Three Nights of Horror' (5 November, p. 4; see Hand). On the 12th, the paper quoted Conrad, who repeated the statement he had made to the *Evening Standard* on the 8th.

[2] Where, if we are to trust *Don Quixote* or *The Saragossa Manuscript*, anything may happen.

[3] This note accompanied Conrad's draft of an advertisement for *The Rover*, dated 9 November 1922. See the previous letter to Pinker.

In reference to what Dick told me about me consenting to let a person publish some pamphlets I assure you it is perfectly fantastic. No communication on that or any other matter was made by me to the person in question for months.[1] Lately I sent 2 pamphlets (the receipt of which has not be[en] acknowledged) – that's all.

Regards from us both

Yrs.

J. Conrad

To the Revd Neville Ridgeway

Text TS/MS Private collection; Unpublished

[letterhead: Oswalds]

Nov. 10th. 1922.

Dear Mr Ridgeway.[2]

I am not quite easy in my mind about the suitability of John's glasses. Will you let him go to Maidstone to have his eyes tested again by Dr G. Potts who is a very good man? His address is: – Bower Cottage, Maidstone, and his telephone number 381 Maidstone.

No doubt he will be able to give an appointment on any day you may suggest, so as to interfere as little as possible with John's work for the week.

I thought at first of waiting till the holidays; but in such a delicate matter as eyesight a month may make a difference. I want him made comfortable for work during the holidays. I am making arrangements for his attending a class for conversational French in Canterbury every day. I will make him converse and read aloud with me. I am thinking also of asking Mr Goodburn to give him at least ten hours' work at maths between the 1st and 20th of January.

Arrangements will be made for him to go to France, out of all sound of the English tongue, during the Easter holidays.

I can't tell you how profoundly grateful I am to you and the Headmaster of Tonbridge for suggesting this loophole.

Our love to you both

Always yours

J. Conrad.

---

[1] John Quinn had asked to do so but had been rebuffed in March 1920. Conrad had sent him copies of *The Dover Patrol* and *John Galsworthy* on 27 October 1922.

[2] Having graduated from Oxford, the Revd Neville Vibart Ridgeway (1883–1973) was ordained in 1905. He taught briefly at Elstree and then, from 1906 to 1940, at Tonbridge School, save for an absence from 1917 to 1919 when he was a chaplain in France. During the 1940s, he was an assistant master at Merchant Taylors' School. He lectured at the University of Maryland in the 1960s and was attached to the diocese of Bermuda where he spent his last years.

I am writing to Dr Potts to warn him he may hear from you in the course of next week. Please give John his expenses.

To Walter Tittle
Text MS Texas; Unpublished

[letterhead: Oswalds]

10 Nov '22

Dear Mr Tittle.

This is only to warn you that M^r & Mrs Allan Wade will be travelling with you in the same train on Sunday. My wife has written to them about you, in order to prevent any slight awkwardness when you all discover that you are to pile in together into the same car. There'll be plenty of room.

Looking forward to seeing you

Yrs

J. Conrad.

Wade is connected with the theatre-world tho' not an actor by profession. His wife is french and we think that she is very nice.

To Eric Pinker
Text TS/MS Berg; J-A, 2, 280–1 (in part)[1]

Oswalds

Bishopsbourne

Kent.

Nov. 11th. 1922

My very dear Eric

I had seen very well how much you took to heart the success of the play and all I can say is that you are a good friend to have by one in a tight place. I felt that all the time.

Thanks for the two letters. The one from Bennett coming from a man of distinct achievement in letters and great sanity of mind was a great pleasure to read. It did not cheer me up because I was not cast down, but it has made me happy. Of Mr. Percy Spalding[2] I know only the name but I appreciate immensely this testimony volunteered by an impartial mind and a cultivated intelligence. Since you have sent me the letters with the permission of the writers I feel I ought to drop them a line each, which I intend to do on Monday. I don't do it at once because I have undertaken to write a 1000

---

[1] Jean-Aubry stops with 'the sun comes out'.
[2] See the letter to Frank Swinnerton of [mid-November?].

words article for the Man[chest]^{er} Guardian, at the request of James Bone[1] who is the brother of the "Brassbounder." I have about 400 words more to do and I want to do them today because Tittle (the American official portraitist of the Washington Conference)[2] is coming tomorrow for the day, together with Allan Wade and his missus. I have known A. W. for six or seven years now. Talking to me on that memorable Friday he expressed his conviction that every line of that play was "eminently actable." That was absolutely all he said that evening, during his visit, and that really comforted me very much because it was exactly what I tried to make them.

I assure you, my dear, I would have come up to see the play at least once. The cough alone prevented me. You have seen yourself what it is like. I simply hadn't the pluck to travel with it and go to the theatre with it. I feel better this morning but that may not mean much.

You may take it as a fixed general rule that whatever you do, and especially in respect to the play and the cinema rights in it, will be approved by me. B[enrimo] and Co. really deserve that something should be done for them in that way. This as you say yourself is not a case for us to stand on the letter of the agreement.[3] I have answered Benrimo's last letter (as I told you I would) with renewed messages of thanks to my interpreters. I daresay you are right about the rehearsals. But this short study system has sprung up only lately, since the rent of theatres has gone up in an extravagant manner.

The cinema gleam is the lining to the cloud. I trust you will make hay when the sun comes out. In view of the proportion you mention as what you think of conceding to Benrimo I would of course be satisfied to be credited with 70% of what we may get from the aforesaid lining. Only let me tell you that whatever concession we make it must not encroach upon your proportion of the proceeds which you must have in its entirety (as agreed between us verbally) in matters of this sort. All deductions must come out of my share.

Yes, the pamphlets are printed and disposed of. I am sending you your copies under a separate cover. As you know there is nothing suitable for Beaumont's proposal,[4] which otherwise might have been considered.

Affect^{ly} yours

J Conrad.

---

[1] 'Outside Literature', published on 4 December. James Bone (1872–1962) was the paper's London editor. He was the brother of Muirhead, the artist, and David, sailor and author of *The Brassbounder*.

[2] The Washington Conference on the Limitation of Armament, held from 11 November 1921 to 6 February 1922 in Washington, DC.

[3] Which was to present 'Not less than 50 perf: within 12 months after the first perf: If fail to do so shall pay the author sum equal to royalties of perf: not given' (Hallowes, p. 226).

[4] The Beaumont Press (established 1917), a small press specialising in fine printing, published a limited edition of *One Day More* in January 1919. They had apparently enquired about other possibilities.

This wire arrived Sat ev^g. Will you deal with it for there may be something in it. If not please cable for me *Impossible*. Love to Willard c/o Copley Theatre Boston.[1]

To Arnold Bennett
Text TS/MS UCL Ogden MS 96; J-A, 2, 281–2

[letterhead: Oswalds]
Nov. 11th. 1922.

My dear Arnold Bennett.[2]

Your letter to Eric which he sent on here did not comfort me, for indeed I was not cast down; but coming from such a master (amongst other things) of the absolute "truth of presentation" it has made me happy and – I hope not unduly – proud.[3]

As to the words you have written, well, my dear Bennett, one can't very well thank a man for his native generosity (and yours shines in every page you have written in all these years); one can only be deeply moved by it and thank one's stars for having been led in its way. As I write it strikes me that I have lost count by now of all the occasions you have given me to thank my stars.

Two years ago after finishing the play I felt I had written "actable" lines. More I did not know. You put your finger on the spot in your remarks on the third scene of the 2nd Act. It was re-written three times. I could not argue myself out of the notion that I must let in some outer air into the close atmosphere of the Verloc household; and, also, that unless I showed Mr Vladimir in his "milieu" he would remain too incredible. That notion was honest and perhaps artistic but it was not apparently "du bon théâtre", or was not done in the way it should have been done.

As to the last act, the defect you point out is the outcome of the weakness of my character. I did not like to lose anything capable of visual presentation in my desire to squeeze every ounce of tragedy out of the story of Winnie Verloc. I also reckoned on the assistance of mere curiosity – for after Mr V. is stabbed nobody can tell what will happen next. I simply lost for the moment whatever I may have had of the "stage-sense" in me.

---

[1] Catherine had now begun what was to be a highly successful North American career.

[2] Enoch Arnold Bennett (1867–1931) won widespread recognition as the prolific chronicler of Staffordshire, London, and cosmopolitan life. His Naturalist approach to fiction and financial success made him the butt of Modernist writers such as Virginia Woolf and Ezra Pound, yet his taste in Conrad was impeccable. Bennett was also active as a playwright, and like Conrad was a client of J. B. Pinker.

[3] Bennett told Eric Pinker that *The Secret Agent* was too modern and too good for London: 'It is, artistically, a most disturbing play, for the reason that it shows up, in a way that nothing but a first-rate work of art can do, the superlative fatuity, futility, infantility, and falsity of even the respectable better-than-average English plays that we talk seriously about in this here city' (Hand, p. 9; MS Berg).

Your letter has untied my tongue, and it is a great relief to be telling these things to you – who think this an honest and not altogether inept piece of work – of which I never have spoken freely with anybody.

Always, with the most affectionate regard,

Yours

Joseph Conrad.

To Frank Swinnerton

Text MS Arkansas (damaged); Unpublished

[letterhead: Oswalds]

11. Nov. 22

Dear Mr Spalding.[1]

I was glad to read your letter which E. P[inker] sent on to me. It came with a welcome human note of kindness and intelligence through the impression of a noisy parrot-house which the reading of the newspaper-cuttings left with me.

I appreciate very much your praise as well as your critical remarks which both together form a judgment remarkable in its consistency, and more than flattering to a beginner in the art of the theatre.

What gratifies me most is to feel [. . .] cultivated and impartial mind. And for that, especially, pray accept my sincere thanks.

To Major Gordon Gardiner

Text MS Harvard; Unpublished

[letterhead: Oswalds]

[c. 12 November 1922][2]

My dear Gardiner.

I ought to have thanked you before for your extremely comforting letter. I would not however have you think that I was cast down – in any sense – by my theatrical adventure. Its echoes still ring in the "Great Inane"[3] where the

---

[1] See the letter to Frank Swinnerton of [mid-November?] for the person Conrad meant to address. Percy Spalding (1854–1930) was the senior partner of Chatto & Windus, the publishing house to which Conrad had directed his letter and for which Swinnerton worked as a manuscript reader and editor. Conrad and Swinnerton were not personally acquainted: 'I never saw ... Joseph Conrad ... I had two unsolicited letters from Conrad, first because he had been shown a note of mine by the person to whom it had been addressed, and second because he liked an article I had written': *Swinnerton: An Autobiography* (Garden City, NY: Doubleday, 1936), pp. 112–13.

[2] The next letter's reference to Gardiner and the letters to Bennett and Swinnerton at this juncture suggest the placement.

[3] The early antecedents of this expression for the void are in Latin poetry. In English, it goes back at least as far as John Locke's *An Essay Concerning Human Understanding* (1689): 'the great inane, beyond the confines of the world' (2.15). During the late nineteenth century, the phrase became popular again, for example in Lucas Malet's *The Carissima, A Modern Grotesque* (1896): 'Immediately, Leversedge appeared to be in the very heyday of success ... He had made his

newspaper-press has its flimsy being. A large batch of press-cuttings came every day – and even yesterday. Regrets, explanations, recriminations, critics lecturing each other and so on. I wonder what it would have been if there had not been the motor-show and the Gen. Elec^{on1} to take up space. All this is kindly meant, no doubt, but, with a few exceptions, resembling the sort of noise one hears in a parrot-house any day in the Zoo.

The experience was disagreeable for the moment – a short moment. I am surprised myself at the slight effect it produced on me. The fact is my dear friend that I foresaw what was going to happen; even scandalising and hurting young Pinker by giving 3 performances as the limit. I have in me a "sense of reality" which is not easily deceived. Benrimo was justified in taking the play off in the total absence of all "ahead bookings". That is the only test. What I regret is the chance of making a little money which I wanted badly. But it was like taking a Hamburg Lottery ticket.[2] One is a little ashamed of doing it, one does not believe in it, and yet one is vexed when the virtually "Impossible" fails to happen.

What was warming and comforting in your letter was to see (black on white) that one was so thoroughly understood by a friend like you – capable to see under the imperfect surface the not unworthy intentions and – well – even the ambition of the artist working with his eyes open to all the risks for the sake of being himself come what may. I agree fundamentally with all your remarks and prize immensely your appreciation in all its significance and extent.

Ever my dear Gardiner most affectionately and gratefully Yours

Joseph Conrad.

To Eric Pinker

Text MS Berg; Unpublished

[letterhead: Oswalds]
[12? November 1922][3]

My dear Eric.

A letter went to you yesterday and now I am sending you your copies of pamph's.

By this same opportunity – or envelope – I send you Gordon Gardiner's letter. It is only one from a good few communications I received in the same

---

pile. The elephants and ostriches and South Africans, white or black, had receded into the Great Inane.'

[1] The Sixteenth Annual Motor-Show was held at Olympia and White City from 3 to 11 November. Parliament was dissolved on 26 October, and polling took place on 15 November.

[2] This lottery in what had long been an independent city-state dates back to the late seventeenth century. Its popularity has always depended on the abundance of its prizes and the honesty of its administrators. Buying tickets was theoretically illegal in England, but the Conrads had always been partial to such enterprises.

[3] This letter enquires again about the cable mentioned to Pinker on the 11th.

tone (I don't mean in laudation but in the strongly expressed surprise) so that I myself cannot at last defend myself from wondering whether B[enrimo] has not been a bit "previous".

But even if he has been I understand too well that a man must sometimes cut his losses dead short to be in the least affected. But if, as at least 5 different people let me know (not that I wanted it) the audiences they saw (after Monday) were large and most attentive, and if the one paper (Herald) I think was correct in reporting the houses on Tues: Wed & Thursd: full – well then it is a breath-catching sort of adventure. Something like leaping just short and finding yourself in a ditch. Finis.

Have you answered the cable for me? Or least dealt with it in any way? I enclose also a lecture-agent letter. Will you answer him for me that it is for me physically impossible.

Affct^{ly} Yours

JC

To Violet Tweedale
Text MS Rosenbach; Unpublished

[letterhead: Oswalds]
12. Nov. '22

Dear Mrs Tweedale.[1]

Your charmingly compunctious letter brings home to me the sense of my unworthiness. Pray imagine a defiant sinner; for all this screeching had almost persuaded me that I was a sinner – not exactly of the "habitual" kind, but in this particular instance. Since reading your letter, however, I begin to feel considerably less black than the press has tried to paint me. And to feel less black is very pleasant and comforting.

Thus, you see, besides doing a very gracious thing you have acted charitably, in a spirit worthy of your descent and of that Scots humanity which in gentle and simple alike I have always found so tolerant, so kindly towards strangers, so delicate often under the roughest envelope; and to which I have given my affection years ago.

Pray believe me, always, Your very faithful and obedient Servant

Joseph Conrad

---

[1] Violet Tweedale (née Chambers, 1862–1936), a Scotswoman by birth, and her husband Clarence, whom she married in 1891, were Kentish neighbours of the Conrads. She was a writer of popular novels, such as *The Beautiful Mrs Davenant* (1920), and also wrote ghost stories. She had an interest in psychic phenomena, and Sir Arthur Conan Doyle wrote a preface for her *Phantoms of the Dawn* (1924).

To Richard Curle
Text MS Indiana; Curle 102¹

[Oswalds]
14. Nov. '22

Dearest Richard.

We were pleased to hear from you in that cheerful tone.

Jessie went to bed yesterday. It is not much – an internal chill – getting better to-day; but she will have to be careful as to exerting herself for a few days.

I am afraid next Sat: is an impossible day – or else nothing would please us more. The Camerons will be in and out all that day (both Sir M. and Lady C)² to look for some rooms in Bi[r]ch[in]gton or R[ams]gate³ to transport Miss Kinkaid* to. We promised to help – with the car and they will sleep here. Vexing – but this is the sort of thing one can't put off.

The discussion in the papers goes on the critics telling each other "You have made rather an ass of yourself" "Look at the fine drama that's in it" "What a shame" and things of that sort.

I feel that all this affair is perfectly asinine including B'mos funk. The public was beginning to come after only one blank day.

Really the only person that need not feel an ass is me. I tell you this in all modesty.

We must have you and L. C.⁴ next week if it can be done.

In haste for post

Ever affec^ly Yours

J. C.

Jessie's love

To Eric Pinker
Text MS Berg; Unpublished

[Oswalds]
15.11.22.

My dear Eric.

I send you back the documents. I do believe that of us two it is you who take the failure most to heart. I wrote as I did simply not to appear as if I

---

¹ Curle omits 'including B'mo's funk'.
² Major Sir Maurice Alexander Cameron (1855–1936; knighted 1914) was a former civil servant in the Straits Settlements whom Conrad met through Hugh Clifford in 1903. They became reacquainted in Corsica. Long a widower, he married his second wife, Frances Mary Perkins, in 1920.
³ Seaside resorts on the North Kent coast.
⁴ Lady Clifton: Elizabeth Adeline Mary Bligh (1900–37; 17th Baroness Clifton), author and journalist.

did not take interest from vexation. I had a notion that the houses must have been paper.[1]

Affec[ly] Yours

J. C.

To Frank Swinnerton

Text MS Arkansas; Unpublished

[letterhead: Oswalds]
[mid-November? 1922][2]

My dear Swinnerton.[3]

I dispense with the M[r] and hope to be forgiven.

I hope also you will not cast me out for a hopeless ass.[4] The tenour,[5] the phrasing, the very handwriting seemed to [me] the most unlikely to come from that quarter. But I did not know of your connection with that house.[6] There was the heading – the initials of the senior partner – your F. S. of which the first letter looked to me like a P! What was I to do? – and yet even as I wrote Doubt stood at my elbow.

If you have seen that misdirected communication I hope your fine taste has savoured the cautious tone of my solemn acknowledgments of the incomprehensible favour.

As I must hurry up to catch this post I have only the time to tell you now what I feel without any doubt whatever and that is that the appreciation of a man like you is something eminently worth having; and that I am very grateful to you for allowing Eric to send me what you have been moved to say about my play.

Believe me with great and cordial regard

Yours in Letters

Joseph Conrad

---

[1] I.e., the theatre was packed with people holding complimentary tickets.
[2] A speculative dating, on the assumption that, having heard of the confusion, Swinnerton wrote to Conrad very soon after, prompting a swift reply.
[3] Frank Arthur Swinnerton (1884–1982), novelist, reviewer, publisher's reader for Chatto & Windus, was a chronicler of London literary life, particularly in *The Georgian Literary Scene* (1935), and had a great affection for the Kentish countryside. He reviewed Conrad sympathetically.
[4] See the letter of the 11th, misaddressed to Percy Spalding.
[5] An old-fashioned spelling.   [6] Chatto & Windus.

To F. Tennyson Jesse
Text MS Berg; Unpublished

[letterhead: Oswalds]
16. Nov. '22

Dear Miss Tennyson Jesse

Ever so many thanks for the little book of fancy and charm and sharp irony seasoning the tragic story of poor Loveday, who had no other name.[1] If there was such a thing as a jewel casket in the house I would put this clear sapphire with its decorative rustic setting into it with the other "preciosa". And your story of its reviewing I would (if I had it) put into the safe for historical documents to preserve for the joy of posterity. It's a gem in its way.

But as to the fly-page – that is frankly unsatisfactory. For if it is an attempt at forging a signature then – let me tell you – it is poor, very poor. I think it is only kind to warn you that you will never make your living at it. You had better (precarious as that is) stick to literature and even to the theatre. But if [it] is only that you have a horror of seeing your name on the same page with mine then that, in my opinion, is pushing the love of respectability to the morbid extreme. My own impulses were always and are still respectable. I won't say I haven't betrayed innumerable maidens and murdered innumerable men. But I have never done it publicly. I would have been on the Stock Exchange years ago only I was give to understand that they did not want me there. And as a child I wanted to be a priest on the mere chance of being elected Pope some day. If that is not a respectable ideal – I want to know what is?

Pray consider these things with an open mind and remove the slight from me by coming down here to put your signature on that fly-leaf on the very first opportunity.

Ever Your faithful servant

J. C.

---

[1] Heinemann published *The White Riband; Or, a Young Female's Folly* in 1921. This satirical fable directed against vanity, snobbery, and privilege is the tale of Loveday Strick, an illegitimate orphan, 'who gave her life for a piece of finery'.

To Wilfred G. Partington

Text TS Williams; Partington (in part)

[letterhead: Oswalds]
Nov. 16th. 1922.

Dear M[r] Partington.[1]

I return to you the proof of the article[2] you have been good enough to send to me. As you have done so, making me thus a party to its publication, you can not in fairness object to the marginal notes I have made in the interest of accuracy and truth. Two of them bear on my personal feelings and I don't suppose for a moment that they will be disregarded.[3] As to the others they may or may not be worth attending to.

———

In regard to the production of "The Secret Agent" on the stage, and the reception of the play, all I can say is this: that having never in the course of my writing life answered or taken notice of criticisms, except to acknowledge particular instances of kindness and sympathy in the way it was expressed, I do not intend to begin on this occasion. First of all I think that anything of the kind would be incorrect; and, what is more, it seems to me that one could not enter into any such controversy without dragging to light all the intimacies of creative process which are purely the artist's private concern and, frankly, too delicate to be offered to the world which, very properly, would be indifferent to them. The critics judge the finished product. They write what they think, and I think – what I think. I am not under an obligation, as the critics are, to give publicity to my thoughts. Taken at the lowest it would be idiotic after offering a piece of work to public judgment for one to start arguing about it into the empty air, as it were. This, my dear Mr Partington, is my sense of the situation, and in view of its negative character I can't think that you will find it worth while to give it publicity. Nevertheless I appreciate the

---

[1] Wilfred George Partington (1888–1955) worked in London and Birmingham before joining the *Bombay Gazette* in 1912. After serving in the war, he edited the *Bookman's Journal & Print Collector* until 1931. His books include an anthology in praise of tobacco (1924), works on Sir Walter Scott, and, with Hugh Walpole, *Famous Stories of Five Centuries* (1934). A book collector and bibliographer, he was instrumental in documenting and exposing Thomas J. Wise's forgery of literary rarities. He issued a privately printed edition of Conrad's *Laughing Anne* in 1923.

[2] Thomas Moult's 'Joseph Conrad as Playwright' for *Bookman's Journal & Print Collector*, 7, 15 (December 1922), 65–6, the proofs of which are preserved with the letter. This article and Conrad's comments on it appear in *Documents*, pp. 177–84.

[3] Conrad objected to quoting a letter to Ford (then in Wise's possession), to suggesting that he would 'in future doubtless work more in accord with the playwright's general custom', and to announcing that he would adapt *Almayer's Folly* for the stage.

proposal contained in your letter, which is evidently dictated by a friendly feeling towards the unsuccessful dramatist for which I thank you cordially.

Believe me, with Great regard,

Yours

Joseph Conrad

To Eric Pinker

Text MS Berg; Unpublished

[Oswalds]

16.11.22

My dear Eric.

Many thanks for Your letter advising payment into bank.

I do not want to worry you unduly but please have you thought of those pp of the play on which we made our cuts. And also one or two I sent to Benrimo previously with a request to preserve them carefully. Will you administer a stimulant to B's secretary?

E^r Yrs

J. C.

Enc^d copy of M'r G'an. article.[1] I reserved US. rights. Perhaps you will do something there if the thing itself seems to you worthwhile.

To Edward Garnett

Text MS Free; G. 317–18

[Oswalds]

17.11.'22

Dearest Edward.

I am truly glad to know that your leg is improving.

It was dear of you to write to me again after seeing the play for the second time.

Your letter is very comforting. Of course a failure is disagreeable; but this one has affected me very little. I am myself surprised at my indifference. And to tell you the truth I foresaw what was going to be said – even to the very words and tones. It isn't very strange after all. If you know the vocabulary of a hundred learned parrots you will know what they will screech out at you when you open the door. I knew the vocabulary. It isn't very extensive – you know.

A "man of the theatre", a producer,[2] assured me that every line I wrote was eminently "actable". He also told me that to his mind the play was altogether

---

[1] 'Outside Literature' for the *Manchester Guardian*.
[2] Allan Wade (see the letter to Pinker of the 11th).

mis-cast. All this matters nothing now. I suppose every playwright that ever failed has been told something of the kind. I don't think I will again court failure in that way. It would be an objectless thing to do, for from the nature of things I can not hope to affirm myself in the end. More press cuttings are pouring in. There seems to be a sort of controversy started on the merits and effects of theatrical criticism.

Jessie sends her dear love.

Ever Yours

J. Conrad.

To Evelyn Stainton
Text MS;[1] Unpublished

[letterhead: Oswalds]

17 Nov. '22

My dear Sir.[2]

Before your friendly determination to complete my wife's set I can do nothing but surrender gratefully.

You have of course spoiled your set for a time – or for all time. In any case I assure you that my offer to sign the whole set was perfectly genuine and stands awaiting your pleasure.

With kindest regards to Mrs Stainton and yourself

pray believe me very faithfully yours

Joseph Conrad.

To Eric Pinker
Text TS/MS Berg;[3] Unpublished

Oswalds,

Bishopsbourne,

Kent.

19th. Nov. 1922.

Dearest Eric.

The London office of the M[anchester] G[uardian] have not acknowledged my MS which was dispatched to them on Tuesday.[4] The man in charge is James Bone. As far as I know they intend it for their Annual Literary Supplement and they asked for the copy to be delivered no later than the 20th. As your letter of enquiry has reached me this morning I think, my dear Eric, that the quickest thing would be for you to get on the phone and

---

[1] Formerly in the Sutton collection, current whereabouts unknown.
[2] (Nathaniel) Evelyn William Stainton (born c. 1864) of Barham Court, Kent, and his wife, Nora Mary Dorothea (died 1942), were Kentish acquaintances of the Conrads.
[3] 'Ger[rard] 1279', the telephone number written beneath the date, is not in Conrad's hand.
[4] The 14th.

get the date of publication from them direct. You could also mention that Conrad is surprised that the receipt of his MS has not been acknowledged.

I don't know why Melrose is in such a state of mind. If he had not written to me about the appearance of the book[1] with a sentimental allusion to the labour and sorrow he had in getting it out (and also sent me a copy which I did not want) I would have let the appearance of the thing pass without comment. I would send you a copy of my letter, only I haven't got one. My feelings about this matter were perfectly well known to him. Many years ago at Miss Capes' request I gave most reluctantly, my permission for that sort of Anthology with its absurd title. That publication was suppressed under circumstances which I never investigated, but which apparently arose from M. not obtaining permission from my various publishers. It looked uncommonly like a "try-on". That of course irritated me since it may have been surmised that I was materially interested in this affair; whereas I gave the permission to Miss Capes only with a view of her being remunerated for her work in a decent manner. Had it been a question of profit to myself I would have certainly never have given my consent to a publication of that kind. Well, the little book vanished, and I thought we had done with that spec[ulation] for good. Then about three years ago Miss Capes re-opened the matter, to my great consternation.[2] But Miss C.'s means are very straitened and with this always before my eyes, and having once given permission, I did not like to refuse. (Note that, neither on the previous nor on this occasion or at any time between, had I any direct communication with Melrose on that particular matter). I said that she might go on and I said that, I am afraid, ungraciously. Later, probably incited by M., she wrote to me proposing I should furnish a Preface for the damned thing. I wrote very plainly what I thought of that proposal, which seemed to me, if suggested by M. (and what else could I think) bordering upon impudence and a desire to get something for nothing, regardless of my well-known feelings as to the appearance of that book. I simply did not want to hear anything more about it. Neither did I hear anything of it till the copy was sent to me with Melrose's triumphant letter, utterly uncalled for, with a sort of triumphant note of the see-what-I-have-done-for-you kind. It was about a week ago. Having then my nerves a little jangled I admit that instead of merely letting it pass without any notice I wrote to M., in effect, that: "the receipt of the vol. did not give me any pleasure"; and in view of his boasting of his exertions, as it were in my cause,

---

[1] Melrose had just reprinted Miss Capes's *Wisdom and Beauty from Conrad* (1915).
[2] See the letter to her of 17 November 1920.

I pointed out "that I never thought that taking the plums out of an author's work was any benefit to him; and as to the publicity there may be in it, an advertisement for which people have got to pay six shillings before they can look at it is a fantastic proposition".

Those are the material phrases, with the addition of one other to the effect that: "I hoped that Miss Capes has been properly remunerated for making her excellent selection".

Really my dear, I am sorry you are troubled with this thing but I could not conceal my irritation at the atmosphere of the whole transaction as far as M. is concerned. Knowing my regard for Miss Capes he pushed her on (the poor woman is infatuated with the charm and goodness of Melrose) in order to get something for nothing. Having got it the decent thing was to keep quiet about it, instead of trying to make the thing appear as a friendly service which he is rendering to me as it were. What adds to my annoyance is the intimate conviction that Miss C. will derive precious little benefit after all. As to him getting rid of the book I really don't understand what it may mean. Does it mean anything? He has published the thing. It is out. Is it worth our while, my dear Eric, to trouble what he does or doesn't do with it? I never negotiated with him about the book. It was always a matter between Miss C. and myself, while he stood behind and refrained scrupulously, either through Miss C. or by himself, to hint at any terms; which would have been only a decent thing to have done. And this attitude he has tried to camouflage in sentiment; and what irritated me was that he seemed to think that I would be deceived by it.

The above my dear is confidential as to my comments. As to facts it is just a statement.

Affect^{ly} Yours

J. Conrad.

To Elbridge L. Adams

Text TS Doheny; J-A, 2, 283–5

[letterhead: Oswalds]
Nov. 20th, 1922.

My dear Adams,[1]

It was very pleasant to receive your good letter with its good news about yourselves and the Flower of your house. My love to her and her charming mother.

---

[1] Elbridge L(apham) Adams (1866–1934), was a New York City lawyer whose acquaintance with Conrad began in 1916. During the visit to the USA in 1923, Conrad spent two days at the Adams's country house in the Berkshire Hills of Massachusetts. Adams also admired the works of Bernard Shaw and published his letters to Ellen Terry at his own Fountain Press.

I am extremely pleased to know that you have made the acquaintance of Hugh Walpole and that you are displaying towards him your characteristic kindness. His novel, *The Cathedral*,[1] has been received here with universal applause, as the phrase goes. As a matter of fact I have been very pleased and impressed by the appreciation of this, as they all say here, his biggest effort. I feel rather guilty at not having written yet to him about the book, but he knows me well and we understand each other thoroughly, so I am not afraid of him being angry with me. Pray give him our love when you see him next. He will probably get a letter from me by the next mail.

I have had a letter from Mr. Lee Keedick*[2] on the subject of the lectures of which you speak. I have directed Eric Pinker to write him that it is impossible, for the moment, at any rate. And I don't know that, on consideration, it is a thing ever to be done. In your friendly anxiety, my dear Adams, you forget the deplorable state of my voice, which has been affected by a severe attack of gout in the throat some years ago.[3] Then, apart from the danger of being faced by "extinction" in the middle of a lecture, I will tell you frankly that I am not very anxious to display my accent before a large gathering of people. It might affect them disagreeably, to my disadvantage. And no man ought to be condemned for shrinking from that kind of risk. I will disclose to you that this really is the sorrow of my life; for if it were not for that shrinking I would love nothing better than to give readings from my works, for I know that I can read expressively and dramatically and with good effect if it were not for those obstacles to any sort of public appearance. It costs me something to meet the suggestion of such a warm friend as you are by a negative, and I want you to believe that it is not unreasonable shyness or mere obstinacy, but something in the nature of very reasonable caution that causes me to assume that attitude. I don't mention laziness because that was never my failing, and in this particular instance would have had no chance because, God knows, I want the money. And it is not greed either. You must remember, my dear Adams, that success came to me in the material sense only in 1913, after eighteen years of steady writing.[4] I at once devoted myself to paying off old debts and meeting old obligations. This was of course the first duty. Then came the war, checking the normal development of that material prosperity to a great extent and bringing no end of calls upon my earnings, calls the strength of which one could not resist and indeed never thought of resisting.

---

[1] Published in October, it was dedicated 'To Jessie and Joseph Conrad with much love'.
[2] Lee Kedrick (1880–1959) headed a New York lecture bureau handling famous personalities and writers.
[3] During his breakdown in 1910.
[4] The very lucrative American edition of *Chance* appeared in October 1913, though its financial rewards did not, of course, show up immediately.

And now the years are creeping on me with absolutely nothing laid by. So the position is serious enough to make me turn to any prospect of making a little money in an honest and dignified manner – as long as my faculties last. For my faculties are the only capital I have.

I am telling you these things because I believe in the absolute warmth of the friendship you have for me, which I appreciate immensely and return with an affection and regard not to be measured by the few occasions on which we have met. You are very much in my thoughts always, and I care for your good opinion. I don't want to appear before your eyes as careless or negligent of my opportunities, assuming a pose of disdain or superiority. Neither would I like you to think me unduly timid. But I put it to you that no man can be blamed much by weighing the chances of failure against a possible advantage. I have had an experience of it lately in the non-success of my play which was put on at the Ambassadors Theatre and was withdrawn at the end of a week. It was very disagreeable; though I am neither vexed nor cast down by it, because I am perfectly certain that it had qualities enough to make it not an unworthy performance, and that it deserved a better reception, which, under different circumstances, it might have had. However, this is all over now; and even the disagreeable impression did not last more than a few days.

The idea of your writing an article, of a more intimate character than anything that has been written before on me in America,[1] pleases me vastly; for I do really believe that you understand me better than anybody from your side that I ever met. Under all our outward and obvious differences, such as origins, life history, experiences and activities there exist, I believe, deep similitudes of character and temperament in us two which make me look forward with confidence to anything you may judge proper to write about me. If that thing is to be done (and I don't say it ought not to be), I would much sooner you did it than any man I can call to mind now. Your characteristically considerate offer to send me the paper to look at before publication is not one that can be declined. But as I have said, my dear Adams, I have a perfect confidence in your judgment, in your tact and your sympathy; so, pray, don't do it unless it can be done without putting you or the editor to any inconvenience as to the date or other arrangements connected with the publication. Of course you will see to it that the number of the *Outlook* is mailed to me by the very first packet that sails.

We have just emerged here from the very moderate and indeed remarkably mild turmoil of the General Election. The Labour party has attained

---

[1] 'Joseph Conrad – The Man', *Outlook* (New York), 18 April 1923, 708–12. This article was all the better for Conrad's help with it.

by its numbers to the dignity of being the official Opposition, which, of course, is a very significant fact and not a little interesting. I don't know that the advent of class-parties into politics is abstractly good in itself. Class for me is by definition a hateful thing. The only class really worth consideration is the class of honest and able men to whatever sphere of human activity they may belong – that is, the class of workers throughout the nation. There may be idle men; but such a thing as an idle class is not thinkable; it does not and cannot exist. But if class-parties are to come into being (the very idea seems absurd), well then, I am glad that this one had a considerable success at the elections. It will give Englishmen who call themselves by that name (and amongst whom there is no lack of intelligence, ability and honesty) that experience of the rudiments of statesmanship which will enable them to use their undeniable gifts to the best practical effect. For the same reason I am glad that they have not got the majority. Generally I think the composition of the House is good. The outstanding personalities are not so promising. The majority of them – to be frank about it – are somewhat worn out; therefore one looks forward with great interest to those unknown men yet, who, before long, are bound to emerge.

My wife joins me in warmest wishes for the prosperity of you all, big and little.

Always my dear friend very faithfully yours
Joseph Conrad.

To Richard Curle

Text MS Indiana; Unpublished

[letterhead: Oswalds]
20. Nov. '22

My dear Dick.

Jessie finds it very difficult to word a direct invitation to Lady Clifton. For really if it is to be done "without your knowledge" there is no reason in the world why we should invite her here in that sans façon manner.[1] It isn't that Jessie does not want to see L. C. here; but I can see her difficulty. For even the friendliest feeling on L. C.'s part for us would not give us the right to assume that she would be glad to come on demand as it were. Don't forget that we hardly know her. The diffuculty* is to "motiver" the invitation. And even writing: "Richard Curle is coming – won't you come too, for the day" would be an awkward thing to do.

---

[1] 'Unconventional' or 'improper' manner.

Jessie is writing to you, asking you to convey our invitation if you think it proper to do so. Your conveying the invt^{on} would *not* mean that you suggested it. The thought is our own. Of course you know that we are both anxious to do what you wish.

Ever Yours

J. Conrad.

To Eric Pinker
Text MS Berg; Unpublished

[Oswalds]

[20–22? November 1922][1]

Dear E.

Just heard that the play will be put on in Warsaw about the 20 March.

Winawer who writes tells me he has seen Observer, Times, Dly News and Mchest Guard:. The things which struck him most are what he calls the old-fashioned stage-notions of our critics here.

What I want to ask you especially is this: in case W and Angela are approached by some german theatre for the rights, would you object to me giving my consent (on the basis of a comm[issi]^{on} to those two) to the negotiations. Of course it would be the play *as performed in Poland*.

My view is that we are not likely to be approached by Germany here.

As W is the translator the comm: would have to be at least 20% – it seems to me.

All this "in case". Very likely it will not arise.

Ever Yrs

J. C.

To Agnes Ridgeway
Text MS Leeds; Unpublished

[letterhead: Oswalds]

20. Nov '22

My very dear Agnes

Thanks for Your charming friendly note with its sympathetic appreciation and judicious remarks.

I am sorry You could not stay to the end – and I think it very good of you both to have taken a journey on purpose to see the play. Of course a failure is always disagreeable, but I was neither vexed nor cast down.

---

[1] Conrad's receipt of Winawer's letter on the 20th (to Winawer, 23rd) and acceptance on the 23rd of the proposal mentioned here suggest placement.

The controversy in the press (including the great provincial papers) was considerable, critics reproving other critics for a change. I had two charming letters from Henry Arthur Jones, from actors and actresses such as Esmé Berenger*[1] (for instance) and one from an experienced producer whose opinion is that the play was miscast altogether! I would not go so far as that.

Well, all this is over!

Our dear love to you both and the children.

Always Your affect[te] friend and Servant

Joseph Conrad.

To Richard Curle
Text MS Indiana; Curle 103

[Oswalds]

[21 November 1922][2]

Dearest Dick.

I return the proof[3] in which I pulled together the phrasing here and [there] but have altered nothing.

It arrived this morning and now at 5 pm after meditating over it I came to the conclusion that no addition (of the sort I myself contemplated for a moment) would be fitted in without looking suspect — or at any rate tactless, out of place — if it were to be more than the three lines inserted on the margin of the last page. And even that I leave to your judgment.

If you reject the insertion then take care to transfer the semi-colon after *tales* to after the word *earth* — when the page will read just as correctly as to punct[on] as with the insertion left in.

Jessie is better. She sends her love.

I think next Sat: can be managed.

Ever affec[ly] Yours

J. C.

Yes my dear the pref: as you wish to offer it to me in pamph: form will fetch something which especially now after the play-failure would be of help. I think the Serial[on] of Rover will have to be given up too.

---

[1] Esmé Beringer (1875–1972) enjoyed a long career in modern drama, Shakespeare, and the music hall.

[2] Date from postmark: Curle gives [17 November].

[3] Of Conrad's preface to *Into the East*. Curle brought out the preface as a pamphlet in December, three months prior to its appearance in his book.

To Christopher Sandeman
Text J-A, 2, 285–7

Oswalds.
21 Nov., '22.

Très cher ami,

Your letter reached me this morning, bringing warmth and light to my spirits gloomied by the November sky and chilled by the November temperature of this Blessed Isle. As to the story of this household, it is soon told: "*Nous avons vécu.*"[1] This saying of a Frenchman (Abbé Sieyès, I think) may be supplemented and coloured by the saying of an American (name unknown): "Life is just one damned thing after another."[2] The longer I live the more I feel that the above *est une très belle généralisation*. Children and savages are alone capable sometimes of such illuminative sayings.

Talking of children, I may just as well tell you here that one of mine is now with the Daimler Co. on the administrative-trading side; and the other (John) is still at Tonbridge School, trying to crawl out of the classic side on to the modern (for which he hankers, having certainly a "technical" mind). From them by an easy transition I come to their mother, who was the first to spot your handwriting in the pile of letters and begs to be remembered to you with her kindest regards. She has regained her walking powers almost completely – though of course she cannot expect to ever be as active as the "undamaged" of this world.

I of course have arrived at the time of life when one lets the years come and go without caring much. My latest accomplishment is incipient asthma, which I fancy will develop into something remarkable before long. At present it is almost negligible. Last July between the gasps, coughs and groans I managed to finish a comparatively short novel – which certainly is not remarkable. It will be published next spring. I am at work at another – because I must. But that is nothing new. Several "damned things" of a rather pronounced type happened to me during the last 12 months, and I duly cursed them. But when the "series" stops – where will I be? Not that I care; it's only the stupidity of the whole thing that irritates me.

Oh! yes! my dear Sandeman. The theatrical world! I felt more than ever how much *la vida es sueño* and what *fantoches* we become the moment we step on to the stage.[3] I was there like a man in a dream of a particularly squalid kind,

---

[1] See the letter of 22 September 1922.
[2] Elbert Hubbard (1856–1915), writing in *The Philistine* (1909).
[3] 'Life is a dream': the title of Pedro Calderón de la Barca's play set in Poland (1635). 'Fantoches' are puppets.

my very lines sounding hollow and utterly contemptible. And yet I may say to you without false modesty that the play is certainly not contemptible. I felt disconcerted at every step – and yet amused. And that faculty of detachment saved me from dying of rage on several occasions. However, I went only three times to the theatre. Jessie went to the première and confessed that she had the evening of her life, never having spoken to so many people she didn't know, before.

La chute a été retentissante.[1] Reading the press-cuttings was like being in a parrot-house. Of course a failure is always disagreeable, but that impression wore off at the end of 3 days. The play will be put on in Warsaw about the 23rd March. I had letters expressing surprise, mostly at the old-fashioned notions of the London critics.

Thanks, my dear Sandeman, for your most friendly invitation. I do not think I can get away this winter – or else nothing would give me greater pleasure than to accept your hospitality offered with such charming *camaraderie* in the Palazzo.[2] I am one of those that can only work in their workshop. And this novel[3] *must* be finished by April.

I've lately read nothing but Marcel Proust. But I share your opinion of the historians who have treated of the Second Empire.[4] What an astonishing atmosphere that time had!

Never doubt of our affectionate remembrance.

To Wilfred G. Partington
Text MS Williams; Unpublished

[letterhead: Oswalds]
23 Nov '22

My dear Sir

Thank you very much for your letter. I am glad you agreed with me that one or two words had not a nice ring (the intention of course was quite harmless) and were good enough to delete them.[5]

Believe me always very faithfully

Yours

J. Conrad

---

[1] 'It was a resounding fall.'
[2] El Palacio Sandeman in Jérez de la Frontera, Spain. [3] *Suspense.*
[4] The period of Napoleon III, Emperor of the French from 1852 to 1870.
[5] See the letter to Partington of the 16th.

To Eric Pinker

Text TS Berg;[1] Unpublished

[Oswalds]
23rd. Nov. 1922.

Dearest Eric.

Thanks for your letter in which I note you have no objection to negociations in Germany being undertaken by the Polish translators after the
performance in Poland, which, I see from a Warsaw paper received to-day,
is in the programme for the winter season of the Polish Theatre. The point
may never arise; but it is a fact that the German producers come over to
see new productions in Warsaw, and the thing is not altogether unlikely. It
is possible that the Warsaw production may produce a good effect on some
Boshe*.

In respect of book publication by Methuen:[2] I want to prepare the text
for book-form, taking for basis the privately printed copy; but I have none
by me, neither in type nor in print. Even the "proof pages" which I have
are not complete, since I have sent some of them to Benrimo and he has
not sent them back to me yet, notwithstanding my original request and your
reminders. What do they want to stick to them for? Have they lost them?
I am horribly annoyed at not getting them back. Can't you do something
more to get them back for me? It's a matter of some importance, for the
reason you know.[3]

As to preparing the text for Methuen I can do nothing unless you have a
text you can send me. Perhaps you have a typescript copy? If you haven't,
the only way I can see is that you should send me one of the priv. printed
copies and debit me with £5 for it; which is the price Father paid me
for them. Whatever you can do, my dear Eric, pray do it at once as I
should like to have this business off my chest. In any case when we get
back the pages from Benrimo I would not like to have to send them to the
printers.

+Have you had a request from Miss H[allowes] for a copy of "Rover"
TS? We will send it back to you in two or three days, but I must settle the
book-text of "The Rover" including *all* the corrections.

In this connection: could you cable Doubleday (at cheap rates) to send me
another set of galleys. They have only sent me one set. I should like to have

---

[1] Postscript in Miss Hallowes's hand.
[2] Nothing came of this with Methuen. The play was privately printed by T. Werner Laurie; see
     the letter to Pinker of [26 December].
[3] The price they would fetch from Wise (see the letter to him of the [29th]).

another from which, ultimately, the English Ed. could be set, so as to have the text in both countries exactly alike.

Ever affect^ly Yrs

J. Conrad

+P. S. Typescript just arrived. Many thanks.

To Eric Pinker
Text MS Berg; Unpublished

[Oswalds]
[late November 1922?]¹

My dearest E.

I quite see the inner meaning of your letter and the answer is meant to be shown, if you like. I expect all your support.

My dear, no man having the slightest sense of his value and, I may say, position would allow himself to be dismissed in such airy fashion.

Ever Yrs

JC

Sorry to worry you – but just consider! . . .

To Bruno Winawer
Text TS copy Yale;² J-A, 2, 287–8 (in part);³ *Głos* (114); Najder 282–3

Oswalds,
Bishopsbourne,
Kent.
Nov. 23rd. 1922.

My dear Sir,

Please excuse my writing in English but my hand is painful and I am compelled to dictate – doing so in Polish would mean spelling it out letter by letter.

Thank you very much for your letter received three days ago and for the newspaper page which came by to-day's post.

---

¹ Catalogued as from November. Possibly related to the Melrose affair (see the letter of the 19th)?
² Typing errors not reproduced or signalled. The greeting, first paragraph, farewell, and signature, not in the Yale copy, are from Najder, who reconstructs them from quotations in Polish in a letter from Winawer to Jean-Aubry of 23 October 1924 (Yale).
³ Jean-Aubry omits the first paragraph.

Any failure is disagreeable, but in this case I was not unduly affected and I do not think of it now except as a curious and, to me, novel experience. I will also tell you that I anticipated what has happened, for reasons which were not exclusively connected with the defects and the difficulties of the play itself. The reading of press cuttings gave me the impression as of being [in] a parrot-house. Same tones, same words, same noises. Personally I was treated with great consideration; it is a pity that a little more consideration has not been given to the play. If it had been a criminal act it could not have been more severely condemned. There were however a few notable exceptions from the first, and, afterwards, a certain controversy arose upon the manner in which dramatic critics should exercise their function.[1]

All this is over now. As to the production I will not enter here upon the subject, except from a practical point of view. The play was presented in Three Acts, the Drawing room act becoming the third scene of act second, and the Fourth Act being then called the Third. That certainly gave a better balance to the composition. I made severe cuts (after the first night) in Scene I (with the Professor), and Scene II (Insp. Heat) and, as to that last, I was very glad to do it, because those two parts were so badly cast that the less those people had to do and say the better, I thought, it would be for the play as a whole. As a matter of fact I wanted to make those cuts during the rehearsals but was not allowed then to have my way. But, upon the whole I should like you to understand that I have practically nothing to do with the production. I did not go to the premiere or any other of the ten performances.

I have no remarks or suggestions to offer as to the production in Warsaw. All that will have to come from you; and I am perfectly certain that you will do everything that can be done to make the play acceptable on the stage. But an appeal to a public is like an appeal to the Olympian gods – whose tempers were uncertain and the tastes capricious.

I was very much interested in the theatrical announcements and the program of the Polish Theatre. Your little article on queues as a social function, on the mobility of tastes, on the education of the nouveau riche, and other public matters, made a delightful reading.

Warm regards and a handshake
Jph Conrad.

---

[1] See the letter to Eric Pinker of the 9th and its annotations.

To Aniela Zagórska

Text MS copy Yale;[1] *Ruch*;[2] Najder 284

Oswalds,
24.11.1922.

My dear Aniela,

I am sending you my photograph to use for the translation of *Almayer*. I am very sorry that you had so many difficulties and annoyances, but I am glad that publication has been arranged and that the book will come out soon.

Since our return from London three weeks ago, I have been feeling a bit better. Jessie is well too, but the pain in her legs returns from time to time – I perhaps feel it more than she does. I would be glad if after so many years her sufferings ceased.

The controversy in the papers about the fate of *The Secret Agent* has already ended. We will see what Warsaw has to say. Mr Winawer wrote to me that the première will take place towards the end of March.[3] I regret I have not been able to do anything with his play in London. I'm beginning to lose hope.

My dear! Thank you for Pożoga.[4] C'est très, très bien. It seizes hold of and interests one as much by its subject as by the manner of its writing. And as a documentary it also has great value for the writer knows how to observe and has a soul that is grandement humaine. To say nothing of a style that reflects all her sincerity and courage – toute la tonalité du récit me charme par la note de simple dignité qui est admirablement soutenue.[5]

Jessie embraces you.

Always affectionately yours

Konrad.

---

[1] The copy is a French translation from the Polish. Words underlined in the copy were originally in French and are given here in that language.

[2] Wrongly dating the letter to 1923.

[3] Winawer's translation, *Tajny agent*, opened not in Warsaw but at the Teatr Bagatela, Cracow, on 23 March 1923.

[4] Zofia Kossak-Szczucka's *Pożoga: Wspomnienia z Wolnia 1917–19* (1923 [1922]). It appeared in English in 1935 as *The Blaze: Reminiscences of Volhynia 1917–19*. Volhynia was a part of what is now Ukraine.

[5] 'The whole tonality of the story charms me by its simple dignity, which is admirably sustained'.

To Eric Pinker

Text MS Berg; Unpublished

[Oswalds]
25 Nov. '22

Dearest Eric.

Thanks for the parcel of the two cop. of The Secret Agent: one priv: print: and one of the same kind which was used *for prompt:* copy.

The pages you and I worked at on that memorable Friday are there too. What is wanted are the pages which I sent to B[enrimo] before the dress rehearsal in consequence of his letter asking me to make cuts in the Vlad-Verloc scene. I did ask for them to be preserved; but I would not insist if it were not for the hope of disposing of my *personally* correc^d copy of S. A. (print) to some collector. (those pages are 13 & 14)

It was my intention to come up on Monday to have a talk with you in any case. So I will be with you between 12.30 and one. Should you have a lunch engagement I will stay for the afternoon or the night if necessary. We ought to settle all these matters without delay.

Ever Affect^{ly} Yours

J. Conrad

To Thomas J. Wise

Text MS BL Ashley 2953; Unpublished

[letterhead: Oswalds]
[29 November 1922][1]

Dear Mr. Wise,

The enclosed First Draft is of an article I wrote lately for The M'ster Guardian for the Annual Literary Supplement 1922.[2] It will appear about the 5th Dec.

It is in exchange for the MS of the Preface for R Curle's book, you have been good enough to give him.

I hope Mrs Wise and yourself are well. We here are tolerable . . .

My wife joins me in kindest regards.

Always faithfully yours

Joseph Conrad.

Will you care to have complete set proofs of the play (as priv^{ly} printed) charged with additional corrections for the stage and containing the cuts that were made.[3] I've been asked for it but am giving you the option. (£20?)

---

[1] The date '29.11.22', pencilled on the letter, is presumably from a now lost envelope.
[2] Originally published as 'Notices to Mariners', this tribute to the 'ideal of perfect accuracy' in language appears in *Last Essays* as 'Outside Literature'.
[3] *The Secret Agent: Drama in Four Acts*, printed in November 1921.

To J. C. Squire
Text TS/MS Indiana; Najder (1970); Karl facsimile after 722

[letterhead: Oswalds]
Nov. 30th. 1922.

My dear Mr Squire

I do not like to sign collective tributes, though I admit that Mr Pearsall Smith's text is very nice.[1] I have heard first of Marcel Proust[2] either in 1913 or 1914, and I admire him immensely, but not for reproducing[3] Parisian or French provincial life, which has been done by others admirably before, and, in a certain sense, made Marcel Proust's work understandable to us here; nor yet because he has reproduced for us our own past, for our pasts have been very different and we have felt them differently. I should rather admire him for disclosing to us a past like nobody else's and thus adding something memorable to the general experience of mankind. What compels my admiration for M. Proust's work is that it is great art based on analysis. All his greatness lies in that. Where he is unique and for ever memorable is in this: that he is a prose writer (to put it in French since we all have read him in French) "qui a poussé la force de l'analyse jusqu'au point ou elle devient créatrice".[4] The phrase seems absurd and incredible like the statement of the properties Ether must have to make so much of natural science intelligible in theory. I don't know much about Ether,[5] but my phrase about Proust states an obvious fact. All those beings have been created by the force of analysis, of a most minute, penetrating and, as it were, inspired kind. If his Françoise, for instance, (the devoted servant of a middle-class family, which has been done admirably many times before) doesn't live by the mere force of analysis and of nothing else, then I am willing, in the words of that other creation, Falstaff, "to have my brains taken out and buttered and given to a dog for a New Year's gift".[6]

Mr P. S. speaks of beauty in that work. And it is indubitable. But the marvellous thing is that Proust has attained that beauty "par un procédé

---

[1] (Lloyd) Logan Pearsall Smith (1865–1946), American-born man of letters, resident in London, wrote short fiction, verse, and biographies, and was a noted anthologist. The tribute he was putting together did not appear in the *London Mercury*, which did, however, publish an obituary of Proust.

[2] Who had died on 18 November.

[3] In the TS, the next word is a superfluous 'in', which someone has tried to scratch out.

[4] 'Who has pushed the force of analysis to the point when it becomes creative'. The phrase recurs in the letter to Scott Moncrieff of 17 December.

[5] The supposed medium that conducts electromagnetic radiation across otherwise empty space. The Michelson-Morley experiment of 1887 cast doubt on the existence of this centrepiece of nineteenth-century physics; the theoretical work of Lorentz (published in 1904) and Einstein (1905) finished it off.

[6] *The Merry Wives of Windsor*, 3.5.17–18.

tout-a-fait étranger a toute espèce de poétique. Dans cette prose, si pleine de vie, il n'y a ni rêve, ni émotion, ni ironie, ni chaleur de conviction, ni même un rythme marqué"[1] – to charm our fancy. And yet it lives in its tuneless, almost monstrous, greatness. I don't think there is in the whole creative literature an example of the power of analysis such as this; and I feel pretty safe in saying that there will never be another.

I write you all this because you have, in a manner, asked me what I thought of M. P. You have only yourself to thank for that outbreak. But I know you will bear me no grudge for wasting your time.

That day at the Hudson meeting[2] I could not stay a moment. I was already late for an appointement* of some importance – to me. Otherwise I would not have gone away without exchanging if only a bare greeting with you. I hope I am forgiven.

Believe me always, with cordial regard,

Yours

Joseph Conrad.

I have sent the signed copy of the message to Mr Pearsall Smith direct.

To Eric Pinker
Text MS Berg; Unpublished

[Oswalds]
[1 December? 1922][3]

Dearest Eric –

Let me remind you that Karola$^{x)}$'s quarter begins a month earlier than the regulation time i.e. Nov^{er}.

Will you if not done yet make her the last pay^t under the old scheme.

I am writing to her to say that I am compelled to reduce her all^{ce} to ten pounds p. m. as it was originally. Thus she will have 3 m's notice. (for one year more)

---

[1] 'By a method altogether alien to poetic effect. In that utterly vital prose there is no revery, no emotion, no irony, no warmth of conviction, nor even a marked rhythm'.

[2] A committee had formed to erect a memorial to Hudson in Hyde Park. Garnett and Cunninghame Graham were also members. The result was Jacob Epstein's hotly debated statue of Rima, the heroine of *Green Mansions*.

[3] This letter bears the date '1. Dec.', but the hand is not Conrad's. Although the dating is not firm, the contents make it feasible, and the manner of addressing Eric Pinker rules out an earlier year. The allowance was paid in February, May, August, and November, around the 20th of the month (see the letter to Pinker of 14 May). The traditional quarter days fell one month later, keeping 'regulation time'; thus, if the date is right, Conrad reminds Pinker that, far from coming due three weeks hence, payment was over a week late. Conrad's desire to abandon the 'old scheme' may stem from the financial worries outlined to Curle in the letter of the 8th.

I have not yet heard – and did not expect to – from you. I hope you did not mind me sending my last comm[unicati]on to your private address.

E^r Yrs

J. C

^x)17. Viale Monforte, Milan.

To Thomas J. Wise
Text MS BL Ashley 2953; Unpublished

[Oswalds]
2 Dec '22

Dear Mr Wise.

Thanks for your letter with the cheque for the set of proofs of the play (£20).

You are very prompt; but I am not quite ready to send it to you as there are 2 pp wanting which are in London. I expect them by Mond: morning's post.

I am very sorry to hear you have been suffering from a chest affection* of a gouty nature. Strangely enough I have been worried also in that way. Mine takes the form of a most exhausting cough with, now and then, asthmatic symptoms. I am however getting better, and I do hope that you too will improve soon. As far as I've observed the weather has little or nothing to do with it.

I have had lately a letter from M. Janvier (Baltimore)[1] asking for a MS for a client and hoping that the F[irst] D[raft] of The Rover, is disposable. It gives me particular pleasure to think I[t] has been disposed of to you – for I am sure I could not have found a more appreciative and sympathetic collector-friend, and a finer library for these memorials of my work to rest in.

Always sincerely yours

J. Conrad

To Richard Curle
Text MS Indiana; Curle 104 (in part)[2]

[Oswalds]
Tuesday. [5 December 1922][3]

My dear Dick

I am coming up to-morrow Wed^y by the 9.53 to lunch with Doubleday at 1.30 and will be at the R[oyal] A[utomobile] C[lub] about noon.

It would be nice to get a sight of you, the more so as there are developments of which I could talk to you. When you come here with Lady C[lifton] we won't be able to be alone much.

---

[1] See the letter of [17 December].
[2] Curle omits the second paragraph's second sentence.   [3] Curle supplies the date.

However it is not pressing desperately.
You might phone a message to R. A. C.
Love

                                    Yours

                                                        J. C.

To Richard Curle
Text TS/MS Indiana; Curle 105 (in part)[1]

                                                Oswalds
                                                Bishopsbourne
                                                Dec. 8th. 1922.

My dear Curle.

I am sending you here now the case on which I should like to get the
opinion of your tax recovery people. My case is very simple. All my income
comes out of my inkstand, partly from royalties on old books and serial
rights of new books, advances on royalties which mean large sums paid at
once before the book actually earns them, and suchlike ways which you will
be just as well able to explain as myself. My income, except for a small part of
it, comes to me irregularly, the amounts each year depending for their bulk
on the dates of book-publications or the serial appearances. We may take
the steady part of my income at £2000 or a little less. As you know yourself
there are years in which I publish no book, or a book of very small money
value. In this current year, for instance, I have earned nothing but have been
assessed for tax and super-tax on the rendering of three very good years to
the amount of nearly £1800, which is really killing me completely.

All my monies coming from England and America have been for years
passing through the hands of J. B. Pinker, who always made out my statement
of income, after, I suppose, deducting his commission (a variable quantity).
I think that J. B. has always deducted £200 for my secretary's salary, and
I believe managed some two years ago to make them admit the claim of
about £300 or so for travelling expenses. Eric Pinker told me that the Inland
Revenue people can't make him show them his books; they have only the
firm's undertaking to let them know of all the amounts they pay me, which
are above £20.

This, as far as I know, is the situation. I ask myself whether deduction
is made of the interest I pay on monies which from time to time I owe to
Pinker in the general process of his financing me through any given year. But
I suppose it is so. Certain payments, like, for instance, for [the] Edition de

---

[1] Curle omits the last sentence of the second paragraph, the last paragraph, and the postscript.

Luxe in 1921 which swelled the total receipts to £10,000 and only occurred once, have been treated as income and came into the average for assessing my income for 1922–3. The same thing happened in 1919 when payment of £1200 for Arrow's serial rights was treated as income and swelled the average of the assessment for 1919–20. The "Rescue" which earned nearly £3000 serial rights, did the same for 1920–1.

This is the present situation.

I would also like to know what effect it would produce on my liability to tax and super-tax if I were to live in France; which I would do in any case, for my position is not good and two years economising abroad would put it right. Of course, if my taxation were reduced on account of me taking up my domicile in the South of France somewhere, it would certainly hasten the recovery and permit me to take up my domicile in England again. It is only sheer necessity which drives me to contemplate living abroad for at least nine months in the year for the next two years.

Many thanks in advance for the trouble you are willing to take in this matter.

Jessie understands perfectly the objections to realising the Maupassant book.[1] She sends her love.

Ever Yours

J. Conrad.

I will look out all my Hudson 1st Ed*ons*

To F. N. Doubleday

Text TS/MS Princeton; *Listy* 433–4; Original unpublished

[letterhead: Oswalds]
Dec. 8th. 1922.

Dear Mr Doubleday.

I had an interview yesterday with Mr J. M. Dent. He was very helpful and friendly in his suggestions as to getting over the difficulties raised by Mr Fisher Unwin,[2] whose attitude is more uncompromising, I think, than the circumstances warrant. I don't enter into his motives in assuming it. The question is how to meet it in as firm a manner as possible; and to that end, dear Mr Doubleday, you would render the greatest possible assistance if you could prevail with the proprietors of the Pictorial Review to alter their serial programme in such a way as to permit "The Rover" to be published in book form in the autumn of next year (1923). For, if we can secure this we can

---

[1] See the letter to Curle of the 15th.
[2] About including the Unwin titles in Dent's Uniform Edition.

disregard all the threats which Mr Fisher Unwin has judged it opportune to make, regain our complete liberty of action, secure a complete year's run for "The Rover" in book form, and give "The Suspense" time to get serialised and appear in book form in the autumn of 1924. This is all we want; and I don't think there is anything unreasonable in that. The crux of the whole matter is, however, the serialisation of "The Rover" and I know that your word would have immense weight in changing the proposed dates, if it can be done at all. I am therefore very grateful to you for the offer you have made to me in the matter. I have been very much touched by your readiness in proffering your help in this difficulty. Friendship, indeed, is not a vain word with you and I beg you to believe that it is profoundly appreciated.

It is, of course, no small matter to ask a publication of that standing to alter an arrangements* fixed by a contract, and for an author with whom they have had no dealings before. The only standing I can have is that of one of Mr Doubleday's authors *and* his personal friend. It occurs to me, however, that circumstances may make it impossible. I don't know what is the practice of the Pictorial Review in beginning its serials: whether at the end of a year or at the beginning of a year. Should they begin a serial before the suggestion is put before them with your support, it may not be in their power to entertain it.

By my reckoning of the number of words, "The Rover" could be run through in six months.

There is really much more in it than this. I will tell you *in confidence* that a party of distinguished men and good friends of mine in various countries of Europe are working very earnestly to put my name forward for the Nobel Prize in the near future.[1] Their feeling is that the appearance of a work of mine, like "The Rover", in 1923, would be of great importance for the success of their endeavours.

I lunched with Galsworthy yesterday and told him of your extremely kind invitation to come and stay with you and deliver some lectures of a more or less intimate nature in America. G. thinks very well of the plan. G. has been over more than once and seems to understand the conditions fairly well. He suggested that it would perhaps be just as well for me to land in Halifax and proceed by rail to New York with a view of avoiding excessive publicity. His other suggestion was (and I think G. went considerably into general society on his visits to America) that the type of lecture might be of the kind that is given

[1] The Archives of the Nobel Prize show that Conrad was never officially nominated.

in private houses, as it has been done here for certain personalities from the continent distinguished in music and letters. Quite lately two of my friends: Ravel, the composer,[1] who conducted the performance of one of his works at a private house; and Paul Valery,[2] the premier poet of France (I suppose I may say) who delivered a short lecture in Lady Colefax's[3] house, found it very pleasant and satisfactory. Lady Colefax sent out the invitations and it was understood that the people invited would pay, I believe, a sovereign. I send you here the invitation leaflet to show what I mean. The price mentioned has been erased in my case, as it was not intended that I should pay. My young friend, Powell, the American pianist,[4] used also in the same way to play in private houses, in Lady Beresford's[5] and other drawing-rooms. G. thinks that there are society ladies in America who would lend their houses if properly approached by a person of standing and position; which, if you took charge of me would be indubitably the case.

I mention all this to you because it seems to fall in with your idea of the sort of public that is likely to be appreciative of my work. In this connection I will mention that if you think well of the project of having a limited issue of 250 copies[6] published at the same time as the first edition for the general public, I will be ready of course to number and sign the pages which you would send to me for that purpose.

Pray give my respectful regards to the ladies of the family and my thanks for the charming reception they have been good enough to give me. My cordial greetings to Mr Nelson.

Believe me dear Mr Doubleday with great regard and friendship

Always Yours

Joseph Conrad.

---

[1] Conrad met Maurice Ravel (1875–1937) in July through Jean-Aubry and Madame Alvar.

[2] Paul-Ambroise Valéry (1871–1945). Accompanied by Jean-Aubry, Valéry lunched at Oswalds on Sunday, 5 November: *André Gide – Paul Valéry: Correspondance 1890–1942* (Paris, 1955), pp. 492–3.

[3] Sybil Sophie Julia Colefax (née Halsey, 1874–1950), a London society hostess, mingled in literary and artistic circles.

[4] John Powell (1882–1963), a Virginian, made his professional début in 1907. His own composition for piano and orchestra 'Rhapsodie Nègre', first performed at Carnegie Hall in 1917, was inspired by 'Heart of Darkness' and dedicated to Conrad. Powell's introduction to him came by way of Warrington Dawson.

[5] Mina, Lady Beresford (née Gardner), a society hostess, was the widow of Admiral Charles William de la Poer Beresford (1st Baron Beresford of Metemneh and Curraghmore, 1916). She had died in May.

[6] Of *The Rover*. Doubleday did issue a limited signed de luxe edition of 377 copies but only in November 1923, some months after Conrad's visit to the USA.

To H. M. Tomlinson

Text MS Private collection; Unpublished

[letterhead: Oswalds]

11.12.22.

My dear Tomlinson[1]

Thank you for your sympathy.[2] Of course a failure is always disagreeable, but it would take more than that to cast me down. All this is over and done with.

I had a good many letters, from various people whose judgment ought to count, which gave me some pleasure. And I don't feel guilty in the least.

I hope you are well. My wife joins me in cordial regards.

Yours

J. Conrad

To John Galsworthy

Text MS Forbes; Unpublished

[letterhead: Oswalds]

12.12.22

Dearest Jack.

The pic[re] cards of M'pellier Jessie sent to Ada are not of the sort to give the best idea of that charming town.[3] But it is all we have managed to preserve.

It was very delightful to have a long talk with you. I only hope I have not wearied you with my recital of the Gestae Conradorum.[4] That tribe consists of four individuals (as you know). Well as to one of them: B[orys] arrived here unexpectedly for lunch last Sun[y] and left by the 5.15 train.

Having him here I put the question to him plainly. He met it with a scornful negative and assured me that he even could not remember speaking to the man in question lately. He has taken a prov[ision][al] patent for a glareless headlight of his contriving. What pleases me most is that the device is not mechanical but of a more scientific order depending on the distance of the light from the reflector. My only doubt is whether the diffused beam will

---

[1] Born in Poplar, Henry Major Tomlinson (1873–1958) grew up in London's docklands. In 1904, he left a miserably paid job in a shipping-office to write for the *Morning Leader* (later merged with the *Daily News*). He first made a name for his articles about trawlermen, and a voyage to the Amazon as a ship's purser gave him material for his first book, *The Sea and the Jungle* (1912). He published volumes of essays and memoirs with a Conradian flavour.

[2] Apparently somewhat belated, on *The Secret Agent*.

[3] The Conrads spent part of two winters in Montpellier in 1906 and 1907.

[4] 'The Deeds of the Conrads': a play on *Gesta Romanorum*, the collection of tales so popular in the late Middle Ages. Conrad, a careful Latinist, uses the form *Gestae* by association with the phrase *Res Gestae*.

be strong enough. He assures me it is. The lamp was made in D[aimler]'s workshop and he has tried it, on a friends car, already.

John returned from school about 2 hours ago. For most of that time he has been explain[i]ng to me the principle of a sliding valve of his own design. I must say the drawings (3) of it are beautiful. The storm has blown over at school. He wants to work at Maths during the holiday with the Science Master of King's School.[1] I will have to arrange that for him tomorrow.

The two crocks[2] of the tribe are struggling on and send their love to You both. Let us know how Ada is please.

Ever Yours

J. Conrad.

To Richard Curle
Text MS Indiana; Unpublished

[Oswalds]

Tuesday ev^g [12 December 1922][3]

My dear Dick

I write at once to thank you for your letter. We will set these people in movement in the near future.[4]

Last Sunday Borys arrived her unexpectedly for lunch, and left by the five train on his way to M[anches]'ter. I put the question to him straight. He repelled the statement with scorn tho' I pointed out to him that *this* was the oppor^{ty} to make a clean breast of it. He assured me he had not spoken to that particular man for more than six months and was at a loss as to what could have moved *him* to make such [a] statement.

I take this denial as closing the matter. In fact I must do so. His position is comfortable with the certitude of a raise of salary as soon as he has completed six months service. He is managing per interim the M'chester business. Our love to you.

Yrs

J. C.

---

[1] His regular tutor, Harold Goodburn.
[2] During the 1870s, the old word for a worn-out ewe came to apply to decrepit nags and human beings (*OED*).
[3] The letter of the 12th to Galsworthy gives the date. The designation 'ev[enin]g' suggests that it is the later of the two written on this date.
[4] To resolve Conrad's tax problems, broached in his letter to Curle of the 8th?

To John Drinkwater

Text MS Yale; Unpublished

[letterhead: Oswalds]
13. Dec. 22

Dear Mr Drinkwater

I am sorry that my mistaken assumption should have given you the trouble of seeking for a copy of the ltd edition.[1]

I am delighted to possess it of course tho' of course I ought to feel nothing but remorse. Well the remorse is certainly there; but my strongest feeling is gratitude for your so beautifully perfected kindness.

Pray accept my warmest thanks and believe me with the sincerest regard
Always Yours
Joseph Conrad

Pardon this scrawl. I have a gouty wrist.

To George T. Keating

Text TS Yale; J-A, 2, 288–90

[letterhead: Oswalds]
Dec. 14th. 1922.

My dear Mr Keating

Our warmest and most sincere wishes for health, success, and all that's good for you both and all yours for this festive season and all the years to come. And may they be many!

Thank you for your friendly and interesting letter.[2] How good of you to give me so much of your time and so much of your thought. Your appreciation and your interest in my work are very precious to me. I wish I were a better letter writer, both as to quantity and quality, and then perhaps I could convince you of my gratitude. But when it comes to truth of that sort words fail me as a rule. It's the concoction of artistic lies that is my strong point, as twenty-four volumes of pure fictions testify. However, as you and a few other men I care for, seem to like them I will try to continue for a little while longer on my reprehensible course.

Mencken's[3] vigour is astonishing. It is like an electric current. In all he writes there is a crackle of blue sparks like those one sees in a dynamo

---

[1] See the letter to Drinkwater of 8 November.

[2] Conrad had part of it copied and forwarded to Eric Pinker (TS Berg).

[3] H(enry) L(ouis) Mencken (1880–1956), American journalist, social and literary critic, and magazine editor, was famous for his outspokenness. For Conrad's earlier correspondence with him, see *Letters*, 5, pp. 292–3, and 6, pp. 144–5.

house, amongst revolving masses of metal that give you a sense of enormous hidden power. For that is what he has. Dynamic power. When he takes up a man he snatches him away and fashions him into something that (in my case) he is pleased with – luckily for me, because had I not pleased him he would have torn me limb from limb. Whereas as it is he exalts me almost above the stars.[1] It makes me giddy. But who could quarrel with such generosity, such vibrating sympathy and with a mind so intensely alive. What, however, surprises me is that a personality so genuine in its sensations so independent in judgment, should now and then condescend to mere parrot talk; for his harping on my Sclavonism[2] is only that. I wonder what meaning he attaches to the word. Does he mean by it primitive natures fashioned by [a] byzantine-theological conception of life, with an inclination to perverted mysticism? Then it can not possibly apply to me. Racially I belong to a group which has historically a political past, with a Western Roman culture derived at first from Italy and then from France; and a rather Southern temperament; an outpost of Westernism with a Roman tradition situated between Slavo-Tartar Byzantine barbarism on one side and the German tribes on the other; resisting both influences desperately and still remaining true to itself to this very day. I went out into the world before I was seventeen, to France and England, and in neither country did I feel myself a stranger for a moment: neither as regards ideas, sentiments, or institutions. If he means that I have been influenced by so-called Slavonic literature then he is utterly wrong. I suppose he means Russian; but as a matter of fact I never knew Russian. The few novels I have read I have read in translation. Their mentality and their emotionalism have been always repugnant to me, hereditarily and individually.[3] Apart from Polish my youth has been fed on French and English literature. While I was a boy in a great public school[4] we were steeped in classicism to the lips, and, though our historical studies were naturally tinted with Germanism, I know that all we boys, the six hundred of us, resisted that influence with all our might while accepting the results of German research and thoroughness. And that was only natural. I am a child not of a savage

---

[1] 'Conrad Revisited', *Smart Set*, 69, 4 (December 1922), 141–4, forwarded by Keating. In his letter, Keating had written: 'I know that you don't entirely agree with Mencken's diagnosis of your motives and general psychology.' Conrad wrote in the margin '(I don't)'.

[2] Derived from the archaic form 'sclavonic', used, for example, in Gibbon's *Decline and Fall of the Roman Empire* (1776–88).

[3] He wrote of the 'monstrous stupidity' of Tolstoy's 'Kreutzer Sonata' and the 'fierce mouthings from prehistoric ages' of Dostoevsky, but warmed to Turgenev, with his 'Absolute sanity and the deepest sensibility' (*Letters*, 4, p. 116, 5, p. 70, and 6, p. 78).

[4] Conrad's claim to have attended St Anne's Gymnasium, Cracow, is a vexed one: see Zdzisław Najder, *Joseph Conrad: A Chronicle* (New Brunswick, NJ: Rutgers University Press, pp. 31, 505n).

but of a chivalrous tradition and if my mind took a tinge from anything it was from the French romanticism perhaps. It was fed on ideas, not of revolt but of liberalism of a perfectly disinterested kind, and on severe moral lessons of national misfortune. Of course I broke away early. Excess of individualism perhaps? But that, and other things I have settled a long time ago with my conscience. I admit I was never an average, able boy. As a matter of fact I was not able at all. In whatever I have achieved afterwards I have simply followed my instinct: the voice from outside. Mencken might have given me the credit of being just an individual somewhat out of the common, instead of ramming me into a category, which proceeding, anyhow, is an exploded superstition.

This outburst is provoked of course by dear Mencken's amazing article about me, so many-sided, so brilliant and so warm-hearted. For that man of a really ruthless mind, pitiless to all shams and common formulas, has a great generosity. My debt of gratitude to him has been growing for years, and I am glad I have lived long enough to read the latest contribution. It's enough to scare anyone into the most self-searching mood. It is difficult to believe that one has deserved all that. So that is how I appear to [H.] L. Mencken! Well, so be it.

What more could anyone expect!

I was very interested in your account of dear Hugh's activities on the lecturing platform.[1] I am delighted to hear you like him – that all America likes him! Here his latest book had a great success of a serious, worth-having, kind. Our household misses him immensely, but I most of all. F. N. Doubleday has just left for America. He is, as you know, my excellent publisher, but what's more he is a good friend to have.

Certainly I have a great opinion of Maupassant. I formed a guess from something in your letter that you are sending me a splendidly bound book.[2] I have, I believe, begged you before not to do anything of the kind again. I am a considerably older man than you, and you ought to treat my wishes with deference. But much you care! I suppose I will have to forgive you once more.

---

[1] Keating had heard Walpole lecture on the art of Joseph Conrad. Walpole praised 'The Secret Sharer' as Conrad's greatest story, and *Nostromo* as the most satisfying novel, but he urged his audience to read everything Conrad had written.

[2] Continuing his report on the Walpole lecture, Keating had written: 'he compared your short stories, and entirely favorably, with Guy de Maupassant, and as I understand it you also are an admirer of the French master. I mention this because you may expect to hear from Guy some time.'

I am glad you liked the pamphlets.[1] But you must understand that this is
no present. You have a right to them and to a copy of any others I may yet
publish at some future time. That's how I look at it. A moral right – a friends
right.

My affectionate regards to Mrs Keating and love to the children.

Always affectionately Yours

Joseph Conrad

To Eric Pinker
Text TS/MS Berg; Unpublished

[Oswalds]
Dec. 14th. 1922.

Dearest Eric.

Yesterday I dispatched to you the last[2] batch of corrected TS of "The
Suspense" (by the way we had better consider this title as provisional too.
Something better may occur to me as I go on.) I am sorry I could not let
Doubleday have it before he left, but as it is it will catch him up before he
has been a week at home.

I enclose here the last letter I had from him[3] in answer to a rather long
communication I sent him after my last visit to town. It dealt with the situation
created by Fisher Unwin's attitude. I think that FND wants really to be
helpful, partly from a naturally kindly disposition and partly (I like to think)
because I may be worth helping from a business point of view. As I know
that you must have met Nelson[4] since I saw you last I reckon you know more
about their ideas than I do.

Thank you for warning me of Unwin's intention to deliver an attack on
me. Nothing has happened yet. As any communication of that sort would
have to be answered – unless I take up the attitude of having nothing to do
with him personally, which perhaps would not be wise – I would be glad if
you gave me a hint of the tone you would prefer I should take. I may simply
refer him back to you. Or send a bare non possumus[5] to whatever demands
he puts forward. Or make a conciliatory appeal to his better feelings. Or
write simply in such a way as to gain time till we hear from FND; and that

---

[1] See the letter of 28 October.
[2] Conrad generally uses 'last' to mean 'latest'.
[3] Doubleday promised to ask the *Pictorial Review* about serialising *The Rover* and discussed Conrad's proposed visit to the USA in the spring (11 December, TS Berg).
[4] Doubleday.   [5] 'We can't'.

won't be an easy thing to do. I hope to goodness he won't make a move till after Xmas.

I am sending you by the same post the prepared text of the book-form of the Play. I don't suppose you have any objection to deal with the Nonesuch Press, for, after all, the proposal is not bad and the need for cash is great.[1] My only doubt is whether we are engaged with Methuen deep enough to make the transaction difficult. If we are, couldn't we, perhaps offer some share of the plunder to Methuen as consideration for delaying the publication. The Nonesuch Press offers in effect to pay us £150 for 500 copies. Suppose we offer Meth: 20%. – or, roughly speaking, £31 – it would be not a bad sum to pocket simply for sitting still for a year. Of course you will decide.

I have sent a case for opinion to the Income Tax Claims Ltd. Carlton House, Regent St. They answer that, of course, the three year average assessment is in force, though a Commission has recommended its removal, but that they think it is quite possible that I may be over-assessed; though they can only ascertain that by examination of the accounts. They charge a commission of $12\frac{1}{2}$% on all the money they recover or save. Certainly the Revenue gets money out of tax-payers in many ways which people who know absolutely every turn can frustrate. It may be worth while? As to residence in France or the Channel Islands, their opinion is that taxation on American income would be altogether avoided if the money were sent direct there. In case of it passing through the hands of an agent in England they are not positive. It would be a moot point.

A letter in connection with my article for the Manchester Guardian I had from a man, makes me think that the article has already appeared. I have had no copy sent to me of the Annual Literary Supplement for which it was written, nor any communication from the M. G. whatever. Perhaps they have sent the cheque to you. The agreed amount was £10.10.0. If, or when, they do, please dear E. send me the net proceeds. If *I* get it I will religiously send you one guinea, and freeze to the rest, because this is a job I have done "in my own time". But what you manage to get from America must go to our general account.

Mencken has started writing about me again. Perhaps you may like to see his latest outburst. Once he starts he carries on like an escaped lunatic; but one can't really quarrel with a fellow who is boosting one with such enthusiasm. I send you also a report from one of my American correspondents about Hugh

---

[1] The Nonesuch Press, renowned for the beauty of its publications, offered to publish the dramatised *The Secret Agent* at a royalty of 25 per cent on 500 copies (selling at about 25s.) and with no claims on copyright (letter to Conrad of 6 December, Leeds).

Walpole's activities as far as they touch my work.[1] I don't know whether you will care to read these things but in any case you need not send them back. The same applies to Doubleday's letter which I intend to answer in time for the Saturday packet.

I can't say that I am facing this Xmas-tide cheerfully. But I am not depressed. Health, success, peace and all that's good to you both and all yours. Give your wife our love.

Affect^{ly} Yours

Joseph Conrad.

To Elbridge L. Adams
Text TS/MS Private collection; Unpublished

[letterhead: Oswalds]
Dec. 15th. 1922.

My dear Adams.

This is to send you our affectionate wishes for health, prosperity and all possible happiness for all of you on the occasion of this festive season. I am obliged to dictate because my wrist won't let me write more than two or three lines without acute pain.

It is very nice to hear that Mrs Adams and yourself are coming over next year. You will not find us in this house as I have given notice which expires next September, only, it is true; but if no tenant turns up before that date we will shut up the establishment about May and lead for a time a rather homeless life. However you will be kept informed of our movements and plans which so far are not definite yet.

I will tell you in confidence, that my health and the state of my work permitting, I may come over to your side at the beginning of May on the invitation of F. N. Doubleday, who offered me hospitality for about three weeks. As a consequence of your letter of Nov. 4th, F. N. D., Pinker and I have been discussing the possibility of delivering some semi-private lectures during that time. My health and perhaps also my temperament could not stand a regular course under the direction of a manager in the usual way. Your opinion, however, that a visit from me would produce a good effect on the sales of my books, had enough weight with me to induce me to consider the above plan. I don't go into details but you can see from what I have said what it may be like. What do you think of it? I still have my doubts. Pray keep this news to yourself, in which word I include Mrs Adams, of course. Meantime do please tell me what are the two subjects that you think

---

[1] The passages copied from Keating's letter.

would furnish good material for lectures and which are, as you say, only an expansion of ideas from my books.

Jessie, of course, would not come with me (if I come at all), but would take temporary quarters somewhere, probably near the sea, to await my return. After that we contemplate the possibility of going to live in France, just across the Channel, so as not to be too far away from our schoolboy John. What with the circumstances of the war, the enormous taxation, and two years in which I have done no productive work, my affairs are not in a satisfactory condition. Material success, as you know, came to me late in life and the outbreak of the war interfered with its normal development. Neither Jessie nor I are really very good economists, though neither of us has expensive tastes. Anyway, that is the state of affairs. But a couple of years of strict economy will put the situation right, I have no doubt. Since you saw me last here I finished a novel, with the serialisation of which there is some trouble, I am sorry to say; and I have another half written and I must devote all my energy to finishing it by April. All this is for your ear only.

Since last Augst my health has taken a turn for the better. How long it will last I can't say. Jessie joins me in best love to your wife and yourself.

Always affct^{ly} yrs

J Conrad.

To Richard Curle
Text MS Indiana; Curle 106 (in part)[1]

[Oswalds]
15. Dec. 1922.

Dearest Dick.

Would you mind (since selling it is out of question) sending me the Bel-Ami book.[2] I have an idea that it will serve for a present – in these hard days.

I am (so is Jessie and John) looking forward to your arrival – in just a week's time.[3]

---

[1] Curle omits the first paragraph.
[2] Maupassant's novel, published in 1885. Conrad must have tried to dispose of the inscribed copy that he eventually gave to Ada Galsworthy; see John Galsworthy to Conrad, 8 April 1923, in Stape (2000).
[3] Curle was to spend Christmas with the Conrads.

God knows – I would like to know that your trouble, whatever it is, is off your shoulders – partly or entirely.

Our love to you

Yours

J Conrad.

To F. N. Doubleday
Text TS Princeton; Unpublished

[letterhead: Oswalds]
Dec. 15th. 1922.

Dear Mr Doubleday.

I must thank you for your extremely kind and friendly letter which I had no time to acknowledge before your departure.[1]

I am well aware that the situation submitted for your advice and help presents a special difficulty and is not at all hopeful to deal with. My gratitude is acquired to you, apart from any possible success, for the interest you have displayed and the assistance you have been good enough to offer, whatever may be the outcome of it.

I have managed to put into presentable shape something like forty-five thou. words of the novel,[2] in time for it to catch the ship by which I hope this letter will cross over. It remains for me now to devote all my time and efforts to finishing that work by the end of March next, which, in truth, is not a very long time. Days have a trick of slipping by stealthily and I have no doubt I will be feeling most of the time like a man swimming against the tide with his eyes fixed on a landmark and noting the distance anxiously at every dozen strokes.

My wife joins me in warmest wishes of every possible happiness for Mrs Doubleday, Yourself and all the family.

Believe me very sincerely Yours

Joseph Conrad.

---

[1] Doubleday wrote on the 11th from Heinemann's office (TS Berg). Conrad's comments in the margin were made for Eric Pinker's benefit. Concerning Doubleday's assurance that he would encourage the editor of the *Pictorial Review*, a friend of his, to serialise *The Rover*, Conrad wrote: 'I don't know how you may view this line. Or whether it is to be taken seriously. Anyway it comes friendly.' Doubleday advised visiting the USA in spring, before the hot weather, and added that he would 'consider Conrad's suggestions carefully'. Conrad explained that 'this relates to the visit and my sugges[ti]on to lecture in drawing rooms'.

[2] A sample of *Suspense* to circulate for sale as a serial.

To Meredith Janvier

Text MS Yale; Unpublished

[letterhead: Oswalds]
18[17]. Dec. 22[1]

Dear M[r] Janvier.[2]

I regret very much to say that I have nothing for your client; neither am I in a position to promise you anything of importance for the future. You will understand that having had the placing of my MS assured it had never occurred to me to keep anything back in view of a possible offer. I am very sorry to disappoint your client's expectations and can only thank you for your friendly letter.

With kind regards and best wishes I am

Yours faithfully

Joseph Conrad.

H. L. Mencken has been splendid for years! Such sympathy and recognition are a great reward for one's work – which has not been always easy to do. J. C.

To Eric Pinker

Text TS Berg; Unpublished

[Oswalds]
Dec. 17th. 1922.

My dear Eric.

Your suggestion as to meeting an eventual Unwin's letter to me, falls in with my inclination perfectly. I agree that for me to reply to his letter on its points would be disastrous.

I agree with you about the effusiveness of the Other Side, and I share your view of Doubleday's attitude. It is certainly helpful in intention; and I really appreciate it very much, and also the goodwill of all the others of whom a good many write to me. One's *real* merit is a matter for posterity to find out.

I note what you say about the play, of which the text will be ready in a day or two. I am going to work on it all day to-day.

---

[1] Date from postmark.
[2] Virginia-born Meredith Janvier (1872–1936), after graduating in law from the University of Maryland, practised in a Baltimore firm for thirteen years, whereupon he abandoned law to become a photographer. He was also an amateur strongman. Some twenty years later he again changed professions, becoming a manuscript and rare-book dealer. A contributor to the *Baltimore Evening Sun*, he published two collections of essays, *Baltimore in the Eighties and Nineties* (1933) and the posthumous *Baltimore Yesterdays* (1937), the latter with a preface by H. L. Mencken, with whom he was friendly.

Pray, my dear Eric, don't think yourself bound to tell me things. Of course I am glad always to hear what you have to say, when you feel like saying it. But no silence on your part will induce me to think that you go to your office only to sleep there.

I note all you say about the Tax question.

Ever affectionately yours

J. Conrad.

To C. K. Scott Moncrieff

Text J-A, 2, 290–2;[1] Scott Moncrieff 126–8 (in part)

Oswalds.

Dec. 17th., 1922.

My dear Moncrieff,[2]

I forgive you your "horrible" letter. (You will notice how characteristic of Conrad is this proceeding of answering letters by the end. That is the fault the critics found with my novels. They called it "indirect method." Funny lot, the critics.)

I am brilliant this morning. Some day I will begin a novel like this – with a word in quotes and then a long parenthesis.

The lack of response from the public does not surprise me. And I don't think it surprises very much Messrs. Chatto & Windus.[3] The more honour to them in risking that shot for which no great prize can be obtained. As to you, it is clear that you have done this for love – and there is no more to be said.

In the volumes[4] you sent me I was much more interested and fascinated by your rendering than by Proust's creation. One has revealed to me something and there is no revelation in the other. I am speaking now of the sheer *maîtrise de langue*; I mean how far it can be pushed – in your case of two languages – by a supreme faculty akin to genius. For to think that such a result could be obtained by mere study and industry would be too depressing. And that is the revelation. As far as the *maîtrise de langue* is concerned there is no revelation in Proust.

Of course this is for you. It isn't a statement for a propaganda booklet.

---

[1] Text from Jean-Aubry.

[2] Charles Kenneth Scott Moncrieff (1889–1930), authorised translator of Marcel Proust's *A la recherche du temps perdu* and of Luigi Pirandello, translated Stendhal as well as works from Latin, Old English, and Old French. An employee of *The Times*, he apparently came to know Conrad through Lord Northcliffe. Conrad contributed to his *Marcel Proust, An English Tribute* (1923).

[3] The publishers of Scott Moncrieff's Proust translations.

[4] His two-volume translation of *Du côté de chez Swann* as *Swann's Way* appeared in September.

Now as to Marcel Proust, *créateur*, I don't think he has been written about much in English, and what I have seen of it was rather superficial. I have seen him praised for his "wonderful" pictures of Paris life and provincial life. But that has been done admirably before, for us, either in love, or in hatred, or in mere irony. One critic goes so far as to say that P.'s great art reaches the universal and that in depicting his own past he reproduces for us the general experience of mankind. But I doubt it. I admire him rather for disclosing a past like nobody else's, for enlarging, as it were, the general experience of mankind by bringing to it something that has not been recorded before. However, all that is not of much importance. The important thing is that whereas before we had analysis allied to creative art, great in poetic conception, in observation, or in style, his is a creative art absolutely based on analysis. It is really more than that. He is a writer who has pushed analysis to the point when it became creative. All that crowd of personages in their infinite variety through all the gradations of the social scale are made to stand up, to live, and are rendered visible to us by the force of analysis alone. I don't say P. has got no gift of description or characterization; but to take an example from each end of the scale: Françoise, the devoted servant, and le baron de Charlus – a consummate portrait – how many descriptive lines have they got to themselves in the whole body of that immense work? Perhaps, counting the lines, half a page each. And yet no intelligent person can doubt for a moment their plastic and coloured existence. One would think that method (and P. has no other, because his method is the expression of his temperament) may be pushed too far, but as a matter of fact it is never wearisome. There may be here and there among those thousands of pages a paragraph that one might think over subtle, a bit of analysis pushed so far as to vanish into nothingness. But those are very few, and all minor, instances. The intense interest never flags because one has got the feeling that the last word is being said upon a subject much studied, much written about and of undying interest – the last word of its time. Those that have found beauty in Proust's work are perfectly right. It is there. What amazes one is its inexplicable character. In that prose so full of life there is no reverie, no emotion, no marked irony, no warmth of conviction, not even a marked rhythm to charm our fancy. It appeals to our sense of wonder and gains our assent by its veiled greatness. I don't think there ever has been in the whole of literature such an example of the power of analysis and I feel pretty safe in saying that there will never be another.

This is more or less what I think, or imagine that I think. It is really not half of what I imagine I think. If it is any good to you, you may alter, cut down, expand, twist, turn over and do anything you like with the above lines to make them suitable.[1] It's indubitable that you know much more about Proust than I do, so please strike out (as a friendly service to me) whatever may appear to you absurd in this thing without a name. I mean it!

I hope your health is improving. Are you still on the *Times* then? Is it a great tie? Could you find a day to run down here – for the night if possible? Soon, I mean. My wife sends her kind regards.

Always, my dear Moncrieff, cordially yours

To Walter Tittle
Text TS Texas; Unpublished

[letterhead: Oswalds]
Dec. 19th. 1922.

My dear Tittle.

I am laid up and I must dictate my thanks for the prints which arrived to-day. My wife is going to write to you, I believe, on her own account. The more I look at the portrait the more I like it. Of course the print has not got something that is in the original drawing, but it is a great pleasure to have them.

I certainly do wish the portrait to be published with the uniform edition – that is if Dent does mean to include any portrait at all. I will drop him a line to tell him that you will call on him before Friday.

I hope, my dear Tittle, you will send me a line on your safe arrival home, and that before long we shall see each other again. Bon voyage, and my best wishes for your health and continued happiness in the successful exercise of your art and in the prosperity and good health of all who are dear to you.

Believe me always Your sincere friend
Joseph Conrad

To G. Jean-Aubry
Text MS Yale; *L.fr.* 180

[letterhead: Oswalds]
20 Dec. '22.

Très cher Jean.

Je ne peux pas tro[u]ver l'addresse de vos parents. J'addresse ceci a la N. R. F[2] dans l'espoir qu'ils pourront vous trouver.

---

[1] For his *Marcel Proust, An English Tribute* (1923).
[2] I.e., the Nouvelle Revue Française, the Parisian publishing house associated with Gide and his circle, rather than the magazine.

Mille fois merci pour Votre Lafargue*.[1] Votre introduction est on ne peut plus intéréssante – matière et ton. C'est très, très bien. Le texte de Votre auteur e[s]t curieux. On en sent le charme a travers les faits.

Exprimez je Vous prie mes sentiments les plus amicaux a M & Mme Aubry avec mes meilleurs souhaits de la Nouvelle Année.

Venez nous voir aussitôt que possible après Vtre retour.

Je Vous embrasse bien fort. All luck be with you. Jessie sends you her love and best wishes for all.

Ever Yours

J. Conrad

C[arte] Postale reçue. Merci.

Translation

My very dear Jean.

I can't find your parents' address. I am sending this to the NRF in the hope that they will trace you.

Many thanks for your Laforgue. Your introduction couldn't be more interesting as regards both matter and tone. It is very, very well done. Your author's text is odd. Its charm is felt through the facts.

Pray give my most friendly regards to Monsieur and Madame Aubry along with my best wishes for the New Year.

Please come to see us as soon as possible after you return.

I embrace you heartily. All luck be with you. Jessie sends you her love and best wishes for all.

Ever Yours

J. Conrad

Postcard received. Thanks.

To Eric Pinker
Text TS Berg; Unpublished

[Oswalds]
Dec. 20th. 1922.

Dearest Eric.

Of course I expect to hear from you by to-morrow morning's post, but I can not refrain from enlarging a little on my telegram.[2]

---

[1] Jean-Aubry's introductions to Jules Laforgue's *Berlin, la cour et la ville* and *Poésies complètes* were both published in 1922.
[2] Sent from Bridge that morning (Berg).

I am, of course, anxious to sign such an excellent agreement, but I want to call your attention to that aspect, of the case. F. N. D. is being made use of at present and may be made use of in the future; and he certainly loves Limited Editions and has been talking to me very much about them, in relation of course to the next two novels. He is not a bad fellow; and I should think that by giving him notice of the thing[1] it would avoid giving him offence. You know how sentimentally touchy those people are.

Always affectionately Yours
J. Conrad.

P. S. I am only waiting for your opinion to sign, naturally, and the text of the play is practically ready and will be sent on to you before New Year's Day, which will be quite early enough.

To Eric Pinker
Text MS Berg; Unpublished

[letterhead: Oswalds]
25.12.22.

Dear Eric

Thanks for MS of Suspense received 2 days ago.

I wrote to Dent telling him he has every right to include the prefaces in the uniform edition. The line in H[einemann]'s advert[*] is vague. No subscriber will have any ground of complaint.

I hope you all had a good time. I had my regulation winter fit of gout (hand) but am almost wholly recovered.

You'll hear from me again soon.

Always affect[ly] Yrs
J Conrad.

To John Everett
Text MS Private collection; Unpublished

[letterhead: Oswalds]
26.12.22

Dear M[r] Everett.

Thanks for the photographs, the letter accompanying them[2] and for your good wishes with* I warmly reciprocate.

---

[1] The script of *The Secret Agent* in the proposed Nonesuch edition of 500 copies.
[2] Of the 20th (Stape and Knowles, pp. 196–7).

I am sending the set to Pinker today by registered post together with your letter. You may rest assured that both he and I feel about the matter exactly as You do.[1] The thing must be settled as soon as possible; and every effort will be made in that direction.

Not having heard for a long time as to the state the negociations are in I can not tell you more here. I have no doubt however that You will hear from Eric Pinker before long and I hope that it will be something definite at last.

Believe me very sincerely Yours

Joseph Conrad.

To Eric Pinker

Text MS Berg; Unpublished

[letterhead: Oswalds]
[26 December 1922][2]

Dearest Eric

I enclose here a letter from Everett whom I have answered in a soothing mood; assuring him that he will hear from You before long, and that we both have the affair of the ills[d] edition of the M of the S at heart as much as himself.

The other letter is from W. Laurie[3] whom I do not want to get into correspondence with. Still I have answered, and I enclose my answer in an open envelope for you to see and send on. Unless you would prefer to answer for me in that sense.

I am sorry to say I have been laid up but I am now better. You will have the text of the play on Monday.

Affect[ly] Yours

J Conrad.

Have I acknowledged receipt of MS of *Suspense* safely received?

To Sir Sidney Colvin

Text MS Private collection; Unpublished

[letterhead: Oswalds]
28.12.22.

My dear Colvin.

I was laid up and unable to write when your dear letter arrived. Thank you my dear friend for your warm appreciation of *Chance*. It has made me

---

[1] Everett wanted Heinemann's to make up their minds about publishing an edition of *The Mirror of the Sea* illustrated with his pictures: 'I cant either reproduce them or exhibit them. I cant afford to sit on them much longer' (*ibid.*).

[2] The previous letter and the note of the 25th fix the date.

[3] T(homas) Werner Laurie (1866–1944) was interested in publishing the dramatised *Secret Agent*. He had worked for T. Unwin Fisher before establishing his own publishing house in 1904.

happy to hear that the book (which seems so far away) stood re-reading so well.[1] Your and Your dear Wife's friendship and sympathy are most precious to me.

I won't be able to come up to town for some time yet, I fear. I feel rather shaken. Of course my first visit will be for you.

I kiss dear Lady Colvin's hands and commend myself to her memory.

Ever Yours

Joseph Conrad

To André Gide
Text MS Doucet; Vidan (1970–1)

[letterhead: Oswalds]
28.12.22

Mon cher Gide.

Je Vous envois nos meilleurs souhaits de la Nouvelle année a Cuverville ou j'éspere ils Vous trouveront "en residence" – comme on dit.

Je sais que, comme correspondant, je suis un être méprisable et même indigne de vivre. Tout de même je crois que Vous ne jetterez pas ceci au feu sans le lire. Ce n'est pas parce que j'ai des choses intéressantes a Vous dire mais parce que je sais que Vous êtes un homme charitable.

Les exemplaires des traductions que j'ai reçu cette année-ci m'ont fait le plus grand plaisir. Et c'est le seul plaisir de ce genre que j'ai eu; car je n'ai rien publié en 1922. J'ai mal travaillé – ou, plutôt, peu travaillé en 21 et 22. J'ai tout de même fini en août un roman "*The Rover*". Je crois qu'il faudra traduire cela par "*Le Forban*".[2] Sujet français – côte de Med'née. Pas très long; a peu près comme l'*Agent Secret*. Epoque 1799–1804. J'ai l'idée que ça pourra Vous plaire. Je ne sais pas quand ça paraîtra en volume. Cela depend des arrangement que l'on pourra faire aux Etats Unis pour la "Serial publication" – une affaire de deux milles livres que je ne peux pas sacrifier a mon désir de paraitre en vol: le plus tôt possible.

J'ai eu dernièrement le très grand plaisir de faire la connaissance de Ravel et de Paul Valery.[3] Ils ont été charmants tous les deux pour moi. Je me suis pris de réelle affection a première vue pour Valery. Je ne peu pas Vous en parler longuement car j'ai mal au poignet comme le prouve cet affreux gribouillage. L'année 1922 sera memorable pour moi par le jour noir de ma

---

[1] Colvin had reviewed it (*Observer*, 18 January 1914, p. 5).
[2] Jean-Aubry's translation appeared in 1928 as *Le Frère-de-la-côte*.
[3] In July and early November, respectively.

pièce. La-dessus j'ai eu un accès de rage qui a duré 24 heures, pas plus. C'est drôle, le theatre vue de près.

Voilà mon cher Gide le bilan de l'année passée. Comme Vous voyez cela n'est pas fameux. Je suis en train de travailler a un roman dont la moitié a peu près est faite. Je Vous embrasse bien affectueusement

Tout à Vous

Joseph Conrad.

J'ouvre l'enveloppe pour Vous dire que Votre lettre[1] vient d'arriver. Merci mon très cher. Croyez en mon affection et a ma reconnaissance pour l'amitié que Vous me temoignez.

Translation

My dear Gide.

I send you our best wishes for the New Year to Cuverville where I hope they will find you "in residence," as the saying goes.

I know that as a correspondent I am a contemptible being and not even fit to live. None the less I think you will not throw this into the fire unread – not because I have interesting things to tell you but because I know you to be a kind man.

The copies of the translations I received this year gave me the greatest pleasure. And the only pleasure of that kind I had because I published nothing in 1922. I worked badly – or rather worked little in 21 and 22. I none the less finished a novel, *The Rover*, in August. I think that should be translated as *Le Forban*. A French subject – Mediterranean coast. Not very long – about the length of *The Secret Agent*. Time period 1799–1804. I have an idea that it will please you. I don't know when it will appear in book form. That depends on arrangements for serialisation in the United States – a question of £2000 that I can not sacrifice to my desire to appear in book form as soon as possible.

I recently had the very great pleasure of making the acquaintance of Ravel and Paul Valéry. I found both of them charming. I felt a real affection for Valéry at first sight. I can't tell you more because I have a bad wrist as this wretched scrawl proves. 1922 will be memorable to me for that black day my play had. I had a fit of anger about it that lasted 24 hours, not more. Seen close up, the theatre is a funny thing.

---

[1] Of 26 December; see Stape and Knowles, pp. 197–8.

That, my dear Gide, is an account of the past year. As you see, it's not impressive. I am now working on a novel, which is about half done. I embrace you affectionately.

Yours truly

Joseph Conrad.

I opened the envelope to let you know that your letter has just arrived. Thank you, my dear. Believe in my affection and in my gratitude for your friendship.

To Eric Pinker

Text TS/MS Berg; Unpublished

[Oswalds]
Dec. 29th. 1922.

Dearest Eric.

I have written to Dent about the Author's Notes for his Uniform Edition. These Prefaces could in no sense have been written specially for the Ed. de Luxe. Two of them, as you know, are contemporary with the first editions, more than twenty-four years ago.[1] Four others were written (if for anybody) for Dent himself; that is for his reprints of Lord Jim, Youth, A Personal Record and Nostromo, long before the matter of the Ed. de Luxe was settled. As to the phrase in Heinemann's advertisement about these Notes, I have taken the advice of Dick Curle who was here for Xmas, and his opinion is that it does not amount to anything on which any subscribers to the Ed. de Luxe could found the slightest grievance.

I told J. M. D[ent] to go ahead and obtain the plates. As a matter of fact I want those Author's Notes to be included. I do not think that the American plates made for the Limited Ed. were destroyed. I know that Heinemann's type has been distributed. I am of Dick's opinion, that the sentence you quote from Heinemann's prospectus is really too vague to get us into hot water with the subscribers; and besides, when you consider that six of those Prefaces were published long before the Limited Ed. came into being I really think we are on firm ground.

I wonder what you think of the Werner Laurie request. I hope you approve of my attitude. I feel extremely reluctant to talk at all about the play under present circumstances. Later, when the vol. of *all* the plays appears (as we planned it), in the usual course, I may write an Author's Note for the lot.

---

[1] Those to *Almayer's Folly* and *The Nigger of the 'Narcissus'*.

As to Powys Evans' portrait[1] I really do not like it. He has given me there an immensely thick nose which I haven't got, and a disagreeable expression which I don't think is natural to me, though it may have been there while he was working at the portrait. I was feeling anything but well that afternoon.

Affectiona^{tely} Yours

J. Conrad

To C. K. Scott Moncrieff

Text J-A, 2, 292–3

Oswalds.

Dec. 29th, 1922.

My dear Scott Moncrieff,

We shall be glad to see you either on the 8th or 9th, but I must warn you that John – the boy you have seen when you were here last with Lord Northcliffe – has developed mumps, which is, I believe, an infectious disease. However, I will be able to keep him out of your way if you come for the day.

You give me a job there to think of a title for the flowering young women of poor Proust.[2] It will take some thinking out and I am afraid the solution will be in abandoning it altogether. However, we might talk about it when we meet.

I am sorry to see from your letter that your health is obviously far from good. We hoped that there was a marked improvement. Please drop us a line fixing the day and the train by which you will come, if you do decide to take the risk. Of course the car will meet you in Canterbury.

Warm regards

---

1   In the *London Mercury* (December 1922), p. 119 (see Plate 1). Powys Arthur Lenthall Evans (1899–1981) was a caricaturist, graphic artist, and painter.
2   According to Jean-Aubry, Conrad suggested *In the Shade of Blossoming Youth* and *In the Shade of Young Girls in Bloom* for Proust's *A l'Ombre des jeunes filles en fleurs.*

To Tadeusz Żuk-Skarszewski

Text Krzyżanowski (1958);[1] Najder 285

Oswalds,
Bishopsbourne,
Kent.
Dec. 29th. 1922.[2]

Dear Sir,[2]

I regret to have to dictate my thanks for your friendly communication of Dec. 18th, relating to some of my family relics now in the possession of Madame Orlikowska.[3]

I should of course be very glad to have them. I regret if it is going to cause any trouble to Madame Orlikowska. I will write to her to the address you mention and I hope that our Legation in Warsaw will consent to take charge of the parcel.

Believe me, my dear Sir, with warm regards to Mrs. Skarszewska[4] and yourself.

Very faithfully yours,
Joseph Conrad.

You will make me happy by sending me your works of which you speak in your letter.

To Eric Pinker

Text TS/MS Berg; Unpublished

[Oswalds]
Dec. 30th. 1922.

My dear Eric.

The signed Agreement with Laurie was (by entry in Miss H[allowes]'s post-book) sent to you on Dec. 21st,[5] and the receipt has been acknowledged by postcard from your office.

---

[1] Text from Krzyżanowski (1958). The original is in English apart from the postscript (given here in Najder's translation).

[2] (Jan) Tadeusz Żuk-Skarszewski (1858–1933), a Polish neo-Romantic novelist, was an acquaintance of the Zagórska sisters. He resided for some time in England, where in 1897 he married Kate Hadley, who returned to Poland with him and worked as a translator.

[3] Maria Magdalena Orlikowska (née Kopernicka), the daughter of a physician who treated Conrad's uncle and guardian Tadeusz Bobrowski.

[4] Kate Żuk-Skarszewska (née Hadley, 1868–1950), English translator and painter.

[5] The agreement, undated, is summarised in Hallowes.

I am glad you sent on my letter to Laurie. I don't know when he means to publish but you will see to it that I get the sheets for signature in good time; as there will be a thousand of them to do, which is a considerable amount, I should like to take my time over it.

Thank you very much for your enquiries about the scheme of living in France from the Income tax point of view. You are perfectly right in thinking that I would not like it, and what's more I don't think Jessie would like it; but it is not only avoidance of taxation but also other considerations that made me think of it. There is the obvious advantage in the matter of exchange, as well as other considerations. But I have not made up my mind on that matter at all, and it need not be considered for some time yet. I won't say any more here because I can open my mind to you better in conversation next time we see each other. Meantime, to the end of March I'll put all those matters out of my mind, if possible, to concentrate on my work.

I hear that the translations of my books in France are having a success and attracting general attention. There will be of course not much money in it; but a fuss being made there is valuable from the point of view of an eventual Nobel Prize, which, being an annual thing, offers more chances than one.

Affect[ly] Yours

J. Conrad

Text of play for printer is going to You reg[istere][d] by to-night's post.

To Aniela Zagórska
Text MS copy Yale (incomplete); Najder 285

Oswalds,
30.XII.22.

My dear Angela,

I begin by dictating and telling you in English my impression of the translated Almayer,[1] the copy of which reached me two days ago.

I have read it twice with great care and in a thoroughly critical spirit. I am perfectly satisfied and even more than satisfied. As far as I can judge the atmosphere is rendered in a wonderful way and I assure you, my dear, that I am very grateful to you for this faithful interpretation of my work. The appearance of the book, too, pleases me very much and I hope with my whole heart that it will have with the Polish public a success at least as great, as the French translation had in France.[2]

---

[1] Her recently published translation *Fantazja Almayera.*
[2] As *La Folie Almayer* (1919), translated by Geneviève Seligmann-Lui.

SILENT CORRECTIONS TO THE TEXT

The following slips of the pen have been silently corrected.

Missing full stop supplied

1920: 4 Jan.: after 'address'; Thursday [15 Jan.?]: after 'good purpose'; [mid-Jan.?] (to Grace Willard): after 'as possible'; 27 Jan.: after '2 vol'; 5 Feb.: after 'question'; 15 Feb.: after '"wait and see"'; 21 Feb.: after 'having my way', after 'sorry'; [mid-March?]: after 'in advance'; [17 March, PS]: after '*serial rights*'; 21 March: after 'correct'; 23 March: after 'till Friday'; [25 March] (to Jean-Aubry): after 'le plus'; 31 March: after 'long'; 1 April: after 'very good'; 3 April (to Otolia Retinger): after '3.4', after 'evening', after 'wishes'; 4 April (to Garnett): after 'her love'; Tuesday [6? April]: after 'Dedi^{on}'; 8 April (to Curle): after 'blow', after 'work'; 8 April (to Eric Pinker): after 'yesterday', after 'safely'; 15 April (to Graham): after 'suggest'; 15 April (to Holland): after '*fully* survive', after 'go sooner)'; 17 April: after 'regards to you'; 27 April (to Lady Colvin): after 'looking well'; 27 April (to Pinker): before 'Five more'; [11 May] (to Jean-Aubry): after 'amitiés'; 11 May (to J. B. Pinker): after 'heavens fall'; 17 May: after 'Samedi'; 20 May: after 'keeping well'; 24 May: after 'opportunity'; 26 May: after 'think'; 3 June (to Wise): after 'encl^{re}', after 'difficult'; 8 June (to J. B. Pinker): after 'remember them'; 24 June (to Wise): after 'enquiries'; 9 July (to Dawson): after 'join'; 11 July (to Garnett): after 'soon'; 19 July (to J. B. Pinker): after 'out of them', after 'Luxe Ed^{on}'; 22 July: after 'semaine'; 25 July (to Northcliffe): after 'long screed'; 25 July (to Holt): after 'various ships'; [30? July]: after 'do it again'; 1 Aug. (to Wise): after 'wishes', after 'o'clock'; 4 Aug.: after '"top hole"'; 7[5] Aug. (to Symons): after 'thereabouts'; 18 Aug.: after 'its 3 chap', after 'utterance', after 'part of Aug^t'; 19 Aug.: after 'other day', after 'great fisherman'; 23 Aug. (to Rothenstein): after 'Sept^{er}', after 'little'; 26 Aug. (to Jean-Aubry): after 'jusqu'a lundi'; 31 Aug. (to Mary Pinker): after 'house', 'after heart', after 'F & M'; [early Sept.?]: after 'grounds', after 'possession'; 9 Sept.: after 'Bishopsbourne)'; 21 Sept.: after 'rank and decorations'; 23 Sept.: after 'John to school'; 28 Sept.: after 'that House'; 6 Oct. (to Sutherland): after 'now'; 9 Oct.: (to Curle): after 'Nov^{er}'; [mid to late Oct.]: after 'Film'; [24] Oct. (to Wise): after 'anything for you'; [8 Nov.]: after 'effet'; 9 Nov.: after 'some people'; [10 Nov.]: after 'this mor^{ng}'; 22 Nov.: after '10 o'clock'; 15 Dec. (to Mackintosh): after 'right', after 'days'; [20 Dec.]: after 'perfect Gentleman'"; 30 Dec. (to Poradowska): after 'bien tendrement'.

1921: [2 Jan.] (to Gardiner): after 'Wed^{ay}'; 22 Jan. (to Curle): after 'friend of ours'; 22 Jan. (to J. B. Pinker): after 'century or more', after 'America', after 'without delay'; [22 Jan.]: after 'just to hand'; 26 Jan.: after 'and solitude'; 30 Jan.: after '"matériel"', after 'R[alph]'; 5 Feb.: after 'cross-examined him yet'; 23 Feb. (to Jean-Aubry): after 'l'edition'; 23 Feb. (to Robins): after 'in book form'; 24 March: after '*Numidia*)', after 'with the story'; [11 April] (to Garnett): after 'end of time'; [mid- or late April?]: after ed^{on}; [23 April]: after 'my dearest'; 25 May (to Pinker): after 'are necessary'; [27 May]: after 'macadam surface'; 21 June: after 'in London'; 27 June (to Pinker): after 'difficult to find', after 'nor drama', after 'not "light"', after 'the translator'; 27 June (to Sanderson): after 'perhaps'; 1 July: after 'trouble'; 4 July: after 'much the nicest'; [14 July] (to Pinker): after 'by request'; 20 [or 21] July: after '*at 8.30pm*'"; 1[2] Aug.: after 'weekend'; 15 Aug.: after 'into account'; Monday. 6pm. [15 Aug.]: after 'roy^{ies}', after 'refer to you'; 31 Aug.: after '(Sept.)'; [15 Oct.]: after 'roy^{ies}', after 'ago'; 22 Oct.: after 'without interruption'; 11 Nov. (to Pinker): after 'next week'; 22 Nov.: after 'sale-room'; 23 Nov. (to Curle): after 'prevents'; [26? Nov.]: after '*good* one'; Monday [28 Nov.?]: after 'arrangements'; 6 Dec. (to Ford): after 'town'; 9 Dec. (to Pinker): after 'visitor'.

1922: 3 Jan. (to Pinker): after 'Short Serial'; 4 Jan.: after 'Scient^{ic}C^o'; 24 Jan.: after 'insur^{ce}', after 'everybody'; 21 Feb.: after 'not impatient'; 23 Feb.: after 'disconnected scrawl'; 3[2] March: after 'consequence'; *Jeudi* [16 March]: after 'un petit mot'; 23 March: after 'forgot'; [early April?]: after 'of that kind'; 7 April: after 'Enfin', after 'au lit'; [10 April]: after 'de Vous voir'; 24 April (to Pinker): after 'school *acct*'; 27 April: after 'remember'; [25 May]: after 'train'; 27 May: after 'aurez le temps'; 30 May (to Pinker): after '"clean copy" typing'; [12 June]: after 'have it'; 11 July: after 'whole lot home'; 20 July (to Pinker): after 'approval'; 20 July (to Tittle): after 'ticket'; 22 July (to Rees): after 'meeting'; 25 July (to Curle): after 'is understandable'; 6 Aug.: after 'Hearst Mags'; 7 Sept.: after 'your note'; 22 Sept.: after 'finir'; 1 Oct.: after 'grasped'; [15 Oct.] (to Jean-Aubry): after 'intelligente'; 15 Oct. (to Pinker): after 'Mch '22', after 'be present'; 19 Oct. (to Wise): after 'Patrol'; 20 Oct.: after 'good cause'"; 23 Oct. (to Fitz-Herbert): after 'do now'"; [2 Nov.]: after 'circles for tomorrow', after 'use to you'; 6 Nov. (to Pinker): after 'whole thing'; 7 Nov. (to F. Tennyson Jesse): after 'this morning'; 7 Nov. (to Jones): after 'sans phrases'"; [9? Nov.]: after '"first copy"'; 11 Nov. (to Pinker): after 'Sat ev^g', after 'in it'; [20–22 Nov.?]: after 'not arise'; 25 Nov.: after 'Vlad-Verloc scene'; [1 Dec.?]

(to Pinker): after 'Nov^{er}', after 'address'; 2 Dec.: after '(£20)'; 11 Dec.: (date) after '11'; 20 Dec.: after 'vos parents', after 'retour', after 'you'.

Dittography

2 June 1920: a second 'and' after 'for this reason'; 5 July 1920 (to Doubleday): a second 'joins me' after 'My wife'; 26 Aug. 1920 (to Garnett): a second 'to' before 'meet my uncle'; 31 Aug. 1920 (to Mary Pinker): a second 'in' after 'highly and'; 1 Oct. 1920: a second 'you' after 'If you'. 1921: 3 Jan. 1921: a second 'a' after 'was dictated', a second 'me' after 'willing to give'; 8 June 1921: a second 'the' after 'doubts as to'. 20 July 1922 (to Pinker): a second 'US' after' 'complete the'; 2 Sept. 1922: a second 'has' after' 'your wife'; [22-23] Oct. 1922: a second full stop after 'etc etc.'.

Bracket supplied

15 April 1920 (to Holland): after 'go sooner'; 1 Oct. 1920: after 'high road'. 24 March 1921: after 'her quarter'.

Capital letter supplied

20 Jan. 1920 (to Colvin): before '*Rescue*'; 4 April 1920: after 'done in a'.

Colon supplied

10 Aug. 1921 (to Winawer): after 'divided as follows'.

Comma supplied

18 March 1920 (to Curle): after 'to be sure'; 5 April 1920 (to Ernest Dawson): after 'miner'; 30 Dec. 1920 (to Warrington Dawson): after 'Rouen'. 22 Jan. 1921 (to Curle): after 'Ajaccio' (replacing full stop); 22 Nov. 1921: after 'suppose'. 20 March 1922: after 'morning'; 24 Sept. 1922: after 'Believe me'; [16 Oct.] 1922: after 'Nettlefold'; 30 Oct. 1922 (to Sanderson): after 'good fortune'.

Question mark supplied

8 April 1920 (to Curle): after '(about £50)'; [2 Dec.]1920: after 'to town for me'. [18 Nov.] 1921: after 'Sunday'. 25 July 1922 (to Curle): after 'tomorrow (Wed:)'.

Quotation marks supplied

5 July 1920 (to Quinn): after 'Writing. Quinn.'; 1 Nov. 1920 (to Wise) (PS): after 'return of the'.

Dash supplied

26 April 1920: after 'most detest'; 7[5] Aug. 1920: before 'Bridge'. [27 March] 1921: after 'Versailles'.

Emendations to copied or dictated letters

1920: 22 Jan.: 'to' for 'tr' after 'my decision as'; 24 Jan. (to J. B. Pinker): 'don't' for 'hon't' after 'nuisance because'; 25 Feb.: 'enclosed' for 'enclooed' after 'received the'; 2 March: 'gauge' for 'guage' before 'the possible depth'; 31 May: 'or' for 'of' after 'either my hand'; 5 July (to Quinn): 'in' for 'on' after 'take charge', 'advance' for 'advanced' after 'Doubleday sent you'.

1921: 10 Oct. (to Kinkead): 'Club' for 'Clunb' after 'at the Garrick'; 25 Oct. (to Waldo): 'in' deleted before 'the perception of a beautiful'.

1922: 19 Jan.: full stop after 'for me'; 19 Feb.: full stop after 'to a writer'; 25 March: 'Eric' for 'Eeric' before 'I think it would be'; 3 April (to Candler): 'meteorologically' for 'meteorogically' before 'speaking, no amount'; 8 April: 'clearer to you' for 'cleares to tou'; 9 April: comma after 'glad, however', 'begins' for 'begings' after 'workman's clothes'; 2 May (to Pinker): 'every one' for 'everyone' before 'of my publishers'; 24 May (to Russell): full stop after 'thoughts'; 2 June (to Dawson): 'megalomaniac' for 'megolamaniac'; 21 June: 'Notes on Life' for 'Notes of Life'; 30 June: 'it' for 'iy', 'McKinnel' for 'McKinnell'; 25 July (to Hammond Clark & Daman): 'a' removed before 'the berth of'; 26 July: 'chance' for 'chamce'; 12 Sept. (to Dent & Sons): 'offers' for 'offeres'; 19 Oct. (to Benrimo): full stop after 'paper'; 27 Oct. (to Benrimo): full stop after 'Exactly'; 19 Nov.: 'remunerated' for 'renumerated', 'afraid' for 'afriad'; 30 Nov.: comma added after 'ni ironie'; 8 Dec. (to Doubleday): quotation marks added after '"The Rover'; 15 Dec. (to Adams): 'be' changed to 'me' after 'Jessie joins', full stop after 'wife and yourself'.

CORRIGENDA FOR VOLUMES 6–7

Volume 6

xlii and 160, n. 1: *Les Caves du Vatican* appeared in 1914.

123, n. 1: James Lithgow was born in 1883.

182: 'many people of all sorts and conditions': a variation on 'all sorts and conditions of men' from the 'Collect or Prayer for All Conditions of Men' in 'Prayers and Thanksgivings upon Several Occasions' from the *Book of Common Prayer.*

194: the censor's official title was Examiner of Plays.

218, n. 2: Conrad signed the visitors' book at the library on 30 July 1914.

261: *The First News, an Essay*: published without the sub-title.

536: 'Vous qui comprenez tant de choses...': 'You who understand so much may perhaps be able to forgive me this weakness.' Conrad echoes the familiar phrase 'Tout comprendre, c'est tout pardonner', attributed to Madame de Stael.

(Index II): add 'Horace, 511'; change the grave accent to an acute in 'Mazatlán'.

Volume 7

lx (biographies), 8, n. 4, and 223, n. 2: according to their passports, Catherine Willard was born in 1898, and Grace Willard (née Robinson) in 1879, both in Ohio.

172, n. 3: Oenone Pinker married Captain Cyril Gowland in 1926.

514 (Wicken): Eric had married a Dane, Margit Vibege Watney (née Dietrichson).

INDEXES

In Index I, which identifies recipients, only the first page of each letter is cited. Letters to multiple recipients are indexed under each name and marked ††.

In Index II, an index of names, run-on pagination may cover more than one letter. References to ships are consolidated under 'Ships'; to battlefields, units, and sites associated with the war under 'First World War'; to newspapers and magazines, under 'Periodicals'; to London and its localities, under 'London'; to Parliament and the Civil Service under 'British (or UK) Government'. References to works by Conrad, uniform editions, and selections from his writing appear under his name.

INDEX I. RECIPIENTS

INDEX II. GENERAL